AF568169

RETHINKING A MILLENNIUM

Perspectives on Indian History
from the Eighth to the Eighteenth Century

RETHINKING A MILLENNIUM

Perspectives on Indian History from the Eighth to the Eighteenth Century

ESSAYS FOR HARBANS MUKHIA

Edited by
Rajat Datta

RETHINKING A MILLENNIUM
Edited by RAJAT DATTA

First Published, 2008
Reprinted 2021

ISBN 978-81-89833-36-7

Published by
AAKAR BOOKS
28 E Pocket IV, Mayur Vihar Phase I, Delhi-110 091
Phone : 011-2279 5505 Telefax : 011-2279 5641
aakarbooks@gmail.com; www.aakarbooks.com

Printed at
Sapra Brothers, Noida.

CONTENTS

Preface

When the editors of the *Medieval History Journal* (*MHJ*) declared in its inaugural issue (January–June 1998) that 'as ever newer landscapes of historical problematics are mapped, questioning the premise of received analytical categories—including periodisation—comes centre stage', they were expressing a new disquiet with the standardised approaches of studying the phenomenon of the 'medieval' in history. Harbans Mukhia, whose enthusiasm was the moving force behind the *MHJ* embodies this restless spirit: his work has been characterised by a deep skepticism towards all dominant notions of historical 'truths' without compromising his commitment to the veracity of a historical (i.e. a source-legitimated) explanation. Therefore, when I thought of celebrating his career in 2004, in the form of an international seminar on rethinking India's medieval millennium— the period between the eighth and the eighteenth centuries—my major concerns were a basket of themes which would appeal to him and enable the participants to reconfigure this period by raising new questions through a stringent but imaginative interrogation of their sources. This volume is the outcome of that seminar, and a symbol of our appreciation of Harbans Mukhia's work over the last four decades.

This volume makes no self-congratulatory claims of revising or rethinking all aspects of India's medieval past. It builds on some major historiographical shifts in this direction, which have already taken place over the last fifty years. From the earlier preoccupation with the history of personalities or the grand narrative of dynastic changes, history-writing has moved on to the analysis of institutions and structures. Economic history has revealed the existence of high levels of commercial growth, while social history has shown that conflicts between intersecting social classes were critical in the distribution of the fruits of this growth. Therefore, instead of seeing history as a view from the top, there is now an emphasis on its multipolarities and a greater recognition of human agency and volition in the making of their own histories. Substantial modifications have occurred, for instance, in our understanding of imperial processes, and to see the decline of empires as disjunctures within broad processes of continuity and transformation instead of a breakdown or a regression into chaos. Over the last three decades, explorations in some new directions, broadly called the history of mentalities— or the intersections between cultural practices and economic processes—have extended the frontiers of historical scholarship on this millennium. Environmental histories have begun indicating close links between ecology and ethnicity and the forests are being perceived as more than huge swathes of wooded areas.

Much still needs to be done. Histories of political processes, communities, constructions of gender and patterns of cultural diffusion still need to be written. Even the economy, which at first glance appears an overcrowded field, needs the infusion of fresh perspectives as many economic transactions were rooted in cultural practices. There is also a need to take a fresh look at periodisation itself by questioning the applicability of this seamless term 'medieval' for a period stretching over a millennium, as many of the assumptions which have gone into such a characterisation have been discursive, arbitrary and binary. A historian cannot function without a sense of periodisation or a linearity of perspective, but there is an urgent need for disaggregating this millennium from its present dyadic division of 'early medieval', and 'medieval' into a triptych with the 'early modern' constituting its third dimension. Only then will we begin to get a more refined sense of the dynamics involved and to question dominant binaries, for instance, the one between modernity and pre-modernity.

The contributors to this volume are singularly positioned to shed light on these multi-dimensionalities. None of them is enamoured of any of the standardising explanations—the reigning orthodoxies—of India's medieval past. Nor are they enthralled by any one group of sources, particularly those generated in the Persian language by a fawning or a disgruntled set of courtiers; and even when they use this body of sources, their interpretations of the historical processes are at variance from the state-centred and homogenising interpretations which have characterised much of the history-writing of this period. This is already a big move forward in a direction which will no doubt elicit some approval from Harbans Mukhia.

When I organised this seminar in 2004, I had hoped for its early publication. Unfortunately, that was not to be. Illnesses and bereavements prevented me from devoting my full attention to this volume over 2005 and 2006. Some participants were unable to send their revised manuscripts because of prior commitments. On top of this there were delays caused by the late arrival of revised versions. But these eventually came, unlike a few, who delayed either by not responding to repeated reminders or by adopting the more familiar method of requesting for extension of deadlines and then reneging on their promises. Without their cooperation, this volume would have been published at least a year earlier!

Those who sent in their papers and then waited uncomplainingly, I thank them profusely for their fortitude and hope they will find their patience vindicated. I also thank the Indian Council of Cultural Relations (ICCR) and the Indian Council for Historical Research (ICHR), without whose generous financial help the 2004 conference could not have been held. Mr. K.K. Saxena of Aakar Books has been a delight to work with, and Ms. Ritu Singh has been a patient and efficient copy-editor.

Ratna has also been patient and optimistic in believing that this book would actually see the light of day.

A NOTE ON TRANSLATION AND TRANSLITERATION

Unless stated otherwise in the notes, all translations into English have been rendered by individual authors. The transliteration of non-English words or diacritical marks has also been done by the authors and we have not interfered with them to the greatest extent possible, except while standardising the spellings of some Indo-Persian names.

Introduction*

INDIAN HISTORY FROM EIGHTH TO EIGHTEENTH CENTURIES: PROBLEMS, PERSPECTIVES, AND POSSIBILITIES

Rajat Datta

Even for historians who otherwise flit between centuries, a millennium is a long and a daunting span of time. Since such lengths of time do not brook seamless chronologies or universalising labels, they upset the comfortable cocoons of discrete period specialisations we historians love to claim for ourselves within the profession. However, a millennium is not without its uses: it has *longue duree*, and if considered judiciously, it provides, as Dirk Kolff says (in his essay in this volume), 'choice material' to rethink the history of a country. My essay seeks to do both. The 'choice material' has been provided by the articles in this volume and my task is to extract relevant issues (and relevant is a relative term) and then weave them together into a comprehensible narrative that traces continuities and transformations within a long process of historical transition.

The task, I daresay, is not easy and more worthwhile people have tried their hands at it.[1] But an uneasy sense also arises because their analyses are homogenising and 'big' European historical structures, for instance, feudalism or capitalism, foreground their perspectives. For instance, while the 'feudalism' in India thesis has its share of supporters, it has also been criticised for its structural inappropriateness in the Indian context,[2] and for its essential Eurocentrism because it applies a linear model of European economic progress to Indian conditions marked by enormous diversities and overwhelming complexities. In accounts which seek to by-pass these modal traps, Europe still looms

* Unless stated otherwise, authors and page numbers indicated in parentheses in the text are from this volume.

large. Even for those historians for whom feudalism is not a substantive issue in India's past, classifying 'pre-colonial India' only proceeds by specifying India's *economic difference* from Europe, which is 'in respect of the details of [its] property relations and the pace at which [social] contradictions matured...'.[3]

One is also struck by the fact that such apparently dynamic analytical categories, like states, classes and contradictions, yield a surprisingly static picture of Indian history over much of this millennium. The assessment of the economy of northern India between the thirteenth and the seventeenth centuries in the *Cambridge Economic History of India, volume 1*[4] illustrates this. A certain degree of stratification and conflict in society is recognised, but this is posited within a surprising degree of changelessness in the larger context. In the long period between the thirteenth and the eighteenth centuries, 'two phases or cycles' of state formation, are identified: one in the thirteenth and fourteenth centuries, and the second in the sixteenth and seventeenth centuries. Both the cycles were determined by the ability of the state to refine its tax-assignment systems, which, in both instances, fell regressively on society and subverted 'superior cultivation, while it simultaneously increased the distance between the rich and poor in the countryside'. Stasis is implicit in this explanation because it ascribes one single cause to explain the same sort of change over six centuries: in other words, the more India changed, the more it remained the same.

The collection of essays in this volume will hopefully make a departure in a different direction, the quest for which has been set out under three thematic components. The first rubric comprises explorations in the realms of politics, legitimacy, and political culture. The second studies communities, gender, and cultural transmission. The third component deals with commerce, crafts, and the countryside. Taken together, these seek to provide new entry points beyond the standardised and monochromatic views of medieval Indian history and create space for a more nuanced and interconnected look at the millennium. We hope to see, for instance, the connections between politics, community formations and tensions in the countryside; trace the links between cultural transmission and craft production; and follow the complex interface between politics and cultural diffusion as vital elements in shaping the millennium under consideration. Instead of a linearity of perspective, these interfaces allow us to conceive of historical processes as a continuum characterised by ambivalences and negotiations between multiple, albeit asymmetrically situated, sets of agencies.

The Frame of Politics: States or Processes?

One striking feature of the millennium is the centrality of the 'political' and it is therefore fitting that this volume should begin with a set of essays examining its various dimensions. A long view shows that much of the millennium saw phases of expansion and realigning political configurations occurring almost autonomously of the state, though periodically they could be subsumed under it only to be regain their autonomy when the latter weakened. If we follow the logic of Kolff's argument, these multiple convergences and divergences arose from traditionally embedded conceptual as well as praxis-based separations between politics, as power unfolding over multiple nodal points, and states as the *periodic* reifications of that power, with points of intersection between the two being constituted by a dialogic process between state-action and social practice. The traditional Indian state was the upholder of law but not its legislator—that sphere was located in the realm of *dharma*, a dyadic zone shared by secular sovereignty and a religio-moral brahmanical order created by the sacred texts. *Dharma* was a prescription of public action as well as a lived moral order which determined the boundaries of individual volition. It was also an elaborate mechanism of social control because it enjoined upon individuals to accept their positions in society on the basis of the castes into which they were born. The norms for that caste, as enunciated by the authors of the Law Books, imparted a degree of stability in the social order[5], which perhaps facilitated the task of statecraft to an extent which was not possible after the thirteenth century. *Rajdharma* enjoined upon the king to combine authority with an adherence to a normative world of moral codes, making statecraft an uneasy balancing act amongst three spheres: that of virtue, practical dominion and a dynamic *ordre vécu* of a lived in world 'with its evolving customs, shifting loyalties and survival strategies' [Kolff, p. 58].

Did the Islamic intervention turn things around from the thirteenth century? An influential version of the Sultanate sees the thirteenth century as a watershed characterised by intrusive centralisation, durable institutions of rule characterised by the *iqtā'* system and different norms of governance[6]. This interpretation is a somewhat straightforward rendition of the Persian chronicles generated in the courts of the sultans which were state-centred in orientation[7] with a linear discourse about the unfolding success and novelty of these conquest-regimes.[8] Variant readings of these same Persian sources suggest greater degrees of vulnerability and inchoateness. For Andre Wink, the Persian-language chronicles show the Sultanate as a 'a sum of its *iqtā's*—defined not as local territorial units, but as garrisoned urban centres (*khitta*) with dependent areas (*muzafat*)—and some *khalisa* or "crown" holdings of minor proportions'[9]; whereas for Sunil Kumar the Sultanate appears as a 'loose assembly of urban centres with marginal control over their hinterlands' constantly threatened by hostile forces [Kumar, p. 149]. Despite some differences in their interpretations, both Wink and Kumar have viewed the Sultanate as a negotiated entity, subjected to multiple pulls and pressures from diverse quarters, where moments of intrusive centralisation were interspersed with equally acute moments of divisiveness and fissures. By the early fifteenth century, the sultans were barely able to impose their authority either on their own *muqta's* or on local Hindu princes,[10] and this denouement had a long pre-history, as can be seen from Ziya' al-din Barani's lament about the continued persistence of *kufr* (unbelief) and his anxieties about the flourishing state of powerful Hindu landed, literate and commercial intermediaries—'*rais, ranas, thakurs, sahas, mehtas,* and *pandits*' under the Muslim sultans [Raziuddin Aquil, p. 183].

These sultanist regimes were susceptible to more political vicissitudes as compared to those they supplanted and the one that replaced them. One reason why they continued to be vulnerable and unstable appears to lie in the change they introduced in the norms of governance because of the formal identification of their power with scriptural Islam. Notwithstanding the many syncretic and inclusionist dimensions of medieval Indian cultures, for the conquerors and their ideologues Hindustan was a land of *kufr*. Henceforth the traditional intersections between *niti* (policies based on legal precepts), *dharma* and *rajdharma* were broken and replaced by the notions of *dar ul-Islam* and *jahandari* as abiding principles of state-action. The earlier consensus (and stability) of a moral and transcendental order of things was now replaced by deep anxieties, founded in reality, of subversion and sedition—*fitna*—in these subjugated lands. *Fitna*, as Wink defines it, was not merely underhand subversion; it involved overt contesation of power 'by competing warrior households leading ethnic outsiders which [sic] were recruited in cash'[11]. Court historians of the Sultans and the Mughals perpetuated this anxiety by harping on the existence of seditious and rebellious subjects [Kumar, p. 141], though this anxiety was not limited to *kafirs* but included Muslims as well. For instance, Abul Faz'l, the great courtier-historian of Akbar, portrayed the Afghans as unreliable since the 'treachery' of their leader Sher Shah had temporarily deprived the Mughals of their empire in Hindustan.[12] Kolff, who takes issue with Wink on the admissibility of this term for the semi-autonomous 'little kingdoms', nevertheless concedes that *fitna* was used as a rhetorical strategy by the 'early modern, military-fiscalist' states in the eighteenth century to ride roughshod 'over the hundreds of minor but autonomous princes' on grounds that these were 'corruption-, disloyalty-, treason-, in short *fitna*-ridden'[Kolff, p. 60].

It would thus appear that changes introduced in norms of governance in the thirteenth and fourteenth centuries may have actually exacerbated rather than resolved tensions between the ruling regimes, their *muqta's* and *amirs*[13] and the subordinated magnates,[14] which a state-centric reading of the chronicles would tend to gloss over. Therefore the argument made in respect of the Mughals that 'conquest did not imply the erasure of older fiscal institutions or the older elite and their substitution on the basis of a unique imperial blueprint'[15] would perhaps apply to the Sultanate with greater relevance, considering the rapidly shifting fortunes of the ruling dynasties in this period. Another suggestion that a historian's focus ought to lie not in describing the structure of states (i.e. its ruling or extractive institutions), but in the processes of state-building[16] may be a more pertinent way of approaching the politics of these times because this allows space for looking at the persistence of anterior institutions and power-nexuses and their simultaneous incorporation and transformation in the new dispensations. Quite obviously the ideologues of the Sultanate were grappling with these issues. For instance, Barani continuously struggled with the contradiction between the Islamic prescription of establishing an ideal-typical *shari'a*-oriented polity in the lands of unbelievers and the pragmatic impossibility of imposing such a rule in India. His solution was a state which would enforce a kind of hierarchy where an aristocracy (i.e. Muslims of noble birth and genealogy) would be rewarded and the baser elements (both Hindus and the low-born or newly converted Muslims) would be ruthlessly subordinated, while silently conceding the impossibility of achieving either of these two latter objectives. The latter was reflected in his pungent criticism of Ala'ud-din Khilji that he, despite being a powerful sultan, had allowed worthless and base people to rise to high positions.[17]

One potent example of accommodation within conflict with anterior systems could be the notion of a semi-divine kingship (the shadow of God), which occurred sporadically under the Sultanate and was later revived and strengthened by the Mughals. Divine roots of kingship, though recognised, were weakly articulated in the classical Indian tradition. 'Divinity', remarks Basham, 'was cheap in ancient India. Every brahman was in a sense a god, as were ascetics with a reputation for sanctity. Householders sponsoring and financing sacrifices were in theory raised to divinity...'; and even if 'gods were fallible and capable of sin'[18], the all-pervasiveness of divinity was deeply embedded in the Indian psyche. Therefore a notion of semi-divine sovereignty, though starkly un-Islamic from a puritanical perspective, may have found a fertile soil in India. Attempts at establishing a divine basis for kingship during the Sultanate were intermittent and indifferent, but it was reinvented and reinvigorated by the Mughals, as exemplified by Abul Faz'l imbuing Akbar with the radiance of divine light (*nur parwarda-i izdi*) thus transporting the Mughals from the confines of nebulous and ideologically combated notion of Islamic divinity into the transcendental realm of 'universal divinity'[19]. While the Mughal notions of a universal divinity were easily incorporated into the greater Indian traditions, it is conceivable that even the Sultanate notions of divine kingship may have found some responsive chords, despite the fractious nature of the relations between the domains of imperial and locality-based politics. Zeigler points us towards the acceptance of the warrior-aristocratic Muslim as part of the *jati*-nexus within which medieval Rajput cultural traditions articulated concepts of 'rank, power and sovereignty' and in this the Muslim emperor in particular, held a position of high rank and esteem: 'the traditions often equate him with Râm, the pre-eminent Ksatriya cultural hero of the Hindu Rajputs'[20].

Fractiousness and political accommodation therefore seem to have proceeded hand in hand. Medieval Rajput textual traditions reflect both these processes. While one strand of this tradition was replete with images of the '*turak*' (the Turk or the Muslim) conqueror as the defiler of temples and idols—as the proverbial *mlecchas*, another went as far as portraying a marauding sultan like Ala'ud-din Khilji as Shiva, the god of destruction himself.[21]

Such ambivalent processes were not limited to textual traditions alone. They occurred at the highest levels of the political organisation, at the level of the state itself, and were not limited to any conceivable 'core' area of political dissemination. The great medieval empire in peninsular India, that of the Vijaynagara, was situated at the cusp of these transactions. Vijayanagara was a Hindu-sultanate (*Hinduraya-suratrana*) in the Deccan, which incorporated liberally from the brahmanical traditions of a *dharma*-based polity and deeply implicated itself in the 'Muslim' politics of the other Deccani kingdoms—Bijapur versus Bidar, and Ahmadnagar versus Bijapur. Though this ultimately had disastrous consequences for the future of that empire, it also resulted in the increasing 'Persianisation' of the peninsula with the slow incorporation of Iranian and Deccani Muslims, or Arab seafarers into the fabric of the state and its commercial world [Richard Eaton, p. 102]. Telugu chiefs and Brahmans collaborated with the Muslim Golconda regime, whereas Muslims supported Vijaynagara in Rayalseema.[22] The collapse of Vijayanagara did not put an end to this process as the Deccani sultanates, and later the Mughals continued to engage in the slow incorporation of ethnically and linguistically diverse elite strata through concurrent processes of coercion and compromise.[23]

Modes of Legitimacy and Political Cultures

What therefore had deeper resonances in shaping political processes over the millennium were not the ebb and flow of state-systems but patterns of legitimacy and political cultures which were generated by such countervailing forces over the subcontinent. The acceptance of Islamicate norms of governance by Hindu kingdoms—like Vijaynagara or the Rajput lineage-chiefs—could occur because of the separation between the 'sacred' and the 'royal' spaces within these formations to which Eaton draws our attention [Eaton, p. 101]. While the sacred space could continue to be the scriptural reserve of the imperial household: 'the land of *dharma*, of the gods, of food charities, of the god-like Brahmans' according to the *bakhar* of Ramoji Tirumala Harikara [Sumit Guha, p. 86], the 'royal' space was the open-access window through which norms of governance could be subtly or even overtly modified and a new political culture created. Significantly, this political culture, like its counterpart in the social world, was refractive: it incorporated as much as it got incorporated. In this context, Mukhia draws our attention to a significant change in gender-relations in the Mughal household from the time of Akbar, when from a relatively open-ended arrangement where women enjoyed a fair degree of autonomy, there occurred a slow conservative turn against that freedom, especially their sexuality and an increasing segregation from the public sphere, partly because of the percolation of Rajput morality into Mughal domesticity.[24]

The royal courts were important sites for political cultures and modes of legitimacy to work themselves out. These courts were 'personal residences and administrative centres'— 'households'—of kings and their magnates 'who had the wealth and means to imitate them'; and one distinctive feature of these households seems to be the crystallisation of distinct corpuses of gestures, carriage and deportment in them, and therefore the formation of a 'coherent' courtly-culture in early medieval northern India [Daud Ali, pp. 75–76]. By focusing on gestures and bearing as 'autonomous instruments of social interaction' which 'embody hierarchy', Ali shows how new forms of 'bowing, standing and prostration...were seamlessly incorporated into the larger mental systems operative in court society' [Ali, p. 78]. Following upon this, one can postulate that one of the most distinctive political processes in medieval India was the development of a courtly culture at the cusp of three axes—the sacral, the household and the public (or royal) domain. These innovations, initially designed in the regional kingdoms of the early medieval complex, were incorporated sporadically at a pan-

Indian level by the Sultans of Delhi, and finally raised to ethereal heights by the imperial Mughals. Political cultures and modes of legitimacy were thus inextricably linked in two major forms: one form (as Ali shows) incorporated the symbolic world of gestures and visage, hence proximity and distance from the royal presence; and the other, discussed by Stephen Blake in this volume, manifested itself in gifting and festivity.

Prostration in various complicated postures before the king was made into a courtly ritual by the early medieval kings and the footstool (*pādapītha*) became an important part of royal paraphernalia in these post-Gupta polities, both in the north (Ali, pp. 77-78) and in the peninsula.[25] Ali draws our attention to another court ritual—the veneration of the king's or the superior's feet—as an early medieval innovation designed to express 'subordination and loyalty', plus a device to socialise a class: 'a sort of education of the bodily *habitus* among elites' [Ali, p. 78]. The rituals of *zaminbos* (kissing the earth before the sultan) or *paibos* (kissing the sultan's feet) or prostrating before the sultan (*sijdah*) in the courts of Balban and Ala' ud-din Khilji may have had an Indian genealogy rather than a Sasanid one, as most historians believe.[26]

Gifting and festivity became medieval court rituals *par excellence*. Once again, the incorporation of long-standing traditions of *dana* and *dakshina* (morally-purposeful prestation)[27] involving ritualised transactions in the sacred and quotidian spheres of domesticity were elevated to the status of the royal action (*mahadana*). In northern India, such gifts were made to a range of individual recipients, though brahmans appear to have been the main beneficiaries,[28] while in the peninsula the early medieval practices of gifting seems to have gravitated out of an individual brahman-oriented system to sacred institutional complexes like temples.[29] Gifting thus constituted the nub of elaborate patron–client networks across sacred and profane spaces, and the Sultans of Delhi and their Mughal successors elevated this to an important artifact of medieval political culture. Though grants of revenue-free lands to sacred institutions and pious individuals continued,[30] the imperial courts from the thirteenth century both in the north and in the peninsula [for the latter, see Sumit Guha, pp. 111–112] became centres where clients would expect social elevation by the gifts they received from the king. These could include many material objects, but the ones the elite coveted were robes of honour (*khilat*) which usually accompanied a promotion in rank or accretion of authority.[31] If the emperor gave, he also received—material return-gifts as symbols of loyalty and subordination [Blake, pp. 122, 126].

The great difference however, between the earlier norms of royal gifting and the ones established by the Mughals (at least up to the reign of Aurungzeb) seems to have been the connection they established, perhaps for the first time, with courtly society, gifting and festivity. For instance, Blake shows how the prolonged celebrations around the festival of *nau-ruz* at the Mughal court under Akbar were partly designed to 'open up the cultural climate of the court' [Blake, p. 125] and involved an elaborate division of the way in which the emperor would spend time in the company of different people, almost conceived as concentric circles of varying proximity, with the emperor's household, the most intimate circle of the imperial presence, coming last. Power, culture and legitimacy, webbed in both hierarchic and concentric fashions, were renewed periodically 'on a scale that would appear theatrical to an outside observer either in space or time'.[32] In Vijaynagara, such festivities, marked by elaborate feasts and exchanges of fine cloths and money, implicated the king and his 'captains' over eleven days in the month of October.[33] Festivities thus regenerated paternalism and absolutism as the two pillars of medieval India statecraft.

Early Modernity and the Military-Fiscal Formation

There was a third pillar which has not received as much attention in standard versions of medieval Indian history even though most of them deal with histories of land-revenue administration. This was the phenomenon of military-fiscalism as a differentiator in the political traditions of this millennium and a symptom of early modernity [Kolff, pp. 60–62]. Fiscalism in Europe historically meant the systematic attempt of a state to increase government revenues regardless of the objectives of economic or social policy; in other words, 'the endeavour to maximize the public revenues at all times for other than economic purposes'[34]. Drawing from the eighteenth-century British and French experiences,[35] studies have emphasised the close relations among war, state-building and tax collection as the fiscal markers separating the medieval from the early modern regimes of the subcontinent. The main arguments are that the rising costs of running the state and waging war, plus the expansion in trade and market-networks[36] made governance hinge around the collection and rationalisation of taxes in cash, a process which usually involved local commercial elements (like bankers and merchants) who also financed the state in exchange for a greater role in the management, for profit (including tax farming) of the state's fisc.[37] A great example of this early modern military-fiscalist state comes from Guha's translation of the *bakhar* giving an account of the demise of Vijayanagara. I quote this evocative passage in full since it describes a military-fiscalist state preparing for war.

> The next day the nobles sent messengers with the musters.The aggregate count was: horses 350,000, he-elephants 9778, she-elephants 7318, rockets amounting to 4,609,575, infantry with muskets 148,915, *tapaa* 1184,378,

> spearmen 12,053, *rambana* Rama's arrows (fire arrows?) 231,320, *karalbarani* 250, rockets with fire-pots 11,120, western cannon 3928, arrow makers (?) 3049, musket makers (?) ..938, armorers 27,850, *khurd* (?) 3300, iron helmets 27850, *zabarjang* (blunderbusses?) .. 2200, explosive pots 1,343,870, single combatants 8000, senior headmen (*vadgaudani*) 58,910, armoured horses 14,000, blacksmiths 1090, armoured elephants 1800, craftsmen 3004, hunting dogs 709, *panbude* (pontoons?) 1800, basket-rafts 200, gunpowder 749,208,524 *shers*[38] [Guha, p. 114]

Notwithstanding its hyperbole, what distinguishes this account from a mere description of the military might of any anterior medieval kingdom are the references to the extensive use of gunpowder, which was a revolutionary innovation in the art of war that seems to have occurred simultaneously in Europe and India in the sixteenth century.[39] The other differentiator is the way in which the king raised taxes through a system of levies from the subordinated 'great captains' (*nayakas*)— magnates and revenue-farmers—who held resources worth 'a million and a million and a half *parados*, others a hundred thousand *parados*' and so on[40]—great households who provided the king with his army and paid him enormous sums of money as tribute during the annual cycles of feasting and festivity each October, and who, as Stein argues, combined military services, agro-commercial enterprises and revenue-farming depending on the ecological context of their lands.[41]

Friction, Accommodation and Construction of Communities

A brief overview of the political processes through our millennium has drawn attention to a dynamism arising out of the intersection of three strands—fractiousness, incorporation and synthesis. Another strand, which is the concern of this section, are the processes of social construction through which people having distinctive life-styles and religious beliefs were slotted into monolithic blocs or communities; how a significant part of that community was gendered through texts written by men; and how imperial and regional states and their communities became active sites of cultural transmission.

While the construction of the cultural 'other' was vital in the self-perception of a community, the salient point about cultural construction is that is embroiled in ambivalence and fluidity. By about the end of the first millennium, inscriptional and literary evidence indicates that the perception of the 'Muslim' in India was along two lines: first, as a member of a community such as Tajika or Turuska, 'who is not a raider or a political adversary but a resident, as an active member of the local community', and second, as a 'sovereign ruler' who happened to be of foreign or Turuska descent.[42] There was simultaneously an adversarial reckoning too—the Turk as the conqueror-plunderer and the violator of sacred spaces. This was expressed by al-Biruni when he says that the people of Hind 'declare *us* to be devil's breed and *our* doings as the very opposite of all that is good and proper'. For al-Biruni, this hatred originated from the conquests of Mahmud of Ghazni, who 'utterly ruined the prosperity of the country, and performed these wonderful exploits, by which the Hindus became like atoms of dust scattered in all directions... Their scattered remains cherish, of course, the most inveterate aversion towards all Muslims' and then adds in a truly modernist-secular discourse that this antagonism 'receives more and more nourishment both from political and religious sources'[43]. On the other hand, Sanskrit *praśastis* extolling the virtues of 'Sri Hammira Gayasadina' (Ghiyas al-din Balban, r. 1295–1315 CE) and 'Kuddi Alavadina ('Ala al-din Khilji, r. 1295–1315 CE); or the Qutb Minar being described by workers as a *jayasthmaba* (victory pillar) erected by 'Sri Suratrana Pherojashahi by the grace of Visvakarma', show the efforts being made for a sustainable 'intercultural translation' between the two communities.[44]

Such simultaneously fractious and synthetic ambivalences resided in Muslim perceptions too. The words 'Hindu' and '*qaum*' (community) were already in vogue in Muslim texts by the early decades of the fourteenth century [Aquil, p. 191]. Al-Biruni's moderate and self-critical introspection was drowned by the official accounts of the triumph of Muslim conquerors being churned out from the courts of the Delhi sultans. Barani, (whose narrative constitutes the focal point of Sunil Kumar and Raziuddin Aquil's papers in this volume) represented the aggressive edge of this discourse. For Barani, Hindustan, the land of *kufr*, had to be converted into a Dar al-Islam for which tyranny and violence were justifiable means to an end; but till the end of his life he could not reconcile the contradiction between the scriptural prescriptions and legal disputations about *kufr* and the pragmatic dimensions arising from the need to incorporate the idolatrous *(butparastān)* Hindus into the fold of the *zimmi* (protected people) in an Islamic dispensation. Amir Khusrau, though hostile to *kufr* and the *kafir*, was willing to concede some ground to the sun-worshipping Brahman as part of God's creation [Aquil, pp. 186-87]. One interesting sociological dimension of Barani's critique, which emerges from Aquil's study, is that while he was able to comprehend that Hindu society was composed of a landed aristocracy—the *rao, rana* and the *thakur*, a ritual-literate gentry—the brahman or the pandit, and a group of people functioning as merchants and provisioners—the *mehta* and the *saha* [Aquil, p. 183], he had no inkling about the social or cultural foundations of the normative order of castes *(varna)* among the Hindus.

On the other end of the spectrum were Muslims who were willing to treat the Hindu religion with a great deal of sympathy. For instance, Mahmud Balkhi, a traveller from the Central Asian region of Balkh visited Mathura in 1625, which he says was the seat of 'Kishan' or the 'tenth *avatar* of the Hindus'. He then goes on to describe the 'wonderful' temple dedicated to that God where 'beaming with joy, men and women, without shame mixing together but committing no impropriety, try to outdo each other in performing their rites, *rasoī* and all the *false* prayers', which Balkhi found to be such a 'sense-enhancing sight' that *'one might lose the rein of Islam and become a follower of the Hindus'* [emphasis added]. After this there follows a very rare account of the actual worship which was composed of sermons by 'Brahmans, Bairagis, Bishen (Vaishnavas) and other men of learning', followed by musicians (Kalawants) singing '*badi* and *dhrupad*' which led the congregation to 'ecstasy and great excitement'. Following a night of such devotional music, people made their ritual offerings to the temple the next morning and then returned to their 'respective homes' to engage 'in their daily affairs'[45]. Unfortunately, even such a candidly appreciative account gravitates solely around the practice of idol-worship ('false prayers') and provides nothing by way of an engagement with that society.

However, dialogic attempts to grapple with each other were not absent, as is evident from Eknath's, the sixteenth-century saint from Maharashtra, dialogue with a 'Turk' in his drama-poem *Hindu-Turk Samvād*.[46] The Muslim interlocutor accuses the Brahman (as emblematic of the Hindu) that his religion is false because they give their gods a form ('hands and legs'), worship idols ('stone statues'), and reprehensible because men and women 'all stand together' and worship, while maidens follow 'naked sadhus, clad in lemon leaves'. The *Vedas* are 'impotent books', and without exception 'your verses are unworthy'. 'You make such a hubbub when you worship. You must think God is unheeding, neglectful'. The Brahman responds by claiming the omnipresence of God 'in water, in places, in wood, in stone'. Thus 'the absolute and the image are one', but the Turk not knowing this 'is an undiscriminating fool'. The Turk shouts his devotion facing a particular direction: 'are all other directions barren?' 'You have deceived yourself about your scriptures. You have made a one-direction God'. The dialogue goes on in this fashion till both the Brahman and the Turk realise their folly through the intervention of Eknath and agree about the essential unity of being, 'oneness' of God, and self-knowledge as the path to 'great bliss'—classic tropes of medieval Bhakti syncretism.

An interesting dimension of this dialogic process was the absence of a number of markers which characterised elite discourses of Hindu–

Muslim relations: conquest, kufr, iconoclasm, and conversions. Quite clearly, fractious and accommodative discursive strategies as means of constructing community-identities emanated from two ends of the social hierarchy—the elite and the plebeian; the latter being also linguistically identified fairly early on by use of Hindavi[47] as opposed to Persian which was the language of the court and the clerics. Clearly again, the two communities struggling to carve out commonly shared spaces were not monolithic; nor were the religious precepts guiding these communities so definitive or inflexible. This was certainly true of the Muslims in the thirteenth century who, as Sunil Kumar shows, lived amidst strong sectarian conflicts between the *Sufi pir* and the 'Ulama on questions of 'praxis and dogma' and the 'authenticity of their religious practices' [Kumar, p. 151]. They were, as both Kumar and Aquil show, caught in the cleft of an elite discourse about the connection between ethnic and genealogical purity and being a good or bad Muslim. While a normative sense of what it was to be a Muslim must have been laid out quite early on [Aquil, p. 187], large numbers of the newly converted would certainly have been bereft of this and could thus easily have empathised with Eknath's *Samvād*.

Engendering Medieval India

I have referred earlier to the Turk in Eknath's *Samvād* castigating the Hindu religion for allowing women to worship with men in the open and to keep the company of semi-naked *fakirs*, and I think this provides a good backdrop to investigate the issue of gender-relations and representations of women in medieval India. The Turk's anxiety arose quite clearly from the possibility of women subverting a masculine activity like public worship by their presence or by their innate sexuality. One can then conceive of at least five patriarchal spaces where women were constructed and their 'selves' represented: the domestic, the sacred, the quotidian, the royal, and the sensual. As regards the domestic, scattered references suggest that the family was polygamous and extended, and concubinage was an accepted part of that elastic domesticity.[48] Women in aristocratic families, irrespective of their religious affiliations, were neither to be seen nor heard. This process of gender segregation had started earlier in the regions, as can be seen from Madhu Trivedi's account of the sequestered world of the love-struck *virahini* pining for her warrior-lover/husband in the *dhorahar*, the uppermost structure on top of the mansion, her designated place of residence in aristocratic families [Trivedi, p. 206][49], a norm which was incorporated into the imperial household of the Mughals late in the sixteenth century.[50] Within the family, mothers held positions of authority and reverence which had a double derivation: from brahmanical norms of deference in elite households where women were seen as emblematic of the sanctity of the family's honour, lineage and caste[51] and from the *Chingizi* custom (*buzurgdasht)* of paying obeisance to one's mother,[52] possibly for the same set of reasons with the exception of the caste-consideration. Marriages were endogamous, except in cases of men wishing to marry a woman of a lower caste[53] and made usually for political or social alliances ,and thus 'obligatory and politically instrumental in character'[54], though love could sometimes occur; but, as Trivedi shows, feelings of love or desire by the woman had to be kept firmly under control and confided only to a close circle of female confidants [Trivedi, pp. 206-207]. It would thus appear that this millennium saw the evolution of new norms of patriarchy seeking to exercise greater control over the domestic sphere by forcing an increased gender-segregation within a polygamous family. Though we have numerous references to women subverting these restrictions among a variety of social classes,[55] these acts only legitimised the existing structure of patriarchy.

The scriptural sacred space was the reserve of men. The only reference to the female gender in Al-Biruni's account of the sacrificial rituals in early medieval India is that of a mare being used in the *aśvamedha* sacrifice.[56] But the Turk's snide reference to women devotees in public gaze shows the existence of another sacred space—that of piety and popular worship where women could find a voice (for instance, Mirabai) or be represented (as in the Sikh discourse in medieval Punjab)[57]. Therefore the discursive structure of the Bhakti movement seems to have permitted some latitude for women to negotiate zones of ambiguity between patriarchal values and religious beliefs; but it is unclear as to what extent it allowed autonomous agency to the woman. Mirabai subverted the paradigm of conjugality by refusing to cohabit with her husband, but faithfully replicated the notions of wifely devotion in her love for Krishna and accepted all the patriarchal prescriptions of proper behaviour for women: faithful, deferential and pious (for married women), and austere, celibate and ascetic (for widows).[58] The Sikh discourse allowed more space to women by protesting against the gender-discriminatory practices in brahmanical society and enabled their direct access to God, but glorified motherhood (the 'maternal image' in Sikh texts) and embellished the discursive strategy 'with an abundance of bridal imagery'[59] which may have actually resulted in a substantial vindication of existing norms of patriarchy. Notions of love and fidelity, even when couched in divine terms, implicate and perpetuate patriarchy.[60] Madhu Trivedi's paper provides enough information to show how such ideas, so deeply embedded in the *Sufic-hindavi* texts, transposed the idiom of divine love into the corporeal world and created a specifically medieval conception of love as devotion (*seva*), and sublimation to a marital structure (*suhag*) of patriarchy.

In the quotidian world the situation was characterised by greater ambivalences. For instance, among the rural gentry in the Punjab, women's rights of inheritance were honoured, and we have instances of Hindu and Muslim women inheriting zamindaris which they were free to sell or mortgage as they chose.[61] Invidious gender-segregation seems to have been relatively weaker at the relatively lower ends of society. In Rajasthan, widow remarriage (*nata*) among artisanal communities appears to have been in vogue though its scale and effect on the position of widows in general appears uncertain.[62] In the normative world of the Indian household, the *grihasti*, the male was the head,[63] but social conditions of labour ensured a substantial degree of labour-related convergences between the genders. With the growth of nucleated villages and expansion in individuated peasant-farming, which characterised medieval Indian agriculture, the basic prop of production became the labour and resources of the entire household. Naturally, a gendered-segregation between the home (for women) and the world (for men) was not always possible in this context. While some critical functions of domesticity—like motherhood or child-rearing—could have only been a woman's prerogative, social activity seems to have been more gender-friendly, though it has been recently suggested by Sahai that domestic chores tended to relegate women to the invisible margins[64]; but that could break down periodically as women and men had to work shoulder-to-shoulder in the fields. The men tilled and ploughed, while women sowed, weeded, threshed and winnowed the harvest. The more commercialised the product, the more presumably would be the demand on women's labour to produce it.

There was another aspect of peasant production which worked against the segregation of women, as was the wont in elite households. Practically each peasant household combined agriculture with some degree of craft production. Spinning and cotton-ginning were done at the peasants' homes exclusively by the women. Women artisans like *chippi* (dyer) were vital in dyeing the fabric, *kumharan* (potter) kneaded and prepared the clay, and the *chamarin* (leather-worker) embroidered intricate designs on leather goods like shoes and saddles.[65] We also come across womenfolk of indigent Brahmins in rural Bengal constrained to eke out an existence by spinning thread, a vocation usually practised by the lower caste peasant-women of there area.[66] Here again, there were some limits on the extent women could enter the world of the artisanal production. In the textile sector, which expanded remarkably in this period, women could act as dyers and printers, but the actual process of weaving was a male preserve [Vijaya Ramaswamy, p. 284]. A functional gender-segregation existed in the craft sector on grounds of certain rules of purity and the belief that an infringement would destroy the success of a cycle of craft production.[67]

However, these ambivalences in the quotidian posed no challenge to existing patriarchal structures so long as the *organisation* of production remained patriarchal [Ramaswamy, pp. 283-285]. The medieval state reinforced patriarchy by not allowing women the autonomy of litigating disputes on their own and by grading marriages in a way where remarried widows were not assigned a similar status as the wife from the primary marriage.[68]

Gender relations in the royal domain straddled the domestic and the sacred worlds, both of which have been discussed earlier. Mirabai is symbolic of the two worlds—the domestic world of 'feudal' patriarchy and the sacred world of a masculine devotionalism. Gender-exclusion into the deep interiors of the household, polygamy, child-marriage, prohibitions on widow remarriage and *sati* were some of the bridge-areas between the domestic and the sacral in the royal households of medieval India.[69] Muslim households could be differentiated from Hindu ones perhaps only on the basis of the non-prevalence of *sati* in them.

However, one may note two developments in this millennium which had a direct bearing on the construction of the woman in the sensual world. The first, as Daud Ali shows, occurred in the early medieval courts, when bodily attributes of 'grace and playfulness' were integrated into courtly conceptions of romance. This involved the construction, in contemporary dramaturgical literature, of a 'feminine' space embodying *lila* (grace) and a masculine space of *vilasa* (sportiveness) and its combination in a 'common code of courtship and romance, which entailed a set of playful "sportive" gestures' [Ali, p. 86]. The second, as developed by Madhu Trivedi, was the elaborate construction of love (*ishq*) in the Sufi *Premakhyans* composed between the fourteenth and the sixteenth century. Taken together, these constitute the sensual, which constructed a woman of refinement through a set of mundane devices—the passions of the nubile, the ideals of a married woman, and the anxieties occurring in a society given to polygamy.

The ultimate embodiment of *lila* was the woman characterised in such texts as *padmini*, who 'with a body of golden hue and divine radiance' embodied all the 'sixteen' graces (*solah kala*) of ultimate womanhood. But the ultimate woman was also meant to control her sexuality, and here the early medieval notions of a 'sportive' love seems to have morphed into a medieval notion of love as the 'devoted service of *sati*' [Trivedi, p. 207]. The recurring theme of these texts is the existence and controlling of desire.[70] The sexual longing of the young woman (*joban*) was to be strictly controlled and sublimated only though the institution of marriage, where the woman loved though service (*seva*) of her man, which set the framework of her happiness (*sukh-bhog*), leading to the ultimate consummation (*kam-lila*) after an elaborate range of sportive activity which included dice and coquettish conversation and gestures [Trivedi, p. 209]. A change seems to have occurred over the medieval centuries whereby the immensely sensual and public (dramaturgical and courtly) conceptions of love where metamorphosed into a domestic activity.

Trivedi's evidence thus shows what these male authors of Sufic literary texts construed to be the ideal woman or the perfect man–woman relationship. Her evidence is also rich with indications of the 'other' women—the obverse of the devout *padmini* of these narratives. The idea of the *parkiya*—a woman who had sexual dalliances with married man, seems to have become everyone's fantasy, considering she became a major theme in contemporary paintings. *Paturs* entertained by singing and acting (*swang*, *bahurup*, etc.), while the *ganikas* sold sexual services for a price. Despite its plebeian origins, *paturbazi* became incorporated into the culture of the medieval north Indian elite [Trivedi, pp. 214–217], thus bestowing some sort of legitimacy on plebeian femininity and demonstrating the multiple points of cultural transmission in medieval India.

Cultures: Emulation, Transmission and Diffusion

In his classic study, 'Diffusion of Cultural Patterns in Medieval Europe'[71], Georges Duby had shown how cultures display many-ended modes of existence and what appears to be homogenous and monolithic at one stage may actually be a product of a slow and non-hierarchic incorporation of multiple strands. Our millennium offers numerous examples of the multiplicities of cultural transmission. For instance, a whole linguistic world existed between the Persianate paradigms of the court and the world situated outside of it. Learning Persian was desirable, but the literate world of medieval Indian was not seamlessly Persian. To be a *pandit* one needed to know 'Sanskrit, Prakrit, Pali, Apbhransh, Dingal and Pingal' [Trivedi, p. 201] and not Persian. Hindu and Muslim gentries in rural or semi-urban areas of eastern Awadh spoke *theth* (pure) Awadhi, 'an idiom practically free from Arabo-Persian vocabulary'[72], which may have created an intermediate cultural space inhabited indiscriminately by both communities, whereas *hindavi* both written (*likhi*) and spoken (*goi*) enabled textual traditions like the *Premakhyans* to emerge as shared cultural spaces between such groups and the plebeians over much of northern India. Therefore the much-celebrated cultural syncretism of this millennium seems to have occurred from the intermeshing of high, intermediate and the folk (even plebeian) cultures and their diffusion in each other.

Even the rarefied heights of the imperial court were not immune to such cultural cross-flows. The charisma of the emperor, his god-like visage as he sat in the *jharoka*, and the 'overt sensuality' of some of the festivities at the Mughal court (for example, the celebration of the spring festival of *Holi*), were all derived from folkloric traditions. So was the great faith that all emperors had in soothsaying, astrology and prognostication. The propensity of emperors to visit Sufi *khanqas* and the assemblies of Hindu *jogis* implicated them with folk traditions.[73]

At the top, cultural trends were, like fashion, hugely aspirational. What the emperors did in Agra or Shahjahanabad was intently watched and emulated in the provinces. If the emperors built gardens, palaces and hospices, their satraps did the same in the regions; if the emperors patronised libraries or ateliers of artists, so did their Muslim and Rajput nobles [Catherine Asher, pp. 223–226]. The emulations did not mean cultural cloning. For instance, Asher draws our attention to the Govinda Deva temple constructed at the behest of the Kacchwaha chief Man Singh, which had vaults and pillars along the lines built at Fatehpur Sikri with motifs in red sandstone, but 'were more innovative' in execution than the Akbari model [Asher, p. 226].

Emulation also had a time lag and involved subtle inversions. For instance, Enhbom argues that the style of painting in Mewar did not incorporate Mughal influences till the 1650s despite the very close proximity between the Kacchwahas and the Mughals, and even when it did, it was tilted more towards the Akbari model rather than the Shah Jahani style in vogue by that time.[74] If Akbar's Muslim noble Abd al-Rahim Khan i-Khanan patronised Persian, Man Singh patronised Sanskrit. Further away from the centre such inversions could go deeper. Man Singh's palace at Rohtas used Akbari motifs and had a *hammam*, which was a Muslim not a Rajput tradition; it also had a *jharoka*, but in a Sanskrit inscription in the same building Man Singh invoked his authority as the chief of the Kacchwaha Rajputs and omitted Akbar's name altogether [Asher, p. 227]. Sometimes the emulation-inversion syndrome was quite in the face. Jai Singh conceived of a new capital to emulate Shah Jahan shifting his capital from Agra to Shahjahanabad, but he consecrated his new city of Jaipur with Vedic rituals and two *aśvamedha* sacrifices. His documents did not use the Mughal honorific Mirza Raja as it denoted a kinship relation with the Mughals, but instead declared allegiance to the deity Sita Ram, and not to any Mughal overlord [Asher, p. 236]. This was not *fitna* as the loyalty of Kacchwahas was never questioned, but it was instead, what Asher calls, 'code-switching, that is wearing multiple hats concurrently' [Asher, p. 236], a common activity among the regional magnates of the eighteenth century.

Yet the new city of Jaipur was planned and built to house 'multi-religious communities' and was populated by providing incentives of free land without favouring one community or discriminating against another. It is here that one gets a living example of the transmission of the Mughal *urbane* ethos into a regional setting. Mughal cities like Agra or Delhi were not designed as Islamic cities but were conceived, as Stephen Blake argues, as symbols of the empire's patrimonial spirit—as pluralist havens to all communities who were the subjects of the Emperor.[75] The city of Jaipur had an 'ecumenical spirit' [Asher, p. 239] which was both plural and inclusive: a place that allowed space for all communities to live and worship and no primacy was assigned to a single faith. But it was commissioned by a Hindu ruler who saw no contradiction between his vision of a *dharmic* city and the idea of a secular habitat, just as there was no contradiction between the Jami' Masjid in Shahjahanabad and the inclusive nature of city's layout.[76] Jaipur is testimony to the momentous significance of the patterns of cultural diffusion and cultural vibrancy of the millennium.

The World of Commerce

Vibrancy and accommodation characterised maritime trade of early medieval India, argues Ranabir Chakravarti and provides a critique of the perception of the Indian economy as moribund and closed before the arrival of the Turks in the thirteenth century. He shows instead a certain reorientation in the oceanic profile in early medieval India which was characterised by the decline of some important ports in eastern, peninsular and western India; and by a simultaneous rise of new trading centres and ports in these same places. A further sophistication is suggested by the emergence of the *mandapika* or *mandi* as a 'new type of exchange centre' and as a point of intermediation between the village market—the *hattika,* and the urban markets—*pattana* or *velakula* [Chakravarti, pp. 255–256]. Chakravarti also rejects the characterisation of this trade as peddling activity, or of its insignificance on grounds that it was overwhelmingly oriented towards luxury goods. He shows instead that trade comprised a diverse range of commodities, including basic staples and horses, and was being conducted by a whole range of merchants, starting from merchant-princes at the top to petty itinerant *vyaparis* at the village level [Chakravarti, pp. 257–260]. The brahmanical prohibitions against crossing the seas were only normative, as Indian merchants from the western coast and the peninsula sailed in a great arc from the western end of the Indian Ocean (*bahr Larvi* of the Arab seafarers) to its eastern end (the *bahr Harkal*).

Inscriptional and textual evidences are replete with words like *mahanavika*, *navikarmakra*, *sitapatra* and *nauvittaka*, which show that maritime activity was a durable occupational and wealth-generating occupation [Chakravarti, pp. 263–265]. The other striking aspect which Chakravarti delineates is that the Indian Ocean was bound together by four points of unity—by the monsoons, by ships made of wooden planks and held together by coconut coir, by the striking ethnic mix of people trading in these waters, and by the economic and cultural centrality of India in this entire complex. All this changed from the sixteenth century, when European intrusion into the high seas ruptured the earlier 'pluralist, tolerant and assimilative' tenor of the Ocean and replaced it with violent, monopolistic and coercive methods of trading [Chakravarti, pp. 266–267].

The centrality of the Indian Ocean in pre-industrial maritime trade is no longer in question and Chakravarti's essay amply testifies to its long antecedents, and as far as our millennium was concerned, this long-term and incremental process of maritime involvement gives it a specific historical uniqueness. Historiographically, it allows rethinking on two fronts: first, the idea that the early medieval was a period of economic and commercial contraction; and second, the Turkish irruption marked a qualitatively different break in the Indian tradition.[77] One must remember that by the thirteenth century, the Indian Ocean was already deeply implicated in Islam's political, commercial and urban structures stretching over the vast swathes of territory in west and central Asia. Therefore, apart from the Jewish *nakhuda* (ship owner) being replaced by the Muslim Karimi merchant [Chakravarti, p. 263], the establishment of the Delhi Sultanate barely altered the structures and processes of maritime activity up to the sixteenth century. But the post-thirteenth century phase did see a quickening of the pace of India's maritime commerce, particularly along the western coast, with spice trading now emerging as the big commercial venture and with craft techniques and knowledge brought by emigrating Muslim artisans striking deeper roots with increasing conversions of local communities to Islam along the coastal frontiers.[78] Trade, particularly in spices, brought in good money, but costs of state-building and the import of horses took it out in equal measure, and only successful plundering raids over western and southern India by the Sultans could have brought about much of the acclaimed monetisation of the thirteenth century.[79] It was not before the end of the sixteenth century that the silver shortages characteristic of the first seven hundred years of this millennium were actually broken by the 'discovery' of the 'New' World which converged with the expanding output of silver from the Japanese mines.[80]

It is this huge monetary expansion due to the availability of silver bullion from the sixteenth century onwards that makes me somewhat sceptical about arguments regarding the negative impact of European seafaring. The Portuguese were entirely dependent on pre-existing networks and Indian merchants cooperated with them to take advantage of their presence. On the whole, Portuguese intrusion caused only a minor disturbance on the Ocean's placid waters,[81] and once the waves caused by their carracks had settled, the Indian Ocean trade, particularly Gujarati shipping on both its ends expanded considerably. Surat, Acheh, Bantam and Macassar emerged more vigorously as focal points of a vigorous Asian commerce. This was an age of 'partnership' in the Indian Ocean and all partners—Asian or European—abided by the traditionally established commercial rules and practices. The European presence did not alter this *structure*. The carrying trade was never monopolized; it was, on the contrary, shared by all concerned.[82] Indian ports continued to play a central role in these networks, and they were also its main beneficiaries: the silver which circulated in the Indian Ocean came to India and was used for Indian ends.

Artisans and Manufacturers

It is in this context that one has to locate the massive expansion in artisanal activity, one of the concerns of Vijaya Ramaswamy's essay, which occurred for two reasons: first, the massive expansion of European commerce and second, the rise of a new class of consumers—nobles and officialdom—in Vijayanagara and in the Deccani sultanates [Ramaswamy, pp. 276–277]. European demand stimulated manufactures for export, while the indigenous elite in these Deccani kingdoms 'brought new styles into fashion such as doublets, embroidered jackets and turbans' and stimulated the manufacture of metalware and diamonds [Ramaswamy, p. 278][83]. With the expansion as a backdrop, Ramaswamy's main concern shifts elsewhere—in a historical sociology of the artisans, particularly the double articulation of caste and community in peninsular India. Expanding commercial economy and production systems touched different sections of manufacturers differently.

She proposes a social separation between artisans and craftspeople as 'two different kinds of economies' since they represented two different kinds of manufacturing processes in pre-colonial India. The artisans were more skilled, were socially mobile and had better access to technology compared to craftspeople who 'lived in the village community with a certain degree of relative physical immobility, socio-economic security and comparatively static living standards' [Ramaswamy, p. 278]. The former were composed of different *jatis* but jointly constituted the Viswakarma *kula* (community) and reaped the maximum social and economic benefits from expanding overseas trade, a consolidating temple-economy and expanding clientele in the peninsula.

Taking issue with the idea that caste was a barrier to technological or other forms of productive innovation, Ramawamy sees a more filtered response by the artisans to new technology as the appropriate way of understanding the problem. According to her, artisans rejected or accepted new technologies on their assessment of what was appropriate to specific environmental conditions [Ramaswamy, p. 287], and the standard response of artisans to expanding economic opportunities was a proliferation of occupational sub-groups (*jaitis*) which made the caste system flexible and adaptive to new techniques and technologies [Ramaswamy, p. 290]. Economic enrichment allowed the Vishwakarma community to wrest some social privileges under Vijayanagara rule, and they emerged as temple donors for the first time; but these were never enough to pacify their aspirations. The latter led to two further developments: first, the growth of tensions between the artisanal *jatis*, for instance, between the Kamalars and the Kaikolars taking the form of the famous left-hand/right-hand (*idangai-valangai*) disputes, and second, the rise of successful social protest movements like the Vira Saivites and the Lingayats against the caste system [Ramaswamy, pp. 291–294].

Ramaswamy's essay places the peninsula squarely within a range of similar developments occurring elsewhere in India and thus allows us to see the pan-Indian nature of the commercial and manufacturing expansion between the sixteenth and the eighteenth century. The literature on the expansion of manufacturing, particularly textile manufacturing, in this period is huge and growing[84] and its connection with European trade is indisputable. European ships sailed out of India twice a year (once in September and another between January and March) and thus lengthened the weaving season by creating two peak seasons instead of the one which had prevailed so far for the weavers.[85] The economic implications of such massive expansion in trade have yet to be worked out for India as a whole, but they are likely to have been positive. On the basis of Dutch records of the early eighteenth century, Om Prakash visualises the impact as an expansion of 'income, output and employment' at the subcontinental level. In Bengal alone, he estimates that full-time employment opportunities in the artisanal sector increased at least by 10 per cent by the middle of the century.[86] Though he discounts any inflationary impact of this massive influx of bullion, a rise in prices of commodities like rice and sugar is suggested in the prices of provisions listed in the purchases made by the English

Company around Calcutta in the eighteenth century.[87] This would suggest that increases in money supply occasioned by larger and larger amounts of silver-bullion being pumped into the economy might have led to a *simultaneous* rise in output and prices in Bengal and elsewhere, since Parthasarathi has recently detected a similar tendency on the Coromandel from the 1720s.[88]

Thus a massive expansion of output was achieved without major improvements in technology in the textile sector, but the Indian artisan was not averse to the absorption of new technologies. With the possible exceptions of book printing and the blast-furnaces, most of the other technological innovations that spread across the globe (like weaving, cotton printing, paper, gunpowder, firearms and so on) and improved manufacturing capacities in the early modern period found an immediate acceptance in India or were disseminated with a small time-lag.[89] Even in the more remote areas of that time, like Jharkhand, tribal ironsmiths were using bellows and furnaces to make iron implements and weapons.[90]

From the point of view of production, one important feature of the economy of India was the dispersal of a multitude of productive and commercial functions below the level of the town and their concentration in centres scattered over a wide variety of intermediate townships (*qasbas*) and in the larger villages (*dehat* or *gaon*), which together comprised a web of interconnected production centres dotting the face of the country across interwoven trade routes. Together, these gave to a rise to a rural-commercial economy that incorporated the village and the intermediate, or 'rurban' economies into a composite whole. Under such conditions of expansion, the separation between artisans and craftspeople (i.e. between urban and rural artisans) which Ramaswamy introduces to delineate almost two worlds of aritsanal activity would not have worked or would have certainly broken down. Its continued existence would have required a degree of isolation of the countryside and of the rural craft-producer from the impulses of the external world, which in the case of India in the period between the sixteenth and eighteenth centuries seems highly unlikely.[91]

Such processes created their own tensions. Ramaswamy documents intra-community and inter-community stresses which, in the peninsula at least, seem to have assumed significant proportions. Weavers and petty-artisans constituted the base of popular movements protesting against caste and other forms of social exploitation which erupted over much of northern India in the same period. These social reform movements were radical and their discursive strategies were admirably non-partisan and pluralist, and yet, with the exception of the Sikhs, these monotheistic and radical movements were transitory and failed to make a dent in the caste system. A recent survey of these movements suggests that their failure lay in their combined institutional and organisational failure against which the apparent success of the Sikhs at creating a *panth* stands out in striking contrast.[92] An earlier explanation of their failure had suggested that the internalisation and assimilation of the ideology of the ruling classes by these protestors had sapped these movements[93] thus impeding the growth of more subversive strategies; but the Sikh movement suggests that such a breakout was possible, though the extent of its success against caste divisions is open to question.[94] Perhaps equally germane would be to ask whether there were certain other constraints in the modes of protest and resistance in pre-colonial India which militated against such structural inversions.

Protest, Resistance and the Power of Silence

Dilbagh Singh's paper provides a good empirical context to examine this issue. Singh uses resistance, particularly the 'everyday forms of resistance' adopted by rural communities as a way of examining 'the material basis of class relation and class struggle'. He argues that though the material context of such forms of resistance may be as mundane as the urge to enhance income, they land up questioning the legitimacy of the state/ruling class [Singh, p. 301]. In the context of eighteenth-century eastern Rajasthan, he finds that almost all sections of rural society were defaulting on their financial obligations to the state, 'thereby raising the question of real magnitude of land revenue and relationship between the state's claim over surplus produce and its actual payment in practice'. This was facilitated by three reasons: first, multiplicity of methods of assessment; second, the existence of several categories of cultivable land in villages; and third, inter-cropping as a dominant form of agricultural production [Singh, p. 303]. The more affluent cultivators, which also included the village headmen (*patel*) and the merchant-moneylenders (*bania*), cultivated cash-crops and primary staples at the same time, but used the inter-cropping loophole to keep the benefits of the former to themselves. Lower down the social scale, village artisans and menials (called *kamins*), who were given lands at concessional terms of revenue also colluded with the upper caste peasants to avoid paying taxes which were due from them [Singh, pp. 304–306].

Cheating the state thus appears as an all-caste, all-community practice. It took various forms, and was deemed a perfectly justified way of resisting the state's demands by the cultivating classes even though it was strictly illegal in the eyes of the former. For the peasants defaulting on the state's revenue by understating the area under cultivation, or the crops grown on it, or by colluding with the state's revenue officials were means to enhance income and thus of enrichment.

On its part, the state tried to prevent such acts by exhorting its officials to be more vigilant, gathering information about peasants and their resources, and by levying hefty fines as when such cases were detected. Significantly, Singh's essay shows that coercion, physical torture or eviction are conspicuously absent from the list of state action against such erring peasants.

Though conflicts over the distribution of the surplus were as much a part of peasant existence as the agricultural cycle dictated by the monsoons, they have not received as much attention as they ought to have by modern historians since their preoccupation has mostly been with overt forms of resistance—specifically, armed peasant rebellions—towards the end of the seventeenth century. The other assumption is that of an inert, impoverished peasantry crushed under the burden of the heavy fiscal hand of the state, revolting only when the pressure became unbearable.[95] Quite apart from the irreconcilable problem of balancing this image of an impoverished peasantry with the picture of an expanding *agricultural* and commercial economy in the Mughal period, the evidence from the regions seems to point in a contrary direction: that of a stratified peasantry, reaping the benefits of an expanding economy and resisting the state in a myriad of ways including an axis of interests with the rural landed-gentry (the *zamindar*) in order to protect these gains.[96]

What do we fathom from the nature of these conflicts? They can be understood in two ways. First, following Harbans Mukhia, we see that conflicts in medieval India, whether silent or violent, centred on the sharing of the surplus between the state and the peasant and did not at any stage involve the redistribution of the means of production because of the specific nature of property-relations in India. Despite the many external constraints on them, the Indian peasants were 'free' in an economic sense because they were the owners of what they possessed and there was no extraneous control over their *processes* of production, unlike medieval Europe, where both were situated under the lord's domain. There the conflicts were more class-oriented (in an orthodox Marxian sense)[97]. In India, violent conflicts led to the further consolidation of older forms of property (as happened in the eighteenth-century regimes), whereas silent struggles allowed the cultivators to enhance their income (as Singh argues in his essay). In either case, the external appearance would that be of long-term stability.

In any case, the relationship between the state and its subjects, particularly in the countryside was a combination of fractiousness and accommodation, as I had argued earlier, and Singh's essay points to the quiet existence of both in the countryside. For the state, its fiscal interests were primary and manifested themselves in a 'growing extraneous interference and control over the process of production' [Singh, p. 308], but whether an intrusive fiscality and concern for revenue is the same as exerting extraneous control of the 'process' of production remains a moot point. Ujjayan Bhattacharya's analysis of the early British fiscal regime provides enough ground to situate an explicit difference between the two.

The second way lies in conceptualising the medieval producer as a member of a social collectivity first and an individual later.[98] This set the boundaries of social action and conflicts and introduced corporate mechanisms to reconcile these conflicts within the framework of reciprocal obligations and norms of acceptable behaviour. Recent research has argued that tensions in rural society were often resolved through more participative and collaborative processes in which the state and communities interfaced within a framework of caste-specific qasi-judicial institutions, the *jati panchayats*. The administration saw these organisations as essential to maintain social order. They were routinely consulted by the state in all disputes and their powers enhanced to preserve social stability.[99] These *jati panchayats* were not seen as competitors by the state but as devices of collaboration, which enabled the state to exercise power over communities by allowing them safety-valves to resolve tensions within the twin frameworks of caste and customary practices. This ensured that conflicts seldom assumed uncontrollable proportions. It is quite possible that these safety-valves were momentarily ruptured during the closing years of the seventeenth century with disastrous consequences for the Mughal state.

Perhaps it is significant that even under the severe disposition of early British rule, when the norms of governance were being inexorably turned around from custom to the tyranny of an impersonal law [Kolff, pp. 63–64], we find official sources in Bengal in the 1780s discussing the existence of a village 'oligarchy' being led by a person—a headman—known as *mandal*, who was 'elected' by consensus among the village elders, and this choice was later ratified by the *zamindar*. They were to hold their office as long as they enjoyed the confidence of the general body of the villagers, failing which they could be dismissed by the *zamindar*. The chief functions of this person were to assist in the preparation of village accounts, to oversee the conduct of members of the village community, and 'chiefly to prevent any offence against their caste'. In addition, in eastern India at least, all marriages and other 'civil' ceremonies were to be held in the presence of the *mandal* who was paid a specified fee (usually revenue-free land) for his services.[100]

But there was now a major difference. In their anxiety to pacify the countryside, early British administrators perceived these institutions as conflict-mongering instead of conflict-resolving and thus unleashed processes to annihilate them. As a recent study of the Rangpur *dhing* (uprising) of 1783 has shown, there was nothing specifically anti-colonial about the intentions of the rebels. The rebellion was 'merely one instance in the everyday process of engagement with a range of competing points of authority', and the peasants believed that the political order which the Collector oversaw depended on his ability to fulfill their expectation of justice; but during the course of the *dhing* the 'peasant's fluid and pluralistic way of conceiving the rural world' collided with a completely different way of perceiving and structuring power and authority in rural Bengal.[101] This was a new feature, and by no means an easy process, but the fiscal logic of early colonialism[102] would achieve it by reorienting state-society relations, particularly in rural Bengal, in most fundamental of ways. This was a very significant moment and fittingly has come to occupy a significant position in standard interpretations of this transition.

The Colonial 'Break'

Two questions arise: did the conquest of eastern India by the English East India Company mark an abrupt closure of the social trends over this millennium; or did some of these trends modify and reconfigure themselves to suit this new dispensation? Ujjayan Bhattacharya's essay enters into the core of the Company's efforts to craft a new type of military-fiscal edifice and brings centre stage the intermeshing of politics, land-revenue, indigenous gentry and the financial imperatives of the Company which together constituted, to use Wilson's words, a 'complex set of contingent forces that constituted the [early] colonial encounter'[103].

Bhattacharya traces the consolidation of a 'non-traditional revenue-receiving gentry' who, through a combination of commercial ventures and revenue farming emerged as the 'new' landed-proprietors in post-1760 Bengal. Such people began their intrusion in the 'old' world of landed property through revenue farming (*ijaradari*) but they 'prefaced their ventures', since the early 1740s, by a prior process of 'accumulating substantial assets in land', directly through purchases in order to 'establish their reputations as men of substantial wealth, credit and goodwill in society' and used the already existing 'institutional structures for transactions relating to landed property' [Bhattacharya, pp. 316-317]. As to what motivated such people, who had 'wide options with regard to their investment and careers' to invest in revenue-farming and acquisition of land, Bhattacharya looks at 'exogenous' and 'endogenous' explanations: 'capital accumulated through commerce was invested in revenue management (the exogenous factor) and that capital chose to move into this direction because land had a value (the endogenous factor) due to an expanding agrarian economy within which acquisition of property on a substantial scale meant a degree of power to control rental receipts' [Bhattacharya, pp. 318–319].

Bhattacharya takes a close look at one such 'new' family—the Ghoshals of Bhukailash—who moved through the commercial world (as salt traders under the Nizamat) into the Company's fiscal apparatus and used both to leverage massive acquisitions of landed property all over Bengal. In the post-1760 phase, commercial families like the Ghoshals (and there were many such families in Bengal) latched on the new opportunities being provided to diversify their businesses into land by using a reciprocal arrangement with Bengal's new masters: 'rendering of service and acceptance of assignments as rewards'. Men like Gocul Ghoshal 'were quick to realise the economic potential of their agrarian assignments and acquired as much as they could [and] the Company assisted their ventures with sufficient legal cloaks, unless stretched beyond the limits set by their own norms', and Bhattacharya's study shows that these 'norms' were indeed very flexible, thus allowing families such as the Ghoshal(s) to acquire extensive landed properties in various parts of Bengal (and of course in Calcutta) [Bhattacharya, pp. 332–335].

Bhattacharya's essay documents the formation of landed-gentry in early colonial Bengal and provides a forum to consider one of the most vital problems of the eighteenth century in Indian history: that of persistence and transformation under early colonialism. Bhattacharya's study shows that the problem of gentry-formation in the late eighteenth century can hardly be explained though the application of some perverse norms of revenue maximisation.[104] Rising agricultural prices throughout this period knocked-off pressures of uncertain assessments[105] and the Company's policy from the 1780s shifted, as Bhattacharya says, towards a 'hunt for resources': looking for productive assets within a small area through measurement that could secure a [landholder's] profits and facilitate collection of revenue without incurring high costs' [Bhattacharya, p. 328]. The capitalised value of landed property continued to appreciate. Zamindaris and *talluqdaris* could fetch five times the *jama* (assessed revenue) while the sale of revenue-free land (*la-kharaj*) could easily be worth ten times its estimated produce, prices which appear strikingly high in a situation where a sale price equal to two years *jama* was considered to be of good value in the market.[106] Some proprietors became bankrupt and many properties disintegrated, but new ones were formed with equal speed.

That post-1760 Bengal had many routes, perhaps more than before, which allowed fresh entrants into a traditionally exclusive club of landed proprietors is summed up in the somewhat introspective note of the Board of Revenue that no matter what, 'a new set of men will be set up, who will claim property to which they have no title, at the expense of those who are already admitted to possess, or supposed to have, a right in the soil.[107] Thus on the eve of the Permanent Settlement, enterprising people could enter through 'purchases, misrepresentations, evictions and usurpations'; corruption came easy in a situation where new money was looking for profitable outlets; but *'long custom & possession'*[108] still continued to have a strong sway, as did purely economic considerations of investing in something which appreciated in value over time. There are thus reasonable grounds to argue that the early colonialism continued older forms of property but widened the net of property owners who saw land as a capital asset and a viable commercial option. Therefore could early colonialism be a part of early modern capitalist processes in India?

Early Modernity, Capitalism and the End of the Millennium

In an innovative essay, Prasannan Parthasarathi invokes a question, which expended vast amounts of historical energies in the 1970s, viz. was there capitalism in pre-British India? For Parthsarathi, this question is important from three historiographical concerns: first, a growing discomfort with the 'seamless' notion of the medieval from eighth to eighteenth century; second, an increasing uneasiness with the traditional notions of long-term economic stability in India compared with the rapidity of changes in the world after 1500; and third, a new sense of convergence between developments overtaking Europe after 1500 which 'ran parallel' with changes in India [Parthasarathi, p. 345]. The fourth issue, which lies embedded in the question Parthasarathi raises, is the validity of the term 'capitalism' itself for the world before 1800.

To get his markers in order, Parthasarathi argues that the timeline of the genesis of capitalism as a world-system from the sixteenth century *pace* Wallerstein[109] cannot hold because structural conditions of production were still largely pre-capitalist in form. An agriculture, where peasants were 'smallholders', and a 'largely household-oriented' production system still dominated the economy. Huge unemployment or underemployment existed, and productivity increases could occur only through more intensive work regimes in post-Enclosure Britain and not because of sustained improvements or capitalisation. Agricultural productivity could not meet demands for food, which had to be imported, leading to a decline in the living standards of wage earners [Parthasarathi, pp. 347, 352].

In India, high commercial levels were characteristic of the same period. The economy was highly monetised and there was no shortage of cash or credit to push businesses forward. However, long-term economic trends were characterised by the 'apparent stability of both the agrarian and manufacturing sectors', partly (and here Parthasarathi agrees with Mukhia), because of high agricultural fertility and low subsistence levels, and partly because the state played a major role in agriculture by providing capital, incentives and concessions, which became the means 'by which political authorities and dominant classes managed conflict in the countryside' but were less involved in 'managing the impact of the world economy' [Parthasarathi, pp. 354–356][110]. This, for Parthasarathi, was the *differentia specifica* of Europe's trajectory in the early modern phase. Here the state emerged as the greatest manager of an expanding world economy by actively inserting itself as the defender of domestic industries, by legislating in favour of private property and business enterprises, and by enacting laws limiting wages, apprenticeship and contracts in favour of employers or owners. The state encouraged local manufacturing with imported raw materials by enacting protectionist legislations, and the greatest advantages were seized by the cotton and iron industries in Britain [Parthasarathi, pp. 352–353]. In contrast, India's massive participation in the world economy 'reinforced agrarian stability', with the Mughal state doing nothing more than being a passive bystander, and therefore becoming a 'political failure' [Parthasarathi, p. 357]. If capitalism is a misnomer in the case of early modern Europe, it is a case of missing the bus in early modern India.

The innovativeness of Parthasarathi's essay makes it an apt case to look at the closure of the millennium in an economic sense, and to ask whether the late eighteenth century made a difference. There is no doubt that the world was much more coeval before the nineteenth century. Recent revisions in British economic history suggest that an effective spurt in industrial growth occurred only after 1815, and not in the 1760s and 1770s, once considered the conventional starting points of the Industrial Revolution.[111] Spain hardly invested the treasure it acquired in the development of the Spanish economy, losing sometimes as high as 40 per cent of its American wealth directly to the Philippines,[112] while those countries, like England and Holland, which became the core areas of Europe's economic expansion, hardly engaged in the colonial extraction of bullion. France, for instance, was scarcely affected by the excitement of New World silver: 'gold was never used. Even silver coinage was sometimes too strong a currency'; billon currency circulated sluggishly.[113] While European currencies suffered periodic bouts of debasement, leading to severe short-term increases in the price of goods, (a fate which even China could not escape in the seventeenth century)[114], the silver currency of Mughal India was never debased between 1556 and 1707,[115] not even during the massive monetary crisis which convulsed much of Eurasia in the mid-seventeenth century.[116]

A convergent understanding informs Kenneth Pomeranz's impressive comparative study of economic conditions prevailing in early modern Europe and China which strongly refutes entrenched ideas of the innate superiority of north-western Europe from the more advanced regions of Asia (particularly China, Japan, India and south-east Asia) in terms of life expectancy, wages, standards of living, and patterns of consumption of both preciosities as well as ordinary goods. He further shows that property rights in land and processes of mercantile accumulation from commerce were coeval, and that markets and market-transactions had a very close and significant bearing in determining the fate of economies. What made the difference swing in favour of Europe, and that too quite late in the eighteenth and early nineteenth century, was Europe's *conjunctural* ability to break free of ecological and technical constraints posed by the hiatus between limited quantities of productive land and a rising population. 'Europe's escape' says Pomeranz, 'required... various favourable global conjunctures...'. The two elements of this conjuncture were: the use of its abundant supplies of coal which allowed the use of greater funds of energy to be harnessed in critical industries like iron production and transportation; and the New World metal and plantation complex, which provided Europe with the windfall of silver, along with cheap calories in the form of sugar and sources of raw cotton for the mills in Lancashire and Manchester.[117]

Obviously, the state would have a minimal presence in these conjunctural moments but would be instrumental in causing a successful conversion of the conjunctural into the structural by facilitating, what Marx called, 'the historical preconditions for the formation of manufacture', namely, 'the growth of the market, the accumulation of capital, the modification of the social position of the classes [and] a large number of persons being deprived from their source of income'[118] something with the Mughals state patently failed to do.

But notions of long-term stability based on low subsistence levels have their own problems for various reasons. First, society was stratified. Though the principal axis of stratification was caste, there are enough grounds to show caste restrictions did not impede capital accumulation or technological innovations. In fact, Ramaswamy's essay provides ample opportunities to visualise the accumulation of sizeable capitals in the hands of intermediate caste groups, and there can be no doubt about merchant and artisan capital underpinning the great economic expansion in the seventeenth and the eighteenth century. Second, systems of land tenure based on private ownership and a reasonably brisk market in land and in rights over land had been securely established over the millennium. Third, favourable land–labour ratio pushed cultivation into lands with high intrinsic fertility, capable of replenishing themselves with the minimum of effort and supported by high levels of animal fertilisation. As a result, per acre yields were perhaps substantially higher than those generally prevailing in the later nineteenth century.[119] Fourth, subsistence levels were market-related and varied according to social status. Scattered evidence from Bengal in the eighteenth century suggests that expenditures on food were inversely related to incomes—poorer people spent more on food (sometimes as high as 83 per cent of the household budget) than the rich who could afford to spend 80 per cent of their income on 'consumer' goods.[120]

The principal reason for the cheapness of manufactured goods also seems to lie elsewhere. Despite the massive influx of silver in the economy, India seems to have escaped the trauma of a price inflation in the sixteenth and the seventeenth century. Commodity prices were largely stable, or if they rose, the increase was very gradual and hardly noticeable in the seventeenth century.[121] In this respect, India's experience was unique not only in contrast to Europe but also with respect to China where the combined effects of Spanish and Japanese bullion created cyclical inflationary and deflationary phases.[122] India's escape from such cyclical problems was not because of some perverse economic behaviour (like hoarding), but because each increment in the country's monetary stock was absorbed by the expansion of the manufacturing sector and in the growth of monetized transactions.[123] Low and stable agricultural prices gave a competitive edge to Indian manufactures, particularly textiles, because producers could turn out enormous quantities of cheap manufactured goods.[124] This they could without compromising too much with their standards of living. The situation changed in the eighteenth century, leading immediately to a clamour of increasing costs of manufactured goods and 'necessities of life' and the deteriorating living standards of the artisans.[125]

Finally, a sustained monetization of the economy substantially altered the relations of production. The existence of privileged social groups in the countryside as well as rich peasants situated cheek by jowl with the poor, landless and the menials meant that the circuits of capital and its intervention in the labour process could proceed autonomously, that is, independent of the macro-level transference of tribute from the regions to the imperial centre. With the expansion of the market and increasing demand for Indian goods, the context of production both expanded and changed. There was simply an enormous need for working capital, which, at least in the textile sector, even a well-to-do weaver did not possess. In such a case, individual merchants and later the European free traders began extending finances to such producers. *Paikars* or rural agents of town-based merchants went to the houses of the weavers, extending money to them, as per the contract. Apart from the amount paid for the purpose of weaving, the weaver was also paid his wages by contracting-moneylenders (*mahajans*). These were directly proportional to the skills and the quality of the cloth produced by him, and while the merchant had his own assistant, the weaver was assisted by his.[126] Wage labour had not yet developed in agriculture, but paid labour was certainly used during the peak season and cultivators depended on grain merchants to provide them with working capital.[127]

All these features provide sufficient reason to suggest that despite the failure of the state to manage the economy, the impulses of an expanding world-economy had seeped into the economy and proto-capitalist features had begun permeating both manufacturing and agriculture by the end of the eighteenth century. While these became the preconditions for a massive market-expansion, the regime of the East India Company and the political-economy of Company rule in Bengal intensified this process by forging a regionally integrated market in the province, not only for high-value commodities like cotton or silk, but for basic foodgrains. Appropriation of revenue in cash was now factored into the expansion of Bengal's internal market through a rising demand for consumables at prices which were now linked on a provincial scale, and with the increase in the cultivation of indigo and opium the pace of commercialisation speeded up. Since these were primarily meant for export, even villages were further integrated into the fluctuations of a capitalist world market. While this expanded the scope of capital accumulation among traders and landed people, it also increased the economic vulnerability of the producers.

On the whole, the first fifty years of British rule in eastern India seems to have also been a period of vastly expanding commercial opportunities in the countryside. My study of grain trade has shown how traders in Bengal used the new grid of factors—rising prices, increasing demand, inflexible revenue, and periodic subsistence crises—to batten on to the peasants through a combination of subsistence and consumption loans given at high rates of interest. Production and the pace of agricultural reclamation increased, as did debt bondage and a sharecropping peasantry whose vulnerability deepened with each cycle of loan repayment or adverse weather which upset the returns of their harvests.[128]

As far as capitalist relations were concerned, it would appear that the early colonial regime was bent on a course correction. Dirk Kolff has drawn our attention to this in the sphere of law and legal regulations which henceforth supplanted regimes of custom and moral codes. The new system brooked no negotiations but operated through elaborate sets of court procedures grounded on the *inviolability of private property*. Recent studies of textile production in South India and Bengal show that Company legislations transformed the easy negotiability between capital and labour in the manufacturing sector into legal regimes which were patently skewed in favour of owners (capitalists?) and harshly coercive against labourers.[129]

Thus, at a programmatic level, the establishment of British rule buttressed regimes of private agrarian and commercial properties but at the cost of increasing the vulnerabilities of workers and labourers who could now even be expropriated. The functioning of capital was transformed and its reach deepened under the new dispensation on a scale which had never occurred before. One good example of this was the Permanent Settlement. This was a great feat of mercantilist social engineering whose end purpose was to stabilise Bengal's revenue under a class of improving landlords securely ensconced in their private domains by virtue of law. Under its terms the Mughal rights of taxation, traditionally devolved upon the zamindars by the state were now fused to their *milkiyat*, their 'private' domains, both of which could now be sold. In south India, the *ryotwari* settlement broke the nascent forms of private property in the jointly-held village lands and community-oriented processes of production (which had characterised *mirasi* tenures in the past) and instead consolidated the position of the leading *mirasidars* as private village contractors. These *mirasidars* henceforth combined cultivation with revenue farming and local-level agrarian management, and used their new control over land, labour and various commercial assets to accumulate financial resources that enabled them to contract for village revenues. But these were accompanied by drastic changes in the social conditions of the less privileged groups who were pushed into social and economic subordination.[130] Thus the 'rule' of 'property' was now fully enshrined, but the flexibilities which had characterised economic and social transactions under the 'old' regimes were henceforth irrevocably shattered.

The' medieval' millennium was over!

Whatever happened in the Millennium?

Looking back from the vantage point of the eighteenth century, I find it difficult to conceive of neatly demarcated chronologies (or comprehensive labels like feudal) as sufficient grounds for understanding the thousand years which had gone by. For instance, what was so definitive about the thirteenth century to call it a watershed?

Or what was so disruptive about 1757 to call it the end of medieval India? The three features which have been ascribed to explain these dates as ruptures are conquest, political centralisation and fiscal systems. In both instances, it can be shown with equal ease that the extent of territories *actually* controlled by these new states was limited; that conquest was a protracted process since opposition was bitter and hostile; and that the fiscal demands or the pitch of taxes in both regimes were precarious and not unknown in the subcontinent.[131] In all respects, the vulnerabilities of the Muslim conquerors and the fragility of their states did not end till the sixteenth century, and a colonial regime subordinating the economy of India did not emerge till the 1830s.[132] What made the difference towards the end of the eighteenth century was that colonial intervention gave a definitive (i.e. structural) swing to an early modern economy which had been slowly consolidating itself through the sixteenth and seventeenth centuries. Therefore, historical processes and a sense of continuum, not arbitrary dates, may be the better way to approach the division of this millennium into periods.

What were these processes? Unfortunately, historians have the habit of conflating processes with structures, and nothing is more emblematic of this than the conflation of non-economic forms of coercion in landed-estates with feudalism in early medieval India; or the conflation of politics with state systems for the subsequent centuries. For me, the first lesson of the first five hundred years of the millennium is that decentralised *politics* (in the early medieval complex) spawned fairly stable regional *polities* and court-cultures, whereas the so-called centralised states (or rather, a sequence of dynasties) in the post-thirteenth century were buffeted by recalcitrant subjects and a *fitna*-ridden elite. The emergence of regional kingdoms in the eighteenth century showed parallel tendencies—a strife-torn centre and stability in the provinces. By processes I therefore imply the play of political forces which involved accommodations *in* conflict in a continuously evolving saga of subordinations, subversions, and negotiations. No state, not even the Mughal state, simply had the fire-power to bypass these processes. These negotiated settlements provide the context of understanding the three-pronged strategies of rule which formed the single unifying political thread through the millennium: *the paternal, the patrimonial and the despotic*, which were tried in various combinations, depending upon the context and conditions.

While states failed, legitimacies and political cultures survived. The organising principles of both in the post-thirteenth century were the court and a royalist idiom, whose roots went deep into the early medieval kingdoms. Legitimacies operated on a number of axes—ascriptions of divinity, gifting and festivity, derivations from folk traditions, scriptural approval (though that was perennially uncertain), stylised norms of behaviour and deportment, and the fiction of the ruler's charisma.[133] Since they had such multiple derivations, these were pluralist in their externalities (shown for instance, in the creation of multi-ethnic ruling classes by central powers and regional kings alike) and synthetic in content (i.e. no single scriptural orthodoxy could determine their formation). These legitimacies and cultures were socialised into a commonly shared ruling-class ethos across regions, across political affinities, and across ethnicities. Rajput chiefs, Vijaynagara rulers, Maratha sardars, leaders of Sikh warrior-bands and Tipu's Mysore—all were participants and beneficiaries of this ethos.

Multiplicity, ambivalence and friction were central both to the formation of communities and to their perception by other communities between the thirteenth and eighteenth centuries. For the Muslims living and trading in India prior to the formation of the Sultanate, the rhetoric that Islam was to be the ideology of the new state and its ruler would certainly have been an unsettling experience, as much as it was for those who genuinely believed that this ought to be so. For both, the pragmatic concerns were how to function in a country where they were in a minority and where *kufr* was not eradicable by force of arms. Nor was being a Muslim easy, even within regimes that swore by denominational Islam. Deep aristocratic prejudices against plebeians did not spare the baser members of their own communities. The uneasy truce between the Sufi Shaykh and the scriptural 'Ulama, fashioned in the trying times of the thirteenth century, must have exerted contrary pressures on the community, as they did with the Hindus caught between the scriptural thrall of brahmanical traditions and the liberating air of the *bhakti* saints.

The medieval era seems to have been a little stifling for women for two reasons: first, while polygamy continued as of yore, a greater conservatism seems to have been crept into the elite strata, which now began tilting towards more invidious forms of gender segregation, which involved their sequestration in the inner recesses of the 'domestic' sphere (which included the royal *harams* or the *dhorahar* in Rajput households) and the translation of feminine desires and love into a service (*seva*) to please the male. Emulation at the lower levels may have followed quickly: the understanding among peasants that the 'domestic' was an exclusively feminine space; remarried widows not being assigned the same status as the woman of a first marriage; women not being allowed to handle devices which involved the use of 'technologies' in artisan families; and a substantial number of foreign travelers describing women committing *sati*[134] seem to be important markers of these changes. Telling perhaps was the growing conservatism towards women in the Mughal imperial household at the same time. With apologies to women who may find this to be a comparison of dubious quality, even this conservative turn was the result of cultural seepages in a multiple of ways.

Emulation and cultural seepages had their happy dimensions too, and these are particularly noticeable from the sixteenth century onwards. The empire and its regions— the emperor and his satraps—partook of a commonly shared 'ecumenical spirit' of pluralism and inclusion, which became the dominant principle influencing how such 'big' people construed 'public' spaces (i.e. the cities) that they commissioned; and there is no doubt that they commissioned a lot of cities, particularly in the eighteenth century when regional kings or *nawabs* built their capitals or redesigned existing cities to suit their purposes.

Economic trends over the millennium show similar processes of expansion and incorporation. The standard argument that the period between the eighth and the thirteenth century was economically static and closed, and the post-thirteenth century saw a sudden spurt in economic activity is considerably at variance from the evidence of agricultural expansion and commercial growth in the earlier period. However, here a big change is noticeable from the sixteenth century when the economic impulses from the Iberian-Atlantic complex began to stimulate an expansion in the Indian economy. There was a phenomenal expansion in the volume and value of Euro-Asian trade as well as a major diversification in the composition and the origin of the Asian cargo entering this trade. This conjuncture began a new phase in this millennium. An aggregative expansion in production, growth of military-fiscal state apparatuses, a cultural world characterised by pluralist-ecumenism, the diversification of mercantile activities and the growing sophistication of peasant and artisan production systems—all indicate a new *proto-capitalist* configuration in Indian history. The sixteenth century ended the 'medieval' and ushered India into a global world of early modernity.[135]

Early modernity also saw early problems. The nature of the intersections between the European (particularly, the English) and Indian commercial worlds began changing from the eighteenth century. There may have been some metropolitan interests in Britain pushing for the conquest of India, though the extent of that is not very clear for the eighteenth century.[136] Also, conquest did not end the participation and incorporation of anterior structures and agencies in the new dispensation. But a difference was visible within these broad patterns of persistence. The early colonial system was deeply implicated in commerce, and its programmatic thrust had fundamental commercial consequences. The proto-capitalist economy of the early modern phase was transformed, but the ecumenical world which had bridged the medieval and the early modern was irreversibly ruptured.

REFERENCES

1. Even if I discount some of the good textbook type of surveys, it would be absurd to even try to list some of the more representative studies of this millennium. The formidable scholarships of R.S. Sharma and Irfan Habib have been profoundly influential. Irfan Habib particularly has tried to trace long-term structural patterns which begin much before and end much later than this millennium (for instance, see his writings on landed property, caste and peasantry in his *Essays in Indian History: Towards a Marxist Perspective*, New Delhi, 1995). The corpus of their collective scholarship constitutes the benchmark which historians, even if they disagree with them, have to acknowledge with a sense of awe.
2. See Harbans Mukhia, 'Was there Feudalism in Indian History?' *The Journal of Peasant Studies*, vol. 8 (3), 1981; idem., 'Peasant Production and Medieval Indian Society', *The Journal of Peasant Studies*, vol.12 (2-3, 1985); B.D. Chattopadhya, *The Making of Early Medieval India*, New Delhi, 1994.
3. Irfan Habib, 'Classifying Pre-colonial India', in Harbans Mukhia (ed.) *The Feudalism Debate*, Delhi, 1999.
4. Irfan Habib and Tapan Raychaudhuri (ed.), *The Cambridge Economic History of India, vol.1: c.1200-c.1750*, Delhi, 1982 (original, 1982).
5. Romila Thapar, *Ancient Indian Social History: Some Interpretations*, Delhi, 2006 (first published, 1978), p. 27.
6. Irfan Habib, 'Economic History of the Delhi Sultanate—an Essay in Reiterpretation', *Indian Historical Review*, vol. 4, 1977; Irfan Habib, 'Formation of the Sultanate Ruling Class in the Thirteenth Century', in idem., (ed.), *Medieval India 1: Researches in the History of India, 1200-1750*, Delhi, 1999.
7. On the court-centred biases of the Persian, see Peter Hardy, *Historians of Medieval India: Studies in Indo-Muslim Historical Writing*, London, 1966; Harbans Mukhia, *Historians and Historiography During the Reign of Akbar*, New Delhi, 1976; Sunil Kumar, *The Emergence of the Delhi Sultanate, 1192-1286*, Delhi, 2007.
8. Kumar, *The Emergence of the Delhi Sultanat*.
9. Andre Wink, *Al-Hind: the Making of the Indo-Islamic World. Volume II: The Slave Kings and the Islamic Conquest 11th-13th Centuries*, Delhi, 2001 (first published, Leiden, 1997), p. 212.
10. Peter Jackson, *The Delhi Sultanate: A Political and Military History*, Cambridge, 1999, p. 323.
11. Wink, *Al-Hind*, Vol. II, p. 183.
12. Raziuddin Aquil, *Sufism, Culture and Politics: Afghans and Islam in Medieval North India*, Delhi, 2007, p. 28.
13. On this see Jackson, *The Delhi Sultanate*, Chapter 5.
14. See for instance, Aziz Ahmad, 'Epic and Counter-Epic in Medieval India',

in Richard Eaton (ed.), *India's Islamic Traditons, 711-1750*, Delhi, 2003 for epical representations of Hindu tales of resistance to Muslim invasions.

15. Muzaffar Alam and Sanjay Subrahmanyam (eds.), *The Mughal State, 1556-1707*, Delhi, 1998, p.11.
16. *Ibid*, p. 6.
17. Irfan Habib, 'Ziyā Baranī's Vision of the State', *The Medieval History Journal*, vol. 2 (1), (hereafter, *MHJ*), January–June 1998.
18. A.L. Basham, *The Wonder that was India*, Delhi, 1999 (first published, 1954), p. 86.
19. This is the substance of the argument put forward by Harbans Mukhia, *The Mughals of India*, Oxford, 2004, pp. 45–46.
20. Norman P. Zeigler, 'Some notes on Rajput Loyalties during the Mughal Period', in Alam and Subrahmanyam (eds.), *The Mughal State*, pp. 201–202.
21. Ramya Sreenivasan, 'The "Marriage" of "Hindu" and "Turak": Medieval Rajput Histories of Jalor', *MHJ*, vol.7 (1), January–June, 2004.
22. Burton Stein, *The New Cambridge History of India 1.2. Vijayanagara*, Cambridge, 1994, pp. 75–77.
23. The fiscal and institutional arrangements of this slow incorporation are analysed by Alam and Subrahmanyam (eds.), *The Mughal State*, pp. 33–39.
24. *The Mughals of India*, pp. 135-146.
25. Cynthia Talbot, *Precolonial India in Practice: Society, Religion, and Identity in Medieval Andhra*, Delhi, 2001, p. 145.
26. For instance, Mukhia, *The Mughals of India*, p. 78.
27. See Romila Thapar, *Ancient Indian Social History*, pp.104–108 for an explication of these traditions.
28. R.S. Sharma, *Perspectives in Social and Economic History of Early India*, Delhi, 1995 (first published, 1983), p. 272 ff.
29. Talbot, *Precolonial India in Practice*, pp.88-90.
30. See Irfan Habib, *The Agrarian System of Mughal India, 1556-1707*, Delhi, 1999, pp. 342–363.
31. For a detailed discussion on the courtly rituals of gifting, see Mukhia, *The Mughals of India*, Chapter 2; on *khilats*, see Stewart Gordon, *Robes of Honour:* Khil'at *in Pre-Colonial and Colonial India*, Delhi, 2003.
32. Mukhia, *The Mughals*, p. 74.
33. Vasundhara Filliozat (ed.), *Vijayanagar*, Delhi, 2001 (first published, 1977), p.110 citing the account of Domingo Paes written circa 1520-22.
34. Jacob Van Claveren, 'Fiscalism, Mercantilism and Corruption', in D.C. Coleman, (ed.), *Revisions in Mercantilism*, London, 1969, pp.140,142.
35. Burton Stein's 'State Formation and Economy Reconsidered', *Modern Asian Studies*, 19(3), 1985 derived extensively on Martin Wolfe's, *The Fiscal System of Renaissance France*, New Haven, 1972; and C.A. Bayly, 'The Military-Fiscal State and Indigenous Resistance: India 1750-1820', in Lawrence Stone (ed.), *The Imperial State at War*, London, 1994, based himself substantively on John Brewer's, *The Sinews of Power: War, Money and the English State, 1688-1783*, London, 1989.

36. For a discussion of the expansion in trade and market-networks in eastern India in the eighteenth century, see Rajat Datta, 'Markets, Bullion and Bengal's Commercial Economy: An Eighteenth Century Perspective', in Om Prakash and Denys Lombard (eds.), *Commerce and Culture in the Bay of Bengal, 1500-1800*, Delhi, 1999.
37. While most of such studies have tended to cluster around western and southern India, particularly around the Marathas, the nawabi of Arcot and the Tipu Sutan's Mysore, the argument has also recently been advanced to cover Bengal where a process of aggressive centralisation of fiscal resources at the regional level leading to a large-scale reorientation in the rights over revenue and agrarian management was said to be underway in the twenties of the eighteenth century (Alam and Subrahmanyam (eds.), *The Mughal State*, pp. 46–53) and continued through the century reaching its apogee with the fiscal system set up by the early colonial state (for this argument see Rajat Datta, 'Commercialisation, Tribute, and the Transition from late Mughal to Early Colonial in India', *MHJ, vol.6 (2),* July–December, 2003*).* It is thus plausible to argue that tribute and fiscalism fused in early modern India in the form revenue because it embodied both the *political* supremacy of the state and the *commercial* (that is, mediated through the market) extraction of the surplus from the producer.
38. Guha adds here in parenthesis: 'about 700,000 tonnes if we take the *sher* at 900 grammes'.
39. Geoffery Parker, *The Military Revolution: Military Innovation and the Rise of the West, 1500-1800*, Cambridge, 1987; and for southern India see V. Narayan Rao, David Shulman and Sanjay Subrahmanyam, 'The Art of War under the Nayakas' , and Iqtidar Alam Khan , 'Early Use of Cannon and Musket in India' for a the negligible evidence of the use of gunpowder in India before the sixteenth century, both in J.L. Gommans and Dirk H.A. Kolff (ed.), 2001, *Warfare and Weaponry in South Asia, 1000-1800*, Delhi, 2001.
40. The account of Domingo Paes in Filliozat (ed.), *Vijaynagar*, p.109.
41. *Ibid.*, pp. 126–130.
42. B.D. Chattopadhya, *Studying Early India: Archaeology, Texts, and Historical Issues*, Delhi, 2005, p.203.
43. *Al-Beruni's India*, vols. I and II, (ed.), Edward C. Sachau, reprint, New Delhi, 2003, pp. 3, 5.
44. Sheldon Pollock, 'Rāmāyana and Political Imagination in India', in David N. Lorenzen (ed.), *Religious Movements in South Asia, 600-1800*, New Delhi, 2005, p.189.
45. Cited in Iqbal Hussain, 'Hindu Shrines and Practices', in Habib (ed.), *Medieval India 1*, p. 145.
46. Eleanor Zelliot, 'A Medieval Encounter Between a Hindu and Muslim: Eknath's Drama-Poem Hindu-Turk *Samvād*', in Eaton (ed.), *India's Islamic Traditions*, pp. 64–82.
47. Charlotte Vaudeville, *A Weaver Named Kabir: Selected Verses with a Detailed Biographical and Historical Introduction*, New Delhi, 1993, p.125.

48. Mukhia, *The Mughals*, pp.114ff.
49. As can be seen from Madhu Trivedi's account (in this volume) of the sequestered world of the love-struck *virahini* pining for her warrior-lover/ husband in the *dharohar*, the uppermost structure on top of the mansion, which was her usual place of residence in aristocratic families [Madhu Trivedi, p.195]; also see Varsha Joshi, *Polygamy and Purdah: Women and Society Among the Rajputs*, Jaipur, 1995; Ramya Sreenivasan, 'Honoring the Family: Narratives and Political Kinship in Pre-colonial Rajasthan', in Indrani Chaterjee (ed.), *Unfamiliar Relations: Family and History in South Asia*, Delhi, 2004.
50. Mukhia, *The Mughals*, pp. 130–135.
51. Uma Chakravarti, 'Conceptualizing Brahmanical Patriarchy: Gender, Caste, Class and State', *Economic and Political Weekly*, 27, no.14, 1993, pp. 579–85.
52. On the latter, see Mukhia, *The Mughals*, pp. 114–15.
53. *Al-Beruni's India*, p. 444.
54. Kumkum Sangari, 'Mirabai: the Female Voice and Oral Compositions', in J.S. Grewal (ed.), *Religious Movements and Institutions in Medieval India*, New Delhi, 2006, p.233.
55. Mukhia, *The Mughals*, pp. 133–35; Nandita Prasad Sahai, 'The "Other" Culture: Craft Societies and Widow Remarriage in Early Modern India', *Journal of Women's Studies*, vol.19 (2), Summer, 2007.
56. *Al-Beruni's India*, p. 430.
57. Kamlesh Mohan, 'Women in Sikh Discourse: Liberation or Ambivalence?', in Irfan Habib (ed.), *Religion in Indian History*, New Delhi, 2007.
58. These points are based on Kumkum Sanghari, 'Mirabai'.
59. Mohan, 'Women in Sikh Discourse', pp. 192–93.
60. As Georges Duby's classic work shows, notions of love and fidelity in medieval Europe emerged out the rationalisation of inter-personal relationships and intimacies within an unfolding saga of feudal patriarchy (*Love and Marriage in the Middle Ages*, Oxford, 1994).
61. Indu Banga, 'Gender Relations in Medieval India', in J.S. Grewal (ed.), *The State and Society in Medieval India*, New Delhi, 2005.
62. Sahai, 'The "Other" Culture', pp. 48–50.
63. This is the impression one gets from reading the description of the family life and business ventures of a seventeenth-century Oswal jeweller Banarasidas in the *Ardha Kathanak* (*Indica*, vol.7, nos. 1 and 2, March and September 1970); also, Ronald Inden and Ralph Nicholas, *Kinship in Bengali Culture*, Chicago, 1977; and Dilbagh Singh, 'Regulating the Domestic: Notes on the Pre-colonial state and the Family', *Studies in History*, vol.19 (1), January–June 2003.
64. Sahai, 'The "Other" Culture', p. 44.
65. On these issues, see Vijaya Ramaswamy, *Textiles and Weavers in South India*, (second edition), New Delhi, 2006, and Nandita Prasad Sahai, *Politics of Patronage and Protest: the State, Society, and Artisans in Early Modern Rajasthan*, New Delhi, 2006.
66. The commercial and revenue records of the English East India Company

in eastern India contain many references to women spinners belonging to poor Brahman families.

67. Asha Shukla Choubey, 'Technology and Culture among the Iron Workers of Bihar during the Seventeenth and Eighteenth Centuries', *MHJ*, vol.6 (1), January–June, 2003, pp. 104–5.
68. Sahai, The "Other" Culture, p. 49.
69. Sangari, 'Mirabai: the Female Voice and Oral Compositions'.
70. On this, see Aditya Behl, 'The Magic Doe: Desire and Narrative in a Hindavi Sufi Romance, circa 1503', in Eaton (ed.), *India's Islamic Traditions.*
71. *Past and Present*, no. 39, April 1968; reprinted in Harbans Mukhia and Maurice Aymard (eds.), *French Studies in History*, vol. II : *The Departures,* Delhi, 1990.
72. Vaudeville, *Kabir*, p.125.
73. These aspects are discussed by Mukhia, *The Mughals*, pp. 156–171.
74. Daniel J. Ehnbom, ' "Passionate Delineation and the Mainstream of Indian Painting": The Mughal Style and the Schools of Rajasthan', in Richard Barnett (ed.), *Rethinking Early Modern India*, New Delhi, 2002, p.183.
75. The patrimonial nature of the state was implicit in the vision of a state being run as extension of the emperor's household: a paternalistic system, based on personal bonds of dependence on the monarch instead of an imperial-bureaucratic system run on impersonal rules. As Blake's essay in this volume shows, the abiding vision of the Empire was that of an elaborate household, in which bureaucratic norms of governance were to be subsumed under the persona of the emperor. Such an edifice was in consonance with the power equations prevalent in India at that time. The existence of powerful social groups and communities meant that a full-scale centralisation of authority was never an option for the Mughals. The option was instead a combination of paternalism and semi-bureaucratic norms of governance. This was the essence of the flexibility and pragmatism of the so-called 'Islamic' state in India, matched by the flexibility and pragmatism of the regional Hindu kingdoms under it. (also see, Stephen Blake, *Shahjahanabad: the Sovereign City in Mughal India, 1639-1739*, Cambridge, 1993; and for an account of the innately pluralist nature of this city even in its dying moments, see William Dalrymple, *The Last Mughal: The Fall of Dynasty. Delhi, 1857,* New Delhi, 2006).
76. Catherine Asher, 'Piety, Religion and the Old Social Order in the Architecture of the Later Mughals and their Contemporaries' in Barnett (ed.), *Rethinking Early Modern India*; also see, Nurul Hasan, 'The Morphology of a Medieval Indian City: A Case Study of Shajahanabad', in Indu Banga (ed.), *The City in Indian History: Urban Demography, Society, and Politics,* New Delhi, 1991; Urvashi Dalal, 'Shahjanhanbad : An Expression of the Mughal State's Legitimacy', *Islamic Culture,* vol. 74 (4), October, 2000.
77. R.S. Sharma and Irfan Habib are two of the most prominent historians who have developed arguments for a pre-thirteenth century economic contraction and a thirteenth-century political and economic revival respectively in a formidable body of scholarship too vast to be listed here.

78. Simon Digby, 'The Maritime Trade of India, c.1200-1500', in Irfan Habib and Tapan Raychaudhuri (ed.), *The Cambridge Economic History of India, vol.1;* Richard Eaton, *The Rise of Islam and the Bengal Frontier, 1204-1760,* Delhi, 1997; Kenneth McPherson, *The Indian Ocean: A History of People and the Sea,* New Delhi, 2006 (first published, 1993), particularly pp. 102–110. Irfan Habib's argument that the slaves and skilled migrants expanded the scope of artisanal activity with the establishment of the Sultanate assigns more productive energies than existing levels of technology would allow to such absurdly small numbers of people (see Irfan Habib, 'Economic History of the Delhi Sultanate'). The expansion could only have occurred because of the quick absorption of these techniques by Hindu artisans and by the percolation, through conversions, to Islam.
79. On this, see Digby, 'Maritime Trade'; and John Deyell, *Living Without Silver: The Monetary History of Early Medieval North India,* New Delhi, 1999 (first published, 1990), pp. 218–31.
80. Possibly the best account of both these events is still J.F. Richards (eds.), *Precious Metals in Later Medieval and Early Modern Worlds,* Durham, 1983.
81. M.N. Pearson, 'Merchants and States', in James D. Tracy (ed.), *The Political Economy of Merchant-Empires: State Power and World Trade, 1350–1750,* Cambridge, 1997, p. 97.
82. Asin Dasgupta, *The World of the Indian Ocean Merchant,* New Delhi, 2001, pp. 35, 42, 124–25.
83. On diamond mining see Ishrat Alam, 'Diamond Mining and Trade in South India in the Seventeenth Century', *MHJ,* vol.3 (2), July–December, 2000.
84. Some recent studies are Om Prakash, *European Commercial Enterprise in Pre-colonial India,* Cambridge, 1998; Prasannan Parthasarathi, *The Transition to a Colonial Economy: Weavers, Merchants and Kings in South India,* 1720–1800, Cambridge, 2001; Eugenia Vanina, *Urban Crafts and Craftsmen in Medieval India (Thirteenth-Eighteenth Centuries),* New Delhi, 2004; Ramaswamy, *Textiles and Weavers in South India;* and Smritikumar Sarkar, 'Social Organization of Artisan Production: Changing Role of Market, Technology, and Merchant-Creditor—18th to 20th Century', in B.B. Chaudhuri (ed.), *Economic History of India from Eighteenth to Twentieth Century,* Delhi, 2005; Nandita Prasad Sahai, *Politics of Patronage and Protest: the State, Society, and Artisans in Early Modern Rajasthan,* New Delhi, 2006.
85. See, for instance Parthasarathi, *The Transition to a Colonial Economy.*
86. *European Commercial Enterprise in Pre-Colonial India,* Chapter 8.
87. See Rajat Datta, 'Markets, Bullion and Bengal's Commercial Economy', and 'Commercialization, Tribute and Transition'.
88. *The Transition to a Colonial Economy,* p. 37.
89. Vanina, *Urban Crafts and Craftsmen,* p. 72.
90. Sarkar, 'Social Organization of Artisan Production', p. 213.
91. In eastern India, there was a significant expansion of textile-producing centres in rural areas which functioned as the procurement hinterlands of the main urban and production centres in the seventeenth and eighteenth centuries (Om Prakash, *European Commercial Enterprise in Pre-*

colonial India, p.197). Various metal-working crafts also expanded in eastern India (see Sarkar, 'Social Organization of Artisan Production' for a thorough overview of the trends in the metallurgical sector); in Bihar, iron workers (*lohar*) in the villages were becoming 'small-scale commodity producers' in the seventeenth and eighteenth centuries, servicing both rural and urban areas through a network of markets controlled by merchants (Choubey, 'Technology and Culture among Iron Workers', p. 94).

92. Grewal (ed.) *Religious Movements and Institutions in Medieval India*, pp. 383–476.
93. Harbans Mukhia, 'Ideology of the Bhakti Movement: the Case of Dadu Dayal' in D.P. Chatopadhyay (ed.), *History and Society: Essays in Honour of Professor Nihar Ranjan Ray*, Calcutta, 1978, reprinted in idem., *Perspectives on Medieval History*, Delhi, 1993.
94. As Mukhia does when he reflects on the 'the effortlessness which characterised the re-instatement of caste among the Sikhs' (*ibid.* pp. 63–64).
95. The classic case here is Habib, for both these views (*The Agrarian System*, Chapter 9). Non-confrontationist forms of resistance are dismissed by him in one page (p. 384) as tending to 'cloud or obscure' the 'class nature' (consciousness?) of these protests.
96. See Mukhia, 'Was there Feudalism in Indian History?'; and 'Peasant Production and Medieval Indian Society'; J.F. Richards, *The Mughal Empire*, Cambridge, 1993, esp. pp.185ff.; and the collection of essays in Alam and Subrahmanyam, *The Mughal State* for helpful starting points. More detailed studies from which such a view can find enough substantiation include Andre Wink, *Land and Sovereignty in India: Agrarian Society and Politics under the Eighteenth Century Maratha Swarajya*, Cambridge, 1986; Muzaffar Alam, *The Crisis of Empire in Mughal North India: Awadh & the Punjab*, Delhi, 1997; Stuart Gordon, *The Marathas, 1600-1818*, Cambridge, 1998; J.S. Grewal, *The Sikhs of the Punjab*, Cambridge, 1999; and Sumit Guha, *Environment and Ethnicity in India, 1200-1991*, Cambridge, 1999. I have shown the persistence of a differentiated nature of rural enrichment even under the intrusive fiscality of the early colonial regime in Bengal (*Society, Economy and the Market: Commercialization in Rural Bengal, c.1760-1800*, Delhi, 2000).
97. See Mukhia, 'Peasant Production in Medieval Indian Society'.
98. I have in mind Marx's description of pre-capitalist production systems as being 'rural patriarchal systems', organised along a 'communal' (i.e. communitarian) form of existence, which caused individual labour to appear rather as the 'direct function' of a collectivity rather than as the labour of an individual (Karl Marx, A *Contribution to the Critique of Political Economy*, London, 1970, (original, 1859), p. 33–34).
99. Sahai, *Politics of Patronage and Protest*, pp. 88–124.
100. Datta, *Society, Economy and the Market*, pp. 99–102.
101. Jon Wilson, ' "A Thousand Countries to go to": Peasants and Rulers in Late Eighteenth-Century Bengal' *Past & Present*, no.189, November 2005, p. 85.

102. On this aspect, see Datta, 'Commercialisation, Tribute, and the Transition' pp. 285–91.
103. Wilson, 'A Thousand Countries to go to', p. 103.
104. In fact, the extent to which revenue actually increased in the 1757–1790 period can be questioned by adopting a different set of chronological markers (see Datta, *Society, Economy and the Market*, Appendix 1, pp. 333–341).
105. Datta, 'Commercialisation, Tribute, and the Transition' pp. 274–285.
106. Datta, *Society, Economy and the Market*, pp. 146–147 and passim.
107. British Library, Oriental and India Office Collections (herafter, OIOC), Proceedings of the Board of Revenue, P/71/26, 4 June 1790.
108. Ibid; emphasis added.
109. *The Modern World-System. Capitalist Agriculture and the Origins of the European-World Economy in the Sixteenth Century*, New York, 1974.
110. See Mukhia, 'Peasant Production in Medieval Indian Society' for this view of long-term stability.
111. N.F.R. Crafts, *British Economic Growth During the Industrial Revolution*, Oxford, 1985; Gary Hawke, 'Reinterpretations of the Industrial Revolution', in Patrick O'Brien and Ronald Quinault, *The Industrial Revolution and British Society*, Cambridge, 1993.
112. John J. TePaske, 'New World Silver, Castile and the Philippines, 1500-1800', in Richards (ed.), *Precious Metals*, pp. 434, 442–45.
113. Jean Meuvret, 'Monetary Circulation and the Use of Coinage in Sixteenth- and Seventeenth-Century France', in Peter Earle (ed.), *Essays in European Economic History, 1500-1800*, Oxford, 1974.
114. William S. Atwell, 'Notes on Silver, Foreign Trade, and the Late Ming Economy', *Ch'ing-shih wen-t'i*, 3(8), 1977.
115. Compare N.J. Mayhew, 'Population, Money Supply, and the Velocity of Circulation in England, 1300-1700', *Economic History Review*, 48(2), 1995, with Irfan Habib, 'A System of Trimetallism in the Age of the "Price Revolution": Effects of the Silver Influx on the Mughal Monetary System', in J.F. Richards (ed.), *The Imperial Monetary System of Mughal India*, Delhi, 1987.
116. Jack Goldstone, 'East and West in the Seventeenth Century: Political Crises in Stuart England, Ottoman Turkey and Ming China', *Comparative Studies in Society and History*, 30(1), 1988; also see Niels Steensgaard, 'The Seventeenth Century Crisis and the Unity of Eurasian History', *Modern Asian Studies*, 25(4), 1990.
117. Kenneth Pomeranz, *The Great Divergence: China, Europe and the Making of the Modern World Economy*, Princeton, 2000; quotations are from Kenneth Pomeranz, 'Political Economy and Ecology on the Eve of Industrialization: Europe, China and the Global Conjuncture', *American Historical Review*, April 2002, p. 426.
118. Karl Marx, "The Poverty of Philosophy', in Karl Marx and Frederic Engels, *Collected Works*, vol. 6, Moscow, 1976, p. 186.
119. Habib, *Agrarian System of Mughal India*, Chapter 1.
120. Datta, *Society, Economy and the Market*, pp. 191–195.

121. Om Prakash, *Bullion for Goods: European and Indian Merchants in the Indian Ocean Trade, 1500-1800*, Delhi, 2004; Habib, *The Agrarian System*; Joseph J. Brenning, 'Silver in Seventeenth Century Surat: Monetary Circulation and the Price Revolution in Mughal India', in Richards, (ed.) *Precious Metals in Later Medieval and Early Modern Worlds*, Sanjay Subrahmanyam, 'Precious Metal Flows and Prices in Western and Southern Asia, 1500-1750: Some Comparative and Conjunctural Aspects', in Idem, (ed.), *Money and the Market in India, 1100-1700*, Delhi, 1994.
122. William Atwell, 'International Bullion Flows and the Chinese Economy *circa* 1530-1650', *Past & Present*, Number 95, May 1982; Atwell, 'Notes on Silver, Foreign Trade'; William S. Atwell, 'Some Observations on the "Seventeenth Century Crisis" in China and Japan', *Journal of Asian Studies*, 55(2), 1986.
123. Om Prakash, *Bullion for Goods*; Subrahmanyam, *Money and Market*, 'Introduction'.
124. For a similar point, Prasannan Parthasarathi, 'Rethinking Wages and Competitiveness in the Eighteenth Century: Britain and South India', *Past & Present*, No. 158, February 1998.
125. Writing in 1769, Harry Verelst noted that prices of 'provisions' had 'considerably advanced within these twenty years' (Verelst Papers, OIOC, Mss. Eur. F 281/6-10/9, f.279). In 1776, Warren Hastings also noted that '...the price of coarse rice which forms the principal consumption of the people was 5½ times cheaper in the time of Shuja Cawn [1728] than it is now' (OIOC, Bengal Revenue Consultations, P/49/66, 29 November–31 December 1776, 29 November 1776). In 1789, the rise in prices of the 'necessaries of life' had pushed up the prices of 'every article of manufacture' in the textile producing centres (OIOC, Bengal Commercial and Shipping Consultations, P/155/74, 28 March 1789). For an overview of the impact of prices on the agrarian economy of Bengal, see Datta, *Society, Economy and the Market*, pp. 196–200.
126. In Bengal, one anna and a half per day was paid to the weaver who prepared the thread for the loom; 2 to 3 annas per day to those who wove plain muslins; and 11 annas per day to those who wove flowered muslins (D.B. Mitra, *Monetary System in the Bengal Presidency, 1757-1835*, Calcutta, 1991, pp. 40–41).
127. Rajat Datta, *Society, Economy and the Market*, pp. 217–220
128. *Ibid*, Chapter 4.
129. Parthasarathi, *The Transition to a Colonial Economy*, pp.132-140; Om Prakash, 'From Negotiation to Coercion: Textile Manufacturing in India in the Eighteenth Century', *Modern Asian Studies*, vol. 41 (6), 2007.
130. P.B. Mayer, 'The Penetration of Capitalism in a South Indian District: the First Sixty Years of Colonial Rule in Tiruchirapali', *South Asia: Journal of South Asian Studies*, vol. 3 (2), 1980; David Wshbrook, 'Land and Labour in Late Eighteenth-Century South India: the Golden Age of the Pariah?' in Peter Robb (ed.), *Dalit Movements and the Meanings of Labour in India*, Delhi, 1993.
131. These arguments are irreverent of all canonical orthodoxies, and will be

soundly condemned, but compare Mukhia, 'Was there Feudalism in Indian History' and 'Agricultural Technology in Medieval North India' (in idem., *Perspectives on Medival History*) for a critique of the thirteenth century as a watershed; and Datta, 'Commercialization, Tribute, and the Transition', for a critique of conquest and taxation as a sufficient conditions of an early colonial rupture.

132. On this, see C.A. Bayly, *Rulers, Townsmen and Bazaars: North Indian Society in the Age of British Expansion, 1770-1870*, Cambridge, 1983; Parthasarathi, 'Rethinking Wages and Competitiveness in the Eighteenth Century'; Tirthankar Roy, 'Economic History and Modern India: Redefining the Link', *The Journal of Economic Perspectives,* vol.16 (2), Summer 2002; Peter Harnetty, ' "De-industrialization" Revisited: the Handloom Weavers of the Central Provinces of India, c.1800–1947', *Modern Asian Studies,* vol. 25 (3), no. 3, July 1991.
133. J.F. Richards, "The Formulation of Imperial Authority under Akbar and Jahangir', in Alam and Subrahmanyam, *The Mughal State;* Mukhia, *The Mughals of India.*
134. On the latter, see Andrea Major, ' "Eternal flames": Suicide, Sinfulness and Insanity in "Western" Constructions of *Sati*', 1500–1830', *International Journal of Asian Studies,* vol. 1 (2), 2004.
135. While early modernity as a specific period of the post-fifteenth century European and Eurasian complexes is now widely accepted, the insular world of Indian historiography is slowly waking up to an engagement with it parameters. Notable in this direction are J.F. Richards ('Early Modern India and World History', *Journal of World History*, vol. 8 (2), 1997); Burton Stein, *(A History of India*, New Delhi, 1998); Sanjay Subrahmanyam (*Penumbral Visions: Making Polities and in Early Modern South Asia*, New Delhi, 2001), Richard Barnett, (*Rethinking Early Modern India*), and David Washbrook, ('India in the Early Modern Word Economy: Modes of Production, Reproduction and Exchange' *Journal of Global History,* vol. 2, 2007).
136. See P.J. Marshall (ed.), *The Eighteenth Century in Indian History: Evolution or Revolution?* New Delhi, 2003, pp. 23–28.

SECTION I

Politics, Legitimacy and Political Culture

Chapter 1

A Millennium of Stateless Indian History?

Dirk H.A. Kolff

If, looking at a single nation, one can perhaps think in terms of decades, the fate of continents may be measured by the century. The millennium, however, should be reserved for something even greater, for civilisations, that is for comparative and world history. It is perhaps not unnatural for a European like me to realise that most of the centuries as it were preferentially allotted to his continent and its 'expansion' have run their course, and to feel it is time to look beyond the centuries and beyond Europe to the millennia and to world history. But that is easier said than done. The concepts and scenarios that Europe once lightheartedly imposed on one continent after the other, now prove, with few exceptions, to be blunt tools, incapable of doing justice to the historical patterns that emerge amongst the main civilisations outside the old continent. The language that so many Europeans thought was universal or close to it, turns out to have allowed them a grip on only part of non-European realities. Their loss of power, in other words, is parallelled by a loss of conceptual control. For the Indian and the European historian to agree, even bilaterally, on a common angle of observation and to balance what they have in common with the features that are unique to both of them, seems quite suddenly beyond the discipline they belong to. Perhaps historians as a group are not as yet quite up to the challenges of millennial history.

That, at least is the opinion of Jack Goody, the anthropologist of Africa, who looks at the whole of the Eurasian land mass as that part of the world that, having undergone, during the Bronze Age, an intensive transformation of urbanisation and social stratification, is characterised by a number of common features. These common features, of which he singles out for analysis those of rationality, calculated behaviour (for instance, with the help of writing and, more specifically, bookkeeping), and the structure of the family, render their civilisations basically similar and, therefore, comparable. In the Bronze Age and in Africa, Goody has found Archimedean points in time and in space respectively that allow him to argue convincingly, that what distinguished the Eurasian subcontinents of Europe and India is, historically speaking, recent, a divergence of not more than a couple of centuries that, already, is coming to an end. The difference was due to the contingent configuration of the last few hundred years only, not to substantially different cultural traditions, at least not as far as the structure of the family and the much-hallowed Western rationality were concerned. If ever there was a reason to write condescendingly about or 'primitivise', as Goody puts it, the East, that time is over now. None of us is off the track anymore and, as far as comparing the dynamics and creativity of civilisations is concerned, we should realise that we are just where we were in the first millennia since the Bronze Age, that is before 'the rise of the West'. And Goody blames the historical profession for not facing these facts.[1]

There is, in my opinion little arguing with this rejection of theories about, for instance, the supposedly superior qualities of the Western nuclear family over the Indian extended family. The extended family in India can be, and is, a great help in entrepreneurship, as it once was and still, to an extent, is in Europe. The collectivist spirit of the Chettiars of South India, says Goody, quoting David Rudner, is as successful in its own context as the individualist spirit is elsewhere in another context. In India, the wider participation of kin has often been a positive advantage, in spite of the Western myth that this phenomenon constituted 'a drag' on development and that the nuclear family was universally crucial as a key to progress. Arguing along similar lines, Goody does away with the exclusive European claim on rationality.

Once we have expelled from our mental image of the past millennium the myth of the unique and inalienable genius for progress of the West, however, we have not explained away the temporary configuration that made Europe dominant for a—better left unspecified—number of centuries. If it was neither the genius for guns and sails, nor the family or rationality, something else must have been at work. I will argue that other, crucial cultural differences must be looked at in this connection, differences that perhaps are, after all, of a millennial character and are still at work today, even though they play much less of a role now than they did, let us say, in the eighteenth century. I refer to what we call 'territorial law' and its younger sister, the 'sovereign state'.

The legal system of India perhaps represents the oldest living tradition of written law in the world and it is certainly more extensive and diverse even than that of classical Rome. But whereas in the experience of Europe 'the state' and 'the law' seem to be condemned to jointly create the phenomenon of a territorial rule of law, in India law and state appear to be capable of separate existences. In India, as a result, in spite of the weakness and frequent collapse of political power, the legal system seems to have been immune to any negative effects that this might have had on its authority. Also, in the history of the rulers and kingdoms of South Asia, little is found of what in Europe is called an autonomous public sphere, that is kept alive by a 'state' by means of legal and judicial provisions. In the ideal typical European state, on the other hand, such a public sphere is in place and, unshaken by the fickleness of shifting alliances, is capable of resisting the pressures of faction and patronage. The reason is that Indian law was clearly not meant to impose, through the medium of royal power, on society an impersonal, territorial, rule of law and did not require the creation and maintenance of a 'public' domain separate from that of the 'private' interests of clientele and kinship, as the European state was expected to do. Indian law kept a permanent distance from the sphere of royal power. It emanated from an independent source of authority and held fast to an orientation that was transcendent and ethical, rather than directly geared to the management of party conflict or the promotion of political order for its own sake. It never had the ambition to impose itself on the bustle of party rivalry that was the business of kings.[2]

Significantly, the oldest written sources of the law in India are to be found neither in royal decrees and legislation, nor in customary law. The point of departure is not the throne or the judges of a so-called 'early state', but must be looked for in the oldest Vedic schools of the brahmans. There, far from the stir of power and violence, were born notions concerning the natural and eternal order of things—which even the gods are subject to —as well as norms with regard to virtue and proper behaviour that came to be summarised under the term *dharma*. It is true that norms of this nature could and can be adopted and be declared as valid by dynastic rulers or other power brokers whenever they failed, even on pain of sanctions, to settle rivalries of a disturbing nature by negotiation and compromise. Yet, this practical application of the law by the wheelers and dealers of this world did not contaminate its authority with the impurity of compromise, because its source, its origins, were outside the domain of power and, therefore, beyond the grasp of those who wielded power. *Dharma* is born in a sovereign domain where the king's foot cannot tread. Those who wield power have only indirect access to this sovereignty and are autonomous only when managing a province such as taxation that is indifferent from the point of view of *dharma*, because it represents a competence that is not concerned with the dharmic issue of what is ethically pure.

Initially, legal prescriptions in the modern sense of the term had hardly a place among the multitude of traditions preserved by the Vedic people and cherished by the brahmans whose duty it was to transmit them to the next generation. Those on the ritual of the all-important sacrifices were imparted in the form of *sutra*s, very compact aforisms in prose, apparently meant to be learnt by heart by the disciples of a master in a Vedic school and to serve as mnemonic assistance to those initiated in their use. Among these texts, the so-called *dharma-sutra*s set out the rights and duties of the Arya, that is the Indo–European speaking elite of householders. In this way, rules for correct social relationships and behaviour were gradually formulated. Probably in each of the great Vedic schools, collections of *dharma-sutra*s that were not limited to the treatment of ritual duties, came to occupy, albeit a minor, place in the curriculum. They tended to what Europeans later would convince themselves was 'early law'. The didactic, advisory voice, typical of the ethical manual, however, would remain typical of these and later legal texts. They would never, until the British period, assume the prescriptive tone of a lawyers' law of the kind the West was familiar with.

During the next phase of the history of the law, more specialised legal disciplinary schools came into being, independently of the old all-inclusive Vedic schools. The *dharma-sutra*s were systematically studied there. The literary deposit of the new legal discipline now emerging is known as the genre of the *dharma-shastra*s, texts arranged in a strict order, so that, later on, British administrators did not hesitate to assign the status of 'codes' to them. But in India, unlike Europe, there was no place for rulers acting as 'law givers', legislating about each and everything. In cases where the learned brahmans could not find a Vedic (i.e. *sruti* or revealed) text that elucidated an issue or confirmed a tradition, it was considered reasonable to assume that an underlying original text had once existed and was lost. The brahman authors of the *dharma* (i.e. *smrti* or traditional) literature, who must have been excellent people, must have been well acquainted with the lost original and could be trusted to represent an almost spotless line connecting the contemporary legal discipline with the Vedic past. Such reasoning, which was conditional on kings and rulers never infringing upon the autonomy of the law schools, left room for multiple interpretation and would be resorted to throughout Indian legal history. The flexibility in the construction of the law remained one of the features and also one of the strong points of the Indian legal system. It must be regarded as an intrinsic element, in a sense even the core, of the oldest Indian practice of law finding. But it could flower only thanks to the Indian legal discipline having an existence independent of politics.

This is not to deny that the learned brahman interpreters of the *sruti* texts, of the legal literature and of good custom (*achara*) were, already at an early stage of what we are used to call 'state formation', welcome advisors at royal courts and that they put their expertise to good use as judges of ethical issues. Yet, in the last analysis, the brahmans's primary, even their only concern was the virtue of householders and people's hopes of a reward after this life. All the rest was derivative. The brahman was not subject to any king, but only to *dharma* and to Him who is the regulator of sacrifice. Therefore, only he knew what, in each case, is sin and what is not and only he knew the adequate expiation. As long as he maintained his link with the transcendent sphere of sovereignty, did he retain the competence to advise those in power in such matters. The king, in his turn, could inflict punishment, either on the brahman's indication or, if his only concern was the secular management of the affairs of society, in his own right. In this restricted sphere, outside the sovereign realm of *dharma*, lay his power and his duty of independent action. For him to claim 'sovereignty', would be blasphemous and tantamount to a desertion of his position in society.

In all this, ample room was left for a dialogue with social practice. The king, while faithfully keeping in touch with brahmanical values and injunctions, for instance, concerning the *varna* model of society, was supposed to take into consideration the customs of his people. How the king and his court performed this balancing act, was of no direct concern to the learned lawyers: they were only thinkers and systematisers, deeply involved in questions of virtue and order, though with an understanding of what was practical and what wasn't, and of what one could reasonably demand from the average king and judge. Therefore, though academic questions continued to belong to the province of the brahman *literati*, the latter left the executive aspect of their recommendations to the king, who remained immediately responsible for social harmony while, at the same time, presiding over, and often being involved in, the conflicts within his realm. The lawyers were respected as the providers of second, third, and ultimate opinions, but could never be held responsible for the executive outcome of the particular issue reviewed by them. It was the king alone who could translate brahmanical advice concerning penitence into a criminal verdict. That role was not conceded or delegated to him as a kind of rest category of the law that the brahmans did not care about. To maintain society in a state of order was explicitly endorsed as his most special duty, his so-called *rajadharma*. How else could one attempt to live one's life according to the prescriptions of one's birth and in such a manner that one retained hope of a future existence? On the other hand, only as long as the *raja* refrained from interference with sovereign *dharma*, could a man receive the guidance he needed to keep his family on a course away from sin. Political correctness, one could say in this connection, was a contradiction in terms. What is political is in one sphere, what is correct in another. In this sense, if in no other, the *raja*, from the European perspective, was no more than a 'little king'.

In Europe, the legal profession used its great prestige and expertise with regard to the 'reception', interpretation and reformulation of ancient law to, as it were, penetrate the state, then to support it and confer on it a degree of legitimacy that came to be termed sovereignty. Lacking an independent sovereign authority of their own (of the kind possessed by the Indian lawyers), they could only assist this state through authoring what in their civilisation became known as 'positive' law. This positive law expressed the sovereignty and political correctness of the European state. As a result, a high degree of juridification became a distinctive feature of the European political system. In India, on the other hand, the sovereign domain of the law ultimately remained beyond the socially disruptive influences of the conflict-ridden world of power.[3] There, the purity of the law and the virtue of man were too important matters to be left to kings and their necessarily vagarious fortunes.

There was nothing rigid or artificial in this duality. It was true, that, in the final analysis, the justification of the brahmanical legal injunctions could only consist in their maintaining the transcendentally fixed order as given to man at the time of creation and that the message simply was, that to violate universal order was sin. As to practice, however, the endless variety of historical forms that emerged in India, is proof enough of the vitality of the system.

Therefore, though clearly distinguished from each other, individual penance and executive punishment, *dharma-shastra* and royal decrees, abstract good manners and daily jurisprudence jointly developed an inexhaustible array of social forms. The exchanges between the brahmanical schools and the royal courts, the two centres of, respectively, transcendental authority or sovereignty and immanent or executive power, were not even the only engines at work. Much of what is crucial in Indian history consists of the unceasing negotiations of each of them with the world of diverse and endlessly evolving custom. The result of this tripartite dialogue is not primarily the taking shape of a unified legal system, let alone a process of 'legislation'. Dialogue, not systematic agreement, was what was aimed at. The brahmanical, the royal and the customary might occupy confronting positions and express themselves in different idioms. Yet, they kept going a conversation about all the social issues that presented themselves. The king's *rajadharma* assigned him a role not only in policing the country and in the maintenance of *dharma*, but importantly also in facilitating exactly this process of negotiation. Characteristic is the absence of statute law that imposes itself. The term 'state formation', used indiscriminately by historians as if it were a millennial, world-historical phenomenon, blurs this important feature of the Indian model of civilisation.

This is not to deny that gradually, brahman counsellors, as their attention shifted from the family to the administration, got involved in the executive dilemmas that dominated the minds of those at the king's court. Typically, whereas the *sutra*s, in a language meant for insiders only, spoke to the disciples resident in the old Vedic schools, the *shastra*s, with clarity and distinctly, addressed all those in society who bore responsibility, in particular the king as ruler and as judge. Yet, it is true to say that the *shastra*s, in spite of this shift in direction, were, first and foremost, concerned with the moral content and the merit of the behaviour they discussed, not primarily with its punishability or administrative desirability. Practically in none of these texts does the compiler or author take the risk of giving himself away as an observer of particular historical events such as the emergence of Buddhism or the rise to power in North India of the Maurya dynasty. Clearly, such references would have detracted from the timeless character that these texts, in spite of their intention to be useful, needed to claim in order to retain their authority. Yet, the increased following of sects, like that of the Buddhists and the emergence of kingdoms that, more than ever before, were intensively involved in the fiscal and forensic affairs of their clients and subjects, could only have led to a greater administrative demand for authoritative legal opinion. This demand the brahmans had to meet if they were to maintain their strong position in the field of the law. The royal courts, moreover, would have more to offer in the way of patronage than the pious donors on whom the old Vedic schools depended.[4]

To sum up, what is striking in the case of ancient India, and to an extent also in medieval India or even to the present day, is that the authoritative re-interpretation of the maxims of the Indian art of living or civil morality, remained exclusively and firmly in the hands of learned lawyers or, in any case, beyond the grasp of rulers. This feature of the history of India must be understood as the natural corollary of the belief, strongly held in India even today, that power corrupts and that whoever claims authority or wants to keep it, must keep away from power and government. I do not argue for a Dumontian view, according to which a domain of brahmanical clean hands 'encompasses' and tolerates a sphere of dirty conflict and royal violence. Rather, as suggested already, what we see at work is a triple and equal alliance of, first, a sovereign sphere of virtue, which is the special domain of the renouncers and the learned, i.e. of those having access to the universal and transcendental, then an entirely different sphere of practical dominion and royal order, indispensable if one desires to maintain society in a state of civil virtue, and, finally, the dynamic *ordre vécu*, that is lived-in world or *Lebenswelt*, with its evolving customs, shifting loyalties and survival strategies. The dynamic of Indian society consists in the dialogue in which these three are continuously locked.[5] The difference with the dynamics of Europe seems to me to consist in the fact that in the case of India, unlike the European case, the dialogue is not necessarily dominated by a 'state', but is equally balanced between the domains of power and custom on the one hand and a more legitimate and sovereign sphere of values and ethics on the other. This suggests an Indian polity to which the term state in the European sense can hardly be applied, at least, as I will argue in a minute, until the arrival of the so-called 'early modern state'. Or, to put it differently, to suggest that states invariably form the backbone of the Indian *ancien regime* and to force Indian history into the straightjacket of 'state formation' would be an even more reductionist exercise than it is in the case of European history.

Much attention has, during the last few decades, been given to the historically more visible participant in this perennial Indian dialogue, the sphere of royal order, or, as it is commonly termed, 'the little kingdom'. The term is an academic invention. Of course, 'no king in the history of India ever defined himself a little king or spoke of his little kingdom.'[6] Yet, the expression may be used, provided its un-Indian origin is recognised. The sharing of the resources of the kingdom and the legitimacy derived from it and, for instance, from temple patronage, which makes the raja the sacral vice-regent of the god, have been shown, by Nicholas Dirks and other ethnohistorians, to be essential features of the Indian kingdom. Recently, a number of German anthropologist-historians, pupils of Hermann Kulke, have significantly contributed to this field of studies, which, as a result, assumes an increasingly sophisticated character.[7] Taking into account the work of, for instance, Jan Heesterman and Jean-Claude Galey on classical Indian kingship, they have even addressed the question whether Indian kingship and royal power can be understood in a way that is of help in writing not only the pre-colonial and colonial history of India, but even in interpreting political power in independent India. This may be too ambitious. I agree with Georg Berkemer that 'the end of the old regime is also the end of the little kingdom.'[8] Margret Frenz suggests that, if we adopt a concept of Indian kingship that is more dynamic and contextual than hitherto applied, it will be more useful to historians who, like herself, aim at doing away with eurocentric models of the state. Studies like those of Berkemer, Frenz, and Burkhard Schnepel contribute in a most constructive manner to the historisation of the model of the 'little king'. One of the results of such an approach of historisation and bringing down to earth the model is that, more often than not, we no longer see any significant difference between the kingship of a 'little king' and that of any Indian raja, whether great or small. I have suggested above a dynamic and contextual tripartite model that may be of use in further historicising our image of classical and medieval Indian kingship and enhancing our understanding of the continuities in Indian forms of rulership during the millennium discussed in this volume. But this would surely not be enough.

It is of overriding importance that, groping for an idiom that does justice to Indian history, we must be aware of the need to avoid all European terms and accept Indian ones if, because of their contextual quality, they do justice to India where European terminology does not. The term sovereignty, for instance, understood as the freedom to decide one's behaviour independently of others and to establish it as unshakably legitimate in its own right, is bound with European, sixteenth-century ideas about the unassailable authority and claim to power of the indivisible European state. Yet, as I have argued above, if there is sovereignty in India, it applies to the domain of an august and transcendentally legitimated *dharma*, not to that of political management. The European notions of the sovereignty of states clash with the flexible, shared, and negotiable nature of interests and ritual rights in the Indian *riyasat*. There, even consecrated rajas possess no more than a basketful of rights that represent as many claims to participate in judicial, ritual, fiscal and redistributive politics. Such a basket is of a size and has a content different in the case of each of them, whereas its weight diminishes or increases as the wheel of fortune recycles the rights contained in it. To think of ways to retain the term sovereignty through the invention of all sorts of different fragments of, for instance, 'ritual', 'political', 'parcellised', or 'shared' sovereignty, as is sometimes done, is hardly helpful.[9] Is not what we really see, if we look at Indian kingship, a participation in the rivalry for power and resources with a certain room for manoeuvre and a continuously refurbished claim to act as patron? It is a process that, if it may be empasised again, of itself produces no sovereignty, but is in the last resort subject to the teachings of *dharmic* referees who speak from a domain that is wholly separated from that of politics. Rather than sovereignty, what seems to present itself seems to be a field in which different measures of autonomous agency make themselves felt and are engaged in dialogue (whether tripartite or even more complex than that) with each other.

This means that, if we speak of the British colonial onslaught on India in the eighteenth century, it may be preferable to say that the British introduced the (European) concept of sovereignty and imposed it on the princes of India rather than that they wrested sovereignty from the rajas. The rajas were not so much asked to hand over sovereignty (a concept they would not have understood) to the British as denied the agency, the patronage, both sacral and secular, the resources and the autonomous negotiating position that, according to *rajadharma* and prevailing practice, were the essence of their kingship. When their right to receive gifts at festivals was stolen from the baskets of powers that represented their political capital, one of the bases of the Indian redistributive political system was removed. A term like sovereignty, which suggests a positive legality in the manner of European constitutional law, can only confuse things.

Another alien, though not a European, expression adopted to describe eighteenth-century India by many, mostly non-Indian, historians, is *fitna*. This Perso-Arab term, proposed by Wink, confuses rather than elucidates historical events surrounding the 'little kingdom'.[10] Now little used in India, and then only in a pejorative way (*fitna uthana*, to cause mischief), in the eighteenth century the term belonged to the vocabulary, or rather the propaganda, of the military-fiscalist or 'early modern' state builders, like the newly independent governors of Mughal provinces, the Maratha warlords, and men like Haidar Ali and Tipu Sultan of Mysore. It is abundantly clear, that well before the onslaught of colonialism, rulers emerged in Indian history who led their subjects on the road to modern army formation and the maximisation of taxes. As Harbans Mukhia has brilliantly shown in his comparative work, intensive fiscalisation is as typical of the Indian polity as intensive juridification is typical of the European state.[11] Norbert Peabody has convincingly argued that the military-fiscalist aspect of the Indian kingdom must indeed be considered essential to our understanding of the early modern period of Indian history.[12] The *fitna*-label was employed by the rulers of the military-fiscalist or early modern states to denounce the political culture of alliance and negotiation so characteristic of the 'little kingdom', the raja's polity or *riyasat*, whose place in legal Indian history we have discussed. More than the Mughals, the early modern states of India were keen to brand as rebellious and illegitimate the hundreds of minor, but autonomous, princes of India as corruption-, disloyalty-, treason-, in short *fitna-*, ridden. By uncritically embracing this term of abuse—rather fruitlessly, because in itself it doesn't explain anything—in modern studies, one unwittingly places oneself in the camp of these early modern, military-fiscalist state builders and even, by extension, in that of the all-too-modern, but equally military-fiscalist, British colonialists.

As an 'ideal type', the military-fiscalist state, characterised by the attempts of a central ruler at maximising (often through tax farming) the resources of as wide as possible a region and using them, with the help of a costly standing army, to monopolise power, is the antithesis and arch-enemy of the 'little kingdom' or *riyasat*, that is 'the *jajmani* system writ large' (Dirks), based on the exchange, sharing and redistribution of resources. Therefore, one cannot adopt the slogans of the conquerors and, at the same time, be fair to the Indian *ancien régime*. To that *ancien régime* the early modern states did not belong, whereas the Indian rajas, great and small, represented the essence of it. It seems inevitable to recognise, that the continuous easing of and tightening of alliances denounced by the military-fiscalists, constitute perhaps the central features of the political culture of the millennium of Indian history we are discussing.[13] Compared to the political tradition of Europe, the millennium's main characteristic was the Indian kingdom with its concentration on executive, situational compromise and practical solutions. It was, as noted above, a polity that ultimately refreshed its norms at *dharmic* values that were rooted in a sphere that was not situational, but absolute and immune from the imperfections of royal compromise. The Indian kingdoms were in no need of a *trias politica*, a separation of the legislative, the judicial and the executive, which, in the European state, all came within the purview of the 'sovereign' ruler. The reason is that the first of this European trinity, the legislative, was never entrusted to the Indian polity and remained safely beyond its power. The tripartite model I proposed and of which the Indian *riyasat* is but one of the components, is based not on the distinction of different royal functions, but on the autonomy of a function that is external to royalty.

There is indeed nothing dishonourable or amiss about the chemistry of Indian royal alliance politics and it deserves a better label than the rather nasty, un-Indian one of *fitna*. To borrow this military-fiscalist predator's tag in describing the admirable negotiating skills and survival talents of their preys, India's 'little kings', is not only unjust, it is also a distortion of history. The term *fitna* is indicative of the incapacity of the early modern and, for that matter, the colonial modern, world to yield to or to recognise the legitimacy of the maxims of the Indian *ancien régime*. The reaction of Indian kings to the attacks launched against them by the early modern, including the early colonial, states can only be understood in terms of the norms of their *rajadharma* and its embeddedness in the civilisation it was part of. The British, however, as noted by Frenz, could see in their behaviour no more than an overreaction, an extreme, but misguided, love of freedom and free agency.

This being said, and however healthy it may be to disembarrass the two opposite models, that of the 'little kingdom' and of the early modern state, of concepts that mix them up and thus fail to explain them, it is true that eighteenth-century Indian history saw a number of polities that partook of the qualities of both. Peabody has shown, from the example of the state of Kota, how the interaction of these models and the dialogic entrepreneurship along the 'fault-lines' of their idioms of legitimacy and power, produced historical complexities that determined important features of the British federal empire. The point is well-argued and well taken. Still, I am not one of those who want to do away with the precolonial versus colonial divide of Indian history or, in other words, with the terminus ad quem of the millennium we discuss.

The differences between the Indian early modern and the colonial enemies of India's *ancien régime* are far too important for that. To the disciplinarian tools of sophisticated and overwhelming military force and fiscal penetration of agrarian society, characteristics of the Indian early modern, as well as of the—pathologically modern—colonial states, the servants of East India Company added a third one. I refer to their insidious procedures, the so-called 'rules and regulations', as the classic configuration of which the Cornwallis Code of 1793 must be regarded. An understanding of this instrument of rule which ran the roost of much of India during almost forty years— between 1793 and 1830—and remained largely in place after that, is, to my mind, the more important as the administrative and social history of the period has been largely skipped by historians so far.

This Code, or colonial constitution, consisting of 48 regulations, running into 387 pages of print already in 1793, had as its main purpose to create a distance between the servants of the colonial state and its subjects. The means to do so was to force the population into the role of 'citizen', defined as a 'permanently settled' holder of landed property, whose possessions were legally secured to him. The government granted him the right to act as a legal person, whenever he chose to do so, provided he left the path of the freely negotiating agent and subjected himself to an elaborate set of court procedures. The Company assumed that their new subjects, in their search of justice, would in the end find their way into the many intricate channels of the government's impersonal, that is non-situational, but 'transparent' judicial machinery. This allowed the British rulers to eschew executive rule, to retain clean hands and to forego the need to empathise with and enter into the complex inner world of their Indian subjects. The East India Company thus imposed on India a social contract by which it abdicated practically all executive responsibility, simply referring their subjects to the colonial courts of law. No longer as negotiators, but as tax payers and litigants would the colonial state take notice of them. In fact, apart from the military-fiscalist side of it, colonial rule almost entirely limited itself to the administration of a system of justice which would, because of its sheer 'transparency', set right all things. In this way, moreover, the Company could continue to denounce the Indian political culture of alliance and compromise, where everything was contextual, situational, i.e. lacking transparency, and stigmatise it as a world devoid of principle and, therefore, in decay. It followed inexorably, that India's 'little kings' were hopeless relics of the past.

Early British rule, therefore, culminated in 1793 in a constitution that was, first of all, an institutional onslaught on India, one that attempted to impose a set of judicial rules and procedures, deemed 'modern' in Europe at the time, even enlightened, but basically at variance with the culture of contextual negotiation and flexible alliance that was of the essence of Indian political culture. In the first regulation of the Cornwallis Code, which declared permanent all earlier land settlements in Bengal, the Company relinquished agrarian society to the forces of the market and to the courts of justice. The courts would uniformly protect tenants and owners and, if allowed time, they would, undisturbed by executive interference, through the perspicacity and clarity of the regulations, transform agrarian society and propel it to ever increasing progress. The Code abolished the revenue courts which had been closely linked to the former fiscal administration of Bengal, established a completely independent judiciary, and transferred all suits to it. The major principle of rule was henceforward for the government to distance itself from the management of agrarian affairs and to avoid 'infringing' upon the legal autonomy conferred on the new citizen-proprietors. 'Government must divest itself', declared Regulation 1, 1793, 'of the power of infringing, in its executive capacity, the rights and privileges which, as exercising the legislative authority, it has conferred on the landholders'. This craving for colonial hygiene is found throughout the Cornwallis Code. In a 'corrupt'—the Company's term for the '*fitna*' of the Indian military fiscalists—environment, the reasoning went, the only clean-hands policy was a hands-off policy. The government even, in its own words, 'has determined to divest itself of the power of interfering in the administration of the laws and regulations in the first instance, reserving only, as a court of appeal or review, the decision of certain cases in the last resort' (Regulation 2, 1793; Regulation 3, 1793). The agency of the procedures of a highly mechanistic system of adjective law would render superfluous all human agency. Nothing could be further removed from the spirit of *rajadharma*: here we meet a government that refused to arbitrate the rivalries and contrasting interests of its people on a daily basis or taking into account their personal and historical contexts. Instead, it committed the blasphemy of claiming leadership in the moral domain of *dharma* itself.

Essential in all this was the creation of a homogeneous civil service, consisting primarily of a judiciary that would be imbued with a single rhetoric and idiom of rule: that of the Cornwallis constitution. This service would then spread to the farthest corners of Bengal a culture of abiding trust in the formalities of the law. Thus, the Cornwallis Code was to ignite the engine of progress, start the bottom-up regeneration of India, the irreversible Indian pursuit of happiness and freedom. Court procedure would be the oil to ensure the smooth running of the wheels of an otherwise self-propelling machine. The new spirit of enlightened citizenship and trust would take over from the stagnation and factionalism of the *ancien régime* in India as it had done elsewhere in the world. The administration would limit itself to maintaining and improving a skeletal structure based on a legal ethos such as was taken to be universally beneficial to mankind. The Company's success would thus depend on its having as little as possible to do with anything specifically Indian.

This, however, did not mean that Indian agency or Indian law had no place in the colonial state as devised by Cornwallis and his associate in all this, Barlow. On the contrary, they rejected any ambition to impose a new substantive law on the country. The law was in no need of change; it needed 'regulation'. It would be sufficient to enable the people of Bengal to bring to the courts their own legal notions and arrange for their laws to be explained there by their own representatives, the pandits and muftis who were the learned doctors of the country. India had her own substantive laws which should not be interfered with. But they were in need of a system and proper procedure; they must be made modern by the removal of all internal inconsistencies. Only European judges, steeped in the niceties of modern adjective law, could be trusted to preside over the process. They would cook the raw victuals that those seeking justice would bring to the kitchens of their courts, the refineries of Indian civilisation. And, according to the Company's scenario, these courts would, in their turn, leaven and saturate India with the juices of universal fairness and impersonal civility.

This, of course, would never happen. The situational fairness of Indian justice that characterised the executive tradition of the Indian polity, would indeed be largely stamped out, at least, for the time being, from the judiciary apparatus, perhaps to find a refuge elsewhere, in a kind of alternative or fragmentary little kingdoms, so to say, beyond the reach of the state. But the claim of the colonial centre to be the ultimate judge of values and ethics, claimed emphatically in the Cornwallis Code, would irreparably disqualify the Company's authority in India, because in the Indian order of things that claim invaded the realm of *dharma*, which is something any genuinely Indian state could do only at the peril of self-extinction.

In September 1824, when the Upper Doab was devoid of East India Company troops because of the Burma War, a rumour spread in the area that the British and their state were about to go, '*aap se*', as it was said. A century later, Gandhiji had a similar vision. And two years ago, Ranajit Guha identified as the essence of the European onslaught on Indian history the spread of the idea of the State as the embodiment of all that gives direction to world history and leads it to its destiny.[14] Europe's contempt for Indian institutions and, based on this disdainful attitude, her justification of the imposition of the modern colonial state on India have much in common with Hegel's delegitimation of all social forms in Europe that didn't deserve to be exercised in the name of the state. Yet, institutions of the kind envisaged by Hegel or Cornwallis could never strike root in Indian society and remained, therefore, in the last analysis, devoid of sovereignty. The modern state could not legitimately claim to be the basis on which India's history would progress. There is ample justification for Ranajit Guha's question to Indian historians as to how they think they can liberate themselves from the terror of the Hegelian, that is European, concept of the state, so that they will, again, be able to turn to Indian society and the complexities of it that no state can encompass.

Already in 1993, Partha Chatterjee, in his *The Nation and its Fragments*, rejected all scenarios of nation and state formation and started on his search for niches, fragments of society, uncontaminated by the terror of the modern state, where the sovereignty of what was the genuinely Indian Geist (to use the Hegelian term) still reigned. It was an attempt at piecing together a cultural domain that could be the source of unpolluted norms of public behaviour.[15] And in the year 2000, Dipesh Chakrabarty's *Provincialising Europe* fulminated against the first-in-Europe-then-with-you or first-happened-elsewhere models of world history, which are not world history, but nothing else than Western projections on the world.[16] All these historians try to escape from the public-versus-private dichotomy that has dominated European historiography since Aristotle. The last thing that they aspire to is to be reduced to the role of a citizen of an all-too-European state. At the most they are content to act as a voters, because in that capacity you at least don't lose your dignity. These authors are looking for a civil society that will not condescend to serve the state as its social basis, but one that is autonomous and makes the state shrink and assume the form of a somewhat littler kingdom. Or, at least, they look the other way and have their certainties in places where the state cannot reach.

Such ideas are not unrelated with the question of the sovereignty-less Indian *riyasat* or polity that characterised the millennium we discuss in this volume. In her keynote address to the European Conference of Modern South Asian Studies held at Heidelberg in 2002, Susanne Rudolph drew attention to Gandhi's radical rejection of the separation of the private and the public. Gandhi's *ashrams* meant to be subaltern, genuinely autonomous, moral institutions of private persons who transformed themselves into the servants of a hopefully ever more civil society and who never craved for the power vested in 'the state'. In Gandhi's vision, Rudolph remarked, the Indian state is morally too weak, even incapable, to be the arena of the common weal. Real legitimacy is vested elsewhere. In this interpretation of Gandhi, in terms of what I said before, a state emerges that carries limited legitimacy and is given a say only outside the sovereign sphere of supreme justice.[17]

Goody is right in pointing out the basic similarities between India and Europe. Yet, there are features of the Indian and the European civilisations that should not, in an exaggerated urge to wipe out all difference and colour and choice that distinguish civilisations, be ignored. On the contrary, such differences can, for the two subcontinental provinces of Eurasia, have great mutual explanatory value. And why not rejoice in the fact? Although India and Europe, as civilisations and unions have, for perhaps a thousand years, chosen different trajectories and have tried to solve in different ways the insoluble problems involved in our search for a balance between relationships and individuality, for ways out of conflict towards security and for strategies that produce social trust, can nonetheless perfectly understand and do justice to each other, intellectually as well as in other respects.

Or, in other words, if we provincialise Europe and see its history as unique, as happened-only-there, we will at last be able to see India as a sister province of Europe and her history as well as happened-only-there, as unique to India. Surely the millennium we are discussing offers, perhaps more than the periods that precede and follow it, the choice material to do this.

REFERENCES

1. Jack Goody, *The East in the West*, Cambridge, 1996.
2. This and the following paragraphs are based on my 'Early Law in India', in F.J.M. Feldbrugge (ed.), *The Law's Beginnings*, Leiden/Boston, 2003, pp. 11–22. For perhaps the best introduction into the subject, see Robert Lingat, *The Classical Law of India*, Berkeley, 1973.
3. I refer to the work of J.C. Heesterman, for instance, his *The Inner Conflict of Tradition*, Chicago, 1985.

4. One can only agree with Lariviere that *dharma-shastra* represents law in a very real sense, though what 'real' means in the Indian cultural and historical context is a different question, as we have tried to show above. Richard W. Lariviere, 'Dharmasastra, Custom, "Real Law" and "Apocryphal Smrtis", in Bernhard Kölver (ed.), *Recht, Staat und Verwaltung im klassischen Indien*, München, 1997, pp. 97–110.
5. See my 'The Indian and the British Law Machines: Some Remarks on Law and Society in British India', in W.J. Mommsen and J.A. de Moor (eds.), *European Expansion and Law: The Encounter of European and Indigenous Law in 19th- and 20th-Century Africa and Asia*, Oxford/New York, 1992, pp. 201–35.
6. Heiko Frese, 'The Great Afterword', in Georg Berkemer and Margret Frenz (eds.), *Sharing Sovereignty: the Little Kingdom in South Asia*, Berlin, 2003, p. 245.
7. See especially the articles in the volume mentioned in the preceding note. Burkhard Schnepel, *The Jungle Kings: Ethnohistorical Aspects of Politics and Ritual in Orissa*, Delhi, 2002; Margret Frenz, *From Contact to Conquest: Transition to British Rule in Malabar*, New Delhi, 2003.
8. Georg Berkemer, 'Little Kings or Little Kingdoms? Some Unresolved Questions', in Berkemer & Frenz, *Sharing Sovereignty*, p. 241.
9. See for these distinctions, Burkhard Schnepel, *The Jungle Kings*, pp. 37, 45, 51. Peabody coins 'overlapping, layered, and non-exclusive sovereignties' (p. 83) and later adds 'multiple' and 'interlaced' ones (pp. 156–57)); with him the term seems to lose most of its European resonance and to stand for 'competence', which, after all, is perhaps a preferable term.
10. André Wink, *Land and Sovereignty in India: Agrarian Society and Politics under the Eighteenth Century Maratha Svarajya*, Cambridge, 1986.
11. Harbans Mukhia, 'Was there Feudalism in Indian History?', *The Journal of Peasant Studies*, vol. 8 (1980–81), pp. 289ff. This article was republished in Harbans Mukhia, *Perspectives on Medieval History*, New Delhi, 1994, pp. 91–152; there, see esp. pp. 118ff.
12. Norbert Peabody, *Hindu Kingship and Polity in Precolonial India*, Cambridge, 2003, pp. 80ff.
13. For a first analysis on my part of the Indian art of the management of shifting alliances and the negotiation of compromise, see my dissertation *An Armed Peasantry and its Allies*, Leiden, 1983, later revised as *Naukar, Rajput and Sepoy: the Ethnohistory of the Military Labour Market of Hindustan, 1450–1850*, Cambridge, 1990.
14. Ranajit Guha, *History at the Limit of World-History*, New York, 2002.
15. Partha Chatterjee, *The Nation and its Fragments: Colonial and Postcolonial Histories*, Princeton, 1993.
16. Dipesh Chakrabarty, *Provincializing Europe: Postcolonial Thought and Historical Difference*, Princeton and Oxford, 2000, pp. 180–213.
17. Susanne Hoeber Rudolph and Lloyd I. Rudolph, 'The Coffee House and the Ashram', Keynote Speech at the 17th European Conference of Modern South Asian Studies, Heidelberg, 9–14 September 2002, p. 26.

Chapter 2

Aristocratic Body Techniques in Early Medieval India*

Daud Ali

This essay seeks to contribute to the small field of studies on etiquette and comportment among elite societies in pre-colonial India, a topic to which Professor Mukhia has recently drawn our attention.[1] Most of this literature has focused on Indo-Persianate culture as it evolved under the Mughals, though there are ample sources available for reconstructing courtly manners in earlier centuries. The essay here will be concerned with the Sanskrit sources of early medieval India. It will focus on a related realm of social history which has been scarcely touched on at all by scholars, though there have been a handful of studies in mostly European contexts: the history of bodily postures and movements, what may be conveniently called 'gesture'.[2] The topic of gesture is a potentially vast one, including a variety of types of history and sources, but this study will focus on codes of bodily movement among the noble and service classes which emerged in various royal courts throughout the subcontinent in the centuries following the Gupta empire. Even then, due in part to the fragmentary nature of the evidence and in part to limitations of space, it is not possible here to provide anything like a comprehensive survey of the material relating to the etiquette of gestures among the aristorcratic classes—though such a project remains a desideratum. The goal instead will be to present a synoptic view of certain gestures and their uses among the courtly elite as well as to explore a few key 'body techniques'and their wider conceptual moorings. The paper will be divided into four sections. The first will explore theoretical and methodological problems attending the study of gestures in pre-colonial Indian history. The second section will review the evidence of and principles lying behind several key gestures performed at court, which became standard protocols in the centuries following the Gupta era. The third section will examine the role of bearing and posture in courtly representations—how people of different classes and ranks were expected to move and carry themselves. Building on the observations of sections two and three, the final part will explore an important family of body concepts and techniques current among the sections of the nobility, which may usefully be understood as 'gracefulness', and which reveal an important relationship between aesthetics and power.

I

Considering the wide diversity and manifest complexity of the sources used in this paper and the almost completely neglected theme of gesture in current historiography, it may be germane to begin with a few theoretical and methodological considerations to set the stage for the analyses which follow. It is probably not contentious to assert that many apparently 'natural' bodily inclinations and gestures in all societies are in fact 'learned', either consciously or unconsciously, by individuals. It has also been widely recognised that while some gestures and movements of the body tend toward the technical or functional, others have a distinctly communicative or semiotic dimension, often replacing, supplementing or even contradicting speech. By extension, it may be admitted that not only are an individual's bodily proclivities and gestures 'learned' in specific social contexts, they themselves form an important means by which social relationships are structured and experienced on a day-to-day basis. But in spite of such apparently common sense acknowledgements, historians have typically placed bodily gestures, when treated at all, in what Marcel Mauss famously noted in the case of sociology as the 'rubric of the miscellaneous'.[3]

To remedy this negligence, Mauss proposed the concept of 'technique' to describe actions which are both 'effective', having some practical outcome, and 'traditional', transmitted between agents through conscious instruction or unconscious imitation. It was thus possible, according to Mauss, to suggest typologies and principles of specific body techniques according to gender, age, efficiency, function, and the like. Equipped with this perspective, the sociologist was everywhere faced, according to Mauss, with 'physio-psycho-sociological assemblages of series of actions'.[4] From a semiotic point of view, the coherence of these 'assemblages' suggests a further proposition, that a society's collective array of gestures and body movements are ordered by a variety of structuring principles that give meaning to particular acts and movements within specific environments—there is, in other words, a set of underlying 'grammars' or *langues* of the body. Any single gesture takes on meaning through its relation to the totality of other gestures within a system, the 'grammar' of which provides both actors and viewers with rules of deployment and a framework of meaning. These grammars are fractured and multiple, their totality being a set of complex overlapping codes through which individuals interact with one another. The potential for misrecognition, ambiguity, and dissemblance is considerable, and is compounded by the fact that gestural meaning may be generated and interpreted with or without the full intention of the agents concerned. Further, gestural codes coexist not only with one another but with other sign systems like speech and dress, with which they have their own complex relations. Medieval Indian literature presents numerous instances where bodily gestures or demeanour contradict sumptuary and cosmetic appearance. So a courtier, though dressed in the finery appropriate to his station, reveals an internal vice or low origins by incessant and excessive attention to his ornaments with his hands. A woman dressed in bark cannot conceal her noble birth, which is suggested by her placid and graceful gait.

The non-intentional dimension of bodily technique and expression has been of particular importance for sociologists. Mauss argued that the reason why a series of bodily techniques took root in any given individual was because they were 'assembled by and for social authority'.[5] Mauss saw the totality of these techniques as composing a *habitus*, the embodiment of collective 'practical reason'. Pierre Bourdieu has further refined the idea of *habitus* to denote a pre-conscious yet socially mediated realm of inclinations and habits (in both mind and body), which at once created the horizons of individual choice and facilitated the reproduction of specific social relations.[6] The advantage of this approach for the sociologist and historian is that it enables power relationships to be conceived not merely in institutions and doctrines, or 'ideologies', but in the most intimate bodily, psychical and affective tendencies of the individual. This gives far greater force to the proposition mentioned above that bodily techniques form a realm through which individuals unconcsiously experience, enact and reproduce social relationships.

Body techniques were crucially important aspects of public interaction in pre-bureaucratic and pre-print societies. If gestures and movements in such societies were often explicitly recognised 'status-attributes', forming parts of what Habermas called 'representative publicity'—where lords and leaders represented not abstractions but their own social being through demonstrable bearing, conduct and insignia—then they were also necessary instruments of 'communicative interaction'. Legal, financial and diplomatic relationships were often incomplete without mutually recognised gestures. In early India, gifts to Brahmans, for instance, were accompanied by various actions which culminated with the gesture of pouring water on to the donee's hand.[7] Verbal interactions like greetings and farewells were accompanied by specific gestures of deference and respect. Even written documents were 'performed' in a similar manner.[8] Overall, the extent to which such conventions structured both the bodily responses and innermost texture of individual behaviour—the reflexive responses of shame, deference, anger, loyalty and love which were the affective sinews of political and social life—has hardly been appreciated.

Some uncertainty about the value of studying gestures in medieval India certainly proceeds from their elusiveness in the historical record. This is no doubt because in India, as elsewhere, it is not gestures themselves, but representations of gestures—in various sources—which have survived in the historical record. In India, these representations—whether figural, iconographic, normative, or descriptive—have tended, like portrayals of the body itself, to be highly stylised and conventional. Sometimes it is difficult to know how such representations were enacted in social practice. Indeed, the relationship of such representations with the lived experience of men and women remains an important interpretive problem for the historian. But the problems which face the historian in the case of gesture should not be exaggerated, for they are not so different from those which attend the reconstruction of other domains of history—they in fact proceed from the same types of source material. Mainstream historical concerns like the chronology of dynastic transactions, the structure of polity, or the history of communities, have most often been derived from the same 'conventionalised' sources which provide us with information about bodily gestures. Compared to some historical concerns, the study of gestures may in fact have the advantage of being an explicit preoccupation in many of the early medieval sources. Their absence in historical analysis, thus, points to a limitation in some of our existing analytical frameworks.

As far as sources are concerned, the early texts on dramaturgy form a particularly interesting case in point—for they provide a tantalising source for the study of gestures in medieval India whose historical potential is perhaps as unique as it is problematic. Texts like the *Nāṭyaśāstra*, *Abhinayadarpaṇa*, and *Nāṭyadarpaṇa*, in providing directors, actors, dancers and audiences with directions for bodily movements on the stage (*āṅgikābhinaya*) provide an obvious source for the historian interested in reconstructing the social world of gestures. For it is obvious that one goal of such directions was to make actors on the stage immediately recognisable to audiences through gestures and postures.

It would be hasty, however, to generalise about the social currency of such gestures in real life. In fact, these texts seem to present a number of gestural repertoires whose relations with social conventions off the stage was complex. If we take the gestures of the hand alone, it is possible to perceive at least four types of gesture: those which were direct representations of conventions off the stage; those which indicated off-stage conventions in abbreviated form; those which were entirely conventional and symbolic of actions states and external objects; and finally those which had no symbolic or off-stage referents at all, being entirely ornamental—flourishes to supplement dance and other movement. It is clear here that all gestures were not conceived of as similar, and the degree to which wholly conventional or dance gestures on the stage had resonances with movement in everyday life requires further research.

Jean-Claude Schmitt, in his magisterial history of gesture in medieval Europe, distinguishes between three planes, or 'axes', through which gestures may be viewed: as signs expressive of internal states, as forms of non-verbal communication, and as both practically and symbolically efficacious actions.[9] Though there is considerable overlap between these categories, they provide a useful heuristic with which to approach some of the Indian materials. The vocabulary and concerns around gestures in Sanskrit texts are diverse.[10] Along the axis of expressivity we may place a variety of concerns. There were gestures which, like bodily attributes, indicated one's general social rank. For aristocrats, we must remember, being noble was not simply social category, but a way of living, thinking, and, indeed, moving. In Sanskrit drama, characters of noble rank are able to recognise one another immediately by observing carriage and demeanour. Gestures could also indicate particular virtues, qualities, or internal characteristics—haughty and humble men walked differently. Also under this axis were those particular gestures which revealed transient but crucial inner states and dispositions. The concern of correlating certain gestures with particular emotional states is found not merely in dramaturgical texts, but in a number of other genres which indicate the widespread importance of a sort of 'hermeneutics' of gesture. Judges, for example, were to ascertain the guilt of accused criminals by close attention not only to their speech, but to their bodies and facial expressions.[11] Princes, courtiers, and lovers were all to observe each other closely for outward changes which indicated inner disposition. Kāmandaki's eighth-century 'Essence of Policy' advises that a courtier be 'capable of reading either the attachment or indifference of his master expressed through physical gestures (*iṅgita*), expressions (*ākāra*) and signs (*liṅga*)'.[12] The art of discerning inner dispositions through outward signs, reinforced by the interpretive demands of Sanskrit drama, was essential to the practice of politics at court. Indeed, it may be argued that the reading of gestures and the like as the outward signs of others' intentions formed a crucial part of the lore of *nīti* in early medieval India, as Geib has argued.[13] Consider the jackal-courtier Damanaka's advice to his companion Karaṭaka in the *Pañcatantra*: 'even a beast grasps the sense of the spoken word; horses and elephants advance when commanded; but wise men discern even what is unspoken; Fathoming another's demeanor is the reward of a keen mind.'[14] Finally, the observation of involuntary gestures (usually the throbbing or spasms of the eye or limbs) either on one's own or another's body as portents of favour, disfavour, good and bad fortune, linked gestures to a vast science of bodily prognostication.

Under the second rubric may be placed a wide variety of bodily movements which signified particular ideas, concepts and objects. These uses equated particular gestures, sometimes suggestive and sometimes arbitrary, as supports or surrogates for verbal communication. Knowledge of these could be limited or sometimes even secret or obscure, as they tended to be used as specialised sign-systems. They occur frequently not only in dance and iconography, but also in everyday contexts, where for various reasons gestures may have been more expedient than words. The eleventh-century manual for lovers, known as *Nāgarasarvasva*, for example, details 'bodily signs' (*aṅgasaṅketa*) through which lovers could communicate their designs discreetly to one another. Touching various parts of the body suggested levels of affection, and hand and finger movements the times and directions for meeting.[15]

Many gestures in the above categories may also be viewed as symbolically and practically efficacious, particularly when they became so wedded to their social meanings that they tended to function as autonomous instruments of social interaction. Importantly, a large number of such gestures in early medieval India were shared between both 'secular' and 'religious' spheres, or more precisely, between the spheres of both human and divine lordship. Such actions often formed part of court and temple ceremonial, where their proper performance was seen to have more or less successful outcomes. These could include gestures of submission, purification, beneficence and grace. This final dimension of gesture, I believe, points to a feature of systems of body movements in general—that while they were inherited structures, they could also to certain degrees be manipulated and deployed by those within their confines. This suggests an important caveat to the sociologist's tendency to associate bodies and psychic states with some 'deeper' or 'unconscious' level of social conditioning. While this might be true in modern societies, with their pretensions to legalistic abstraction and individualism, it is perhaps less the case in societies where gesture and emotion were *explicitly* acknowledged elements of public life and political theory. In such worlds, where gesture was formally constitutive of social relationships, its very negotiability made it less 'obscure to itself', to borrow Bourdieu's phrase.

II

In this spirit, that gestures were both hermeneutic systems as well as individually learned body techniques consciously deployed, I wish to turn to the system of bodily gestures which prevailed at royal courts in early medieval India. By 'royal courts' I mean the households of imperial kings and the greater and lesser lords and officials who had the wealth and means to imitate them. These men formed the most powerful agents of a class of landed lords, who rose from diverse backgrounds between the fourth and seventh centuries but who adopted an increasingly common set of behavioural norms. I have argued elsewhere that these noble households formed the context in which much classical Sanskrit culture grew up in the first millennium of the Common Era.[16] It is important to note that courts, so defined, were at once personal residences and administrative centres. They typically consisted of the living quarters of not only the king or lord, but kin, service personnel and men and women on permanent retainment—making them large clusters of dwellings. Here men of rank conducted the business of rule—they assembled with their dependents, collected tribute from subordinates, met supplicants and announced policy. Many of these activities occurred in a public hall of audience, or *sabhā*, prominently positioned within the household, which served both as a place of meeting for visitors and barrier beyond which few outsiders were allowed. Courtly manuals from the eleventh and twelfth century elaborate in great detail the protocols which were to be followed in these assembly halls, but sources from Gupta times indicate many other places within the household where personal conduct was also highly regulated, including halls for bathing and adornment, military grounds, gardens and women's quarters, to name some of the most prominent. To a large extent, the lordly household was moveable, as kings often travelled through their domains accompanied by large domestic and military retinues and conducted their affairs from these encampments. This wider spatial arena, then, formed the immediate context of most of the behaviours and norms which I will be examining in the remainder of this essay.

The system of gestures prevalent at these courts cannot be considered a historically or socially self-contained totality. Their origins were diverse and heterogeneous. Some gestures, like those of respect and deference, and various body concepts, particularly those associating virtue and bodily perfection, had very early and often non-courtly origins. Others, like the gestural emphasis on walking and standing postures, seem to have been largely confined to courtly sources. In many cases the courtly materials are characterised by a heightened articulation, calibration, and/or re-orientation of practices which already existed among various social classes. Prognosticatory knowledges relating to the body, for example, though undoubtedly of great antiquity, gained new meaning and prominence when they were subsumed into a newly formulated and court-oriented astronomical knowledge by Varāhamihira in his 'Great Compendium' (*Bṛhatsaṁhitā*) in the early sixth century. Some protocols of the royal household were very limited in their provenance, while others stretched far beyond the court. Despite such caveats, it is the contention here that the culture of these royal courts, as embodied in inscriptions, collections of verses on policy, aesthetic treatises, courtly poetry, coins, and changing styles of temple sculpture (which often drew from courtly vocabularies), do, in fact, present a coherent system of gestures from the Gupta period.

The argument of this paper will be twofold. First, it will attempt to demonstrate a hieratic assemblage of body-concepts through the exploration of three types of gestures mentioned repeatedly in courtly sources: bowing, standing and walking. The first of these, bowing, formed a specific premeditated movement and hence may be conceived as a conscious instrument of social interaction. It subsequently developed a complex repertoire and ethics. While the latter two activities could also have this character, being consciously 'learned' or 'imitated' by people of rank or those who aspired to it, they were typically conceived as innate and internalised tendencies of movement. The analysis here will demonstrate how principles of courtly hierarchy were 'embodied' in these gestures and to highlight some of the implications that such embodiments had on related realms of life. In all cases, the essay will rely on both descriptions of the aristocratic classes gleaned from contemporary inscriptions and literature, as well as the significant and revealing directions in dramaturgical texts for imitating the behaviour of these people on the stage. The second strand of argument in this paper develops a theme raised in the analysis of courtly modes of standing and walking—namely, how a certain principle of bodily movement, organised around the concepts of gracefulness and sportiveness, functioned within the overall logic of gesture at court. This cluster of movements has not been properly understood to date, either in its internal gestural economy or its external sociological context.

Bowing or prostration was quite an early practice, conspicuous since at least early historic times, as is evident from the railings of Buddhist stūpas which contain many bowing and prostrating figures, and the dharmaśāstras which contain some details on bowing and saluting.[17] The basic gesture was a bending of the head and/or waist, denoted by the Sanskrit root √*ñam* (sometimes prefixed by *pra-* or *ava-*).[18] This was supplemented (or sometimes replaced) by a gesture involving the clasping the hands together at the chest or the head known as *añjali* (√*kṛ*). The contexts for these actions were diverse, as they formed part of salutations and greetings, but they were prominently performed in the assembly halls of kings in royal households. We know that bowing formed part of the requirements of subordinated kings by the Gupta period. Samudragupta's famous pillar inscription is the first public edict to document the importance of prostration at court, in its mention of 'bowed approaches' (*praṇāmāgamana*) among the requirements of kings defeated by the emperor.[19] According to the twelfth-century text, the *Mānasollāsa* of Someśvara, each man entering the king's court, excepting the royal preceptors and certain priests, was to bow before the king.[20]

By the seventh century, it is that clear that the gestures of prostration had been greatly elaborated in the courtly context. While the *Nāṭyaśāstra* sets out three varieties of *añjali* for the interaction with different social groups, made above the head, in front of the face, and on the chest, literary texts by the seventh century represent a number of different styles of prostration performed by nobles within the context of the royal court alone.[21] Bāṇa's seventh-century romantic poem, *Kāḍambarī*, records four types of prostration performed by kings at court: a simple bow, the placement of the hands in *añjali* on the head, the touching of the forehead to the floor, and the touching of one's crown to the footstool of the king.[22] The principle which lay behind these movements, as with non-courtly bowing, was the lowering of the highest and purest part of one's own body toward the lowliest part of a superior's body. The types of prostration were differentiated by the degree to which the body was lowered, particularly the head, towards the feet of one's lord. The touching of the head to the ground mentioned in *Kāḍambarī* is widely attested in other sources from the Gupta period, as the *pañcāṅga* or 'five limbed' prostration, referring to the toūching of the two feet, two hands and forehead to the ground. In Bāṇa's seventh-century court narrative, the *Harṣacarita*, the princes Mādhavagupta and Kumāragupta appear before Prabhākaravardhana and his sons and bow by touching their four limbs (feet and hands), as well as their heads, to the ground.[23] Daṇḍin's roughly contemporary text, the *Daśakumāracarita*, describes a similar gesture with the hands folded in *añjali* pressed to (literally 'kissing') the head.[24] We also hear of the 'eight-limbed' (*aṣṭāṅgam* or *sāṣṭāṅgam*), prostration in other texts, comprising the two feet, two knees, two hands, forehead and chest. The most extreme prostration was called the 'staff', (*daṇḍavat* or *daṇḍapraṇāma*), where the entire body was straightened on the ground before one's lord.[25]

The emphasis on types of prostration from Gupta times was accompanied by an expansion of ritualised protocols in the royal household. Sumptuary manuals began to set out various types of thrones, daises and footstools for different ranks of nobles and kings.[26] At court, the king sat on an elevated throne with his feet resting on a footstool or *pādapīṭha*, effectively raising him entirely from the ground and elevating him above others present at court. Indeed, elevation and spatial positioning developed into complex organising principles in court routine, and, along with size and height, become important indicators of status and hierarchy in sculpture and statuary. This is clearly depicted at Gupta sites like Deogarh and Udayagiri (Figure 1). Judging from the evidence, it would seem that at court, supplicants bowed before the king at some distance, and when signalled, approached the throne to prostrate themselves at his feet, which were elevated by a footstool and dais. In Bāṇa's *Harṣacarita*, when the emissary of Bhāskaravarman arrives at Harṣa's court, he first enters and performs a *pañcāṅga* bow with his five limbs touching the ground, and then, when signalled by the king, rushes forward to the throne to rub his forehead on a footstool where the king's feet rested.[27] The footstool, or *pādapīṭha*, formed an important aristocratic paraphernalia in the Gupta period. Both Samudragupta and Candragupta II are depicted on their coins as seated on royal couches with footstools (Figures 4 and 5)[28] and the Bhitarī pillar inscription depicts the majesty of King Skandagupta as seated on the throne, 'having his left foot placed on the royal footstool'.[29] The very prominence of the footstool paralleled the growth of rituals related to the honouring of the feet of one's superiors—ministrations that were often performed with great fanfare. The *Mānasollāsa* speaks of the washing, anointing and adornment of the feet among the ritualised 'enjoyments' (*upabhogas*) of a king.[30]

The prominence of prostration and foot rituals is underscored by the actual language of devotion and favour used within courtly circles. From the fourth century, we find common reference in inscriptions to men being 'devoted to' (*bhakta*), or even more commonly 'meditating upon' (*anudhyāta*), the feet of their superiors, both secular and religious. The Allahabad pillar inscription, for example, claims to have been executed by a military retainer (*mahādaṇḍanāyaka*) named Tilabhaṭṭaka, who 'meditates on' the feet of the Gupta emperor.[31] Another Gupta inscription, dated nearly a hundred years later, proclaims that the king Kumāragupta himself meditated on the feet of his predecessor,

Candragupta II, in his Karaṁdaṇḍa inscription.[32] Such phrases in the inscriptions indicated the loving devotion of a son to a father, or a vassal to his overlord, and usually carried the implication of some special relationship, which entailed privileges. Favour, maintenance or subsistence was similarly expressed in this language. Men were 'accepted by the feet' (*pādaparigṛhīta*) of their lords. In the Dāmodarpur grant of the time of Kumāragupta in eastern India, one Chirātadatta expresses publicly that he was appointed as *uparika* of Puṇḍravardhana by the emperor through the phrase that he had been 'selected by his majesty's feet' (*tatpādaparigṛhīte*).[33] The courtier Āmrakārdava of the Sanchi stone inscription claims that his livelihood (*jīvita*) has been 'augmented through the favour of the feet (*pādaprasādāpyāyita*) of the prosperous *mahārājādhirāja* Candragupta (II)'.[34] Courtiers were commonly referred to as 'dependents' (*upajīvin*) 'on the (favour of the) feet' of their lords.[35] In sum, the subordinate repaired to and concentrated on the 'feet' of his lord, who in turn deigned to accept him at his feet. These are no doubt the relations implied in episodes like the famous Varāha relief panel at Udayagiri and countless other sculptural depictions of lords and devotees from Gupta times.[36] In literature, poetry and public documents, the theme of prostration to the feet was amplified into a rich and complex language of power.[37] Students of Sanskrit *kāvya* and epigraphy will be well-familiar with the vast imagery developed in post-Gupta India around royal and divine feet. According to the courtly descriptions, the king's feet were brushed and scratched by the crowns of prostrating kings, showered and illumined by jewels set in and even falling from their crowns.[38]

The seemingly endless variations on this theme in royal *praśastis* and courtly *kāvyas* across the epigraphic record in medieval India suggest two points. First and most obviously, relations of subordination and loyalty, domination and submission came to be conceived, embodied, and expressed in strikingly physical ways among the emerging and established medieval elite, and particularly through the gestures toward a superior's feet. And second, the proliferation of this terminology throughout the scores of inscriptions in the fifth to seventh century,[39] represents not only a newly consolidated way of speaking about and conceptualising political relationships, rooted in gestural protocols of the court, but a sort of education of the bodily *habitus* among elites.This is to say, the adoption of the manners and ways of aristocratic life by emerging elites also marked a more or less gradual transformation of bodily movement, both at the level of formally learned gestures like bowing and prostration as well as in the development of psycho-physical tendencies and value systems, gestures being seamlessly incorporated into the larger mental systems operative in court society.

At court, prostration and the physical tendency toward lowering one's posture were closely connected to courtly ethics, particularly the dynamics of pride and humility. As a gesture of submission, it will be recalled, the act of bowing was a potentially demeaning act, as the highest and purest part of one person's body was placed at or inclined toward the lowest part of another's body. Numerous inscriptions and courtly poems praise their patrons by recounting how enemy kings were defeated and made to demonstrate their submission through public acts of prostration. Accounts like that of the sixth century Aulikāra king Yaśodharman are typical, and reveal a clearly agonistic aspect to the gesture: the Hūṇa king Mihirakūla is described as being forcefully and painfully compelled to bend his forehead in obeisance, honouring the feet of king Yaśodharman with the flowers in his hair.[40] The large number of didactic verses which grew up in courtly circles from the eighth century on the topic of 'royal service' (*rājaseva*) present a similar picture from the vantage point of the lower aristocracy and service classes, lamenting the conditions of dependence through frequent reference to the demeaning gesture of prostration.[41] Counterbalancing such assertions, however, were many courtly adages which praised acts of prostration as signs of devotion or humility. Both servants and lords had occasion in different contexts to exhibit deferential behaviour of varying degrees to strangers, to their equals or to their superiors. In these cases postures of deference were not only deemed appropriate but were also seen as a mark of the highly valued quality of humility. To the extent that the court as an institution relied on the dynamics of respect and honour, bowing and the virtue it signified were an integral part of every man's bodily education. Kālidāsa tells us that soon after the young prince Raghu learned to utter words and walk as a child, he also learned to bow and prostrate himself, a gesture which caused great joy to his father.[42]

That there indeed was an 'ethics' of gesture is quite clear from the the emphasis in courtly sources on the judicious and nuanced display of deference through the use movements like prostration and the like. It is this consideration which lay behind the adage, put into the mouth of the crow-minister Āḍīvin in the *Pañcatantra*, that 'a man's shadow will lengthen when he bows, like that of a stick when tilted, but if inclined too much will actually disappear.'[43] Suitable deference, in other words, increased a man's stature; but too much brought its diminishment. How young men came to acquire such skills remains an open question, but courtship, with its exaggerated codes of courteous interaction—where supplication was highly ritualised and errant lovers constantly fell at the feet of their beloveds—may have formed a sort of hypertrophied sphere where young men learned such skills.[44] Courtly sources are filled with descriptions of how men deftly and skilfully exhibited humility before the court. Suitable humility, effectively manifest in one's demeanour, had the effect of exalting a man's character and reputation, and was the zenith of refinement in manners. The psycho-physical dynamics of humility, thus, were folded back into the logic of power. A particularly illustrative example of this, from Bāṇa's *Kādambarī*, depicts the arrival of the young prince Candrāpīḍa at the residence of his father's chief minister, Śukanāsa. Upon entering Śukanāsa's household, the prince, accompanied by his companion Vaiśaṁpāyana (Śukanāsa's own son) approaches the minister, who is seated among many subordinate kings. Candrāpīḍa bows with his head 'very low' (*durāvatena*) and Śukanāsa arises from his seat, advancing 'respectfully' (*sādaram*) to meet the pair. At this point, the subordinate kings immediately leave their own seats and stand in apprehension. With tears in his eyes Śukanāsa embraces Candrāpīḍa, and then his own son Vaiśampāyana. He offers Candrāpīḍa a jewelled seat, which the prince refuses, instead lowering himself to the bare ground, once again followed by Vaiśampāyana. This act causes the entire assembly of kings in turn to abandon their own seats and likewise assume positions on the ground.[45] The poet's depiction of the prince is clearly concerned as much with the onlooking kings as it is with the reactions of Śukanāsa. Here we see not only how gestures of prostration and the logic of positional elevation (being lower and higher) were used to demonstrate humility, but also how humility could be a powerful display of power.

III

I want to turn now to the more elusive but equally important body techniques involved in the activities of standing and walking at court—what might more accurately be called 'bearing' or 'carriage'. Here I turn to the dramaturgical texts, which provide interesting evidence on these themes, through the directions given to actors playing characters of different social classes. The texts divide characters into 'high' (*uttama*), 'middling' (*madhyama*) and 'low' (*adhama*), each of which were to walk, gesticulate, and speak differently. The *Nāṭyaśāstra* admonishes the playwright not to confuse or misapply the physical bearing of one of these classes with another.[46] The presence of noble-born characters or heroes and heroines on the stage, even when disguised, was often apparent to the discerning eye both in the audience and on the stage by their physical appearance and movements.[47] Below I would like to explore the dramaturgical directions not so much as specific 'regulations' for the movement of men and women, but instead as ideas current among elites about what constituted (and differentiated) low and exalted bearing. In the end I hope to illustrate certain principles of movement and posture which informed the body techniques of the elite.

In dramatic performances, according to the *Nāṭyaśāstra*, as the curtain was drawn away from the stage at the outset of the drama, the characters entered in specific gaits (*gati*) and assumed particular standing postures (*sthāna*),[48] which indicated their position as superior, middling or low characters.[49] Though during the course of the play characters combined a variety of other movements and gestures to convey different emotional states and sentiments, the 'natural' (*svabhāva*) gait of the characters reflected their innate dispositions.[50] The stride (*kṣepa*) of the step for kings and gods (high characters) was to be four *tālas* (a measurement of space) in length, for middling characters, two *tālas*, and for women and inferior characters, one *tāla*.[51] The time for each stride was correspondingly to be measured to four *kālas* (a division of time) for high characters, two *kālas* for middling, and one for inferior.[52] Finally, the tempo (*laya*) of the high character's gait was to be firm and calm (*sthita*, *dhairya*), that of low characters fast (*druta*) and copious (*pracura*), and of middling character's in between.[53] The height of the step was also a sign of ranking, as the highest category lifted their knee in striding to the waist.[54]

The idea behind these assignments was the higher the character, the longer the stride, the slower the gait, and the firmer and calmer the step. It is in this context that we may understand the common likening in *kāvya* of the walking of men and women to that of the elephant, as this creature, along with the lion, was considered the strongest and most eminent of animals, its natural gait being slow, placid and firm.[55] Steadiness and deliberation of gait were counterposed to uncontrolled and agitated movement. The movements of lower characters were copious, hurried and excessive. The *Nāṭyaśāstra* advises characters playing ministers and merchants—middling characters—to refrain from moving excessively (*parivāhitam*) and stiffly (*stabdham*).[56] The example of the *śakāra*, known from the *Mṛcchakaṭika* of Śūdraka, is instructive. This figure, the brother of a lesser wife of the king, appears as a villainous character, dominated by cruelty and pride. These faults were choreographed into his manner of walking. The *Nāṭyaśāstra* describes him like this: 'his gait will be with presumption (*sagarvita*) and while walking, due to incessantly touching and looking at his clothes and ornaments, and because of the scattered agitation of the movement of his limbs, his garlands and the drapes of his garments move to and fro.[57] The Śakāra's vanity and preoccupation with his appearance caused both excessive and sudden, jerky movement. Excessive movement was a sign of clumsiness or internal agitation, and suddenness and stiffness of gesture suggested intoxication, surprise and lack of control.[58] These states, deemed highly undesirable in one's general carriage, may be directly opposed to the value placed upon ease, economy and dexterity of movement.

Posture, or how one held the body while standing, was generally denoted by the terms *sthāna* or *sthānaka*. The most exalted posture, according to the *Nāṭyaśāstra*, was the stance relating to the god Viṣṇu, or *vaiṣṇava sthāna*. This stance, in which the feet were two and a half *tālas* apart, with one foot level and the other obliquely placed with its shank bent, was to be assumed in the course of conversation *(saṁlāpa)* and activities that were innate (*svabhāvaja*) to the upper and middling characters.[59] The *Nāṭyaśāstra* advises that the high and middling characters should assume this stance of the feet while the upper limbs were to be in the *caturasra* posture, where the breast was raised (*samunnatam*) and shoulders at rest (*prasanna*) and not raised too much (*nātyutkṣipta*), and the arms held at navel and the waist.[60] The limbs in the *vaiṣṇava sthāna* were to have a certain 'excellence' or 'beauty' in carriage (*sauṣṭhava*): they were unwavering (*acañcalam*), uncrooked (*akubjam*), at ease (*sanna gātram*), not too raised (*atyuccam*), and not collapsing (*calapātam*).[61] The waist, ears, elbows, shoulders and the head were to be in the normal or even (*sama*) position, and the chest, as in the *caturasra* pose, was to be raised.[62] We may compare these recommendations with the posture of the servants (*ceṭa*) and low (*nīca*) people, who were to walk with one of their sides, their heads, or a hand and foot lowered.[63] The famous Kashmiri satirist Kṣemendra, who wrote a treatise on the relations between servants and masters in the eleventh century, dwells at length on the shrinking postures of servants, whom he describes as having 'drooping faces (*adhomukha*) from their loss of honour' (*māna*).[64]

Bearing also had the quality of signifying the presence of inner virtues, and even physical well-being. In this regard, Bāṇa's description of the emperor Harṣa is illustrative: he is described as having 'a glance not defective and soiled by the deadly poison of selfishness...postures not stiff due to the loss of consciousness in the epilepsy born out of astonishment, his change of feelings not agitated by the paroxysm of inflammatory fever arising from unrestrained self will, and his movements not rigid or jerky from the derangement of the three humours from pride'.[65] In each case, the king's bearing is seen to be free of a physical affliction which is rooted in one or other vice: selfishness, surprise (an emotion which suggested lowness) impetuousness, and pride. What we may learn from such descriptions is the close 'readings' which men of the court applied to bodily gesture and bearing, and by extension, how they attempted to correlate the cultivation of their own inner virtues with ways of moving and acting.

Taken together, then, elevated bearing for those of superior rank may be understood through a series of oppositions:

stiffness of motion	ease of movement
agitated, jerky movement	calm, even movement
hurried movement	slow, deliberate movement
lowly carriage	elevated carriage
excessive movement	economic movement
inflated posture	calm and relaxed posture
drooping, broken limbed	raised and firm limbed
crooked posture	straight and upright posture

These oppositions present a set of subtle distinctions: the body was to be elevated, yet not puffed up; firm, but not stiff; calm, but not drooping; straight, but not rigid; slow, but not heavy. The combination of these opposing poles into a 'golden mean', often the basis of elaborate poetic conceits, may be usefully understood as forming an ideal of 'graceful' or 'elegant' bearing. One of its obvious principles was moderation. The dictum of 'not overly' or 'not too much' (*nāti*) precedes many of the directives for courtly movement. Too much curvature or a collapsing, drooping posture was a sign of lowness, and too erect a bearing was a sign of arrogance and pride. The ideal was a gentle curvature of the body, captured by words like *añcita*, which meant 'graceful', but derived from the root √*āñc*, 'to bend [slightly]'. A gentle curvature and relaxation in posture was the hallmark of 'elevated' (*audārya*) bearing.[66]

These principles of posture and carriage are also quite apparent in the evolution of figural iconography, both royal and religious, from Kuṣāṇa through post-Gupta times. Not only do the more muscular physiques of Kuṣāṇa–Mathurā sculpture give way to increasingly slender bodies with smoother surfaces and rounded angles during the early Gupta period, but postures also become more fluid and relaxed.[67] Relaxed and reposing postures, only occasional and sporadic in pre-Gupta art, become increasingly widespread from the fifth century in the depiction of both men and gods—and by the seventh century are clearly the norm of representation. Typically, standing figures show a slight flexion of the torso and gentle thrust of the hip to one side as a result of the body's weight being supported on one leg. This trend is clearly illustrated in the royal portraits on the coins of northern India from the first to the sixth centuries (Figures 2 and 3). While the coins of the Kuṣāṇa kings typically present rulers in rigid postures with angular shoulders, those of the Guptas show a fluidity of movement and flexion of the body.[68] From the post-Gupta times, nearly all standing sculpture has this pronounced flexion of the body. This emphasis in figural sculpture, often perceived negatively as overly mannered and stylised, lacking the natural balance and 'grace' of classical art, should instead be seen as the extension and elaboration of the bodily dynamics set out in the Gupta period, not their abandonment.

IV

Gracefulness at one level was the expression of 'balance' between exalted and humble bearing. The moderate postures and fluid movements of graceful comportment were a desideratum for both men and women, and were thought to differentiate the most accomplished men and women, not only from those of low birth, but also from the rank and file of the nobility from which they came. There is another conceptual element to graceful bearing, however, which came from a different direction and which seems to provide an interesting counterpoint to the gestural logic we have been reviewing so far. This is the idea of 'playfulness' or 'sportiveness'—an important and polyvalent concept denoted by a large lexical set, including various derivates from the verbal roots √*krīḍ*, to play; √*lal*, to play; √*ram* to rejoice or play; (*vi* +) √*las*, to shine, glitter, or frolic; (*vi* +) √*nud*, to pierce, play (a musical instrument), or entertain; and perhaps, most important, the noun *līlā*, sport or play, from which the denominative verb *līlāyati* was derived.[69] These terms have most often been connected to the religious doctrine of 'divine play', but their prevalence in courtly contexts suggests a wider range of meanings. In the courtly context, these terms could refer to specific games, contests, and entertainments enjoyed by men and women individually or collectively (the chief of which, as we shall see, was the game of romance), but also, partly by extension from this, a sort of physical inclination and even behavioural disposition.[70] In either case they amounted to a style of movement or bearing, and words like *vilāsa*, *ramaṇa*, *lalita* and *līlā*, could refer variously to an exuberant playfulness, mirthful spontaneity, or a charming insouciance.

This family of terms would seem to introduce a somewhat contradictory element into the otherwise finely calibrated hierarchy of courtly protocol. Indeed, these concepts suggest a carelessness, frivolity or even 'transgression' with regard to the solemn demeanour, which typified much of the protocols of movement and bodily interaction at court. Yet they form an unmistakable element in representations of the protagonists of courtly literature, a point which begs some explanation. Consider Bāṇa's description of the emperor Harṣa. When he first glimpses the emperor, seated on a finely wrought couch of stone cooled with sandalwood water, he notes that Harṣa is not seated rigidly, but rather rests his weight on one arm placed at the edge of the seat, with his foot dangling gently on to a brilliant sapphire and ruby footstool. This relaxed posture, which differentiated the king from his companions, immediately evokes an image of 'ease' for Bāṇa, who says that he seemed to be 'playing' (*ramamāṇam*) with his subject kings in a vast canopied lake composed of the light emitted from his body, with his foot, 'sporting' (*salīlam*) on the jewelled footstool as if he was Kṛṣṇa dancing on the head of the demon Kāliya.[71] Such conceits are meant to suggest the astonishing power of such men through the *effortlessness* of their actions, a quality which the poet derives in the first instance, from the king's posture. Bāṇa concludes his description by summing up the qualities evoked by the king's bearing: 'though foreboding, unfathomable, and full of *gravitas*, the emperor was at the same time open, gracious, sportive and delightful'.[72] Bāṇa's conceit in this final summation is significant because it begins from the apparently contradictory or antithetical relationships which these families of terms had with one another—the one set indicating the values of majesty, solemnity, and authority, and the other its opposite, ease, play, and abandon.[73]

Such descriptions, applied generally to the most powerful people at court, connected up to a conception of lordship which I have elsewhere called 'irenical'—one ideologically centred on fructification and happiness, and stressing lordly prerogatives as sublime enjoyments—which gained currency among royal courts from early Gupta times. It is in this context that we should place the persistent emphasis in courtly circles on pleasure and dalliance. Thus it is not so much in the interest of any subversion of authority or transgression of protocol that such disposition and bodily principles were celebrated; they in fact formed an integral image of authority itself. This is perhaps better understood when we consider that Bāṇa's depiction of Harṣa sitting on his couch was emphatically one of public authority. Here Harṣa's manner of sitting was partially reclined and even reposeful. This posture, which grew in the first centuries of the Common Era, and became popular during the Gupta period, when various emperors portrayed themselves on their coins sitting precisely like this, relaxed, sometimes playing the lyre, with one leg raised, the other extended on to a footstool, was shared by both courtly and religious sources, and later came to be known as the 'sportive recline' (*lalitāsana*) (see Figures 4 to 6).[74] On the one hand it was powerful and benefactive, indicated in religious contexts by the hand-gestures of assurance and favour (particularly on religious images). On the other, it was 'reposeful', signified by a relaxed or reclining torso with legs in different positions, one extended playfully on to a footstool.

The garden and domestic scenery of the reclining courtier in Figure 6 suggests another arena where playful grace was particularly prominent—in the comportment that men and women were to take toward one another in courtship and romance. Once again, the texts on dramaturgy provide us with important clues as to how grace and playfulness were integrated into the courtly conception of romance. They introduce a number of the terms mentioned above to describe behavioural accoutrements or 'ornaments' to be displayed by heroes and heroines in courtship as represented on stage. These lists appear first in the *Nāṭyaśāstra*, and are notably conspicuous in later *alaṅkāraśāstra* literature.[75] According to the *Nāṭyaśāstra*, the term *līlā* in a woman designated the delightful and affectionate imitation (*anukṛti*) of her beloved's speech, gestures and qualities; *vilāsa*, the appearance of relevant changes in standing, sitting, and walking postures and particularly the actions of the hands, eyebrows and eyes [when seeing or meeting the lover]; *lalita*, the position of the hands, feet and body, along with the eyebrows, eyes, and lips produced by tender and beautiful gestures; and *vicchitti*, the beauty that arose from a slight (*svalpa*) disregard in the arrangement (*anādaranyāsa*) of garlands, clothes, ornaments and unguents.[76] For men, relevant concepts were *vilāsa*, which was marked by the straightforward movement of the eyes, smiling when speaking and a graceful (*añcita*) walk like a bull; and *lalita*, romantic gestures and expressions which were undeliberate and grew out of a tender nature (*sukumāra-svabhāvaja*).[77] Despite the fact that women and men tended to inhabit these 'graceful' modes in quite different ways—revealing a strong gender differentiation which could be read into the slightest movements of the body[78]—the point I would like to stress here, and one which is equally significant, is their similarity, the fact that proper courtship for both the hero and heroine, entailed a set of playful, 'sportive' gestures which themselves were deemed beautiful and alluring.[79]

One theme that emerges from these terms as they appeared in the directions for courtship, and which embodies a wider courtly sensibility, is the valorisation of 'naturalness' and 'spontaneity'; gestures and sartorial demeanour were to be 'undeliberate' (literally, *abuddhipūrvakam*, 'not conceived before') and slightly careless. This was enough to demonstrate that one's appearance was not over-arduous, premeditated, or 'staged'. The irony of such apparent exhortations to spontaneity is only partly attributable to their obvious function as dictums for actors on stage, for the 'play' concept which lay behind them implied not only a commitment to grace and spontaneity, but an acknowledgement of its boundaries and limits as well. This is clearly demonstrated if we compare the playful disregard of heroes and heroines, deemed 'graceful', with the violation or ignorance of them due to moral failing or low birth. The stiff demeanour and maladjusted clothes of the character of the *śakāra* is instructive. For, unlike the heroes and heroines of the drama, his dishevelment suggested vanity and presumption rather than ease and spontaneity.

I would suggest that the concept of grace indicated by these terms did not denote a true disregard for protocol and hierarchy, nor any ecstatic abandon. Rather, it is clear, given the context I have explored in this paper, that they presumed and embodied the highest forms of self-control and discipline by people of the court. Indeed, like much other courtly gestures and speech, they were only deemed comprehensible by men and women of superior refinement. A verse from a fifteenth-century anthology pities the fate of a sophisticated woman approached by a man who cannot understand her urbane manners, her slow (and graceful) gait, the indirection of her speech, and her playful side glances, but instead preferred vulgar village girls.[80] Such references to *śakāras* and vulgar 'rustic' men suggests not merely a sort of 'policing' of the boundaries of good society, but more probably a set of ever-present mechanisms of internal differentiation—distinguishing those of superior sophistication from their lesser counterparts. Grace so conceived was a body-technique of the highest order, operating well within the protocols of respectability and received expectations of bodily carriage, which, perhaps not unlike the Italian Renaissance concepts of *sprezzatura* and *disinvoltura* (a comparison which begs closer inspection), referred to a sort of cultivated spontaneity, a premeditated frivolity which was at once a sign of beauty and mark of power.

REFERENCES

* This essay has benefited from discussions with Taru Dalmia and Jessica Bath.

1. Harbans Mukhia, *The Mughals of India*, Oxford, 2004, pp. 72–112; for an earlier study, see John Richards, 'Norms of Comportment among Imperial Mughal Officers' in Barbara D. Metcalfe, ed., *Moral Conduct and Authority: The Place of Adab in South Asian Islam*, Berkeley, 1984.
2. Marcel Mauss, 'Techniques of the Body', *Economy and Society*, Vol. 2, no. 1 (1973), pp. 70–87. More recently, see the work Georges Vigarello, 'The Upward Training of the Body from the Age of Chivalry to Courtly Civility', in Michael Feher, Romana Naddaff, and Nadia Tazia, eds., *Fragments for a History of the Human Body*, New York, 1989, part two, pp. 149–199; Jean Claude Shmitt, 'The Ethics of Gesture' in Michael Feher, Romana Naddaff, and Nadia Tazia, eds., *Fragments for a History of the Human Body*, part two, pp. 128–47; and idem., *La Raison des gestes dans*

l'Occidente Médiéval, Paris, 1990. See also the individual studies in Jan Bremmer and Herman Roodenburg, eds., *A Cultural History of Gesture: From Antiquity to the Present Day*, Cambridge, 1991.

3. Mauss, 'Techniques of the Body', p. 71.
4. *Ibid*, p. 85.
5. *Ibid*, p. 85.
6. See the discussion in Pierre Bourdieu, *Pascalian Meditations*, trans. Richard Nice, Cambridge, 2000, pp. 168–174; for Bourdieu's now famous discussion of habitus, see *Outline of a Theory of Practice*, trans. Richard Nice, Cambridge, 1977.
7. See P.V. Kane, *History of Dharmaśāstra*, Poona, third ed., 1997, vol. 2, pt. 2, pp. 854–55.
8. Despite the fact that from Gupta times it would seem that royal courts and local officials were known to have kept records, the handling and transmission of documents was not yet 'rationalised' in the manner of modern bureaucracies. Literacy remained partial and and publicly recorded transactions were typically accompanied by bodily, sumptuary and material symbology. Royal orders, for instance, were typically received with great fanfare and ceremony—indicated in the first instance by a gesture of obeisance by local officials performed to the document itself. The royal orders of the Chola kings, for example, called *tirumukam*, or 'sacred face', were received by local lords and notables as an embodied presence—they lifted them to their heads, processed them on a female elephant—before having them inscribed on copper or stone. See the Tamil portion of the Tiruvāḷaṅgāṭ plates, issued during the reign of Rājendra Chola, *South Indian Inscriptions*, vol. 3, pt. 2 (1929) pp. 383–439.
9. Jean-Claude Schmitt, *La Raison des gestes dans l'Occident Médiéval*, Paris, 1990.
10. A number of terms are used to denote bodily gesture and movement in Sanskrit: *ceṣṭā*, denoting an action or movement of the body; *iṅgita*, a conscious or unconscious change in the body; and *ākāra*, a general appearance or facial expression.
11. See *Mānavadharmaśāstra*, ed. J. Jolly, London, 1887, 8.25–26. According to Manu, the interiority of the mind (*manah*) is perceived through changes in the eye and face (*netravaktravikāra*), by gestures (*iṅgita*), facial expression (*ākāra*), movements (*ceṣṭā*) and speech (*bhāṣita*).
12. *Nītisāra*, ed. and trans. Rajendralal Mitra, Calcutta, 1961, 5.34.
13. See Ruprecht Geib, *Zur Frage nach der Urfassung des Pañcatantra*, Wiesbaden, 1969.
14. *Pañcatantra*, ed. and trans. Fraklin Edgerton, New Haven, 1924, 1.18.
15. See *Nāgarasarvasva* 6.1 ff. Gestures were to be used along with symbolic language and objects (usually parcels).
16. Daud Ali, *Courtly Culture and Political Life in Early Medieval India*, Cambridge, 2004.
17. *Vasiṣṭhadharmasūtra*, ed. A. Führer, Bombay, 1882, 13.41-46; *Gautamadharmasūtra*, ed. Chinnaswami Sastri, Benares, 1934, 6.1-11; *Āpastambadharmasūtra*, eds. Chinnaswami Sastri and Ramanatha Sastri, Benares, 1932, 1.4.14.7-24, 1.2.5.18.

18. The verb √*vand* tended to be used for bowing and salutation to gods and brahmins, see *Kādambarī*, p. 156 and *Vikramorvaśīya* 2.0+
19. *Corpus Inscriptionum Indicarum* [henceforth *CII*] 3 (1981), no. 1, p. 213.
20. *Mānasollāsa*, ed. Shrigondekar, 3 vols, Baroda, 1925, vol. 3.1207–1242.
21. The *añjali* was to be made on the head for the gods (*devatā*), at the face for venerable persons (*guru*), and on the chest for friends (*mitra*). Kings are conspicuously absent from this list. See *Nāṭyaśāstra*, ed. Manmohan Ghosh, Calcutta, 1967, 9.127–8.
22. Mentioned by Vaiśaṁpāyana in describing the majesty of King Tārāpīḍa to his son. See *Kāḍambarī*, ed. M. R. Kale, Delhi, 1968, pp. 190–91. V.S. Agrawala, in his study of Bāṇa's works, has distinguished a similar list, see *The Deeds of Harsha*, Varanasi, 1969, p. 155.
23. *caturbhiraṅgairuttamāṅgena ca gāṁ spṛśantau namaścakratuḥ*, *Harṣacarita*, ed. K.P. Parab, Bombay, 1925, ch. 4, p. 140.
24. *pañcāṅgaspṛṣṭabhūmirañjalicumbitacūṭa*, *Daśakumāracarita*, ed. M.R. Kale, Delhi, 1966, ch. 8, p. 194..
25. See *Daśakumāracarita*, ch. 2, p. 25; also *Mānasollāsa* 3.1235, where kings seeking protection were to 'bow and fall to the ground like a staff' (*praṇata daṇḍīabhuvi*).
26. See Varāhamihira's *Bṛhatsaṁhitā*, ed. and tr. M. Ramakrishna Bhatt, Delhi, 1981, 79.1 ff. For the base (*padmabandha*) and socle (*upapīṭha*) of the lion throne, see *Mayamata*, ed. and tr. Bruno Dagens, Pondichery, 1970, 32.14.
27. See *Harṣacarita*, ch. 7, p. 214.
28. For the 'lyre type' coins of Samudragupta and 'couch type' coins of Candragupta, see John Allan, *Catalogue of the Coins of the Gupta Dynasties and of Śaśāṅka, King of Gauḍa*, London, 1914, nos. 51 and 102.
29. *kṣitipacaraṇapīṭhe sthāpito vāmapādaḥ*: *CII* 3 (1981), no. 31, p. 315.
30. Both anointment of the feet (*pādābhyaṅga*) and the wearing of sandals (*pāduka*) are included by Someśvara among the twenty royal enjoyments treated in his *Mānasollāsa* (3.954-58; 1630-38).
31. *CII* 3 (1981), no. 1, p. 215.
32. *Ibid*, no. 21, p. 281.
33. *Ibid*, no. 22, p. 285.
34. *Ibid*, no. 9, p. 250.
35. See for example, the Majhgawan plates of the Parivrājaka king Hastin and the Deo-Baranārk inscription of the later Guptạ king Jīvitagupta II, *CII* 3 (1888), nos. 23, 46, pp. 106, 216. See also R.S. Sharma, *Indian Feudalism*, Delhi, 1980, p. 79.
36. Michael Willis has pointed out the polyvalent meanings of this important Gupta relief: See Michael Willis 'Archaeology and the Politics of Time' in Hans Bakker, ed., *The Heritage of the Vakāṭakas*, Groningen, 2005, pp. 33–58.
37. This cultural development goes some way toward explaining the truly remarkable and perhaps unparalleled obsession with feet in the religious and courtly culture of medieval India. Equally remarkable is the almost total neglect of the subject in secondary literature, save the recent and exceptional study of Jutta Jain-Neubauer, *Feet and Footwear in Indian Culture*, Ahmedabad, 2000, esp. pp. 16–79.

38. Instances are copious, but see, for a literary example, Bāṇa's description of the emperor Harṣa's feet in *Harṣacarita*, Ch. 2, p. 72. In traditional *kāvya* style, Bāṇa begins his description of the king with his feet and ends with his crown. It should be noted that this 'upward' descriptive movement is also the sequence of vision of one prostrating before a lord.
39. The terminology of 'meditation' or 'devotion' to a superior's feet as an expression of loyalty, first found in the records of the Guptas and Vākāṭakas, is taken up by numerous courts from the fourth century. For Gupta uses, see *CII* 3 (1981), nos. 1, 9, 21, 22, 24, 31, 38, 40, 41, 44, 45, pp. 215, 250, 281, 285, 289, 315, 336, 344, 348, 355, 358. For the Vākāṭakas, see *CII* 5 (1963), no. 2, p. 7, no. 8, p. 36. For select specimens from dynasties between the fourth and seventh centuries see *CII* 3 (1888), no. 3, p. 25 for the Śanakānikas; *CII* 3 (1888), no. 24, p. 111 for the Parivrājakas of Bundelkhand; *CII* 5 (1963), nos. 21-22, pp. 91–2; *CII* 3 (1888), nos. 26–31, p. 117 ff. for the kings of Ucchakalpa; *CII* 4 (1955), nos. 8–9, pp. 24, 27 for the Traikūṭakas; *CII* 5 (1963), no. 19, p. 85; *CII* 3 (1888), no. 81, p. 295; *Epigraphia Indica* [henceforth *EI*] 7 (1902–3), no. 13, p. 104, for the Somavaṁśis of South Kosala; *CII* 3 (1888), nos. 40–41, pp. 193, 198; *EI* 9 (1907–8) no. 39, p. 283, for the kings of Íarabhapura; *EI* 9 (1907–8), no. 7, p. 58; *EI* 31 (1955–6), no. 1a, p. 4; *EI* 31 (1955–56), no. 1b, p. 9; *EI* 25 (1939–40), no. 7, p. 46, for the Śālāṅkāyanas of Veṅgi; *EI* 17 (1923–4), no. p. 332; *EI* 12 (1913-14), no. 17, p. 134; *EI* 4 (1896–7), no. 25, p. 196, for the Viṣṇukuṇḍins of Śrīpārvata/Veṅgī; *EI* 28 (1949–50), nos. 16, 31, 39, 47, pp. 84, 178, 235, 302; *EI* 3 (1894–5), nos. 3, 20, 21, pp. 18, 128, 131; *EI* 12 (1913–14), no. 2, p. 5; *EI* 23 (1935–6), no. 8, p. 60; *EI* 24 (1937–8), no. 17, p. 135, for dynasties of Kaliṅga; *EI* 15 (1919–20), no. 16i-ii, pp. 289–9; *EI* 2 (1894), no. 4iii, p. 23; *EI* 10 (1909–10), no. 16, p. 74; *CII* 4 (1955) , nos. 12–14, pp. 41, 45, 49, for the Kalachuris of Western India; *EI* 15 (1919–20), no. 11b, p. 254; *EI* 8 (1905–6), no. 15, p. 162; *EI* 24 (1937–8), no. 18, p. 141 for the Pallavas of Kanchi; *EI* 16 (1921–2), no. 4, p. 18; *CII* 3 (1888), no. 39, pp. 174–8 for the Maitrakas of Valabhi; *CII* 3 (1888), no. 46, pp. 215–6, for the later Guptas of Magadha; *CII* 3 (1888), no. 47, p. 220 for the Maukharis of Kanauj; *CII* 3 (1888), no. 52, p. 232, for Harăavardhana; *CII* 4 (1955), nos. 28–29, pp. 129, 134, for the early Chalukyas of Gujarat; and *CII* 4 (1955), no. 26, p. 121, for the Íendrakas of Gujarat.
40. The idea being that the Hūṇa king made an offering of flowers with his head, *CII* 3 (1888), no. 33, p. 147. See also the eighth-century Maitraka inscription of Kharagraha which describes him as causing his sāmantas to bow before him 'violently subdued (*sarabhasavaśikṛta*) by excessive attachment (*atiprakṛṣṭānurāga*) (for him)' *CII* 3 (1888), no. 39, p. 177.
41. For example, 'Victory and salutations to those whose heads don't improperly meet the dust of the road in the ingnominy of the affliction of service, and whose head-jewels do not fall when saluting their master' from Kṣemendra's poem on the subject, *Sevyasevakopadeśa*, in Rāghavācharya and Padhye, eds, *Kṣemendralaghukāvya-saṅgrahaḥ*, Hyderabad, 1961, v. 33.
42. *Raghuvaṁśa*, ed. and tr. G. R. Nandargikar, Dehli, 1982, 3.25.

43. *Pañcatantra* 3.4.
44. One may recall the famous Bhāṇa of Śyāmilaka, entitled *Pādatāḍitakam* or 'Small Kick', in which a royal scribe complains bitterly before an assembly of urban sophisticates (*viṭas*), or *goṣṭhī*, that his paramour, the courtesan Madanasenikā, has meted out to him the greatest of humiliations by kicking him in the head, and seeks redress. He becomes the laughing stock of the assembly because, it is announced, he is too foolish to understand that 'being received' by the feet of one's lover, like that of a king, was not a humiliation but an honour, and an expression of favour. Implicit also is the suggestion that the young man has too much pride. See the *Pādatāḍitaka of Śyāmilaka*, ed. and tr. G. H. Schokker and P.J. Worsley, Dordercht, 1966.
45. *Kādambarī*, pp. 156–7.
46. *Nāṭyaśāstra* 13.34.
47. See Harṣa's *Priyadarśikā*, ed. and trans. G.K. Nariman, A.V. Williams Jackson, Charles J. Ogden, New York, 1965, 2.6+; and Kālidāsa's *Mālavikāgnimitram*, ed. and trans. R.D. Karmarkar, Delhi, 2002 repr., 1.5+.
48. It is not clear exactly how this was to be sequenced. Perhaps the character entered the stage in his assigned gait and assumed this posture.
49. *Nāṭyaśāstra* 13.3 ff.
50. Literally, their movement was 'independent' (*svacchandagamanam*) of the constraints of anger, and other sentiments, *Nāṭyaśāstra* 13.29–30. For the use of *svabhāva*, as 'natural' or innate movement, see *Nāṭyaśāstra* 13.15.
51. *Nāṭyaśāstra* 13.9–10.
52. *Ibid*, 13.10–11.
53. *Ibid*, 13.12–13.
54. *Ibid*, 13.15.
55. Having a slow, elephant-like walk was a common epithet for people of rank. For men, see *Raghuvaṁśa* 4.4; for women, see Harṣa's *Ratnāvalī*, ed. and tr. C. R. Devadhar and N. G. Suru, Poona, 1925, 4.3. For inscriptional references, *EI* 8 (1905–6), no.8, p. 60; *CII* 3 (1888), no. 49, p. 224; *CII* 4 (1955), no. 26, p. 120.
56. *Nāṭyaśāstra* 13.78.
57. *Ibid*, 13.148–9.
58. See the mid-fifth-century inscription of Kumāragupta and Bandhuvarman at Mandasor, where the brahmins of Daṣapura are described as 'free from surprise' (*asmayita*) and king Bandhuvarman as 'never carried away by intoxication (*mada*), surprise (*smaya*) and other faults', *CII* 3, (1888), no. 18, p. 82.
59. *Nāṭyaśāstra* 11.51–3; see also 13.4–7.
60. For the assignment of the *caturasra* with the *vaiṣṇava sthāna*, *Nāṭyaśāstra* 13.4. The definition of the *caturasra* is given in *Nāṭyaśāstra* 11.91–2.
61. Elsewhere, ministers and merchants are urged to avoid drooping (*niṣaṇṇa*) limbs, *NS* 13.78.
62. *Nāṭyaśāstra* 11.88–91.
63. *Ibid*, 13.147–8.
64. *Sevyasevakopadeśa* 18.

65. *Harṣacarita*, ch. 2, p. 54. The description is conveyed from Harṣa's brother to Bāṇa through the emissary Mekhalaka. All of these diseases are attested to in the medical literature except the first. See editorial note in P.V. Kane's edition, p. 251.
66. The cow and bull are typically associated with these relaxed postures. See the *Nāṭyaśāstra* 24.33 which recommends a graceful (*añcita*) walk like that of a bull, for the male hero. Cf. *Raghvaṁśa* 2.18, where the slightly bent gaits (*añcitābhyām gatābhyām*) of Nandinī and Dilīpa decorate their path home from the forest.
67. See the remarks of Susan Huntington, *The Art of Ancient India: Buddhist, Hindu, Jain*, New York, 1985, pp. 190, 201.
68. Compare the gold stater of Kaṇiṣka depicting the emperor standing in rigid posture (see Robert Göbl, *System und Chronologie der Münzprägung der Kusanreiches*, Wien, 1984, type 71) to the gold coin of Candragupta, showing the emperor standing with bow (see John Allan, *Catalogue of the Coins of the Gupta Dynasties and of Śaśāṅka, King of Gauḍa*. London, 1914, archer type, no. 63).
69. For a discussion of the origin of these terms with an alternative understanding of their significance, see Johan Huizinga, *Homo Ludens: A Study of the Play Element in Culture*, Boston, 1955, pp. 31-32, *et passim*.
70. Many of the sixty four 'arts' (*kalā*) detailed in the *Kāmasūtra* were later called 'entertainments' (*vinoda, krīḍā*) in the sumptuary manuals like the *Mānasollāsa*.
71. *Harṣacarita*, Ch. 2, pp. 70, 72. In this conceit the footstool is compared to the dark-jewelled hood of the demon Kāliya and the darkness of Kali age. The touch of the left foot was humiliating.
72. *Harṣacarita*, Ch. 2, p. 77.
73. Bāṇa uses the figure of speech known as *virodha*, where seemingly antithetical descriptions are revealed to be compatible.
74. The first known sculptural depiction of this posture is perhaps not surprisingly, of the Buddha at Amarāvatī (first or second century CE), though its nomenclature is apparently much later. I thank Akira Shimada for bringing this to my attention.
75. These are detailed in texts like the *Nāṭyadarpaṇa*, *Sāhityadarpaṇa*, and *Abhinayadarpaṇa*. They are also recognised in some kāmaśāstra texts to denote particular behaviours of women who were to be courted.
76. *Nāṭyaśāstra* 24.14–16, 22.
77. *Ibid*, 24.33, 37.
78. Female grace often emphasised delicacy, weakness, or unsteadiness, which at its best was deemed charming, but also had a negative side. It was often taken as a sign of frivolity and inconstancy. For men, by contrast, tenderness and sportive grace were usually combined with *gravitas* and fortitude in bearing which reflected their stronger inner constitution. The common image used to denote this contrast was that of the tree and the creeper, both tender in different ways, but one stable, firm, and supportive, the other delicate and unsteady. In *kāvya* the common characterisation of women was that they more easily 'lost control' in love play, becoming

vulnerable to indiscretion, intoxication and even wildness, thereby breaking codes of grace. Yet even this weakness was deemed the particular charm of women in love-play.

79. In courtship, the transgressive element raises itself again, and perhaps quite signficantly, for while the largely male world of the *sabhā* tended to view such terms as part of a rather uncontested icon of graceful power, the representation of courtship tended to be far more reciprocal and apparently 'transgressive' allowing it to be invested—courtship as 'battle'—with a full range of courtly anxieties.
80. *Mahāsubhāṣitasaṁgraha*, ed. S. Bhaskaran Nair, Hoshiarpur, 1999, vol. 7, no. 11673.

Chapter 3

From Kalyana to Talikota: Culture, Politics, and War in the Deccan, 1542–1565

Richard M. Eaton

In his volume entitled *Vijayanagara*, Burton Stein noted the many books on South Indian history whose titles include the phrase 'to the fall of Vijayanagara'.[1] The reference, of course, is to the Battle of Talikota, in which four sultanates of the northern Deccan joined forces and destroyed the army of Vijayanagara in January 1565. After the battle, the allies then marched down to the sprawling metropolis of their defeated enemy and spent six months plundering the city.

There is no denying that the debacle at Talikota caused a political rupture for the Vijayanagara state. The destruction of the city deprived the ruling dynasty of its status as 'protector' of Pampa and Virupaksha, whose ancient temples by the banks of the Tungabhadra River long predated the Vijayanagara state itself. Nor could its rulers continue to patronise the many monuments with which the kingdom's sovereignty had become closely associated—most important, the Vitthala temple complex, whose central shrine and image were apparently desecrated in the course of the city's destruction following the battle.[2] The defeat at Talikota also led to the collapse of the third dynasty at Vijayanagara and the advent of the fourth and last dynasty, the Aravidu, which for another century maintained a tenuous hold over fragments of the kingdom's earlier realm, from successive capitals that migrated ever southward—first to Penukonda, then to Chandragiri, finally to Vellore.

But the phrase 'to the fall of Vijayanagara', to which Stein referred, implies much more than just political rupture. For many modern historians, Talikota represented a total break, in fact a civilisational rupture, on the assumption that before Talikota the Vijayanagara era had been a Hindu 'golden age', and that after that battle, it became a *lost* golden age. Such thinking, argues Stein, lies in 'the attribution of a spurious nationalism to the Vijayanagara state'[3]—a state often construed as the vessel of a pure 'Hindu' essence, or even as India's last 'independent Hindu state' before an advancing Muslim tide completely swamped the subcontinent. In short, Talikota has had to bear a great deal of ideological freight. In this essay, I wish to re-examine that battle and suggest an alternative perspective on its meaning.

The roots of the Battle of Talikota go back several decades, to 1542. In that year Rama Raya, the great general from southern Andhra, rode in triumph through the gates of Vijayanagara, acclaimed as the hero who would save the kingdom from its political chaos. By his side were his two loyal brothers, Tirumala and Venkatadri, and the sole remnant of the ruling dynasty to have escaped a general massacre in the kingdom's recent civil war. This was the prince Sadasiva, whom Rama Raya had spirited away to an interior fort during the recent turmoil in the capital. He would now serve as Rama Raya's ticket to supreme power. Abandoning the notion of seizing the throne for himself, Rama Raya arranged for Sadasiva to be formally crowned king, with himself as regent.

This arrangement lasted until 1550, when Sadasiva tried to assert his own right to rule. In response, Rama Raya simply imprisoned his charge, allowing him to make a public appearance but once a year. Whereas inscriptions now identified the former regent as co-ruler with Sadasiva, in fact the kingdom had become a patrimonial state, with Rama Raya appointing his own kinsmen as commanders of the principal forts in the realm, as high officials at court, and as governors over territories as distant as Sri Lanka. The final stage was reached around 1562, when Rama Raya discontinued even the formality of allowing the hapless Sadasiva his annual public viewing. Though he stopped short of having himself crowned, Rama Raya had emerged as an autocrat.[4]

Historians are in basic agreement with these facts respecting Vijayanagara's internal conditions in the days of Rama Raya. It is with the state's external relations, and especially with Rama Raya's relations with the five sultanates of the northern Deccan, that we encounter difficulties. Here, most historians argue that from 1542 to 1565, Rama Raya cynically exploited the mutual rivalries of the five sultanates of the northern Deccan, to the point that the rulers of those states, in the name of Islamic solidarity, combined to overthrow their 'infidel' enemy to the south in the fateful Battle of Talikota (1565). The conventional view was best captured by the historian Robert Sewell, who in 1900 characterised Vijayanagara as 'a Hindu bulwark against Muhammadan conquests.'[5] From this perspective, Talikota represented a decisive moment in India's religious history, since it saw Sewell's 'Hindu bulwark' overwhelmed by the advancing tide of Islam.

A scrutiny of Rama Raya's behaviour vis-à-vis his northern neighbours, however, reveals motives that were not at all religious in nature. Departing radically from the traditions of any of the three houses that had theretofore governed Vijayanagara—the Sangama, Saluva, and Tuluva—Rama Raya associated himself with the mighty Chalukya dynasty of Deccani kings, and also with that dynasty's capital city of Kalyana. Although long-defunct, the imperial Chalukyas, who had dominated the peninsula from the Narmada River clear down to the Tamil country between the late tenth century and the mid-twelfth century, were in Rama Raya's day still very much a living memory.

Consider the rhetoric of Vijayanagara's court poets. Between 1543 and 1547, during his early years as regent, Koneru Natha Kavi praised Rama Raya's family with the extraordinary titles 'Chalukya Emperor' (*Calukya-cakravarti*), 'Founder of the Kingdom of Kalyana' (*Kalyana-rajya-sthapanacaryundu*), and 'born in the Chalukya line' (*Calukya-anvaya-bhava*).[6] Yet these boasts had no basis in fact since Kalyana, located some forty miles west of Bidar and far to the north of Vijayanagara, had for several centuries been controlled by Muslim rulers — first the Tughluqs, then the Bahmanis, and from 1543 by Amir Barid, the sultan of Bidar, which was one of the five successor-states of the Bahmanis. Quite remarkably, Rama Raya's family was thus identified as lords over a city that in fact had long been ruled by 'Turks,' as they were known in Vijayanagara.

Titles assigned to Rama Raya by the late seventeenth-century Telugu poet Andugula Venga Kavi may well have been inherited from Rama Raya's own day, or they might have been subsequently added to his repertoire. In any event, they make specific claims as to the territorial reach of Rama Raya's authority. Heading them all is the exalted 'Radiant King of Kalyana' (*Kalyana mahipalabhaswari*), followed by 'Lord of the Excellent City of Kalyana' (*Kalyana puravaradhisvara*) and 'The One who Captured the City of Kalyana' (*Kalyananagara sadhaka*). Respecting cities to the north of the Krishna River other than Kalyana—that is, cities beyond Vijayanagara's actual reach — Rama Raya is said to have 'protected' (*poshana*) Warangal, 'captured' (*harana*) Sagar, 'occupied' (*samakranti-dhira*) Daulatabad, 'chastised' (*dushana*) Golkonda, and 'terrified' (*bhishana*) Bijapur, Bidar, and even Delhi. By contrast, with respect to forts that Vijayanagara had controlled for a long time, such as Udayagiri, Kondavidu, Gutti, or Mudgal, the same poet described Rama Raya as only a 'ruler' (*rajyapalaka, dharandhara, nayaka*), and not a 'lord'. In sum, among all the important political centres on either side of the Krishna, including metropolitan Vijayanagara itself, the only cities over which Rama Raya was declared 'lord' were Kalyana (*puravaradhisvara*) and his family's power base in the Tamil plain, Chandragiri (*rajyadhisvara*).[7]

From Kalyana to Talikota

We should not dismiss as mere hyperbole Rama Raya's titles such as 'Chalukya Emperor' or 'Lord of Kalyana', as trumpeted by court poets, whether they were contemporary with Rama Raya or not. For, turning from the rhetoric of his poets to the record of his own deeds, we find that his actions in fact confirmed their words. For more than twenty years, Rama Raya endeavoured to ensure that whichever northern sultan he was at the moment allied with *also* controlled Kalyana, as though that sultan were an intermediary between himself and the old Chalukya capital.

Thus in 1543, soon after his triumphant return to the capital, Rama Raya was invited by the sultan of Ahmadnagar to participate in a joint invasion of Bijapur, then allied with the sultan of Bidar, who in turn controlled the nearby fort of Kalyana. Agreeing to the proposition, he sent his brother Venkatadri at the head of a large army to join the action, out of which Vijayanagara gained both land and treasure. Kalyana, however, remained in Bidar's control. Three years later, Rama Raya induced his ally Ahmadnagar again to invade Bijapur, but that campaign failed. Then in 1549 the sultan of Bijapur, angry at Rama Raya's intrigues against him, threatened Vijayanagara's ambassadors residing at his court, whereupon these men fled to their capital and complained to their master of their mistreatment. An enraged Rama Raya now resolved on punishing Bijapur by urging Ahmadnagar very specifically to attack Kalyana, which had been ceded to Bijapur by Bidar several years earlier. Following these urgings, the sultan of Ahmadnagar launched a dawn attack on the fort, and in line with Rama Raya's intentions, the former Chalukya capital fell into the hands of his ally, the sultan of Ahmadnagar.[8]

In 1558, when the sultan of Bijapur died and his successor 'Ali 'Adil Shah resolved to recover Kalyana, the new sultan appealed to Rama Raya for help in the project, riding virtually alone down to Vijayanagara to make his case, and also to convey personal condolences on the death of Rama Raya's son. On this occasion the two men exchanged robes and feasted; Rama Raya's wife even called the sultan her own son (*farzand*). The upshot of their friendly meeting was that Rama Raya agreed to attack the new ruler of Ahmadnagar, Sultan Husain Nizam Shah, and to restore to Bijapur both Kalyana and the fort of Sholapur.[9] So in 1559 'Ali 'Adil Shah and Rama Raya joined forces and marched straight to Kalyana, which they besieged.

Outnumbered, Husain retreated to his capital at Ahmadnagar, which the invaders now besieged with a combined force of 100,000 cavalry. Husain then retreated to the town of Paithan just beyond the Godavari river, only to be pursued by one of Rama Raya's generals. From Paithan the fugitive king sent an urgent message to the sultan of Berar pleading for help, and in response the latter sent his intrepid general Jahangir Khan to relieve the siege of Ahmadnagar. In late 1561, with Kalyana threatened, Ahmadnagar besieged, and himself holed up in Paithan, a desperate Husain sued for peace with Rama Raya. But Vijayanagara's stubborn generalissimo informed Husain that he would agree to peace only when three conditions were met. First and foremost, Husain must cede Kalyana to his ally 'Ali 'Adil Shah of Bijapur. Second, Jahangir Khan must be executed for interfering with the siege operations at Ahmadnagar. And finally, Husain himself must personally come to Rama Raya's headquarters and eat *pan* (betel nut) from his hand.[10]

Swallowing his pride, Husain submitted to each of Rama Raya's humiliating demands. First, he ordered Jahangir Khan executed. Then he proceeded to the Vijayanagara camp outside Ahmadnagar's fort and entered Rama Raya's tent. Rising to his feet, Rama Raya took the defeated sultan by the hand. But Husain, offended at having to touch the skin of his enemy, called for a basin of water to wash his hands. Enraged at this breach of etiquette, Rama Raya turned aside and muttered in Kannada, 'If he were not my guest, I would cut off his hands and hang them round his neck.' Calling for water, he too washed his hands. Husain then gave the keys to Kalyana fort to Rama Raya. At that moment the Vijayanagara ruler was indeed, if only briefly, the 'lord' of Kalyana, his sovereignty unmediated by any other ruling authority. But he immediately sent the keys to his ally 'Ali 'Adil Shah of Bijapur. Then, for his final and most humiliating act of submission, Husain ate *pan* from the hand of Rama Raya.[11]

If the city and fort of Kalyana had all along been the focus of Rama Raya's policies in the northern Deccan, it now became an obsession for an embittered and humiliated Husain Nizam Shah. In 1562, determined to recover Kalyana from Bijapur, but also needing allies for the project, Husain cemented an alliance with Golkonda by offering his daughter in marriage to the sultan of that kingdom. To dramatise the centrality of the issue of Kalyana, the wedding ceremony was actually held beneath the walls of that fort, just beyond range of its cannon. As soon as the marriage celebrations were over, the forces of Ahmadnagar and Golkonda set about laying siege to the fort. Again 'Ali' Adil Shah of Bijapur marched to Vijayanagara to request assistance, and again Rama Raya mobilised and marched to Kalyana, this time to help his northern ally defend the fort.

For a second time Husain was forced to lift his siege of Kalyana and retreat to Ahmadnagar. Rama Raya pursued his adversary to the walls of Ahmadnagar, and again Husain was forced to abandon his capital, this time fleeing to the fort of Junnar, north of Pune. Rama Raya pursued him there as well, but in June 1563 monsoon rains forced him to turn back to Vijayanagara. En route he gratuitously plundered and seized several districts of Golkonda and even some others belonging to his 'ally' Bijapur.[12] This perfidious behaviour snapped whatever tolerance the rulers of those kingdoms might still have had for their powerful neighbour to the south. Meanwhile, Sultan Husain of Ahmadnagar, whom Rama Raya had repeatedly humiliated and hunted, burned with a desire for revenge, which he would soon take.

Such was the background to the Battle of Talikota of 1565, in which four kingdoms of the north—Ahmadnagar, Bijapur, Golkonda, and Bidar (Berar abstained)— combined to challenge the grand army of Vijayanagara. It was Rama Raya's last battle. During the conflict the octogenarian suffered a spear wound and fell from his horse. Captured by some Nizam Shahi troops, he was taken to Husain who, confronting his bitter adversary for the last time, ordered him beheaded on the spot, and his head stuffed with straw.[13] Vijayanagara's army now completely disintegrated; soon, its great capital city was destroyed.

Rama Raya's preoccupation with Kalyana appears to have played a key role in the events leading up to Talikota, to his own death, and to the destruction of the capital. But why was he so preoccupied with possessing 'lordship' over Kalyana in the first place, even if only a symbolic or indirect lordship? For one thing, that city, occupying the very centre of the plateau, had been ideally situated for the imperial ambitions of Chalukya kings. With their capital straddling the fault lines between the Marathi, Telugu, and Kannada linguistic zones, Chalukya sovereigns could make claims to imperial rule that transcended the linguistic space defined by any one of those vernacular languages. In fact, all three houses that ruled the Deccan from the twelfth to the fourteenth century — the Hoysalas, Kakatiyas, and Yadavas — carved out linguistically-based regional kingdoms by rebelling against their imperial Chalukya overlords. Rama Raya's claimed ties to the Chalukyas therefore signalled a return to a much earlier conception of authority, one whose spatial reach had extended from Kalyana over the *entire* Deccan plateau, both north and south of the Krishna River.

It is also likely that Rama Raya's claims to having conquered and ruled Kalyana evoked the memory of the bitter rivalry between two of the mightiest empires of medieval India — the Chalukyas of the central Deccan and the Cholas of the Tamil coast. In 1045, Rajadhiraja

Chola had attacked and plundered Kalyana, taking back to his own capital a large stone door guardian as a trophy of war; subsequent Chola rulers made similar claims of having mastered or humiliated the Chalukya rulers of Kalyana.[14] Inasmuch as Rama Raya's own power base was centred on the fortress of Chandragiri, on the Tamil plain near the Chola heartland, his claims to lordship over Kalyana would have recalled Chola deeds of glory vis-à-vis their perennial adversaries. Moreover Rama Raya, who lacked royal blood of his own, had usurped power, and had withheld the state's reigning sovereign from public view, needed some means to legitimate his rule. By mimicking Chola claims of mastery over their Chalukya adversaries, he would have attained at least a vicarious connection with a legitimate dynastic authority.

Vijayanagara and Persian Culture

The conventional idea that the Battle of Talikota represented a 'clash of civilisations' in which Hindu sovereignty sustained a blow, is seriously flawed. For one thing, Rama Raya's diplomacy vis-à-vis his northern neighbours appears to have been motivated far more by his preoccupation with lordship over Kalyana than with a concern with Hindu *dharma*. What is more, during the two centuries prior to 1565, states on both sides of the Krishna river had assimilated so much Persian culture, and had experienced so much cultural interaction, that their mutual struggles were practically reduced to the usual rivalries over territory and forts, and not over matters of 'civilisation'. Architectural historians of metropolitan Vijayanagara have noted the spatial separation between the city's Sacred Centre and Royal Centre. In reality, this separation reflects a conceptual compartmentalisation of the kingdom's 'sacred' and 'royal' domains, which was what enabled rulers to assimilate so much exogenous culture in the royal domain without affecting the sacred domain.

For example, most of the political culture of both Vijayanagara and its northern neighbours was Persian, whether elements of that culture had originated in Iran itself or had been transmitted through Iran en route to India. Most monarchs of Vijayanagara adopted the title 'sultan,' as in the formula 'Sultan among Indian kings'. Meaning 'all-powerful ruler' in Arabic, the term entered Persian, was carried to India by ethnic Turks, was then assimilated into Sanskrit as '*suratrana*,' and in the Deccan became naturalised in Telugu and Kannada, among other vernaculars. This migrant orphan, which Phillip Wagoner has analyzed as part of a wide range of Vijayanagara's cultural borrowing from the Persian world, presents a classic instance of an idea, and a term that resisted appropriation by any single language or ethnic group. Virtually every ruler at Vijayanagara included 'sultan' among his other titles. And while most were content with 'Sultan among Indian kings,' Rama Raya went further and styled himself 'Sultan of the World' (*gola suratranuakunu*), a title even more inflated than 'Chalukya Emperor' (*Calukya-cakravarti*).[15]

As for the visual arts, metropolitan Vijayanagara, especially the Royal Centre, is saturated with Persian architectural elements: domes, vaulted arches, parapets of merlons, corner finials, fine plasterwork, and so forth.[16] The same holds for the city's layout. As Wagoner has further noted, Vijayanagara's citadel does not appear in the centre of a concentric *mandala* pattern, as is prescribed in classical Indian texts, and is actually seen in the Kakatiya capital of Warangal. Rather, it appears off to one side, a design that finds antecedents in Indo-Persian citadels such as those of Daulatabad (1326–27), or a few years earlier in Tughluqabad (1320–23). Similarly, whereas Vijayanagara's north-facing throne hall has no known precedent in classical Indian courts, it does find antecedents in most Persian or Persian-inspired courts — such as at Bidar, Tughluq Warangal, Tughluqabad, and Samarqand — extending clear back to ancient Persepolis, capital of the ancient Persian Empire. To that famous site, too, can be traced the widespread tradition of royal halls with forty columns, a hundred columns, or even a thousand columns. These are found in courts throughout the Iranian plateau and South Asia, as in Delhi's 'Hazar Sutun' (1343) built by Muhammad bin Tughluq. Moreover, Vijayanagara's multi-columned 'House of Victory' and 'Great Platform' find striking correspondences to the Throne Hall and Apadana of Persepolis. As on the Apadana, sculptural reliefs carved at the base of Vijayanagara's Great Platform depict processions of figures bearing tribute to the enthroned king.[17]

Further linking Vijayanagara with the wider Persian world were the thousands of Iranian or Deccani Muslim mercenaries who took up service with the court and were accommodated in a large quarter of the capital — such as the 10,000 'Turks' hired by Deva Raya II in 1430, or the 3,000 Middle Eastern soldiers that Rama Raya himself employed when these had been dismissed by the sultan of Bijapur in 1535. To these may be added the many Arab or Persian long-distance merchants, especially those involved in the international horse import trade, memorialised in bas-relief sculptures along the base and exterior walls of numerous Vijayanagara monuments, sacred and secular. As a result of such contacts, a wide spectrum of Arabo-Persian words infiltrated spoken Telugu and Kannada, while courtly dress increasingly conformed to fashions set in the Middle East and Central Asia.[18]

In sum, the quickening pace of peninsular India's commercial and cultural interaction with the Iranian plateau in the fifteenth and sixteenth centuries had the effect of drawing the *whole* Deccan into the orbit of

Persian culture, which was widely perceived as prestigious, cosmopolitan, and readily portable across ethnic frontiers. In 1443 'Abd al-Razzaq Samarqandi, a Timurid ambassador from Central Asia, visited Vijayanagara and found a court steeped in Persian culture. Wearing a green satin robe, Deva Raya II was seated on a magnificent golden throne set in a north-facing throne hall that 'Abd al-Razzaq called a *chihil sutun* ('forty columns'). The ambassador's use of that Persian term suggests that he recognised in Vijayanagara the same sort of multi-columned hall already familiar to him from Middle Eastern courts. And during his interview with the king, 'Abd al-Razzaq was closely questioned about Timur's nobles, army, number of horses, and the cities of his realm, such as Samarqand, Herat, and Shiraz — all indicating Deva Raya II's avid interest in the Timurid court.[19] In fact, the ambassador's experience illustrates Marshall Hodgson's remark that by the sixteenth century Vijayanagara had found itself 'more or less enclaved' in what he called an 'Islamicate' world, that is, a domain characterised not by religious identity but by standards of taste already established in the Middle East.[20]

Summary

In his own day, Rama Raya was understood in many ways. To his subjects he was son-in-law of Krishna Raya, powerful general, godfather of a sprawling patrimonial state, saviour of that state from civil war, patron of Telugu literature and of the Venkateswara temple at Tirupati. The sultans of the northern Deccan viewed him either as a powerful ally or as a feared, 'infidel' enemy, depending on whether they were allied with him or against him.[21] Rama Raya appears to have seen himself as, among other things, 'lord' of Kalyana—simultaneously conqueror of that city and heir to the Chalukya imperial tradition.

No evidence, however, suggests that his contemporaries saw him as a defender of Hindu *dharma* or the Deccan itself as a region permanently divided between a Muslim north and Hindu south. Like other soldiers, Rama Raya served rulers on both sides of the Krishna river; and like other rulers, he employed soldiers from both sides of that river. In a word, his career exemplified the remarkable extent of élite mobility that in the fifteenth and sixteenth centuries was occurring throughout the Deccan plateau, enabled in large part by the diffusion of a common, Persian culture in the region.

From this perspective, then, the Battle of Talikota, while a political disaster for the Tuluva dynasty, was hardly the watershed event for the Deccan's cultural history that historians from Sewell on have maintained. More than anything else, it was the tragic outcome of one man's obsessive preoccupation with retaining a symbolic or indirect 'lordship' over Kalyana, the ancient Chalukya capital.

REFERENCES

1. Burton Stein, 'Vijayanagara and the Transition to Patrimonial Systems,' in Anna L. Dallapiccola (ed), *Vijayanagara — City and Empire: New Currents of Research*, Stuttgart, 1985, p. 73.
2. It was customary for military victors in pre-modern India to desecrate the principal temple of a defeated enemy, in this way detaching the latter from the most visible representation of his state-deity. By 1565 Vitthala, not Virupaksha, had become the deity before whom important documents were witnessed and authenticated. This seems to be why, of all the monuments in Vijayanagara, the Vitthala temple suffered the most damage when the city was sacked, whereas the Virupaksha escaped desecration. See Anila Verghese, *Archaeology, Art and Religion: New Perspectives on Vijayangara*, New Delhi, 2000, p. 108. See also Pierre-Sylvian Filliozat and Vasundhara Filliozat, *Hampi-Vijayanagar: the Temple of Vithala*, New Delhi, 1988, p. 29.
3. Burton Stein, 'Vijayanagara and the Transition to Patrimonial Systems,' in Dallapiccola, *Vijayanagara*, pp. 73, 74.
4. Henry Heras, *The Aravidu Dynasty of Vijayanagar*, Madras, 1927, pp. 32–38.
5. Robert Sewell, *A Forgotten Empire (Vijayanagara): a Contribution to the History of India*, 1900; reprint, Delhi, 1962, p. 1.
6. Konerunatha Kavi, *Padya Balabhagavatamu*, in C.V. Ramachandra Rao, *Andugula Vengakavi Ramarajiyamu leka Narapati Vijayamu mariyu Doneru Konerunatha-kavi Padya Balabhagavatamu, Dvidpada Balabhagavatamu (Araviti Rajula Prasamsa)*, Nellore, 1995, pp. 67, 73. My thanks to Phillip Wagoner for drawing my attention to this work.
7. Andugullavenga Kavi, *Ramarajiyamu* [also known as *Narapati Vijayam*]. Extracts in Krishnaswami Ayyangar (ed), *Sources of Vijayanagar History*, 1919; reprint Delhi, 1986, pp. 182–83.
8. John Briggs (tr), *History of the Rise of the Mahomedan Power in India till the year AD 1612, Translated from the Original Persian of Mahomed Kasim Ferishta*, 1829, reprint Calcutta, 1966, vol. 3, pp. 56, 62–63, 141–43.
9. *Ibid*, pp. 71, 145–46.
10. *Ibid*, p. 146–47, 241. T. W. Haig (tr), 'The History of the Nizam Shahi Kings of Ahmadnagar', *Indian Antiquary*, April, 1921, pp. 105–6.
11. Briggs, *Rise*, vol. 3, pp. 147–48.
12. *Ibid*, pp. 74, 148–50, 243–44.
13. *Ibid*, p. 248; G. T. Kulkarni and M. S. Mate (eds and trs), *Tarif-i-Husain Shah Badshah Dakhan*, Pune, 1987, pp. 199–205.
14. Richard H. Davis, *Lives of Indian Images*, Princeton, 1997, pp. 51–3, 76–82.
15. Phillip B. Wagoner, 'Sultan among Hindu Kings: Dress, Titles, and the Islamicization of Hindu Culture at Vijayanagara', *Journal of Asian Studies*, vol. 55 (4), Nov. 1996, pp. 851–80.
16. Koneru-natha Kavi, *Padya Balabhagavatamu* (1543), in Ayyangar (ed), *Sources*, p. 204.

17. George Michell, 'Royal Architecture and Imperial Style at Vijayanagara', in Barbara S. Miller (ed), *Powers of Art*, New Delhi, 1992, pp. 175. See also Catherine B. Asher, 'Islamic Influence and the Architecture of Vijayanagara', in Dallapiccola, *Vijayanagara*, pp. 188–95.
18. Phillip B. Wagoner, 'The Islamicate Contribution to the City Plan of Vijayanagara', Paper at a symposium 'Hindu and Muslim in Precolonial South Asia,' University of Texas, Austin, 13 Nov. 1998.
19. Wagoner, 'Sultan among Hindu Kings', pp. 851–80. 'They have breeches after the order of the Turkes', remarked Cesare Federici, who visited Vijayanagara in 1567. Samuel Purchas, *Hakluytus Posthumus, or Purchas his Pilgrimes*, 1625, reprint Glasgow, 1905, Vol. 10, p. 99.
20. W. M. Thackston (tr), *A Century of Princes: Sources on Timurid History and Art*, Cambridge MA, 1989, pp. 310–14.
21. Marshall Hodgson, 'The Role of Islam in World History', *International Journal of Middle East Studies*, Vol. 1 (2), April 1970, p. 118.
22. The only contemporary description of the Battle of Talikota was composed by Aftabi, a court poet of Sultan Husain Nizam Shah. Aftabi refers to Rama Raya, the enemy of his patron, as a 'useless infidel' (*kafir-i nabakar*). But when describing the battle scene, Aftabi resorts to stock poetic tropes appropriate for any powerful and respected adversary: 'Ram Raja was Rao of Bijanagar. He was with tied waist and wore a crown. When he arranged his army of swordsmen and archers, its lightening-like flash reached the clouds. Because of movement of iron shoes of animals, the swords and the tent poles, the earth was shaken up from its very foundations. Due to the loud cries coming from ambush, the sky appeared to be thrown down on the earth.' Kulkarni and Mate, *Tarif-i-Husain Shah Badshah*, pp. 173, 183.

Chapter 4

Literary Tropes and Historical Settings: A Study from Southern India

Sumit Guha

> 'Broadly speaking, a literary text, one already recognized as such, is an objective given, however open to multiple readings and interpretations. But historical contexts do not exist in themselves; they must be defined, and in that sense constructed, by the historian before the interpretive work of producing meaning, of interpreting the past, can begin.' (*Gabrielle Spiegel*)

The problems addressed by Gabrielle Spiegel are not unique to the European middle ages and vernacular histories of that time. They arise even more sharply in the context of South Asian history. Spiegel points out that 'the historian functions as a "writer" in the sense of composing the basic historical narrative out of which significance will flow, while the literary critic stands in relation to the literary object primarily as a "reader" ... the task facing the one is largely constructive; the other, largely deconstructive.'[1] This means that texts of the past are addressed in radically different ways by the two disciplines.

This was of course a challenge to an increasingly popular view that has over the past forty years sought to assimilate the literary and historical approach to texts. One of its earliest manifestos was published by the hugely influential Hayden White in 1966. He wrote that a historical 'explanation need not be assigned to the category of the literally truthful on the one hand or the purely imaginary on the other, but can be judged solely in terms of the richness of the metaphors which govern its sequence of articulation. Thus envisaged, the governing metaphor of a historical account could be treated as a *heuristic rule which self-consciously eliminates certain kinds of data from consideration as evidence.*'[2] It would follow then different accounts could legitimately select evidence to prove a wide, if not infinite set of narratives in the same way as a set of children's blocks can be made into various shapes. Indeed no historian could historian challenge another with the charge that relevant evidence had been omitted, since the criteria of relevance (heuristic rules) are separate from the evidence and indeed determine its selection. White of course, sought to maintain this position for some decades but then found himself in the decidedly un-chic (and academically hazardous) position of seeming to endorse denial or affirmation of the Jewish Holocaust as being equally valid positions with David Irving (say) merely exercising his right to *eliminate certain kinds of data*. Such an endorsement would logically follow from White's position. A leading historiographer, Georg Iggers pinned White on this point in article published in 2000. Iggers pointed out that White 'admits that the [Holocaust] took place.' Iggers added that White 'distinguishes between events which are real and facts which are constructs but then uses the two terms interchangeably.' In his response Hayden White sought to retract without appearing to do so.

Iggers finds untenable my view 'that every historical account, provided it does not violate fidelity to the facts, possesses equal truth value. 'Did I say that? Maybe. Actually, I wanted to say...' [3]

The last decades of the nineteenth century saw the beginnings of major efforts by members of the Indian intelligentsia to contest the colonial narratives that dominated Indian history at the time. The search for indigenous primary sources was a central part of this effort.[4] Scholars were all too ready to seize on Indian-language narratives and to accept everything they said as descriptively true, omitting only the magical and supernatural element. In this search for factual information, the literary qualities and internal features of texts were neglected in favour of mining them for evidence for inspiring narratives. This approach still has its votaries in India. Romila Thapar recently wrote that historical consciousness is often analogous to 'a particular vein embedded in rock ... in that such consciousness is not always visible and has to be prised from sources which tend to conceal it. Within the vein lies information purporting to relate to events of the past, and enveloping this vein is the commentary which arises from concerns of the present.'[5] In her view, therefore, the historical is merely enveloped by the ideological and therefore, they can in principle, be identified and separated.

The text that I will discuss came to light as a part of the effort at recovering indigenous histories. The incomplete Marathi text of this narrative was first published by Go. Ka. Chandorkar in the third annual volume of the *Proceedings of the Bharata Itihasa Samshodhaka Mandala* in 1914. He lacked the first few pages and they have never been found. By the 1990s, not only the original manuscript but even the Nagari transcript presumably supplied by Chandorkar to printer were also untraceable. Therefore the printed Nagari text of 1914 is the only available copy of the Marathi version.[6] In 1925, S. Krishnaswamy Iyengar located a Kannada manuscript titled *Ramrajana Bakhairu* in the Oriental Manuscripts Library at Madras (now Chennai). He suggested that the Marathi was an abridged translation of the Kannada original which was itself written within a year of the great battle itself.[7] The Kannada text was printed in 1922. Since the Marathi part apparently follows the Kannada *Bakhairu*, (or vice versa) I present it below. I am unable to access the Kannada text, but will depend on a paraphrase cum translation published by Na. Shri. Rajpurohit in 1929.[8] This work titles itself '*Ramarayana bakhairu*' (the *bakhar* of Ramaraya).

In 1952 Gramopadhye produced a small volume of selections from different *bakhars*, including this one.[9] It was probably intended for the use of University students in Maharashtra. In editing his selection, Gramopadhye largely omitted what he must have viewed as the 'non-historical' or perhaps 'fanciful' parts of the texts. This led to the omission of portions such as the emperor's visits to the palaces of his three principal queens and the highly imaginative list of the fruits that he distributed. Perhaps for the sake of brevity, he also omitted the names of nobles who were killed and wounded on both sides and the list of nobles dispatched to different fortresses before the battle. The evidently embroidered list of military equipment is included as Gramopadhye evidently assumed it to be accurate.

Gramopadhye follows an earlier editorial tradition, which as Wagoner describes it, mined texts 'for whatever veins of historical data it might contain embedded among more legendary and fanciful strata.' But, as Wagoner goes on to point out, such sifting (by the editors of the 1919 volume of *Sources* and the 1946 volumes *Further Sources* of Vijayanagara history) eliminated 'the very passages that would have provided the keys to understanding the *Rayavacakamu*'s unique vision of the past...' In his anxiety to find an authentic source from the Vijayanagara side, he also chose to ignore the various inconsistencies that simply make it unlikely that it dates from 1565. In his edition, he largely excised these elements of the narrative. He thereby also eliminated the internal clues that would have enabled an accurate dating of the work. Overall, these omitted portions would have enabled a proper understanding of the text as an account from a much later time, mediated through the sensibilities of its own setting.[10] Spiegel has called for the placing of texts in context: and no context can be more important for historians than the chronological one. As we shall see, later users of that edition have fallen into the trap that he inadvertently constructed.

My research on this *bakhar* is at an early stage and I cannot claim to possess anything like the massive erudition and subtle understanding that Wagoner brought to bear on his text. But I will try to show below that the *bakhar* is in many ways analogous to the *Rayavacakamu*, a later text anachronistically presented as a news-report written within a year or so of the battle. Anglophone scholars of early modern India have been introduced to this *bakhar* via the cursory consideration of Gramopadhye's abbreviated text found in the recently published *Textures of Time* whose authors chose not to use the full text. They follow Herwadkar (1994) in stating that the 1914 text was based a copy made in 1614 CE.[11] This date is based on a statement in the concluding pages of the text that attributed the first copying to Venkaji Narayana Kulkarni in *Anandanama Samvatsara, Phalgun*, second day of the bright half.[12] But this is merely the name of a year in the sixty-year astronomical cycle[13] and could therefore refer to 1613-14 but also to 1673-4, 1733-4 and so on. They also note the massive error in the narrative's placing the Mughal emperor Akbar among the rulers in the confederation attacking Vijayanagara, but add: 'Yet this should not bother us overmuch ... the location of Akbar on the battlefield is not without its deeper significance for a coherent transition in sovereignty between Vijayanagara and the Mughals.'[14] But in fact the later portions of the text, as the reader will see, essentially present the Adilshah as the successor to Vijayanagara both descriptively and in the symbolic narrative of the emperor asking that Adilshah, whom he had made his son, should kill him. Furthermore, in 1614, Mughal dominions hardly extended beyond the Tapi valley well to the north of Vijayanagara while the Adilshahi and Qutbshahi were actively acquiring the former territories of the Vijayanagara empire. Finally, Gramopadhye's abbreviated text omits the concluding scribe's notation that the copying was completed on 11th Jamadilakher Hijri year 1095 or May 26, 1684. It is therefore quite possible that the *Ananda Samvatsara* of the copyist was in fact 1673-4, a year of great importance in the Marathi-speaking world, because Shivaji was crowned Chhatrapati in that year.

I felt that a complete translation of the whole text as currently available may be of some value to historians. That empire of Vijayanagara dominated the Southern peninsula for two centuries until it began to decline following the defeat at Rakshas-Tagdi and the subsequent sack of its capital by a coalition of the Dakhani Sultanates in 1565. By the mid-seventeenth century, its former territories had been parceled out among various successor states. The fall of Vellore in 1649 is the conventional date for the extinction of the third dynasty of Vijayanagara.

But the Vijayanagara empire remained a point of reference and origin for successor states south of the Krishna river for the next two centuries. Local histories and family pedigrees of south India harked back to it. Its great sixteenth-century ruler, Krishnadevaraya passed into folklore. The significance of the tradition of Vijayanagara as far south as the city of Madura was shown by Phillip Wagoner's brilliant analysis of the *Rayavacakamu* which he edited, analyzed and translated.[15] He shows that a text claiming to be an eyewitness report from Vijayanagara was actually written at least seventy-five years after the event as a contribution to the construction of legitimate political authority for the rulers of Madura hundreds of miles south of Vijaynagara. The text that follows has all too often been read as a simple contemporary narrative of Vijayanagara, written from the defeated side. In my opinion, it is far more likely to be a complex pastiche composed many decades later with a different agenda in mind. Whatever its object, I present a complete text that may advance our understanding. I begin with the 1929 Marathi paraphrase/translation of the Kannada text printed in1922.

It declares the author to be Ramaji Tirumala Harikara and states that he was in the entourage of Ramaraya, the emperor of Karnataka. Ramaji then describes the origin of the war as follows:

> A distinguished courtier came to the Vijayanagara emperor as envoy from Alli [sic] Adilshaha of Bijapur on some business. He was given audience and the matter had begun to be discussed when a troupe of traveling Dombari entertainers arrived. Some hours elapsed while the court watched them perform. When the time came for them to rewarded and dismissed, they said "Pray gift us some pigs." They were immediately presented with ten excellent village swine in the court. The Bijapur envoy who was seated there ejaculated "How can Hindus eat these filth-eating beasts?" The emperor retorted "Muslims eat chickens, which is like eating dirt." Whereupon the envoy responded "You are low-caste eaters of filthy animals."
>
> This enraged the emperor who had many swine gathered from the streets of the city, shut up in a large building and fed large amounts of millet grain. During the night the pigs defecated profusely. The next morning some chickens were brought to the place. When released, they began to pick out the undigested grains from the pig feces and eat them. The emperor showed this to the envoy and said "We eat pigs. But you people eat chickens that live by picking food out of pig feces. That being so, whose is the superior caste?" The envoy was deeply upset and sought to leave immediately. But the emperor calmed him, saluted him and then bade him farewell.
>
> Then the envoy went to Alli Adilshah at Bijapur and took off his turban and wound the cloth around his neck and said "Today the Muslim empire stands ruined. The emperor has insulted the Muslim faith and grabbed the whole Karnataka. Therefore it is essential that an expedition be sent to set him in his place." But the Adilshaha responded: "I call myself the emperor's son; therefore it is not right for me to raise a hand against him." Enraged

by this response, the noble went off with out the Adilshaha's permission and came to Jahlnapur. Jalaluddin Akbar, Kutubshaha and Nizamulmulk [sic] were gathered there for a banquet. The courtier made his complaint to them. They responded: "You are a servant of the Adilshaha. Why have you come to us without asking him?" The courtier responded "I told him this. But he merely said that he was the emperor's son and could not go against him. Therefore I have come to you to redress." Hearing all this, the three kings were inflamed with rage and resolved to campaign in the Karnataka. All three ordered their ministers and generals to prepare their armies. Timaji Bhimaji, an envoy from Vijayanagara was at Jalnapura. He sent a messenger to the emperor with a letter informing him that three kings were going to invade the Karnataka. After Vijayadashami, the emperor held his court in a beautiful garden grove and summoned the eight ministers, the Dalavai's etc [and] all the 72 *niyogis* [office-holders] and all his subordinate chiefs, told them the news and motivated them to fight bravely.

When the three kings learned of the preparations at Vijayanagara, they sent an ambassador to the Adilshaha with the following message: "We three are embarked on a campaign of conquest against Vijayanagara. You should permit us to march through your dominions with our armies. We should all unite to invade the Karnataka." The Adilshaha told the ambassador to say to them: "The emperor is like my own father. It is impossible for me to betray my lord (*svami*)." This news reached the emperor at Vijayanagara. Thereupon he honored the Adilshaha by sending his army commander, Bisalappa Nayak with valuable robes, a pearl head-ornament, jewel necklace and horses. The Adilshaha happily accepted these gifts.

Rajpurohit adds that the rest of the narrative is as in the Marathi version.

The translation below follows that Marathi text. Chandorkar deciphered some words and phrases from the damaged portions of the menuscripts. I have translated them wherever it has been possible to produce a coherent sentence from them. Omissions have been marked by ellipsis; but I have not omitted any complete sentence of the available text. Obsurve terms and epeculative translation are indicated by question mark.

The *bakhar* of Rakshasa Tagdi

On the third day spies had taken the news to Akbarshah padshaha Jalaldina Jalnapur padshah and Imanpru [lik patshaha] Varad desha and Nizamashaha Bahiri padshaha. These three collectively sent an envoy to the Aliyedilshaha (saying) "We will [invade?]... the Karnataka ... you should give us passage through your kingdom and provide supplies for our armies. Aliyadilshaha replied :"the emperor has called us his son, and therefore no passage will be afforded to you." He gave the envoy gifts of armbands, robes, two *tezi* (Arab horses?) and an elephant canopy and sent him back. This news came in a sealed letter. The emperor then sent Bisalya [to the Adilshah]...with the message "you are my son. Arrange that the three kings do not cross through your territory." The Adilshaha gave the envoy Bisalaya a private audience and then dispatched him with a gift of robes and a horse and hand-parasol back to Vijayanagara. When the emperor heard the news from the envoy, he ordered all the ministers to assemble and consider the news. They bowed deeply and said "You are the king of 90 million, the repository of valour, sole lord of heaven. … rich gifts from the treasury .. deeds of manhood will be performed." The emperor bestowed perfumes and fruit and betel leaf and then went quickly into the Queens' section (of the palace). In the palace of the senior queen, he sat down on a couch studded with the nine types of gem and sent for the bales of goods from his ancestors' time and gifted the queen gem-studded gold ornaments waistbands, rings and armlets. He then went to the palace of the second queen, Devacintamani Trivegal and they sat together and called the dancing girls to perform. He then gave the dancing-girls 5000 *phalam* [*fanam*] and pearls weighing one *khandi* 5½ *man* 3½ *ser*[16] and five yellow cloths. Then the third queen, she of enchanting form, took him to her own palace, put a cloak (?*baladuri*) round him and took him to her palace where she entertained him much. Thereupon the emperor ordered the following fruits as listed to be brought from the Royal garden:

Amritphalen
[? Fruit of immortality]
135,000
jackfruit
352
pomegranates
about 500,000
apples
30,000
almonds by weight
1200 *sher*
coconuts
about 21,300
khalal khurma [??]
1½ *khandi*? Or 1200 *sher*
sweet limes
890,000
walnuts by weight
1200 *sher*
raisins by weight
1520 *sher*

oranges
1750
watermelon
840
grapes by weight
63 *sher*
musk melon by weight
1331 ½ *sher*
young sugarcane [?]
178,200
charoli fruit by weight
2480 *sher*
bananas
about 8000
sweet seeds by weight
1400 *sher*
figs
about 138,300
list complete
0 [sic][17]

These were distributed in all the quarters of the Queens' section. Then the emperor went to the queen-mother's palace where she gifted him an abundance of gem-adorned garments and robes *baladuri* and taking him into her palace entertained him royally. Then the emperor told her all the news that four kings were advancing on the kingdom. "This is a land of *dharma*, of the gods, of food charities, of the god-like Brahmans, may this not be destroyed. So I go to assemble an army, give me advice and bid me farewell." He fell at her feet. Thereupon the queen-mother was deeply disturbed and said "Your son the prince has almost grown from prince to emperor in my care. Do not let any disturbance come from the Turks. If it comes, they commit great excesses. Negotiate with them through envoys to conciliate them." She spoke at length to change his heart.

But he did not heed her and got up and left the place. Then she bade him an agreeable farewell. Then the emperor went into the hall of music and fell asleep on a couch. He dreamed that night that the pearls from his ears were being snatched away; that his throne was taken even while he sat on it. An envoy came and stood arrogantly before him. Seeing this, he awoke in consternation. He sent for great and wise astrologers and Vedic scholars and city priests who had been there for a long time. When he told them his dream they reassured him and calmed his mind, saying:

"Your enemies wherever they come from will be destroyed. You will reign as long as Markandeya." He then bestowed gifts of cloths on them and dismissed them. Then he distributed five thousand *hons* among Brahmans. Then the astrologer having calculated the auspicious moment, the King's steed was brought for him and at the eleventh hour he left the throne of Vijayanagara and advanced northward, pitched his pavilion and halted. The cavalry and elephants and camel corps and the tent establishment and the hunting establishment and weapon collection and the beverage preparers and the commissariat and the carpet-keepers and *ambarkhana* and everyone advanced and halted all around. In the city of Vijayanagara, it was proclaimed by beat of drum that not one horse or soldier was to remain in the city, all were to join the camp. All came out and camped. The treasury was opened and its distribution placed in the hands of … from Srirangastana, Sadasivappa Naik treasurer, Gopalpa the judge and Komararau the treasurer. Details of what was given to each noble (*vazir*) also what was given to others—their emissaries were summoned and was paid into their custody as follows:

zademol honu	ramacandrapantmole
3748460	153914
sivrai	acyutrai
1873220	10790
adhormole	ghutmole
44971	500,000
hakeri honu	chanrai honu
800,000	400,000
mekhi honu	venkatesh mole
800,000	400,000
velur hon	madhuri mole
400,000	60,000
ananta mole	nagara phani honu
15,000	107,000
mahisvala	*hosmole [hoskote?] hon*
12,000	18,000

vengati honu	hanmant mole honu
16,000	26,000
anigondi	raghunath mole
219,360	2387,833

In total, *hons* amounting to 12,357,411 this amount was handed over the deputies of the nobles gathered at the court. The nobles were enjoined to dress the horses in armour and the horsemen in armour and helmets and armour the elephants and mount them after weighing [themselves?]. The next day the nobles sent messengers with the musters. The aggregate count was: horses 350,000, he-elephants 9778, she-elephants 7318, rockets amounting to 4,609,575, infantry with muskets 148,915, *tapaa*. 1184,378, spearmen 12,053, *rambana* Rama's arrows [fire arrows?] 231,320, *karalbarani* 250, rockets with fire-pots 11,120, western cannon 3928, arrow makers [?] 3049, musket makers [?] ..938, armourers 27,850, *khurd* [?] 3300, iron helmets 27850, *zabarjang* [blunderbusses?] .. 2200, explosive pots 1,343,870, single combatants 8000, senior headmen [*vadgaudani*] 58,910, armoured horses 14,000, blacksmiths 1090, armored elephants 1800, craftsmen 3004, hunting dogs 709, *panbude* [pontoons?] 1800, basket-rafts 200, gunpowder 749,208,524 *shers* [about 700,000 tons if we take the *sher* at 900 grammes.].

Apart from this, the contingents of chieftains and feudatories and leaders were impossible to count. They filled up the jungles and ravines and the Karnataki camp covered the lands of seven or eight townships. The emperor moved his camp across the Tungabhadra and the advance guard held the bank of the Krishna. There the emperor inspected the elephants and clad them in armour [the names of 92 elephants are listed here][18]. Then long muskets and blunderbusses were mounted on them and they were placed on the river bank. The emperor placed the camp between the towns of Tavargiri and Kundarapivayel and erected his pavilion. Selected cavalry and camp-followers camped near Muski.

Nizamshaha Padshaha holder of the Marhata [Maratha] throne of Daulatabad came from Bhimrathi camped near Ferozabad. And Akbar Jalaldin padshaha camped near Shahadurg. And Ibrahim Kutubashaha holder of the Telangan throne Golkunda camped between Mudgal and Raichur. On all sides of the Muslim kings, the soldiers and plunderers and Vanjaris (grain-carrying pastoralist—also given to marauding) and robber horsemen camped along the river. They began to enter the territories of the emperor and carry off plunder and slaves. The entire territory began to be abandoned by its inhabitants. The emperor placed four thousand horsemen and fifty thousand footmen to guard the camp and ordered all the nobles, royal princes [*rajbida*] and bravoes and betel carriers and Rajputs and *kshatriyas* and commandants to gather near Rakshasa Tagdi. Armoured carts and western cannon were to be joined together and the rocket men —there were 80,000 rockets—each bullock carried 18; in addition other rockets transported on camel-back were to be arranged alongside. Around the carts horses and footmen were to be deployed. [text here exceptionally confused. It appears that the scribe missed a line or two in copying].

They took positions near Rakshasa Tagdi. This news was carried by spies and messengers to the Muslim kings. Then the Muslim kings came and placed themselves five kos away. Nizamshaha of the Marhatha kingdom and Kutabshaha of Telangan separated and advanced around a lake. Seeing this, the emperor formed up an infantry contingent and developed an attack. Ali Yedalshaha of the Kannada folk gathered all his forces and took up a position. Imamammulik Padshaha of Varad desha gathered his whole army and prepared to advance. As all the three or four kings stood in formation, the Karnataki infantry and horsemen advanced with the fortified carts and began to attack the Nizamshaha and Kutabshaha. Rockets and arrows were fired on both sides. Many fell dead and wounded on both sides. Nizamshaha of the Marhatha kingdom and Kutabshaha of Telangan retreated one and a half kosa; Ali Yedalshaha of the Kannada folk and Imamanmulik king of Varad still held to their positions. They advanced into combat. The wounded and fallen [nobles] were as follows:

Belonging to King Nizyamshaha Bahiri were killed:

Sivaji Kate
Alamkhan
Bairagi
Akvalkhan Total – 4
Were captured:
Kale Mandur
Basvaji
Kheroji Bhosle Listed 3
Belonging to King Kutubshaha of Telangana were captured
Isankhandola
Kesavarau
Antaji
Satvaji Total – 4
Were killed :
Motirau
Agirau
Yesajirau
Devaji Kurap Total – 4
On the Emperor's side:
Wounded:
Raghuvir Komar
Somana Dalvi
Miriya the Treasurer
Gholpa the banker
.... [missing]
Rama the superintendent of the store
Sekh Ali Total – 6

And as for the infantrymen who fell, both Karnataki and those belonging to Nizamshaha and Telangana—so many fell that their number is beyond count—they lay all over the fields and forests.

Wounded – Devinaik   Total - 1

Learning of these casualties, the emperor sent out robes for the nobles and all other men on his side and instructed them not to fight until he gave the word. He said, "Otherwise there will be heavy losses. When everyone has been gathered together we shall fight manfully." He sent this message to all the Bhosle *dalvis*. Then he sent Chhariyepa naik as an envoy to Ali Yedalshaha padshaha of the Kanadas with the message: "You came of your own accord and were seated in my lap and called a son. And you were given Rayechur and Advani on the promise that you would not advance against me. That being so, you gave the three kings passage through your realm and have joined them with your entire army. That is very well. What will happen even if four kings join together? What will happen to you in future?" Then Ali Yedalshah replied that: "The three kings came into my kingdom with their armies by force. I lacked the force to oppose them. They were ruining my people and army. I have not joined this league. I am not betraying the compact made [by the fact] that I sat in your lap and swore oaths of loyalty. Do not be disheartened."

This he said to the envoy in private and sent him back with rich gifts of robes and a fine horse and armlets and a pair of pearl ear-rings. And the ten men who had come as his escort were given a shawl each and they were given betel and sent back. A *harkara* named Sivaji Gopinath was in the service of Yedilshaha. He talked in private with the envoy for two hours and gave him a large parcel of clothing and a pearl ornament and a sash. He entertained him royally. Ali Yedilshaha also sent a sword and a valuable sash. This news reached Nizamshaha Bahiri and Kutubshaha Telangan and Akbar Jalaldin Mogli padshaha—spies wrote to them saying that Ali Yedalshaha was engaged in some diplomatic manoeuvre. The three kings sent a messenger to him: "We have gathered for a campaign of conquest. It is not good if you engage in separate diplomacy in the midst of the war. We should all speak together. There will be no success by separate diplomacy. Even if you place yourself in the middle we will not give up the campaign—we will attack manfully. Come and consult with us."

Thereupon Yedilshaha sent the message "I am with you. Whatever is in your hearts is acceptable to me." Then he gave the messenger a respectful send-off.

The emperor formed up near Rakshasa-Tagdi. The battle-pillar was planted in the fields of Rakshas-Tagdi. The entire Karnataka army gathered there. Fighting raged for seventeen days. Mogals, Karna Rajput Rahathod [Rathor?] of Jalaldin Akbar padshaha of the throne of Jalnapur formed up in Nalatvadi and skirmishes were fought daily in the vicinity of Rayabagh. Karnataki nobles and Yainalmuluk and Ankushkhan, commander of light cavalry (*bargir*) deserted to the Yedilshaha. Jalaldin Akbar padshaha, Nizyamshaha padshaha Bahiri and Kutubshaha Telangan advanced together in a great army. The imperial princes, cavalry and infantry gave battle. Fighting raged from the first to the eleventh hour. Men fell on both sides. The emperor summoned the bodyguards and the other nobles and held a council. All of these now respectfully said: "The armies of the Muslim kings are advancing together. Let us make a stand. Victory depends on valor.

Ali Yedilshsha and Imamanmulik, these two kings have advanced from their position. They are both fully engaged in combat. We shall seize them by a stratagem. They will not know. Just post ten thousand horse and fifty thousand foot before them. We shall work stout-heartedly. We shall trick both these royal armies."

At dusk the emperor gave out gifts of clothing and dismissed the nobles. Then he dispatched dependable men to each of his fortresses; these were:

Ramachandra Narttakasi to Chandragad
Lakshmana Naik Treasurer to Rayegad
Chikanna Naik to Shahadurg
Thalavenkati to Torgal
Giriyeppa Naik to Tadpatri
Nagpadevar to Anegodi
Yelaveduru to Bankapur
Bisalapa Vedru to Krishnagad
Virapa Naik to Ilori
Amrit Naik to Kadnoli
Bhojraj to Chandavar
Venkatapa Naik to Nadi Alasi
Girikrishna guru Veda to Chichalgala
Rayeppa Naik to Salaripattana
Gopal Naik to Madhra

They were all given ceremonial robes and sent off. The royal armies met in battle. Nizyamshaha Bahiri and Kutubshaha Telangan were defeated. Then the Mogals of King Akbar Jalaldin were attacked. No one moved to support him. The beaten Nizyamshaha Bahiri and Kutubshaha Telangan sought to consolidate their forces in one place. They challenged the Karnataki forces as they returned to the field. The Karnatakis fired 4,000,000 thousand [sic] rockets simultaneously. The armies of the two kings suffered huge losses. Shaken, they halted. The Mogals came back and attacked again. The Karnatakis suffered great losses. After this protracted combat the emperor's army returned to its camp. The emperor mounted a howdah firmly on his elephant and advanced with the entire army against the enemy kings. The big guns were loaded and a heavy barrage began. The enemy army suffered a setback. Much pleased, the emperor returned to his pavilion and alighted. The Karnatakis having scattered the armies of three kings had returned carelessly to their camp.

At this point Ali Yedalshaha and Imamanmulik king of Barad desha launched a well-prepared cavalry attack on the emperor. His howdah had been taken off his elephant and was unprepared for the attack. The soldiers had gone off to prepare their food. They panicked and scattered. The emperor Ramraj fell into the hands of Ali Yedalshah of the Kannadas, and said to him: "You had called yourself my son. Then you suddenly seized me by treachery. Now what can I say? My whole army is slain." He dressed himself in fresh clothes, a Portuguese *daiva* [?], placed a rose formed of gems and pearls in his cap and wrapped on a *mavishala* [?]. Then having called on his god, he sent a message to Ali Yedalshaha saying: "come alone and sword in hand and fight me; no one else is to lay a hand on me." He made his promise this. Then Ali Yedalshaha came alone and cut off his head. This news was published by the four kings. The entire Karnataki army scattered and fled. Elephants and horses, camels, stores and supplies, the treasury—all were plundered. The armies jointly advanced on Vijayanagara. The emperor's mother and his three queens set the palace on fire when they heard the news. The Muslim armies advanced together and systematically ransacked the city in search of gems and jewels for a total of 14 days. Huge amounts of property were found. The three kings conducted raiding expeditions. The army of Akbar Jalaldin Padshaha went back. And Imamanulmulk went back to his own territories. Nizyamshaha Bahiri went back to his own kingdom. Ali Yedalshaha continued on the path of conquest. He besieged Pingouda. The latter held out for three months. Then the fort was seriously weakened and he surrendered it.[19] Then Yedilshaha besieged Torgal. Venkati resisted him and did not allow him to capture anything. Then Ali Yedalshaha left an army there and returned to Vijyapur. Raktakshi *samvatsara Vaisakha dark half, 8th day Monday 10th hour Shravana nakshatra* the moment named *bhimasima* [boundary of fear?] Ramraja lost his life. This became known to the kings previously subordinate to the Karnataka emperor. Ali Yedilshaha gave a grand entertainment to the four kings. They were delighted and departed. The Yedilshaha sent the Raja's head to Kasi. He is sending horsemen into the latter's provinces in order to seize forts and strongholds. As more news is received it will be transmitted as reported. Today is sent the news current up to the 25th day of Moharam. It is being reported (by) Ambaji Kamadi reporter (*jasud*) and warden (*naikvadi*) may it be known. This *bakher* is complete. Copied by the pen of Venkatadri Takel writer, district Sampgaum, subdivision Hubli. Venkaji Narayana Kulkarni of little learning [self deprecatory epithet] ... Ananda samvatsara bright half of Phalguna, 2cd day completed copying.

A new entry [sic orig.] Appa[nna] ji [20] Joshi headman, district Parenda it is complete 11th day month of Jamadilakher year thousand (*sic*) 1095. [1684]

I began this essay with a citation emphasising the importance of placing text in context as the only historically sound way of approaching it. This effort has revealed significant discrepancies between the internal truth claims and the external corroboration of the text. If there is a singular reality located in a unified time, then the text is a much later retelling or reinvention of traditions relating to the fall of Vijayanagara. The overhasty adoption of it by twentieth-century historians is a reflection on the political and ideological currents within the profession.

REFERENCES

1. Gabrielle M. Spiegel, *The Past as Text: The Theory and Practice of Medieval Historiography* Baltimore, 1997, "Introduction", p. xix.
2. Hayden White, 'The Burden of History', *History and Theory* 5, 2 (1966) p. 130.
3. Georg G. Iggers, 'Historiography Between Scholarship and Poetry', *Rethinking History* 4,3 (2000), p. 383; Hayden White, 'An Old Question Raised Again: Is Historiography Art or Science? A Response to Iggers', *Rethinking History*, 4,3 (2000), p. 399.
4. For a fuller consideration of this issue, see Sumit Guha, 'Speaking Historically: The Changing Voices of Historical Narration in Western India c.1400–1900', *The American Historical Review* 109, 4, p. 1084–1103 (2004).
5. Romila Thapar, 'Society and Historical Consciousness: The Itihasa-Purana Tradition' in *Interpreting Early India* 1992; Corrected fifth reprint, Delhi, 1999, p. 137.
6. This information is derived from the introduction to the reprinted text in Avinash Sovani ed. *Aitihasika Bakhari- Khand pahila* Pune: Shabdavesha Prakashan 1998, pp. 12 (preface); 13–23 (text). I am indebted to Prachi Deshpande for also checking the original 1914 printed version and confirming that there was no additional prefatory matter beyond that reprinted in Sovani.
7. Rajaram V. Herwadkar *A Forgotten Literature: Foundations of Marathi Chronicles,* Mumbai, 1994, pp. 12-13; idem, *Marathi Bakhar* Revised enlarged edition Pune, 1974, pp. 40-41.
8. Na. Shri. Rajpurohit, 'Rakshah-Tangdiya rananganaca sthalanirnya', *Bharata Itihasa Samshodhaka Mandala Traimasika*, vol. 10, no. 1 (1928-29), pp. 17–22.
9. G. B. Gramopadhye ed. *Marathi Bakhar Gadya,* Pune 1988 (first published 1952). He titled it '*Rakshes Tagdicha Ranasamgrama*'–the Battle of Rakshes Tagdi. pp.17–22; annotation pp.170–71.
10. Phillip. R. Wagoner, *Tidings of the King, A Translation and Ethrohistorical Analysis of Rayavacakamu,* Honolulu, 1993, pp. 5–9.
11. See n. 14. Rajaram V. Herwadkar *A Forgotten Literature: Foundations of Marathi Chronicles* Bombay, 1994, pp. 11–12. This booklet draws upon Herwadkar's much more substantial analysis in Marathi - *Marathi Bakhar* Revised and enlarged edition, Pune, 1975.
12. Herwadkar, *Marathi Bakhar,* p. 40.
13. Every sixty years, the planets return to a particular configuration and the cycle resumes. Each year has a specific name—the first being *Prabhava* and the last *Akshaya*.
14. *Textures of Time,* pp. 227–28.
15. Phillip B. Wagoner *Tidings of the King;* Also V. Narayana Rao 'Epics and Ideologies: Six Telugu Folk epics' in Stuart Blackburn and A.K. Ramanujam eds. *Another Harmony: New Essays on the Folklore of India,* Berkeley, 1986.
16. 1,223 ½ *sher* or perhaps about a thousand kilograms.

17. A clerical notation to balance a list and indicate that it was complete. The units of weight are not specified in the text. I have consistently assumed them to be ordered in the usual *khandi-man-sher-pavsher* and then calculate the number of *sher*. This last was usually around 2 lbs.
18. The first (1914) editor omitted these names.
19. In the printed text we have a period after the word *dilhe*. Then follows a fragment *nahi*. Obviously if we read it as *dilhe nahi*, then it means was not allowed to capture it. Pingouda may also be a corruption of the famous fort of Penukonda.
20. [anna] is added by the original editor. In my opinion the name was most likely Appaji. Appanna-ji would be a clumsy doubling of two honorifics.

Chapter 5

Nau Ruz in Mughal India

Stephen P. Blake

Although the Safavid Empire in Iran (1501–1722) was neither the military nor the economic equal of the Mughal Empire in India, its cultural influence was substantial. Persian poets, calligraphers, architects, painters, and tile workers found patrons and opportunities in early modern India, influencing the artistic life of the subcontinent. Beyond material productions for the court and market, however, Iranian influence penetrated the customs and activities of everyday life. The festival of *Nau Ruz*, marking the beginning of spring (March 20 or 21) and of the Iranian New Year, held an important place in the Mughal calendar. To examine this festival is to uncover a different but equally significant impact of Safavid Iran on the culture of Mughal India.

NAU RUZ IN IRANIAN CULTURE

The Iranian New Year, commemorated on the vernal equinox (March 20 or 21), predated the introduction of Islam by centuries, being established as the most important day of the year under both the Achaemenids and the Sassanids. While *Nau Ruz* is usually associated with the prophet Zoroaster (ca. 628–551 BCE), scholars now think that the celebration actually preceded the establishment of the Achaemenids (550–331 BCE) and was an ancient pan-Iranian custom. After Zoroaster appropriated this festival and reconsecrated it as the most important ritual observance of the year, it came to be associated with the legendary Iranian king, Jamshid, who ruled the country in a golden age that would, according to the legend, eventually be restored. As the beginning of spring and of the new year, *Nau Ruz* was both a remembrance of the golden past and a promise of the paradise to come. Under the Sassanids the common people donned new clothes and exchanged gifts while at court the kings conferred titles and ranks on the noble and wealthy and received in return gifts and presents.[1]

While the day remained central to Iranian life from the time of the Achaemenids, the mode of celebration varied. During the Sassanid period (224–638 ACE), as part of an effort to reform the calendar, the length of the celebration changed several times but was eventually set at six days. The first day of the celebration (March 21) coincided with the first day of the first month (Farwardin) of the ancient Iranian calendar. On the equinox itself the people bathed and anointed their bodies with oil to ward off disease and misfortune. On the sixth day, the day of hope, fate was thought to distribute each person's portion of happiness.[2] According to al-Biruni, the eleventh-century traveller and scholar, the emperor held court for six days: the first day he opened the festival and announced his intention to bestow benefits; the second day was for men of high rank and their families; the third day was for warriors and priests; the fourth day for the Emperor's family, relations, and domestics; the fifth day for his children and clients; and on the sixth day, having fulfilled his public obligations, he celebrated the festival in private with his intimates.[3]

According to the French traveller Jean Chardin, the festival ordinarily lasted for eight days under the Safavids. It was called Nau Ruz-i Sultani (i.e. the Emperor's New Year) to distinguish it from the first day of the Islamic or Hijri year, which was lunar, and unconnected to the movements of the sun and the seasons. The exact beginning of the festival was determined by the court astrologers and announced by cannon fire and the crash of bands. The ordinary people brought out new clothes, visited friends and relatives, and exchanged gifts. At court the emperor established a schedule for the festivities—bestowing benefits and accepting gifts: the first day was for the common people; the second for scholars and astronomers; the third for the ulama; the fourth for magistrates and officials; the fifth for nobles; the sixth for other important people; and the seventh and eighth for the wives and children of the emperor. Parades, fireworks, and music marked the celebrations in Isfahan and other large cities.[4]

Although Chardin gives us a general description of the celebration in the mid-seventeenth century, there were variations over the two hundred years of Safavid rule. In 1603, for example, Shah Abbas I organised a large celebration in the Naqsh-i Jahan Garden in Isfahan. He allotted space along the stream that ran through the park to the important people of the city, and they put up elaborately decorated tents. Abbas's festivities, however, lasted for only three days.[5]

In mid-nineteenth-century Iran, the first day of spring remained the most important holiday of the year. In the family of a Qajar merchant the preparations started a month in advance; the house was cleaned and the entire family outfitted in new clothes. The celebrations and merry-making lasted for thirteen days.[6]

Despite the efforts of the Ayatollah Khomeini to abolish the festival in the first years after the revolution, *Nau Ruz* retained its importance in the Islamic Republic. In present-day Iran, first-grade textbooks answer the question 'Who is an Iranian?' by referring to both geography and culture. An Iranian is someone who lives within certain geographical borders and who shares with his neighbours a common culture, defined in part by the celebration of a common festival—Eid-i Nau Ruz.[7]

NAU RUZ IN MUGHAL INDIA

The celebration of *Nau Ruz* during the Mughal period (1526–1739) reflected the complex cultural relationship between Iran and India in the early modern world. While it ended up being the most popular festival in India during the middle years of Mughal rule, under the emperors Akbar, Jahangir, and Shahjahan, it was slow to be adopted by the first two emperors (Babur and Humayun) and it was abolished by the last of the great Mughals (the emperor Aurangzeb).

Zahir al-Din Babur (r. 1526–30), the founder of the Mughal Empire, was a direct descendant of the great Central Asia conqueror, Timur, and in the early years of the sixteenth century was engaged in an ultimately unsuccessful effort to win back his ancestor's lands in Transoxiana. While he was, like his ancestors, a Sunni Muslim, he also desired the help of the newly-victorious Shah Ismail in trying to defeat the Uzbegs and regain his Central Asian kingdom. According to contemporary chroniclers, Babur had to meet certain political and religious conditions in order to secure Ismail's support: he had to strike coins bearing Ismail's name, have the Shiite version of the *khutba* read in the Friday service, and don at Ismail's court the Qizilbash dress, including the distinctive Safavid cap (conical, red, and twelve-pointed, symbolising the Twelve Imams).[8] With Ismail's help Babur was able, in 1511 to briefly capture the former Timurid capital of Samarqand. However, the Safavids withdrew their support, the populace turned against him, and in 1512 the Uzbegs returned and recaptured the city. In 1505, before he had turned to the Safavids, Babur wrote a poem commemorating the unusual convergence of *Nau Ruz* and Id al-Fitr, marking the end of the month-long Ramadan fast.[9] Whether or not Babur celebrated *Nau Ruz* during his brief Shiite phase, we have no evidence. What we do know is that in March 1526, exactly a month before he defeated the Afghan ruler Ibrahim Lodi at Panipat (April 21,

1526), Babur refused to celebrate the New Year's festival because it was not sanctioned by the Sharia.[10]

For the Mughal Emperor Humayun (r. 1530–40, 1555–56), Babur's son and successor, the decision to celebrate the Iranian holiday seems also to have been affected by his relationship with a Safavid ruler—this time Shah Tahmasp, Ismail's son and successor. It is doubtful that Humayun had the leisure or the resources to celebrate *Nau Ruz* during the hectic first years of his reign (1530–40), when he unsuccessfully attempted to consolidate his hold over the fledgling empire his father had bequeathed him. However, several contemporary historians noted that Humayun patronised Iranians, attracting many adventurers from the Safavid Empire. In fact, one historian wrote that after his defeat by the Afghan Sher Shah in 1540, a number of Humayun's commanders deserted him on the grounds that he had favoured the Shiite immigrants. Humayun's experience in Safavid Iran, like that of his father before him, appears to have tempered his enthusiasm for things Iranian. After wandering in the province of Sind, Humayun sought the help of Shah Tahmasp. In Herat in 1544, Humayun celebrated *Nau Ruz*, presiding over the festivities with Tahmasp's officials and commanders in attendance, but it is clear that he was simply playing a role in a larger Safavid-orchestrated pageant. Like Ismail, Tahmasp also required a sectarian commitment and Humayun, like his father, found the public ceremony shocking and humiliating. Tahmasp presented Humayun with a robe of honour, the wearing of which indicated political subjugation, and with the Shiite cap, signifying membership in the Safaviyya order. Two years later in Kabul, after escaping the protection of Tahmasp, Humayun banned the celebration of the spring festival. Because, however, the *Nau Ruz* of 1546 coincided with the circumcision ceremony of the child Akbar, Humayun relented and a subdued version of the festivities took place.[11]

It is Akbar, however, Humayun's son and successor, and the creator of the mature Mughal state, who established the format for the celebration of *Nau Ruz* in early modern India, a format that was followed for the next seventy-five years. Akbar came to the throne in 1556 as a callow, untested 13-year-old, under the thumb of his guardian and prime minister, Abd al-Rahim Khan-i Khanan. Not until 1560, was he able to free himself and to begin his rule. In his first capital, Agra, he erected a palace-fortress and the beginnings of a new city. Over the following nine years, however, none of Akbar's wives was able to provide him with a son and heir. In 1569, therefore, the emperor sent his pregnant Rajput wife to Sikri, a village twenty-three miles west of Agra, where the leader of the Sufi Chishti order, Shaikh Salim Chishti, had his *khanqah* (hermitage). Akbar had been a frequent visitor to the shrine of the Sufi saint, Muin al-Din Chishti, in Ajmer, and he hoped that the Shaikh Salim's presence would prove auspicious. And so it turned out, when several months later Akbar was presented with a son, Salim, who later ruled as the emperor Jahangir.

In 1571, when Jahangir was two years old, Akbar began construction in Sikri of a new capital—named Fatehpur Sikri. While the official histories point to the birth of Jahangir and the presence of Shaikh Salim Chishti as the controlling factors in Akbar's decision, the desire for a new imperial centre—as the site for the far-reaching political, religious, and economic changes he was introducing—must also have played a role. In 1572 Shaikh Salim Chishti died and in 1573 Akbar finished his conquest of the rich province of Gujarat. In 1574, construction on a magnificent congregational mosque was completed and in 1575 work began on the Ibadat Khana (House of Religious Discussion). In 1585, a mere fifteen years after founding the new capital, Akbar left Fatehpur Sikri for Lahore and the northwest, to meet the threat of the Uzbegs. For the remaining twenty years of his reign, he never returned to his new capital for any significant period.

The fifteen years in Fatehpur Sikri (1571–85) were a momentous but turbulent period. Akbar reorganised the political system. He established an elaborate hierarchical system of ranks and offices (called the *mansabdari* system) and required officials to supply a certain number of men and horses—the horses were branded to insure accountability. Akbar overhauled the fiscal basis of the largely agrarian empire—measuring the land and establishing crop rates, allowing him to more easily collect taxes and pay his men. He also opened up the *mansabdari* system to men of talent and ability, whatever their religion, tribe, or nationality—Hindus (Rajputs and Khatris, primarily), Afghans, and Iranis. And, finally, partly from curiosity and partly as a way of opening up the cultural climate at court, the emperor promoted a wide-ranging discussion of religious ideas and practices—both Islamic and non-Islamic. It is within this context of change and controversy that Akbar's decision to establish the Iranian New Year as a major Mughal festival must be examined.

In his history of Akbar's reign, Abd al-Qadir Badauni, a disappointed office-holder, places the first extended celebration of *Nau Ruz* in Ajmer on 21 March 1574. This celebration lasted for six days—the emperor put out an elaborate feast and distributed Rs.100,000 to the nobles and officials.[12] Four years later (21 March 1578), when describing Akbar's first celebration of the Iranian festival in his new capital, Badauni offers his interpretation of the Emperor's motivation:

> The accursed Birbar [a Rajput commander and supporter of Akbar] tried to persuade the Emperor, that since the sun gives light to all, and . . . supports the life of mankind, therefore that luminary should be the object of worship and veneration; that the face should be turned towards the rising and not towards the setting sun [i.e., toward Mecca], which is the west; that man should venerate fire, water, stones, and trees, and all natural objects, even down to cows and their dung; that he should adopt the sectarian mark, and Brahmanical thread. Several wisemen at Court confirmed what he said, by representing that the sun was "the greater light" of the world, and the benefactor of its inhabitants, and the patron of kings, and that kings are but its vice-regents. This was the cause of the worship paid to the sun on the Nau Ruz-i Jalali, and of his being induced to adopt that festival for the celebration of his accession to the throne.[13]

Badauni goes on to relate that, in addition to Birbar, there were Zoroastrians at court who also revered the sun. Thus, on this first celebration of the New Year's festival in Fatehpur Sikri, Akbar 'prostrated himself before the sun, and before the fire in public, and in the evening the whole court had to rise up respectfully when the lamps and candles were lighted.'[14]

Whenever Akbar found himself in his new capital, he appears to have celebrated the New Year in an elaborate manner. In March 1582, for example, Father Monserrate, the Portuguese Jesuit, witnessed a lavish celebration. The next year, 1583, the festivities were expanded, and assumed the form they would take for the next seventy-five years or so. The festival lasted for nineteen days, and the high-ranking amirs competed with one another in decorating the public buildings of the palace fortress. On the first and last days of the celebration, Akbar held a grand assembly and presented the amirs and officials with horses, robes of honour, and increases in rank and salary. On the other days the emperor visited the mansions of the great amirs, one after another. Responsible for one day's entertainment, the noble offered rich cloth from India, Khurasan, and Iraq; pearls, rubies, and gold; and elephants, camels and Arabian horses.[15]

This elaborate expansion of the New Year's festival seems to have been part of Akbar's effort to transform the Mughal state. The emperor invited the Iranian scientist and intellectual, Amir Fathullah Shirazi, to develop a new solar calendar, based on that devised by Omar Khayyam for the Seljuk ruler, Sultan Jalal al-Din Malik Shah (1072–92). The months of the year were Persian and the start of the year was, of course, the vernal equinox. In addition to a new calendar, Akbar also introduced on 21 March 1584 a new era (the Ilahi or Divine). At this point, Amir Fathullah recalculated and renumbered the early years of Akbar's reign—thus 1584 became the year 19 of the Divine Era rather than year 992 of the Hijri era. Since the emperor's accession had occurred in mid-

February 1556, it was decided to make the vernal equinox the date both of his accession and of the start of the new era.[16] An important reason for the expanded celebration was that now on March 21, two important events had to be commemorated: the accession of the emperor (*jashan-i julus*) and the new year (*jashan-i nau ruz*).

Why did Akbar introduce the new calendar and the new era? Abul Fazl, Akbar's apologist, ideologue, and court historian, stated that the emperor introduced the solar calendar primarily for economic reasons. In an agrarian economy it was important to have the official calendar coincide with the seasons. Since the solar calendar is 11 days longer than the lunar calendar, there are approximately 31 lunar years in every 30 solar years and, as a result, the peasants under the Hejira reckoning would be asked to pay an extra year's tax. In discussing the new era introduced by the Il-Khanids in Iran, Abul Fazl wrote:

> Before its adoption the state records bore the date from the Hejira . . . By this means the road was opened to grievous oppression, because 31 lunar years are equal to only 30 solar years and great loss occurred to the agriculturists, as the revenue was taken on the lunar years and the harvest depended on the solar. Abolishing this practice Ghazan Khan promoted the cause of justice by the introduction of this era.[17]

Abd al-Qadir Badauni, however, had a completely different explanation:

> The era of the Hijrah was now abolished, and a new era was introduced, of which the first year was the year of the Emperor's accession. . . The months had the same names as at the time of the old Persian kings . . . Fourteen festivals also were introduced corresponding to the feasts of the Zoroastrians; . . . Reading and learning Arabic was looked on as a crime; and Muhammadan law, the exegesis of the Quran and the tradition, as also those who studied them, were considered bad and deserving of disapproval. . . In the same way every command and doctrine of Islam, whether special or general, as the prophetship, the harmony of Islam with reason, the doctrines of . . . the details of the day of resurrection and judgment, all were doubted and ridiculed.[18]

For Abul Fazl the introduction of the solar calendar was a way of bringing order and justice to the administration of the land revenue system; for Badauni, on the other hand, it was part of a wholesale attack on Islam.

Under Jahangir (r. 1605–28), Akbar's son and successor, the New Year's celebration followed the routine established by Akbar. Lasting for nineteen days and commemorating both the coming of spring and the accession of the ruler, the preparations were extensive and the celebration lavish. In the Diwan-i Am (Hall of General Audience) in the Agra palace the emperor's men erected a magnificent tent; the walls were hidden by tapestries of velvet and silk and carpets of silk and gold covered the ground. The emperor held court sitting on a magnificent throne. In the open courtyard beyond the hall the great amirs pitched smaller tents. The emperor visited each tent, accepting presents from his ranking officials and nobles. On the first and last days of the festival Jahangir bestowed titles, promotions, and gifts in a general audience.

The tents of the nobles also served as the shops in a make-believe fancy bazaar. During the day the emperor strolled from tent to tent, admiring the rarities, and chatting with his nobles but in the evening the bazaar was only open to women. The wives of the great amirs served as shopkeepers, and the emperor and the ladies of his harem strolled past the tents, stopping to admire, haggle, and buy.[19] To ensure that the festivities would be lively, Jahangir lifted the Islamic prohibitions on wine and drugs:

> I gave orders that whoever might wish for the intoxicating drinks and exhilarating drugs should not be debarred from using them.[20]

The scale and expense of the celebrations are suggested by Jahangir's statement:

> As my mind was inclined towards the comfort and ease of the army and subjects, I this year let them off their gifts with the exception of a few from my intimate retainers, which I accepted in order to gratify them.[21]

Jahangir's son and successor, Shahjahan (r. 1628–58), epitomised the wealth and power of the Mughal Empire. Builder of the Taj Mahal and the magnificent new capital in the Delhi area (Shahjahanabad), Shahjahan celebrated the Iranian New Year on a lavish scale. Occupying the throne on 14 February 1628, Shahjahan, like his father and grandfather, chose, as the official date of his accession, the next vernal equinox—21 March 1628. On this first *Nau Ruz* imperial workmen erected a great tent beneath the Hall of Public Audience in Agra. Brocaded velvets from Europe, China, and the Ottoman Empire lined the tent walls and rich carpets covered the floors. In the general audience Shahjahan distributed honorary robes, cash, and increases in rank and salary to nobles and officials. Thousands of rupees were given to the poor.[22]

For the first ten years of his reign, Shahjahan celebrated the holiday in the usual fashion.[23] Sebastian Manrique, who visited India in the mid-1630s, was fascinated by the lights that outlined the towers and minarets of the imperial palace-fortress on the eve of the equinox. On the first day of the festival, four thousand cavalrymen in full dress and six hundred heavily-decorated elephants lined the road leading to the palace-fortress. In the evening animal fights and fireworks displays were arranged in the great open courtyard.[24] Shahjahan had the famous Peacock Throne moved from the palace to the imperial tent for the duration of the festival. Studded with jewels, surrounded by railings of gold and silver, and covered with silken canopies, the royal seat was, in the words of the contemporary historian, the New Year's (*Nau Ruz*) throne.[25]

For reasons that aren't entirely clear, however, Shahjahan decided, halfway through his tenth reignal year (in October 1637), to drop the solar calendar and the Ilahi era and to return to the lunar calendar and the Hijri era. As a result the accession festival (*jashn-i julus*) was no longer held on the vernal equinox but reverted to the actual Hijri date. Thus, the eleventh regnal year began on 21 October 1637 instead of on 21 March 1638. Muhammad Amin Qazwini, who wrote the official history of Shahjahan's first ten years, suggested that the shift was prompted by the complaints of the conservative ulama who felt, like Badauni fifty years before, that the solar calendar was a pagan innovation. Why, however, Shahjahan was swayed by this argument at precisely this time is a mystery.[26]

Nevertheless, despite the uncoupling of the two events (accession and vernal equinox), Shahjahan continued to celebrate the new year on 21 March rather than on Muharram 1, the first day of the Hijri calendar. And his celebration was no less lavish than that of his predecessors—the full nineteen days and the usual distribution of money and gifts. In fact, one of the most lavish examples of the entire Mughal period occurred on 21 March 1650—the first *Nau Ruz* celebrated in the new capital of Shahjahanabad.[27] Two English factors in Agra wrote to their superiors in Surat on 21 Feb. 1650:

> Some other piece goods to hand [sic] from the same source will be sent as soon as possible to Ahmadabad; we suppose on camels, carts being of very difficult procury [sic], by reason that the king hath commanded vast sums of money to be carried to Dely, no less than 200 lakhs of rupees, and many other things for the celebrations of the Nau Ruz shortly at hand; whereby all carts are taken up for that service.[28]

The Emperor Aurangzeb (r. 1658–1707), the last of the great Mughals, was a man of austere temperament, pious and abstemious. The contrast between him and Akbar could not have been more stark. The comparison, however, is not that of modern-day Indian journalism: the one liberal, open to religious diversity, the patron saint of secular India; the other narrow, bigoted, and fundamentalist, the champion of right-wing nationalist Hindus. Rather, we need to see the changes in court culture from the late-sixteenth to the late-seventeenth century in the context of individual agency, more a matter of temperament than of policy. Aurangzeb's legalistic turn of mind, his lack of interest in artistic matters, and his piety accounted for the shift in style. In 1659, the second year of his reign, Aurangzeb abolished the celebration of *Nau Ruz*. Soon after, he increased the grants and gifts to the ulama and the money donated to the poor. In the eleventh year the practice of weighing the emperor on his solar and lunar birthdays was discontinued. He also forbade the playing of music at court and the selling of clay images on Islamic festivals, and he banned the visits of women to the shrines of saints. In 1679 he reimposed the jizya, the canonical tax on non-Muslims, which the Emperor Akbar had abolished in 1564.[29]

Why did Aurangzeb discontinue the celebration of *Nau Ruz*? The historian Khafi Khan saw Aurangzeb's order to abolish Akbar's new era intimately connected to his decision on *Nau Ruz*—to abolish the solar calendar was to abolish the solar New Year. Since, as we have seen, Shahjahan and his historians had already (in 1638) retired the Ilahi era and the solar calendar, it is not entirely clear why the matter should have been revisited. Perhaps since Aurangzeb, unlike Shahjahan, wanted to abolish the celebration of *Nau Ruz* as well, he needed to stress its connection to the non-Islamic mode of marking time. And Khafi Khan did state that it was the festival's Zoroastrian origin that made it anathema to the emperor.[30]

With the elimination of the solar calendar and *Nau Ruz*, Aurangzeb had to choose a new date on which to celebrate his accession. Unlike Shahjahan, who chose to celebrate his accession on its original Hijri date, Aurangzeb, the pious Muslim, chose Ramadan 1, the first day of the canonical fast. This meant that any celebrations were postponed until the *Id-ul-Fitr*, the last day of the month. Eventually the separate accession celebration was phased out, absorbed in the larger religious festivities.[31]

A letter Aurangzeb wrote to his second son, Prince Muhammad Muazzam, provides an additional perspective. On hearing that the prince had recently celebrated *Nau Ruz,* Aurangzeb wrote:

> In any case, as this day is one of the festivals of the fire worshippers [*ayad-i majus*], and further, as it is, according to the Hindus of India [*kuffar-i Hind*], the anniversary of the accession of the accursed Bikramajit and marks the beginning of the Indian era [*mbada-i tarkih-i Hind*] , there must be no repetition of this stupid act.[32]

It is important to note that Aurangzeb, despite his reputation as a strict Sunni, criticised the festival for its non-Islamic roots and not for its connection to the culture of Shiite Iran. In fact, in discussing the role of Iranis in the Mughal Empire, he is surprisingly judicious:

> ... for the position of *mutasaddis* (clerks and accountants) there are no more suitable people than the Persians. And in war too, from the days of Humayun up to the present time, no Persian has ever deserted or acted unmanfully. Further they have never been guilty of sedition or treason. But as they are extremely jealous of their honor, it is not easy to get along with them. However this may be, it is essential to put up with these things.[33]

And again on the same theme:

> Muhammad Amin Khan .. . once submitted a petition. . . stating, "Both of the paymasterships have been conferred on the heretical demon-natured Persians. If one of the paymasterships be given to this old and devoted servant, it would be a means of strengthening the [Sunni] faith and of snatching away employment from accursed misbelievers." The emperor in his order on the petition, queried, "What connection have worldly affairs with religion? and what right have matters of religion to enter into bigotry?" and praised the Persians for their steadfastness on the battlefield.[34]

Conclusion

The story of *Nau Ruz* in Mughal India—its introduction, rise, and eclipse—is not a simple one of cultural appropriation, the wholesale adoption by one culture of an element from another. Rather, in early modern India the Iranian spring celebration took on a new role and had new and different meanings.

Akbar, the architect of the mature Mughal state, introduced the festival. While contemporary historians suggested that the humiliating experiences of Babur and Humayun at the courts of Ismail and Tahmasp accounted for their aversion to *Nau Ruz*, it seems more likely that the unsettled, chaotic conditions in which these men ruled were more important factors. A complicated, lavish, and expensive celebration like that of Akbar and his successors demanded a certain level of peace and stablity, a relatively sedentary life style.

Akbar's decision to interject the popular Iranian festival into Mughal court culture was the result neither of a blind infatuation with things Iranian nor of pressure from Shiite immigrants. For Akbar the elevation of *Nau Ruz* to the central place in the ritual calendar was inseparable from his desire to adopt a new era based on a new calendar. This decision had both a symbolic and an economic aspect.

Akbar's interest in promulgating a new era and a new calendar was part of a larger effort to reorganise and revitalise the Mughal state. Babur had been almost completely absorbed in trying to achieve military dominance in northern India, and Humayun had only just returned from a fifteen-year exile in Iran and Afghanistan. It took the teenaged Akbar fifteen years (1556–71) to discipline his followers and defeat his major enemies. As a result, the political, economic, and religious restructuring of the new state had to await his move to Fatehpur Sikri. That the expanded nineteen-day celebration, inaugurated in 1583, and the new solar calendar, begun in 1584, were both set at the very end of the fifteen-year period of state building suggests that Akbar intended his new era as a symbolic capstone to his recently revitalised state: a new era for a new empire.

An additional factor in Akbar's decision to establish a new era and a new calendar was the approaching end of the first Islamic millennium (the year 1000 of the Hijri era occurred in 1592). The first seventy-five years of the sixteenth-century witnessed an upsurge in revolutionary, religious movements within Indian Islam. The leaders of these heterodox sects challenged the political as well as the religious orthodoxy of the day. Abul Fazl quoted the poet Nasir-i Khusrau:

> I saw in 992 [1584] two conjunctions,
> I saw the sign of the Mahdi [Rightly Guided One] and that of the Antichrist:
> Either politics must change or religion.
> I clearly see the hidden secret.[35]

For Akbar then a new era would inaugurate not only a new empire but a new millennium as well.

In addition to these symbolic factors, Akbar was also motivated by economic considerations. Making the official calendar solar was part of his larger effort to organise and systematise the collection of taxes in the largely agrarian economy of early modern India.

Both the new era and the new calendar structured the official life of the Mughal state for the next fifty-four years. Although in 1638 Shahjahan abolished the solar Ilahi era as the chronological framework for his reign and reinstated the lunar Hijri era, he continued to celebrate *Nau Ruz*, though by this point it was neither the beginning of a new year nor the anniversary of his accession. However, the fact that in 1659 (21 years later) Aurangzeb again ordered the abolition of the Ilahi era suggests that perhaps Shahjahan's earlier edict hadn't extended much beyond the court historians. It seems possible that the state functionaries—the accountants, court reporters, newswriters, chancellery officials, and secretaries—had continued to use Akbar's era and calendar.

While there were elements of sectarian bigotry in Mughal India (especially among disappointed officeholders and conservative court ulama), the decision to abolish *Nau Ruz* by Aurangzeb (the most orthodox of the great Mughals) appears not to have been an anti-Shiite, anti-Safavid decision. Rather, for Aurangzeb the problem was the festival's un-Islamic character: its origins were pagan, Zoroastrian and Hindu.

It is worth noting that, despite Aurangzeb's order, *Nau Ruz* continued to be celebrated in many parts of India throughout the eighteenth and nineteenth centuries. In the late eighteenth century, for example, in the north Indian state of Awadh, the Urdu poet Mir wrote of the Hindu and Muslim festivals celebrated at court:

> Asafuddaulah, the wazir, plays Holi
> The festival of Nau Ruz of Hindustan[36]

For this poet, *Nau Ruz* was the defining celebration of the ritual year, the one by which all others were judged. Fifty years later, in the 1830s, *Nau Ruz* continued to be a major festival in Awadh—the Nawabs celebrating with presents, feasts, visits, and merry-making.[37]

In Safavid Iran, *Nau Ruz* was certainly an important festival—during the reign of Shah Abbas and after. However, its primacy appears to have been challenged during the seventeenth century as the Safavid effort to convert the populace to Shiism gained momentum. With the spread of Shiism the commemoration of the death of the Imam Husain during the first ten days of Muharram came to rival *Nau Ruz* as the defining celebration of the civilisation. In Mughal India, on the other hand, *Nau Ruz* played a different role in a radically different cultural universe. In Mughal India, interestingly enough, *Nau Ruz*, while indisputably Iranian, was not identified as a Shiite, Safavid festival. For Akbar, the festival was the linchpin of new era based on a new solar calendar and that calendar while Iranian was not at all Safavid. Akbar's calendar was based on that of Omar Khayam, devised by the poet and mathematician for the eleventh-century Seljuk sultan, Jalal al-Din Malik Shah. Even Abd al-Qadir Badauni, a conservative Sunni and rabid anti-Shiite, a man who attacked Amir Fathullah Shirazi (the deviser of Akbar's new era) for his Shiite prayers, excoriates Akbar's new era and his new calendar for its Zoroastrian and Hindu elements—not because its inventor was Shiite. The same holds true for Aurangzeb, who abolished *Nau Ruz* not on the grounds of its Safavid connections but because of its association with the coming of spring, the vernal equinox being a pagan celebration of the Zoroastrians and the Hindus.

REFERENCES

1. 'Iranian Festivals', in Ehsan Yarshater (ed.), *The Cambridge History of Iran: Vol. 3: The Seleucid, Parthian, and Sassanian Periods*, Cambridge, 1983, pp. 793–811.
2. C. Huart, *Ancient Persian and Iranian Civilization*, M.R. Dobien (trans.), London, 1927, p. 191.
3. J.S. Hoyland and S.N. Banerjee (trans.), *The Commentary of Father Monserrate, S.J. on His Journey to the Court of Akbar*, London, 1922, p. 174.

4. Jean Chardin, *Voyages du Chevalier Chardin, en Perse...*, L. Langles (ed.), 10 vols, Paris, 1811, vol 2, pp. 249–69; Engelbert Kaempfer, *Am Hofe des persischen Grosskings, 1684–85*, W. Hinz (trans.), Tubingen, 1977, p. 190.
5. Roger M. Savory (trans.), *Tarikh-e Alamara-ye Abbasi: History of Shah Abbas the Great by Eskandar Beg Munshi*, 2 vols. Boulder, 1978, vol. 2, p. 825.
6. Shireen Mahdavi, 'The Structure and Function of the Household of a Qajar Merchant', *Iranian Studies* 32 (1999), pp. 557–71.
7. Golnar Mehran, 'The Presentation of the "Self" and the "Other" in Post Revolutionary Iranian School Textbooks', in Nikki R. Keddie and Rudi Mathee (eds.), *Iran and the Surrounding World: Interactions in Culture and Cultural Politics*, Seattle and London, 2002, pp. 232–53.
8. Riazul Islam, *Indo-Persian Relations*, Tehran, 1970, p. 8.
9. Zahir al-Din Muhammad Babur Padshah, *Babur Nama (Memoirs of Babur)*, Annette Susannah Beveridge (trans.), New Delhi, 1970, p. 236.
10. Zain Khan, *Tabaqat-i Baburi*, S. Hasan Askar (trans.), Delhi, 1982, p. xxxiii; Mohibbul Hasan, *Babur: Founder of the Mughal Empire in India*, New Delhi, 1985, p. 162.
11. Muhammad Azher Ansari, 'Court Ceremonies of the Great Mughals', *Islamic Culture* 35 (1961), pp. 183–97; Sukumar Ray, *Humayun in Persia*, Calcutta, 1948, pp. 12–13; Islam, *Indo-Persian Relations*, pp. 24–36; P.N. Chopra, *Life and Letters under the Mughals*, New Delhi, 1976, pp. 83–4; Gulbadan Begam (Princess Rose-Body), *The History of Humayun (Humayun-Nama)*, Annette S. Beveridge (trans.), Delhi, 1972, pp. 179–80.
12. Abdul Qadir bin Muluk Shah, known as al-Badauni, *Muntakhab-ut-Tawarikh*, George S.A. Ranking (trans. and ed.), 2 vols., Karachi, 1976, vol. 2, p. 175.
13. *Ibid*, Vol . 2, p. 268.
14. *Ibid*, Vol. 2, p. 269.
15. Abul Fazl, *The Akbar Nama*, H. Beveridge (trans.), 3 vols, Calcutta, 1902, vol. 3, p. 589; *Mukatabat-i'Allami (Insha' I Abu 'l Fazl) Daftar. Letters of the Emperor Akbar in English Translation*, Mansura Haidar (ed.), New Delhi, 1998, pp. 85–6.
16. Abul Fazl, *The Ain-i Akbari*, H. Blochmann (trans.), 3 vols., Calcutta, 1927-49, vol. 2, pp. 1–2; 29–32; Abu al-Fazl, *Akbar Nama*, vol. 2, pp. 15–18.
17. Abul Fazl, *A'in*, vol. 2, p. 28.
18. Badauni, *Muntakhab*, vol. 2, pp. 316–17.
19. Muhammad Azher Ansari, 'Court Ceremonies of the Great Mughals', *Islamic Culture* 35 (1961): 183–97; Mubarak Ali Khan, *The Court of the Great Mughals based on Persian Sources*, Lahore, 1986, p. 50; Beni Prasad, *History of Jahangir*, Allahabad, 1962, p. 38, 89; *The Embassy of Sir Thomas Roe to the Court of the Great Mogul, 1615–19*, William Foster (ed.), 2 vols, London, 1899, vol. 1, pp. 142–44.
20. *The Tuzuk-i Jahangiri or Memoirs of Jahangir*, Alexander Rogers (trans.), Henry Beveridge (ed.), 2 vols., New Delhi, 1968, vol. 1, p. 49.
21. *Ibid*, pp. 187–88.
22. Muhammad Azher Ansari, 'Court Ceremonies', pp. 185–6; Khan, *The Court of the Great Mughals*, p. 50; Inayat Khan, *The Shah Jahan Nama of Inayat*

Khan, edited and completed by W.E. Begley and Z.A. Desai, Delhi, 1990, pp. xvii–xix.

23. Khan, *The Shah Jahan Nama*, pp. 37–8.
24. *The Travels of Fray Sebastien Manrique 1629–1643. A Translation of the Itinerario de las Missions Orientals*, C. Eckford Luard and Father H. Hosten (introduction and notes), 2 vols. Oxford, 1927, vol. 2, pp. 190–94; *The Travels of Peter Mundy in Europe and Asia, 1608–67*, Richard Carnac Temple (ed.), 2 vols., London, 1914, vol. 2, pp. 237–38.
25. Chandar Bhan Brahman, 'Chahar Chaman, Qawaid-i Saltanat-i Shajahan', British Library, Oriental Manuscript Collection, Or. 1892, pp. 62–3.
26. Inayat Khan, *The Shah Jahan Nama*, pp. xviii–xx, xxiii–xxiv.
27. *Ibid*, pp. 446–48; Muhammad Salih Kanbo Lahauri , *Amal-i Salih or Shahjahan Nama.*, G. Yazdani (ed.), 3 vols, Calcutta, 1912–46, vol. 3, pp. 107–08.
28. William Foster (ed.), *The English Factories in India, 1648–50*, Oxford, 1914, pp. 299.
29. Khan, *The Court of the Great Mughals:* p. 51; Rafat M. Bilgrami, *Religious and Quasi-Religious Departments of the Mughal Period, 1556–1707*, Aligarh, 1984, pp. 95–97, 194–195.
30. *The History of India as told by its Own Historians*, H.M. Elliot (trans.), John Dowson (ed.), 8 vols, Allahabad, 1964, vol. 7, pp. 241–42.
31. Jadunath Sarkar, *History of Aurangzeb*, 5 vols., Calcutta, 1925, vol. 3, pp. 8–10, 82. Saqi Must'ad Khan, *Maasir-i Alamgiri*, Jadunath Sarkar (trans.), Delhi, 1986, p. 14.
32. Riazul Islam, *A Calendar of Documents on Indo-Persian Relations, (1500–1700)*, 2 vols. Karachi, 1979, vol. 1, p. 460.
33. Hamid al-Din, *Anecdotes of Aurangzeb*, Jadunath Sarkar (trans.), Calcutta, 1912, p. 460.
34. *Ibid*, p. 461.
35. Abul Fazl, *A'in*, vol. 1, pp. 207–08.
36. Ishrat Haque, *Glimpses of Mughal Society and Culture: A Study based on Urdu Literature in the Second Half of the 18th Century*, New Delhi, 1992, p. 128.
37. Mrs. Meer Hasan Ali, *Observations on the Mussulmauns of India: Description of their Manners, Customs, Habits, and Religious Opinions made during a Twelve Years' Residence in their Immediate* Society, 2 vols. Delhi, 1832, pp. 284–86.

SECTION II

Community, Gender and Cultural Transmission

Chapter 6

Politics, the Muslim Community and Hindu–Muslim Relations Reconsidered: North India in the Early Thirteenth Century*

Sunil Kumar

Introduction

Historians of medieval India were slow in recognising the perils of trying to encapsulate medieval social sensibilities within a modern, English lexicon. To be sure, in the 1920s the British civil servant and historian, W.H. Moreland, was rare amongst his colleagues in suggesting that the 'translation' of Persian administrative technical terms within British frames of reference interfered with the comprehension of medieval Indian history. Having said that, Moreland did not go further and worry whether the pivotal role he ascribed to administrative institutions and political agents in the shaping of economic life was derived from his own experiences with modernity. As an officer committed to the programme of a bureaucratised colonial regime in India and a historian with a positivist training, he valorised the rationally organised, centralised state introduced by the British.[1]

It is, however, altogether too easy to criticise Moreland, or almost any other turn of the century historian, forgetting for the moment that historians are forced to seize words and terminologies from their own milieu to retrospectively identify problems and periods in history. Today, however, one would expect historians to be more attentive to the subjectivities that they encounter in a post-modernistic world and to rework their terminologies more carefully in the contexts of the medieval past. A few exceptions notwithstanding, the gridlock of a presentist vocabulary has challenged attempts to seize the histories of attitudes and identities of the pre-modern world. A paucity of materials for such a study is a refrain that is sometimes voiced. Indeed, unlike the early modern period, sources that might facilitate the study of individual and collective identities are not easily available to the historian. There are no documentary records of court cases where prescription and proscription were debated, very little pertaining to a public culture where social mores were displayed and reproduced. But equally, the inability to move beyond the narratives of the sources at hand is also a methodological problem, a product of a naive empiricism that follows 'authoritative' sources and their narratives as repositories of dependable and verifiable information.[2]

It is important to bear in mind that even as medieval Persian chroniclers recount the migration of dispersed groups of Muslims into the subcontinent and detail a history of considerable competition and strife amongst these people, the politics of this heterogeneity is not a subject that they choose to develop. They focus instead upon how a cohesive, monolithic Muslim community bravely overcame the challenges of living in an 'alien land'. One historian characterised these narratives as 'epics of conquest', eulogies expanding on the achievements of the victorious Muslim armies. Not surprisingly, these epics of conquest produced 'counter-epics of resistance' in their wake, where the valour of Rajput arms against 'foreign invaders' received their due.[3] There was little historiographical intersection with these materials. Writing at the height of communal polarisation, the distinguished scholar A.B.M. Habibullah concluded:

> [Socio-religious war] was bound to occur in territories which had an unbroken tradition of Hindu rule, and there it was that the Muslim Turks met with real and sustained opposition. Not only were they of an alien race but were followers of a religion which had little in common with that practiced in India. Hinduism had amazing powers of assimilation; it had absorbed countless peoples in the past whose identity is [sic] now lost in the mosaic of Indian society and culture. But not so the Muslims; they resolutely maintained their identity and refused compromise in religion. For the first time in her history, India was to reconcile herself to the existence of a separate culture-community.[4]

A resurgence of communal violence in the 1990s once again drew historiographical interest to the pre-history of communitarian distinctions. Although many historians were by now more careful of presentist readings of the past, they attempted to avoid anachronistic conclusions by being carefully positivistic in their methodologies. Empiricism without any theoretical orientation, however, displayed an extreme naïveté in dealing with medieval sources. Peter Jackson's work on the political and military history of the Delhi Sultanate was noteworthy for its diligent reading of Persian materials on military campaigns and administrative terminology.[5] Jackson could point out biases, exaggerations, even contradictions in his sources, but his terminology — Muslim ruler, Muslim state, Muslim power, Islamic 'religious establishment', heterodox Muslims — reflected the extent to which his narrative remained an uncritical translation of the medieval chronicles. As a result, Jackson's conclusions only stirred and sometimes qualified Habibullah's assumptions:

> ..... the 'Greater' Delhi Sultanate.... functioned as the sole bastion of Muslim power in the Indian subcontinent. ...The Delhi Sultans were first and foremost Islamic rulers.... . Perhaps for them the paramount distinction was not that between Muslim and Hindu (important as that may have been) but between peaceful subject and agent of government on the one hand and troublemaker and rebel on the other.[6]

The serious departures in the study of 'Hindu–Muslim' relations occurred when historians questioned the presence of anachronistic political boundaries separating Muslim invaders/conquerors from their 'Hindu' subjects. John Richards argued that a variety of political and cultural exchanges occurred between contestants and collaborators throughout the Middle Ages across frontiers that were permeable and slow moving in character. The political frontiers of military engagements were in constant flux and changed rapidly, but 'behind them' were processes of social engagements that led to the making of durable Indo–Muslim cultures in Hindustan.[7]

Some aspects of Richards' provocative, if fleeting, ideas were later developed by Richard Eaton in his studies on the process of mass conversions in the Punjab and Bengal regions.[8] Eaton's work was exciting for his insight into the formation of regional Muslim societies — the interaction and exchange between Muslims and non-Muslims over a variety of 'frontiers' — and it also queried the anachronistic premises on which 'Hindu–Muslim' relations had hitherto been studied. But the value of many of his historiographical insights was considerably diluted because of an implicit dichotomy in his work between the 'core' and the 'periphery'. In his diffusionist paradigm, transformations within the Muslim community operated along a horizontal and a vertical plane. The closer you were to the core scripturalist traditions, the greater the distance between the Muslim elites and non-Muslim subject populations. Conversely, more significant 'adjustments' relating to belief and orthopraxis were possible in the peripheral, pre-literate, pastoralist zones, which is why Islam in eastern Bengal and Punjab showed greater innovation in winning adherents. The longer history of autonomy from the Sultanate and Mughal social and political organisation provided these regional societies with enough space to negotiate their own relationships.

In his work on Punjab and Bengal, Eaton had less to contribute to the formation of 'Muslim and Hindu' relationships and identities in the 'core' regions of the middle Gangetic plain. But elsewhere, he remarked that 'creative encounters' between Muslims and non-Muslims occurred more generally in the subcontinent during the fifteenth, sixteenth and eighteenth centuries. These coincided with the period when the Delhi Sultanate and Mughal states had declined, which is why 'imperial visions of Islam were replaced by more localized perceptions'.[9] There was consistency in Eaton's arguments, whether he was discussing Punjab, Bengal or the larger subcontinent: political agency and history were more obviously manifest amongst subject people, Muslims and Hindus both, when the heavy hand of the state was weak. This argument was, of course, cogently supported by medieval Sultanate and Mughal court historians. In their narratives, the hegemony of the state was unquestioned and political initiatives expressed by subject populations were viewed with the gravest suspicion. '*Fitna*', sedition and rebellion, against legitimate political authority, was the extreme representation of political agency by subject people and, not surprisingly, it always carried a negative connotation in the documentation produced by the state. As Eaton put it, while the state was strong it suppressed *fitna* vigorously, but insurrectionary 'creative encounters' were possible during the period of its decline. As a result, even though Eaton researched the slow processes of community formations and argued against bivalent social identities normal to a Cartesian mapping of the modern world, he remained trapped in the juxtaposition between the state and its subjects imposed upon him by the tenor of his sources.[10] Like Moreland before him, he was sensitive to one set of problems historians face in using medieval Persian documentation but was nonetheless restrained by their discourse.

The role of 'frontiers' in the framing of 'Hindu–Muslim' identities was also creatively used by Cynthia Talbot.[11] In Talbot's work, the framing of a Telugu–Hindu identity occurred during the fourteenth through the seventeenth centuries when Sultanate forces intruded into medieval Andhra and established regional states in the Deccan. It was a non-linear process that included conflict, accommodation and the eventual shaping of new ethnic identities. The framing of a Telugu identity was a part of a larger attempt by new elites to cohere fragmented political groups within a homogeneous ethnicity with a shared linguistic, regional and [apocryphal] history. But the framing of an identity of the Telugu 'Self' required the portrayal of a demonised Muslim/Turk 'Other'. These were elite 'strategies aimed at consolidating community allegiance', and if parvenu Andhra warriors and Turkic invaders used religious rhetoric, 'what better way to shore up shaky claims to legitimacy', she asked, 'than to exploit the ancient symbols of their respective religious traditions?'[12]

Less developed in Talbot's work was a recognition that elite strategies of framing self and collective identities were intrinsically violent and hierarchy-generating exercises that had their own local, contextual politics. These were sometimes deliberately obscured in the grander narratives of Hindu–Muslim engagements and state formations. In assuming that 'Hindu–Muslim' encounters propelled the framing of medieval definitions of the self, it was, quite ironically, the politics of the region itself that was ignored by the historian.

The politics of identity formations is integral to the study of local (and large) communities in the Middle Ages. Both Eaton and Talbot recognised correctly that this was the first step in the study of what was altogether too lazily characterised as 'Hindu–Muslim' relations. Despite my disagreements with Eaton and Talbot, it is important to recall that their underlying arguments made two very significant contributions. They questioned (even if they did not always adequately replace) the alternate edges of the historiographical spectrum: one that assumed the presence of fully formed community constructions together with the ahistorical origins of Hindu and Muslim religions. And a second that placed an emphasis on modernity and the colonial encounter as important historical insertions in the making of individual and community identity formations. Eaton and Talbot argued instead for a medieval provenance for these dynamic historical processes, where the expansion of the Delhi Sultanate and Muslim society into the different regions of the subcontinent served as a significant catalyst.

My paper follows a slightly different tack. Its focus is the early thirteenth century, circa 1220–1260, the years when the Delhi Sultanate consolidated its rule over large segments of the middle Jamuna–Ganga plain, the Punjab, Sindh and northern Rajasthan. In the historiography of the period these were the remarkable years, described as the 'Foundation of Muslim Rule in India'. There was intense conflict with Hindu chieftains and the accomplishments of the armies of Islam were recounted in glowing terms in the chronicles of the Delhi court. Virtually ignored about these decades is the manner in which the discourse of a Muslim community in India made its original appearance. My paper studies the manner in which this 'idea' was constructed, the agents involved in its formulation, the politics of its implementation, the resistance and counter-ideologies that it stimulated. For decades after its inception, the identity of the righteous Muslim was hotly contested, with many individuals refusing membership in a community that they felt was misguided by its leaders. Looking at it from a different perspective, I would like to texture the historical context of the early definition of 'a' Muslim community in north India and question the importance of the frontier with the 'Hindu Other' in the fashioning of this consciousness.

Conflict and the Early Muslim Community: two episodes

On the 8th of December 1315 (10th Ramazan, 715 A.H.) Nizam al-Din Awliya narrated an anecdote regarding the Sufi Shaykh Jalal al-Din Tabrizi, who was strongly reproached by the Shaykh al-Islam of Delhi, Najm al-Din Sughra. The conflict between the two snowballed to such an extent that Jalal al-Din Tabrizi left Delhi. Tabrizi migrated to Budaun where one day he had a prescient vision of Najm al-Din Sughra's death. After a funeral prayer for the Shaykh al-Islam of Delhi, Tabrizi remarked to his companions: 'If the Shaykh al-Islam of Delhi expelled me from the town, my Shaykh expelled him from this world!'[13] Although Nizam al-Din Awliya's narrative remained enigmatic about the reasons for Jalal al-Din's exile, his disapproval of Najm al-Din Sughra's conduct was evident enough to his listeners.

As the Shaykh al-Islam of Delhi, Najm al-Din Sughra was involved in another case of expulsion, this time of the Sufi Shaykh Qutb al-Din Bakhtiyar Kaki. This story was first narrated in the mid-fourteenth century biographical encyclopedia, *Siyar al-Awliya*. The anecdote started with a reminder to the audience about the close friendship between Mu^c^in al-Din Chishti (the spiritual master of Qutb al-Din) and Najm al-Din Sughra. It was in the context of the friendship between the two protagonists that Mu^c^in al-Din was struck by Najm al-Din's haughtiness and coldness during one of his rare visits to Delhi. Mu^c^in al-Din wondered if the change in the latter's demeanour was because of his appointment as Shaykh al-Islam. When queried, Najm al-Din explained his sense of injury at Mu^c^in al-Din's decision to leave a disciple such as Qutb al-Din in Delhi. Mu^c^in al-Din immediately understood the nature of Najm al-Din's complaint and resolved to take Qutb al-Din back with him when he left for Ajmer. But the story did not end here. The climax came when Najm al-Din's efforts at purging Delhi of another Sufi Shaykh were thwarted by the spontaneous intervention of the residents of the city and Sultan Iltutmish, who begged Mu^c^in al-Din to leave his pupil behind with them.[14]

The two incidents, themselves, were historical: Jalal al-Din did indeed leave Delhi for Budaun and eventually Lakhnauti and, evidently, there was considerable animosity between Qutb al-Din Bakhtiyar Kaki and Najm al-Din Sughra. Qutb al-Din, at any rate, did not suffer expulsion and he spent his last years in Delhi. Exile from Delhi meant dishonour and expulsion from the community of Muslims resident in the town. This was an extremely serious affair, of particular significance because the people involved were not commoners but individuals well known for their piety.

Notably, both incidents were first narrated over a century after the event, in texts that belonged to the Chishti mystical tradition — and, even later, in a Suhrawardy one — and they were all hostile in their depiction of Najm al-Din's conduct.[15] The records of these moments of disharmony within the Muslim community in Delhi were disrupted by later efforts to reformulate these incidents: Najm al-Din was a petty man and his jealousy provoked the malicious incidents against the Shaykhs of Delhi. These texts went to some extent to suggest that Jalal al-Din Tabrizi was not exiled: he left, instead, on his own accord because he did not want to be further sullied by the corrupt environment of Delhi. Nizam al-Din Awliya, for example, made the deliberate effort to restore the Shaykh's reputation by suggesting that he was a victim of an unjust punishment. Ultimately, in his narrative, Jalal al-Din's dishonour was avenged by the miraculous intercession of his Shaykh and the death of Najm al-Din.[16] There is the further embellishment in the Suhrawardy account of the *Siyar al-ᶜArifin*, where Sultan Iltutmish was so appalled by his Shaykh al-Islam's conduct that he hurriedly removed him from office.[17] As for Bakhtiyar Kaki, the residents of Delhi belied Najm al-Din's efforts to expel him.[18] In the reformulation, the incidents were reduced into one of personal intrigue and not one where the integrity of the Muslim community in Delhi was disturbed by conflict between some of its major protagonists.

But was it, indeed, such a serious affair? If one goes beyond simple personal jealousies, the Chishti and Suhrawardy narratives of the imbroglio can also be read to suggest that the incidents were a classic example of a conflict between the mystically minded and the scripturalist traditions in Islam; between the more liberal, introspective readings of the Holy Law and the dogmatic computations of its juristic, textually-oriented based versions. It could be argued that the conflict was provoked by the esoteric beliefs of the mystics Jalal al-Din Tabrizi, Muᶜin al-Din Chishti and Qutb al-Din Bakhtiyar Kaki on the one hand and the exoteric practice of the Shaykh al-Islam Najm al-Din Sughra on the other. A modern historiography sometimes installs Sufis and ᶜUlama into antagonistic camps, within two relatively well-hewn groups with very distinct and divergent characteristics. Hence, the argument goes, their recurring disagreements over questions of dogma and practice.[19]

A careful study of Shaykhs and ᶜUlama in this period, however, quickly collapses these distinctions. Najm al-Din Sughra's animosity towards Jalal al-Din Tabrizi or Bakhtiyar Kaki, for example, was not provoked by innate differences between Sufis and ᶜUlama. Neither the ᶜUlama nor the Sufi belonged to a coherent prototype. There were ᶜUlama like Qazi Minhaj al-Din Siraj Juzjani, at one time the chief jurist of the realm, who was renowned for his sermons, knowledge of jurisprudence and, without any contradiction whatsoever, was also inclined towards the mystical path. According to Nizam al-Din Awliya, it was the Qazi who popularised the ritual singing of the Sufis, *samaᶜ*, in Delhi.[20] By contrast, there were Sufis like Baha' al-Din Zakariya whose own conduct was in certain spheres very close to a scripturalist orthopraxis.[21] Other Sufis often criticised him for his ostentatious life-style, his accumulation of wealth and hobnobbing with the military commanders of the Delhi Sultan.[22] The ᶜUlama and the Sufis did not necessarily occupy a juxtaposed terrain. But, at the other extreme, it was not quite an open-ended world either. The mystically inclined jurist, Minhaj-i Siraj Juzjani, could condemn a Sufi like Nur Turk as a heretic and damage his reputation to such an extent that Nizam al-Din Awliya made a special effort to exonerate the Sufi in his teachings.[23] Obviously the practices of only some mystics were acceptable to jurists; others, however, were condemned. By the same token, Shaykhs like Baha' al-Din Zakariya, whose mysticism was strongly influenced by a Sharᶜi orthopraxis, could not abide the pedanticism of some prescriptive rituals. He explained how his personal practice emanated from a superior, intuitive understanding of law.[24] Indeed, Sufis and ᶜUlama extolled and condemned their own and each other's conduct. The distinctions within and between them did not necessarily predispose their reactions one way or the other. This was certainly true in the case of Najm al-Din Sughra. As the sixteenth-century biographical encyclopedia of mystic Shaykhs of the Firdausi fraternity, the *Manaqib al-Asafiya*, brings out, the Shaykh al-Islam of Delhi was actually ***not*** one of the ᶜUlama. He was a mystic with an enviable spiritual genealogy: a student of the great Shaykh Najm al-Din Kubra. Apparently his mystical background did not mute his decision to reproach and harass other Sufis in Delhi nor stand in the way of his appointment by the Sultan as the Shaykh al-Islam of Delhi.[25]

If the animosity between Sughra and the other Sufis was not caused by ingrained ᶜUlama–Sufi distinctions, could it be that these incidents were examples of the intense rivalry amongst Sufis over charismatic precedence and spiritual domains (*wilayat*)? According to many scholars, conflicts over *wilayats* could be quite fierce. Was Najm al-Din, therefore, upset with Muᶜin al-Din's appointment of Bakhtiyar Kaki in Delhi, a domain that he regarded as his own particular *wilayat*? Was this also the reason why Jalal al-Din was forced to leave Delhi?

The *Kashf al-Mahjub*, an eleventh-century Sufi text produced in Ghaznavid Lahore, describes how Sufis identified specific regions as their spiritual domains and the extent to which Shaykhs sought to preserve their exclusive rights to these territories. Reportedly, Sufis were greeted hospitably when they visited the hospices of different Shaykhs but they were not welcome to establish competing mystical fraternities in each other's domains.[26] It has been assumed, of course, that eleventh-century Ghaznavid traditions transposed themselves into the Delhi Sultanate of the thirteenth century, that the administrative organisation, cultural expectations, belief systems and mystical practices flowed quite seamlessly from one regime and time period to another.[27]

The first reference that we have to the presence of exclusive Sufi domains in India is in the conversations (*malfuz*) of Nizam al-Din Awliya that were compiled between 1308 and 1322. This is a relatively late record of Sufi practice and we cannot be sure if Nizam al-Din Awliya was ascribing the politics of his generation to a previous century.[28] Certainly, there is nothing in Nizam al-Din's conversations that would suggest that Jalal al-Din Tabrizi and Bakhtiyar Kaki established flourishing mystical fraternities in Delhi. This was certainly in marked contrast to Nizam al-Din's description of Baba Farid's hospice in Ajudhan in the distant Punjab, or Baha' al-Din Zakariya's assemblies in Multan. Nothing remotely resembling these mystical assemblies in size or influence seems to have existed in Delhi in the first half of the thirteenth century when, despite the presence of several mystics, the city remained strangely devoid of any major Sufi establishments.

While the early thirteenth century saw the presence of local congregations organised around individual Shaykhs in some parts of north India — if not in Delhi — these were not organised as yet around spiritual genealogies (*silsilas*) of past teachers. A tentative outline of the Chishti *silsila* is recognisable for the first time in the teachings of Nizam al-Din Awliya — the *Fawa'id al-Fu'ad* — but this dates only from the turn of the century. Significantly, Mu^cin al-Din Chishti, the Shaykh venerated today as the 'founder' of the order, received only a tangential mention in this account.[29] The history of the Chishti *silsila* was only clearly articulated in the middle of the fourteenth century in the *Siyar al-Awliya*, and of the Suhrawardy's only in the sixteenth-century biographical encyclopedia, the *Siyar al-^cArifin*. The lines of conflict between the Shaykh al-Islam and the other Shaykhs in Delhi in the early thirteenth century was not, therefore, along the combative Chishti, Suhrawardy and Firdausi lines that later sources tried to shape them into. This retrospective organisation of pietistic Muslims into coherent mystical fraternities tends to obliterate the special characteristics of the early thirteenth century when the conflicts between the Shaykhs occurred. Certainly any reading that suggests personality clashes, Sufi–^cUlama conflict or competition amongst Sufi *silsilas* tries to rationalise the conflict between the different Shaykhs in individualistic or sectarian terms. It might help, on the other hand, to use the moment of rupture to analyze further the character of the Muslim community and study the contexts in which the Shaykh al-Islam possessed the ability to threaten and exile eminent Shaykhs.

The Social and Political Context

The incidents that we have been discussing occurred during the reign of Sultan Shams al-Din Iltutmish (1210–36), perhaps in the 1220s or the early 1230s. The *Fawa'id al-Fu'ad* mentions no dates but we do know, even if it is without any degree of precision, that both Jalal al-Din Tabrizi and Bakhtiyar Kaki were in Delhi during the reign of Iltutmish.[30] Its account is also suggestive of the fact that the Mongol excursions into north India had already commenced.[31] This would be post-1221, a decade that witnessed important transitions in the Sultanate of Delhi.

The kingdom of Delhi was originally one of several military outposts established by the Shansabanid Sultan of Ghazni, Muᶜizz al-Din Ghuri (1173–1206), during his campaigns in north India. Its fortunes fluctuated until the reign of Shams al-Din Iltutmish (1210-36) when military campaigns in the first twenty years of the monarch's reign led to the defeat of the surviving commanders of Muᶜizz al-Din and the emergence of a paramount Sultanate of Delhi. With the annexation of these rival settlements by the late-1220s, the authority of Delhi expanded to include a diverse collection of people resident in areas as far away as Sindh in the west and Bengal in the east.[32]

Integrating this dominion as a composite Sultanate of Delhi was a huge challenge. The urban residents of the newly annexed settlements had already experienced several decades of stable political and economic life under their respective commanders. They had few ties with Shams al-Din Iltutmish, their new, and very distant, Sultan of Delhi. But the problems of consolidating the newly conquered territories and subjects within a composite Sultanate of Delhi were further complicated with the beginning of the Mongol invasions in 1221. Through the following decade, cities in north India received a flood of immigrants from eastern Iran, Khurasan, Transoxiana, and Afghanistan. These were 'Muslims' from diverse ethnic, 'class' and regional backgrounds, groups of disassociated people sharing few, if any, social ties with each other. Their arrival in the recently annexed domains of the Delhi Sultan immediately made the composition of his subjects even more complex and compounded the problem of integrating them within a composite Sultanate.[33]

Consolidating the domains of the Delhi Sultan in the 1220s was also a difficult exercise because the Sultanate was still a loose assembly of urban centres with marginal control of their hinterlands. Although this would improve through the decade, the interior of the countryside was still outside the governance of the Sultanate. Hostile forces controlled the vast intervening tracts — a difficult terrain, particularly during the long summer and monsoon seasons — separating Sultanate garrisons.[34] The Delhi monarch retained political control over the more strategic areas in his dominion through elite military slaves (*bandagan*). These elite slaves were primarily of Turkish background and were specially purchased, trained and fostered over a considerable period of time by the Sultan to function as his loyal subordinates. The close, dyadic bonds established between the master and his elite slaves allowed for a political stability that spanned the geographical distances separating the monarch from his territories (*wilayats/iqtas*).[35]

Iltutmish's slave governors were trusted with considerable political initiative and they were also dispensers of patronage and rewards in their own courts. Besides armed personnel, they also recruited secretaries and jurists. Fakhr-i Mudabbir described the compromises that service with these slave patrons entailed:

> .....after the Persian language none is finer and more dignified than Turkish. And now a days the Turkish language is more popular that it ever was before. This is due to the fact that the majority of Amirs and Commanders are Turks. And it is the Turks who are most successful and most wealthy, and so all have need of that language. And grandees of the highest pedigree are in the service of the Turks and from their success derive peace, prosperity and honor.[36]

Other than suggesting that the Turkish military slaves maintained a composite racial, cultural and linguistic identity, Fakhr-i Mudabbir also waxed eloquent about the political power and influence that they commanded within the Sultanate. Despite the eulogistic tone in which his account of the 'Turks' was couched, there was also a series of telling juxtapositions in his observations. The first was between Persian and Turkish languages. Whereas the importance of Persian needed little explanation — its heritage was evident to all — the popularity of Turkish was not derived from a cultural past but a political present. It was the language of the military elite, the current dispensers of service and wealth. The second juxtaposition is somewhat more obscure to a modern audience. Fakhr-i Mudabbir spoke of 'Turks' without clarifying that the people that he was describing were Turkish slaves. Although the reference to slaves as Turks was common in the Persian literature of the Sultanate, it acquired a particular salience when Fakhr-i Mudabbir juxtaposed them against the Persian literati. In contrast to the slaves/ Turks, the literati were described as aristocrats, 'grandees of the highest pedigree'. Hence, according to Fakhr-i Mudabbir, social precedence between aristocrats and slaves was inverted in an interesting way during the early Sultanate. Turkish slaves — implicitly of a menial social standing — commanded power and wealth while Persian aristocrats of learning served them and mastered a foreign language to acquire patronage and honour.[37] It remains to be noted that while this 'social inversion' might have perturbed some of the Persian literati, it did not deter the likes of Fakhr-i Mudabbir himself, or Minhaj-i Siraj Juzjani who invested large parts of their life in the service of Turkish slave masters. The tensions present in this world, however, were captured in verse and recounted by Nizam al-Din Awliya to the congregation present in his hospice — in an environment that was more than a little ambivalent about the grandeur of the Sultan's court. The verse was addressed to Hamid, a Persian secretary who served Tughril, his Turkish master.

> Oh Hamid! why are you standing before this man?.....You are a learned man and he is ignorant, you are a free man and he is a slave, you are a pious man and he is an uncultured sinner.[38]

In a pithy Nizam al-Din captured the flimsy foundations upon which Sultanate authority resided. It may have possessed brute military power but the templates that assessed an individual's worth by his learning, pietistic inclinations and genealogy were unimpressed by the claims of slaves to command by force of arms. Certainly they were not the people qualified to lead the Muslim community as moral exemplars; they were Amirs and Maliks, possessors of wealth and power but not *sharif* or *buzurg*, cultured, respectable elders of the community.

Defining Orthopraxis: the role of the Shaykh al-Islam

If Iltutmish and his slave subordinates lacked the learning and culture to appear as moral exemplars, it made their task of appearing as leaders of their subjects incredibly difficult. It did not lead to a situation, however, where Muslim communities were left without guidance. They recognised Shaykhs and ᶜUlama as learned men, individuals whose training in law, history, theology and mysticism helped in charting a path through which Muslims could reproduce a culture and habitat in north India that was so violently uprooted by the Mongol invasions in eastern Iran and Afghanistan. The cataclysmic destruction of their homelands and the trauma of immigration was for many of them the harbinger of the Day of Judgment. It was during this moment of despair that they turned to their community leaders for reassurance and guidance.

On the face of it there was probably very little to distinguish between these community leaders. Broadly speaking, they had a similar kind of education in the Qur'an and its exegesis, in the *Hadith* and other roots of law. Gaining such an education was a strenuous exercise, not just because of the nature of the curriculum, but also because 'schooling' implied travelling in search of distinguished teachers and gradually piecing together a knowledge of classical texts.[39] At a time when education and literacy was at a premium, any kind of apparent scholasticism earned the individual huge accolades and entry within a scantily populated circle of learned elites.[40] At the same time however, a knowledge of subjects such as jurisprudence, theology, grammar, disputation or history was not necessarily sufficient to guarantee a learned individual social pre-eminence. A lesser-schooled person's introspective, reflective discourses on mysticism, on the hidden meanings of praxis and belief, sometimes touched the heart and soul of Muslims in a manner that a ['pedantic'] scholar could never attain. Sometimes a scholar's knowledge was tempered with an inclination towards mysticism, at other times a mystic may have considerable training in classical jurisprudence, an education that was apparent in the mystic's discourse even while it was deliberately underplayed.[41]

In the context of the twelfth century, Marshall Hodgson has described the complex distinctions in the community of Sunni Muslims and their leaders very succinctly. The first face of Islam, Hodgson noted was 'Shari^ca-minded, concerned with outward, socially cognisable behaviour, accepted as their care by the Shar^ci Ulama; the other was mystical-minded, concerned with the inward, personal life of the individual, accepted as their care by the Sufi pirs. Often the same religious leader was at once pir and Shar^ci scholar, or at least took both sides of Islam very seriously; just as most of the Muslim public respected and took guidance from both pirs and ^cUlama. Always however, there were those who accepted the one face of Islam as genuine and mistrusted the other, or even rejected it as spurious...'.[42] In sum, despite the seeming conformity in the qualifications that Muslims looked for in their community leaders, there was considerable variation in their training and approach to textual traditions regarded as authoritative by most Muslims.

Indeed, Muslim society was hardly monolithic, but what is interesting from our perspective are the social and political dimensions of internal disputes concerning questions of praxis and dogma. Especially in the context of displaced Muslim communities in north India, the differences of class, ethnicities and regions were further underscored by recurring debates concerning the authenticity of their religious practices. For the Shari^ca-minded ^cUlama, a recourse to the textual canons defining 'socially cognisable behaviour' provided a means to challenge the charismatically inspired, divergent interpretations of Islam taught by Sufi Shaykhs. Since the sovereignty of the Shari^ca in the lives of Muslims was beyond question, the Shari^ca-minded scholars focused upon enforcing a social praxis determined by the Holy Law's narrow, textual definition. This restricted the spectrum of permissible conduct and introduced an important element of uniformity to cohere Muslims together into a community of Islam.

Disagreements over questions of praxis in the history of Islamicate societies were of long standing and, as a careful review of the Persian material clarifies, they became the subject of urgent cogitation in north India after the Mongol invasions and the arrival of Muslim refugees in the decades after the early 1220s.[43] It led to sharp debates and conflicts, the memories of which were commemorated in the mystical records of Sufis belonging to a later generation where the piety and resoluteness of their predecessors was praised. Some Persian court historians also had strong mystical leanings and their texts carried sub-narratives recording the [usually ineffectual] efforts of the Shari^ca-minded ^cUlama to curb Sufi practice through *fatwas*, judicial decrees, and *mahzars*, inquisitions (literally, assembly, council). It is, in fact, interesting to note how the number of references to *fatwas* and *mahzars* from Iltutmish's reign remains unequalled until perhaps the reign of Sultan Muhammad Shah Tughluq (1324–51). And it is the ***'public'*** contexts in which debates over questions of social praxis occurred that is particularly illuminating. Private belief or the discreet practice of Sufi rituals by individuals seems to have been generally ignored, but when a Shaykh such as Jalal al-Din Tabrizi or Qutb al-Din Bakhtiyar Kaki tried to gain adherents in the city they faced the hostility of the Shaykh al-Islam. But how exactly were the boundaries of this socially cognisable conduct determined and enforced?

The stray references that we do possess concerning the Shaykh al-Islam indicate that he was one individual whose specific function was to guide the conduct of Muslims in his area of jurisdiction, interact with the pious and, most crucially, scrutinise their texts and teachings. In its normative conceptualisation the function of the Shaykh al-Islam in the reign of Iltutmish does not seem to have differed markedly from its Ghurid predecessor and an anecdote in the *Chahar Maqala* throws fortunate light on some of its features:

> The Shaykh al-Islam ^cAbdu'llah Ansari...conceived a fanatical hatred...(towards the physician Adib Isma^cil)..., and several times attempted to do him an injury, and burned his books. Now this fanatical dislike arose from religious motives, for the people of Herat believed that he could restore the dead to life, and this belief was [injurious to the common folk].[44]
>
> Now the Shaykh [al-Islam] fell ill, and in the course of the illness the death-rattle became apparent. However much the physicians treated him, it availed nothing. They were in despair ...... (and finally appealed to the

physician Adib Isma^c^il. The physician studied the symptoms and prescribed a remedy, which he sent together with this message to the Shaykh al-Islam) .... 'You should study science, and not burn men's books'.[45]

Unlike many sources that ascribe persecution of pious Muslims by the Shaykh al-Islam to purely personal motives, the *Chahar Maqala* went much further and clarified that religious reasons caused this fanatical hatred. The physician's books were burned because they were the font of knowledge through which he had acquired the unholy reputation of 'restoring the dead to life'. This was especially disturbing since the physician's reputed prowess had 'fooled' people into believing that he possessed miraculous powers otherwise associated only with the Prophet Jesus. The Shaykh al-Islam had to curb the activities of the charlatan physician and destroy the texts that empowered the dissemination of such heretical beliefs. At least as far as the Shaykh was concerned, the future integrity of the Muslim community depended upon his success in curbing such false practices.

Several chroniclers have also recorded the activities of the Shaykh al-Islam of Delhi in Iltutmish's reign and many of these accounts are clearly apocryphal. Yet they all harmonise with each other and independently emphasise the Shaykh al-Islam's role as a guide and adjudicator of the conduct of Muslims. In Ziya' al-Din Barani's *Ta'rikh-i Firuz Shahi* (a mid-fourteenth century chronicle of the Delhi Sultans), for example, Balban (1266-86) remembered how the Shaykh al-Islam of Delhi, Sayyid Nur al-Din Mubarak Ghaznawi harangued Sultan Iltutmish about the manner in which the existing customs of governance contravened the traditions of the Prophet. This, according to the Shaykh, inevitably damned rulers to perdition. Subsequently, the Shaykh al-Islam narrated four precepts for the protection of the faith, which rulers should follow.[46] As some historians have clarified, Sayyid Nur al-Din represented the authorial voice of Ziya' al-Din Barani, and, in the light of the responsibilities entrusted to the Shaykh al-Islam, was seen as an apposite choice of character to question and voice aphorisms on moral conduct.[47] That this was no accidental choice can be clarified if we recall the evidence of the *Siyar al-^c^Arifin*. According to the sixteenth-century Suhrawardy text, in the *mahzar*, inquest, held to adjudicate Jalal al-Din Tabrizi's conduct, it was the Shaykh al-Islam Najm al-Din Sughra who was the plaintiff and prosecutor, and the judge was the Shaykh al-Islam, Baha' al-Din Zakariya.

The additional information about the Shaykh al-Islam helps to clarify the nature of the conflict between Najm al-Din Sughra and the several Shaykhs as well. As the Shaykh al-Islam, Najm al-Din was apparently disturbed by their conduct, which is why he persecuted these mystics. Ultimately it was the quality and degree of this 'supervision' that made it impossible for Jalal al-Din Tabrizi to remain in Delhi. The Firdawsi biographical encyclopaedia that praised Najm al-Din Sughra as a 'great man, a saint' also sharply criticised Qutb al-Din Bakhtiyar Kaki for the hold he had acquired over the people of Delhi by the display of miraculous powers.[48] Not only was Qutb al-Din a fraud but in gaining adherents the Shaykh was also endangering Islam and the Shar^c^i principles that cohered the community of Muslims. It is hardly surprising that later Chishti and Suhrawardy texts reacted so strongly to Najm al-Din Sughra's persecution and provided such a hostile account of his conduct. Nor is it shocking to find that the Firdawsi text responded to this assault and tried to restore his credibility.

The evidence from the early thirteenth century does suggest that charismatic Sufis — pious Muslims who claimed a latitude of action and belief because of their special intuitive powers — were particularly persecuted in Iltutmish's reign. In this context we can appreciate the import of Nizam al-Din Awliya's remark that the jurist Minhaj-i Siraj Juzjani should have been a Shaykh al-Islam and not a mere Qazi. Had Juzjani been a Shaykh al-Islam his personal evaluation of conduct would have been influenced more by his well-known Sufi leanings rather than a 'scriptural' understanding of Islam. Nizam al-Din Awliya's wish was a pious hope of a different configuration of forces that would have enabled the triumph of mystical Islam — rather than Shar^c^i orthopraxis — in Delhi.

In reconfiguring the episodes surrounding Bakhtiyar Kaki, Jalal al-Din Tabrizi and Najm al-Din Sughra, the Chishti and Suhrawardy texts were inadvertently highlighting their discontent with the nature of piety dominant in Delhi. The intensity of opposition to the imposition of an 'authoritative' Islam is apparent from the reports of an incident when an armed body of Muslims attacked the congregational mosque in the city sometime in 1236, the end of Iltutmish's reign and accession of Sultana Raziyya.[49] In the earlier, contemporary report of the event provided by Qazi Minhaj-i Siraj Juzjani, a Shi^c^i heretic named Nur Turk provoked the attack. According to Juzjani, Nur Turk was an extraordinary preacher who convinced his followers that the Shafi^c^ and Hanafi ^c^Ulama in the Delhi mosque were misrepresenting Islam and leading the community into error. In the alternative report provided by Nizam al-Din Awliya, Nur Turk was actually a Sufi whose piety was as pure as the dew from heaven. Nizam al-Din Awliya himself glossed over the incident of the armed attack on the mosque and suggested that this was a canard floated by the ^c^Ulama to conceal their sins. Instead, he spoke approvingly of Nur Turk's piety and his public challenge of the worldly demeanour of the ^c^Ulama of the city. By contrast, Qazi Minhaj-i Siraj Juzjani praised the armed dispersal and death of the heretics.[50]

But beyond the conflicting accounts, Nur Turk's attack on the congregational mosque and its keepers revealed the extent to which many Muslims were alienated from the authoritarian structures of governance that controlled the environs of Delhi. The Sultan and his agents were only one of the lineages of power in the early thirteenth century; governance in the larger sense of the word involved other dignitaries as well. Individuals like Najm al-Din Sughra, however, possessed authority but were not, strictly speaking, servants of the Sultan. Their authority resided upon the recognition that the public gave to their learning, decorum and spiritual genealogy; it was not gained purely through the dispensation of the monarch. In fact it was the efficacy of this public respect that led the Sultan to choose Najm al-Din as Shaykh al-Islam and it was precisely this popular regard that facilitated his confident denunciation of Shaykhs such as Bakhtiyar Kaki and Tabrizi. In turn, it was the personal credibility of Najm al-Din that the Chishti and Suhrawardy texts tried to run down.

It is unclear, however, whether this 'supervision' of conduct reflected a wider effort to 'discipline and punish' the practice of some recalcitrant Shaykhs in the latter part of Iltutmish's reign. Judging by the numerous reports of conflict between the ʿulama and Sufi Shaykhs over the validity of mystical practices like *namaz*,[51] *sama'* and *raqs*[52] in towns such as Budaun, Multan and Ajudhan, Delhi does not seem to have been an isolated case. Depending upon the individual jurist's confidence, conflict could occur in a *qasba* as well and Juzjani provided information about Qazi Shams al-Din of Mihir, who persecuted a Turkman derwish called Ayub.[53] Slightly later, in the middle of the thirteenth century and some distance from Delhi, the local Qazi of Ajudhan was frustrated in his attempts to discipline Baba Farid. The Qazi's compatriots in Multan refused to give him a decree, *fatwa*, that he could use to forbid the practice of a Shaykh who commanded great respect in the region.[54] It is not just the Qazi's inability to police the Shaykh's conduct that is worthy of comment. Of equal interest is the jurist's sense of anxiety and his pursuit of 'justice'. The Qazi was unable to make any impression in Ajudhan because the local configuration of power went against him, but his appeal to templates of righteous conduct already in circulation was telling. The enforcement of these structures of orthopraxis certainly restricted the ability of Muslims to negotiate their unique definitions of righteous conduct in the early thirteenth century. It crystallised the sense of an 'orthodoxy', a definition that would circulate in public discourse and remain under considerable dispute.

Although not involved in its framing or implementation, Sultan Iltutmish was complicit in ensuring the dissemination of this textually constructed definition of orthopraxis in his dominion. The Delhi monarch preserved the greatest of decorum in his personal dealings with all the piety minded in his realm and seems to have, in fact, suggested that his accession to the throne was made possible through the divine benediction of great Sufi masters.[55] But, despite the efforts of Sufi texts to suggest the Delhi monarch's leanings towards mysticism and Sufi Shaykhs, Iltutmish appears to have been very careful not to appear as the patron of any Shaykh. Court eulogists might have found spiritual intercession a useful trope to suppress memories of a contested accession[56] and mystical visions of the Prophet added pious lustre to his construction of a community reservoir in the capital.[57] But his public declarations regarding the duties incumbent on all Muslims unequivocally stressed the congregational aspects of Islam and the prescriptive injunctions of the Shariᶜa.[58] He invested huge sums on public projects that could function as centres of community organisation and socialisation. Congregational mosques, schools and *idgahs*, community festival grounds, were constructed in Delhi and other cities of the realm. These were places where social interaction as well as social reproduction could be efficiently engineered. And, as his decision to honour Najm al-Din Sughra as Delhi's Shaykh al-Islam reveals, Iltutmish left little to chance. His support to the structures and agencies that enforced a textually defined social orthopraxis rather than any intuitively inspired interpretation of faith, effectively challenged the foundations upon which many charismatic pious Shaykhs legitimated their teaching of Islam and established their separate fraternities. The condominium of interests between the Shariᶜa-minded pious Muslims and the state served to map boundaries of righteous conduct that also framed the outlines of the Muslim community. A united Muslim community, protected by a powerful state, ruled by a pious monarch served as a powerful contrast to the destruction of Muslim homelands in Iran and Afghanistan. Juzjani tried to get as much mileage out of this imagery as possible, but the Muslims terrified by the impending holocaust were often assuaged by the charismatic Shaykhs, whose miracles testified to their proximity to God. Socially cognisable conduct that abided by the Holy Law was all very well in its own place but at a time when the Hereafter was upon them, many Muslims sought the reassurance of their Shaykh as an intercessor with God.[59]

Politics and Society: Hindu–Muslim relations reconsidered

The literature generated within the circle of the Delhi court made little effort to clarify the processes or justify the imposition of the strictures and boundaries that defined the community of Muslims. It celebrated the emergence of Delhi as the 'Axis of Islam' as a self-evident fact that needed little clarification. Why a diverse body of Muslims dispersed in distant cantonments in north India should regard Delhi as the hub of their lives, a place where Muslims were assured of sanctuary in troubled times, were questions that Sultanate chronicles answered with platitudes regarding the generous patronage available to all in the court of the great Sultan Shams al-Din Iltutmish. Certainly the obscuring of political agency and historical processes in the construction of a Sharᶜi orthopraxis had the advantage of conferring upon it a sense of normalcy and timelessness.

The synchronic nature of Persian chronicles made it possible for their authors to negotiate the politics of their present in a variety of ways. Not the least of the unpleasant realities of their times concerned the deep divisions within the Muslim community and the inadequate qualification of its political masters to cohere its constituent elements. The tenth-century juridical gloss on this world argued that the political sphere of Islam was embodied in the State. It may not be an ideal world, jurists argued, but it was a necessary compromise so that society and religion could flourish in a protected environment.[60] It served the dual purpose of differentiating between religion and politics, and abstracting politics from society. This distancing meant that Muslims remained untouched by the excesses of the Sultan's world. But it also meant that rebellion, or the usurpation of political initiative by subjects, could only be regarded as a fundamental challenge to the social order. Kings and nobles were expected to fight with each other; the subjects were not supposed to intrude into this realm.[61]

Paradoxically, the usurpation of political initiative by subjects — rebellions — was often explained as a consequence of unstatesmanlike conduct from kings and their agents. They had given up the path of 'moderation' and their excesses drove their subjects to this extreme action. Thus, depending upon the political leanings of the chronicler, Shams al-Din Iltutmish could be described as the paragon of moderate virtue, but ᶜAla' al-Din Khalji's ambitious interventions in the affairs of religion and social transactions — his efficient management of public administration notwithstanding — marked him as an irreligious despot.[62] There had been rulers of this nature in the past; history merely recorded the transient impact of human frailties.

The depoliticisation of the Sunni-jamᶜa society made rebellion, *fitna*, abhorrent. The juridical reasoning arguing for the preservation of the Muslim community conjoined stability and consensus together in a milieu that was outside history and debate. Would conditions ever change, making such a compromise unnecessary? Not within the horizon of Sunni-jamaᶜ speculation in India between the thirteenth through the sixteenth centuries.[63] The implications of this theoretical position anathematised internal disputes within the community and left it unreported. The author who chose to recount Jalal al-Din Tabrizi's exile and the events leading up to it had two hypothetical options: he could cast the Sufi Shaykh as a heretic, or portray Iltutmish (or one of his agents) as a prejudiced party guilty of excesses. As it happened, Jalal al-Din's case was never reported in the Persian histories of the day and the Sufi accounts that did carry it, universally ascribed the whole incident to the Delhi Shaykh al-Islam's petty and jealous character. As a result, the pristine, monolithic character of the Muslim community remained untarnished and the whole episode was brushed aside as an example of 'excesses' of a person unqualified to hold public office.

Alternatively, rebellions could also be caused by groups of people who had never accepted the moral legitimacy of the Muslim social world. Conventionally, they were described either as Shi^c^i heretics (Juzjani's Qarmatians), rationalist philosophers or Hindu infidels. Although the former two theoretically were Muslims, they were outside the pale of the Sunni-jama^c^ moral order and their expulsion was a relatively straightforward way of protecting the community. More problematic were the large number of non-Muslim 'Hindus' who could be suffered only if they accepted Islam. Or as the classic Hanafi position allowed: recognise them as one of the 'people of the book', a dependent, subject race who paid the jaziya tax. Both positions were resurrected time and again, debated and used to underline and homogenise 'difference'.[64] An equally classic trope was carried in the recurring admonition in Sultanate texts: rulers could only be great Muslim Sultans if they constantly chastened Hindus and, like the paradigmatic Mahmud of Ghazni, destroyed their temples.[65]

The large-scale reportage of conflict between 'the army of Islam' and non-Muslims was in marked contrast to the discreet acknowledgment of discord within the Muslim community. In the context of the Mongol invasions, non-Muslims were cast as the greatest, if not the only, threat to the community of Muslims and the Sultanate. The Mongols and the Hindus were seamlessly joined together into a composite 'Other' and if Juzjani's exhortation delivered on January 17, 1258 — 'stimulating [Muslims] to holy warfare and the merit of fighting against infidels, to defend the glory of Islam and serve the sublime court and obey the orders of their commanders'[66] — had been less explicit in its contextualisation, the reader could mistakenly assume that the infidels under discussion in this passage were the Hindus and not the Mongols. Ironically, this threat also provided the rhetorical space to demand cohesiveness within the Muslim community. Juzjani's exhortations, for example, were necessary to raise the morale of the believers and galvanise them into superhuman endeavour against the enemy of Islam. In other words, the non-believer, Hindu or Mongol, served the crucial purpose of making the Muslim community more cohesive and pious. The Mughal emperor, Babur's, dramatic renunciation of wine before battle with the unbelievers reflected only one of the ways in which the threat of the external 'Other' could be deployed as a reformist trope to underline solidarity within God's chosen community.[67] But narratives that underlined 'difference' and 'conflict' with people outside the community of Muslims seldom ventured into the complex terrain of discussing similar questions within the Sunni-jama^c^.

With the state as the principal political actor in South Asia and the protection of the community of Muslims as its primary aim, it was always cast in an offensive or defensive engagement with non-Muslims. Modern positivist historiographical methodologies, especially if they belonged to secular traditions, had the greatest difficulty in dealing with these materials. Some of them, like Tara Chand or Khaliq Nizami turned to mystical traditions to suggest that medieval social life was not organised along the bigoted principles reported in most court chroniclers.[68] Power and politics were distant from the concerns of Sufis, it was a search for mystical union that animated their lives. But their arguments consolidated the discrete world of the social and political, religion and the state — the intention of medieval political philosophers in the first place. Other empiricists tempered the accounts of the monolithic Muslim state by suggesting that it engaged in a variety of realistic, pragmatic relationships with the majoritarian non-Muslim population of the subcontinent. While the contingent contexts of pragmatic political relationships helped to complicate the simple accounts of Hindu–Muslim conflicts, it still left Hindus and Muslims as two distinct entities embodied in their respective political formations.[69] Even when more sophisticated interpretations of 'frontier interaction' questioned this scholarship, the heavy hand of the state did not entirely disappear. According to Eaton, creative dialogue and exchange between Muslims and non-Muslims was successful only in the politically peripheral areas, distant from the might of the state and the textual traditions that cohered its subjects. In the core areas of political formations, 'creative encounters' between juxtaposed traditions had to wait for the moment when the power of the state declined.[70]

My own interpretation is squarely rooted in a post-1992 Babri masjid demolition milieu, when essentialist arguments concerning Muslim and Hindu social and political traditions have once again received a wide circulation. Beyond the merits of taking on the iconoclastic depiction of Islam and debating the character of Muslim–Hindu engagements in the pre-modern period, what I find particularly disturbing is the extent to which the ahistorical treatment of Muslim society in the pre-modern period has contributed to the essentialist discourse of modern communal politics. The bulk of research on Muslim identities contesting the notion of a monolithic pan-Indian Muslim community has come from scholars working on the eighteenth through the twentieth centuries. Although it may not have always been their intention, the modern and early modern contexts of their research have tended to link questions of 'identities' and 'communities' with themes of 'modernity' and 'colonialism'. The pre-modern antecedents of 'modern' Muslim identities have, on the other hand, either remained shrouded in obscurity, or, been articulated within largely 'fuzzy' notions of sectarian and regional sensibilities. The unchanging, traditional nature of the medieval world contrasts dramatically with the modern where the history of 'Muslim identities' was propelled not so much by the politics of its own history and discourse, but by the exogenous impact of a modern world. Until historians can recapture the politics of this past and discover how multiple disciplinary formations textured the history of the Muslim community at different times, the presence or absence of the dominant 'Muslim' state will determine the account of 'Muslim–Hindu' relations in the Middle Ages.

REFERENCES

* A slightly different version of this paper titled, "La Communauté Musulmane et les Relations Hindous-Musulmans dans l'Inde du Nord au début du XIIIe siècl: une Réévaluation Politique", *Annales Histoire, Sciences, Sociales*, vol. 60, (2005), pp. 239–64.

1. W.H. Moreland, *The Agrarian System of Moslem India: a Historical Essay with Appendices*, Delhi, 1929 (1968 reprint). Moreland argued that the revenue collection functions of the Muslim state in India were 'the most potent factor in the distribution of the national income; while its action in regard to distribution inevitably reacted on production, so much so that we are justified in concluding that, next only to the weather, the administrator was the dominant fact in the economic life of the country'. See p. xii.
2. Peter Hardy, *Historians of Medieval India: Studies in Indo-Muslim Historical Writing*, London, 1960, (1966 reprint) described the limitations in Sultanate sources at great length, but from a largely Whiggish historiographical perspective. Hardy argued that Persian chronicles were better suited to provide insights into the metaphysical, subjective realm of ideas, attitudes and perceptions but not on the material structures of society. Hardy's positivist leanings (on which, see Velcheru Narayana Rao, David Shulman and Sanjay Subrahmanyam, *Textures of Time: Writing History in South India, 1600–1800*, pp. 217–9 and Sunil Kumar, *Emergence of the Delhi Sultanate*, Delhi, 2007, Chapter 1), made it extremely difficult for him to historicise

his observations. His research on 'violence' or 'duty', for example, remained very Weberian in their formulations.

3. Aziz Ahmad, 'Epic and Counter-Epic in Medieval India', *Journal of the American Oriental Society,* 83 (1963), pp. 470–6, reprinted in Richard M. Eaton, (ed.), *India's Islamic Traditions, 711–1750,* Delhi, 2003, pp. 37–49.
4. A.B.M. Habibullah, *The Foundation of Muslim Rule in India,* Allahabad, 1976 (revised edn.), p. 44.
5. Peter Jackson, *The Delhi Sultanate: a Political and Military History,* Cambridge, 1999.
6. *Ibid,* pp. xiii, 278, 295.
7. John F. Richards, 'The Islamic Frontier in the East: Expansion into South Asia', *South Asia,* 4 (1974), pp. 91–109.
8. Richard M. Eaton, 'The Political and Religious Authority of the Shrine of Baba Farid', in Barbara D. Metcalf, (ed.), *Moral Conduct and Authority: the place of Adab in South Asian Islam,* Berkeley 1984, pp. 333–56, reprinted in *India's Islamic Traditions,* pp. 263–284 and idem, *The Rise of Islam and the Bengal Frontier, 1204–1760,* Delhi, 1993, (1997 reprint).
9. See Richard M. Eaton, 'Introduction', in *India's Islamic Traditions,* pp. 25–7. He noted (p. 26): 'In much of thirteenth-century north India, for example, Islam was associated with the ruling ethos of Turkish conquerors, and the earliest Islamic traditions from this period, such as historical chronicles or Sufi literature of the Chishti order, reflect this ethos. But in the fifteenth and sixteenth centuries, when the authority of the Delhi Sultanate was resisted by local landed chiefs—as also occurred in the eighteenth century in an age of Mughal decline—imperial visions of Islam were replaced by more localised perceptions, which might explain the emergence in these periods of regionally based hagiographies pitting local Sufis against Hindu yogis in competitive "spiritual combat".'
10. I am grateful for this formulation to Shail Mayaram, 'Rethinking Meo Identity, Cultural Faultline, Syncretism, Hybridity or Liminality?', *Comparative Studies of South Asia, Africa and the Middle East,* 17 (1997), pp. 35–45.
11. Cynthia Talbot, 'Inscribing the Other, Inscribing the Self: Hindu-Muslim Identities in Pre-colonial India', *Comparative Studies in Society and History,* 37 (1995), pp. 692–722, reprinted in *India's Islamic Traditions,* pp. 83–117.
12. *Comparative Studies in Society and History,* p. 720, *India's Islamic Traditions,* p. 108.
13. Amir Hasan Sijzi, *Fawa'id al-Fu'ad,* (ed.) Khwaja Hasan Sani Nizami, Delhi, 1990, p. 245. The Persian text in this Persian to Urdu translation is a reproduction (including pagination and critical commentary) of M.L. Malik's edition published from Lahore in 1966.
14. Amir Khurd, *Siyar al-Awliya,* ed. Sayyid Mahdi Ghuri, Lahore, Markaz-i tahqiqat-i Farsi Iran wa Pakistan, no. 23, *Mu'assi-yi Intisharat-i Islami,* 1978, pp. 63–4. This edition is exactly the same as the Delhi, Muhib-i Hind Press, 1302/1885 lithograph. The only difference is in the pagination where the table of contents and the introduction has added ten additional pages to the Lahore edition. Thus pp. 63–4 of the Lahore edition are pp. 53–4 of the Delhi one.

15. The *Fawa'id al-Fu'ad* was completed in 1322 and the *Siyar al-Awliya* in circa 1350. The details concerning Jalal al-Din Tabrizi's conflict with Najm al-Din Sughra were elaborated in the early sixteenth-century *tazkirat* of Hamid Fazl Allah Jamali (d. 1536), *Siyar al-'Arifin*, Delhi, 1311/1893, pp. 13, 166–8.
16. Sijzi, *Fawa'id al-Fu'ad*, p. 245.
17. Jamali, *Siyar al-'Arifin*, p. 168.
18. Amir Khurd, *Siyar al-Awliya*, p. 64.
19. To be fair, these binary distinctions are present in Nizam al-Din Awliya's discourses as well. At one point Sijzi cites him mentioning that Sufis were *'ahl-i' ishq'* (people of love) and the Ulama were *'ahl-i' aql'* (people of intellect). See Sijzi, *Fawa'id al-Fu'ad*, p. 226. In his larger narrative, however, the distinctions between the Sufis and 'Ulama were not nearly so simple or clear. The two practices frequently informed each other's beliefs just as an *'alim* could sometimes chose to be a Sufi. For a further development of these ideas, see below. For the conventional historiographical position, from many examples, see K.A. Nizami, *Some Aspects of Religion and Politics in India during the Thirteenth Century*, Delhi, (1961, 1974 reprint) and M. Mujeeb, *The Indian Muslims*, Montreal, 1967.
20. Sijzi, *Fawa'id al-Fu'ad*, pp. 429, 407–8.
21. On Zakariya's strictness about completing the prescribed rituals associated with prayer, *ibid*, p. 391.
22. Note especially the critical letter written by Jalal al-Din Tabrizi to Baha' al-Din Zakariya concerning his conduct as a 'man of the world'. *Ibid*, p. 172.
23. Minhaj-i Siraj Juzjani, *Tabaqat-i Nasiri*, ed. Abdul Hayy Habibi, Kabul, 1963-4, 2 vols., vol. 1, pp. 461 and Sijzi, *Fawa'id al-Fu'ad*, p. 334. See below for a fuller discussion.
24. Sijzi, *Fawa'id al-Fu'ad*, pp. 399–400.
25. Shu'aib ibn Jalal al-Din Maneri, *Manaqib al-Asfiya*, Calcutta, 1895, pp. 121-2, cited by Simon Digby, 'The Sufi Shaikh as a source of Authority in Medieval India', *Purusartha, Islam et Société en Asie du Sud*, 9 (1986), p. 65, reprinted in *India's Islamic Traditions*, p. 245 where Najb al-Din Kubra in the second instance is a typographical error for Najm al-Din Sughra.
26. al-Hujwiri, *Kashf al-Mahjub*, trans. R.A. Nicholson, London, E.J.W. Gibb Memorial Series, vol. 17, 1911 (1976 ed.), p. 213, Amir Khurd, *Siyar al-Awliya*, p. 71, and for a general discussion see Digby, 'Sufi Shaikh as a Source of Authority', *Purusartha*, pp. 62-3, reprinted in *India's Islamic Traditions*, pp 241-2.
27. Compare the efforts to establish continuity between the eleventh and thirteenth centuries by K.A. Nizami, *The Life and Times of Shaikh Farid-ud-Din Ganj-i-Shakar*, Delhi, 1955, (1987 reprint), pp. 10–14, with Digby's efforts to distinguish between the thirteenth and fourteenth centuries, Digby, 'The Sufi Shaikh as a source of Authority in Medieval India', *Purusartha*, p. 64, reprinted in *India's Islamic Traditions*, p. 244.
28. See Sijzi, *Fawa'id al-Fu'ad*, p. 236 where Baba Farid delineates the extent of his *wilayat* from that of Baha' al-Din Zakariya.

29. Mu'in al-Din Chishti is mentioned incidentally in the context of references concerning two of his descendants. Sijzi, *Fawa'id al-Fu'ad*, pp. 76, 405. For the closest recollection of spiritual transmission, see p. 346 and the reference to Qazi Hamid al-Din Nagauri who was reported as a disciple of Mu'in al-Din Chishti and then Qutb al-Din Bakhtiyar Kaki. See also P.M. Currie, *The Shrine and Cult of Mu'in al-Din Chishti of Ajmer*, Delhi, 1989.
30. Bakhtiyar Kaki died in Delhi in 1235, a year before Iltutmish. Jalal al-Din was expelled from Delhi in Iltutmish's reign.
31. The clearest statement suggesting this comes from an anecdote repeated by Nizam al-Din (Sijzi, *Fawa'id al-Fu'ad*, p. 185) which has Jalal al-Din Tabrizi, Qutb al-Din Bakhtiyar Kaki and Baha' al-Din Zakariya present together in Multan during a Mongol onslaught. The rhetorical intention of the anecdote was to underline the authority of the Sufis against the regnant Amir (Qubacha, in this instance) but the contextualisation had to be convincing enough to carry credence.
32. For the early history of the Sultanate see Kumar, *Emergence of the Delhi Sultanate*, and from a slightly different perspective, Jackson, *The Delhi Sultanate*.
33. The discourse of the court chroniclers ignores this challenge. In their narratives, immigrants fleeing from the Mongols flocked to Delhi where they received generous patronage from Sultan Iltutmish. See Juzjani, *Tabaqat-i Nasiri*, vol. 1, pp. 440–1 and 'Isami, *Futuh al-Salatin*, ed. A.S. Usha, Madras, 1940, pp. 114–5. Secondary literature, following the Persian evidence, has assumed that the infusion of skilled manpower only strengthened the Sultanate. See in particular, Irfan Habib, 'An Economic History of the Delhi Sultanate—an Essay in Interpretation', *Indian Historical Review* 4 (1978), pp. 286–303.
34. Jackson, *The Delhi Sultanate*, pp. 87–8, provides a useful description of the limited control of the Delhi monarch, although his usage of 'centre and the provinces' is unable to capture the manner in which the fragments of the state were cohered.
35. See Sunil Kumar, "When Slaves were Nobles: The Shamsi *Bandagan* in the Early Delhi Sultanate", *Studies in History* 10 (1994), pp. 23–52. From a slightly different perspective: Peter Jackson, "The *Mamluk* Institution in Early Muslim India", *Journal of the Royal Asiatic Society*, (1990), pp. 340–58 and Irfan Habib, "Formation of the Sultanate Ruling Class of the Thirteenth Century", in Irfan Habib, (ed.), *Medieval India I: Researches in the History of India, 1200–1750*, Delhi, 1992, pp. 1–21.
36. Fakhr-i Mudabbir, *Ta'rikh-i Fakhral-Din Mubarak Shah*, E.D. Ross (ed.), London, 1927, pp. 43–4.
37. See Kumar, "When Slaves were Nobles".
38. Sijzi, *Fawa'id al-Fu'ad*, pp. 342–3.
39. The education of the medieval *'alim* has attracted little attention. There are several useful texts for the central Islamic lands amongst which see Jonathan Berkey, *The Transmission of Knowledge in Medieval Cairo: a Social History of Islamic Education*, Princeton, 1992 and Michael Chamberlain,

Knowledge and Social Practices in Medieval Damascus, 1190–1350, Cambridge, 1994. An old article of Richard Bulliet, 'A Quantitative Approach to Medieval Muslim Biographical Dictionaries', *Journal of the Economic and Social History of the Orient*, 13 (1970), pp. 195–211 is useful in drawing attention to the perignations in search of knowledge (and trade!) of the medieval *ᶜUlama*. For South Asia, P.M. Currie, *Shrine and Cult of Mu'in al-Din Chishti*, has shown how stories of Mu'in al-Din Chishti's travels accrued over time (see map in the front end-paper). These were akin to the *hajj*, a pious pilgrimage to sites important to the Muslim experience and they enhanced the reputation of the Shaykh who interacted with a legendary number of pious Muslims scattered in distant areas.

40. The small town, *qasba*, of Patiali, for instance did not have a *Qazi* (judge) or a *mudarris* (teacher). The local school was run instead by the calligraphist Sa'd al-Din Muhammad who also functioned as the *Qazi*. Amir Khusrau, *Dibacha-yi Tuhfat al-Sighar*, cited by Wahid Mirza, *Life and Works of Amir Khusrau*, Delhi, 1974, p. 20.
41. Nizam al-Din Awliya's discourses are laced with quotations from the *Hadith* of the Prophet, traditions that he had learnt while training to become a *Qazi*. An anecdote in the *Fawa'id al-Fu'ad*, p. 46, recalls these ambitions of the Sufi and Shaykh Najib al-Din Mutawakkil's admonition to become 'something else'.
42. Marshall Hodgson, *The Venture of Islam: Conscience and History in a World Civilization*, Chicago, 3 vols., 1974, vol. 2, p. 203.
43. But, note for example, the case of the Shansabanids in the late twelfth century (prior to Mongol invasions) and the bitter conflict between the Karramiya and the Shafic's. See Juzjani, *Tabaqat-i Nasiri*, vol. 1, pp. 362-3. The impact of the Mongol invasions leading to the great dispersal and destruction of the Muslim world cast its shadow over these debates already present within the Muslim community.
44. The translator of the text, E.G. Browne (for full references see below) read this phrase as 'injurious to his own pretensions, *da'wi-ra'* which was based on the BM Ms, Or 2,955 and the Tehran lithographed edition (AH 1305). Browne noted (p. 129, fn. 2), however, that 'injurious to the common folk, *cawam-ra'* was the reading in the oldest manuscript, BM Ms, Or. 3,507. I have preferred the reading of the oldest manuscript.
45. Nizami-i Aruzi Samarqandi, *Chahar Maqala*, trans., E.G. Browne, (London: E.J.W. Gibb Memorial Series XI.2, Luzac and Co. 1921, 1978 reprint), p. 129.
46. Ziya' al-Din Barani, *Ta'rikh-i Firuz Shahi*, Sayyid Ahmad Khan (ed.), (Calcutta: Bibliotheca Indica, 1860–2), pp. 41–4; S.A. Rashid (ed.), (Aligarh: Department of History, 1957), pp. 49–52.
47. The Shaykh al-Islam's aphorisms were central in Barani's didactic 'mirror for Princes', *Fatawa-i Jahandari*, ed. A. Salim Khan, (Lahore: Idarah-i Tahqiqat-i Pakistan, #25, 1972), where they were embellished and discussed in length. See Peter Hardy, *Historians of Medieval India*, p. 29 and K.A. Nizami, *Religion and Politics in the Thirteenth Century*, pp. 161-2.
48. Maneri, *Manaqib al-Asfiya*, pp. 121-2, cited in Digby, "Sufi Shaikh as a Source of Authority", *Purusartha*, p. 65, *India's Islamic Traditions*, p. 245.

49. The ambiguity comes from Juzjani, *Tabaqat-i Nasiri,* vol. 1, pp. 461-2 who places the event in his account of Raziyya's reign whereas ['Isami], *Futuh al-Salatin,* p. 122 suggests that it occurred in Iltutmish's reign. It is likely that the event dates to the turbulent months following Iltutmish's death, Rukn al-Din's dethronement and Raziyya's accession, 633–4/1236.
50. Juzjani, *Tabaqat-i Nasiri,* vol. 1, pp. 461–2 and Sijzi, *Fawa'id al-Fu'ad,* p. 334.
51. From many examples, note the example of Baha' al-Din Zakariya in Multan. According to Nizam al-Din Awliya, Zakariya was very strict about completing the required rituals associated with prayer, Sijzi, *Fawa'id al-Fu'ad,* p. 391. While this would suggest a practice closer to the recommendations of the ᶜUlama, Zakariyya disagreed with Qazi Qutb al-Din Kashani over the rituals of prayer and legitimated his practice on the basis of his 'inner light' *(nur-i batin).* Because of this dispute the mystic never returned to the mosque where the Qazi read his *namaz,* Sijzi, pp. 399-400. See also the dispute between Jalal al-Din Tabrizi and Qazi Kamal al-Din Ja'fri in Budaun, *ibid*, pp. 401-2.
52. *Ibid*, pp. 407-8, for the narration of an early dispute in Delhi regarding *sama'* that involved the Sufis Qazi Hamid al-Din Nagauri and Bakhtiyar Kaki and *ibid*, p. 166, for a reference from a slightly later period. Opposition to Qazi Hamid al-Din Nagauri's practice of *sama'* also received a dramatic notice in 'Isami, *Futuh al-Salatin,* pp. 117–120. For a dispute concerning *raqs* in Ajudhan/Pakpattan that touched the 'ulama in Multan as well see the case of Baba Farid and the Qazi of Ajudhan mentioned below: Sijzi, *Fawa'id al-Fu'ad,* p. 166.
53. Juzjani, *Tabaqat-i Nasiri,* vol. 1, p. 466. This event probably took place in the last years of Iltutmish's reign or very shortly after his death because according to Juzjani, in 1242 Ayub resided in Delhi where he had gained the favour of Sultan Mu'izz al-Din Bahram Shah (1240–2) and eventually succeeded in getting Qazi Shams al-Din executed.
54. Sijzi, *Fawa'id al-Fu'ad,* p. 166.
55. Both Juzjani and 'Isami report that the adolescent Iltutmish was promised the throne of Delhi by Sufis. See Juzjani, *Tabaqat-i Nasiri,* vol. 1, p. 442 and 'Isami, *Futuh al-Salatin,* pp. 118–9.
56. It is frequently ignored that Iltutmish seized the throne of Delhi from his master, Qutb al-Din Ai-Beg's, son, Aram Shah (see, for example, Jackson, *The Delhi Sultanate,* p. 29). For the manner in which the details of the event were obscured, see Juzjani, *Tabaqat-i Nasiri,* vol. 1, pp. 418, 443 and Sunil Kumar, 'Service, Status and Military Service in the Delhi Sultanate: Thirteenth and Fourteenth Centuries', in Richard Eaton and Indrani Chatterjee, (ed.), *Slavery and South Asian History,* Bloomington, 2006, pp. 90–7, and idem, *Emergence of the Delhi Sultanate,* Chapter 3.
57. The reservoir is mentioned and described in a number of sources but these do not report Iltutmish's vision of the Prophet instructing the Sultan to construct the *Hauz-i Shamsi* (See, for example, Amir Khusrau, *Qiran al-Sa'dayn,* abridged trans., S.A.A. Rizvi, *Adi Turk Kalin Bharat,* Aligarh, 1956, p. 286, Ibn Battuta, *Rehla,* trans., Mahdi Husain, Baroda, 1953 (1976 reprint), p. 28. The earliest reference that I have found to the story is in Jamali,

Siyar al-'Arifin, p. 25. 'Isami, *Futuh al-Salatin*, p. 118, has an elaborate version of Iltutmish's consecration of the *Hauz-i Shamsi* with the hallowed *zamzam* waters from Mecca.

58. For a discussion of Iltutmish's constructional and epigraphic agenda, see Kumar, *Emergence of the Delhi Sultanate*, Chapter 3 and Sunil Kumar, 'Qutb and Modern Memory', in Suvir Kaul, (ed.), *The Partitions of Memory*, Delhi, 2001, pp. 140–182, reprinted in idem, *The Present in Delhi's Pasts*, Delhi, 2002, pp. 1–61.
59. This is succinctly brought out by Digby, 'Sufi Shaikh as a Source of Authority', *Purusartha*, p. 62; *India's Islamic Traditions*, p. 241.
60. The most influential articulation of this idea was by al-Mawardi, *Ahkam al-Sultaniyah.* See H.A.R. Gibb, 'al-Mawardi's Theory of the Caliphate' and 'Some Considerations on the Sunni Theory of the Caliphate' in H.A.R. Gibb, *Studies on the Civilization of Islam*, (eds.) S.J. Shaw and W.R. Polk, London, 1969, pp. 141–65 and, more generally, Louise Marlow, *Hierarchy and Egalitarianism in Islamic Thought*, Cambridge, 1997.
61. These sentiments are clearly expressed by Baihaqi, the Ghaznavid chronicler, in the context of the Seljuqid threat to the town of Nishapur and Balkh. The Nishapuri residents wondered whether they should resist or submit and were advised by Qazi Sa'id: '...Organizing warfare is not the business of subjects *(ra'iyyat)*. You have a ruler, Amir Mas'ud who has adequate forces. If this province means anything to him at all, he must necessarily send someone and secure his rule here' ...[the example of the Nishapuris was upheld by Mas'ud for the residents of Balkh. The Sultan told them:]... What have subjects to do with war? ...If any ruler proves himself stronger [at a given moment] and demands taxes from you and protects you, you must hand over the taxes and thus save yourselves. Why do you not consider the example of the men of Nishapur and of other cities, who submitted? They acted quite right in doing that, so that no plundering took place'. See C.E. Bosworth, *The Ghaznavids: their Empire in Afghanistan and Eastern Iran, 994–1040*, Beirut, 2nd edition, 1973, p. 253.
62. For an uncritical collation of material regarding the pious qualities of Sultan Iltutmish, see K.A. Nizami, 'Religious Life and Leanings of Iltutmish' in *Studies in Medieval Indian History and Culture*, Allahabad, 1966, pp. 13–40. On 'Ala' al-Din Khalaji, see the depiction of Ziya' al-Din Barani analyzed in Sunil Kumar, 'Assertions of Authority: a Study of the Discursive Statements of two Sultans of Delhi', in Muzaffar Alam, Françoise 'Nalini' Delvoye, Marc Gaborieau, (ed.), *The Making of Indo-Persian Culture*, Delhi, 2000, pp. 37–65. More generally, see Peter Hardy, *Historians of Medieval India*.
63. See Muzaffar Alam, "Shari'a and Governance in the Indo-Islamic Context" in David Gilmartin and Bruce B. Lawrence, *Beyond Turk and Hindu*, Florida, 2000, pp. 216–245 and his, "*Akhlaqi* Norms and Mughal Governance" in *Making of Indo-Persian Culture*, pp. 67–95.
64. For a discussion of the juridical position of 'Hindus' as 'people of the book' see Jackson, *The Delhi Sultanate*, pp. 281–7.
65. A useful analysis of Ghaznavid renditions of Mahmud's Somnath expedition is now available in Richard Davis, *Lives of Indian Images*, Delhi,

1997 (Indian reprint 1999), pp. 88–112, 186–220 and Romila Thapar, *Narratives and the Making of History: Two Lectures*, Delhi, 2000, pp. 24–50.
66. Juzjani, *Tabaqat-i Nasiri*, vol. 2, p. 76.
67. Zahir al-Din Muhammad Babur, *Babur-Nama*, trans. A.S. Beveridge, New Delhi, 1921-2 (1989 reprint, 2 vols.), Vol. 2, pp. 553–6.
68. Tara Chand, *Influence of Islam on Indian Culture*, Allahabad, 1976, K.A. Nizami, *Religion and Politics in the Thirteenth Century*.
69. Compare the approach of Jackson, *The Delhi Sultanate*, with Shantanu Phukan, ' "Through throats where many rivers meet": the Ecology of Hindi in the world of Persian', *Indian Economic and Social History Review*, 38 (2001), pp. 33–58.
70. Eaton, *Islam and the Bengal Frontier*; idem, ed., *India's Islamic Traditions*. Much anthropological work that studies the 'folk-technology' of Islam rooted in its local modern South Asian contexts has also remarked upon the distance of this 'lived Islam' from textual praxis. See Veena Das, 'For a Folk-technology and Theological Anthropology of Islam', *Contributions to Indian Sociology*, 18 (1984), pp. 293–300. Shahid Amin's recent work on the histories of Ghazi Miyan is far more nuanced in attempting to develop the historical and political dialectical processes of these belief systems. See Shahid Amin, 'On Retelling the Muslim Conquest of North India', in Partha Chatterjee and Anjan Ghosh, ed., *History and the Present*, Delhi, 2002, pp. 24–43.

Chapter 7

On Islam and *Kufr* in the Delhi Sultanate: Towards a Re-interpretation of Ziya' al-Din Barani's *Fatawa-i Jahandari**

Raziuddin Aquil

This paper is part of an attempt to examine the diverse representations of non-Muslims, often condemned as *kafirs* (infidels),[1] in medieval Indian Islamic literature, including court chronicles, Sufi texts and literary compositions. The divergent images of non-Muslims in the sources reflect the attitudes of various Muslim groups such as the rulers (including the *umara*), *'ulama* or religious scholars, Sufis and the poets towards them, which may be located in the historical processes of the period. The aim of this paper is limited to the study of the views expressed by one author—Khwaja Ziya' al-Din Barani—in one text—the *Fatawa-i Jahandari*. Though recognising the possibilities of analytical gains that may be derived from what Stuart Hall calls the 'conundrums of theory' in Cultural Studies,[2] we shall prefer to locate such depictions in the formation of ideas about Muslims and non-Muslims in classical Islamic political thought. The aim is to make sense of the problems and put them in perspective, as our author Barani himself has adapted his ideas from the 'grand tradition' of Islam, which was informed by the Qur'an, Traditions of the Prophet, practices of the rightly-guided caliphs, and the attempts by the early Muslim jurists and political thinkers to address a variety of issues emerging in different times and locations.

Contrary to the established position, I would like to think that Barani's *Fatawa-i Jahandari* is not exactly a typical example of what is referred to as the 'Mirror for Princes' literature. This is at least for three reasons: First, the views expressed by Barani in the *Fatawa* are not merely abstract, normative ideas, even though parallels can be drawn from the works of classical Islamic political theory, some of which was known to him. The writer has all along located his position in, and compared and contrasted with what was happening in the Delhi Sultanate. Second, the opinion expressed by him on many issues, for instance, the status of non-Muslims in the Sultanate are to be found scattered all over the pages of the *Tarikh-i Firuz Shahi*. It is possible that the author himself or somebody else extracted and put together Barani's views in the form of *nasihats* or counsels attributing many passages to Sultan Mahmud of Ghazna and others for greater acceptability. This is not exceptional for Barani, as the extant versions of the *Tarikh-i Firuz Shahi* also contain many passages attributed to some well-known figures. In fact, in the Introduction to his *Tarikh-i Firuz Shahi*, Barani himself writes: 'If readers peruse this compilation as a mere history, they will find recorded in it the actions of great sultans and nobles; if they search in it the rules of administration and the means of enforcing obedience, even in that respect it will not be found deficient; if they looked for warnings and admonitions to the rulers, that is also very well elucidated'.[3] Third, the tone of the views expressed in the *Tarikh* is not very different from that of the *Fatawa*. Indeed at several places, the language of Barani's *Tarikh* is harsher than the one in his *Fatawa*. All these can perhaps help us resolve the question as to why the *Tarikh* was frequently mentioned by early Muslim writers, whereas they are silent about the *Fatawa*. It may also be clarified that an inter-textual comparison of Barani's writings should not necessarily take away the beauty of the *Tarikh* as a Persian classic.

The Background

Courtier-turned historian and political theorist of the Delhi Sultanate, Khwaja Ziya' al-Din Barani belonged to a family which was known for its association with the sultans of Delhi at least from the latter half of the thirteenth century.[4] His maternal grandfather, Husam al-Din was appointed as the governor of Lakhnauti, the stronghold of Muslims in Bengal, by Sultan Ghiyas al-Din Balban (r. 1266–87). His father Mu'ayyid al-Mulk was administrator of Baran in the first year of the reign of 'Ala' al-Din Khalji (r. 1296–1316).[5] His paternal uncle Malik 'Ala' al-Mulk was *kotwal* of Delhi and a prominent counsellor of 'Ala'-ud-Din Khalji. With this kind of background Barani was able to move around Delhi's ruling circle, was known to be an entertaining conversationalist and friend of poets and courtiers, Amir Khusrau and Amir Hasan, and probably through them became close to the leading Chishti Sufi of the capital, Nizam al-Din Auliya. Though apparently a late starter in Sultanate government service, Barani went on to be a *nadim* or boon companion of Muhammad Tughluq (r. 1325–51) for nearly eighteen years.[6] It may also be important to keep in mind that as a prince Muhammad Tughluq was a disciple of Nizam al-Din. According to the

Chishti tradition, the latter had predicted bestowal of kingship to the prince shortly before his death in 1325.[7] The sultan's reign was full of turmoil and as a boon companion Barani must have keenly observed the turn of events even though he was unable to exert much influence on the ruler.

At the beginning of the reign of Firuz Shah Tughluq (r. 1351–88), Barani was banished from court and imprisoned in the fortress of Pahtez (Bhatnir). He was possibly associated with the attempt of Khwaja Jahan Ahmad 'Ayaz to place a minor son of Muhammad Tughluq on the throne soon after the death of the sultan during the expedition against Thatta in Sind.[8] Though he was released from prison subsequently, Barani reportedly spent the remaining years of his life in a miserable condition. At the time of his imprisonment, he was nearly seventy years old (according to the lunar calendar). Yet he used the free time to emerge in a new avatar as a writer and went on to produce several books, including *Sana-i Muhammadi* (or *Na't-i Muhammadi*), *Salat-i Kabir*, *'Inayatnama Ilahi*, *Ma'asir Sadat*, *Tarikh-i Firuzshahi*, *Hasratnama*, *Tarikh-i Al-i Barmak* or *Akhbar-i Barmakiyan* and *Fatawa-i Jahandari*. Some of these have survived.

Modern, 'secular' historians have been very critical of Barani for his provocative views on many issues, which, according to them, smack of 'communalism'. Even in the most balanced and serious writings, Barani is condemned as a 'fanatic' or 'bigot'. The communalists and other vested interests, on the other hand, have tried to misuse his writings for their own agenda. Notwithstanding the interest in Barani's works, no matter from whatever perspective one was trying to read them, the author still awaits a modern biographer. The only serious attempt in this connection is by Mohammad Habib. However, Habib's strong commitment to secularism prevented him from appreciating the career and views of this courtier and intellectual in his own context. Also, it was his ire against the partisan scholarship of British administrators and their constant projection of medieval India as a period of Muslim oppression from which British colonialism had delivered (Hindu) Indians that animated Habib's formidable scholarship.[9] Accordingly, Barani's views on the ideal Muslim polity and the position of non-Muslims and people from non-aristocratic background in the Sultanate came in for sharp criticism from Habib. His account of Barani's life is full of disparaging remarks about the author. An attempt has been made not only to chastise Barani, but also to completely sanitise his understanding of Islam. Habib has, however, given sufficient illustrations from Barani's writings to prove his 'fanaticism'.

In his Introduction to *The Political Theory of the Delhi Sultanate*, incorporating portions of translation from *Fatawa-i Jahandari* by Afsar

Umar Salim Khan, Mohammad Habib does not think highly of Barani as an author. According to him, the cynical and frustrated old man could write on the basis of his memory, could translate, write a book of his own on the basis of the work of another writer, or he could put in logical order the ideas that had been developing in his mind over a period of time. But, Habib firmly believed, Barani was not capable of undertaking any investigation or research.[10] The question of how Barani could write two of the 'greatest works' of the Sultanate period, *Fatawa-i Jahandari* and *Tarikh-i Firuz Shahi*, is not adequately resolved. (Scholars of Persian language also claim that the language of the *Tarikh* is excellent). Habib further notes that there may have been three reasons for this impoverished person to turn to writing: (a) to gain recognition from Firuz Shah Tughluq and his nobles; (b) to achieve salvation; and (c) for the guidance of the future generations of the high-born Muslims. Habib's conclusions in this connection are cryptic: Barani had failed in his first mission, but probably succeeded in the second and the interest in his writings even after six hundred years shows that he was at least successful in his third objective of guiding the *ashraf* or the Muslim elite.[11]

Habib also notes that Barani was an unparalleled recorder of contemporary events, which is proved by the 'excellence' of the *Tarikh-i Firuz Shahi*. (Habib seems to ignore the fact that the *Tarikh* is a work of history and not merely a record of contemporary events). He was a good scholar of Arabic and knew the main events of the period of the Prophet and the 'rightly-guided' caliphs. But in Habib's opinion, 'of the rest of Islamic history he knew little and what he knew was all wrong'. In the Introduction to his *Tarikh-i Firuz Shahi*, Barani refers to some books (characterised by Habib as 'bogus') and also to the works of the following well-known writers—Tabari, 'Utbi, Baihaqi, Firdausi and Minhaj al-Siraj. In Habib's judgment, 'Barani had either never read the works of these authors in the original or else had completely forgotten them. The former alternative is more probable', that is, Barani was lying. This remark is unjust as it not only casts doubts on Barani's credentials, but also devalues his writings.

By contrast, the method adopted by the author in writing the *Tarikh-i Firuz Shahi* may be taken into account. Barani has himself noted that he had planned to write a general history, beginning with Adam and his two sons, but when he recalled the value of that 'marvelous' work, *Tabaqat-i Nasiri* of Minhaj al-Din Siraj Juzjani, he realised that those who have read Juzjani's history will derive no advantage from reading his (Barani's) book. On the contrary, if he tried to amplify or abridge the narrative of that illustrious and venerable religious leader and scholar, it might be considered disrespectful and rash, besides creating doubts and difficulties in the minds of the readers. He therefore decided to concentrate on the history of the later sultans of Delhi from the point where *Tabaqat-i Nasiri* left it, that is, from the reign of Ghiyas al-Din Balban.[12]

Further, for Habib, the works referred to in *Fatawa-i Jahandari* 'were either cheap and worthless fabrications, which have not survived to our days or else existed only in the imagination of our author'.[13] Habib laments that it is on the basis of his acquaintance with the bogus, fabricated literature of the Delhi Sultanate that Barani claims himself to be a historian: The *Historical Illustrations* in the *Jahandari* are sufficient proof of this. Barani's ignorance of history is appalling even with reference to the basic authorities available in the Delhi of his days. In making such a statement, Habib ignores the citation of a number of standard works, besides the Qur'an and Traditions of the Prophet. Not satisfied with the alleged ignorance of Barani concerning the history of classical Islam, Habib has added that the writer's ignorance of geography is even more shocking.[14]

Habib also questions Barani's understanding of the Sultanate polity. According to him, the author's 'application of the principle of contradiction to monarchy is unfortunate. After condemning monarchy as un-Islamic and sending kings to Hell-fire, he goes to the opposite extreme and makes the king a partner in "the contradictory qualities of God" and declares him to be God's "deputy" and "agent". No educated contemporaries of Barani would have seriously agreed with this assertion'.[15] This remark is surprising because the concept of the sultan as the shadow of God had already been in wide currency in medieval Islamic political thought. The writings of the mystically-inclined theologian Imam Ghazali[16] and the Saljuqid *wazir* and noted political theorist Nizam al-Mulk Tusi[17] may be mentioned here. But then the trouble is that Habib is very dismissive of Nizam al-Mulk, who is condemned as a Sunni fanatic, again, with 'little regard for historic truths'.[18] Moreover, Barani's friend and senior colleague, Amir Khusrau has also called 'Ala al-Din Khalji the shadow of God on earth in his *Khaza'in ul-Futuh*. In his translation of the work, Habib plays down the symbolic significance of the use of the expression by mentioning in a note that the 'sultan was styled the "Shadow of God" (*Zillullah*)'.[19]

Further, representing the interest of the high-born Muslim elite,[20] Barani was against the low-born.[21] He noted that the merits and demerits of men were apportioned at the beginning of time and allotted to their soul.[22] He opposed the idea of educating the low-born and giving them important positions in the Sultanate. Barani particularly hated the traders, who were counted as lowly creatures. Habib trivialises Barani's views by remarking that the shopkeepers may 'have refused to supply him commodities on credit!'[23] For Barani piety was the attribute of the high-born. If a man is pious, there must have been some elements of aristocracy among his ancestors. However, if his low birth is proved, then his piety is a mere pretence. In Habib's opinion, another expression of the same attitude is Barani's condemnation of persons who had accepted Islam through personal 'free-choice'. Habib concludes that for Barani 'Islam, like good wine, must have matured in the muscles and tendons of a man's ancestors; to be spiritually effective, Islam must be hereditary'.[24]

Habib further writes that God had denied to Barani the virtues of charity, tolerance and forgiveness; he hated and hated intensely and considered his hatred a virtue. Among the Muslims his hatred was directed against philosophers, scientists, heretics, all low-born Muslims and particularly those who had risen to occupy high offices.[25] Concerning Barani's attitude towards non-Muslims, Habib comments: 'He hated all non-Muslims and particularly the Hindus, and in order to justify "an all-out war against Hinduism", which the kings refused to undertake, he even misrepresented the doctrines of Imam Shafi'i', the founder of one of the four schools of Sunni jurisprudence (*mazahib*). Habib portrays Barani as having really gone mad. He writes that as the author was unable 'to abuse those who had injured him personally, he found a spiritual consolation in cursing those who had done no harm'.[26]

Habib does not think that Barani's connections with some influential Sufis of Delhi was of any use. He writes that though the author was a disciple of Nizam al-Din Auliya and 'claimed to be an intimate friend of Amir Khusrau and Amir Hasan, the teachings of the great shaikh and the mystic literature of the day had not touched even the periphery of his soul'. Habib further notes that Barani's conception of Islam was formal, mechanistic and earthy. For Habib, Barani was a complete stranger to the spiritual elements of Muslim life and must not be considered a representative of contemporary Muslim religion and culture.[27]

Habib's position may be compared with the account of Barani's career in the fundamental Chishti text of the Delhi Sultanate, the *Siyar al-Auliya* of Amir Khwurd. The author has included Barani's life amongst the prominent disciples of Nizam al-Din Auliya, the leading Chishti saint of Delhi. He noted that Khwaja Ziya' al-Din Barani was unrivalled in grace, pleasing to the spiritual minded and was admired by both the noblemen and the common people. He was full of wit and humour and at every gathering in which he was present, he stole the show with his soul-refreshing words. He had a great collection of humorous stories and anecdotes (*majma' al-lata'if wa jawama' al-hikayat*). He had the good fortune of being in the company of the *'ulama*, Sufis and poets.[28] This was facilitated by his father, who belonged to a noble family. He was blessed with the discipleship of Sultan al-Masha'ikh, that is, Nizam-ud-Din Auliya, settled down at Ghiyaspur (where the shaykh's hospice was located) and obtained a position of status and nearness to the shaykh as he himself noted in his *Hasratnama*.[29]

Amir Khwurd also records that owing to his elegant mind, Barani, later on, had no equal as a boon companion of Muhammad Tughluq and achieved high status in the court. This is despite the fact that the world around him was full of fraudulent, deceitful and faithless elements. As a septuagenarian, Barani retired from active political career. He received an allowance from Firuz Shah Tughluq for his creature comforts and devoted himself to writing his unrivalled books, which include *Sana-i Muhammadi*, *Salat-i Kabir*, *'Inayat Nama-i Ilahi*, *Ma'asir-i Sada'at*, and *Tarikh-i Firuz Shahi*.[30] It may be pointed out that Amir Khwurd has not included *Fatawa-i Jahandari* and some other titles in his list of Barani's works.

Amir Khwurd goes on to add that this saintly person (*buzurg*) spent much of his time in the company of the sultan of poets Amir Khusrau and the chief of scholars Amir Hasan (who had compiled *Fawa'id ul-Fu'ad*, an authoritative collection of Nizam al-Din's *malfuzat* or utterances) and obtained great benefits from them.[31] Mohammad Habib translates the word *buzurg* as 'gentleman'.[32] This does not appear to be an accurate rendering of the word as originally used by Amir Khwurd in his work. The author has also used the words Khwaja (lit. a man of distinction, teacher, preceptor, lord, master) and Maulana (a Muslim religious scholar) to address Barani. A Sufi who was given permission to enroll disciples in a particular *silsila* (brotherhood) was called a shaykh. As Habib has himself noted, if the shaykh were a *sayyid* or descendent of the Prophet, he could be referred to as Khwaja.[33] (This suggestion needs substantiation). The Chishtis addressed themselves as Khwajagan. Further, the *Siyar al-Auliya* is devoted to saintly figures associated with the Chishti order and the chapter in which Barani's *tazkira* or biographical note is included is focused on the leading disciples of Nizam al-Din Auliya, though many of whom, including Barani, Amir Khusrau and Amir Hasan, were successful as courtiers as well.[34] Amir Khwurd further notes that in addition to the above-mentioned merits, the love for the descendents of the Prophet was firmly rooted in Barani's heart (This statement indicates he was not a *Sayyid*, though he mentions in the *Tarikh-i Firuz Shahi* that his grandmother was a 'pure' *Sayyid*). Eventually, after a short illness Barani departed from this world to the next like a lover of God (*mardana wa ashiqana*). At the time of his death, there was no *dang* or *daram* with him. He had even distributed his clothes to the extent that his dead body was lying on a gunny-bag (*boriya*) and was covered with a piece of cloth.[35] Thus, according to Amir Khwurd, the influence on him of the company of Sultan al-Masha'ikh Nizam al-Din Auliya ultimately dominated over that of the kings. His end was good as he left this world in poverty (a Sufi ideal). He was buried in the tomb complex of Nizam al-Din Auliya at the foot of the grave of his noble father.[36]

Elsewhere in *Siyar al-Auliya*, Amir Khwurd has also drawn on Maulana Ziya' al-Din Barani's account, in his *Hasratnama*, of Nizam al-Din Auliya's reaction over the *mahzar* or judicial inquest at Ghiyas al-Din Tughluq's court over the legitimacy of the shaykh's practice of listening to music (*sama'*).[37] Barani had reportedly noted that after his return from the *mahzar* the shaykh called him along with Maulana Muhy al-Din Kashani and Amir Khusrau and lamented the disregard for the tradition of the Prophet by the Hanafite 'ulama of the capital city of Delhi and cursed them.[38] It is important to note here that the shaykh had defended *sama'* in the light of a tradition of the Prophet which is not taken into account by the Hanafites in their condemnation of music. In doing this, Nizam al-Din followed, according to Amir Khwurd, Imam Shafi'i's interpretation, which considered music as lawful (*mubah*) even when accompanied with instruments.[39] This reference to Imam Shafi'i is important as Barani also refers to the jurist's position concerning the status of non-Muslims in Islam in the *Fatawa-i Jahandari*. Thus, unlike the official 'ulama of the Delhi Sultanate who called for a blind following (*taqlid*) of Imam Abu Hanifa, the Chishtis and the larger circle of their followers were much more eclectic in their attitude towards the four schools of Sunni jurisprudence. In certain situations, they may not have refrained from borrowing a saying of fourth caliph Hazrat 'Ali, cousin and son-in-law of the Prophet, or from the Shi'ite-Ja'fri interpretation of Islam.

Thus, the condemnation of Barani in modern scholarship as a fanatic *'alim* or theologian needs to be reconsidered. His contemporaries counted him amongst the close disciples of Nizam al-Din Auliya. This is also testified by his burial in the compound of the grave of the 'great' shaykh, along with his other friends and companions, including Amir Khusrau. Sufi memory continued to view Barani's association with Nizam al-Din with respect, even veneration. 'Abdul Haqq Muhaddis Dehlawi has included Barani's life in his *Akhbar al-Akhyar*, considered to be the most authoritative collection of biographies of Muslim holy men in medieval India. 'Abdul Haqq notes that Barani, the author of *Tarikh-i Firuz Shahi*, was a disciple of Nizam al-Din Auliya. The compiler then goes on to summarise Amir Khwurd's account of Barani's attributes and career. He however differs a little from Amir Khwurd to note that he was buried at the foot of the grave of his mother at Nizam al-Din shrine complex.[40] This indicates that both of his parents were buried there, further confirming the family's proximity to Nizam al-Din, as not everybody could be interned there. 'Abdul Haqq then goes on to quote a lengthy account from *Hasratnama*, citing *Siyar al-Auliya*, of why Nizam al-Din had opened the gate of discipleship for the common people, unlike other shaykhs who were very choosy about it.[41] Ziya' al-Din Barani's reference again occurs in the next entry in *Akhbar al-Akhyar* on Khwaja Ziya Nakhshabi. 'Abdul Haqq records that it was said that during the time of Nizam al-Din Auliya there were three persons whose name was Ziya. First was Ziya Sanai, who was an opponent of the saint. Second, Ziya Barani, a disciple and faithful friend of the shaykh. Third, Ziya Nakhshabi, the author of a number of works including *Silk al-Suluk* and *Tutinama*, was neither an antagonist, nor a follower.[42] The above examples should guard us against the misconception that Barani was a lonely, fanatic *'alim* and that his utterances are not important for understanding the fourteenth-century Muslim attitude towards non-Muslims. Even if Barani was exceptional in taking an extreme position, it will be worthwhile to consider his ideas rather than dismiss them altogether.

Before we move forward, it would be pertinent to point out the method adopted by Habib and Afsar Umar Salim Khan in translating the *Fatawa-i Jahandari*. Habib himself informs us in the Introduction that the translation was done keeping in mind the following: (i) Barani's long historical illustrations, unless relevant to the main theme, 'were to be drastically summarised'; (ii) repetitions were to be ignored; (iii) expletives which Barani repeats were to be translated only once or twice, but it was to be indicated clearly that such abuses were habitual (One cannot identify any vulgar words as the narrative is completely sanitised, some adjectives remain despite the censor); (iv) unnecessary adjectives were to be eliminated wherever possible; (v) Barani's confused arguments were to be restructured in logical form; (vi) where Barani's discussion was long and tiresome, it was to be summarised within square brackets; (vii) and finally, translation was to be made as readable as possible and an attempt was to be made to give it 'the strength' which Barani would have certainly given to the original had he written it eight or ten years earlier.[43] One wonders what the theorists of translation have to say about such a subversion of the text. Habib, however, claims that the project was undertaken 'while remaining sternly faithful to the original'.[44]

The end product then is not exactly a translation of *Fatawa-i Jahandari* as visualised by Barani, but a *Political Theory of the Delhi Sultanate* as conceived by Habib himself with Barani serving as a whipping boy. The entire project at times gives a bizarre picture with

Habib highlighting those of Barani's passages he likes, often stopping his narrative, deleting paragraphs and writing his own views on the subject under discussion within the text. Sometimes Habib's initial 'H' is there at the end of the paragraph to know who is the author. (Nineteenth-century colonial administrator-scholars did the same while working with such 'Oriental' texts. Habib clearly followed their style to counter their readings). To give an example of the method adopted by the learned scholar, Barani's reference to Sultan Mahmud's two unfulfilled dreams may be mentioned here. Instead of the direct translation, Habib gives his own interpretation. According to Barani, Mahmud's first project was to capture the Abbasid capital city of Baghdad and remove the rampant heresy there by slaughtering the philosophers, heretics and opponents of the *shari'at* or Muslim law. Habib intervenes to point out that this information is not historically correct and that Baghdad was no longer a centre of innovations in the field of religion during the time of Mahmud. The sultan's second wish was to attack Hindustan again to eliminate Hindu religion completely. Barani thought that Mahmud commanded enough military power to invade Hindustan with the purpose of putting to sword some two or three lakh Brahmins, who had kept the traditions of infidelity on this vast land alive. He would then have given the rest of the Hindus the option of death or Islam, as recommended in Shafi'i Islam practised by Mahmud. Habib interrupts to note that 'There was no point in translating and re-translating Barani's fanatical words. On the matter of the Hindus, Barani was mentally unsound'. Habib has also asserted that Imam Shafi'i's views on Muslims and non-Muslims were diametrically opposed to those of Barani's. The jurist believed in freedom of peaceful religious preaching based on the Prophet's practice following the Treaty of Hudaibiya.[45]

Clearly, there is a need to go back to the *Fatawa-i Jahandari* again for Barani's views on the *kafirs*/Hindus. Barani's career, in general, also needs a careful study. In this regard, it might be useful to keep in mind not only the writer's family background and the political context of the Delhi Sultanate, but also his connection with the Sufi fraternity of Delhi. Though Habib's formulations, which are fraught with problems as we saw above, continue to dominate existing scholarship on Ziya' al-Din Barani, there have been some attempts to evaluate him as a historian[46] and to interpret his ideas on norms of governance.[47] The next section of this paper aims to reconsider the author's views on non-Muslims as delineated in his *Fatawa*, which may be compared and contrasted with those of his contemporaries as also, in a measure, the theorists of classical Islam.

Islam and Infidelity

Barani addressed the sultans in his *Fatawa-i Jahandari*: Sons of Mahmud and sultans of the Muslim world should know that the activities of the ruler were not merely limited to satisfying physical requirements. His responsibilities include governance, which makes him share the attributes of God. The ruler's salvation and spiritual progress is not possible unless he takes appropriate measures leading to the establishment of truth at the centre and enhancement of the status and honour of the religion of the Prophet.[48] The ruler should also know that the establishment of truth at the centre doesn't mean that falsehood is completely wiped off and truth prevailed in the kingdom. God Himself states: everything is created in pairs. That is, every created thing has an opposite: truth/falsehood, peace/violence, virtue/evil, piety/sin and submission/rebellion. To substantiate this further, Barani gives some other examples of dyadic creations: night/day, light/darkness, earth/sky, religiosity/heresy and theism/polytheism.[49]

The above examples serve to illustrate that the establishment of truth does not mean that falsehood is completely overthrown. In Barani's opinion, even if all the prophets and Muslim sultans had worked in tandem to liquidate and eliminate falsehood, which includes infidelity (*kufr*), anarchy, sin and wickedness, so that only truth (Islam, peace, obedience and virtue) prevailed in the world, they will not succeed. It is beyond the limits of imagination that the world is free from sinners and infidels. The evil must survive, as Islam distinguishes itself with the existence of infidelity and devotion for God comes to the fore in contrast to idol-worship. So, the distinction between truth and falsehood, Islam and infidelity, and every other thing is identified with reference to its opposite. Further, falsehood, which denotes wickedness, infidelity, idol-worship, anarchy, and sin were deliberately created to make the truth intelligible.[50] Thus, for Barani, difference, though tolerated/despised, must be highlighted to establish superiority/domination.[51]

Further, difference and indifference, hostility and toleration can coexist in a diverse, multi-cultural society. There may not be bloodshed all the time.[52] Early Muslim settlers of the Delhi Sultanate seemingly deployed a number of strategies. Whereas some confrontationist *'ulama* wanted the Hindus to choose between the options: Islam or death, the attitudes of the Sufis, who straddled many worlds, reveal their insularity, angry silences, critical appreciations, and argumentative or combative stance depending upon the context and their own temperament.[53] Our author Barani chose to take on the 'other' by thoroughly condemning it even as he lacked power to check or subdue it altogether.

Barani reiterated that the teachings of the prophets and the power and authority of the Muslim sultans couldn't remove the evil completely, as human nature comprises contradictory features. It is full of praiseworthy elements as well as meanness. On the day of creation itself, God had registered the deeds of those who were supposed to follow the path of Islam or infidelity. The binaries include virtue/wickedness, guidance/error and obedience/sinfulness. Thus, according to Barani, it is impossible to think of complete eradication of the evil. The real meaning of the establishment of truth is to ensure that truth overpowers falsehood so that polytheism and infidelity are humiliated and disgraced and the triumph of Truth of Islam is vindicated.[54]

Barani believed that a well-meaning sultan could use his power and authority and the support of his well-wishers and followers to suppress the sinners and criminals and establish the supremacy of Islam. He could ensure that the Sayyids, religious scholars, Sufis, saintly Muslims, ascetics, recluses and the devotees of God attain eminence, honour and distinction. Compare this with Barani's master images of the 'other': ignorant, mischievous, faithless, shameless, and those slack in praying to God. All of them were to be downgraded, despised and humiliated. Barani further added that under a just Sultan, the holy-warriors participating in *jihad* and campaigns were stimulated with the desire to achieve martyrdom. The religious people and the protectors of the faith achieved higher status and positions, while those with bad intentions, bad faith and bad religion, founders of innovations and enemies of faith became contemptible, destitute, worthless and of no account. The good deeds of the faith were established and those who had no respect for the *shari'at* were suppressed.[55]

Further, Barani appreciates, under a just sultan, God-fearing and honest officers are promoted, while the cheats and swindlers are dismissed. High-born people belonging to established families are given positions of power and lowly creatures are ignored. Hypocrisy, jealousy, evil speaking and ill-will are scratched out from the minds of the people and virtues occupy its place. Mosques, schools, *khanqahs* or Sufi hospices and feasting places for the poor flourish. On account of the laws of the *shari'at* and the punishments meted out by the sultans, all those things which smack of injustice are prohibited, disapproved and rejected by the people and ultimately the prevalence of rampant sins is replaced with all-round respect for religion.[56]

Barani goes on to suggest that the Muslim sultan cannot establish the supremacy of Islam in Hindustan unless he makes concerted efforts to overthrow infidelity and destroy its leaders, called Brahmins. He should make a firm resolve to overpower, capture, enslave and degrade the infidels. The full strength of the sultan and the warriors of Islam should be devoted to religious campaigns and *jihad*. They should put their lives on stake during the campaigns so that the faith succeeds in uprooting false creeds. Thereafter, it will appear as if false beliefs never existed, because their magic or glamour will have been destroyed. On the other hand, if the Muslim sultan, despite all the power and position that God has granted to him, is satisfied with the collection of taxes like *jizya* and *kharaj* from the Hindus and allows the infidels and infidelity to exist and avoids taking risks to destroy it, then in such a situation there will be hardly any difference between the sultans of Islam and the chiefs of the infidels. This is because even the *kafir* rulers who share the false religion of the Hindus collect the taxes and fill up their treasury. In fact, they collect a hundred times more taxes.[57] Barani must also have been aware of the fact that practical considerations prevented the collection of the *jizya* on a regular basis. The concept seemingly lost its specific legal sense during the Sultanate period and was used as a general tax or tribute.[58]

Further, if the sultans of Islam, despite their royal power and authority are contented with letting the infidels and infidelity continue in lieu of the payment of *jizya* and *kharaj* then how could the tradition of the Prophet be implemented which says: I have been directed by God to fight wars with those who do not conform to the Truth, that is, 'There is no God, but Allah'. Once they testify to this, their lives and property are protected in accordance with the laws of Islam.[59] Barani reiterates that the purpose behind sending one lakh twenty-four thousand prophets was to eliminate the infidels and infidelity and this has been the objective of the sultans of ancient and recent past. Since Prophet Muhammad was the seal of the prophets, the liquidation of infidelity through the teachings of the prophets is no longer possible. The only way the infidels and polytheists can be overthrown and disgraced is by the sultan deploying all his might with necessary preparations, so that the supremacy of Islam is established and heavenly blessings procured.[60]

It would be inaccurate to say that Barani was unique in speaking in such a language. His contemporary and near-contemporary authors like Sayyid 'Ali Hamadani and Fakhr-i Mudabbir also offer similar formulations. Much of the views expressed in these works appear canonical in the sense that, in many cases, they are attributed to the second rightly guided caliph 'Umar ibn al-Khattab. Indeed, classical Islam had already formulated the status of the *Ahl-i Kitab* or the *zimmis*[61] in an Islamic dominion. The *zimmi* is defined as against the Muslim and the idolater (*kafir*). Originally only Jews and Christians were involved. Subsequently, it became necessary to consider Zoroastrians, a number of minor faiths in Central Asia and the Hindus in the subcontinent. The inhabitants of India were treated as *zimmis*, though classical Qur'anic exegesis did not regard them as *Ahl-i Kitab* or the

People of the Book. This expansion of the concept entailed a compromise with idolatry that was not acceptable to all the schools of jurisprudence (*mazahib*). The Shafi'i and Hanbali jurists (*fuqaha*) counted only Jews, Christians and Zoroastrians as *zimmis*. On the other hand, the Malikites and the Hanafites included among them all non-Muslims (even idolaters) who were not Arabs or apostates (*murtad*). The preponderant Hanafite position enabled medieval Indian rulers to legally justify a tolerant policy or attitude towards the Hindus. Significantly, the decision to categorise Indian idolaters as *zimmis* is attributed to Muhammad bin Qasim, the early eighth-century Arab conqueror of Sindh, who had reportedly stated that the idol-temples of the Hindus were similar to the churches of the Christians, synagogues of the Jews and fire-temples of the Zoroastrians. Despite occasional demands for strict regulations, the status of the Hindus as *zimmis* was not questioned in a serious way.[62] Yet, the 'virtual consensus' on the legal standing of the Hindus did not preclude the emergence of great variations in Muslim attitudes towards them in a more general sense. These attitudes range from 'utmost hostility to almost total acceptance of Hindu religious beliefs'.[63]

Further, it would be important to keep in mind the fact that the evolution of ideas in this regard in classical Islamic thought has shown two aspects at once different and interdependent. On the one hand are the doctrinaires, found mainly among the jurists and the judges, who have interpreted the regulations in a restrictive way seeking to develop a programme which, if not one of persecution, is at least vexatious and repressive. From time to time a sovereign, either through Islamic zeal or through the need for popularity amongst Muslims, ordained measures to the doctrinaires' satisfaction. Sometimes, also, there were outbursts of popular anger against the *zimmis*, which in some cases arose from the places occupied by them in the higher ranks of administration, especially that of finance. Several examples can be given in the medieval Indian context of the articulation of such protests, for instance, by Barani, 'Abdul Quddus Gangohi, 'Abdul Qadir Badauni and Shaykh Ahmad Sarhindi. But indeed, on the other hand, current practice fell very much short of the programme of the purists, which was hardly ever implemented. Moreover, the different schools of jurisprudence are not all in agreement and some of them reiterate rules without any practical effect.[64]

For Barani, it was possible that the sultans should first strengthen their administration and then with high resolve risk their power, prestige and dignity so that the religion of truth defeats and prevails over falsehood, Islamic customs are elevated and as designed by God truth prevails. But the sultans should realise as to what is the meaning of the establishment of truth so that they dedicate their lives in the struggles to establish them, consider them as the most important objective, and be prepared to sacrifice their lives and those of their supporters endeavouring to achieve what was the aim of the prophets, caliphs, friends of God, the truthful men as well as the earlier sultans. For their struggles and sacrifices the sultans will get prestige in this world, which will last till the Day of Judgment. Subsequently, in heaven, their status will be at par with the prophets and saintly Muslims and they will receive blessings of God.[65] Barani further exhorts the rulers: If you want not to be ashamed before God and the Prophet and your record of life is full of virtuous deeds, then you should use your royal power to uproot the infidels, polytheists and heretics, and humiliate them.[66]

According to Barani, the majority of religious scholars and intellectuals of both early and later times were convinced that the Muslim sultans enjoyed enough power to ensure that the true religion gained a proper ascendancy over false creeds, the Word of God was respected, the customs and traditions of infidelity and polytheism weakened and Muslims were favoured and honoured. The rulers could also see to it that the infidels and the irreligious were impoverished and disgraced. The rules and orders of illegal kingdoms and opposing believers can be removed, the laws of *shari'at* implemented and the enemies of God and the Prophet condemned, banished, repudiated and terrorised.[67] Sounds like a 'pre-fascist' agenda, but the fact remains that the sultans of Delhi like Shams al-Din Iltutmish and Jalal al-Din Khalji felt helpless to give the *kafirs* the option of Islam or death. They were not even in a position to prevent the Hindus of the capital from publicly professing their faith and taking out religious processions. The frustrations of Jalal al-Din Khalji are noted in the *Tarikh-i Firuz Shahi* by Barani himself.[68]

Barani however lamented that the reality was that truth could not be established, the supremacy of the Word of God was not possible, and the true religion was not able to keep the people of bad faith in check, because despite seven generations of Muslim power and rule in this land, the kings of Islam were allowing the customs of infidelity to flourish in their capital and other Muslim cities. Idols were worshipped openly and the people were following the tradition of infidelity with greater insistence than before. The *kuffar* were engaged, openly and without fear, in the teaching of their false creeds. They decorated their idols, beat drums, sang and danced while celebrating their festivals. After paying a few *tankas* as *jizya*, they continued with the practice and teaching of the instructions in their books of falsehood. In such a situation it was impossible to effectively implement the rules and regulations to raise the traditions of Islam to an exalted position, to establish piety, and prevent evil.[69]

Barani was convinced that the hearts of the Muslim sultans of Hindustan were free from the desire and passion to overthrow and knock down the *kafirs*, idol-worshippers and polytheists. On the contrary, in view of the fact that the heathens paid *kharaj* and were treated as *zimmis*, they were honoured, distinguished, favoured and achieved eminence. The sultans honoured them with gifts of drums, standards, jewels, gold-embroidered robes, armoured horses, governorship, and high ranks and positions. The Muslim sultans not only allowed this to flourish in their capital, the grandeur of which was a model for other Muslim cities, but were also pleased to see that the infidels, polytheists, idolaters and cow-dung worshippers constructed their houses resembling palaces, wore clothes of brocade, and rode Arab horses caparisoned with gold and silver ornaments. They had thousands of resources of power and strength, led luxurious lives, employed Muslims in their service and made them run before their horses. In the capital of Islam, which was the source of Islam's prestige, they were called *Rais*, *Ranas*, *Thakurs*, *Sahas*, *Mehtas* and Pundits. In such a condition, how could the Faith emerge victorious over false-creeds and truth be established?[70]

In condemning the 'wretched cow-dung worshipping' Hindus who were enjoying power and prestige in the Sultanate, Barani was evidently invoking the doctrinaires' suggestions on the question of the position of *zimmis* in an Islamic state. It would be useful to point out here that in classical Islam *zimmis* and Muslims were not treated equally. Apart from the *jizya* to be paid in a submissive manner, the *zimmi* was not allowed to marry a Muslim woman, though a Muslim could marry a *zimmi* woman. Similarly, a *zimmi* could not own a Muslim slave, although the converse was permitted. Also, according to the doctrine going back to the Ummayad caliph 'Umar bin 'Abdul Aziz, the *zimmi* was supposed to wear distinguishing articles of dress, the original intention of which was reportedly to prevent administrative errors but which gradually came to be regarded as a sign of humiliation, and was accompanied by complementary restrictions such as the prohibition of fine cloth, noble steeds, uncut forelocks, etc. Muslim authors like Ziya' al-Din Barani and later Mulla 'Abdul Qadir Badauni wanted such rules to be implemented by the rulers. Badauni, who wrote a counter-narrative to Akbar's 'inclusive' programme of *sulh-i kul* or 'peace with all' in the latter half of the sixteenth century, referred to the regulation imposed by his previous master Husain Khan Tukariya. As a governor of Lahore under Akbar, Husain Khan had ordered the Hindus to stitch a patch of cloth of a different colour on their garments near the bottom of the sleeve so as to be able to distinguish between Muslims and *kafirs*. This earned him the sobriquet 'Tukariya', derived from that piece of cloth or *tukra*. The Arabic word for *tukra* is also given: *ghiyar*,[71] any piece of dress or uniform which distinguishes soldiers or sects of people; a strip of yellow cloth worn by Jews in Persia.[72] This served as a distinguishing badge, which makes a person *ghair* (different) from others.[73] According to Badauni, on another occasion Husain Khan had ordered that the *kafirs* should not ride on saddles, but should sit on a pack saddle, claiming his injunction to be the requirements of the Muslim law.[74]

Islam tolerated the religion of the *zimmis* subject to the following restrictions: it was forbidden to insult Islam and to seek to convert a Muslim. Both the preacher and the apostate could receive death penalty. Existing places of worship were protected, construction of new buildings forbidden and reconstruction of old buildings fallen into decay opposed by the rigorists. There were also various limitations on the outward expression of worship, such as processions and the use of bells, though these were not strictly implemented in the early centuries of Islam. The same is true for the Delhi Sultanate. But in the contemporary Mamluk state, due to pressures from various factors including the Crusades, Mongol invasions and the campaigns by Muslim religious leader like Ibn Taimiyya, various regulations concerning the *zimmis* were implemented with varying degree of success. This included a distinguishing type of dress, mounts were to be reduced to nothing better than a donkey and a new restriction, with an Italian parallel, forbade them to possess houses higher than those occupied by Muslims.[75] This may perhaps explain generally the nondescript nature of Hindu places of worship in medieval India, compared to the grandeur of mosques, tombs and palaces of the Muslims. In the Muslim context, the building of the mosque should be higher than those of the residential quarters of the neighbourhood.

The above reference to Ibn Taimiyya also is not without value. A messenger of the Egyptian religious reformer had indeed visited the court of Muhammad Tughluq and Barani may have met him. This again shows that Barani was not an isolated figure thinking aloud about the cause of Islam in the evening end of his life. He must have developed his ideas over a long period of time reading the books he has cited as also through his interactions with contemporary intellectuals, writers and religious leaders. Barani's insistence on the recruitment of responsible *muhtasib* also reminds one of the classical theorists' suggestions in this regard. The official was not only to be entrusted with the maintenance of order in the streets and markets, but was also to supervise the control of the *zimmis*.

The Sunnite doctrinal position, though not necessarily conforming to one or the other schools of jurisprudence, is also reflected in Barani's instructions concerning the need to govern the Muslims in the light of the teachings of the Prophet. He wrote that if the sultans were free from the desire to protect the faith and establish the pious laws of the Prophet, then the Muslims might get the freedom to indulge in impious and sinful trade and profession. Wine-shops, brothels and gambling dens would be opened in every market and street. There would be no restriction on organising music parties everywhere. The sultans were satisfied with imposing taxes on them. The result was that the sinners and upholders of vice and immorality flourished without fear on every street, market and locality of the city. The sultan, whose responsibility was to ensure pious activities to flourish and crush evil was doing the contrary. In such a condition, Barani again wondered how truth and justice could be established and the banner of Islam flutter.[76]

Barani insisted that the world was full of wicked people who could be kept in control only through the power and authority of the king and not through the teachings of the Prophet. The rightly guided caliphs could rule for some time by strictly following the Traditions of the Prophet, but three out of four of them were killed by their Muslim opponents. That was so soon after the death of the Prophet, whose own style of governance was a miracle in itself. If a contemporary Sultan tried to follow the Tradition of the Prophet for ruling over the area under his control, his kingship would collapse then and there. It is only through the terror of the power of the king that the people could be kept in check and prevented from committing oppression against one another. Such views were already expressed by theorists like Ghazali and Tusi. Barani also noted that neither Islam nor such a Muslim survived two hundred years after the death of the Prophet who could rule the way Abu Bakr and 'Umar ruled over their subjects.[77] Barani therefore proposes the need to evolve secular/extra-religious state laws called the *zawabit*, deriving and adapting rules for governance from diverse traditions, including pre-Islamic Sasanid Persia, with public protestation of respect for the *shari'at*. Barani's reference to corruption in Islam is significant as his preceptor Nizam al-Din Auliya also kept lamenting the deteriorating character of Islam and Muslims since the time of the rightly guided caliphs. Like Barani, Nizam al-Din had also lamented the lack of moral integrity amongst the Muslims of his time.[78]

For Barani, to control the society then a strong arm of rule was required. If the sultans appreciated and continued to allow the philosophers and other heretics, who were the enemies of the faith and the Prophet, they would be emboldened to preach their books openly. Barani pointed out that they called Greek sciences, which was critical of the teachings of ancient and the last of the prophets, as *'ilm-i ma'qulat* (rational sciences) and the sciences of the *shari'at* was characterised as *'ilm-i manqulat* (traditional knowledge). They believed in, and declared that the world was eternal. They did not believe in resurrection of the dead, Day of Judgment and in hell and heaven, and questioned the limits of God's knowledge. According to Barani, these fundamentals of the faith were stressed in 360 revealed books of the prophets. The heretics not only preached their doctrines but also refuted the fundamentals of Islam in their argumentative tracts. If such people were allowed to live in the capital of the king with dignity and honour, spread their doctrines, privilege rationalistic over traditional knowledge, then the true religion would not be able to emerge victorious over false creeds, the supremacy of Islam and truth could not be established, the instruction to do good and prohibit the evil could not be carried out.[79] It is not a coincidence that Nizam al-Din Auliya was extremely critical of the rationalistic views of the Mu'tazalites.[80] The latter might have been crushed or subdued, but their books and ideas were still in circulation, and therefore a cause of anxiety for the torchbearers of Sunni Islam.

Such concerns were voiced by Muslim writers from time to time. A number of contemporaries of Barani also appreciated the sultans' efforts to dispatch the infidels to hell. Indeed, the court chronicles record a series of violent conflicts between the Muslims (led by the Turks, Afghans and the Mughals) and non-Muslim chieftains, like the Rajputs. These conflicts, mainly for political power and prestige, have been projected in the sources as *jihad* with the *ghazis* (victorious soldiers) and *shahids* (martyrs) involved in large-scale loot and plunder, including destruction of temples, gaining thereby rich rewards both 'here' (in this world) and 'hereafter' (in the next). The claims of demolition of temples might have been greatly exaggerated,[81] but the rhetoric in the Persian accounts cannot be dismissed as unimportant altogether. Assuming that the reports are not relevant for understanding even the contexts in which they were written, then at least they point to the 'personal' views, temperament or interests of the authors concerned.

The case of Amir Khusrau may be mentioned here. His 'court-chronicles' are full of 'hostile references to the Hindus and unreservedly condemns them as infidels'.[82] Khusrau celebrated the sultan washing the earth clean with the blood of the impure idol-worshipping Hindus and Pharaohs of infidelity.[83] Secular historians have tended to ignore or justify Amir Khusrau reporting on the countless infidels being sent to hell for the satisfaction of the sultans. Instead they highlight Khusrau's 'patriotism' (if not 'nationalism', though indications are to this effect also), by quoting all the appropriate words expressed by the court-poet and closest disciple of Nizam al-Din Auliya about the goodness of Hindustan and achievements of its people in various fields. Aziz Ahmad has pointed out that Khusrau's glorification of India was related to the

Muslim supremacy and splendour of Islam. Khusrau appreciated the reports that the strong men of Hind were trodden under foot and were ready to pay tribute, and that Islam was triumphant and idolatry was subdued.[84] Friedmann has suggested that Khusrau was convinced that religious truth was to be found in Islam alone: 'In this he does not differ from the consensus prevailing among the Muslims in his time and place'.[85]

Barani certainly did not differ with Khusrau on this question. It is important to note, however, that Khusrau's approach towards the Brahmins worshipping the sun, stones and some animals was different from Barani. For the latter, all these smacked of polytheism, while Khusrau explained that these are not considered as similar to God, but only a part of His creation. Khusrau would go to the extent of saying that as a religious group the Hindus were better than many others, including Christians.[86] Evidently, there is a need for a fresh study of Amir Khusrau's vast writings.[87]

Another set of sources, Sufi literature records a large number of anecdotes of miraculous encounters between the Sufis and non-Muslim miracle-workers or spiritual power-holders such as the yogis, *sanyasis*, gurus, and Brahmins. Provoked by the competing claims to territorial authority, these stories are significant for a more informed understanding of the religious complex and the processes of diffusion of Islam in India.[88] Sufi interaction in Indian environment was not always marked by conflict however. Interactions between diverse religio-intellectual traditions at various levels were distinguished by the concern to learn about/from each other and carve out a modus vivendi. This is reflected in music, painting, architecture, growth and development of vernacular literature, and evolution of 'syncretistic' cults that incorporated beliefs and practices common to Islam and other religious currents.

Conflict and Accommodation

There is hardly any attempt in existing scholarship on medieval India to take into account the views expressed by Barani and like-minded Muslim intellectuals of medieval India. The detailed passages quoted from Barani's *Fatawa-i Jahandari* throw up a number of questions. Who were the *kafirs* in medieval Indian context? How did Muslims characterise idol-worshipping non-Muslims? Did they know and identify them as Hindus? Were these Hindus categorised as *kafirs* or as *zimmis*? If there were ambiguities on this question, in what contexts and the categorisation change from *kafirs* to *zimmis* and vice versa? How much *jizya*, from whom, when and who collected it? How many temples were destroyed, by whom and when? How many temples could survive, were maintained and constructed in medieval India? What do these speak of Islamic iconoclasm and monotheism? Did all Muslims think alike on the question of classifying non-Muslims and on treatment to be meted out to them? If not, what were the different views? To what extent Muslim rulers were receptive to the 'agenda' of these different groups of people, say mainly the *'ulama* sodality? What were the limitations of the political authorities? Was *shari'at* inadequate to address the problems faced by the rulers? Even if the proverbial 'gates of *ijtihad*' were not closed and the *shari'at* could be re-interpreted to deal with new questions in a new setting, could it be implemented as the law of the land? To what extent did the ruptures within Indian Islam—the struggles between the different *mazahib* or the schools of jurisprudence, sectarian divisions, differences between the *'ulama* and the Sufi orders, and between traditionalist and rationalist Muslims—limite the scope for creating conditions in which a monolithic Islam could construct and deal with a non-Muslim 'other'?

These and many such questions of crucial import for the study of Muslim attitudes towards non-Muslims need to be addressed and resolved. On the other hand, the equally important question is as to how the vast majority of non-Muslims/Hindus responded to the advent of Islam in India. What were the strategies they adopted when successive generations of Turks, Afghans and Mughals wielded considerable political power, or how did they perceive Muslim rule? What were the factors that opened up avenues for non-Muslims to join the political process? What were the opportunities offered to them? Or were they completely unaffected, silent all the time, and shut themselves up altogether? If not, what were the sites of interaction? Did Muslims and Hindus consider themselves as separate communities? Did religious identities exist? If yes, in what forms? Finally, can the formation of community identities be understood only in terms of colonialism and modernity, or there can be some alternative ways of looking at the problem? Our ignorance about the above questions does not prove their irrelevance. Many of these issues may have contemporary resonance, but they are legitimate research questions.

Modern scholars have not addressed these themes adequately. The most influential and dominant pluralist and left-oriented scholars deny the existence of separate Hindu-Muslim identities prior to the British rule. The historians of this 'school' almost apologetically hold that the incidents of temple destruction were limited to a very short period of early encounter, the motivation being economic aggrandisement and not iconoclasm. They also assert that the Hindus were in no way denigrated. Finally, condemning the British for their alleged 'construction' of communalism in India, they suggest that the medieval period presented a fascinating picture of communal harmony. Alongside, there has existed a 'separatist' Muslim scholarship with its rigid assumption that Hindus and Muslims are two different 'nations', and that their separate history may be traced back to Muhammad bin Qasim's conquest of Sindh. Also, the 'agents' of 'Hinduism', such as Kabir and Akbar had almost destroyed the distinct character of Islam in India, but the timely intervention of the Naqshbandi Sufi Shaykh Ahmad Sirhindi, known as Mujaddid Alf-i Sani, saved the situation in the early seventeenth century. Not surprisingly, there also exists another stream of scholarship with its overt pro-Hindu tinge. The basic premise in the literature produced by this latter group is that medieval India under Islamic rule, with large-scale destruction of temples and constant humiliation of the Hindus, was a dark phase in an otherwise glorious history of Hindu civilisation. Related to this is the suggestion that much of the evils facing the Hindu society today are basically a legacy of Muslim rule in India.

Obviously, the variety of discourse indicates the various points of vantage from which the scholars have studied the theme. Our own reading of a portion of the sources suggests that the diverse views summarised above need to be reconsidered and revised in a large measure. It appears that religious identities, in their various forms, did exist in medieval India. It is also clearly visible that in the conflict over political control of a territory mobilisation on religious lines was not uncommon. Also, religious symbols were frequently used for political purposes. Muslims seemed to be engaged in a long-drawn *jihad* against the *kafirs*, or infidels/Hindus in India. However, the Muslim rulers with all their pretensions of following the *shari'at* had not converted the conquered territories into *dar-ul Islam* or the abode of Islam in the strictly orthodox sense of the term, nor did they force the entire 'local' population to embrace Islam. The non-Muslims were allowed to stay peacefully by paying *jizya,* mostly in the form of annual tributes to be paid by the chieftains (referred to by Barani and other Muslim writers as zamindars, *rais*, *muaqaddams*, *chaudharis*) who controlled the regions.

The conquered people, however, had not fully reconciled themselves to a subordinate position. The Hindu resistance in the period appears to be both overt/open (that is, in the form of armed struggle) and covert/ 'everyday' variety (reflected in an increased religiosity, *bhajan*, *kirtan*, peaceful monotheistic movements, etc.). Sixteenth-century Marathi Bhakti poet Eknath's presentation of a hard-hitting argument between a Hindu and a Muslim in his drama-poem, *Hindu-Turk Samvad*, may be mentioned here. The aggressive Muslim protagonist was made to realise that both Hindus and Muslims were created by God. Their 'goal is one', though 'the ways of worship are different'. Eknath's Hindu character also castigates the Muslim who is supposed to catch a Hindu and convert him to Islam: 'Did God make a mistake in making a Hindu? Is your wisdom greater than His?' The practices and rituals of the Sufi shrines are also questioned: 'You tell us we worship stones. Why do you place blocks of stone over the dead?'...'You cover the stone with flowers and silk cloth; you burn incense before it!' More punching is the criticism of the popular veneration or 'worship of a *haji* of stone (Ka'ba in Mecca)'. The drama ends on a consensus: 'The argument was about oneness. The argument became agreement'.[89] The consensus does not dissolve the question of identity. It only shows the author's concerns to illustrate the commonality of certain beliefs and rituals, and resist conversion of Hindus to Islam. On the other hand, at times, the Muslims also manifested an extraordinarily magnanimous attitude in their treatment of the Hindus. Yet it is clear that the Muslims, at least the elite who have left their works in the Persian language, were conscious of the presence of an 'other' in the person of the Hindu. It is in this context of a perceived overwhelming presence of an, often dangerous, 'other' that the process of formation of community identities of Muslims in India needs to be examined.

It has been suggested recently that the 'development of strict orthodoxy' in Indian Islam in the midst of 'idolatrous and polytheistic population' was diametrically opposed to 'the attempt to find a common denominator for the two civilisations, to establish a mutually acceptable modus vivendi for their respective adherents, though the conciliatory trend was always weaker than the orthodox one'.[90] The above formulation is fraught with problems. The use of the expression 'two civilisations' presupposes non-Muslims and Muslims as two biologically, racially, even culturally different sets of people. It ignores the vast majority of Indian converts to Islam. It may be kept in mind that conversion did not happen in one day, except in individual cases. Several communities or groups of people underwent a long process of Islamic acculturation. Diffusion of Islam in the regions also unleashed the emergence of a large number of 'syncretistic' cults/communities. Politics determined their classification as 'Islamic' or 'Hindu' and even pushed them to be identified as part of Islam or what is termed as 'Hinduism', or may be as something new: Sikhism for instance, though attempts to appropriate Sikhism into Hinduism continues.

It does not mean, however, that politics always created conflict in society. The attitude of Muslim rulers towards their diverse subjects differed, basing on reasons such as personal temperament and political expediency. It could be ambivalent, pragmatic and in a few cases even programmatic. If the juristically inclined *'ulama* wanted an all-out war against the *kuffar*, the Muslim attitude towards the latter was tempered by the more politically correct position taken by a large number of Sufis of a variety of spiritual lineages. Many Sufis who mingled freely with people adhering to diverse formal/informal religious traditions largely considered it unadvisable to use political power for spreading Islam by forcibly bringing non-Muslims to its fold. Some of them would refrain from converting people without a proper 'introduction' to Islam, through personal interaction over a long period of time. The most powerful and articulate argument on the question came from the influential Chishti saint and Barani's preceptor Nizam al-Din Auliya, who asserted that no amount of force could change the heart of these people. In this context, the words 'Hindu' and '*qaum*' are used already in the early decades of the fourteenth century. They should spend time in the company of good Muslims to be transformed into good Muslims themselves.[91] Conversion then would become a matter of formality. Thus, it was through a long-term association with Sufi centres like hospices and shrines, facilitated by a number of attractions, that many individuals and groups of people embraced Islam. Colonial enumeration may have played a role in sharpening of categories such as Muslim or Hindu. This does not mean that they did not exist altogether in medieval times. To deny this is to ignore the views of medieval Muslim intellectuals like Ziya' al-Din Barani, who clearly identified himself with one political and, shall we say, cultural group as against many others. Barani has shown contestations were involved in what constituted a community or *umma* of Islam in relation to the *kafirs*. It is also clear that the self-righteous, privileged group amongst Muslims wanted to utilise all the tools of dominance to subdue those who belonged to a different group within a socially-stratified and sectarian-conflict ridden society referred to by the generic term Islamic. Barani wanted the *kafirs* to be sent to hell, even as he condemned the rise of Islam's internal 'others' such as the converted Indian Muslims in the Delhi Sultanate as a complete perversion.

REFERENCES

* **Acknowledgement:** The paper has benefited from discussions with Muzaffar Alam, Rimi Chatterjee, Rosinka Chaudhuri, Anjan Ghosh, Sanal Mohan and Tilottama Mukherjee. I am also grateful to the participants in the 'Rethinking a Millennium' conference, especially Najaf Haider and Sunil Kumar, for their insightful comments on an earlier version. I take this opportunity to express my deep sense of gratitude to my teacher, Prof. Harbans Mukhia, for encouraging me to ask all questions and not one set of them only.

1. Originally used in the sense of 'obliterating', 'covering', 'concealing' in old Arab poetry and in the Qur'an, the word *kafir* is applied to the unbelieving Meccan 'infidels', who endeavoured to refute and revile Prophet Muhammad. In the early Meccan period a waiting attitude towards the idolators is recommended, but later Muslims are ordered to keep apart from them, to defend themselves from their attacks and even to take the offensive against them. In most passages of the Qur'an the reference is to the unbelievers in general who are threatened with God's punishment. Later sources also refer to them as unclean and *jihad* (holy war) against the unbelievers of a *dar al-harb* (enemy land) is obligatory. For more information, see W. Bjorkman, 'Kafir', *Encyclopaedia of Islam*, New Edition, Vol. 4, Leiden, 1978, pp. 407–09.
2. Stuart Hall, 'Cultural Studies and its Theoretical Legacies', in Lawrence Grossberg, Cary Nelson and Paula Treichler, (eds.), *Cultural Studies*, New York and London, 1992, pp. 277–94.
3. Ziya' al-Din Barani, *Tarikh-i Firuz Shahi*, Saiyid Ahmad Khan (ed.), Calcutta, 1862, p. 23.
4. Barani may have been born not later that 1285 and probably earlier as he was old enough to remember the convivial parties and to have read the whole of the Qur'an in the reign of Sultan Jalal al-Din Khalji (1290–96), Peter Hardy, 'Barani', *Encyclopaedia of Islam*, New Edition, Vol. 1, Leiden, 1986, pp. 1036–37. For a detailed treatment of Barani's career with a lot of adverse remarks, see Mohammad Habib, 'Life and Thought of Ziyauddin Barani'. The work has been printed several times. I have used the one in *Politics and Society During the early Medieval Period, Collected Works of Mohammad Habib*, Vol. II, Delhi, 1981, pp. 286–366. I shall also refer to the reprint in (*Politics and Society*, Vol. II, pp. 418–432) of Mohammad Habib's 'Introduction' to *The Political Theory of the Delhi Sultanate* (Including the translation of Ziauddin Barani's *Fatawa-i Jahandari* circa, 1358–9 A.D.) by Mohammad Habib and Afsar Umar Salim Khan, Allahabad, n.d.
5. Baran is the old name of Buland Shahr, an ancient town situated on the main road from Agra and Aligarh to Meerut in Uttar Pradesh. The name Baran was derived from its legendary founder, Ahirban. Discovery of copper plate inscriptions of the fifth century C.E. and coins of much older dates establishes its antiquity. The town is familiar to the students of the history of Islam in India as the birthplace of our author Ziya' al-Din Barani. Its earliest recorded association with Muslims dates back to its conquest by Sultan Mahmud of Ghazna in 1018, see A.S. Bazmee Ansari, 'Bulandshahr (Baran)', *Encyclopaedia of Islam*, New Edition, Vol. 1, Leiden, 1986, pp. 1299–1300.
6. Mohammad Habib writes that Muhamad Tughluq appointed Barani as his *nadim* or courtier in late 1334. Curiously, Habib notes that it was an office of much profit and no responsibility and not suited to a man of self-respect. He then goes on to quote the account of the courtier's position and duties as recorded in Nizam al-Mulk's *Siyasatnama*. It is noted that Nizam al-Mulk's description matched with 'Barani's own confessions'. Nizam al-Mulk wrote that there were some advantages in employing the

courtier. First, as a friend of the king he was with him day and night, and was in a position of a bodyguard of the king and if danger arose he would sacrifice his life and makes his body a shield for the king. Second, it was possible for the king to say a thousand things, in jest and seriousness, to the courtier, which was not possible for him to say to the wazir and to the great officers of his government for they were holders of high posts and managers of his affairs. Third, like spies, they informed the king of the actions of his *maliks*. Fourth, they could speak boldly about the good and bad matters of state policy. The *nadim* ought to be well born, accomplished, good in manners, pleasant in appearance, orthodox in faith, worthy of confidence and pure in his ways. He should be able to tell plenty of stories, jocular as well as serious. He should be the king's companion in drinking, enjoyment, *majlises*, hunting and playing, *Politics and Society*, Vol. II, pp. 339–40, citing *Siyasatnama*, ed. Agha Abbas Iqbal, Tehran, 1320 A.H.

7. Muhammad Jamal Qiwam, *Qiwam al-'Aqa'id*, Urdu trans. Nisar Ahmad Faruqi, Rampur, 1994, pp. 96–97.
8. Barani admits that when he was imprisoned in Bhatnir fort after the death of Muhammad Tughluq, his enemies complained to Firuz Tughluq and accused him of using a thousand kinds of poisonous words. According to Habib, the complaint may be true: 'Barani as a writer is too fond of abusive phrases, many of which are only intelligible when translated literally from Persian into plain Hindi. But while in the *Firuz Shahi* there is some literary flavour about his abuses, in the *Jahandari* they are merely coarse', *Politics and Society*, Vol. II, p. 420.
9. Shahid Amin, 'Alternative Histories: A View from India', SEPHIS – CSSSC lecture, Amsterdam/Kolkata, 2002, p. 7, commenting on Mohammad Habib's Presidential Address, Indian History Congress, December 1947.
10. *Politics and Society*, Vol. II, pp. 422–23.
11. *Ibid*, Vol. II, p. 419.
12. *Tarikh-i Firuz Shahi*, pp. 20–21.
13. *Politics and Society*, Vol. II, p. 421.
14. *Ibid*, Vol. II, p. 422, emphasis original.
15. *Ibid*, Vol. II, p. 429.
16. Defending the rule of the sultan, Imam Ghazali wrote that the decline of the caliphate does not mean that the people should stop obeying the law, dismiss the *qazis* (jurists), declare all authority to be valueless, and pronounce the acts of those in high places to be invalid. The office of government in different regions was legally executed by the sultans, who professed allegiance to the caliph, by mentioning the latter's name in the sermons (*khutba*) and the coins (*sikka*), and maintained stability and order. Ghazali also recommended support for and submission to even an unjust and ignorant ruler, as the attempt to depose him might prove counter-productive. Further, Ghazali also effected a fusion of the Islamic ethic and the Sasanian norms of governance. For a detailed exposition of Ghazali's views on good governance, see F.R.C. Bagley, *Ghazali's Book of Counsel for Kings*, Oxford, 1964. The noted historian Ibn Khaldun also defended the transformation of the caliphate into kingship, as the qualities

of the caliphate survived in the preference for Islam and its ways, and adherence to the path of truth. The only change that became apparent was in the restraining force which had been in religion and was now changed into *'asbiyat* (lit: party-spirit; love of kindred or country) and the sword, (Lambton, *State and Government in Medieval Islam*, p.173). For Ibn Khaldun's life and works, see also M. Talbi, 'Ibn Khaldun', *Encyclopaedia of Islam*, New Edition, Vol. 3, Leiden, 1971, pp. 825–31.

17. Like Ghazali, Nizam al-Mulk Tusi also attempted to combine something of the Islamic ideal with the Persian notion of the ideal ruler, see, *The Book of Government or Rules for Kings, The Siyasat-nama* or *Siyar al-Muluk* of *Nizam ul-Mulk*, translated from the Persian by Hubert Darke, London, 1960.
18. *Political Theory*, p. 28.
19. M. Habib, 'The Campaigns of 'Alauddin Khalji Being the English translation of "*The Khaza'in ul-Futuh*" of Amir Khusrau', reprinted in *Politics and Society*, Vol. II, pp. 149–270, esp. pp. 149, 152, 163 (n. 3).
20. Barani wrote that the noble, free-born, virtuous, religious, of high genealogy and pure birth were worthy of offices and posts in the government of the king. They alone were capable of virtues like kindness, generosity, valour, good deeds, truthfulness, keeping of promises, protection of other classes, loyalty, clarity of vision, justice, equity, recognition of rights, gratitude for favours received and fear of God, *Political Theory*, pp. 97–98.
21. For the author, the low born, who practised baser arts and meaner professions were capable only of vices such as immodesty, falsehood, miserliness, misappropriation, wrongfulness, lies, evil-speaking, ingratitude, dirtiness, injustice, cruelty, non-recognition of rights, shamelessness, impudence, blood-shedding, rascality, jugglery and Godlessness, (*Political Theory*, p. 98).
22. *Ibid*, p. 97.
23. *Politics and Society*, Vol. II, pp. 419–20.
24. *Ibid*, Vol. II, p. 420.
25. *Ibid*, Vol. II, p. 420.
26. *Ibid*, Vol. II, p. 420.
27. *Ibid*, Vol. II, p. 430.
28. Amir Khwurd, *Siyar al-Auliya*, Lahore, 1978, p. 322.
29. *Ibid*, p. 323.
30. *Ibid*.
31. *Ibid*.
32. *Politics and Society*, Vol. II, p. 288.
33. *Political Theory*, p. 18, n.13.
34. For the Chishti Sufis' relations with the sultans of Delhi, see Raziuddin Aquil, 'Sufi Cults, Politics and Conversion: The Chishtis of the Sultanate Period', *Indian Historical Review* (hereafter *IHR*) Vol. 22 (1-2), 1995–96, pp. 190–97; idem, 'Miracles, Authority and Benevolence: Stories of *Karamat* in Sufi Literature of the Delhi Sultanate', in Anup Taneja, (ed.), *Sufi Cults and the Evolution of Medieval Indian Culture*, Delhi, 2003, pp. 109–38.
35. *Siyar al-Auliya*, p. 323.

36. *Ibid.*
37. For a recent discussion on the Chishti practice of music, see Carl W. Ernst and Bruce B. Lawrence, *Sufi Martyrs of Love: The Chishti Order in South Asia and Beyond*, New York, 2002.
38. *Siyar al-Auliya*, p. 541.
39. *Ibid.*
40. 'Abdul Haqq Muhaddis Dehlawi, *Akhbar al-Akhyar*, Urdu trans. Subhan Mahmud and Muhammad Fazil, Delhi, 1990, p. 222.
41. *Ibid*, pp. 222–24.
42. *Ibid*, p. 225.
43. *Politics and Society*, Vol. II, p. 431.
44. *Ibid.*
45. *Political Theory*, pp. 5–6. Treating Sultan Mahmud as his 'hero', Barani addresses the later Sultans as Mahmud's sons and attributes many statements on good governance and the cause of Islam to the former. According to Habib, Barani knew little or nothing about Sultan Mahmud of history. In fact, 'his ignorance is appalling. But Mahmud has to bear the whole burden of Barani's philosophy, though he would have repudiated it from A to Z', *Politics and Society*, Vol. II, pp. 420–21. It may be mentioned here that Habib himself prepared a completely sanitised account of Mahmud's career and his Indian campaigns, first published in the form of a book in 1927, reprinted in *Politics and Society*, Vol. II, pp. 36–104. For a more insightful study, see Romila Thapar, *Somanatha: The Many Voices of a History*, Delhi, 2004.
46. Harbans Mukhia, *Historians and Historiography during the Reign of Akbar*, Delhi, 1976, Chapter one.
47. For a recent example, see Muzaffar Alam, '*Shari'a* and Governance in the Indo-Muslim Context', in David Gilmartin and Bruce B. Lawrence, eds, *Beyond Turk and Hindu: Rethinking Religious Identities in Islamicate South Asia*, Delhi, 2002; idem, *The Languages of Political Islam in India, c. 1200–1800*, Delhi, 2004.
48. *Political Theory*, p. 43.
49. *Ibid*, pp. 43–44.
50. *Ibid*, p. 44.
51. It is suggested by some scholars, though in a different context, that domination must exist within a relationship. The dominant groups, in their exercise of domination, do not consume and destroy the dominated classes, for then there would be no relation of power, and, therefore, no domination, Partha Chatterjee, 'Peasants, Politics and Historiography: A Response', *Social Scientist*, 11: 5, May 1983, pp. 58–65.
52. Scanning a complex or unfamiliar scene, the individual tries to sort it out rapidly in terms of images which fall into simple and general categories, drawing on social stereotypes. Encountering a black man or an Arab on the street, a white person registers threat, and does not look more searchingly. The judgment is instant and the result surprising; thanks to the classifying powers of what Roland Barthes has termed as 'image repertoire', people shut out further stimulation. Confronted with

difference, they quickly become passive. By using an image repertoire to withdraw from others, the individual feels more at ease. For a discussion on these issues in a very different context of the city of New York, comprising all kinds of individuals and social groups, see Richard Sennett, *Flesh and Stone*, London, 1994, pp. 355–59, 365–66.

53. For the Chishti Sufis attitude towards non-Muslims, see Raziuddin Aquil, 'Conversion in Chishti Sufi Literature (13th-14th Centuries)', *IHR*, Vol. 24 (1–2), 1997–98, pp. 70–94.
54. *Political Theory*, p. 44.
55. *Ibid*, pp. 44–45.
56. *Ibid*, pp. 45–46.
57. *Ibid*, p. 46.
58. Yohanan Friedmann, 'Islamic Thought in Relation to the Indian Context', first published in 1986, reprinted in Richard M. Eaton, (ed.), *India's Islamic Traditions, 711–1750*, Delhi, 2003, pp. 50–63, esp. p. 52.
59. *Political Theory*, p. 46.
60. *Ibid*, pp. 46–47.
61. Cl. Cahen, 'Dhimma', *Encyclopaedia of Islam*, New Edition, Vol. 2, Leiden, 1991, pp. 227–31.
62. Friedmann, 'Islamic Thought', pp. 52–53.
63. *Ibid*, p. 53.
64. Cahen, 'Dhimma'.
65. *Political Theory*, p. 47.
66. *Ibid*.
67. *Ibid*. Sharing similar sentiments, later Shaykh Ahmad Sarhindi also suggested that the honour of Islam required the humiliation of the infidels, who must be oppressed, treated like dogs and mercilessly subjected to the *jizya*. In utter disregard of Hindu sensitivities, Sarhindi emphasised that a very effective way of establishing the supremacy of Islam was the slaughter of cows, which was 'one of the most glorious commandments of Islam in India', Friedmann, 'Islamic Thought', p. 61.
68. For a more detailed discussion of relevant issues, see Raziuddin Aquil, 'From *Dar-ul-Harb* to *Dar-ul-Islam*: Chishti Accounts of Early History of Islam in Hindustan', International Seminar on Assertive Religious Identities, New Delhi, 16–18 October 2003.
69. *Political Theory*, p. 48.
70. *Ibid*.
71. 'Abdul Qadir Badauni, *Muntakhab al-Tawarikh*, Vol. II, English trans. W.H. Lowe, reprint, Delhi, 1973, p. 227.
72. F. Steingass, *A Comprehensive Persian-English Dictionary*, reprint, New Delhi, 1996, pp. 899–900.
73. *Muntakhab al-Tawarikh*, Vol. II, p. 227, note 5.
74. *Ibid*, Vol. II, p. 228.
75. Cahen, 'Dhimma'.
76. *Political Theory*, p. 48.
77. *Ibid*, pp. 39–40. For a criticism of Barani's views that *shari'at* could not be implemented as the rule of law, see Syed Sabahuddin Abdur Rahman,

Hindustan ke Salatin, 'Ulama aur Mashaikh ke Ta'lluqat par ek Nazr (Urdu), Azamgarh, 1964, p. 37

78. *Fawa'id al-Fu'ad*, conversations of Shaykh Nizam-ud-Din Auliya compiled by Amir Hasan Sijzi, Persian text with an Urdu translation by Khwaja Hasan Sani Nizami, Delhi, 1990, Vol. IV, 40th Meeting.
79. *Political Theory*, pp. 48–49.
80. *Fawa'id al-Fu'ad*, Vol. II, 23rd Meeting.
81. Richard Eaton, 'Temple Desecration and Indo-Muslim States', in *Essays on Islam and Indian History*, Delhi, 2002.
82. Friedmann, 'Islamic Thought', p. 55.
83. Several examples can be given from Amir Khusrau's *Khaza'in al-Futuh*, ed. M. Wahid Mirza, Calcutta, 1953. See also, M. Habib, 'The Campaigns of 'Alauddin Khalji Being the English translation of "*The Khaza'inal Futuh*" of Amir Khusrau', reprinted in *Politics and Society*, Vol. II, pp. 149–270.
84. Aziz Ahmad, 'Epic and Counter-Epic in Medieval India', first published in 1963, reprinted in Eaton, (ed.), *India's Islamic Traditions*, pp. 37–49, esp. p. 39.
85. Friedmann, 'Islamic Thought', p. 55.
86. *Ibid*, pp. 54–55.
87. M. Wahid Mirza's work and subsequent writings though well researched and noble in their intentions need considerable revision. See M. Wahid Mirza, *Amir Khusrau* (Urdu), Delhi, 1986; Zoe Ansari and Abul Faiz Sahar, eds., *Khusro Shanasi* (Urdu), Delhi, 1989.
88. Aquil, 'Conversion in Chishti Sufi Literature'.
89. Eleanor Zelliot, 'A Medieval Encounter Between Hindu and Muslim: Eknath's Drama-Poem *Hindu-Turk Samvad*', first published 1982, reprinted in Eaton, ed., *India's Islamic Traditions*, pp. 64–82.
90. Friedmann, 'Islamic Thought', pp. 50-51. Aziz Ahmad also refers to the 'two mutually exclusive religious, cultural and historical attitudes, each confronting the other in aggressive hostility', Aziz Ahmad, 'Epic and counter-Epic', p. 37. As Eaton has pointed out Ahmad's classification, prepared not long after Partition, of Muslim epic of conquest and a Hindu epic of resistance and of psychological rejection, which grew in mutual ignorance of the other, likely reflected the hardened political and ideological positions that had crystallised with the creation of independent India and Pakistan, *India's Islamic Traditions*, p. 35.
91. *Fawa'id al-Fu'ad*, Vol. IV, 40th Meeting.

Chapter 8

Images of Women from the Fourteenth to the Sixteenth Century: A Study of Sufi *Premakhyans*

Madhu Trivedi

This paper will attempt to represent the images of women one finds in *Chandayan*, *Mirgavati* and *Padmavat*, three texts composed between the late fourteenth to mid sixteenth centuries. These narrative poems, popularly known to us as Sufi *premakhyans*, enjoyed immense popularity amongst the learned and the common folk alike, were adaptations of popular tales of love and ballads for expressing the soul's mystic yearning for God in allegorical terms. *Chandayan*, the earliest extant work in the Sufi tradition, was written by Maulana Daud during the reign of Sultan Firuz Shah (r.1340–1385) in 1379 at Dalmau (a town in Rae Barely district). He was a disciple of Shaikh Zainud Din and patronised by Khan-i Jahan, the *vazir* of Sultan Firuz Shah Tughlaq.[1] *Mirgavati* was written in 1503 by Qutban under the patronage of sultan Husain Shah Sharqi (r.1458–1505) of Jaunpur. He was a disciple of a renowned Sufi saint, Shaikh Burhan of Kalpi, of the Chishti *silsila.*[2] Badayuni and Banarsidas, in *Muntakhab ut Tawarikh and Ardhakathanak* respectively attest to the great popularity of these two.[3] *Padmavat* belongs to the reign of Sultan Sher Shah (r.1540–1545) and was written in 1540-1 by Malik Muhammad Jayasi who was also a disciple of Shaikh Burhan and composed this work due to his inspiration.[4]

Of these, *Chandayan* and *Mirgavati* belong to an old and well-established Indian genre of narratives, *katha*, rendered by a class of wandering musicians or mendicants. Maulana Daud refers to one such love ballad, *Geet-Chandraval*, performed by a *bajur* (a wandering musician) who captivated his listeners by his singing. Qutban also refers to a *jogi* playing *birah biyog* on his *kingri* (*kinnari-vina*) and moving the listeners with his performance. The fact that, like these two ballads,

Chandayan was also a versified *katha* and meant for musical rendering is mentioned clearly by Maulana Daud:

tau re kaha main yahu khand gaun
katha kabit kai log sunaun[5]

Maulana Daud has also mentioned that the impact of his recital of the *katha* of Lorak and Chanda, which he had versified, was immense and created tumult in the hearts of the listeners:

daud kavi chandayan gai
jei re suna so ga murjhai[6]

Similarly *Mirgavati,* also meant for performance, was a refined literary version of an earlier *katha* in *hindui* and presented by someone in *turki,* i.e. the language of the *turuks*, a generic term used for the Muslims in India. However, here Qutban means Persian, as *turki* is the commonly used expression for this literary language in the vernacular literature in medieval north India:

pahle hindui katha ahi
funi re kamhi turki lai kahi
funi ham khol arath sab kaha
jog singar vir ras aha[7]

At another place he says:

to ham ek katha yah kahi
jo hamre seu suvani ahi[8]

Padmavat, the only *prem-katha* focusing on the historical background to some extent, was also meant for performance. At many places we find Jayasi addressing an imagined audience:

sinhaladip katha ab gavon
auo so padmini barani sunavon[9]

In the concluding part also, he appears in the manner of a *sutradhar* to relate to the audience the essence of the story.[10] That the tradition of rendition of these epics continued during the seventeenth century is attested by Banarsidas who used to recite *Mirgavat*i and *Madhumalti,* another poem of the same class to a group of people who gathered at his place at night.[11] *Ramcharitmanas*, which is written in the same *chaupai-doha* format and to some extent follows these epics in respect of language, continues to be tunefully recited even today. There is a major departure, however, from Indian tradition of oral epics in one respect that these ballads were written in a large narrative framework, *masnavi* form (a poem of rhyming couplets) and in Persian script. Maulana Daud mentions it clearly that *Chandayan* is a poem written in *turki* script and rendered in *Hindui* (*hindavi*) language (*turki lipi likh hindui gri).*[12]

These poetic works present a blend of the stylistic and poetic concepts of Indian and Islamic tradition. While they adopt the Persian model, the *masnavi* form, the stylistic features for the most part are from indigenous poetry, which are used efficiently in the fabric of the *masnavi*. The layout of the prologue, called *stuti-khand*, is in the fashion of Persian *masnavi*s, the imagery and mystical idioms are typically of the Nath-yogis,[13] whose language virtually served as the lingua franca to an audience, composed of people of mixed cultural locations from diverse social groups and communities, for whom this poetry was intended. There is, thus, only a structural similarity with *masnavi* tradition; the artistic and rhetorical tools are indigenous. Also, what amazes one is the fact that while their script is Persian, there is a striking absence of Persian words in the language of these works. Very rarely do some Persian words appear and that too in an Indianised version[14] such as *bekarara* or *sir ta pai*.[15] They use Hindu vocabulary to define Islamic concepts.

The metric pattern, which is known as *karvak* and employed generally in the *apbhransh kavya*, is also in accordance with indigenous poetry. It comprises two types of verses, a unit of five *chaupai*, and in some cases seven, followed by a *doha* or similar poetic metres such as *arilla* or *arrillaka*, *gatha* and *sortha*.[16] The use of *doha*[17] is more frequent especially in *Padmavat*. In it the unit of seven *chaupai* is concluded by a *doha* and very rarely by a *soratha*.[18] It appears that some sort of *khand* division also existed at least in *Chandayan*, which is the earliest extant poetic work in the Sufi tradition, and in this respect it is akin to the *prakrit* and *apbhransh* poetry.[19] It retains the traits of oral epics and the art of *qissa-khwani* more than any other narrative of this type composed during the period under review. The following verses are instances in this regard:

kahu kabitu man bhayo giyanu
kahat suhavan sunahu dei kanu[20]

… … … …

nathan malik dukh bat ubhari
sunahu kan dei bahu guniyari[21]

One may notice here the expressions, *sunahu dei kanu, sunahu kan dei* (listen with concentration), which are part of the performance strategies in north Indian oral epics, *dastans* and *qissa-khwani*.[22] Gradually, however, the literary overtone became dominant as one finds in *Mirgavati*, and *Padmavat*. Qutban represented his age and displayed great erudition and the grandeur of the language. He chose his diction in accordance with the scholarly tradition of his period and he was conscious of the fact. Regarding his diction and ways of expression, which was weighted with high-flown Sanskrit words as well as a great deal of *desi,* he opines that a person will be a *pandit* on his own after reading his work:

sastri aakhar bahu aaye
auo desi chuni chuni sab laye[23]

... ...

khat bhaka jo ienhai bancha
pandit binu puchhat ho sancha[24]

We also find here the continuity of the *khat bhaka* tradition, i.e. the knowledge of six languages deemed necessary to become a *pandit,* which included Sanskrit, Prakrit, Pali, Apbhransh, Dingal and Pingal. This tradition in notional form continued till the end of the seventeenth century in the *riti* poetry.

Chandayan was undoubtedly a very popular work. Mulla Abdul Qadir Badauni remarks about it:

> In the year 772 (1370 CE) Khan-i Jahan, the *vazir*, died and his son Juna Shah obtained that title; and the book *Chandayan* which is a *masnavi* in Hindi language relating the love of Lurak (Lorak) and Chanda, a lover and his mistress, a very graphic work, was put into verses in his honour by Maulana Da'ud. There is no need for me to praise it because of its great fame in that country, and Maulana Shaikh Taqiu-d-Din Waiz Rabbani used to read on some occasions poems of his from the pulpit, and the people used to be strangely influenced by hearing them, and when certain learned men of that time asked the Shaikh saying, what is the reason for this Hindi *masnavi* being selected? he answered, the whole of it is divine and pleasing in subject, worthy of the ecstatic contemplation of devout lovers, and conformable to the interpretation of some of the *Ayats* of *Qu'ran,* and the sweet singers of Hindustan. Moreover by its public recitation, human hearts are taken captive.[25]

Badauni's observations are extremely significant. They testify to the trait of compositeness that is so typical of medieval north Indian culture. Even though the Turko-Persian art forms and literary genres found vogue during the sultanate period, Indian genres too existed side by side and were equally adhered to by the Muslim literati and they used the Indian metric pattern quite efficiently. Badayuni does not react to the fact that that a love-ballad composed in *Hindi* and representing typical Hindu culture was rendered from the pulpit *(mimbar)* and some of its position were found suitable by a Maulana to explain the *Ayats* of the holy *Quran*. This prompts us to think about the notion of orthodoxy of the class of *'ulama* Badauni belonged to. This also brings out the vibrant resilience of Indian traditions in the cultural setting of the sultanate period, and the emergence of a common culture. There was an interruption in the process for some time due to a fresh wave of Persianisation under the early Mughals, who conformed to the cultural traditions of Hirat, but it regained its pace under Akbar.[26]

Chandayan acted as a model for later Sufi poets like Qutban and Jayasi, who adopted its poetic format and elements as well as thematic concepts and composed their romances in *Hindui (Hindavi)*. A comparison of these works reveals that though these poets differed in the selection of their stories, their narrative strategies as well as the metaphoric idioms were similar.[27] While Maulana Daud's story, has relevance to real-life situations, Qutban borrows a fairy tale with magical tricks from the stock of north Indian oral epics and *dastans*, and *Padmavat* describes a historical event in fictional mode. In spite of it they have thematic and structural similarities to the extent that sometimes the sequence of scenes and narrative elements are the same, as may be seen in *Chandayan* and *Padmavat*. They blend well the theoretical concepts of Indian philosophy and Islamic mysticism in an Indian story and provide us a fuller portrait of Hindu society. Indirectly, however, they tell a lot about the elite Muslim culture. These *akhyans* thus echo the spirit of the age wherein these were created.

These works contain a plethora of information about north Indian art and culture. Here we find vibrant sketches of the urbane and sophisticated society as well as folk culture, the activity of a busy town and that of a tiny village *haat*, where performances such as *chharhanta-pekhan* (a sort of *indrajal*), *bhamnagri* (tricks and stunt) were staged. They describe the Indian city as an imaginary world, the trade routes as the *prem-path*, and provide factual details in the fashion of professional story-teller (*dastan-go* and *qissa-khwan*). *Chandayan* is extremely rich in this respect.[28]

I

As is evident from the titles of these epics as well as the structure of the stories, women characters play a dominant role in these narrative poems.

Chandayan is a story of a beautiful young princess Chanda of Govara who is married to one Siohar at a very young age. Her husband, called Baman (*vaman*, a dwarf) due to his short stature, does not pay attention to her sexual needs and she returns to her parental house. Meanwhile a *bajur* (wandering musician), captivated by her beauty, describes her *nakh-shikh* (appearance from top to toe) in the court of Raja Rupchand. The Raja lays siege to Govara and demands Chanda. The hero Lorik, who is known for his skill in the martial arts, is called by the father to assist in the battle and he defeats Rup Chand. During the *jevnar* (banquet) following the victory Lorik sees Chanda, and is fascinated by her beauty. Chanda is also inclined towards him. On the advice of the *dhai* (wet nurse) of Chanda, Lorik goes to the temple in the guise of a *jogi* and tells Chanda about her love. Both meet secretly at night at her *dhorahar*. The secret is, however, revealed and Chanda elopes with Lorik and they stay in Hardipattan. Lorik's valour and love are put to the test in many adventures during this period, which only deepens his love for Chanda and they live together happily. Lorik, however, returns to Govara after receiving a message sent by his wife Maina through a *nayak* of a *tanda* who tells Lorik about the sufferings of his wife pining away in separation. It is not clear from the text, which ends abruptly, as what was the end of the story.[29]

Qutban also presents his story in a fairy-tale setting and elaborates the *katha* of Mirgavati, the princess of Kanchannagar and Prince Raj Kunwar, the son of King Ganpatidev of Chandragiri. Prince Raj Kunwar is fond of playing *hinguri* (polo) and hunting, and one day, in the forest, sees an unusual doe adorned with ornaments. He follows her but it disappears in a lake (*Mansarovar*). The prince waits for her for a year and one day he finds out that the doe is in fact a beautiful fairy Mirgavati and falls in love with her. He steals her *chir* on the advice of her *dhai* and Mirgavati is unable to fly. Mirgavati lives with the prince for some time and is attracted towards him. One day, however, she succeeds in getting hold of her *chir* and returns to her father's capital, which is located in a distant island in the ocean. The prince becomes a *jogi* and goes in search of her. During this period he also rescues a princess, Rupmani, from a demon, and her father forces him to marry her. The prince escapes from there and after facing many hardships he succeeds in reaching Kanchannagar. Finally Mirgavati, Rupmani, and the prince are united.

The story of *Padmavat* is woven around a princess of exquisite beauty, Padmavati, the daughter of Gandhavsen, the king of Sinhaldip. Ratansen, the king of Chittor, after listening to the *nakh-shikh* from a talking parrot, Hiraman, goes to Sinhaldip in the guise of a *jogi* in search of Padmavati and sends a letter to her, written with his blood and tears, through Hiraman expressing his feelings how his love for her has taken the life out of him and he can only be revived when he gets an opportunity to meet her. Hiraman delivers the letter to Padmavati that kindles the fire of love in her. She sends him a reply that she can accept him only when she becomes sure of the sincerity of his love and he should show that he is ready to die for his love and come to her palace. Ratansen proves the sincerity of his love and tries to enter the *kot* (the fortress) but is made captive along with fellow-*jogis* by the guards and taken to the stake with his companions. However, he is released by the king who comes to know about his royal status by a bard, who is in reality Lord Shiva, and he gives Padmavati's hand in marriage to him. Ratansen, after listening to the sufferings of his separated wife Nagmati, through a message conveyed by a bird, returns to Chittor with Padmavati. He is, however, made captive by Sultan Alauddin who wants to possess his beautiful wife, but released through the valour and strategy of his warriors Gora and Badal. Meanwhile a rival king Devpal tries to win Padmavati's favour, and is attacked by a furious Ratansen who dies in the duel and Padmavati and Nagmati become *sati* with the king.

All these narrative poems are not mere tales of love; the Sufi poets lay emphasis on their allegorical meaning and their portrayal of love is based on the concept of mystical love (*ishq; prem-marg*). The central figure in these epics is a woman, who is the symbol of divine love. *Ishq* is the final goal of the hero who symbolises the soul's yearning for God and the attainment of the love of the woman symbolises the mystical union with God. The representation of women in allegorical terms is more pronounced in *Padmavat*. The union of Padmavati and Ratansen, for instance, is depicted as the union of the moon and the sun. Jayasi uses the Nath-yogi imagery of the mystical union as the merging of the two heavenly bodies.

Jayasi further elaborates the allegorical symbols:

nagmati yeha duniya dhandha
bacha soi na ehi chit bandha[30]

That Nagmati represents the concerns of this world; one whose mind is bound by this is not free.

tan chitaur man raja kinha
hiya singhal budhi padmini kinha

The body is Chittor, the mind its king, the heart is Sinhala, the wisdom can be seen as Padmavati.[31]

However, the concept of divine love and such other themes appear to be treated in a casual manner by these poets. For instance, after returning to Chittor, Padmavati no longer remains the object of mystical love. These tales, as Qutban points out, delineate other sentiments also apart from *jog* such as *vir* and *singar*.[32]

It is not the religiosity of the woman that matters for these Sufis, that is probably the least described theme; there are only casual references to the observance of religious rituals by ladies. On the contrary, they describe pure mundane matters, which brings out graphic images of women in all shades and hues: the carefree life and youthful passion of the young girls; the ideals of wedded women and the real-life situations faced by them in a society given to polygamy; the allurements and the love affair of a *parkiya*, as one finds in *Chandayan*; the performing women and the women of free love of which we get vivid depiction in *Mirgavati* and *Padmavat*. The *duti*, a go-between used by lovers and probably chosen from the class of skilled entertainers, emerges as a prominent figure in these epics; however, the delineation of women companions and slave girls is scanty. The *dhai*, however, appears to have occupied an important place in the households of the princely families. Maulana Daud has the ability and fluency to add more details to his story and that these details are realistically vivid may be seen in his representation of women. Daud employs the verbs from the popular stock and the idioms of the common women folk to a considerable extent. Only *Masnavi saharul bayan* of Mir Hasan Dehalwi in Urdu is as imposing in such details as *Chandayan*. Daud provides us glimpses of the life of common people and provides us an opportunity to know about the spoken dialect of the womenfolk in the countryside of the Awadh region during the fourteenth century. Qutban's and Jayasi's female characters, however, represent urban women who converse in a sophisticated language.

It may be noted here that the evocation of beauty by these poets presents a blend of the convention of *Kamasutra*, the Nath-yogi tradition as well as the concept of beauty that originated in the medieval cultural surroundings. The term *nayika-bhed* is not used in these *akhyans*. The description of four types of women (*Stri-bhed*) by Raghav: the *hastini, shakhini*, *chitrini* and lastly the *padmini*, a class of woman of exquisite beauty is in the mould of *Kamasutra*, but certain new traits also appear in the description. Padmavati of Chittor is in all respect such a perfect woman with a body of golden hue and divine radiance.[33] The association of the perfect woman *padmini*, who has sixteen marks of beauty, also brings in the connotation of the religious idioms of the *Jogi*. In this tradition *Sinhaladip* is the place where a *jogi* goes for the attainment of *siddhi* and it is also the centre of the women of the *padmini* category. Not only the queens, even the *paniharis* in the palace of the king Gandharvsen of *Sinhaladip* were of *Padmini* variety:

pani bhare aavahi panihari
rup sarup padmini nari
padumgandh tinha ang basaahi
bhanvar laagi tinh sang firaahi[34]

However, *nakh-shikh*, i.e. description of beauty from top to toe, conventionally of a woman is a poetic convention borrowed from the *apbhransh* poetry and the enumeration of sixteen marks of beauty, and *battis-lakhan* (*lakshan*, sign) is of typical medieval Indian origin.

Significantly, the metaphors used in the description of *nakh-shikh* bring out some interesting details about north Indian religious practices. In a vivid description of the beauty/demeanour of Padmavati from her hair, which is like a tress of black snakes, to her lotus-like feet where all the ascetics want to put their head, Hiraman refers to *karvat* and other practices in this context.

Daud provides interesting details about the sartorial styles of the fourteenth century. The articles of female attire were *phundiya, sari, meghvaana, kusiyaara, chir, pataangi, mungia, mandila, chundari,* etc. Of these, only a few varieties are traceable. The varieties of cloth used in the making of such attire were *chokaria, doria, chandrota, abjaaru, pator* and *khirodak.*[35] *Pator* is frequently mentioned and it was an expensive variety of silk. The leather slippers were known as *ghai-pai.* The hair-do was usually in the *patravali* style that remained in fashion till the first half of the twentieth century and known as *patti bithana. Barah ahrann* (twelve ornaments) and *solah singar* (marks of beauty) are described by Qutban in conventional mould.

II

The heroines of these epics are queens and princesses leading a lavish lifestyle. They live in palaces, usually seven storeys high. *Chandayan* provides a rare glimpse of the interior of a palace, where Chanda used to live, located in the midst of an *ambrai* (a mango orchard) with a *phulwari* in the front and four *panvari* (entrances). It was an ensemble of *maan-khand* (probably guest room), *batsaar* (*baithak*), *sain-mandir* (bedroom) and *oberi* (?), and *attaris* (*atta, attalika)* on all four sides decorated above with a *chaukhandi,* i.e. four-storeyed domed structure with its walls worked in mural paintings in gold on a vermilion background.[36] It appears that princesses' generally used to live in the *dhorahar,* which was the uppermost structure on the top of the mansion.[37]

Jayasi provides us the images of the youth of women, the freedom of the unwedded girls to move around and carefree life in their parental house; their budding sexual desires and their anxiety about their life in a new environment in the house of their in-laws after their wedding; all these aspects are illustrated at the time when Padmavati goes to the lake with her *sakhis*. There they bathe and discuss their future marriages:

jau lahi ahai pita kar raju
kheli lehu jaun khelahu aaju[38]
dhani so khela khelahin rasa pemaa
rautaai au kusal khema[39]

One is amazed at the boldness in these comments of the young companions (*sakhi*) who intended to play the game of love (*khelahin rasa pemaa*). The way Padmavati frankly reveals her heart before Hiraman *sua* and her *dhai* and expresses her desire and longing (*kamanurag)* for a lover, reminds us of the courtesan culture of the early medieval period, of which we find vivid delineation in the Sanskrit plays and *akhyayikas*. She goes to the temple along with her friends to worship and pray for a good match on the occasion of *Shri Panchami;* here she meets with Ratansen (who is in the guise of a yogi) who faints when he sees her beauty. She smears his chest with sandal paste and inscribes a message on it.[40] Even at the time of her wedding, when Padmavati meets Ratansen for the first time, she does not behave like a *mugdha nayika*. She behaves in the fashion of an accomplished courtesan, plays *sari pancha.*

The young girls of the princely families and of the upper strata were placed under the supervision of a *dhai* who took care of their needs, related them stories and so on.[41] She was a sort of governess; reliable and dedicated to the well-being of her ward. Sufi *akhyans* portray the *dhai*'s faithfulness in two ways: she is the one who fulfills the wish of her mistress at any cost, as we find in *Chandayan*. The *dhai* Birespati asks Chanda to reveal her feelings about Lorik without any hesitation:

rajkunwari tu kaani na karain
haun so dhai mori laaj na dharai[42]

She makes arrangements for their meeting in the *devra* (temple) as well as *dhorahar* of the palace. She asks Lorik to disguise himself as a *jogi* and encourages him to go to the *dhorahar* at night. *Padmavat*, however, brings out her other side. The advent of the spring-festival 'unleashes' the youthful passion and sexual desire in Padmavati, she is burning with the desire for her beloved and shares her feelings with her *dhai*. The *dhai* asks her to restrain herself till she meets her true match and warns her of the force of *joban* and converts her longing into the devoted service of a *sati;* she also advises her to endure the pain of love like a *sipi* (oyster) who lives in the ocean yet retains its thirst until it gets water in the *swati* (*nakshatra)*. She asks her to control herself:

joban turai haath gahi lijai jahan jai tahan jai na dijai
joban jo re matang gaj ahai gahu giyan jimi ankush gahai
abahin bari tum prem na khela ka janasi kas hoi duhela

Keep that stallion, i.e. youth firmly under your control and do not let it go wherever it wants to go. The youth is like a rutting elephant; check it with the hook of wisdom. You are still a girl and have not played the game of love yet; (and thus) you are ignorant of the sufferings it can cause'. The *dhai* advises her to remain firm in her *sat* (fortitude) when she feels the passion of love:

kahesi pema jaun upanaa bari
bandhu satta man dol na bari[43]

Interestingly, from *Mirgavati*, it appears that the princes also confided in their *dhai*s more than in any other person.

III

The ideal of love assumes a distinct form in a society depicted by these poets wherein polygamy was an established tradition amongst both Hindus and Muslims. Love is not a bond of togetherness between husband and wife, but it is a kind of *seva* performed by the wife. The man with several wives enjoys the love of his women as worship.[44] The longing of a woman is converted in to devoted service of a *sati*.

Sat (from Sanskrit *sattva*) denotes truth and faithfulness. The concept of *sat* is demonstrated in various episodes. When Ratansen is captured by Sultan Alauddin Khalji, a rival king Devpal tries to take advantage of the situation and sends a *duti* to win over Padmavati in his favour. Padmavati keeps her *sat* and remains faithful to her husband and is not carried away by the deceitful talks of the *duti*. When Ratansen dies defending her honour against Devpal, both the queens become *sati* in expectation of the final union in the paradise. *Sati*, the rite of self-immolation, is described by Jayasi in detail:

padmavati nai pahari patori   *chali sath hoi piya ki jori*
suraj chhpa raini hoi gai   *punivan sasi so amavas bhai*
chore kesa moti lar chhute   *janahun raini nakhat sab tute*
sendura para jo sis ughari   *agi laga janu jag andhiyari*
...   .
dipak priti patanga jeun janam nibah kareun[45]

After giving alms they took seven rounds of the pyre and then they mounted the *khat* (bier) with the hope that now they could behold the *shiv-lok* (i.e. heaven).[46] Both Nagmati and Padmavati immolated themselves on the funeral pyre of Ratansen. The *maha sat* (i.e. *satitva)* of both the women was held in high esteem by the *sati* women who were accompanying them.

One may refer here the *pariksha* (test) of true love carried out by the female deities. Parvati, the consort of Shiva, assumes the form of an *achhari* (*apsara*) and make all sorts of allurements to Ratansen who, however, remains true to his love. Similarly at the time of his return from the isle of Sinhala, Ratansen's ships are caught in the storm.

Padmavati and Ratansen are rescued with the help of Lakshmi, the daughter of the ocean. She also wants to test the 'steadiness' of Ratansen's love and takes on the form of Padmavati and tries to allure him and finally becomes convinced of his sincerity. This motif is borrowed from the medieval folklore. The women characters and dieties in medieval folklore present a queer combination of courtesan and *sati*.

IV

Woman as the Beloved

The women in these epics are generally bold. Take the example of Badal's newly-wed wife. She approaches her husband who is ready to go to Delhi for the rescue of the king. She does not behave like a *nai-naveli* and sits humbly till his return. Instead, she grabs her waist and asks him why he is going when they have not yet met. She tries all tricks to attract him, falls at his feet and tells him that she has also come prepared for the battle of love and she will fight with the weapons that are provided by her beauty. Badal, however, leaves her saying that the *seva* to his lord is more important than the love to his wife.

On the day of the wedding, Padmavati seems worried about the coming night as she is inexperienced in love and does not know what her husband would expect. The *sakhis* wake up Ratansen telling him that Guru Gorakh has come for the pupil. Padmavati, feeling shy, hides her face in the *ghunghat*. However, she soon recovers her wit and accuses Ratansen of not being a serious lover. Ratansen, using the metaphor of betel proves the sincerity of his love for her.[47] Padmavati proposes to play *saripansa* (the game of dice) with Ratansen to test his love and all aspects of love are presented by her in the terms of the game of dice. Ratansen replies in similar terms. He also uses the imagery of the *rasayani* (a sect of *jogis*) such as *para* (mercury) and *gandhak* (sulphur) for displaying the depth of his love. Padmavati finds that his love is true and then relates her own feelings for the king, offers her body to Ratansen and merges with her lover in body and soul. Padmavati does not behave like a *mugdha* or pretend shyness. Instead she tells her *sakhis* that she has learnt the secret of love. The next evening, Padmavati, dressed in beautiful attire and ornaments, goes to Ratansen and earnestly urges him to fight the battle of love. Ratansen conquers her, employing his skill in the *chaurasi-aasan* of *kam-kala* (eighty-four codified arts of lovemaking) and both enjoy the company of each other and the beauty of the six seasons.[48] All this description prompts us to suggest that it was not only the elite patrons and literati had familiarity with *Kamasutra*,[49] its memory survived at popular level in the oral tradition.

Jayasi is rather restrained in his description and he merely refers to the conventions of lovemaking described in the *Kamasutra*. Maulana Daud describes the sex-scenes in great detail without referring to the text.

Depiction of *Sautiya Dah*

The Sufi poets have also provided the images of envious wives. The feeling of envy for the co-wife is known as *sautiya dah*. The fight between the co-wives is a theme wherein Daud and Jayasi shine most. Daud's presentation of the fight-scene is realistic. He virtually takes us to a fourteenth century north Indian household and uses the expressions of the womenfolk, which are still used by the women coming from lower strata, especially from the rural background, in north India. On the occasion of the *Somnath-puja* performed in the month of *Asarh*, Chanda meets Maina and irritates her by her biting comments as to why Maina looked so sad. Was it due to her fight with the mother-in-law or because her husband was not sleeping with her or her husband suspects her of adultery:

hasi kai chhandai maina bujhi kai   sasurei huti aayihu jhujhi
… … … …
kai saain nisi sej na aavai   tei santap dukh raini bihavai
… … …
kai sungaai kahu seu apjas aani charaav[50]

These comments infuriate Maina and she retaliates in similar terms, using expressions such as *baanguri*, *besa* and *dari*:

dekhau baangari kiru dhithaai   aai so bujhati baat sugaai
jasi aapan tasi avrahi jaanai   jasi chhinar tasi suugi bakhaanai
… … … …
tain kaadiikhi haun besa dari   chitt sugaai dinhi mohi gari[51]

The fight of Chanda and Maina is not confined to words only; the two women physically entangle with each other, pouncing like cats, using their nails and ripping off each other's clothes. Chanda tears away the *chandrota-choli* of Maina and Maina furiously removes the *chir* of Chanda and tears her *patangi*. Their hair becomes in disarray during the course of this (*haatha-baanhi*) and earrings and other ornaments are broken.[52] They look like distressed women going to drown themselves in the river. Even the travellers stop to watch to see this *nataramb h* (*natak*?) in the *devra*.[53] Lorak tried to console them and offers them *khandvani* and betel leaves flavoured with camphor and *ek-hkand chhapa sari*.[54]

Jayasi, however, uses this opportunity for pedantic display and uses the negative connotation of *kamal* (lotus flower) in a scornful manner in the scene of the fight between Nagmati and Padmavati. Although in a message to Padmavati, which she sent to her at Sinhaldip, Nagmati declared that she would be satisfied only by just a glance of her husband, implying that Ratansen belonged to Padmavati:

mohi bhog so kaj na bari saunh dishti ke chahanhari[55]

But she begins to burn with anger at the sight of her. After coming to Chittor, Ratansen goes to Nagmati who initially turns him away but he convinces her of his love. [What could she do beyond this? She had to accept it as her fate in those days of polygamy.] In the morning Ratansen returns to Padmavati, who starts crying and tells him that he has left her for Nagmati and preferred a *nag* (snake) over lotus. Thus, from the very first day in Chittor, Padmavati becomes envious of Nagmati and she even goes to fight with her in her *bari* (garden) and an argument develops between them. Nagmati also retaliates, telling her not to be proud of her beauty because the lake where the lotus blooms is filthy, and the smell of the water is so awful that it does not go even if one washes a thousand times. Ratansen forbids them to fight and tells them that through *seva* both can be united with him and enjoy *sukh-bhog,* i.e. his love:

tumha ganga jamuna dui naari likha Muhammada jog
seva karahu mili dunahu au maanahu sukh bhog[56]

Images of *Virahini-Nayika*

The Sufi poets described the images of women suffering from *virah* (the pain of separation caused by the absence of the beloved). The best illustrations are found in the *baramasa*, which is a literary convention of *apbhransh* poetry and woven around the theme of love and vexation caused by the separation of the beloved. This *virah*-motif describing the longing of the waiting wife or beloved, has survived in the folk songs rendered on the occasion of the swing-festival. Maulana Daud used this literary convention in *Chandayan.* The *baramasa* of Maina and Nagmati have the description of festivals that fall in the twelve months of Indian lunar calendar. We can have some idea of the ritualistic dances performed by womenfolk in these *baramasa* such as *diwali* (*parab devari*), and the rendition of *jhumak* by the womenfolk on that occasion; on the occasion of the festival of *hori* (*fag*), *chanhari* (*charchari*) was performed. On the occasion of *vasant panchami,* Jayasi refers to various dance-forms, such as *dhamaris, manora-jhumak* and *charchari*, generally performed in groups.[57] Some of these are still prevalent in rural north India.

Interestingly, we don't find mention of the swing festival in any of these works. In the month of *kuwar* (*ashwin*) the young girls (*bari*) welcome the *nav-ritu* by burning lamps in the *charua*, and preparation of a variety of food, in every household in the *pitar-pakh* (*pitra-paksh*).[58] The *baramasa* of Rupmani is done as a ritual in *Mirgavati*.

Baramasa, describing the *virah* of Nagmati is considered as one of the best literary pieces of the Sufi poetry, and at some places it retains the flavour of *apbhransh*:

saaras jori kimi hari mari gaeu kina khaggi
jhuri jhuri paanjari dhani bhai birha ke laagi aggi

Nagmati, who is pining away as a separated woman for a year, wanders in the forest and asks the birds for the news of her husband. She says:

katha jo kahai aai piya keri   paanvari houn janam bhari cheri[59]

Nagmati endures the pain of separation in the manner of corn in burning sand. She is totally devoid of the feelings of envy and pride, and is only interested in seeking a glimpse of her husband. What is more interesting here is the fact that in the *baramasa,* Nagmati also represents the woman of an ordinary household who sees the arrival of *chaumasa* not as an occasion of enjoyment, but as a cause for worry for her about the repair of the roof to stop rainwater from seeping into the house:

pushya nakhat sir upar aava   hon bin naah mandir ko chhava[60]

Nagmati's character shines most as a *preshitpatika* (one whose beloved is away from her), one of the sixteen types (*nayika-bhed*) described in the *riti* poetry in Brajbhasha and in the paintings of the seventeenth century. A proud woman of beauty and wealth suddenly finds herself in distress as her husband deserts her for another woman.

Padmavati is also sorrowful without her beloved, who is a captive of Sultan Alauddin Khilji. She is scorched with the fire of *virah.* In vain she pours out the *dol* (bucket) of her eyes to extinguish the fire of her heart; for moment her life comes back and the next moment it departs:

naina dola bhari dhaarai hien na aagi bujhai
ghari ghari jiu bahurai ghari jiu jai[61]

The description is, however, done as a ritual in her case. Padmavati emerges as a strong personality at the time of crisis. She does not cry when Ratansen is captured by the sultan. She keeps her cool and tactfully wins over the angry warriors Gora and Badal, and plans out a strategy for release of the king, which shows the strength of her character and her intelligence. She does not cry even at the time of Ratansen's death.[62]

Woman as a *Parkiya*

The concept of a *parkiya* apparently originated during the early medieval period. *Kuttanimatam* by Damodar (written c. ninth century) refers to the practice of *Bandhaki-gaman* (secret love with other person's wife), which is recommended in preference to a *ganika*, who was a devourer of wealth.[63] Whether this practice became popular in fashionable society of the time wherein the courtesans dominated, is not clear. However, the portrayal of Radha as a *parkiya-nayika* in Jaeydev's *Geet-Govindam* became a popular literary convention in medieval poetry. Chanda, the heroine of *Chandayan*, depicts the love of a *parkiya* (another man's wife) in all its shades. She is projected as a *chhinari* (*swairini*).

Chanda becomes restless (*bekarara*) after seeing Lorik and she asks her *dhai* either to take her to Lorik or bring him to her place:

chhand virspat ke paan pari   kaalhi suraju dekhiyun eik ghari
kai ohi more gharen bolavahi   kai moi lai oken dand laavahi[64]

Encouraged by Biraspati, Lorik makes a daring effort to go to the *dhorahar* with the help of the lasso (*barha*, i.e. *kamand*) and finds Chanda sleeping in the *chaukhandi*.He grabs her hand and wakes her and then follows a long conversation and Chanda reveals her feelings to Lorik.[65] Then follow the description of sex-scenes[66] and Maulana Daud concludes by saying:

bhav kar [chitu] upnaa lor madan a [?]ti laag
ati [ras?] rasiku senj funi raave chaanda dey suhaag[67]

Chanda as a *parkiya* became so popular that it became the theme of contemporary paintings. There are many illustrated copies of *Chandayan* painted in the *Chaurpanchashika* style; some folios are in Bhartiya Kala Bhavan, Varanasi.

IV

Strangely, these texts tell us very little about the traditions and practices of the class of performing women; those who acquired skill in one or the other arts for the entertainment of people; or those who had an expert knowledge of the science of love and its ancillary arts and who sold pleasure for profit. There is a casual reference to some female entertainers, *gayan bedini*, *swangi* or *nati*, or the slave-girls (*dasi*, *cheti* or *kanizak-i kinari*), who used to be trained in dance and music and other ancillary arts during our period of study.[68] We also don't find them delineated in the capacity of *dasi* or attendant to the gods or part of temple ceremonials in these *akhyans*.

However, we find *Paturi* (*patur*), the medieval incarnation of *ganika*, delineated at some length in the context of a dance repertoire in *Mirgavati*. *Patur* appears to be a generic term in use for skilled entertainers.[69] Even though sex and love are not referred to in the context of performing women in medieval sources as *kala, shilp* and *tantra,* they were distinct from those who sold virtue for profit. Prostitution was one of the attributes and not the sole aim of their profession.

The *Patur* combined the attributes of a *nati* and a *ganika*. The status of a *nati* as an accomplished stage artiste declined considerably during this period as theatre had no place in the *majlisi hunars* of the elite patrons, who conformed to the Persian cultural tradition. In the new cultural scenario, the theatre became a source of entertainment for the masses. *Ganika* also disappeared from the cultural scene after the establishment of the Delhi Sultanate during the thirteenth century, as the new patrons had no appreciation for her arts. Many traditional arts of the indigenous courtesan were lost as they were no longer profitable for her trade and her memory as well as the ideal of her sixty-four arts now survived only in the oral and literary tradition. Gradually the term *ganika* became a synonym of the woman of free love.

Patur became the custodian of the traditional musical forms and dance as well as expert in the latest styles and techniques of Indian and central Asian music, which found vogue during the period. *Paturs* were skilled entertainers is asserted by the fact that they performed in the exclusive gatherings and generally employed in the *akharas* (musical assemblies) maintained by the rulers and their nobles during the sixteenth century. The *paturs* also had skill, like the *nati,* in the theatre art, which was becoming a popular mode of entertainment in the form of *swang, bahurup* and *bhagatbazi* about this period. Some of these *paturs* acquired skill in different kinds of make-up and the art of disguise and were known as *Swangi*. This class of performing women appears to be well trained in stagecraft and the term *swang* in the context of theatrical show probably originated during this period with reference to them. Jayasi mentions one *patur* of the *akhara* of Sultan Alauddin Khalji who acted excellently as a *jogan.*[70] This also suggests that different kinds of costumes were also used in the musical shows performed in the *akharas*. It appears from Badauni's description that the nobles of the Sultanate period were fond of *Paturbazi* and many of them kept *akharas.*[71] He does not elaborate the term *akhara* for the reason that it was well known in Hindustan. However, he mentions that some Sanskrit works on this type of entertainment were translated into Persian during the reign of Sultan Firuz Shah Tughlaq, which were then called *Paturbazi.*[72] The term *akhara*[73] was becoming popular during the sixteenth century and it was used in various contexts: a playhouse, a musical assembly and a group of performing women.

Qutban provides a fairly good picture of the dance repertoire of the *paturis* (*paturs*) in a royal gathering. After the betel leaves were served to the guests, arrangements were made for *naach. Natsar ka saj* or the paraphernalia of *natyashala* for the show was brought in and a stage was improvised. Then arrived the performers which included *natwa, paturi, nayak, pakhawaji, upangi, jantkar* and performers on *bramh-bin, sur-bin, avdhuti* and *rudra-bin, shabd-sura, surmandal, bans, pinak, sarangi, maadar* (*mardal*) and *kahal*. The instrumentalists and percussionists enchanted the listeners with their string play and *shabd*, i.e. the rhythmic patterns respectively.[74] The performance of the vocalists, who rendered six *raags* and thirty *bharjas*, was followed by the *naach* of the *paturi* who were attired in *dakhni kachhani* and *chandan-choli* and wore ankle bells. They began the dance with all sorts of blandishment (*kam-cheshta*) and coquetry. Music was provided by *gayans* who started rendering *maantha, dhauras* and *jhumra prabandhs* and the dancers performed accordingly in unison.

Qutban gives a graphic description of their repertoire:

sarab nil rupak chhand au chaali   dekhi jat panvar iktali
atth-talo pattalo naachi   tal dihinh, janaun dhar taachi
sis niyar kudai manh monti   daha dihinh chakr bhanvahi urdhuti
saro akanch khargai dhara   maan lehi par tal nipara[75]

Among the dancers the performance of one Mahendri was found superb and she was rewarded handsomely. Besides the *payand* (the travel expenses) she was given a hundred horses as well as *mundari, toders* (*tora*?), *kanthhar*, as well as *paat, pator*, and *chir* and *taanka* (*tankas*) in abundance. Other *paturis* were also laden with ornaments from top to toe (*pa lehi neiur sar maang*) in reward.[76] This is one of the rare instances when we find a skilled entertainer mentioned by name during the period under review.

These details are extremely useful in understanding the context of the contemporary practices of north Indian dance. The term *natsar ka saj* reminds us of the pre-sultanate days when *sangit* was an amalgam of acting, dancing and singing, and knowledge of stagecraft was deemed essential for the entertainers and the patrons.

The term *sudhang* (a phonetic degeneration of *shuddha-ang*) is not found in the Sanskrit musicological literature. The Persian musical treatises of the fourteenth and fifteenth centuries also do not mention it. However, we find its description in *Tuhfat al- Hind* as a dance form wherein the units of *tals* were performed accompanied with graceful body movement (*kichol*) and expressive and suggestive postures (*ada u andaz*). In it a variety of *angs* were performed. Mirza Khan has also provided valuable details about some of these *angs* which, according to his description, were numerous.[77] Interestingly, this dance-form came to be known as *thai thai naach* during the late eighteenth century among the masses.[78] Later on it was integrated in *Kathak Natwari Nritya* at Lucknow, the capital of the kingdom of Awadh.

The term *prabandh* continued in the professional parlance during the fifteenth and early sixteenth century.

In Jayasi's description of *singarhat* (the market of beauty), some details are found about the *besa* (*veshya*), the women of free love and her arts and wile, which she adopted to earn profit. She indulged in all kinds of flirtations (*hav*) to capture the heart of her clients and to secure a livelihood. Contrary to *patur*, who were generally employed by the kings and the nobles, the *Vaishya* (*besa)* was a freelancer and operated her trade in the *singarhat*, a busy marketplace in an urban area where sellers of cosmetic items, florists, perfume sellers (*gandhis*) used to trade. One could also get hold of performing artistes including the storyteller, dancers, puppet masters, and stage artistes who had expertise in *natak* and *chetak*.[79] Amidst these the *besa*, clad in *kusumbhi* (deep orange) attire and decorated with all kinds of make-up and jewel-embedded *khunbhi* (earrings) and betel leaf in her mouth, carried on her profession and targeted her customers with coquettish glances. Jayasi refers to their great expertise in gambling and in playing the *bin* (*vina*).[80] The *bin* was gaining prominence as a melody-making instrument during the sixteenth century.[81] One is prompted on the basis of a reference in *Padmavat* that the *bin* (*vina*) also used to be played by the elite women:

gahei bin maku raini bihaai   sasi bahan tanhi rahai onaai

These Sufi poems also illustrate the image of *duti* (a messenger). A sharp, ready-witted eloquent woman with an expertise in perceiving the innermost thoughts of others was employed as a *duti* and she was probably recruited from the class of performing women. The service of a *duti* was deemed essential by a courtesan during the early medieval period, as it was not considered appropriate to approach a desired customer directly. During our period of study, however, her services were required on a large scale. Her types were described in detail by Pundarika Vitthala during the late sixteenth century and many musical treatises in Persian, like *Rag Darpan* mention her along with *nayak-nayika* and *sakhi*.[82] We find one *Swangi* from the *akhara* of Sultan Alauddin Khilji sent as *duti* to Chittor in the guise of a *jogan*. Devapal, a rival king sent a *duti* to win over Padmavati in his favour, she pretended to be an old friend of Padmavati and tried to convince her that she was wasting her youth by remaining true to her husband and induced her to go to Devpal:

haar chir tan pahirahi sir kar karahi sambhar
bhog mani le din das joban ke paisar

She further says:

jani tum baari karasi asa jiu *jau lahi joban to lahi piu*
purukh sinh aapan kehi kera *ek khai dosareha munh hera*

... ...

kit pavasi puni joban rata *maimamt carha syam sir chhata*
joban bin biridha hoi nau *binu joban thakasi sab thaau*[83]

Where will you get this passionate youth, it comes riding on an elephant with a black parasol, i.e. black hair above its head; without youth old age appears; without youth you will be stuck everywhere. Padmavati does not give in and discovers the true nature of the person who pretended to be her friend. She declines her proposal saying that it will be like putting *masi* on my face. At this the *duti* uses the word *masi* in such a way that implies the positive meaning of the word. This shows that a *duti* required communication skill besides expertise in the art of disguise.

These Sufi *premakhyans*, thus, project varied images of woman as beloved, in all its shades—as an ideal woman, a *parkiya,* and also as a woman trained in the tradition of skilled entertainments. Aspects of her family life are not portrayed in this kind of literature. A complete picture of women in that age will emerge only when we explore other vernacular literature of the period.

REFERENCES

1. *Chandayan*, Mataprasad Gupta (ed.), Agra, 1967, *karvak*, 10, 11, 17. See also *Ardhakathanak*, Mataprasad Gupta (ed.), Allahabad, 1943.
2. *Mirgavati*, Parmeshwarilal Gupta (ed.), Banaras, 1967, *karvak*, 8; 'Abdu'l Qâdir al-Badâûnî, *Muntakhab al-Tavârîkh*, ed. by Ahmad 'Ali Sahib, Introduction and Notes Tofigh H. Sobhani, Tehran, 2001, p. 11.
3. Badâûnî, p. 172; English Trans., George S.A. Ranking, Delhi, Reprint, 1973, Vol. I , p. 333.
4. See *stuti-khand*, of *Padmavat* in *Jayasi Granthavali,* ed. Ram Chandra Shukla, Varanasi, *samvat* 2035, 1978, *karvak* 20, p. 6; from *Padmavat* it appears that Jayasi was also deeply attached to Shaikh Ashraf Jahangir of the Chishti *silsila* (see *stuti-khand*, karvak 8, p. 6), and that like his *pir* Shaikh Burhan, he also believed in the *Mahadawi* tradition (*'guru mohdi khevak mein karva'* (*karvak*, 20, p. 6).
5. *Chandayan*, *karvak* 329, p. 327.
6. *Ibid*, also see *karvak*, 61,143, 259, pp. 59, 140, 251–52.
7. *Mirgavati, karvak*, 398, p. 431.
8. *Ibid, karvak*, 14, p. 121.
9. *Padmavat*, *Singhaldip varnankhand, karvak*, 1, p. 20.
10. *Padmavat*, *karvak* 1, p. 245. He further says to think about this *prem-katha*

(love story) in the way he perceived, and to make clarifications in case of any ambiguity in this regard:
prem katha ehi bhanti bicharahu bujhi lehu jo bujhai parhu (*ibid*.).

11. Benarasidas, *Ardhakathanak* (ed.) Mata Prasad Gupta, Prayag, 1943, verse 335, p. 25.
12. *Chandayan, karvak* 9.
13. The use of the natha-yogi elements in Sufi poetry shows that they played a central role in north Indian popular religion. The Naths came to be the followers of a legendry guru Gorakhnath. The main centre of the cult was Gorakhpur but the graves (*samadhis*) of many famous local Naths and Siddhas developed into important regional centres of pilgrimage and devotion. Sinhala dip was the *siddha pitha* for the *gorakhpantis*.
14. *Chandayan, karvak* 138, p. 135.
15. Jayasi says:
adi ant jasi katha ahai likhi bhasha chaupai kahai
turaki arabi, hindui bhasha jeri adhi
see *Padmavat*, I, p. 245.
16. Qutban says; *gatha doha arilla racha* I *sortha chopahinhkai saja* II (*Mirgavati, karvak*, 13, p. 120).
17. *Doha* is a self-contained verse-form generally used for lending rhetorical force to the stanza.
18. For details see Introduction by Mata Prasad Gupta, *Chandayan*, p. 14; Parmeshwarilal Gupta, *Mirgavati*, p. 44; Jâyasi Malik Muhammad, *Padmâvat*, in *Jâyasî Granthâvali*, ed. Ram Chandra Shukla, Varanasi, *samvat* 2035/1978, p. 148.
19. For instance, *rau rupchand bola bahuri eihai khand gau* (*Chandayan, karvak*, 64, p. 258); The Persian heading at one place, *aakhir bishar khand chand sukhan farmudan bai maulana naththan*, also denotes that the narrative had the scheme of *khand* division.
20. *Chandayan, karvak*, 18.
21. *Ibid, karvak*, 329. He refers to some portion of his poetry as *khand* (section).
22. This trait persists even in the early nineteenth century in *Bagh u bahar*, a literary work in Urdu prose produced at Fort William College, Calcutta. Mir Amman begins his work in the style of a narrator asking his audience to be attentive. '*main apne qisse ka aghaz karta hun, zara kan dhar kar suno*', p. 1.
23. *Mirgavati, karvak*, 13, p. 120.
24. *Mirgavati, karvak*, 431, p. 398.
25. Badauni, tr. Ranking , vol. I, p. 333.
26. See Madhu Trivedi, 'Imperial Agra as a Cultural Node: Late 16th to early 17th century', paper presented in a Seminar on Qazi Nurullah Shustari, held on 18th–20th January, 2003 at Agra.
27. See S. Wadley, 'Choosing a Path, Performance Strategies in a North Indian Epic', in Blackburn et al. ed., *Oral Epics in India*, where she describes the drums, melody prose and poetry as the tools of an oral performer.
28. For details, see Madhu Trivedi, '*Art and culture as reflected in the Sufi Premakhyans: Chandayan and Mirgavat*', paper presented in a seminar on

'Culture Economy and Social Change in Medieval India 12th–18th century', held on 5–7 January, Aligarh, 2002.

29. The text suggests an early death of both Lorik and Chanda. According to the folk version of the story Chanaini and *loriki*, prevalent amongst the *Ahir* community, the news is spread that Maina was away with someone at night and one infuriated family member kills Lorik, thinking him to be another man. Chanda and Maina become *sati*. According to another version, Lorik died by performing the rite of *karsi sijhana*, a form of self-immolation by putting a pile of *karsi* (dung-cakes) all around the body which slowly burnt him, see *Chandayan*, ed. Mata Prasad, p. 33.
30. *Padmavat*, I, p. 245.
31. For details see Th. De Bruijn, *The Rubi hidden in the Dust, A study of the Poetics of Malik Muhammad Jayasi's Padmavat*, Leiden, 1996.
32. *Mirgavati*, *karvak* 431, p. 398.
33. *Padmavat*, *stri-bhed varnan khand*, *karvak* 1–4, pp. 169–70.
34. *Sinhaladip varnan khand*, *karvak*, 8, p. 10.
35. *Chandayan*, *karvak*, 81, 83, 139, 265, pp. 79, 81, 136, 258.
36. *Chandayan*, *karvak*, 39, 135, 193, 264, pp. 37, 132, 188. *Mirgavati*, *karvak*, 39, 377, pp. 136; 366; Jayasi uses the term *amraau* for a mango orchard (see *Padmavat*, *karvak*, 3, 4, pp. 8, 9).
37. *Chandayan*, *karvak*, 39, pp. 37, 188; also see *Sinhaladip varnan-khand* in *Padmavat*, *karvak*, 24, p. 15:
    saat khand dhorahar saaja uhei sanvari sakei as raja
    hira eit, kapur gilava auo nag laai sarag lai aava
    bha kataav sab anvat bhaanti chitra kori kai paantahi paanti
    laag khamh-mani-manik jare nisi din rahei dip janu bare
38. *Mansarodak-khand* in *Padmavat*, *Karvak*, 6, p. 20.
39. *Ibid.*
40. *Padmavat*, *janam khand*, *karvak* 7, p. 17; *Padmavati viyog khand*, *karvak*, 2. p. 59; *Basant khand*, *karvak* 3, p. 68.
41. See *Chandayan*, *karvak* 172, p. 167, where Chanda asks Viraspati to tell a *saras-kahani*.
42. *Chandayan*, *karvak*, 139, p. 146.
43. *Padmavat viyog khand*, *karvak*, 3–5, pp. 59–60.
44. *Ibid*, *Nagmati Padmavati vivid khand*, *karvak*, 13, p. 161; *Padmavati viyog khand*, *karvak*, 3, p. 60.
45. *Ibid*. *Padmavati Nagmati sati khand*, *karvak*, 1, p. 244.
46. *nagmati padmavati rani* *duvau mahasat sati bakhanim*
    duvanum sati chhari khat baithi *au sivlok paraa tinh dithi*
    baithau koi raja au pata *ant sabai baithai ehi khata*
    … … … …
    sar rachi dan punni bahu kina *sat bari phiri bhanvari linha*
    eka bhanvari bhai jo re biyahin *ab dosari dai gauhan jahin*
    lai sar upar khat bichhai *paumrihin duvau kant kantha laai*
    … … … …
    au jo ganthi, kant tum sang jori aadi ant dinh jai na chhori
    … … …

kaah jo acchai na ehi jag ham aathi tumha naah duhun jag sathi
(see *Padmavat*, *karvak*, 3, p. 244)

47. Interestingly, these imageries are also used in *Indarsabha*, a play written by Mirza Amanat during the early 19th century.
48. *Padmavat*. For details, see *Padmavati Ratan Sen bhent khand*, pp. 109–13.
49. The *Kamasutra* is a treatise on sex and love by Vatsyayan who, as Moti Chanda opines, deals with his subject from a 'purely mundane point of view'. He incorporated various thoughts on the subject and the entire range of topics on the science of love 'with a cold scientific thoroughness' so much so that it appealed to the ease-loving and pleasure-seeking members of the upper layers of society and became a source of inspiration for artists, poets, sculptors and *ganika* of the early medieval period.
50. *Chandayan*, *karvak*, 250, p. 242.
51. *Ibid*, *karvak*, 259, p. 251.
52. *Ibid*, *karvak*, 260, 261, 265 pp. 253, 253, 255. For details, see *chand Maina vivad khand*, *karvak*, 244–265, pp. 237–259.
53. *Ibid*, *karvak*, 262, p. 255.
54. *Ibid*, *karvak*, 265, p. 258
55. *Ibid*, *Nagmati sandesh khand*, *Karvak* 3, p. 131.
56. *Ibid*, *karvak* 10, p. 155; *Karvak* 13, p. 161.
57. *Jayasi granthavali* (*Basant khand* of *Padmavat*), pp. 65–6.
58. *Chandayan*, *karvak*, 343, 345, pp. 341, 343.
59. For details, see *Nagmati sandesh khand*, *karvak*, 1–15, pp. 130–34.
60. *Ibid*, *Nagmati viyog khand*, *karvak*, 4, p. 124. The way Jayasi paints her sufferings is unparallel in the whole of Hindi literature Ram Chandra Shukla, ed. *Jayasi Granthavali*, p. 29.
61. *Ibid*, *Padmavati Nagmati vilap khand*, *Karvak*, 1, p. 215.
62. See *Padmavati Nagmati sati khand*, *Karvak*, 1–4, pp. 243–44.
63. *Kuttanimatam*, verse, 822, p. 162.
64. *Chandayan*, *karvak* 140, p. 137.
65. *Ibid*, *karvaks* 193, 211, pp. 188, 205. There is a caption in Persian also *guftan-i Chanda hikayat-i ishq-i khud bar Lorik ra.*
66. *Ibid*, *karvak*, 215, pp. 209.
67. *Ibid*, *karvak*, 216, p. 210.
68. Following the practice of the hereditary classes of entertainers, the slave girls in India also began to be trained in many forms of art, which required a vigorous training schedule. Shihabu'ddin al 'Umari, an Arab traveller who came to India during the time of sultan Muhammad bin Tughlaq, tells us about the great care taken in the refinement of Indian slave girls and their good breeding; they could write, recite verses and stories, play chess and backgammon (*shatranj u nard*), and they excelled in music and playing the lute. Their price amounted to 20,000 *tankas* and more (see *Masalik ul Absar fi Mumalik ul Ansar*, English Trans. Otto Spies, Shaikh 'Abdu'r Rashid and S. Moinul Haq, Aligarh, 1943, pp. 45–6). For details, see Madhu Trivedi, *'Court patronage in the Indo-Persian Context: Evolution of Hindustani Music* (13th–19th Centuries)', Paper presented at the international symposium on 'The History of North Indian Music, 14th–

20th centuries', Rotterdam, 18–20 December 1997; Madhu Trivedi, 'Female Performing Artistes in Northern India: A Survey', *Art and Culture : Painting and Perspective,* vol. 2, eds. Ahsan Jan Qaisar and S.P. Verma, Delhi, 2002.

69. William Crook, *The Tribes and Castes of the North Western Provinces and Oudh,* 1896, Delhi reprint, 1974, Vol. II, p. 498.
70. *Padmavat, Badshah duti khand, karvak,* 1, p. 223.
71. Badauni records that by an order of Islam Shah, all the *paturs* were taken away by force from those *amirs* who maintained *akharas* (Badauni, I, p. 496).
72. *Ibid*, Vol. I, pp. 32, 496.
73. Abul Fazl has described the *akhara* in detail in the context of a musical assembly. See *Ain*, Vol. III, p. 273.
74. *Mirgavati, karvak,* 250, 254, pp. 276, 288.
75. *Ibid, karvak,* 256, p. 290.
76. *Ibid, karvak,* 257, pp. 290–91.
77. *Ibid*, Vol. I, p. 440; For details, see Madhu Trivedi, 'Hindustani Music and Dance: An Examination of some Texts in the Indo-Persian tradition', in *The Making of Indo-Persian Culture: Indian and French Studies,* eds. Muzaffar Alam, Francois 'Nalini' Delvoy and Marc Gaborieau, New Delhi, 2000, pp. 281–306.
78. Mir Amman, *Bagh u Bahar* (1803), Urdu, Calcutta, Delhi edition, 1995, p. 153.
79. *Padmavat, Singhal Dip varnan khand*, p. 12.
80. See '*hath bin suni mirig bhulaahi nar mohahi suni pain na jaahi*' (*Ibid, karvak,* 14, p.11).
81. Yahya Kabuli, *Lahjat-i Sikandarshahi*, ed. Shahab Sarmadee, New Delhi, 1999, pp. 470–78.
82. Faqirullah Saif Khan, *Rag Darpan*, ed. Nurul Hasan Ansari and Shatrughan Shukla, Delhi, 1981, p. 51.
83. *Padmavat, Devpal duti khand, karvak,* 16, p. 222.

Chapter 9

Excavating Communalism: Kachhwaha *Rajadharma* and Mughal Sovereignty

Catherine B. Asher

In the spirit of Professor Harbans Mukhia's work, this paper is concerned with tensions in pre-modern Indian history that are often read—or should we say, misread—as communal issues. The scholarly community over the last twenty some years has recognised that the commonly perceived Hindu–Muslim binary is inaccurate and especially that the application of this binary to states' allegiance misses the political dynamics that, in fact, prevailed. The alliance of states might shift over time in barely perceptible ways or sometimes in patently obvious ways. I seek to apply this notion of shifting alliances to Kachhwaha– Mughal relations and in particular to explore how this was manifested in artistic and architectural production. The paper commences with the late sixteenth century, when the highest-ranking nobles in the Mughal system promoted the official Mughal policy of *sulh-i kull* (universal toleration) through the patronage of the visual arts. Continuing this exploration of Mughal–Kachhwaha relations, I consider a third party, the Sisodiyas, who were purportedly both anti-Mughal and anti-Kachhwaha. Here I will show how this uneven triangular relation worked to stimulate the creation of art and architecture under the seventeenth and early eighteenth century Kachhwaha maharajas, Mirza Raja Jai Singh and Sawai Jai Singh.

The Mughal emperors, Akbar and Jahangir, were among the richest men on earth. They were generous patrons of the arts and could afford the best artists, musicians, poets and artisans. Their artistic patronage had considerable impact on the nobles — such as those of the Kachhwaha and Sisodiya houses as well as Muslim nobles from diverse backgrounds — inspiring them to emulate Mughal tastes. An examination of the patronage of two of the highest-ranking Mughal nobles gives us an opportunity to understand the scope and tastes of roughly contemporary men coming from different backgrounds, each of whom had an unusual familiarity with the court.

Raja Man Singh (1550–1614) was a Rajput Hindu prince whose aunt and sister were married to the great Mughals; he himself had lived and served in the Mughal household since he was twelve.[1] Akbar was fond of Man Singh and called him *farzand*, son, a term used very sparingly by the Mughals. He came to be an important military commander and had a pivotal role in subduing territory in the hinterlands, especially in eastern India where he served the longest. At Akbar's death, he had the highest rank of any noble except the king's own sons.[2]

Abd al-Rahim (1556–1624) was the son of the Turkoman Muslim Bayram Khan, the commander of the army under Humayun and then Akbar; when Akbar acceded to the throne, Bayram Khan became his regent.[3] Four years later he was murdered and Akbar then took the young Abd al-Rahim into the court and asked Man Singh to look after his education. He too found favour with Akbar and also was called *farzand*. Abd al-Rahim was made commander of the entire Mughal army, earning him the title of *Khan-i Khanan* even before he was thirty. He, like Man Singh, by the time of his death had achieved the highest rank possible.[4] Jahangir, the son and successor of Akbar, viewed both Abd al-Rahim *Khan-i Khanan* and Raja Man Singh as nobility of the former court. He tolerated the *Khan-i Khanan*, who nevertheless suffered from intrigue at court. He disliked and distrusted Raja Man Singh, but recognised his importance and so continued to maintain his extraordinarily high rank.[5]

Both these men were major patrons of the arts. The *Khan-i Khanan* himself composed poetry and had mastered a number of languages including Persian, Hindavi, Arabic and Turki; he also knew Sanskrit and Portuguese. Thus it is not surprising that he was famed as far away as the Safavid court for his generous patronage of superb poets including two who had come from Iran, Nasiri and Urfi. The *Khan-i Khanan*'s interest in and patronage of Persian literature actually surpassed that of the imperial court, even though Akbar actively promoted Persian as the court language.[6] Continuing the tradition of his father and grandfather, Raja Man Singh sponsored court poets, commentators and playwrights, although the languages he encouraged were regional ones and Sanskrit, not the Persian of the Mughal court. One expectation of court poets was to write panegyrics for their patrons. Both Man Singh and the *Khan-i Khanan* had poets who sought to laud them in order to gain and maintain patronage. One poet in Man Singh's court, Kesavadasa, managed to praise both his own patron and the *Khan-i Khanan* in a single line, proclaiming them the saviours of Akbar's imperial prestige.[7] Poets composed at least two biographies of Man

Singh, one in 1585 while he was still a prince, and the other in 1613, the year before his death. These biographies extol Man Singh, proclaiming his heroic career, his religious orientations, his lavish architectural patronage as well as his support of other arts, such as enameling and paper.[8]

The *Khan-i Khanan* was the topic of a 3000-page biography by Abd al-Baqi.[9] Here we learn of his library which many scholars visited daily. Following the imperial model, he collected important literary works and presented some to Jahangir, including one that had been copied in 1492-93 by the famous Iranian calligrapher, Sultan Ali. Close to 100 people worked in his library, among them a head librarian, painters, calligraphers and every sort of person needed to make books, for example, gilders, book binders, and collators among others. Seven extant illustrated manuscripts have been traced to the *Khan-i Khanan*'s patronage, although clearly many more unillustrated works formed his collection as well.

Like Akbar, the *Khan-i Khanan* had a range of tastes, for after he saw Akbar's illustrated *Ramayana* (1587/8–1598/9), he too commissioned one of his own. Recent work by John Seyller shows that in spite of a lengthy inscription handwritten by the *Khan-i Khanan* on the flyleaf of his *Ramayana* stating that it was completed in 1591–2, dates on the interior paintings indicate it took over a decade longer to complete.[10] Although Abd al-Baqi claims that the *Khan-i Khanan* took immense personal interest in his painters' progress, it seems unlikely that he would have noted that the manuscript was complete when clearly it was not, if he had paid close attention to the work. The paintings executed in the early phase of the *Khan-i Khanan*'s *Ramayana* are similar to those in Akbar's imperial *Ramayana* and were done by artists who earlier had been associated with the Mughal court. The later paintings are less refined and detailed and were the products of artists who had no training at the imperial workshops. Thus a sub-imperial painting style emerges, which reflects the emperor's taste but is somewhat less sophisticated.[11] To my mind, more significant than Seyller's focus on style is the *Khan-i Khanan*'s patronage of a Hindu text, a subject that reflects his own promotion of official Mughal policy, *sulh-i kull*.

Despite the fact that Akbar engaged in few new construction projects after he departed from Fatehpur Sikri in 1585, his nobles continued to build, doing so on his behalf. Both Raja Man Singh and the *Khan-i Khanan* maintained active architectural projects during the period that Akbar seems to have lost interest in providing buildings. Regardless of the ruler's personal interest, his nobles fulfilled their obligation, one whose roots may be seen as early as the 1570s when Akbar issued orders that mosques and *khanqahs* should be built by his nobility in Ajmer.[12] Indeed they did build, as inscriptions at Ajmer clearly indicate.[13] And when Akbar's production of architecture abated, that of the nobles did not. The expectation that nobles would build is evident at the beginning of Jahangir's reign, for in 1605 he issued 12 accession orders, the first of which stated that it was the duty of the nobility to build in the hinterlands in order to encourage population and stability.[14] He was apparently making official an already established practice.

Our knowledge about the *Khan-i Khanan*'s architectural patronage comes from texts; it is not clear if any buildings of his time survive.[15] John Seyller has proposed that his library was probably portable and not established in a single locale. His provision of a garden in Ahmedabad, a mansion for his own use in Burhanpur, a township for the elite known as Jahangirpura, and a caravan serai on the Delhi–Lahore road as well as a tomb for his wife all were probably the sort of structures expected of a high-ranking noble, especially one such as the *Khan-i Khanan*, whose status and wealth were exceptional. His patronage is largely secular, which is in keeping with the sort of illustrated manuscripts he commissioned. Like his masters, Akbar and Jahangir, he was relatively uninterested in providing structures to further Islam. Nevertheless, he was interested in religion to some extent, for he is credited with repairing a mosque, books of a religious nature were in his library and the mystical dimensions of Islam were of interest to him.[16] Although his father Bayram Khan was a Shia, it appears that the son was a Sunni. Thus this Central Asian-descended Muslim belonged to the majority mainstream Sunni elite.

The position of Raja Man Singh was more complicated. He was a Hindu, a minority among the Mughal elite, and wore two hats; that is, on the one hand he was a Mughal amir and on the other, he was the head of his own ancestral line, the Kachhwahas. If the patronage of literary figures was the passion of the *Khan-i Khanan*, then building was Raja Man Singh's. He erected buildings in part to satisfy his own needs, in part to serve the Mughal house.

Man Singh provided gardens, palaces, temples and mosques in both his ancestral lands and in the larger Mughal territory. His first project, his garden at Wah, was provided when he was serving as governor of the north-western frontier region; today it is in Pakistan.[17] Not far from Islamabad, its location near the ancient Buddhist monastery of Taxila is an area long associated with Hindu and Muslim lore. Set in the foothills of the Hindu Kush mountains, Wah was regarded by seventeenth-century Mughal chroniclers as ranking next only to the famed Shalimar gardens in Kashmir. Today the garden has been considerably expanded, but Man Singh's garden consisted of a large central tank with pleasure pavilions at the tank's far end. Built over a natural spring, water in the tank even today is crystal clear, and descendants of the fish Jahangir observed with admiration can still be seen in the water. Jahangir praised this garden, especially significant since he, unlike his father Akbar, was suspicious of Man Singh.[18] Jahangir suspected him of supporting Khusrau, not Jahangir himself, as the next ruler when Akbar was close to death. Jahangir's praise for the garden suggests that he felt it corresponded to a 'perfect' Mughal pleasure garden suitable for rulers descended from the great Timurids of Central Asia. While I have no disagreement with this interpretation, I would suggest that the garden was perceived in yet another manner by its Hindu patron.

Wah's surroundings — hills dense with trees and water — also match descriptions in classical Indian texts of settings appropriate for temples and for the dwellings of the numerous Hindu deities. These texts relate that temple sites must have plenty of water.[19] They are best if surrounded by forests, rivers, hills and waterfalls. Temples such as these situated close to Man Singh's ancestral lands and hence known to him, for example those at Bijolia, Menal and Badoli, seem a perfect translation from canon to setting.[20] While the tank and setting at Wah were appreciated by Jahangir as an appropriate Mughal pleasure retreat, to Man Singh personally, who knew that the gods were attracted to the waters, waterfalls, trees and spring-fed tanks, this garden must have evoked a more personal response. The garden at Wah thus sets an appropriate stage for the rest of this paper that deals with the patronage of Rajput princes who are also high-ranking officers and administrators in the Mughal court.

Man Singh's best known project is the massive Govinda Deva temple that was completed in 1590, fulfilling a vow the prince made when he was victorious in Akbar's Gujarat campaign of 1572–73.[21] His decision to rebuild this temple at a site then recently identified as Vrindavan, Krishna's birthplace, must have been driven by a larger imperial interest, for Akbar had been investing in this temple's site as early as 1565.[22] Thus, just as the *Khan-i Khanan* commissioned an illustrated Persian manuscript of the *Ramayana*, knowing that doing so would please the emperor, so too Man Singh built at a site favoured by Akbar. The temple, the largest constructed in north India since the twelfth century, was built in red Sikri sandstone favoured by the imperial Mughals for building material; its interior vaults and pillars were stimulated by those used at Fatehpur Sikri and other imperial sites but in fact were more innovative than those of Akbar's own buildings.

Man Singh built several temples that were intended to both celebrate Mughal victories and to commemorate recently deceased family members, including one for his mother, one for his father and one for

Jagat Singh, his heir apparent. (Plate 1) This last-mentioned temple, the Jagat Siromani, built at the seat of the Kachhwaha palace in Amber, is highly unusual in that its exterior is covered with figural sculpture, rare in north India since even before the twelfth century.[23] All the same, the temple's entrance and porch evoke contemporary Akbari architecture. This temple, like the one built for the miraculously revealed image of Govinda Deva, has a large open *mandapa* appropriate for the increasingly popular veneration of Krishna associated with the Bhakti movement. At the Jagat Siromani, the ceiling is composed of a pyramidal vault, thus resembling ceilings of contemporary Mughal buildings associated with imperial presence.[24] By providing temples throughout the domain in a recognisable Mughal style, Man Singh was helping to spread Akbar's official policy of *sulh-i kull* by both the building type and style he employed just as the *Khan-i Khanan* did so by commissioning illustrated *Ramayana*s. To further support the concept of *sulh-i kull,* Man Singh provided at least two mosques and supported the shrine of a Muslim saint.

Man Singh built several palaces, including two in his ancestral lands. But the largest and most important is the one he provided in the eastern Indian capital of Bihar at a hill fort known as Rohtas.[25] The palace remains the largest non-imperial one of the Mughal period, and many features suggest that Man Singh built the palace to reflect his role as Akbar's agent. These include the entrance gate flanked by elephants, recalling those at Fatehpur Sikri, and the presence of a *hammam*, a Muslim tradition not a Rajput one, and a *jharoka-i darshan* (viewing balcony) again recalling the one at Fatehpur Sikri. While it appears that the nobility was not generally permitted to use *jharokas* at this time, there is evidence to suggest that Kachhwaha princes were exempt from this ban, probably because of their special ties to the Mughals.[26]

The size of the Rohtas palace, the presence of a *jharoka* and areas likely used for audiences, all suggest that to Man Singh the palace meant more than a governor's residence. This is bolstered by inscriptions showing that Man Singh recognised his dual role as Mughal governor and Hindu raja. On a large stone slab at the palace entrance gate are two inscriptions, one in exquisitely carved Persian and one in Sanskrit. The Persian inscription's fine calligraphy is unusual in the eastern Mughal hinterlands, suggesting that the text was intended to be noticed and read. It implies that Raja Man Singh built the palace as a servant of Akbar, for it addresses the emperor extensively and makes only a brief reference to Man Singh, the actual patron. But in the companion Sanskrit portion, longer in text but with cramped letters on a smaller slab, Raja Man Singh asserts his own authority as head of the Kachhwaha house, and there Akbar's name is omitted altogether. Instead, Man Singh is mentioned twice, not using his Mughal title, *raja*, but rather identifying himself as '*maharajadhiraja*', that is, king of kings, overlord.[27] The use of his Kachhwaha title, not his Mughal one, on a palace intended to serve both the governor's needs and those of the state, underscores the dual nature of the relationship between the *raja* and Mughal emperor. Under the Mughal state system, serving the emperor included defending one's own religion, honour, and even patrimony if necessary.[28] Thus evoking a title that symbolised Rajput ideals and aspirations did not conflict with Man Singh's role as Akbar's governor, for both were vital to the successful functioning of the Mughal empire. Raja Man Singh, like his contemporary Abd al-Rahim *Khan-i Khanan*, championed Mughal causes by his patronage of the arts, giving visual substance to Akbar's political and social agendas.

Through the mid-seventeenth century Mughal relations with the Kachhwahas remained strong, for Mirza Raja Jai Singh (r. 1622–67), like his grandfather, Man Singh, was a loyal *mansabdar*. He served under Jahangir, Shah Jahan and Aurangzeb, dying in 1667. Until his last failed campaign in the Deccan just before his death, the Mirza Raja's career was generally on an upward trajectory. Also, like Man Singh, Mirza Raja Jai Singh wore two hats. As a Kachhwaha *raja* he was a thoroughly able scholar of Turkish, Arabic and Persian and in particular of Sanskrit literature.[29] He visited Benares when possible and there founded a school for Sanskrit studies. His interest in Vedic studies was keen, a topic of growing interest in much of India, from at least the mid-seventeenth century onwards, and Amber's court pandits played a leading role in deciding the Vedic ritual accompanying the coronation of Shivaji in 1674.[30]

Mirza Raja Jai Singh's patronage of art and architecture selectively reflects contemporary Mughal taste. Paintings commissioned at his court fall into two categories—those that resemble illustrated *ragamalas* of the Mewar school and those modelled on Mughal paintings.[31] In architecture, this dichotomy of style is most evident in two courtyards he added to the Kachhwaha palace in Amber. Within the inner courtyard, entered by a magnificent gate known as the Ganesh Pol, is a pavilion whose top floor is modelled closely on Shah Jahan's *jharoka-i darshan* at his Agra fortified palace.[32] (Plate 2) Like Shah Jahan's *jharoka*, Mirza Raja Jai Singh's pavilion not only overlooks an interior garden but also its *bangla* roof forms a highly visible exterior façade on the palace. Ebba Koch has argued that such curved *bangla* roofs, for example, those found on Shah Jahan's *jharokas,* were the exclusive domain of the Mughal emperor at this time.[33] So its exceptional appearance at Amber, almost surely added before Shah Jahan's fall from power in 1658, is again an indication of the special status the Kachhwahas held for the Mughals.

Within a second courtyard at the Amber palace is a Public Audience Hall provided by Jai Singh.[34] While its pillars are reminiscent of some at Fatehpur Sikri,[35] the overall appearance and layout owe little to any Mughal model. The Audience Hall's double row of pillars along and close to its periphery support an interior pyramidal vault. The interior space created by the pillars and vault is similar to that of the *mandapas* of Man Singh's Govinda Deva and Jagat Siromani temples, allowing the nobility easily to have the king's *darshan* just as a temple's layout allowed *darshan* of the deity.

While the Kachhwahas of Amber were increasingly becoming the most powerful house among the Rajput princes of western India, the Sisodiyas of Udaipur were attempting to counter this authority through their own patronage of the arts and, by extension, of religious ritual. James Tod has provided a romantic image of Sisodiya rule, one that champions their bravery, heroism and tenacious attachment to Hinduism. Jennifer Joffee, however, argues that this view was essentially one invented by the Sisodiya house during the seventeenth century and then promoted in succeeding centuries.[36] Joffee and J. Losty have recognised that artistic production under the Sisodiyas in the mid- to late seventeenth century was a response to Mughal visual production; I would argue that the Sisodiyas were also aware of Kachhwaha production and responded to that as well.

The Sisodiya Rana Jagat Singh (r. 1638–52) commissioned a massive illustrated *Ramayana* under the direction of master artist Sahib Din.[37] Executed in a style and format characteristic of other Mewar painting, the project was radically different from the manuscripts of the same texts produced for Akbar's library and that of the *Khan-i Khanan*. Losty has suggested that the Sisodiya version was intended as a counter to the great illustrated *Namas* of the Mughal court, as if the story of Rama, from whom the Sisodiyas claim descent, were the history of the Sisodiya house.[38] For example, the enemy, Ravana and his entourage are, as Losty observes, depicted in Mughal style tents. Joffee argues that the Jagdish temple in Udaipur, built only two years after the commencement of Shah Jahan's Jami mosque in Shahjahanabad, is a response to that Mughal monument.[39] She observes parallels between their names, Jagdish and Jahan, their prominent placement in each city and the content and location of their inscriptions among other similarities. I would add that its overall appearance — a tall temple covered with sculpture surmounted by a towering *shikhara* — appears to derive from the appearance of the Jagat Siromani in Amber.

The attempts to emulate or surpass Mughal architecture on the part of the Sisodiyas continued after Jagat Singh's death. His successor, Rana Raj Singh (1652–80) excavated an enormous tank at Rajsamand about

80 kilometres north of Udaipur.[40] This was part of a famine relief project inaugurated in 1676. The tank with its exquisite marble pavilions (Plate 3) is clearly modelled on Shah Jahan's marble pavilions at the Ana Sagar in Ajmer. However, the Rana's pavilions are considerably more ornate and the entire platform is studded with inscriptional panels that give a detailed account of the Vedic rituals performed during the tank's consecration. This investment in Vedic practice appears as a response to both Maratha and Kachhwaha interest in the *Vedas*. Only two years earlier, in 1674, the Maratha Shivaji was crowned in an elaborate ceremony whose Vedic rituals were determined by Brahmins at Mirza Raja Jai Singh's court; the *raja*'s interest in Vedic studies, continuing that of his predecessors, was well known. Without belabouring the issue, it appears that artistic production in mid-seventeenth century Sisodiya Mewar was a visual and ceremonial response to cultural and political developments both under the Mughals and Kachhwahas.

In a similar way, the visual culture of the Kachhwaha house drew upon both Mughal and Sisodiya practice. The construction of Jaipur commencing in the early eighteenth century was marked by two trends: a reference to features of Mughal and Sisodiya court art and ceremony and, at the same time, a high degree of innovation. Jaipur is one of India's best-known tourist destinations. Unlike Agra, where tourist lore about the city is matched by corrective scholarship, there is relatively little scholarship on the history of Jaipur's urban fabric.[41] As a result, the common perceptions of Jaipur, the city, reflect James Tod's romantic notions of Rajputana as a seat of Hindu *dharma*, with little regard to its more complex character.

Common assumptions about the walled city of Jaipur, founded in 1727 by the Kachhwaha Rajput ruler, Sawai Jai Singh, to replace the older capital of Amber include: the notion that Jaipur, with its regular wide grid-plan streets, was a conscious attempt on the part of Sawai Jai Singh to build a city based on Shastric texts, which, for most, underpins the assumption that Jaipur was built as a Hindu city by a Hindu ruler for Hindu subjects.[42] That perception is, at best, partly accurate. The city, moreover, is seen as a result of Jai Singh's genius, although, in fact, relatively little of what exists today was complete by his death only 15 years after the city's founding. For example, the Hawa Mahal, often published as an icon standing for the city, post-dates the reign of Sawai Jai Singh.[43] Much of the literature discusses the city ahistorically. Moreover, the role of Sawai Jai Singh's subjects in developing the city is left unexamined; the city is generally discussed only as the result of royal patronage, a view I intend to dispel.

Jai Singh II, later to be honoured with the title Sawai, was born in 1688, a time when the once-strong ties between the Kachhwahas and their overlords, the Mughals, were undergoing strain.[44] Jai Singh inherited the Amber throne in 1700, and then was called to active Mughal service. He served his overlord well, but Aurangzeb was ill-disposed to the Kachhwahas because they had sheltered Shivaji, Aurangzeb's enemy. The situation after Aurangzeb's death in 1707 only worsened.[45] That year Amber was taken by the Mughals as crown land, and not restored to the Kachhwahas until three years later.[46] About 1720, Jai Singh's fortunes with the Mughals began to improve. He proved instrumental in quelling the Jats and Marathas, who were threatening the stability of Mughal rule. His fellow Rajputs also sought his wise counsel, and increasingly Jai Singh became critical in their decisions. In short, Jai Singh's dealings with various groups were based on politics related to his own survival, not on religion. In this, he was not especially different from his near contemporaries, for example, Shivaji.[47] Despite his own increasing independence and importance, Jai Singh never ceased serving his Mughal overlords.

Around 1720, Jai Singh decided to build a new planned city about 10 kilometres south of Amber. Until that city, which came to be named Jaipur, was inaugurated in 1727, Amber remained the capital, except during the period when it was Mughal crown land. Just a year after Amber was restored to Jai Singh, in 1711, a huge map of Amber, about 21 feet square, was produced at the *raja*'s order,[48] a symbol of the authority he had over his natal territory, that is, his birthright. This enormous map is not only remarkably detailed but also instructive about which aspects of the newly planned city of Jaipur were innovative and which were carried over from older tradition. In this cartographic production the architecture is depicted in elevation, and the names of streets and important structures are indicated.

It is clear that Amber was organised from the outset, even if built in successive stages. Inscriptions on the map indicate that neighbourhoods were occupied by members of a single occupation. There was a *mohalla* of barbers, one of dancing girls and so on. The organisation of Amber, probably typical of much of the subcontinent, established a precedent for the future city of Jaipur.

There are a number of reasons to believe that this map is accurate. One is that many of the map's buildings remain standing, so we can see that their depiction on the map corresponds with their actual appearance. One example is the Kachhwaha palace. Its placement and appearance on the map compare closely with the extant remains. For our purposes, the map's most significant feature is the clear depiction of a multi-religious community in Amber, for not only are Hindu temples depicted, but so are Jain temples, mosques and tombs. Amber's religious architecture is decisively and clearly defined. Temples, Hindu and Jain, have prominent *shikharas*, that is, towering superstructures; mosques and tombs are marked with domes. This is quite different from much of the religious architecture in Jaipur, the city that succeeded Amber.

Deciding that Amber had become too crowded, Sawai Jai Singh commenced a new city on the plain to Amber's south. This recalls Shah Jahan's decision to shift his capital from Agra, where he claimed the streets were too narrow for ceremonial processions, to a new planned city, Shahjahanabad. Since Jaipur appears to be a city designed for procession, emulating Shahjahanabad was likely foremost in Sawai Jai Singh's mind. This opportunity to build a city still more regular and ordered than the Mughal capital or the relatively new Sisodiya capital of Udaipur was surely part of his motivation. His competition with the Sisodiya capital may relate to the Kachhwaha–Sisodiya marriage alliance. In 1708, for the first time since the Kachhwahas had aligned themselves with the Mughals, the Sisodiyas gave a princess in marriage to Sawai Jai Singh under the terms of an unorthodox contractual agreement in which a son born to this *maharani*, even though Sawai Jai Singh had more senior wives, would be first in line for the throne.[49]

A Bengali Brahmin, Vidyadhar, had a role in designing the city, although many believe that Sawai Jai Singh was the real mastermind.[50] Construction commenced well before the formal foundation ceremony on November 29, 1727. By then much of the *maharaja*'s palace complex had been completed. Also completed were several of the grid plan sections that today comprise the walled city of Jaipur. The city, since the mid-nineteenth century has grown substantially beyond its eighteenth century walls. Many believe Jaipur's plan was based on Shastric texts, although which particular Shastric text remains elusive.[51] Recently, Vibhuti Sachdev and Giles Tillotson have argued that Jaipur's plan results from knowledge of *vastu* in which a mental *mandala* was placed over the physical terrain.[52]

Although the Shastric basis for Jaipur's organisation might be questioned, Sawai Jai Singh did hold that society's behaviour should conform to that prescribed by religious texts.[53] Moreover, he enacted Vedic ceremony in a more sustained and elaborate manner than had either his Kachhwaha predecessors or his contemporaries from Rajput or other houses.[54] In particular, he was famous for his two performances of the Asvamedha sacrifice, once in 1734 and again in 1741. Each was enacted on the edge of Jaipur's Man Sagar tank just as Rana Raj Singh Sisodiya had performed the Vedic ritual at his especially constructed platform at Rajsamand. As is well-known, this sacrifice, only to be executed by an all-powerful ruler, had not been enacted since about the ninth century. For example, in 1656, Rana Raj Singh Sisodiya gave a white horse to his Brahmin guru in lieu of performing the Asvamedha sacrifice, believing its performance during the Kali Yuga inauspicious.[55] By its performance not once but twice, Sawai Jai Singh flaunted his superiority to all Hindu rulers but especially to the Sisodiyas, once deemed the most powerful of all Rajput houses.

To think of Jaipur as a *mandala* or a city that conforms to Shastric prescription necessitates making the layout and structures conform to an established standard. I propose, rather, to see how the city actually developed. Thus we might start by examining what structures, besides the palace, were built before the formal inauguration of Jaipur in 1727. Among these were the *havelis* of the elite who had been invited to populate the city.[56] A surviving example is the Natani family *haveli* dating around the time of its foundation; today part of the mansion serves as a police station; the rest is a girls' school. (Plate 4) While the elite built their residences according to regulations laid out by the ruler, free land was often provided as an inducement to move from distant locales to the new city.

Accounts of Jai Singh's daily ritual shortly after he established residence in Jaipur indicate that he visited temples, often in an elephant-drawn chariot called the Indra Viman or at times on the back of an elephant.[57] Among the temples that had been constructed during this formative period were one dedicated to Sita Vallabha, a form of the god Rama, and a Rama temple built by the Natani family. (Plate 5)

The Sita Vallabha temple is situated on Sireh Deorhi Bazaar directly opposite a main entrance to the Jaipur palace complex.[58] (Plate 6) Located above shops, the temple is inconspicuous. It has no towering superstructure, unlike earlier ones in Amber. In fact, from the exterior there is no indication that this is a temple. However, when the window is opened, the deity is available for viewing. This permits an elevated viewer such as Jai Singh on his elephant to have *darshan* of the deity, Sita Vallabha, without actually entering the temple. Who installed the image of Sita Vallabha is unknown, but in 1741, in celebration of his second Asvamedha sacrifice, Sawai Jai Singh erected a temple just to the rear of the Sita Vallabha temple, one dedicated to Kalki, the future Vishnu.[59] It has a *shikhara*; however, it is the only temple provided by Sawai Jai Singh inside the city walls with this feature.[60] While the spire is visible when in the temple compound, it is virtually invisible from the street because of its location behind the Sita Vallabha temple. Much more prominent are two temples built in this very early period by patrons other than Jai Singh. One is the Rama temple, constructed by Lunkarna Natani, a wealthy banker.[61] (Plate 5) It is located adjacent to his *haveli* mentioned earlier. It, too, was frequented by Jai Singh even though he did not construct it. Prominently positioned, it is situated on an elevated platform at a strategic point marking the west end of the palace complex. Its dominant *shikhara* indicates clearly that this is a temple. A second Rama temple, built by Jai Singh's foster sister, Vichitra Kumari, marks the eastern perimeter of the palace complex; this one, too, is surmounted by a towering superstructure. These temples are indicated on an early map of Jaipur, marking either end of the palace.[62] Both dedicated to Rama, they reflect the religious preference of Sawai Jai Singh, a Vaishnava who favoured Rama until the later years of his reign, when Govinda Deva became his preferred deity.

After these early temples were constructed, virtually no temple was built with a prominent *shikhara*, as if orders against the construction of this temple type had been issued. Thus the invisible temple type, such as the Sita Vallabha, continued with significant modifications to be the model. From the exterior-most of Jaipur's temples are indistinguishable from the houses and shops that sit on Jaipur's main streets and with which they are interspersed.[63] (Plate 7) The common explanation for this switch is that they were intended to be hidden from Muslim iconoclasts. But this argument is flawed, for Jaipur is a city built and ruled by Hindus. There must be other factors that brought about this change in the appearance of temples. To understand how and why this rather radical transformation in temple appearance transpired, I will focus on the most important temple in Jaipur provided by Sawai Jai Singh, the Govinda Deva temple. (Plate 8)

This Govinda Deva temple was built to house an image that earlier had been installed in a temple of the same name but located in Vrindavan, a temple constructed by Raja Man Singh in 1590. The Mughal emperors had supported Man Singh's Govinda Deva temple in Vrindavan through the initial years of Aurangzeb's reign.[64] But by the late 1660s, two factors, one political and the other religious, came between the Kachhwahas and Mughals, until then close allies. Aurangzeb personally became increasingly orthodox. The Kachhwaha ruler at that time had been, like his predecessors, a loyal *amir* in the Mughal army; however, when he decided to protect Aurangzeb's arch enemy, Shivaji, the Mughal emperor was furious. When Aurangzeb felt betrayed by nobles belonging to families long supported by the Mughal state, he had been known to attack temples built by those families.[65] The Kachhwahas feared for the Govinda Deva image, located not on their *watan jagir* but on crown land.

The temple's custodians moved the image from Vrindavan to various locations over a period of almost 50 years.[66] Around 1716 the Govinda Deva image was transferred to the Jai Niwas garden, the future site of Jai Singh's palace, even before Jaipur was founded; the current Govinda Deva temple, part of the Maharaja's palace, was not established until about 1730.[67] Once the temple was constructed, the Maharaja could see it from his private quarters. Its garden setting was intended to evoke the favoured dwelling of the gods, a landscape with hills, streams and lush foliage.

This temple is a large rectangular single-storeyed building. In plan the temple is divided into three sections, namely service rooms, a central sanctum for the image, and a passage for circumambulation.[68] A passage for circumambulation surrounds the sanctum; however, this passage is not obvious from the temple's front. The temple's plan has little to do with a viewer's perception of its appearance. From the exterior the Govinda Deva temple closely resembles a Mughal Public Audience Hall. In both the Audience Hall and the Govinda Deva temple there is a flat-roofed chamber with a pillared facade behind which the ruler in the Audience Hall or the deity in the temple is enthroned for *darshan*. Here there is a reversal from the situation at Amber, where the temple inspired court architecture; now the temple resembles the Audience Hall. So, too, Jai Singh's own Audience Hall, constructed concurrently with his Govinda Deva temple, draws from a similar source, for it appears like a smaller version of the Govinda Deva temple. The choice of this building type for both the temple and Audience Hall is closely associated with Jai Singh's concept of regal authority as validated by the divine. To obtain *darshan*, be it divine or imperial, it is necessary to approach a structure's threshold. In the case of a ruler, Hindu or Muslim, the *throne* must be approached for *darshan*; in the case of the divine, the sanctum must be approached.

Earlier I suggested that the large *mandapa* of the Jagat Siromani temple, appropriate for crowds of devotees wishing to have *darshan*, was appropriated for the Public Audience Hall at the Amber palace, thus linking the Kachhwaha house with the divine. Jai Singh's construction of a temple that distinctly resembled an Audience Hall results from his attitude toward his state and the deity, Govinda Deva. Sawai Jai Singh, in fact, considered himself a human agent acting on behalf of the deity, Govinda Deva, whom he claimed was the true ruler of Jaipur. As several scholars have noted, the Maharaja's official seal bears the proclamation, "The feet of Sri Govinda Deva [are] Sawai Jai Singh's shelter," indicating that he saw himself as God's minister.[69] Installing the image in a temple that evokes an imperial Audience Hall was a conscious choice, for in this setting Govinda Deva's dual role as ruler and God are understood. It is also appropriate that Sawai Jai Singh's own Audience Hall is similar to but smaller than the god's temple, since this temporal ruler serves at the god's feet.

Like Jai Singh's Govinda Deva temple, nearly all subsequent Hindu temples in Jaipur, whether they are royally sponsored or not, are flat roofed. From the exterior they are indistinguishable from the surrounding structures. Once inside their spacious open courtyards, these temples allow large numbers of devotees to have *darshan* when the image is revealed. However, since the role of these deities inside these temples is not in any way like that of Govinda Deva, the royal deity, the absence of towering *shikharas,* characteristic of north Indian temple architecture might seem curious. However, Jai Singh's perception of Jaipur as well as his attitude toward his own *dharma* and that of his subjects offer an explanation.

Jai Singh was personally very religious and well versed in theology. About the time that he began to construct Jaipur, he received from the Mughal emperor the titles of Maharaja, Mirza Raja and Sawai.[70] Monika Horstmann points out that the title Mirza Raja, which denotes a kinship relation with the Mughals, was not used in his own documents since it did not fit his image as a ruler. She then indicates that by 1727, when Jaipur was founded, a new Kachhwaha seal was adopted that proclaimed allegiance to the deity Sita Rama, not to any Mughal overlord.[71] Her observations are important. However, to see Jai Singh and his relation to the Mughals in terms of binary opposition is to under-read the contemporary political and cultural milieu. Rather, Jai Singh was engaged in a common eighteenth-century activity, code switching, that is, wearing multiple hats concurrently.[72] While Jai Singh's new seal underscored his role as a *dharmic* ruler, he never abandoned Mughal service and until his death remained a major figure in the Mughal *mansabdari* system; his role as a mediator between the imperial Mughals and the princes of Rajasthan remained unprecedented.[73] As James Hastings observes, Sawai Jai Singh, responding to Maratha incursions, organised a Rajput coalition against the Marathas and the threat they made to both Rajput and Mughal territories.[74] Sawai Jai Singh saw himself as a *dharmic* king, a champion of Brahamanical causes and rights, but his state did not promote policies that discriminated against non-Hindus.

Hastings has argued that Sawai Jai Singh perceived himself as distinct from the Mughals, who increasingly had taken an intolerant view of public non-Muslim religious activity.[75] Under the Kachhwahas, Jains, for example, were major administrators;[76] Muslims served the state as well.[77] Jai Singh awarded Muslim amirs with gifts and gave money to *dargahs*, including that of Mu'in al-Din Chishti of Ajmer.[78] Even Europeans lived in Jaipur, some of them collaborating in an attempt to reform traditional Indian astronomy,[79] an interest that doubtless was fed by Sawai Jai Singh's desire for correct timings in the performance of Shastric rite. The court poet Girdhari notes, that Europeans, "have come ... after crossing the oceans. They are very wise and intelligent."[80] When Jai Singh urged the Mughal ruler Muhammad Shah to desist from taking the property of deceased mendicants, he was referring to both *sadhus* and *fakirs*.[81] The poet Giridhari makes it clear that Jaipur was a harmonious multi-cultural city. As he wrote, "Nobody speaks improperly with any person." He then goes on to say that in this city all the 32 weights are quite correct and precise,"[82] meaning that justice prevails. What the poet presents is a city ruled by a Hindu monarch, a city where Brahmins were respected and temples were built, but at the same time a city intended as a universal city with multiple normative communities co-existing peacefully.[83] As the poet then concludes, "Everybody looks to his own religion and all evil deeds are set aside."[84] Consistent with that vision for his city is Jai Singh's exclusion of Muslims from Hindu holy rites and Hindus from Muslim ritual, and his perception of Hindu and Muslim holy men eating together as anti-Vedic.[85] Each to his own faith, as Jai Singh wished, was intended to insure harmony, not hierarchy with Hindus on top. During the period that Jai Singh was planning his city with temples and palaces, other communities built temples within Jaipur's walls; Digambara Jains, in particular constructed many temples. While the community was small, it was highly influential. A number of Jains held ministerial positions, while the overall community controlled considerable wealth.[86]

Several Jain temples were founded when Jaipur's construction commenced or just after the city was inaugurated.[87] These temples are found in a variety of locales within the walled city, reminiscent of Amber, where neighbourhoods were organised by occupation, not religion. Among these early temples is one known as Pataudi Digambara Jain Mandir, founded in 1727. Typical of these temples, it is enclosed by high walls and gates making it invisible from the street. Once inside the courtyard, one can see the flat-roofed temple. It has a small dome over the entrance, the only feature that differentiates it from a house. A similar entrance is seen at the Amber Jain temple of 1657, but there three towering *shikharas* are present as well.[88] In the walled city of Jaipur, no Jain temple has a *shikhara*; moreover, no Jain temple is on a main road, though Hindu temples are there. Many are in the middle of small *chowks*[89] surrounded by the sponsors' *havelis*, thus underscoring a close sense of community.

We know less about early Muslim structures in Jaipur than we do about Hindu and Jain ones. Nevertheless, we know some existed during the reign of Jai Singh, for I have seen Persian documents indicating that by 1739 at least one *dargah* had been established in Jaipur. The *maharaja* himself had donated the land.[90] Moreover, we can surmise something of their appearance if Muslim structures in Amber provide a clue to the appearance of those in Jaipur. For example, the Amber map of 1711 shows domed Muslim buildings like the Amber Jami mosque, built during Akbar's reign, probably indicating that some of those in Jaipur were domed as well.[91]

Muslims now comprise about twenty-five per cent of Jaipur's population, probably about the same percentage as they did in Jaipur's early days. Muslim families were invited to settle in Jaipur to serve in various capacities including the military or as musicians and dancers for Jaipur's many temples.[92] It would thus make sense that some of the city's mosques are quite old. Their ages are difficult to determine because many have been refurbished recently. Still, if we focus on location and general patterns of appearance, we can attempt to understand mosque construction here. Mosques are found throughout the city, for example, the eighteenth-century Rahamiyye mosque is about 300 metres from the *maharaja*'s palace and in the same quarter where Jains built a number of their finest temples.[93]

These Jaipur mosques are quite small. Some are surmounted by multiple domes, for example the eighteenth-century mosque of Maulana Zia al-Din Sahib in *mohalla* Hadipur, while others have flat roofs, such as the mosque at the actual *dargah* of Maulana Zia al-Din in *mohalla* Char Darwaza. Compared to the grand mosques of the Mughals, they appear undistinguished on the urban landscape but no more so than the overall appearance of Jaipur's temples. Jaipur's mosques, it seems, can be located anywhere, but frequently they seem to be in Muslim *mohallas*. Hindu temples, like mosques, can be located on main streets or the back ones. Jain temples, on the other hand, are only located in the back streets and in the cul de sac of neighbourhoods. Use may help explain location. The mosque is, of course, used five times a day, but generally prayer can be performed anywhere—alone or in the presence of others. It is largely on Fridays around noon during community prayer that the mosque is heavily used; thus the mosque must be in a business area, close to where the worshippers will be at that hour. By contrast, both Hindus and Jains require temples in residential neighbourhoods since early mornings and evenings are the timings for *darshan*; however, Hindu worship can be performed from the street if the image is visible. Jains, on the other hand, not only enter temples, but often spend considerable time inside them.[94] Thus Jain temples need to be in residential neighbourhoods, close to the worshippers' homes. The pattern that I have traced here remained the norm for construction in Jaipur into much of the twentieth century, even when mosques and temples began to be built outside the city walls.

Jaipur, uniform and regular with little hint of particular sectarian affiliation in its architecture, was the backdrop for its *maharajas*, who ruled over all subjects, regardless of faith, on behalf of Govinda Deva.

It is in this ecumenical spirit that Jaipur, with its wide and regular streets, was designed for procession. In this setting Sawai Jai Singh and his successors established a bond with all their subjects as these rulers rode forth in elaborate procession on their way to worship in temples and to celebrate festivals.[95] Early photographs of Jaipur document such imperial processions.[96] All subjects, regardless of faith, had *darshan* of the king as he proceeded through his city. That is, the architecture of Sawai Jai Singh and his successors plays out the ecumenical character that Jai Singh sought for his city, one that kept discrete the sectarian affiliation of Jaipur's religious buildings. Despite his personal piety and his devotion to Govinda Deva, Jai Singh wished to establish a city that would not give primacy to the followers of a single faith, something that would not have been possible if the city's many temples and mosques were visually dominant. The change of temple type from those dominant forms used at Amber, the previous capital, expresses Jai Singh's commitment to an economically dynamic — and to use modern terminology, non-sectarian — state.

In spite of the common belief that Jaipur was founded as a Hindu state by a Hindu ruler for the benefit of its Hindu subjects — essentially a communalist reading — Sawai Jai Singh's Jaipur, in fact, was a state that practised considerable more tolerance than did the early eighteenth century Mughal state. Interestingly the lessons of *sulh-i kull* promoted by Raja Man Singh on behalf of Akbar continued to be applied in a modified form by his Kachhwaha successors, including Sawai Jai Singh, who established the cultural agenda for Jaipur state, one that lasted into the twentieth century.

REFERENCES

1. For Raja Man Singh, see R.N. Prasad, *Raja Man Singh of Amber* Calcutta, 1966; G.N. Bahura, *Literary Heritage of the Rulers of Amber and Jaipur*, Jaipur, 1976, pp. 28–35. Also see the following essays by Catherine B. Asher: 'The Architecture of Raja Man Singh: A Study of Sub-Imperial Patronage', *The Powers of Art: Patronage in Indian Culture*, ed. Barbara Stoler Miller, New Delhi, 1992, pp. 183–201 [reprinted in *Architecture of Medieval India: Forms, Contexts, Histories*, ed. Monica Juneja, Delhi, 2001, pp. 370-97.]; 'Amber and Jaipur: Temples in a Changing State', *Stones in the Sand: The Architecture of Rajasthan*, ed. Giles Tillotson, Mumbai, Marg Publications, 2001, pp. 68–77; "Kachhwaha Pride and Prestige: The Temple Patronage of Raja Man Singh," *Govindadeva: A Dialogue in Stone*, ed. Margaret Case, New Delhi, 1996, pp. 215–38; 'Gardens of the Nobility: Raja Man Singh and the Bagh-i-Wah', *The Mughal Garden: Interpretation, Conservation, Implications*, ed. Mahmood Hussain, Abdul Rehman, James L. Wescoat, Lahore, 1996, pp. 61–72; 'Authority, Victory and Commemoration: The Temples of Raja

Man Singh,' *Journal of Vaisnava Studies*, 3, 3 (Summer 1995), pp. 25–36; 'Sub-Imperial Palaces: Power and Authority in Mughal India,' *Ars Orientalis*, 23, 1993, pp. 281–302. These authors cite extensive primary sources.

2. M. Athar Ali, *The Apparatus of Empire: Awards, Offices and Titles to the Mughal Nobility, 1574–1658*, Delhi, 1985, p. 32.
3. For the Khan-i Khanan and his patronage, see M.M. Haq, 'The Khan-i Khanan and His Painters', *Islamic Culture* 5 (1931), pp. 621–30; R.A. Khan, 'The Grand Court of the Khan Khanan', *Lalit Kala* 21, 1985, pp. 27–35; C.R. Naik, *'Abdu'r-Rahim Khan-i-Khanan and His Literary Circle*, Ahmadabad, 1966; Annemarie Schimmel, 'A Dervish in the Guise of a Prince: Khan-i-Khanan Abdur Rahim as a Patron', *The Powers of Art: Patronage in Indian Culture*, ed. Barbara Stoler Miller, New Delhi, 1992, pp. 202–23. Recent interpretive work on the Khan-i Khanan's library by John Seyller includes: 'Model and Copy: The Illustration of Three *Razmnama* Manuscripts', *Archives of Asian Art* 38 (1985), pp. 37–66; 'A Sub-imperial Mughal Manuscript: The *Ramayana* of 'Abd al-Rahim Khankhanan', *The Legend of Rama: Artistic Visions*, ed. Vidya Dehejia, Bombay, Marg Publications, 1994, pp. 85–100; *Workshop and Patron in Mughal India: The Freer Ramayana and Other Illustrated Manuscripts of 'Abd al-Rahim*, Zurich, 1999. Primary sources are used extensively in all these works.
4. Athar Ali, *Apparatus of Empire*, p. 88.
5. Man Singh had supported Jahangir's son, Khusrau, as Akbar's successor and not Jahangir at the time of Akbar's death. Muhammad Nur al-Din Jahangir, *The Jahangirnama, Memoirs of Jahangir, Emperor*, trans., ed. and annotated Wheeler M. Thackston, Washington D.C., Smithsonian Institution and New York, 1999, p. 91 called him 'one of the adversarial old wolves of this eternal dynasty'. Hereafter this will be cited as *Jahangirnama*.
6. Muzaffar Alam, 'The Pursuit of Persian: Language in Mughal Politics', *Modern Asian Studies* 32 (1988), pp. 317–349.
7. Bahura, *Literary Heritage*, p. 29.
8. *Ibid*, pp. 33–34.
9. Schimmel, 'A Dervish in the Guise of a Prince', pp. 202–20; Seyller, *Workshop and Patron*, pp. 45–54.
10. Seyller, *Workshop and Patron*, 73–76.
11. Seyller, 'A Sub-imperial Mughal Manuscript', pp. 76–80. He argues in *Workshop and Patron*, pp. 251–85 that of the six extant illustrated manuscripts belonging to the Khan-i Khanan's library, most are of a similar style except those illustrating classical Persian texts utilise an idiom more akin to classical Persian painting.
12. Abul Fazl, *Akbar Nama*, 3 vols., trans. H. Beveridge, (reprint ed., Delhi, 1972-73), II : pp. 516–17.
13. S.A.I. Tirmizi, *Ajmer through Inscriptions*, New Delhi, 1968, pp. 25–31.
14. *Jahangirnama*, p. 26.
15. Ebba Koch, *Mughal Architecture: An Outline of its History and Development*

(1526–1858), Munich, 1991, pp. 77–78 includes an image of the Khan-i Khanan's tomb in Delhi; there is, however, no epigraphical evidence supporting this commonly believed attribution.

16. Seyller, *Workshop and Patron*, p. 54.
17. For a more detailed discussion of Wah, see Asher, 'Gardens of the Nobility: Raja Man Singh and the Bagh-i Wah', pp. 61–72.
18. *Jahangirnama*, p. 73. Khusrau was Jahangir's son and Man Singh's nephew.
19. Varahamihira, *Brhat Samhita*, 2 vols., trans. M. Ramakrishna Bhat, Delhi, 1981–82, Vol. I, pp. 537–38.
20. For illustrations of these temples see, Chandramani Singh, ed., *Protected Monuments of Rajasthan,* Jaipur, 2002, Vol. xiii, figs. 136–8, 181.
21. There are many illustrations of this temple in Margaret H. Case, (ed.) *Govindadeva: A Dialogue in Stone,* New Delhi, 1996.
22. Tarapada Mukherji and Irfan Habib, 'Akbar and the Temples of Mathura and its Environs', *Proceedings of the Indian History Congress,* 49th Session. Dabolim: Goa University, 1988, pp. 2234–50, and 'Land Rights in the Reign of Akbar, the Evidence of Sale-Deeds of Vrindavan and Aritha', *Proceedings of the Indian History Congress,* Golden Jubilee Session (Gorakhpur, UP): Gorakhpur University, 1990, p. 241.
23. See Asher, 'Kachhwaha Pride and Prestige', plates 10.2–10.24 for illustrations.
24. Asher, 'Amber and Jaipur: Temples in a Changing State', p. 69.
25. See Asher, 'Sub-Imperial Palaces', figs. 10–17 for illustrations.
26. Asher, *Ibid*, pp. 286–87.
27. It reads, '*Sri maharajadhiraja maharaja Sri Mansi[hna]*', M.H. Kuraishi, *List of Ancient Monuments Protected Under Act VII of 1904 in the Province of Bihar and Orissa*, Archaeological Survey of India, New Imperial Series, LI, Calcutta, 1931, p. 168.
28. J.F. Richards, 'Formulation of Imperial Authority under Akbar and Jahangir', *Kingship and Authority in South Asia*, ed. J.F. Richards, Delhi, 1998, pp. 316–17 and Norman P. Ziegler, 'Some Notes on Rajput Loyalties during the Mughal Period', pp. 242–84, in the same volume.
29. Bahura, *Literary Heritage*, p. 38.
30. *Ibid*, p. 39.
31. Asok Kumar Das, 'Court Paintings for the Amber Rulers, circa 1590–1727', *Court Painting in Rajasthan*, ed. Andrew Topsfield, Mumbai, 2000, pp. 44–47. Also see extensive work by Catherine Glynn, 'Evidence of Royal Painting for the Amber Court', *Artibus Asiae* 56/1-2 (1996), pp. 67–93 and 'A Rajasthani Princely Album: Rajput Patronage of Mughal-Style Painting', *Artibus Asiae* 60/2 (2000), pp. 222–64. Also see her co-authored article with Ellen Smart, 'A Mughal Icon Re-Examined', *Artibus Asiae* 57/1-2 (1997), pp. 5–15.
32. Catherine B. Asher, *The Architecture of Mughal India*, rev. ed., Cambridge, 2001, pp. 191, 249 illustrates the two pavilions.
33. Ebba Koch, 'The Baluster Column—A European Motif in Mughal Architecture and its Meaning', *Journal of the Warburg and Courtauld Institutes* 45 (1982), p. 259.

34. Asher, 'Amber and Jaipur: Temples in a Changing State', pp. 72 provides an illustration.
35. They appear as more elegant versions of those at Fatehpur Sikri's Rang Mahal.
36. See Jennifer Joffee, 'Art, Architecture and Politics in Mewar, 1628–1710', unpublished Ph-D. dissertation, University of Minnesota, 2005.
37. J.P. Losty, 'Sahib Din's Book of Battles: Rana Jagat Singh's *Yuddhakanda*', *The Legend of Rama: Artistic Visions*, ed. Vidya Dehejia, Bombay, 1994, pp. 101–116; Vidya Dehejia, 'The Treatment of Narrative in Jagat Singh's *Ramayana*: A Preliminary Study', *Artibus Asiae* 56/3-4, 1996, pp. 303–24.
38. Losty, 'Sahib Din's Book of Battles', p. 102.
39. Joffee, *Art, Architecture and Politics in Mewar*, forthcoming. See Singh, ed. *Protected Monuments* fig. 354, xxxii for illustrations.
40 N.P. Chakravarti and B.C. Ootacumund, 'The Rajaprasasti Inscription of Udaipur', *Epigraphia Indica*, 29/1, Jan. 1951, pp. 1–29; 29/2, April 1951, pp. 212–40; 29/3, July 1951, pp. 41–60; 29/4, October 1951, pp. 61–80; 29/5, Jan. 1952, pp. 81-90; 30/2, April 1953, pp. 91–110; 30/2; 30/3, July 1953, pp. 111–23. I'm grateful to Jennifer Joffee for bringing this to my attention. For an illustration, see Singh, ed. *Protected Monuments*, xxvii, C.
41. A very recent addition is Vibhuti Sachdev and Giles Tillotson, *Building Jaipur: The Making of an Indian City*, London, 2002.
42. For example, see Ashim Kumar Roy, *History of the Jaipur City*, New Delhi, 1978, which is typical of this approach. A notable exception is Joan L. Erdman, *Patrons and Performers in Rajasthan: The Subtle Tradition*, Delhi, 1985.
43. See, for example, the inside cover of Aman Nath, *Jaipur: the Last Destination*, Bombay, 1993, features this structure. I used it as well in my own, *Architecture of Mughal India*, p. 315 as representative of late eighteenth-century Kachhwaha architecture.
44. V.S. Bhatnagar, *Life and Times of Sawai Jai Singh, 1688–1743*, Delhi, 1974, remains the most thorough scholarly work on this ruler.
45. Monika Horstmann, *In Favour of Govinddevji: Historical Documents Relating to a Deity of Vrindaban and Eastern Rajasthan*, New Delhi, 1999, p. 14.
46. Horstmann, *In Favour of Govinddevji*, p. 18.
47. See James W. Laine, *Shivaji: Hindu King in Islamic India*, Oxford, 2003.
48. Susan Gole, *Indian Maps and Plans: from the earliest times to the advent of European Surveys*, New Delhi, 1989, pp. 170–71; Joseph E. Schwartzberg, 'Geographical Meaning', *Cartography in the Traditional Islamic and South Asian Societies*, Vol. 2, Book 1 of *The History of Cartography*, ed. J.B. Harley and David Woodward, Chicago, 1992, pp. 447–48. G.N. Bahura and Chandramani Singh, 'Gardens at Amber and Jaipur: Historical Analysis', *The Researcher*, XVI–XVII (1995–96), pp. 98–110. The map is in the collection of the National Museum of India, New Delhi (56.92.4). I am grateful to Dr Daljeet, painting curator at the National Museum, for allowing me to examine this enormous map (21'8" × 21'2") on several occasions. I am also most grateful to both Chandramani Singh and Joseph Schwartzberg for sharing with me their observations on the map. Dr. Singh spent long hours with me discussing the map's inscriptions.

49. Bhatnagar, *Life and Times of Sawai Jai Singh*, pp. 54–55.
50. Roy, *History of the Jaipur City*, p. 41. Recently, Sachdev and Tillotson, *Building Jaipur*, p. 46-47 have proposed that neither king nor Bengali Brahmin designed the city, but it was executed by unnamed architects skilled in the principles of *vastu vidhya*.
51. Sachdev and Tillotson, *Building Jaipur*, p. 180, note 19 evaluates which authors deny and validate the Shastric origins of Jaipur's plan. In some cases, for example, Roy, *History of the Jaipur City*, they may be overstating the case.
52. Sachdev and Tillotson, *Building Jaipur*, pp. 43–47.
53. James Hastings, *Poets, Sants and Warriors: The Dadu Panth, Religious Change and Identity Formation in Jaipur State circa 1562–1860*, Dissertation, University of Wisconsin, Madison, 2002, 108–12.
54. P.K. Gode, 'The Asvamadha Performed by Sevai Jayasing of Amber (1699–1744 A.D.)', *The Poona Orientalist* 2/3, Oct. 1937, pp. 166–80; V.S. Bhatnagar, 'Savai Jaya Singh's Performance of the Asvadedha and its Significance', *Jijnasa* 1/1–2, Jan.–April 1974, pp. 111–19.
55. Chakravarti and Ootacumund, 'The Rajaprasasti Inscription of Udaipur', *Epigraphia Indica*, 30/2, p. 100.
56. Roy, *History of the Jaipur City*, pp. 44, 52–53. While today the surviving *havelis* and temples are painted pink, until the late 19th century Jaipur's buildings were painted a cream colour.
57. For this information see Bhatnagar, *Life and Times of Sawai Jai Singh*, pp. 331–33. For an 1872 photograph of Sawai Jai Singh's Indra Viman, see Yaduendra Sahai, *Maharaja Sawai Ram Singh II of Jaipur: The Photographer Prince*, Jaipur, 1996, p. 31.
58. The temple is a simple box-like structure on the second floor above shops. It has a centrally placed window overlooking the Sireh Deorhi Bazaar and entrance to the palace. The window's shutters are opened during the timings for *darshan*. I walked past this structure many times without realising it was a temple, not a shop or an office.
59. Roy, *History of the Jaipur City*, p. 229; V.S. Bhatnagar, 'Chronology of Jaipur', *Marg* 30/4, Sept. 1977, np. For an illustration see Singh, ed., *Protected Monuments*, fig. 242.
60. Temples outside the city walls provided by Sawai Jai Singh and his ministers do often have *shikharas*. Among them are the Surya temple provided in 1734 in the Galta Hills and the Varadaraja temple built near the Man Sagar not far from Kanak Bagh.
61. This and the following information are found in personal correspondence from V.S. Bhatnagar to me dated Nov. 5th, 2000; also see Bhatnagar, *Life and Times of Sawai Jai Singh*, p. 332. I am most grateful to Dr. Bhatnagar for the time and energy he spent answering my inquiries.
62. This map, in the Maharaja Sawai Man Singh II Museum, part of Jaipur's city palace, is published in Nath, *Jaipur, the Last Destination*, p. 58, and Sachdev and Tillotson, *Building Jaipur*, p. 19. There is a third temple marked on this map at Ramganj Chopar. Known as the Murali Manohar temple, it is today in a dilapidated condition. Nothing is known about the patron.

63. Catherine B. Asher, 'Mapping Hindu–Muslim Identities through the Architecture of Shahjahanabad and Delhi', *Beyond Turk and Hindu: Rethinking Religious Identities in Islamicate South* Asia, ed. David Gilmartin and Bruce B. Lawrence, 2000, pp. 130–32, and the same author's, 'North India's Urban Landscape: The Place of the Jain Temple', *Islamic Culture,* 73(3), July 1999, pp. 117–18.
64. Irfan Habib, 'A Documentary History of the Gosa'ins (Gosvamis) of the Chaitanya Sect at Vrndavana', *Govindadeva: A Dialogue in Stone*, ed. Margaret Case, New Delhi, 1996, p. 131.
65. S. Moinul Haq, Introduction, *Khafi Khan's History of Alamgir: Being an English Translation of the Relevant Portions of Muntakhab al-Lubab*, trans. S. Moinul Haq, Karachi, 1975, p. xxvii; Shrivatsa Goswami, 'Govinda Darsana: Lotus in Stone', in *Govindadeva: A Dialogue in Stone*, p. 272.
66. Monika Horstmann, 'Sri Govindadeva and his Custodians from 1643 through the Time of Jaya Simha II (1700–1743)', *Govindadeva: A Dialogue in Stone*, pp. 188–92.
67. G.N. Bahura, 'Sri Govinda Gatha: Service Rendered to Govinda by the Rulers of Amera and Jayapura', *Govindadeva: A Dialogue in Stone*, p. 205 states 1739 as its construction date. However, this date, while often repeated, remains uncertain as no supporting documentation accompanies it.
68. For a plan and more detailed description, see Asher, 'Amber and Jaipur: Temples in a Changing State', pp. 69–75.
69. Bahura, *Literary Heritage*, 1976, p. 67; Asimakrishna Dasa, 'Srigovindavarsikadvadasakam: Twelve Verses on the Yearly Festivals of Sri Govinda', *Govindadeva: A Dialogue in Stone*, p. 257. Jennifer Joffee has suggested this may be a response to the Sisodiyas whose state seal indicates they considered themselves as the *diwan* of Ekalingaji.
70. See Horstmann, *In Favour of Govinddevjiji*, p. 18; Bhatnagar, *Life and Times of Sawai Jai Singh*, p. 105.
71. Horstmann, *In Favour of Govinddevji*, p. 18.
72. See the essays in Shushil Mittal, ed., *Surprising Bedfellows: Hindus and Muslims in Medieval and Early Modern India,* (Landam, MD., 2003), for similar attitudes and activities. The essay in this volume by Phillip B. Wagoner, 'Fortuitous Convergences and Essential Ambiguities: Transcultural Political Elites in the Medieval Deccan', pp. 31–54 specifically uses the term code-switching, although his discussion falls into a different chronological frame.
73. Bhatnagar, *Life and Times of Sawai Jai Singh*, p. 197.
74. Hastings, *Poets, Sants and Warriors,* p. 72.
75. *Ibid*, pp. 80–81.
76. See, for example, Roy, *History of the Jaipur City*, pp. 180–83. For a detailed discussion of Jain patronage in Jaipur, see K.C. Kashiwal, *Jaina Bhandars in Rajasthan*, Jaipur, 1967, pp. 43–59, and Anupchand Nayatirth, *Jain Digambara Jain Mandir Parichay*, Jaipur, 1990.
77. Hastings, *Poets, Sants and Warriors,* p. 112; Bhatnagar, *Life and Times of Sawai Jai Singh,* p. 248; G.N. Bahura and Chandramani Singh, *Catalogue of*

Historical Documents in Kapad Dwara, Jaipur, Amber Jaipur, 1988, numbers 354, 505. There are also similar documents held in the Rajasthan State Archives suggesting good and active relations between the state and its Muslim subjects. I shall only cite a few examples. *A Descriptive List of the Vakil Reports Addressed to the Rulers of Jaipur*, Vol. II (Persian), Bikaner, Archives, 1967, nos. 14, 342; *A Descriptive List of the Arzdasts (Persian) Addressed by the Various Officials to the Rulers of Jaipur (1707 to. 1720 A.D.)*, Bikaner: Rajasthan State Archives, 1986, nos. 24, 75, 176, 591, 594.

78. Bahura and Singh, *Catalogue of Historical Documents in Kapad Dwara, Jaipur*, pp. 326, 550. In addition I have been shown Persian documents indicating the support of *dargah* in Jaipur since the time of the city's establishment.
79. David Pingree, 'An Astronomeres Progress', *Proceedings of the American Philosophical Society* 143/1, March 1999, p. 73.
80. P.K. Gode, 'Two Contemporary Tributes to Minister Vidyadhara, the Bengali Architect of Jaipur at the Court of Sevai Jaising of Amber (A.D. 1699–1743)', *Dr. C. Kunhan Raja Presentation Volume: A Volume of Indological Studies*, Madras: Adyar Library for the Dr. C. Kunhan Praja Presentation Volume Committee, 1946, p. 290.
81. Bahura and Singh, *Catalogue of Historical Documents in Kapad Dwara, Jaipur*, pp. 271, 354.
82. Cited in Roy, *History of the Jaipur City*, pp. 235–37.
83. I use the word 'normative' very consciously here as Sawai Jai Singh was actively involved in controlling and subduing armed *sadhus* and others who might cause sedition in Jaipur State. See Hastings, *Poets, Sants and Warriors*, pp. 98–108.
84. Gode, 'Two Contemporary Tributes to Minister Vidyadhara', p. 290.
85. Hastings, *Poets, Sants and Warriors*, p. 112; Bahura and Singh, *Catalogue of Historical Documents in Kapad Dwara*, p. 282.
86. Even today Jains only comprise about five per cent of the population but they control considerable wealth. See statistics provided in Savritri Gupta, *Jaipur*, vol. 27 of *Rajasthan District Gazetteers*, Jaipur, Directorate, District Gazetteers, Government of Rajasthan, 1987, pp. 64–65.
87. See Nayatirth, *Jain Digambara Jain Mandir* for the following temples built during the reign of Sawai Jai Singh. Numbers here refer to the catalogue entry, not pages. These include Sri Digambara Jain Mandir Chaksu (17), Pataudi, (43), Bas Godhan (11), Sangahiji (30), Bara Terah Panti (23) and Jobner (58) among others.
88. This temple is included in K.C. Jain, *Ancient Cities and Towns of Rajasthan*, Delhi, 1972, p. 392. It is also depicted on the 1711 map of Amber. See Singh, ed., *Protected Monuments*, fig. 228 for an illustration.
89. Nayatirth, *Jain Digambara Jain Mandir*, no. 4 (Mandir Godhan) and no. 17 (Mandir Chaksu) are good examples.
90. I am grateful to the custodians of *dargah* Moti Dungree for sharing their documents with me. The custodians of *dargah* Amani Shah, another shrine of Jaipur, reputedly have similar documents.
91. Gole, *Indian Maps and Plans*, plate 91a shows an example.
92. Erdman, *Patrons and Performers*, pp. 56–57; Gupta, *Jaipur*, pp. 64–65. Muslim

families with old ties to the city showed me the original invitations inviting them to Jaipur on the part of the *maharaja* or his agent.

93. *Annual Report on Indian Epigraphy*, 1975–76, D. 154 indicates it is inscribed A.H. 1190/1776 C.E.; however, it has been recently rebuilt as have many of Jaipur's mosques largely from money coming from those employed in the Gulf States. The mosque is on the main road that bisects the city from Chand Pol Darwaza to the Surya Darwaza on the side of the street those interior roads lead to Johari Bazaar, where many of Jaipur's finest Jain temples are located.
94. John Cort, 'Following the Jina, Worshipping the Jina: An Essay on Jain Rituals', *The Peaceful Liberators, Jain Art from India*, ed. P. Pal, Los Angeles, 1994, pp. 49–52 describes Jain worship largely in the Swetambara context; Digambaras do not ordinarily touch the image; the offering of fruit, for example, is not acceptable in the Terapanthi Digambara tradition. Also see Paul Dundas, *The Jains* (London and New York, 1992, pp. 173–79. In my experience, even among the Terapanthi in Delhi and Jaipur there are differences in what offerings are deemed suitable.
95. Joan L. Erdman, 'Jaipur: City Planning in 18th Century India', *Sastric Traditions in Indian Arts*, 2 vols., ed. Anna L. Dallapiccola, Stuttgart, 1989, Vol. I, p. 232.
96 Nath, *Jaipur, The Last Destination*, inside cover; Sten Nilsson, 'Jaipur, in the Sign of Leo', no. 1 of *Magasin Tessin*, Lund, 1987, pp. 41, 47.

SECTION III

Commerce, Crafts and the Countryside

Chapter 10

Visiting Faraway Ports: India's Trade in the Western Indian Ocean, ca. 800–1500 CE

Ranabir Chakravarti

I

The study of India's past during the pre-modern times, spanning several millennia, is endowed with a lively and rich historiography which has experienced several significant shifts and offered new, though occasionally contesting, perceptions of early India (up to ca. 1300 CE). The long-standing economic image of the subcontinent as exclusively agrarian, steeped in insularity and isolation — especially during the pre-modern times — has undergone a significant transformation in the historical researches of late. The distinct possibilities of an active non-agrarian sector of the 'traditional' economy are being increasingly illuminated, although the non-agrarian sector remains firmly rooted to the overarching agrarian material milieu. Sustained scholarly efforts have indeed rendered considerable visibility to urbanisation, crafts production and trade in early India. Tracing the long tradition of commerce in the subcontinent, economic historians have been underlining, roughly from the middle of the 1980s, the significance of the Indian Ocean in the trading activities and linkages of India. The widely believed stigma that early Indians were averse to seafaring with a view to retaining their ritual purity has been effectively negated as such attitudes were available only in the normative Brahmanical lawbooks and at the most, applicable perhaps only to the priestly community. This has resulted in the modification of the dominant historiographical perspective that traditional India was landlocked[1]. 'The argument now made is that there was in pre-colonial times a commercial economy that incorporated many societies of

Eurasia and Africa. The economic impact of this trade was not incidental'.[2]

These preliminaries will help situate better a particular aspect of early Indian socio-economic life, namely India's role in the maritime network of the Indian Ocean in the early medieval period. It is impossible to deny that the material milieu of Indian society has been agricultural over millennia and the bulk of Indian population engaged in agriculture. Without at all belittling the significance of agriculture in India, one also has to acknowledge that trade (*vanijya*) was regularly recognised as one of the major ingredients of economic life from remote times. While nobody can lose sight of the vast continental land mass of India, it is also unmistakable that the subcontinent is washed on its three sides by the Indian Ocean. The other inescapable geographical fact is the almost central position of India (along with Sri Lanka) in the Indian Ocean. The Indian Ocean, the only enclosed ocean in the world, occupies almost 20 per cent of the maritime space of the earth. The map of the National Atlas and Thematic Mapping Organisation shows that the Indian Ocean includes in it two important sea-lanes in the west—the Red Sea and the Persian Gulf—and washes the east coast of Africa ; its eastern sector is marked by the Bay of Bengal (but not the Java and the China Seas); it stretches up to the Antarctica in the south[3]. Though the Atlantic and the Pacific Oceans are larger than the Indian Ocean, the Indian Ocean has been acting as a bridge among numerous communities of Asia and Africa over a very long period of time, with very rich historical consequences. Franz Broeze rightly argues that a long-range view, say spanning the last two millennia, would project Asia and not Europe as the leading maritime zone of the world.[4] The Indian Ocean undoubtedly dominates the sea-face of Asia. It was the seminal researches of Fernand Braudel that established that a civilisation can be related to a maritime space. He repeatedly emphasised that maritime studies do not merely throw light on the sea, but drive home the inseparable unity between a given maritime space and its related land mass.[5] Sea-borne trade is certainly one major facet of maritime history but it is not the sole area of thrust. Maritime history addresses the question of the attitudes and orientation of a given society and polity towards its relevant maritime space and takes a close look at those whose life depends on the sea (e.g. the sailor, the ship-captain, the ship-builder, the fisherman and even the pirate).

The existing historiography of India's position in the Indian Ocean affairs suggests three broad strands of academic interests: (a) the maritime linkages of the Harappan civilisation (ca. 2500–1750 BCE) with Sumer and Akkad through the Persian Gulf; b) India's flourishing sea-borne commerce with the Roman empire through the Red Sea (ca. late first century BCE to CE 250); and (c) the sea change in India's maritime situation with the arrival and consolidation of Europeans in the trade and politics of the Indian Ocean (1500–1800). Needless to explain that the last aspect has received maximum scholarly attention as the historian of these centuries has relatively easy access to the massive quantitative data of the Portuguese empire and the English, French and the Dutch East Indian Companies. The study of these three crucial centuries highlights how India and the Indian Ocean became gradually incorporated into the capitalist world economy and ultimately succumbed to the colonial expansion of North Atlantic powers. In the long chronological range of India's role in the Indian Ocean network, one can easily see a historiographical gap ranging from ca. eighth to the fifteenth centuries CE. It is precisely at this chronological phase that we would like to take a close look in this paper. This phase in Indian historiography is generally denoted as early medieval, the label implying that these centuries witnessed the passage from the early historical to medieval. In at least one genre of historical research, the early medieval phase of Indian history is portrayed as one experiencing crises in social, economic and political spheres, ushering in feudalism in India from 300 to 1200 CE. One of the salient markers of the economic formation characterised as Indian feudalism was the emergence and consolidation of a self-sufficient, enclosed and stagnant village economy which is supposed to have been hardly conducive to trade, especially long-distance overseas trade. The assumed paucity of trade over long distance is said to have brought about widespread urban decay in India and the attendant 'monetary anaemia'. The historiography of Indian feudalism highlights the relegation of trade, especially long-distance maritime trade, to marginalia especially during the period from 500 to 1000 CE. The historian of Indian feudalism suggests some revival of trade, including maritime trade, in India from 1000 onwards.[6] The above portrayal of a sharp decline of overseas commerce of India during the early medieval times has resulted in the much cherished notion of a relatively languishing role of India in the affairs of the Indian Ocean. The above formulation, however, has been effectively contested both on conceptual and empirical grounds[7]. K.N. Chaudhuri in his two monographs presents the patterns of commerce in the Indian Ocean from the rise of Islam to 1750, after which the situation vastly changed because of the domination of the European powers.[8] Chaudhuri's contribution along with some other leading scholars leaves little room for doubt that the rise and spread of Islam was a major fillip to the Indian Ocean commerce.[9]

The very coinage of the expression *'mari Indicum'* (the Indian Sea) by Pliny as early as the second half of the first century CE clearly suggests the familiarity of merchants, sailors and shippers at least with the western sector of the Indian Ocean.[10] The rise and spread of Islam—with a pronounced orientation towards commerce and urban life—resulted in a more intimate association with the Indian Ocean from the late eighth and early ninth century onwards. A perusal of the geographical texts and travel accounts of Arabic and Persian authors reveals the coinage of the expression *al bahr al Hindi*, the near-equivalent of the later English expression the Indian Ocean. In the *al bahr al Hindi* was included *bahr Larvi* (the sea of Lata or Gujarat), corresponding to the Arabian Sea. The Arab authors show a clear awareness of the *aghbab* or the channel separating the southern part of the peninsula from Sri Lanka; this seems to be the same as the Palk Strait. Further to the east, the maritime space was designated as *bahr Harkal* (or Harkand). Harkal is clearly the Arabicisation of the name Harikela, identified with the present Chittagong, Noakhali, and Comilla regions of Bangladesh (south-eastern most Bangladesh to the east of the river Meghna).[11] The coinage of terms denoting the Indian Ocean or different segments of it, especially by Arabic and Persian authors, cannot but demonstrate their regular familiarity and acquaintance with the maritime space in question, obviously in the wake of the burgeoning commerce in the Indian Ocean. It is true that contemporary Indians were content with merely using the terms *purva* (east) and *pascima/apara* (west) to suggest their awareness respectively of the Bay of Bengal and the Arabian Sea.[12] Chinese annals too speak of maritime linkages with India and various areas of the Indian Ocean. But the Chinese authors often used a generic term to point to the Indian Ocean; it was known as *Hsi-hai*, the western sea. The above exercise in the study of nomenclatures of the Indian Ocean is a pointer to the frequent sailings across the vast maritime space.

No less significant an observation regarding another geographical feature of the Indian Ocean is the immense influence of the monsoon wind system on the sailing patterns in this maritime space. Prior to the arrival of steam ships, shipping in the Indian Ocean was largely guided and shaped by the more less predictable alterations of the south-western (June to September) and the north-eastern monsoon (October to January) wind system. The term monsoon is derived from Arabic *mawsim* (plural *mawasim*), which means season. However, in the celebrated navigational manual of Ibn Majid (fifteenth century), the greatest navigator in the Indian Ocean prior to the arrival of the Portuguese, the term *mawasim* stands also for a sailing season to reach a particular destination across the sea.[13] When the Indian Ocean network was at its zenith, its western terminus was situated in Siraf, Kish and Hormuz (in the Persian Gulf) and al Fustat (Old Cairo) under the Fatimid Caliphate in Egypt. The eastern reach of this network stretched to the ports of maritime south-east Asia and China. As it would be impossible for a traditional ship to complete a round trip between the western and the eastern termini in a single year because of the alterations of the monsoon winds, the two seaboards of India—dotted with numerous ports—were ideally suited as stopovers and points of transshipment. This must have proved immensely advantageous to the overseas commerce of India which was also involved in brisk export and import transactions.[14] Contrary to the image of a languishing overseas trade in the early medieval times, evidence available from a wide range of sources strongly suggests India's active and important role in the Indian Ocean commerce. The documentation in use here covers inscriptions, indigenous literary texts, a large number of Arabic and Persian accounts, Chinese texts, the accounts of Marco Polo in the late thirteenth century, and last but not the least, the letters of Jewish merchants (Genizah documents) trading with India from the eleventh to the thirteenth centuries.[15] The information offered by these sources is hardly adequate, often scattered and stereotyped and offers little statistical data. These belong, instead to the category of 'qualitative sources'.[16] The letters of the Jewish merchants, known to us largely due to the stupendous researches of S.D. Goitein, highlight the activities of *musafirun ul Hind* (travellers to India), whom Goitein immortalised under the label, 'India traders'. These unique letters enable us to hear the voices of the merchants directly who actually participated in the Indian Ocean trade; they also occasionally provide some statistical information.

II

The Indian Ocean, especially its western sector, came into great prominence during the first three centuries CE, on account of India's brisk trade with the Roman empire. The maritime network of the western sea-board of India through the Red Sea plays an important role in bringing India closer to the Mediterranean commerce. This far-flung commerce, however, experienced a slump after ca. 250 CE as there was a lesser demand for Indian products in the Roman world in the wake for gradual decline of the Roman empire. The rise of the Sasanid empire in Iran and the eastern Roman empire with its capital in Byzantium again brought the western Indian Ocean to prominence after 400 CE. The maritime commerce of the Eastern Roman empire with India is evident in the coin hoards, largely from south India, yielding many coins of the Byzantine rulers. This was maintained largely through the Persian Gulf which now overshadowed the Red Sea network. The rise of the Sasanids of Iran coincided with their distinct interests in the commerce of the Persian Gulf. In fact, one may discern some rivalries between the Byzantine and the Sasanid powers over the Persian Gulf trade with India. The Indus delta was witnessing the rise of a new port, Debal, mentioned as Daibul in early Arab accounts. Early Arab accounts recounting raids on this port in ca. 627 CE attest to its importance. The descriptions of the first Arab invasion of Sind in early eighth century, narrated in a later source—the *Chachnama*—point to the direct voyages between Daibul and Sri Lanka.

III

The above survey, synoptic and hurried, does not suggest a sharp decline in the maritime trade of India in the centuries succeeding its commerce with the Roman empire. It is, however, true that it does not match in scale with the commerce between the eastern Mediterranean and India. One cannot also deny that around the eighth century, premier ports of the previous epoch, like Broach, Kaveripattinam and Tamralipta, gradually faded out. This may have prompted the historians of Indian feudalism, to infer a period of slump of India's maritime commerce. On the contrary, in the historiography of Indian feudalism, the voluminous evidence available in the Arabic and Persian texts (several of them being composed prior to 1000 CE) has been consistently ignored and sidelined. Impressions left behind by Sulaiman (c. 851), ibn Khuradbeh (c. 882), al Masudi (c. 915), Kitab Ajaib ul Hind (c. 955), the anonymous author of the *Hudud al Alam* (c. 982), al Biruni (1030), al Marvazi (1120), al Idrisi (c. 1162), ibn Battuta (early fourteenth century) speak voluminously of the overseas contacts with India, the importance of Indian ports and the exchange of commodities. To this can easily be added the evidence of Chau ju Kua (1225), who as an officer supervising foreign trade under the Sung dynasty of China wrote a valuable account of commodities and ports of India. Towards the end of the thirteenth century, Marco Polo also informs us about India's role in the commerce of the Indian Ocean. We shall also utilise here the evidence of the Jewish business letters. The Jewish merchants' commercial ventures spanned Tunisia and Levant to Egypt and Aden from where they regularly sailed to ports on the west coast of India.

The establishment of the Abbasid Caliphate in Baghdad paved the way for the growth of trade in the Persian Gulf where stood the premier port of Siraf. After the decline of Siraf since the late eleventh century, Kish or Qays came to great prominence. It is from the thirteenth century that one notes the rise of Hormuz as a port of immense significance in the western Indian Ocean commerce. The Red Sea network seems to have taken a backseat during the period from the seventh to the tenth centuries CE. The rise of Fatimid Caliphate in Egypt in 965 CE once again swung the pendulum in favour of the Red Sea. The Red Sea network further offered linkages with the vibrant Mediterranean maritime trade through Egypt which acted like a hinge between the Indian Ocean and the Mediterranean with momentous significance.

This brings us to another survey of the ports in both the sea-boards of India, active during the period from the ninth to thirteenth centuries. In Sanskrit sources ports are called *velakulas*, in Tamil as *velapuras* and *pattinam/pattanams*. In the Indus delta, the port of Daybul certainly prospered. It seems to have been well connected with Multan and Mansura on one hand and also with the Makran coast on the other. Its remains are found in the excavations at Banbhore.[17]

In the Gujarat coast, Broach was replaced with Stambatirtha, Stambhaka which is the same as the famous port of Cambay. It figures prominently in the Arab accounts under the name Kanbaya and Kambaya. The rise of the Caulukyas as a regional power of Gujarat paved the way for the integration of the coast with the extensive interior by a number of overland routes.[18] Early medieval Gujarat experienced remarkable agricultural growth also. In western India, especially in Gujarat, Rajasthan, Malwa and western part of UP, emerged a new type of exchange centre in the early medieval period. These are known as *mandapikas* (=modern *mandis*) which provided vital linkages between the rural-level market centres (*hatta/hattika*) and larger markets at urban centres and ports (*pattana/velakula*).[19] These were instrumental in the efflorescence of the ports of Gujarat, particularly Cambay. The port maintained coastal linkages with ports in the Konkan and Malabar littorals, as will be evident from the accounts of the Arab writers. Two early medieval Indian texts, *Vastupalamahatmayam* and *Jagaducaritam*, bear clear impressions of the contacts between Cambay and Ardrapura, which stands for Hormuz in the Persian Gulf.[20] The availability of an extensive hinterland and the agricultural prosperity of Gujarat in the early medieval period certainly contributed to the sustenance of Cambay; it was also well served by a few smaller ports in Gujarat and northern Konkan.

These relatively smaller ports acted as feeder ports for the premier Gujarati port. One may enlist in this context Mangalapura (Mangrol in the Kathiawad coast), Diu, Somnath and Ghogha. One of the earliest mentions of Diu is available in a twelfth-century Jewish business letter, which speaks of a voyage from al Manjrur (Mangalore) to al Divi (Diu) in Gujarat from where the ship sailed to Aden.[21] Diu was thus connected with both the Kanara coast and Aden. Though Somnath is principally celebrated in Indian history as a great Saiva sacred centre, it was also a port of some prominence, located at the confluence of the Sarasvati with the sea (*Sarasvtisagarasamprayogavibhusita)*.[22] Al Biruni was one of the earliest authors to have appreciated the importance of Somnath as a port; he states that it was a vantage point of departure for Zanz or Zanzibar in east Africa.[23] We have, however no further corroborative evidence in support of al Biruni's mention of voyage from Somanth to the east African coast. That Somnath did receive ships from Hormuz is proved beyond doubt by a remarkable bi-lingual (in Arabic and Sanskrit) inscription of 1264 from Somnath.[24] *Hurmuji-vahana* or ships from Hormuz also reached the port of Ghogha (*Ghogha velakula*) in Gujarat.

To the south of the Gujarat coast was situated the narrow strip of Konkan, repeatedly figuring in the Arab accounts as Kunkan, Kamkam and Makamkam.[25] At the northernmost fringe of Konkan, almost touching southern Gujarat, was the port of Samyana, Arabicised as Sanjan/Sindan. A port to the south of Sanjan was Sristhanaka or Thana. Thana seems to have come into prominence later than Sanjan. A Jewish business letter of 1145 narrates a coastal voyage from al Manjrur (Mangalore) to Thana wherefrom the ship further proceeded northwards to Barus (Broach). It appears in greater prominence under the name Tana (Thana) in the accounts of Marco Polo in the late thirteenth century. Thana during that period seems to have served as the major port of north Konkan under the Yadavas of Devagiri. Cemulya or Chaul, situated to the south of present Mumbai, was a significant port of Konkan. Already known as Sibor in the sixth-century accounts of Cosmas Indicopleustes, Chaul appears as Saimur in the Arab accounts. Three ports in the southern part of Konkan rose to some prominence in the early centuries of the second millennium CE. These are Balipattana (modern Kharepatan), Candrapura (=Sindabur in Arabic texts) and Gopakapattana (Old Goa). While Balipattana was located in the kingdom of the Silaharas of southern Konkan, Candrapura (Chandore) and Gopakapattana belonged to the realm of the Kadambas of Goa. A close perusal of Sanskrit inscriptions, Arab texts and Jewish business letters brings out a few features of the Konkan ports. Though geographically the Konkan ports were located in the most conducive areas for harbour building, they were less prosperous and prominent than the ports in Malabar and Gujarat. These ports in Konkan neither had rich agricultural hinterland nor commanded regular linkages with the interior because of the geographical barrier of the Sahyadri range between the coast and the mainland. The ports of Konkan witnessed regular settlements of Arab merchants who figure in Sanskrit inscriptions under the category of *Tajjikas*. Al Masudi noted the presence of a large number of Omani, Sirafi and Baghdadi merchants at the port of Saimur or Chaul. The long presence of these Arab merchants explains how and why their names sometimes appear in Sankritised forms in inscriptions, e.g. Mahumata/Madhumati (=

Muhammad), Alliya (=Ali), Shariyarahara (= Shahriyar), etc. A close study of two inscriptions of the Silaharas of south Konkan, one of 1008 and the other of 1094, strongly suggests that ports of Konkan were engaged in looping coastal commerce. This coastal linkage further extended to Gujarat and Malabar. Impressions of long coastal voyages from around Goa to Somnath in the Kathiawad coast are clearly available from the inscriptions of the Kadamba rulers of Goa.[26]

The Arab accounts leave a clear impression that the ports of north Konkan, especially Sanjan and Saimur, derived considerable advantages from their linkages with the Persian Gulf commerce. A few Jewish merchants undertook a voyage from Aden to Sindabur, close to Goa, as known from a correspondence of a Jewish merchant. Sindabur thus seems to have experienced a gradual expansion of its network up to Aden in the twelfth century. To the south of Goa the most important port in the Kanara coast was al Manjrur, sometimes mentioned in the Arab texts, but repeatedly figuring in the business letters addressed to Abraham ben Yiju/Yishu, a Jewish merchant of al Mahdiyya or Tunisia who lived in this port town for more than seventeen years (1132–49).[27]

The southernmost segment of the western sea-board is famous as Malabar, known as Malibar, Manibar, al Mulaybar in the Arabic texts and the Jewish business letters. Three ports deserve special mention: these are Kulam Mali (Quilon), Panatalayani Kollam (Fandarina) and Calicut. The Malabar ports could be reached from both the Persian Gulf and the Red Sea ports by utilising the south-western monsoon in around thirty days. These ports earned their fame for handling the invaluable cargo of spices, especially the pepper of Kerala aptly described as 'black gold'. Calicut does not seem to have attained its great glory prior to the early fourteenth century. Ibn Battuta is one of the first authors to have described its immense importance. He noted that the huge Chinese junks did not sail further west of Calicut and Calicut provided excellent transshipment facilities for Chinese and Arab vessels. Calicut reached its zenith in the fourteenth and fifteenth centuries. The famous Chinese voyages under Admiral Cheng-ho/Zeng he (from 1404–1433) touched Calicut as many as eight times.[28]

IV

These ports in the two sea-boards of India were involved in a lively manner in the exchange of commodities. The sources mentioned above throw considerable light on the items of exports and imports. Among the perennial export items of India were various types of textiles for which India attained legendary fame. Textiles of Gujarat, Malwa and Bengal deserve particular mention in this context. Textile products ranged from the famous and expensive muslin of Bengal to ordinary cotton cloth meant for daily necessity.[29] There was also the expected craze for precious gems and stones in areas abroad. The pearl fisheries of the Tuticorin coast in the Pandyan realm and the diamond mines in Andhra under the Kakatiyas figure prominently in the accounts of Marco Polo.[30] Among spices, the pepper of Malabar was highly prized. The Genizah papers of Jewish merchants are replete with references to regular shipping of pepper in large quantities from Malabar to Aden, and from there through the Red Sea to Egypt.[31] From Egypt, pepper finally reached Italian ports by voyages across the Mediterranean. At the port of Aydhab on the western shore of the Red Sea, ibn Jubayr, an Andalusian traveller, saw huge heaps of Indian pepper (1184).[32] Pepper was a forest product procured in Kerala but assumed the character of a luxury as it reached the markets of the Red Sea and the Mediterranean, fetching very high prices. Two other forest products had wide demand in west Asia, according to the Arabic and Persian texts: aloes wood and teak. The best two varieties of aloes were Multani (from Multan) and Kamaruni (from Kamarupa or upper Assam). Indian teak was regularly exported to the Persian Gulf and Red Sea ports as the basic raw materials for building sea-going vessels for Arab merchants who did not have a local source of durable wood for boat-building.

Along with high value, portable, small quantity luxuries were shipped daily necessities in bulk quantities. The Genizah letters repeatedly tell us about the regular shipment of various types of iron from al Manjrur and other ports of Malabar to Aden during the period from eleventh to the thirteenth centuries. There appears to have been a steady demand for Indian iron in the 'west', possibly for making weapons like swords.[33] A combined testimony of ibn Battuta and Ma huan would reveal Bengal shipped rice to the Maldives, which in return sent out to Bengal cowry shells. Cowry shells functioned as a major currency not only in eastern India, but also in the east African port in Kilwa and the west African kingdom of Dahomey.[34] Huge quantities of cowry shells certainly functioned as small exchanges and also as ballast in the maritime network of the Indian Ocean. This clearly negates the widely held notion that the use of cowry currency in early medieval Bengal was symptomatic of languishing trade and signified only local-level transactions. Cowry currency was part and parcel of and well integrated with the Indian Ocean commercial economy of the pre-modern times. There is a distinct possibility of a regular supply of coconut coir (mentioned as *qinbar* in Arab accounts) from the west coast of India to the ports of the Red Sea and the Persian Gulf. Coconut coir was an indispensable ingredient in the wooden ships of the Indian Ocean which did not use iron nails to fasten the planks. The west coast of India, noted for the regular plantation of coconut since at least second century CE, exported this item in bulk to the ship-building centres in the Islamic world.[35] We have already pointed to the demand for Indian cotton textiles in the Persian Gulf and the Red Sea ports. To this was also closely linked the regular export of Indian indigo to the 'west'. The Genizah documents informs us of an eleventh-century Jewish merchant, ibn Awkal, who maintained meticulous details of correspondence with his agents. While his seat of business was at al Fustat (Old Cairo), his agents spread as far as al Mahdiyya (Tunisia) and the Levant. His correspondence speaks of his dealings in Sanjani indigo; this is certainly the indigo produced in western India and shipped from the port of Sanjan in north Konkan. That the Sanjani indigo competed well with indigo from Amta (in Palestine) and Kirman (south western Iran) is clearly impressed in the correspondence of ibn Awkal. One is therefore not surprised to come across another merchant, involved in the 'India trade', specifically dealing in indigo; hence he is named Sheikh Ali b. Muhammad Nili (*nil*= indigo).[36] This is another instance of the importance of bulk items in the maritime trade of India. It effectively rejects the stereotyped portrayal of India's export of merely high value, small quantity, exotic, luxury/prestige goods.

India received exotic spices and gems from Sri Lanka and south-east Asia as imports, many of which were further shipped to 'western' destinations. This suggests the involvement of Indian ports in transit trade. A case in point is the importation of cinnamon, cardamom, camphor and sandal; the same can be said of the import of ruby from Sri Lanka. Indian imports definitely included precious metals, especially gold and silver, though the actual quantum cannot be ascertained. In at least one Genizah letter, merchants preparing for a sailing to India from the Red Sea port of Aydhab are said to have preferred silver to gold as the form of payment to purchase Indian commodities. In another letter of 1139, the import of silk instead of gold from Aden to al Manjrur is clearly mentioned.[37] That copper was brought to India from West Asia is amply borne out in a few Jewish letters. Among India's imports, a particular commodity demands our attention. This is the horse from Arabia and Fars. India did not have indigenous war horses of the best variety; there was therefore a constant demand for imported war horses. This demand seems to have greatly increased in the early medieval period when there were numerous regional and local powers, engaged in endemic warfare. One of the regular sources of good quality war horses was from the central Asian steppe regions, called Tatari horses in medieval sources. These were brought to India by overland routes through the north-western borderlands of the subcontinent. With the onset of the second millennium, excellent horses from Arabia and Fars began to be sent to India, not however by overland routes but by overseas transportation. These horses were therefore labelled as '*bahri*' (sea-borne) in Arabic and Persian sources and these fetched maximum price. Marco Polo speaks of the shipping of ten thousand horses per year to the Pandyan realm alone from the ports like Shihr, Kish, Hormuz and Aden. Marco Polo's accounts, when read along with those of ibn Battuta, Barani and Abdulla Wassaf, impress upon the enormous price of these horses, each fetching a price of 220 gold coins. The most significant point of disembarkation of these *bahri* horses was the Malabar coast. This coastal zone, significantly enough, was the arena of great activities of Tamil horse-dealers, called *kudiraicettis* of Malainadu (*kudir*=horse, *cetti*= merchant). They were possibly engaged in the distribution of the imported horses to political powers inland, for instance, the Pandyas of Madurai. No less interesting is the observation of Marco Polo that the king around the port of Tana (Thana) colluded with the pirates on the condition that he would receive all the horses from the pirated ship, while the rest of the cargo would remain with the pirates. Polo impresses upon the desperate act of a coastal authority in order to capture by force and fraud the shipload of imported horses which apparently were too costly for him to afford regularly.[38]

The Chinese vessels plying in the Indian Ocean and visiting Indian ports came under the general category of junks. The most and frequently occurring term for a ship in Arabic texts is *markab*. At least in one twelfth-century Jewish letter thus occurs the Arabic term *jahaj*, which however relates to the preparations of fitting out a ship for a long voyage. Three types of ships, *burrama*, *shaffara* and *jashujiyat* were employed by the rapacious king of Kish during a naval blockade around Aden in the early twelfth century, according to a Jewish Genizah letter.[39] The *jilab* was in frequent use in the Red Sea area; ibn Jubayar saw how the *jilab* was always overloaded with passengers in the port of Aydhab. The most important figure on board the Arab ship was the *muallim*, navigator or captain, who figures very prominently in the shipping manual of ibn Majid, himself a great navigator. Right from the beginning of the preparation of a voyage till its reaching the ultimate destination, the *muallim*, according to ibn Majid, was the final authority in the running and maintenance of the ship.[40] Two subordinates under him were the *kardar*[41] and the *tandel*. The *muallim* of ibn Majid closely corresponds to the *sasaka/mahanavika* of Sanskrit sources. Interestingly enough, the Buddha appears as a master mariner having great expertise in bringing in and taking out the ship from the harbour (*aharana* and *apaharana*), according to the Jatakamala of Aryasura. Fascinating stories of sailing, surviving shipwrecks and great dangers of the sea voyage are narrated in the *Kitab Ajaib ul Hind* of Buzurg ibn Shahriyar (ca. 955) who himself was a famous ship-captain. The helmsman figures under the category *karnadhara*. The men who actually manned merchantmen came under the category of *navikakarmakara* (literally engaged in sailing). The sailors belonged to the lower stratum to the *varna-jati* divided society and did not command respectability in the Brahmanical treatises. The term *navikakarmakara* has a correspondence to *al askar* in Arabic, meaning a sailor in general. If the dependence on the alteration of the monsoon wind was a perennial feature of shipping across the Indian Ocean, the other fact of unity lies in the construction of traditional ships of the Indian Ocean with the help of wooden planks, held together by coconut coir. These crafts did not have any iron nails, hence the expression *nilloham* in Sanskrit texts as an epithet of the traditional ship. Though the term *sitapatra* (*siyapata* in Prakrit) stands for sail of the ship, visual representations of early Indian ships rarely display sails.[42] One notable exception to this pattern is the famous painting of the ship in the Ajanta painting. There is little account available of the facilities for passengers. Nahray b. Alan, a prominent Jewish merchant, wrote about his satisfaction having been provided with a *bilij* or cabin in a ship bound for India.[43] Ibn Battuta was mostly very critical of the arrangements of living in the ships of his time; he however spoke in approving terms of Chinese junk where he got a separate cabin for an aristocrat like himself.

VI

Attention now may be paid to merchants engaged in the maritime trade network of the Indian Ocean. The most important figures in this context are the ship-owning merchants. It is from around 1000 CE that ship-owners stole the limelight in the ports on the west coast of India. Sanskrit inscriptions coined the term *nauvittaka* to denote a person whose wealth (*vitta)* was rooted to his ships (*nau*). This exactly corresponds to the Arabic and Persian word, *nakhuda* (*nau*= ship and *khuda*=lord), denoting ship-owning merchant. In some Sanskrit inscriptions the two terms were also abbreviated respectively into *nau* or *nakhu*; sometimes the two terms were also used as synonymous. All these strongly suggest considerable familiarity of the coastal society with the ship-owners. The largest number of such ship-owners comes to our notice in the Jewish Geniza letters. A leading Jewish merchant, Madmun b. Hassan, (the Representative of Merchants/*wakil ul tujjar* at Aden and a close friend of Abraham ben Yiju, the Tunisian Jewish merchant residing in Mangalore) wrote in 1130 of a ship ordered by him for carrying commodities and passengers from Aden to Sri Lanka. This is probably the same craft mentioned as 'the ship of Elder Madmun' in which Nahray b. Allan, another prominent Jewish merchant, sent his goods in

1141. In 1149 ben Yiju informed his brother in al Fustat that he had sent some presents for him in the ship of Madmun. These letters, taken together, indicate that Madmun's ship was operational between Aden and the south western sea-board of India (also with Sri Lanka) for nearly two decades. Though Madmun was not primarily a ship-owner, he seems to have been successful in his shipping business. That is why in a letter to ben Yiju (around 1140) he expressed his desire to launch another ship in Aden in collaboration with four Indian merchants, viz. Sus Siti, Kinbati, Isha and Isaq.

Rich and exhaustive data on shipping and ship-owning merchants prompt us to take a close look at a letter of 1139. Khalaf b. Isaac b. Bundar, a cousin and also a close business associate of Madmun acknowledged the receipt of two *bahars* and one-third of 'refurbished iron' sent by Abraham Yiju to Aden in the ship of *nakhuda* Ibn Abi'l Kataib. Madmun also informed him of the arrival of *nakhuda* Joseph at Aden from Dahabattan or Vallarapatnam (in Malabar) in the ship of Ibn al Muqaddam. While so far we encounter Jewish and Muslim *nakhudas* in this letter, two ships of an Indian shipowner, Fatanswami (= Sanskrit *pattanasvami*) also figure prominently in Khalaf's letter. Khalaf informs of the safe arrival of the smaller ship of the Fatanswami to Aden but announces the terrible news of disaster striking the bigger ship. The pepper in that ship was completely lost, but portions of the iron were salvaged by employing professional divers of the port of Aden. Khalaf continues in his letter to inform that he sent some presents for ben Yiju in the ship of Fadiyar who, according to Goitein was another Indian ship-owner. Another letter from Madmun b. Yiju informed of the shipment of a bag of copper of twenty-three pieces sent in the ship of Ramisht of Siraf, the merchant millionaire of the port of Siraf, also separate consignments of copper in the ships of al Muqaddam and Nambiyar, the last one being certainly an Indian merchant from Malabar.[44] These letters are thus replete with reliable images of close interactions and linkages among Jewish, Muslim and Indian merchants. Abraham Yishu seems to have used the ships of Ramisht on several occasions, though ill luck occasionally struck both Yiju and Ramisht in the form of shipwrecks. In a letter dated in the late 1130s, Joseph b. Abraham broke the news of shipwrecks of two ships of *nakhuda* Ramisht; in those ill-fated ships ben Yiju sent some consignments to Aden. Joseph consoled ben Yiju : 'Do not ask me, my master, how much I was affected by the loss of the cargo belonging to you'[45].

That the Jewish merchants also figured in the coastal network along the western sea-board is visible in a letter of 1145. Mahruz b. Jacob, a *nakhuda* often plying between Aden and Malabar, wrote to his brother-in-law Judah b. Joseph ha-Kohen (sister's husband), who was representive of merchants at the Egyptian capital. The letter was sent through Madmun b. Yiju. Mahruz was greatly disturbed to learn that Judah was attacked by pirates during his coastal voyage from al Manjrur to Tana (=Thana near Mumbai). The letter was originally sent to Thana but Judah had already left that port for Baruz or Broach at the mouth of the river Narmada. Mahruz wrote : 'The boats start presently from your place, from Kambayat and Tana; please set out immediately so that you reach Mangalore with vessels which God willing will soon reach Malibarat, Kayakannur and Mangalore'[46]. The *Geniza* letters thus throw a flood of light on the stellar role of Jewish 'India traders' in the trade with India especially the sea-borne commerce.

From the thirteenth century onwards the Jewish merchants and *nakhudas* gradually faded out from the shipping scenario in the western Indian Ocean in the face of stiff competition from the Islamic *Karimi* merchants who seem to have had a stronger mercantile organisation. Goitein attributes the gradual lessening of the Jewish seafaring mainly because of the ever stricter interpretation and observation of the precepts of Jewish religion. The desecration of the Sabbath was unavoidable for sailors on voyage. Their employers were held responsible for all religious transgressions arising out of their employment. For the scrupulously religious Jews shipping became an increasingly less attractive avenue. The merchants in the Geniza letters were certainly well-off, some of course very rich; but contemporary long-distance trade and shipping in the West was largely financed by the Islamic ruling groups having far greater resources. To this was added the organised business ventures of *al Karim* from the thirteenth century onwards.[47] The prominent role of the Jews in India trade had to give way to other more enterprising and resourceful competitors. It is not difficult to visualise the active presence of several *nakhudas* in the Gujarat coast, especially around Cambay, as revealed by epitaphs. Most of them were Iraqi/Iranian by birth, but settled in and breathed their last in port towns of Gujarat in the fourteenth–fifteenth centuries. Eminently successful and possessing enough wealth, they were leading (*sultan*) merchants and ship-owners and great patrons of the *hajj*.[48] The point to take particular note of is the presence of Indian ship-owners whose ships sailed across the Arabian Sea along with those of the Jewish and Muslim ship-owning merchants. The general perception that Indian ship-owners did not participate in the overseas voyages now needs a revision. Jagadu, a well-known merchant of Gujarat, figures in the Jagaducarita as having sent his ships to Ardrapura or Hormuz from Cambay.[49] He is not described as a *nauvittaka* category of merchants and appears to have invested a part of his fabulous wealth in the shipping business. There were also Indian ship-owning merchants in the west coast of India whose ships mainly operated in coastal voyages. At the port of Balipattana (Kharepatan in the southern Konkan littorals) were active members of a *sresthi* family over three generations, whose vessels operated in the Konkan sector, touching the ports of Cemulya, Nagapura, Candrapura and Sristhanka. They are categorically described as *nauvittakas* or *nakhudas* in the eleventh century inscription from Balipattana. It is quite evident that this *sresthi* family, residing in the port town of Balipattana, was interested in coastal shipping business and invested a part of their wealth in that.[50] In 1145 one comes across *nakhuda* Tinbu whose ships plied between al Manjrur and Thana. His constant interactions with Jewish India traders are writ large in a business later of 1145. This is true not merely in the western sector of the Indian Ocean. A Tamil inscription from Barus in Indonesia (dated 1088 CE), records the presence of *marakkalam* (ships), owners of *marakkalam* and *marakkala-nayan* (ship-captains).[51] The inscription proves beyond doubt the presence of Tamil ship-owning merchants in Indonesia. There is a distinct possibility that the *marakkala-nayan* evolved into the famous Maraikkayan(r) or Maraikkar group of merchants, especially active in the Malabar coast in the sixteenth century.

One is not exactly sure how many of these ship-owners did actually take to the sea; many of them could have been merchants ashore rather than afloat. But many other Indian merchants did undertake overseas voyages by the lure of gain. The brief and hurried survey of voyages undertaken by Indian merchants both in the Arabian Sea and the Bay of Bengal highlights the hollowness of the notion that Indians rarely took to the sea because crossing the sea was forbidden in the *sastras* and brought under the category of *kalivarjya* (proscribed activities during the Kali age). While the Sastric injunctions may at the most speak of Brahmanical ideals and norms, these were not insurmountable and in fact were often transgressed. The ship-owning merchants were undoubtedly the key players in the maritime network in the Indian Ocean.[52] The traditional trade of India did not merely revolve around the ubiquitious pedlars, as van Leur argued so strongly argued. In the *nakhudas, nauvittakas* and *marakkalanayans* one may find the forerunners of Mulla Abdul Ghafur of Surat, the greatest ship-owning merchant of the eighteenth century, immortalised by Ashin Das Gupta.[53]

VII

We have already pointed to two major points of unity in the world of the Indian Ocean, viz. the influence of the alterations of the monsoon winds on the shipping networks and hence on the transactional activities in the ports and their respective hinterlands; and the widespread use of ships made of wooden planks held together by coconut coir without the use of iron nails. A third point of commonality is visible in the role of sea and the maritime merchants as bridges among diverse communities in widely dispersed territories. Merchants and their ships were not merely carriers of commodities, but purveyors of their cultural traditions too. This explains the spread of Buddhism and later the popularity of Vaisnavism and Saivism in many countries of south-east Asia; the same is applicable in the use of Sanskrit and Tamil in south-east Asia in inscriptions. The most eloquent examples are there in the Jewish business letters. These are replete with accounts of rivalries, court cases and complaints against merchants involved in the 'India trade'. But nowhere in the entire range of the Genizah documents does one come across religious intolerance among Indian, Jewish and Islamic merchants active in the maritime trade of the western Indian Ocean. In a letter of 1145, the Jewish trader Judah ha Kohen assured his brother-in-law Mahruz, who suffered an attack by pirates near Thana, to seek any financial assistance from the Hindu ship-owner Tinbu, because between Kohen and Tinbu were 'inseparable bonds of friendship and brotherhood'.[54] There was little difficulty for ben Yiju to marry a local woman from the Kanara coastal society during his stay at Mangalore for seventeen years.[55] Al Masudi noted in the early tenth century that Muslim merchants in the Konkan coast were given excellent support by the Rastrakuta rulers (Balhara kings in the Arab accounts, derived from the dynastic title of the Rastrakutas as Vallabharaja). The result was the construction of mosques in the port towns of Konkan. No less interesting is the information that Muslim Arab merchants were present as witnesses and important members of the coastal community during grants of land to a Durga temple in Sanjan by the Rastrakuta and Silahara rulers.[56] The most celebrated instance in this regard however, comes from Somnath in Gujarat. A bilingual inscription (Sanskrit and Arabic, Sanskrit version more elaborate and Arabic version synoptic) of 1264 tells us of the arrival of a pious Muslim *nakhuda* Nuruddin Firuz from Hormuz to Somnath. The texts of both the versions leaves a clear impression that Firuz probably had made several previous voyages to Somnath and therefore, became well acquainted with the port town and its mercantile population, largely Hindus. With the active support of his Hindu merchant friends, he caused the construction of a *mijigiti* (masjid/mosque) in Somnath where were regularly observed a number of Islamic festivals (*visesapujamahotsava*), typically associated with *nakhudas, nauvittakas* (ship-owners) and *navikakarmakaras* (sailors). These were Baratisabi (Sabe-barat) and Khatamrati (the recitation of the Qu'ran in a single night). The town council of Somanth, headed by a Saiva Pasupatacarya, approved of the procurement of land on which stood the mosque described in Sanskrit as a dharmasthanam. This was then endorsed by the provincial authority Maladeva and finally approved by Baghela Arjunadeva, the king of Gujarat. The Sanskrit inscription recording the construction of the mosque begins with a salutation to Allah (*Om Namastute*) who is given four epithets, *Visvarupa* (Universal), *Visvanatha* (Lord of the Universe), *Sunyarupa* (Formless/Aniconic) and *Lakshyalaksha* (Visible and being anicionic, also Invisible). This is truly emblematic of the role the merchant communities in the Indian Ocean played as bridges among different ethnic groups and religious faiths.[57]

The foregoing discussions would help us recognise the fact that the Indian Ocean had already become a much frequented maritime zone much before the advent of the Portuguese in the late fifteenth century. Vasco da Gama's voyage to Calicut cannot therefore be judged as a marker of the 'age of discoveries' in the Indian Ocean. Such a notion expresses an obvious Eurocentricism and justifies the European claim of inherent supremacy. One also cannot miss that prior to 1500, the Indian Ocean was a theatre of merchants, sailors and even of pirates. But only on very rare occasions did a political power consider the vast maritime space or a part thereof as an arena for establishing or even showing their political and military prowess. The famous Chinese voyages during the Ming period under Admiral Cheng Ho (1404–33) spanned the greater parts of the Indian Ocean at least six decades before the arrival of the Portuguese in the Indian Ocean. But no territorial gains were made, neither were established any naval stations nor was a claim made that the ocean belonged to the Chinese crown. Though the official Chinese annals described that Cheng Ho collected 'tributes' from the countries and ports he visited, a careful reading of the account cannot but suggest that the Chinese official missions were sent with a view to enhancing China's sea-borne commerce. A major exception to this pattern occurred in South India under Rajaraja I (985–1014) and Rajendra (1012–44). The Colas sent several maritime expeditions to conquer and annex Sri Lanka, by conquering which Rajaraja and Rajendra were eulogised as greater heroes than Rama. The Cola fleet also conquered '12000 islands in the open sea' which are usually identified with the Laccadives in the Arabian Sea. In 1025–26 there took place the most daring of the Cola maritime campaigns, the Kadaram campaign. As many as twelve important ports and centres of maritime were conquered by the Colas in the Bay of Bengal and maritime south-east Asia.

Rulers of Asia and Africa did not consider the maritime space as an arena for political contestation. This is not symptomatic of any apathy to the sea, but certainly demonstrates an attitude to the sea different from that associated with the Europeans. This is eloquently borne out by a tractate by a Bishop named William Adams, sometime around 1314/1315 (he died sometime between 1337 and 1341). The tractate is named *De Modo Saracenos Extirpandi*, submitted to the Pope urging him to annihilate the Saracenes or Muslims.[58] The principal thrust is to crush Egypt, which is seen as the stumbling block against Christian forces. The tractate underlines the importance of Egypt from the point of view of its role as a supplier of 'Eastern/Oriental' commodities to Europe. 'Everything that is sold in Egypt like pepper, ginger and other spices, gold and precious stones, silk and those rich textiles dyed with Indian colours and all other valuables, ...all these are brought to Egypt from India'. India is compared with 'head' (actually meaning mouth) through which enters all nourishing food to different limbs of the body, and the simile for Egypt is the stomach. 'If then the head were to be cut off', urges the Bishop in his submission, 'the whole stomach would wither away from the lack of nourishment and other limbs would perish'. With this project in view, the tractate proposes to place four galleys at the island of Socotra, located close to crucial entry point to the 'Gulf of Eden' (Red Sea), to set up a blockade against the flow of commercial traffic from India into that sea-lane. Further proposed is the stationing of galleys at Hormuz, the most significant port in the Persian Gulf, and at Thana (near Mumbai), Cambay, Quilon and Dive Insulide (probably Diu in Gujarat which has already figured in a twelfth-century Jewish trade letter as maintaining contacts with Aden). The text illustrates the attitude to disrupt maritime trade in the western Indian Ocean by imposing naval blockades at crucial and strategic points, something that the Portuguese would translate into practice in the subsequent centuries. No less striking is the correct evaluation of the author regarding the commercial significance of outstanding ports in the-then Gujarat, Konkan and Malabar littorals. Unlike many such Christian tract-writers, who in search for Prester John often confused India and Ethiopia[59], William Adam had a clear understanding of the location of major centres of maritime commerce in the western seaboard of India. In this tractate may be seen the pre-history of the concept of controlling and monopolising the maritime world of the Indian Ocean by means of military force, or in other words, by destroying the freedom of merchants through violence unleashed by the state on the sea. The Portuguese, the Dutch, the French and the English merchants did arrive in the Indian Ocean in the post-1500 phase initially for the lure of profit from trade in spice and textiles, which they ardently sought to import to Europe from the Indian Ocean countries; but on the other hand, the principal export of pre-industrial Europe to the world—including the Indian Ocean world—was violence, as Ashin Das Gupta, Niel Steensgaard and Om Prakash effectively demonstrate.[60] A sea-change in the trading world and politics of the Indian Ocean was in the offing in the centuries succeeding 1500.

NOTES AND REFERENCES

1. Ranabir Chakravarti (ed.), *Trade in Early India*, New Delhi, 2001; Ranabir Chakravarti, *Trade and Traders in Early Indian Society*, New Delhi, 2002; Romila Thapar, *Early India from Origins to c. A.D. 1300*, London, 2002 highlights the importance of commerce in the making of the civilisation and material culture of India.
2. Romila Thapar, 'The Great Eastern Trade, Other Places and Other Times', Vasant J. Sheth Memorial Lecutre, Mumbai, 2002: 2.
3. Julia Gotthold, *A Bibliography of the Indian Ocean*, Oxford, 1987.
4. Franz Broeze (ed.), *Brides of the Sea*, Kensington, 1989, p. 8.
5. Braudel compared this interconnectedness of the land and the sea with the inseparability between the potter's hands and the clay from which the pots get their shapes. See Fernand Braudel, *The Mediterranean and the Mediterranean World in the Age of Phillip II*, in two vols., trans. S. Reynolds, London, 1972.
6. The relative absence of long-distance trade during the early medieval period is one of the major planks of the formulation of Indian feudalism which is said to have brought about a self-sufficient, enclosed and stagnant village society with little impetus to the non-agricultural sector of the economy. See, D.D. Kosambi, *An Introduction to the Study of Indian History*, Bombay, 1956; R.S. Sharma, *Indian Feudalism*, Delhi, 1980; idem, *Urban Decay in India A.D. 300–1000*, Delhi, 1987; B.N.S. Yadava, *Society and Culture in Northern India in the Twelfth Century*, Allahabad, 1974; D.N. Jha ed., *The Feudal Order*, New Delhi, 2000.
7. Debates on this contentious issue are available in B.D. Chattopadhaya, *The Making of Early Medieval India*, Delhi, 1994; idem, 'State and Economy in North India: Fourth Century to Twelfth Century', in Romila Thapar (ed.), *Recent Perspectives of Early Indian History*, pp. 308–46; R. Chamapakalakshmi, 'State and Economy in South India: A.D. 400–1300', in Thapar (ed.), *Recent Perspectives*, pp. 266–307; D.C. Sircar, *The Emperor and his Subordinate Rulers*, Santiniketan, 1982; Chakravarti (ed.), *Trade in Early India* (especially the Editor's Introduction and the Annotated Bibliography); idem, 'Politics and Society in India A.D. 300–1000', in K. Satchidananda Murty (ed.), *Culture, Thought and Society in India A.D. 300–1000*, New Delhi, 2002, pp. 58–171.
8. K.N. Chaudhuri, *Trade and Civilization in the Indian Ocean from the Rise of Islam to 1750*, Cambridge, 1985; idem, *Asia before Europe, Economy and Civilization in the Indian Ocean from the Rise of Islam to 1750*, Cambridge, 1990.
9. G.F. Hourani, *Arab Seafaring in the Indian Ocean during the Ancient and Early Medieval Times*, Beirut, 1951.
10. Pliny, *Naturalis Historia* (VI.XXI.56), trans. J. Rackham, London, 1942, p. 381.
11. B.N. Mukherjee, 'The Original Territory of Harikela', *Bangladesh Lalitkala*, Vol. I, 1975, pp. 115–19.
12. Chakravarti, *Trade and Traders*, the term Vangasagara occurs in the Madanpur Copper Plate of Sricandra of 971CE edited first by R.G. Basak,

Epigraphia Indica (*EI*), XXVIII, 1949–50, pp. 51–58 and later by D.C. Sircar, *EI*, XXVIII, 1949–50, pp. 337–39. None of the epigraphists commented on the coinage of the term Vangasagara.

13. Ibn Majid ,(trans). G.R. Tibbetts, *Arab Navigation in the Indian Ocean before the Coming of the Portuguese*, London, 1971, pp. 34–36.
14. Chaudhuri, *Trade and Civilisation*, has highlighted the commercial advantages of segmented voyages. He also suggests that from around ca. 1000 CE emporia trade grew to the advantage of the Indian Ocean ports, including those in India.
15. Early medieval inscriptions are mainly concerned with political eulogies of rulers and grants of landed property to religious personalities and institutions. Information on trade, especially on sea-faring merchants, appears in these inscriptions only in the shape of incidental notices. The Chinese texts used here are: Fa hsien, *Fu Kuo Chi*, trn. J. Legge, *The Travels of Fa hsien*, Delhi, 1974 (rpt); Hsuan Tsang, *Ta tang His Yu Chi*, trn. S. Beal, New Delhi, 1983 (rpt.); Itsing, trn. J. Tajkakusu, *An Account of Buddhist Religion as Practised in India and the Malay Archipelago*; Chau-Ju Kua, *Chu fan chi*, trans. F. Hirth and W. Rockhill, St. Petersburg, 1911; Ma huan, *Ying-yai-Shen-lang*, trans. J.V.G. Mills, Oxford, 1970. The Arabic and Persian texts include: S. Maqbul Ahmad, trans., *Arab Classical Accounts of India and China* (accounts of Sulaiman and ibn Khurdadbeh), Shimla, 1989; H. Elliot and J. Dowson trans., *The History of India as told by its Own Historians*, ed. by S. Hodivala with a Foreword by Mohammad Habib, Vols. I–III, Aligarh, 1939; Buzurg ibn Shahriyar, *Kitab Ajaib ul Hind*, trans, G.P.S. Freeman-Grennville, London, 1980; Al Biruni, *Kitab ul Hind*, trans. E. Sachau, London, 1910; Al Idrisi (tr. S. Maqbul Ahmad), *India and the Neighbouring Territories*, Leiden, 1960; Ibn Jubayr, trans. R.J.C. Broadhurst, *The Travels of Ibn Jubayr*, London, 1952; Ibn Battuta, *The Rihala*, trans. H.A.R. Gibb, *The Travels of Ibn Battuta in Asia and Africa*, London, 1929; V. Minorsky trans., *Hudud al Alam*, London, 1937; idem, trans, *The Accounts of al Marvazi*, London, 1942. For Marco Polo, see *The Travels of Ser Marco Polo*, tr, H. Yule and H. Cordier, in two vols., London, 1903. The letters of the medieval Jewish merchants were originally deposited in the Genizah (meaning a store house) within a Synagogue in al Fustat (Old Cairo) in Egypt; now the Genizah is completely emptied, the documents having been preserved in various collections. The largest collection lies in the Cambridge University Library. The greatest specialist of the 'documentary genizah' was S.D. Goitein, who devoted considerable attention to the Jewish 'India traders'. See S.D. Goitein, 'Two Eye Witness Reports on the Invasion of Aden by the King of Kais in the Twelfth Century', *Bulletin of the School of Oriental and African Studies (BSOAS)*, XVI, 1954: 247–57; idem, *Letters of Medieval Jewish Traders (Letters)*, Princeton, 1973; idem, 'From Aden to India: Specimens of Correspondence of India Traders of the Twelfth Century', *Journal of the Economic and Social History of the Orient, (JESHO)*, XXI, 1980, pp. 43–66; idem, 'Portrait of a Medieval India Trader: Three Letters from the Cairo Geniza', *BSOAS*, XLVIII, 1987, pp. 448–64; idem, *A Mediterranean Society*, in six vols., Los Angeles and Berkeley, 1967–96. The

present author is grateful to Professors Mark R. Cohen, A.L. Udovitch and Mordechai Friedman for allowing him to use and study the files of the unpublished *India Book* by S.D. Goitein, now in the Dept. of Near Eastern Studies, Princeton University, Princeton. Dr. Roxani Margaritti, of Emory University (USA) was gracious enough to have presented me with her unpublished Ph.D thesis ('Like the Place of Congregation on Judgement Day: Maritime Trade and Urban Civilization in Medieval Aden (ca.1083–1229). Also see Amitav Ghosh, *In an Antique Land*, Delhi, 1990; idem 'The Slave of Ms H.6', Occasional Paper, Centre for the Studies in Social Sciences, Calcutta, 1990; Shaul Shaked, *A Tentative Bibliography of Geniza Documents*, Paris, 1964; Brian Weinstein, 'Jewish Traders in the Indian Ocean—Tenth to Thirteen Centuries: A Review from Published Documents from the Cairo Geniza', *Journal of Indo-Judaic Studies*, IV, 2001; S. Reif, *A Jewish Archive from Old Cairo*, London, 2000.

16. That qualitative data are no less important than statistical information is argued for by A.L. Udovitch, 'Commercial Techniques in Medieval Islam', in D.S. Richard, ed., *Islam and the Trade of Asia*, Pennsylvania, 1970: 37–62.
17. A.H. Dani, *Recent Archaeological Discoveries in Pakistan*, Tokyo, 1989; also see Monique Kervan, 'Multiple Ports in the Mouths of the River Indus: Barbarike, Deb, Daybul, Lahori Bundar, Diul Sinde', in Himanshu Prabha Ray, ed., *Archaeology of Seafaring*, Delhi, 1999: 70–153.
18. V.K. Jain, *Trade and Traders in Western India A.D. 1000–1300*, Delhi, 1989.
19. Chattopadhyaya, *The Making of Early Medieval India*, especially the chapter, 'Markets and Merchants in Early Medieval Rajasthan'; also Chakravarti, *Trade and Traders*, especially the chapter, 'Mandapika as a Centre of Trade in Early Medieval North India'.
20. B.J. Sandesara, *The Literary Circle of Mahamatya Vastupala*, Bombay, 1953; G.Buhler ed., *Jagaducarita of Sarvananda*, Wein, 1892.
21. S.D. Goitein, 'From Aden to India', *JESHO*, XXI; also included in Chakravarti ed, *Trade in Early India*.
22. G. Buhler, 'The Cinra Prasasti of Sarangadeva of AD 1287', *E I*, I, 1892.
23. Al Biruni, *Kitab ul Hind*, trans. E. Sachau.
24. The Sanskrit version of this inscription was first edited by E. Hultzsch, 'A Grant of Arjunadeva of Gujarat, dated AD 1264', *Indian Antiquary*, XI, 1882, pp. 241–45; the same was later studied by Sircar, *Select Inscriptions*, II, pp. 402–09. The Arabic version, shorter and synoptic, was edited by Z.A. Desai, 'Arabic Inscriptions of the Rajput period from Gujarat', *EI, Arabic and Persian Supplement*, 1961–62, pp. 17–24. English translations of both the versions are also extensively quoted in Niharranjan Ray, B.D. Chattopadhyaya, Ranabir Chakravarti and V.R. Mani, *A Sourcebook of Indian Civilization*, Hyderabad, 2000, pp. 644–48. For an analysis see Ranabir Chakravarti, 'Nakhudas and Nauvittakas', *JESHO*, XLIII, 2000: 34–64.
25. S.M.H. Nainar, *Arab Geographers' Knowledge of Southern India*, Madras, 1942.
26. The inscriptions mentioning the port of Samyana and the presence of Arab merchants there were edited by D.C. Sircar, *EI*, Vol. 32, 1955; For other inscriptions of the Silaharas of Konkan see, V.V. Mirashi ed., *Corpus*

Inscriptionum Indicarum, Vol. VI, Delhi, 1978; inscriptions of the Kadambas of Goa are available in G. Moraes, *The Kadambakula*, Bombay, 1931; analyses of these sources for the study of maritime trade have been made by Ranabir Chakravarti, 'Monarchs, Merchants and Matha in Northern Konkan (900–1053)', in Chakravarti ed., *Trade in Early India*; 'Coastal Trade and Voyages in Konkan: The Early Medieval Scenario', *Indian Economic and Social History Review*, Vol. 35, 1998; pp. 97–124; 'Candrapura/Sindabur and Gopakapattana: Two Ports on the West Coast of India (c. 1000–1300)', *Proceedings of Indian History Congress*, Diamond Jubilee Session, Calicut (1999), Aligarh, 2000, pp. 153–61.

27. Amitav Ghosh, *In an Antique Land*, for a fascinating life-story of Abraham ben Yishu. A Jewish business letter clearly describes al Manjrur situated on the 'great sea'; see Brian Weinstein, 'Jewish Traders in the Indian Ocean': 80.
28. A. Appadurai, *Economic Conditions in Southern India* in two vols., Madras, 1936; K.A. Nilkantha Sastri, *Foreign Notices of South India from Megasthenes to Ma huan*, Madras, 1936. It is strange that Himanshu Prabha Ray, *The Archaeology of Seafaring in Ancient South Asia*, Cambridge, 2003 pronounced that 'in the ancient period *no specific terminology for "port"* is in evidence or was for that matter required. Among others, the term *pattana* was used both for a market centre and also a riverine settlement' (p. 22; italics mine). The Sanskrit words *pattanam/pattinam* (also used in Tamil) and *velakula* (in Tamil *velapuram*) figure in textual and epigraphic sources clearly denoting ports. For instance, Tamralipta in the Ganga delta was labelled as a *velakula* by Dandin in his *Dasakumaracarita;* similarly the port of Ghogha in the Gujarat littoral carried the suffix *velakula* which was visited by ships from Hormuz (*hurmujivahana*). One can easily find many references to *velapuram* in Tamil inscriptions (See Noburu Karashima ed., *Ancient and Medieval Commercial Activities in the Indian Ocean: Testimony of Inscriptions and Ceramic Sherds*, Tokyo, 2002, especially those records eulogising the importance of the merchants' body, the 500 *svamis* of Ayyavole, who are said to have regularly visited 32 *velapurams*). Not only is Ray completely off the mark, but even stranger is her statement in the same book (p. 289). Here Ray cites a Rastrakuta inscription from northern Konkan narrating the conquest of chiefs of 'all harbours (velakulas)' in the neighbourhood! Ray's statements on two pages are self-contradictory which in fact suggests a lack of rigour in her handling of relevant primary source(s) and/or source-language(s).
29. Lallanji Gopal, *Economic Conditions in Northern India A.D. 750–1200*, Delhi, 1965.
30. Appadurai, *Economic Conditions*, Vol. II; also K.A. Nilakantha Sastri, *Foreign Notices of South India from Megasthenes to Ma huan*.
31. Among many such letters, a letter of 1139 (Goitein, *Letters*, pp. 185–92) is particularly interesting for information on shipping of pepper from Malabar to Aden. Export of pepper also figures prominently in another letter of 12th century; see Goitein, 'From Aden to India', in Chakravarti ed., *Trade in Early India*.

32. Ibn Jubayr was so impressed by the sight of profuse quantity of Indian pepper at Aydhab that 'so numerous as to seem to our fancy to equal in quantity only the dust'; see the translation of Jubayr by Broadhurst, *The Tranch of Ibn Jabayr*, p. 61.
33. See especially S.D. Goitein, *Letters*, pp. 185–92 and idem, 'From Aden to India', in Chakravarti ed., *Trade in Early India* for the shipment of various types of Indian iron. Some of the letters also show the urgency of Jewish merchants to bring Indian iron to Aden as quickly as possible, as there was a steady demand for Indian iron at Aden and it fetched a good price.
34. J. Heiman, 'Small Exchange and Ballast: Cowry Trade and Usage as an Example of Indian Ocean Economic History', *South Asia*, Vol. 3, 1980, pp. 48–69; the widespread use of cowry currency in pre-modern west and east Africa is discussed by M.D. Newitt, 'East Africa and the Indian Ocean Trade 1500-1800', in Das Gupta and Pearson eds., *India and the Indian Ocean*, pp. 201–02 and Cyril Belshaw, *Traditional Exchange and Modern Markets*, London, 1965, p. 70. The immense importance of cowry currency in the long-distance commerce of the Bengal coast is highlighted by Mukherjee, 'Commerce and Money in the Central and Western Sectors of Eastern India (750–1200)', *Indian Museum Bulletin*, Vol. XVII, 1982, pp. 65–82.
35. Dionisius Albertus Agius, 'Classifying Vessel-types in Ibn Battuta's Rihala', in David Parkin and Ruth Barnes eds., *Ships and the Development of Maritime Technology in the Indian Ocean*, London, pp. 174–208; also Lallanji Gopal, 'Indian Shipping in the Medieval Period', in Lokesh Chandra ed., *India's Contribution to World Thought and Culture, Madras*, 1970, pp. 108–22.
36. Goitein, *Letters*, p. 190.
37. Norman A. Stillman, 'The Eleventh Century Merchant House of Ibn Awkal', *JESHO*, Vol.13, 1971, pp. 15–88; that the Sanjani indigo was exported from Sanjan to al Fustat and eventually to al Mahdiyya (Tunisia) is discussed by Ranabir Chakravarti, 'The Export of Sindani Indigo from India to the "West" in the Eleventh Century', *Indian Historical Review*, Vol. 18, 1996, pp. 18–30.
38. For the importance of the trade in horses in the early medieval and medieval times see, Simon Digby, *Warhorses and Elephants in the Delhi Sultanate*, Oxford, 1971; Ranabir Chakravarti, 'Horse Trade and Piracy at Tana (=Thana, Maharashtra, India): Gleanings from Marco Polo', *JESHO*, Vol. 34, 1991, pp. 189–208; idem, 'Early Medieval Bengal and the Trade in Horses: A Note', *JESHO*, Vol. 42, 1999.
39. S.D. Goitein, 'An Eye Witness Account'.
40. The Red Sea *jilab* was often captained by the *rubban* who however did not enjoy the status and prestige of a *muallim* in the manual of ibn Majid.
41. A *kardal* (=*kardar*) figures in a Jewish trade letter of the 1130s; Goitein, *Letters*: 193.
42. For a catalogue of Sanskrit/Prakrit terms denoting different parts of a sailing craft, see D. Schlingloff, *Ajanta Paintings*, Delhi 1988.
43. Goitein, *Letters*, p. 197.

44. For an elaborate discussion, see Chakravarti, 'Nakhudas and Nauvittaks'.
45. Goitein, *Letters*, p. 193; S. M. Stern, 'Ramisht of Siraf: A Merchant Millionaire of the Twelfth Century', *Journal of the Royal Asiatic Society*, 1967, pp. 10–14.
46. Goitein, *Letters*, p. 63.
47. S.D. Goitein, 'New Lights on the Beginning of Karim Merchants',*JESHO*, vol. I, 1958, pp. 175–84; also Goitein, *A Mediterranean Society*, I, for explanations of the gradual fading out of the India Traders from the Indian Ocean trade in the face of the competition from Karimi merchants.
48. Z.A. Desai, 'Inscriptions from the Prince of Wales Museum, Bombay', *EI, Arabic and Persian Supplement*, 1957–58, pp. 12–13; idem, 'Inscriptions of the Gujarat Sultanate', *EI, Arabic and Persian Supplement*, 1963; M.N. Pearson, *Pious Passengers: The Hajj in the Earlier Times*, New York, 1994.
49. G.Buhler ed., *Jagaducarita of Sarvananda*, Wein, 1892.
50. Chakravarti, 'Coastal Trade and Voyages in Konkan'.
51. Karashima ed., *Ancient and Medieval Commercial Activities*, pp. 235–36 for the text and English summary of the inscription prepared by Y. Subbarayalu and P. Shanmugam. Also N. Karashima, 'Tamil Inscriptions in Southeast Asia and China', in idem ed., *Ancient and Medieval Commercial Activities*, pp. 23–24. For a review article on this book, see Ranabir Chakravarti, 'An Enchanting Seascape, Through Epigraphic Lens', *Studies in History*, Vol. 20, 2004, pp. 305–15.
52. For the *sastric* injunctions on *Kalivarjya*, see P.V. Kane, *History of Dharmasastra*, V, Poona, 1962. In the light of our above discussions it is impossible to accept K.V. Ramesh's indefensible assertion: 'Indians had never displayed interest in sea-faring activities and in building and plying their own ships, as can be inferred from the loud silence about the seas in Indian inscriptions, except in conventional contexts', p. 153 in Karashima ed., *Ancient and Medieval Commercial Activities*. The above opinion lays bare the typical limitations of many epigraphists who are strongly rooted to their texts, but unaware of the contexts. Ramesh evidently did not care to take stock of the existing data in the 'non-epigraphic' storehouse before he embarked upon his ambitious, yet untenable, pronouncement on the maritime trade of India. His comment only highlights the immense influence of the *sastric* paradigm on the study of early Indian society, economy and culture. That the efficacy of the 'epicentric model', is now seriously questioned by many leading historians (e.g. B.D. Chattopadhayaya) has not evidently been appreciated by K.V. Ramesh.
53. Ashin Das Gupta, *Indian Merchants and the Decline of Surat 1700–1750*, Weisbaden, 1974.
54. Goitein, *Letters*, p. 64.
55. Ghosh, *In an Antique Land*.
56. Chakravarti, 'Monarchs, Merchants and a Matha'.
57. An elaborate analysis is available in Chakravarti, *Trade and Traders*, especially the chapter, 'Nakhuda Nurudddin Firuz at Somnath'; also

B.D. Chattoapadhyaya, *Representing the Other? Sanskrit Sources and the Muslims*, Delhi, 1998; Romila Thapar, *Somanatha, The Many Voices of a History*, New Delhi, 2003.

58. The tractate belongs to the *Recueil des Historiens des Croisades*, but included in the second volume of Armenian documents. I am most grateful to Professor Dietmar Rothermund for having drawn my attention to this piece.
59. C.F. Beckingham, 'The Quest for Prester John', in Felipe Fernandez Armesto, ed. *The European Opportunity* (Vol. 2 of *An Expanding World*), Ashgate, 1995: 175–93; Beckingham has also used William Adam's tractate.
60. Om Prakash, 'European Corporate Enterprises and the Politics of Trade in India 1600-1800', in Rudrangshu Mukherjee and Laksmi Subramaniam, eds., *Politics and Trade in the Indian Ocean World, Essays in Honour of Ashin Das Gupta*, Delhi, 1998: 165–82.

Chapter 11

Traditional Crafts, Technology, and Society in Pre-colonial Peninsular India

Vijaya Ramaswamy

The study of crafts in pre-colonial Peninsular India can be problematised in terms of certain specific areas of analysis. The introductory rubric will locate craft history within the broader problematic of researches into the late medieval period stretching from the sixteenth to the eighteenth centuries. The next section seeks to situate the Visvakarma who are the custodians of traditional crafts in the South Indian context. The subsequent rubrics will focus on the following themes: crafts and the artisan community: origin myths of the Visvakarma; crafts and caste; gender issues in crafts, technology, crafts and traditional beliefs; and lastly mobility and conflict among craft communities in the Vijayanagar era.

Crisis or Growth? — Debating the Late Medieval Economy

The sixteenth to eighteenth centuries, especially the eighteenth, in Peninsular India, are very important from the point of view of the economic historian. A study of this crucial phase of South Indian history has given rise to a number of theories and an equal number of questions. The historiography of these crucial centuries has however gone through a paradigm shift in the course of the last four decades of the twentieth century. To those historians of the seventeenth and eighteenth centuries who had viewed the history of these times through the prism of the Mughal empire and its downfall, these centuries constituted crisis years in Indian history. One of the earliest examples of this historiographical position is an essay by Herman Goetz, called 'The Crisis of Indian Civilization in the Eighteenth Century' published in the 1930s.[1] The notion of crisis especially in the agrarian sector with decline in crafts as its scatter effect, began with Irfan Habib's theory of the agrarian crisis in the 1960s. Barun De's Presidential Address to the Indian History Congress in its 49th Session at Dharwad, focused in fact on the 'Crisis' School of eighteenth-century India.[2]

As scholars have made a paradigm shift from a Delhi-centric approach to a more balanced perspective of the regional economies, a trend that is more visible in the last couple of decades, some of them have looked at these centuries as the era of regional prosperity under the regional states. Frank Perlin used the term 'Proto-Industrialization in the Periphery'[3] to describe the economic landscape of the region. Crafts and commerce began to prosper under the Nayaka kingdoms of Madurai, Tanjavur and Ikkeri, the Nizami State of Hyderabad and the princely state of Mysore under the Odaiyars. A counterpoint to the eighteenth century as the era of decline is the collection of essays edited by Richard Barnett, which seeks to look at the vibrant polities of regions, As he outlined his agenda, it was time one moved 'beyond the gloomy paradigm of decline' and savoured the richness and vivacity of the eighteenth century.[4]

The ubiquitous presence of the European companies—primarily the English, the Dutch and the French—foregrounds crafts, commerce and culture in Peninsular India. Craftsmen like the weavers and painters became linked to the larger commercial enterprise of the imperial powers in which Indian merchants became collaborates and crafts and commerce moved away from indigenous production and trade centres into the European 'Black Towns'. The regional kingdoms of the Nayaks and princely states provided competing focal points of power and patronage. The growing demand for craft products in the various regional principalities and the centrality of crafts persons to the economy led many scholars to perceive these years as a boom period followed by the bust in the late eighteenth century. Competition leading to growth in production gradually petered out as Britain established its supremacy over its rivals and emerged as overlord with monopoly over the crafts and commerce of its Indian colony.[5]

In recent years monographs, edited books and articles dealing with the historical and historiographical rigmarole that constituted the eighteenth-century eco-landscape, have multiplied.[6] The Oxford University Press deals with this century in its recent publication[7] under its significant series called 'Debates in Indian History and Society'.

The political and socio-economic milieu of the pre-colonial era in Peninsular India, provides the context for this study of technology, society and traditional crafts. The empire of Vijayanagar witnessed the growing prosperity of certain categories of craftsmen, like weavers and smiths. This was due to a combination of factors such as the emergence of a new class of consumers represented by the nobility and officialdom of the state. The Vijayanagar state played an active role in encouraging both production and commerce. The Deccani Muslim states brought new styles into fashion such as doublets, embroidered jackets and turbans. Textile varieties like *mashroo* and *himroo* owed their existence to the Muslim influence. These varieties have an interesting origin. Islam forbids the use of silk by its adherents. Yet the fashion conscious nobility in the Deccan was keen on using silk in its prayer mats. The result of their peculiar requirement was the *mashroo* which was a silk-cotton mix with the cotton threads on top of the mat, thereby technically fulfilling the Islamic injunction while effectively violating it. *Mashroo* and *himroo* went on to become fashionware not only in the Deccan but also in the Mughal empire and found a lucrative export market in West Asia.[8]

V.I. Pavlov, the Russian scholar formulated the theory of uneven development of craft and industrial production in the pre-colonial era. In his book *Historical Premises for India's Transition to Capitalism,*[9] he speaks of the pre-colonial Indian economy as a 'multi-sectoral' one in which certain sectors such as the textile industry constituted a nascent capitalist pocket whose craft techniques and technology was way ahead of many other craft sectors. In fact, for the textile industry in South India one could speak of proto-industrialisation as a possible stage of capitalist development, as I have tried to show elsewhere.[10] To a lesser extent certain specialised metal crafts benefited from the growing demand both from the domestic elite and the export market, especially West Asia. *Bidri* ware and diamond production in the Deccani States, especially Bijapur and Golconda, would be the best examples of the crafts benefiting from the commercial boom.

Situating the Vishwakarma—The Artisans and the Craftsmen

The socio-economic status of the Vishwakarma as a collective body, as well as the differentiation and stratification that existed among them in pragmatic terms depended upon the nature of their functions, which in turn were linked to their physical location. It would be erroneous to treat craftsmen as a monolithic unit, despite their banding together as the 'Vishwakarma'. The distinction between an artisan and a craftsman may seem fuzzy because of the shifting nature of their occupations but it is nevertheless important to make this distinction. Unless one can be aware of the complex layers that shaped craft development in medieval India, it is possible that one may impose one's own teleological vision, as did the 'Orientalist', the 'imperial' or the Marxist historians, by imaging the medieval craftsman as a static, immobile figure enmeshed within a 'honey-combed' caste structure. One of the ways of breaking up this discourse is to look at the producers of craft objects as distinct from the producers of purely utility commodities. Is the man routinely laying bricks or being employed as a workman in the construction of a dam an artisan or a craftsman? Would the hereditary maker of ploughs in a village, have the same position in economy and in society, as the icon-maker?[11]

In the context of medieval Peninsular India, it can be said that artisanal skills and craftsmanship came to be differentiated economically in terms of the very different dynamics that affected them. Inscriptional evidence clearly indicates that they represented two different kinds of economies, both of which existed parallel to each other. While the maker of ploughs would exist in the village community with a certain degree of relative physical immobility, socio-economic security and comparatively static living standards, the Kammalar or Panchalar craftsmen who had moved out of the custom-determined 'local' market would band together as the Vishwakarma. Benefiting from the temple economy and an expanding clientele, the temple-town-based craftsmen would be more mobile and have greater opportunities for improving their income, while also facing greater risks. The risks would primarily arise from the withdrawal of patronage, or the decline of temple centres with the fall of dynasties, as happened in the twelfth–thirteenth century with the decline and fading out of the Chola State. This situation happened yet again with the fall of Vijayanagar in the sixteenth century. Thus it can be said that while every craftsman was an artisan, every artisan was not a craftsman, the principal distinction arising from their differing relationships to the medieval economy, both in terms of location and role function. More particularly on the latter count, the artisan differed quite significantly from his urban counterpart. To give an example, even among the goldsmiths there were two distinct hierarchical categories. At the lower level was the small-time *tattan* or goldsmith who worked on a piece-wage and lived at the subsistence level, catering to a custom-determined market. These goldsmiths can be seen even today in South India, sitting at street corners and eking out a living by repairing chains or other ornaments, as also piercing ears and noses (a must for women and the girl child among many South Indian communities). At the higher level was the big-time goldsmith referred to in the inscriptions as '*perum-tattan*' (literally 'great goldsmith') indicating master-craftsman employing apprentice goldsmiths, catering to a fairly wide market and forming a part of the urban set-up.

Another question that comes to mind when one looks at the plethora of evidence on the Vishwakarma is the precise character of this grouping. What is the link between the *jati* structure or caste system within which the categories of craftsmen (among others) are said to be located, and the Vishwakarma community which is obviously cutting across caste lines? In this article I have endeavoured to show that the functioning of the Vishwakarma as a community, comprising five socially and economically differentiated *jatis,* shows that the ground situation at least in South India's craft history, was much more complex. The situation was comparatively fluid, and community solidarity in certain situations may have taken precedence over *jati* solidarity. Caste distinctions certainly continued and craftsmen in the rural setting seem to have been known by their individual *jati* affiliation rather than as members of the Vishwakarma *kula.* It is in the context of the urban complex, especially in temple building where these five craft groups worked in such close coordination that the concept of 'Vishwakarma *kula*' seems to have predominated over that of separate caste identities. This can be deduced by the location of the inscriptions referring to the 'Vishwakarma *kula*' in the early medieval times, whether one is looking at the Cholas, Pandyas or Eastern Chalukyas. One unique sixteenth-century inscription from Varikunta in Cuddapah district says that a Boya (tribal community) named Tippana [who was obviously a non-Vishwakarma craftsman] built the local temple for a lumpsum contract of 20 rukas.[12] The inscription is dated 1529 CE, and it points to a certain degree of social flux which was most likely a late-medieval phenomenon.[13]

Having argued for a more open interpretation of craft groups cutting across caste barriers and embracing the wider notion of craft community, one cannot logically push forward this argument to state that the five *jatis* within the Vishwakarma community were exogamous. No evidence is forthcoming, either one way or the other in this regard. However, working backwards from the Kallidaikurichchi inscription of the seventeenth century,[14] which records the legal disassociation of the five *jatis,* one could presume that the five castes may have been exogamous up to that point. If economic status was a factor then the Vishwakarma goldsmith located in the temple town would have much more in common, for instance in terms of forming matrimonial alliances, with the affluent smiths settled there than with his poor village counterpart. Although one can deduce the fluidity of caste boundaries among these crafts, in the absence of more concrete evidence it is not possible to determine how open the 'Vishwakarma community' was to social and familial interaction among the five disparate *jati* categories.

Crafts and the Artisan Community

The primary identity of crafts-persons stemmed from their community rather than their caste identity. The majority of medieval inscriptions emphasise that the artisan belonged to the Vishwakarma *kula* rather than detailing his caste affiliation. The Vishwakarma smiths consisted of five affiliated groups of craftsmen—goldsmith (*tattan*), brass smith (*kannan*), blacksmith (*karuman* or *kollan*), carpenter (*tachchan*) and mason (*silpi* or *kal-tachchan*). Despite belonging to different professions and different *jatis*, these craftsmen claimed a collective entity as *Kammalar* in the Tamil country *Panchanamuvaru* in the Andhra country and *Panchala* in Karnataka. However, in many of the medieval inscriptions they are also collectively referred to as the *Rathakarar* or the *Kammala-Rathakarar*. Today they prefer to use the nomeclature 'Vishwakarma', the divine architect from whom they claim descent.

The smiths have a common mythological origin, claiming their descent from Vishwakarma. Two important inscriptions from Tiruvarur (Tanjavur district)[15] and Uyyakondan Tirumalai[16] (Tiruchchi district) or the twelfth century provide us however with a detailed analysis of their social origins.

It was usually in the context of their role as engravers and sculptors that the names of craftsmen at times accompanied by the panegyrical note on their origins and skills occur in inscriptional records. An inscription from Macherla[17] in Palnad Taluq in Guntur district dated 1111 A.D. states that the smiths were descended from Vishwakarma, who was the son of Brahma. He is also said to be the father-in-law of the sun, converting the rays emanating from the sun into divine weapons like the discus of Vishnu. In terms of understanding the history of craft technology, this inscription is important because it lists a long genealogy of craftsmen and says that they had a proper understanding of their craft in terms of 'grasping the '*kshethra*' (parameters?) involved in the study of *vastu shastras*. They were therefore successful in cutting of '*linga*', preparing divine icons, building four kinds of mansions (*prasada*), etc. One of the longest panegyrics on the Kammalar comes from Alangudi in Tanjavur. Found in the Apatsahayesvara temple, the inscription[18] is dated A.D. 1264 and registers the constructions of a *mandapam* by the Kammala-Rathakarar community and the grant of certain endowments to the temple for its unkeep and maintenance Interestingly, they describe themselves as 'the four kinds of Rathakaras of the six kinds of profession'. Since the workers in the mint have been referred to separately quite often (the *kammatta*), one can presume that they comprised the sixth category of craftsmen.

While the mythological origins of the Kammalar are found in the form of *prashastis* or panegyric usually in those records where the Kammalar feature as temple donors, inscriptions of a general nature sometimes extol specific craftsmen. A record of the period of Rajendra Chola I dated 1018 A.D. from Tiruvalangadu[19] (also called Palayanur in Chingleput district written in Tamil and Sanskrit contains an order in Tamil converting the village from a *brahmadeya* (Brahmin village) to a *vellan vagai* (non-Brahmin) village. The panegyric in Sanskrit states that the four skilled sculptors (*shilpa kovidaihi*)— Aravamurta, Ranga, Damodhara and Purushottama, the sons of Krishna, well-versed in the various forms of mechanical arts, who had their birth in the great city of Kanchipuram, who were clever and wise and born in the Ovi family, engraved the above inscription. One of the earliest eulogical references to craftsmen is found in two inscriptions from Repalli in Tumkur (Mysore) and Ayyangaripalem in Guntur[20] which refer to the architect of the temple of Jalpesa, called Maindarama as *'kalgarabharana acharya'*[21] (meaning an ornament to sculptors) of the fourth (i.e. sudra) caste and the jewel of the Vishwakarma *kula*.

In terms of their social and ritual status, the origin of the Kammala-Rathakarar was defined as being that of a mixed caste, primarily *anuloma,* i.e. born of high-born father and low-born mother. In the Tiruvarur inscription of the twelfth century from Pandyakulantaka Chaturvedimangalam[22] (Tanjavur district) and another record from Rajasraya Chaturvedimangalam from Uyyakondan Tirumalai[23] (Tiruchchirapalli district) of the same period, the Brahmin determined the status, rights and duties of the Kammala-Rathakarar. Based on the *dharma sastras* and the *smritis* of Yajnavalkya, Gautama, Maskara and Bhima, they arrived at the consensus that the Rathakara were primarily *anuloma* being born of Mahisha male (vaisya) and Karana (sudra) female. According to some texts, as *anuloma* they could perform the *upanayanam* (sacred thread ceremony) and *sandhyavandanam* (the special worship of the sun at dawn, dusk and high-noon) but silently (*tushnim eva*). Yajnavalkya however forbids them from reciting all sacred texts relating to architecture and sculpture like Agastya Vastu Shastra and Visvakarmiya, but they had the right to build temples and to sculpt the images of Gods.

The consolidation of these early origin myths of the Vishwakarma community was done sometime in the eighteenth century. The *Visvakarma Puranam* brought together the various oral traditions of the craftsmen. Although the manuscript is undated, one can roughly date it to the colonial period, perhaps mid-seventeenth or eighteenth century on the basis of statements such as the lament of the author that at one time the Vishwakarma conjured up things through their creative imagination and now they were compelled to work according to company musters.

Caste and Crafts

It would be a truism to state that crafts in India were inextricably linked with the *jati* or caste system. The craftsmen in pre-colonial India were organised in corporations. Appadorai has used the term 'caste guilds' to describe such corporations.[24] The nature and scope of these organisations raise a number of ticklish issues. For long, beginning with theorists like Max Weber and Karl Marx, caste has been regarded as a major cause of India's economic and technological backwardness. Karl Marx argued that the influence of the caste system on crafts resulted in the confinement of a craft within a small group. The division of labour, even though it existed, was of several generations of cratsmen living at one time, and working together at the manufacture of a given article, the trades being hereditary. As a result, 'they either petrify into castes or ossify into guilds.'[25] Marx gives the example of the Dacca muslins which he believed were produced 'without capital, machinery, division of labor or any of those means which gives such facilities to the manufacturing interests of Europe.' The classic statement by Marx that crafts in the Indian context 'either petrify into castes or ossify into guilds'[26], was taken up by historians like Irfan Habib[27] for the medieval period and Morris D Morris[28] for modern India, to argue for a situation of technological stasis in the craft structure. Marx, commenting on the fineness of the Dacca muslins, in fact concludes on a note of irony by saying, 'it is only the special skill accumulated from generation to generation and transmitted from father to son, that gives to the Hindu, as it does to the spider, this proficiency[29]!'

Within the historiographical tradition of Indian economic history the inherent strengths of the craft sector was examined by Irfan Habib who attributed the relatively slow pace of technological change to the presence of cheap but skilled craft labour in India.[30] However, the system of working within craft guilds has been interpreted by K.N. Chaudhuri as a 'high quality trap'[31]. To quote him, 'specialisation (in textile technology in India) had gone so far that it would have required very great incentive to induce such men to change their production methods and habits drastically.'[32] Given the level of excellence of the craftsmen and the resulting demand for Indian products, especially among the elite both at home and abroad, there was little incentive to innovate, a situation which was quite the opposite of what pertained in England in the pre-industrial era. To illustrate, the cotton revolution in England in the eighteenth century became necessary only because of the severe competition posed by Indian textiles, especially calico, which was flooding the European markets, including England. Economic compulsions such as high labour costs (in contrast to cheap Indian labour) led to technological innovations and the new production techniques.[33]

I would however like to argue that to perceive the craft guilds as stultified within the caste system is to ignore the dynamics of South Indian society and economy. First the crafts which formed a corporate collectively known as the *Kammalar* or *Panchalar* did not constitute a single caste or a single profession. The caste of the goldsmith was different from the caste of the carpenter, yet they came together under the generic term 'Vishwakarma'. The professions and role functions of the constituent categories of the Vishwakarma—smiths, carpenters and masons/sculptors also varied widely. Yet they had a strong community identity as 'the group of five'. Further, caste in the economy of pre-colonial India did not necessarily play a negative 'petrifying role'. In the course of the seventeenth and eighteenth centuries, specialisations proliferated mainly in response to the western markets and were reflected interestingly in the emergence of new castes. Caingaloon and Mambaloon weavers who are mentioned in the seventeenth-eighteenth century factory records constituted specialist categories. For instance, the Caingaloon weavers were those who wove cloth destined for the Malay Archipelago: the word 'kain' in Malay means cloth and 'gulong' means rolled. The supply of gold thread to the Caingaloon weavers at Armagaon is referred to in an English East India Company letter dated 1629.[34] Similarly, the Mambaloom (Mambalam?) 'painters' were weavers specialising in the production of painted chintz.[35] The Mooree weavers produced superior cotton cloth used as a base for chintz making.[36] The Pattunulkaran or Saurashtra weavers, who became specialists in the tie-and-dye technique, were concentrated in Madurai and rose to prominence in the course of the seventeenth century. Therefore one can conclude that the Indian craftsmen had a dialectic relationship with caste, bending and stretching the caste structure to accommodate new techniques and technologies.[37]

Gender Issues in Pre-Colonial Crafts

An overarching patriarchal framework can be clearly perceived in pre-colonial craft structures. Women by and large functioned in an ancillary or subordinate capacity in the work of the smiths. In the craft of the blacksmiths, the women were allowed to work the bellows while they were not permitted to forge the iron. In jewellery making among the goldsmiths and the silversmiths women were engaged in the tasks of polishing, fine cutting and embellishing the designs but not allowed a primary role in the designing or making of the ornaments. However, among the Gudigara caste in Karnataka, women are said to have taken over the family profession in the case of death of the male member and this included goldsmithy. The goldsmith community, called 'Bayala Akkasaliga', literally 'itinerant goldsmiths' seems to have trained both men and women in the art of goldsmithy.[38] One does not hear of women sculptors at all especially in the craft of icon making. In the context of the wheel-based industry like pottery, much of the activity seems to have been joint, with both men and women being involved in the kneading of the clay and the firing of the pots. However, it was exclusively the work of men to turn the pot on the wheel. The buffing or polishing of the pot was done mostly by women.

Among handicrafts, women seem to have played an important role in the handloom sector. Spinning in South India was done, and is still done, entirely by women while in the north, especially in the hills, men can also be seen spinning on a spindle. While the spinning of thread was also done by housewives, it was by and large the sole occupation of widows and unmarried or destitute women. Such female spinners are referred to in the Sangam literature as '*parutti pendugal*', literally 'cotton women' or as '*kaimai pendir*', literally 'widowed women'.[39] Medieval craft history is also replete with references to women spinners. Within the Virasaivite a number of craft persons are referred to in the medieval work *Shunya Sampadane.* The Shivasharana Jedara Dasimayya belonged to the weaver caste and it is said that his saintly wife Duggali spun the thread that he wove into cloth.[40] Remmavve and Kadire Kayakade Kalavve, both have the prefix '*kadire*' to indicate their professional status as spinners[41] A reference to women spinners during the Vijayanagar period comes from the poet Srinatha in his *Palnattu Viracharitra* where he says that in Palnad, while the farmers ploughed the field, their wives spun thread.[42]

Women were however excluded from the craft of weaving for ritual reasons. For South Indian craftsmen, the loom represented divinity itself and women, because of their periods of impurity could therefore not touch an object that was divine and therefore pure.

The twin crafts of mat weaving and basket making were largely in the hands of women. In fact, the raw material for both, grass weed called *korai* was picked only by women. A folk song of the colonial period records the lament by a pregnant *korai* picker:

> As I come to cut the *korai* growing around my house, my Lord,
> you threaten me as a foolish slut, my Lord.
> Even as I go to pick the *korai* around the lake, my Lord,
> you should know I am heavy with child, my Lord,
> you should know.[43]

In the Andhra and Karnataka regions, the basket weavers belonged to the Medara caste. There is a reference to women basket weavers whose work is known as *kantakara vritti* in the fifteenth-century text *Kreedabhiramamu* of Vallabharaya.[44] The work was apparently very low paid and the Medara women were poor because *Kreedabhiramamu* says that many of these women basket weavers took to prostitution out of compulsion.[45] Besides making baskets and mats out of *korai*, baskets were also made of *panai olai* or palm leaf and bamboo called *moongil.*

The old type of baskets and coconut leaf or palm leaf umbrellas are still a common sight in South India and these are still being made largely by women. Basketry is the specialised craft of the Parava (fisherwomen) of Kerala and in the Tamil country the women of Ramanathapuram are known today for their intricate basket work.

A craft in which women are said to be as skilled as men is pith work called *netti* in South India. The plant, known as *shola* has soft flexible stems with spongy cellular tissues in them and also in the branches making it ideal for crafting things. With *netti* were made flowers, toys, hair decorations especially coronets, temple garlands, etc. The reference to pith work is found in the Sangam and post-Sangam literature. The *Silappadhikaram* refers to the *netti* work done in Pumpuhar and the sale of *netti* products in the markets of the bustling port town of Kaveripumpattinam. *Netti* working has by and large been a craft dominated by women. In Karnataka among the Gudigaras, the men carve wooden figures and idols while women engage in pithwork. The Shimoga district *Gazeteer*[46] which draws largely from the imperial gazetteers and manuals of the nineteenth century such as John Sturrock's district manual of South Kanara, gives very interesting details about women *netti* workers. It says that the women gathered the pith from around Shimoga and Shiralkoppa near the tank area and made beautifully crafted items with just a knife and a pair of scissors. It is said that a woman could make about 20 *venis* (pith strung together of an arm's length called *muzham*) and 20 garlands in a month. The work was done by women in the verandahs of their homes. The account is categorical in stating that pith work was very poorly paid in comparison to sandalwood carving or ivory carving which fetched big sums of money in the market and were entirely male preserves.

Technology, Crafts and Traditional Beliefs

One of the central questions regarding the evolution of crafts is their link with technology. The emergence of new artisanal *jatis* or castes shows that it was in the nature of craftsmen to form new caste groups on the basis of adaption of new craft techniques. However, in the Indian context one also observes that though craftsmen in the course of the eighteenth and nineteenth centuries were exposed to new and perhaps more efficient technologies introduced by the European companies, they often showed a strong reluctance to adopt them, preferring the existing practices. Is this clinging to tradition a sign of reluctance to imbibe new ideas or is it a matter of appropriate technology?

A prime illustration would be the issue of the effort by the Agents of the English East India Company to introduce the coulter both in the Malabar and the Bengal countryside. The iron-tipped plough called the *kozhu* was known to Indian farmers for a long, long time and in fact this term occurs in the Sangam text *Perumpanatruppadai.* However, it was used judiciously, depending the needs of a particular kind of soil and its suitability for farming. For instance, light ploughs were used in fertile areas like the Kaveri basin while heavy ploughs drawn by four or five bullocks were used in the Punjai or dry lands as in parts of Tondaimandalam or Kongumandalam. Madhava's text *Parasara Madhaviyam* refers to the use of a ploughs drawn by six to eight bullocks.[47] The iron-tipped plough was used only in these areas which required intensive ploughing. The *Parasara Madhaviyam,* a fifteenth-century text attributed to Madhava, the minister of the Vijayanagara king Krishnadeva Raya, makes a curious reference to the use of this device:

> *loha sahitena langala mukhena, praninaha*
> *chinnabhinnam bhavantiti matsyavadat papadhikyam uktam*[48]
> A rough translation of this verse would be:
> "with the use of an iron-tipped plough (by the farmer)
> more creatures are killed and greater sin incurred than the killing of (hundreds of) fish."

Here what appears to be a moral injunction is in fact backed by strong economic reasons. The purpose seems to have been to prevent the erosion of the substances present in the surface soil, like alkaline substances and minerals that are beneficial for crops. This would only have resulted in reduced productivity since inferior soil would have come up. It has been noticed that in the deltaic regions of South India, the seed yield ration was as high as 1:12 or 1:20. Hamilton Buchanan; writing about ragi cultivation in the Seringapatam region in the eighteenth century estimated the average seed:yield ratio to be as much as 1:40.[49] This is in striking contrast to the European figures for the same period, which range between 1:4 to 1:6.

In 1820, Mr. Alexander Walker, made this significant observation about the Malabar plough:

> In a climate where the productive powers (of the soil) are so great, it is only necessary to put the seed a little way into the ground. It must be strong proof that the Indian plough is not ill adapted for its purpose, when we see arising out of the furrows it cuts, the most abundant and luxurious crops. What can be desired more than this? The labour and expense beyond this point must be superfluous. The Indian peasantry is commonly well enough informed as to his interest and he is generally intelligent and reflecting. He is attached to his own modes because they are easy and useful...[50]

Dr. Wallick, a superintendent of the English East India Company commented on the attempt to introduce the coulter in the Bengal countryside. Speaking before the committee of the English Commons in 1832, he remarked:

> The Bengal husbandry although in many respects extremely simple and primeval in its mode, yet is not quite so low as people suppose it to be... I have known, for instance, of European iron ploughs (the reference here is to the coulter) being introduced into Bengal with a view to superseding the extremely tedious and superficial turning of the ground by a common Bengali plough. But what has been the result? That the soil, which is extremely beneficent, has generally received the admixture of the undersoil which has deteriorated it very much.[51]

In the case of the coulter at least it is clear that the rejection of the new technological device was not on grounds of lack of initiative on the part of the peasantry but an awareness of what technology would actually be appropriate for this specific Indian situation. In dry areas or the rain-fed *punjai* lands, the coulter was definitely in use. The awareness of varying techniques and technological usages is reflected in two late medieval texts—the *Tiruvarur Pallu of Jnanaprakasanar* (primarily an account of the community of agricultural labourers called Pallar) and the *Mezhivilakkam,* (literally 'an exposition on the plough') which is of unknown authorship.

Another example of appropriate technology can be cited from the textile industry which was one of the strongest traditional industries in the pre-colonial Deccan accounting for a major share of India's exports.[52] The illustration pertains to the attempt by the European Agents to use the reeling and fulling machines in South India. Writing in the nineteenth century, Elijah Hoole[53] remarked on the reluctance of the indigenous textile industry to use the speedier and more efficient reeling machine. This consisted of iron pegs fixed on a frame with slides, around which pegs the cotton yarn was formed into hanks. Interestingly, Hoole himself offers an explanation for the rejection of the device, which was due to the extreme moisture in the atmosphere which tended to rust and corrode everything made of iron in which case the cotton would adhere to the rollers and the whole yarn would be ruined. The fulling machines were introduced around 1607. In this device two heavy wooden hammers were lifted by cams on the shaft turned by the water wheel. As the cam passed the head of the hammer, the hammer would get released and deliver a blow to the cloth in the tank. The reasons for the rejection of this device do not seem to have a specific logic unlike in the case of the reeling machine.

One of the oral traditions highly popular among the Vishwakarma community is the story of the magnetic fort built by them which was impregnable. The story finds a detailed description in the *Visvakarma Puranam.*[54] One common version of this oral tradition is that the five artisans of the Vishwakarma kula were at one time entirely in the service of the gods. Since they were celibate, they possessed the power of creating things by merely imagining them. Their fort made of lodestone was invincible. The location of this fort is said to be on the shore of Ilangapuri (Sri Lanka). As a result of its magnetic powers, the weapons thrown by enemies struck to the fort walls and could not penetrate within. The principal enemy of the Vishwakarma was a king called Karunakaran, who is said to have derived his authority from the Chola *raja*. He planted several beautiful women (in some versions they are Brahmin women) in the fort who married the Vishwakarma, thus destroying their spiritual powers and revealed the secret of the fort to the enemy king. This was the use of a particular kind of grass, which was poisonous and could burn up the fort. The fort was blown up and the Vishwakarma were scattered in all directions and forced to work for ordinary mortals, making weapons, ploughs, houses, temples down to small things like pins and needles.

Certain points of this story are extremely significant to the economic historian or the craft specialists. First, the reference to the lodestone fort. Hamilton Buchanan, for instance, has mentioned the finding of laterite and magnetite, i.e. the lodestone on iron mining sites. Besides the awareness of its magnetic properties, the lodestone also may have been used in the process of smelting iron. A Dutch Scholar, Jan Browner, in his recent survey records the statement of Karnataka smiths that they use lodestone in their smelting furnaces since its melting point is higher than that or iron ore. The second point is the use of grass which is described as 'Haraka' in the Kannada version and 'Varagu' in the Tamil version. This has been identified as a variety of wild millet which can be highly poisonous if not properly processed. After processing, it was eaten in the form of pancakes.[55]

The final illustration in this section comes from iron mining in the eighteenth century in the Karnataka region. Hamilton Buchanan describes the problem of water clogging which nagged the miners often resulting in the loss of lives. He describes the existing technology as 'crude and unthrifty'.[56] After reaching a depth of little more than six feet, the mines would become waterlogged and hazardous. Very often the mines just caved in resulting in, the death of miners. Mining would be eventually abandoned because they failed to find a system by which the water could be drained out and deep drilling could be done.

The poor miners found their own solution to this technological puzzle. Before entering the mines, elaborate worship was offered to a piece of mined rock or iron ore called 'Karikallu Devaru'. This was followed by the worship of Guddada Amma, literally 'The Mother of the Hills'. The miners also had a special protective spirit, the *bhuta* figure Muttarayar. Thus the emergence of mining deities in the Karnataka region had as its root cause a technological problem in mining.

Social Mobility and Conflict in Later Medieval Peninsular India

The dynamics of social mobility, especially among the craft groups has been looked at by social historians of Peninsular India.[57] For the Vishwakarma craftsmen, the great era of gaining and losing royal privileges, of social mobility and conflict, was the Vijayanagar period. Society in the period from the fourteenth to the seventeenth centuries, was in a state of flux. The economic differentiation between the blacksmiths, the carpenter and the village goldsmith on the one hand and the affluent *nagaram* or *pattinam* (town-based) goldsmiths and wealthier *sthapathis* on the other hand, widened.

To state that economic power eventually led to social elevation, either by open or tacit consent, would be a truism. What is interesting are the ways by which the economically prosperous artisan castes sought to achieve social elevation and ritual recognition. The process of social mobility among the more prosperous artisan groups and the dynamics of social change in Vijayanagar society are reflected in (a) the demand for social and ritual privileges; (b) the ascribing of mythological origins and claiming of Brahmanical status; (c) *idangai-valangai* (left-hand-right-hand) conflicts within the Sudra castes; and (d) social protests and participation in the Bhakti movement.

Social privileges mainly consisted of *sangu* (the right to blow the conch shell on all ritual occasions) and *tandu* (the right to ride the palanquin). It could also mean the right to wear sandals, whitewash one's home or even the right to wear certain types of clothes. In the course of the fifteenth and sixteenth centuries, the Kaikkola weavers secured from the Vijayanagar kings the right to *sangu* and *tandu* at Kanchipuram, Tiruvennainallur, Tiruttalur, Tirukkoyilur and Brahmadesam. Apparently, the Kaikkolar of Kanchipuram (a leading textile centre and the headquarters of this caste), were the first to secure these privileges because all subsequent inscriptions state that the weavers in those areas obtained their privileges on the pattern of that at Kanchipuram.[58] It is noteworthy that no inscription refers to their having enjoyed these privileges in Chola times.

An impressive list of privileges enjoyed by the smiths comes from Amaravati in 1437[59] which confers on them the right to insignia like *garudadvaja* (banner), *chamaram* (fans), *sangu* and *tandu* and the use of the five musical instruments—*sringa, tammata, bheri, sankha* and *jayaganta*. They were further allowed to use sandals and to cover their houses with plaster. The Kammalar, or smiths of Tiruvamattur, obtained certain privileges in 1632 which were enjoyed by the artisans at other places such as Padaividu, Senji, Tiruvannamalai and Kanchipuram.[60] In the Vijayanagar period, the goldsmiths appear to have secured exclusive privileges independently of the other sections of the smiths.

Two inscriptions from Pudukottai, both pertaining to the fifteenth century, refer to the conferring of rights and honours on goldsmiths.[61] The almost equal social importance enjoyed by the weavers and smiths was perhaps one reason for such frequent conflicts and rivalry between these two groups. A record from Vriddachalam in South Arcot district of the period of Sriranga (1572–85) registers an agreement entered into by the Kaikkola Mudalis—Kongarayar, Nayinar Kachachirayar and the Nattavar of Idaiyaru—denying the privilege *otpavadai* and *parivattam to* the Kammalar which were enjoyed by the Kaikkolar of Padaividu, Senji and Tiruvannamalai.[62]

The artisans had a very important role to play in the temple towns as these were the nuclei of urban development in the Vijayanagar period. In fact, most of the privileges given to them were those relating to temple rituals. At the car *(ratha)* festival of the deity Raghunayakulu in Udayagiri, according to a sixteenth-century inscription, the smiths were given the honour of going in front of the car with a chisel, a mallet and a sickle in their hands.[63] Important ritual privileges connected with the temple were *pavadai* (the dress put on the deity), and *parivattam* (the headgear of the deity) which were given to the leading citizens. The smiths of some regions secured these privileges as also the additional privilege of *mugamtudai* (wiping the face of the deity after the holy bath or *abhishekant).* However, due to pressure from other social groups these special privileges were eventually withdrawn.[64]

The change in the fortunes of the weavers and the smiths with the advent of the Vijayanagar empire is thus a striking one. Commercial expansion under the active patronage of the Vijayanagar kings was reinforced by the opening up of new markets with the establishment of the East India companies. Cloth, for example, was no longer a primary item of barter for spices or Arab horses as in the Chola period, but a commercial product in its own right. The new-found economic prosperity of the weavers and smiths is reflected in the nature and quality of the donations made by them to the temples, such donations being a primary index of social status in the medieval period. The temples responded by conferring important ritual privileges on these groups and it is significant that while in the Chola period there is not a single instance of the conferring of *sangu* and *tandu* (conch shell and palanquin) honours on the weavers, there are more than a dozen such inscriptions in the Vijayanagar period for the Tondaimandalam region alone between the fifteenth and sixteenth centuries.

The desire for enhanced social status among the artisans was a major factor in the left-hand-right-hand *(idangai-valangai)* conflicts and schisms. Each artisan group claimed for itself ritual recognition and privileges and in this it was challenged by rival caste groups. An artisan caste which had registered its higher status by obtaining flags and symbols, assiduously sought to prevent others from obtaining the same, which led to conflicts. These conflicts took place within the framework of the *idangai-valangai* categories. Just as the *varna* system marks a horizontal division of human society, so the *idangai-valangai* division marks a vertical division of South Indian society. This, however, excluded the Brahmins and was confined to the Vaishyas and Sudras.

Rivalry in the *idangai* was usually between the Kammalar and the Kaikkolar. A record from Vriddachalam (South Arcot district) registers the decision of the Nattavar (the heads of the *nadu)* to withdraw the privileges of *parivattam* and *pavadai* from the Kammalar which they had acquired in imitation of the weavers of certain leading regions of South Arcot like Senji, Padaividu and Tiruvannamalai. This was apparently done on the insistence of the weavers.[65] Dissensions seem to have risen even amongst the smiths during this period, and evidence indicates that the goldsmiths increasingly disassociated themselves from the other sections, a process that is evident in their claim for exclusive privileges. In the early seventeenth century, at Kallidaikurichchi in Tirunelveli district, the smiths finally separated from each other. The inscription records the order of Virappa Nayaka that the Kammalar should not intermingle any longer *(udankoota vendam)*. The writ is said to be a privilege granted to the Kammalar in the presence of their chief, Kulasekhara Asari, indicating that the separation of the smiths was at their own instance.[66] Although the record does not give the reason for this separation it is obvious that the goldsmiths had moved into the more lucrative circle of Company trade and lost the temple links that had bound them with the other participant castes in the Kammalar community.

The seventeenth century saw the rise of the Pattunulkarar, specialists in tie-and-dye weaving in the textile industry in South India, and this had interesting repercussions in the social sphere. The evidence for their emergence as a dominant weaving caste comes from inscriptions and literary accounts of this period. In the seventeenth century the left-hand-right-hand quarrels took on a new dimension. The majority of the conflicts in the Black Towns of the East India Companies (the section of the town where the Indian artisans lived) usually involved the securing of the Companies' contract for cloth.

Not merely conflict but an underlying unity is implicit in the organic metaphor of the right-hand and left-hand. The left-and right-hand castes would unite against a common enemy. Several inscriptions from the fifteenth century, most of them belonging to the reign of Deva Raya II, refer to the combining of the ninety-eight castes of the *idangai* and ninety-eight castes of the *valangai* against enhanced taxation.[67] They also passed orders for the social ostracism of those who had any dealings with the Vellala or Brahmin landlords and fixed the 'just' tax rates on all professions.[68]

The rates were as follows:

Each blacksmith, carpenter, goldsmith silversmith (pertaining to their tools)	5 *panams* including *kottu, kirru arasuperu* (state tax)
Each chief potter	5 *panams* (including *tirigaiayam,* i.e., potter's wheel)
Each chief barber	4 *panams* (including *karuviayam* (shaving kit)
Each chief washerman	4 *panams* (including *kallayam,* the washing stone)
Each brazier	6 *panams*
Each chief oil-monger	20 *panams* (including *karuviayam)*
Each Kaikkolav weaver with one working loom	4 *panams*
Each Kaikkolav weaver with loom that does not work	2 *panams*
On the Saliya weaver on every loom	9 *panams*
Each lace loom in working order	3 *panams*
Each lace loom not in working order	1.5 *panams*

An interesting oral tradition relating to craft unity, cutting across caste differences pertains to the 'Wall Tax Road'. The British colonial masters decided to build a high wall between the 'White Town' and the 'Black Town' in the Fort St. George area. The cost of the structure would be met by raising a levy from the artisanal and merchant inhabitants of the Black Town. However, to their surprise the usually squabbling castes spoke in one voice against this outrageous tax and ensured that the partially constructed wall would never be finished. Even today, the Wall Tax road in the Fort St. George area exists as a telling testimony of imperial folly and native unity.

The claim to social honours and privileges by the more prosperous artisan groups, the Sat-Sudras, was just one facet of a movement fermenting in medieval society. The powerful and influential position occupied by these artisan castes in the economy of the times was hardly reflected in the ritual and normative texts. They tried to improve their social status through ritual recognition, on the one hand by acquiring social and ritual privileges, and on the other by claiming Brahmanical status and ascribing mythological origins to themselves. A common feature of such legends is that they attribute low status to the curse of some god or *Rishi* and the consequent fall from grace. The Kaikkolar attribute their fall to Lord Kartikeya's curse, the Kammalar to the curse of the sage Vashishta and the Teliki to the curse of the sage Visvambar.

It is significant that all these castes claimed Brahmanical status and wore the sacred thread. The attitude of the caste is best expressed in this verse of Sambalinga Murthy, a priest of the Devanga weavers:

> Manu was born in the Brahmana caste
> He was surely a Brahman in the womb;
> There is no Sudraism in this caste
> Devanga had the form of Brahma.[69]

The weavers, smiths and in fact, even the poorer Sudra castes, participated in large numbers in the Vira Saiva or Lingayat movement and the Tengalai Srivaishnava movement. The Lingayat movement originated in the Kanarese country in the twelfth century under the leadership of Basava who is described as an axe to the root of the caste system.[70] Unlike the Brahmanical castes, the Lingayats buried their dead, practised widow remarriage and did not observe any rules regarding ceremonial pollution. The main followers of Basava were the Banajiga and other trading groups, tanners, tailors, weavers and untouchables. Jedara Dasimayya, a famous Lingayat saint, belonged to the Jedara caste of weavers, while another saint, Shankara Dasimayya, was a tailor. Although the Vira Saiva movement began as a protest against orthodox Brahmanism, it soon began to develop social exclusiveness based on the privilege of birth and cleanliness of occupation, much along the lines of Brahmanical orthodoxy. Thus the untouchables among the Lingayats could neither invest themselves with the sacred *lingam* nor perform the eight sacraments. In fact, even the concept of physical pollution was revived. The movement also gave up notions of caste negation and reverted to efforts at caste exaltation. The Lingayats claimed superiority over all groups including the Brahmans and did not mix with the other castes. Probably, even the peculiar practice of burying their dead in a sitting position was adopted in order to appear distinctive.[71]

The Tengalai movement in Srivaishnavism also brought within its fold many of the Sudra artisan castes.[72] When the movement began in the eleventh-twelfth centuries, it did hold ideas of caste negation. Ramanuja maintained, 'If we descend below the four castes and come to the Chandalas who, however lacking in virtue, are true worshippers ... of Vishnu, their servants' servants are my masters and their feet are mine to worship.'[73] But eventually the Tengalai Vaishnavites, comprising mostly Sudras, covertly began to enhance their status and establish their superiority over the Vadagalai or orthodox Vaishnavites. This became the Prabandhic or Tamil school as opposed to the Bhasya or Sanskrit school which gradually had to shift its centre from Tirupati to the Varadaraja Perumal temple at Kanchipuram in the fourteenth and fifteenth centuries, because the Tengalai sectarian leaders managed to gain control at Tirupati. Kuranarayana, the first *jiyar* (head of the *matha*) at Srirangam, and later Alagiya Manavala in the fifteenth century enhanced their power by offering discipleships to the Sudra servants of the temple.[74]

There were several non-Brahmin disciples of Ramanuja, like Pillai Uranga Villi Dasar who was a Malla (the caste of professional wrestlers) or Pattina Perumal. Ramanuja Dasar, another disciple, was a sculptor belonging to the Kammalar caste, while Nambi Eru Tirudaiya Dasar was a Shanar. It is even now believed that Kandadai Ramanuja Dasar, a Sudra Vaishnavite saint of the fifteenth century, who held positions of great importance at Srirangam and Tirupati, was a brother of Saluva Narasimha, the Vijayanagar king.[75] This may or may not be true but it is quite clear from inscriptional evidence that Saluva Narasimha extended considerable patronage to both these temples. At Srirangam, the temple accountant was Vellalar while the ritual of offering a coconut to the deity was done by a Kaikkolar.[76] At Tirupati, Saluva Narasimha publicly proclaimed his patronage of the Sudra worshippers in the temple, for example, through the establishment of *ramanujakutams* (free feeding house for all Srivaishnavas).[77] It has been argued by Arjun Appadorai that the extension of patronage to popular sectarian leaders and the leading artisan groups was a part of the strategy adopted by the Vijayanagar kings to strengthen their rule at the grass roots level.[78]

The upward movement among craftsmen was also reflected in the phenomenal growth of the Amman, or the cult of the mother goddess, between 1300 and 1750. Mariamman, Kamakshimamman and Chandesvaramman are all various manifestations of the mother goddess worshipped by the Sudra artisan castes. Even today, the priests in most of these amman temples are Sudras called pandaram.[79]

Summing Up

Traditional craft industry in pre-colonial India was far from being a monolith in terms of its structures, developments or responses to colonialism. In fact, different crafts were poised differently in terms of their technological development or their potential for industrialisation. Nor would it be appropriate to regard the colonial intervention as the sole marker for understanding the nature of traditional crafts. This is not to deny the impact of colonialism in fostering discriminatory development of the Indian economy but to draw attention to the richly textured differences within the traditional crafts ranging from pottery to weaving to the intricacies of icon making and metal working.

What does emerge powerfully from a study of traditional crafts in pre-colonial South India is the symbiotic link that exists between crafted objects and craft persons. In striking contrast to the standardisation associated with the industrial mode of production, traditional crafts were characterised by asymmetry. In the colonial period, a recurrent phrase in the English Company records, is the injunction to the Company Agents to 'Please make them weave to "the perfection of the pattern" '[80]. 'Perfection of the pattern' went against the very ethos of the craftsmen who could not kill his individuality and creativity through monotonous repetition. Unfortunately, if a weaver or craftsman digressed from the muster provided by the Company Agent, what he produced would be summarily rejected. As he worked on the basis of an advance, this could push him to desperation, even to the extent of committing suicide.

Society in the Vijayanagar period was in a state of flux. The higher artisan castes, the Sat-Sudras, had been the chief beneficiaries of the growth of urbanisation and the expansion of the market, both foreign and domestic. Increasing economic prosperity resulted in their bid for a better social status which revealed itself, unlike the medieval north, not in caste negation but in caste exaltation. This urge operated in a peculiar fashion. While on the one hand the artisans sought to overcome ritual restrictions by raising themselves to the level of the Brahmans, yet, on the other hand, they assiduously tried to maintain differential status and even ceremonial pollution in relation to the lower Sudra castes. This dichotomy is best revealed in the observation of the seventeenth century traveller John Fryer[81] :

> But the most insolent were the artificers; as the engravers, refiners, goldsmiths, carpenters and the like, who behaved themselves not only disrespectfully to their superiors but tyrannically to those of a viler rank. Whereupon they jointly conspired their ruin and with that their own slavery, taking the Moors to their assistance who not only reduced the usurpers to composition . . . but they also took power into their own hands which though despotic the Gentus endure ....

This observation provides a hint of the future history of the artisans in the aftermath of the Vijayanagar empire during the Company period. Fryer's comment can be applied with even greater justification to the rule of the East India Company in the seventeenth century. Exploiting the caste factor was one of the primary the devices through which they maintained their hegemony over the artisans of the Black Town.

REFERENCES

1. Calcutta University Lecture Series, reprint, 1938.
2. Barun De, 'Problems of the Study of Indian History with Particular Reference to Interpretations of the Eighteenth Century', Centre for Studies in Social Sciences, Calcutta, 1988.
3. Frank Perlin in his essay 'Proto-Industrialization and Pre-Colonial South Asia', *Past and Present*, no. 98, 1983.
4. *Rethinking Early Modern India*, ed. Richard B. Barnett, New Delhi, 2002. A thought-provoking review of this book is by Amar Farooqi which has been published in *The Book Review*, Vol. XXVII, no. 3, March 2003.
5. To give a couple of examples of studies of this nature, see Eric Stokes, 'The First Century of British Colonial Rule in India: Social Revolution or Social Stagnation?', *Past and Present*, nos. 58–61, 1973, pp.136-160 for a general survey. Sushil Chaudhury's book *From Prosperity to Decline: Eighteenth Century Bengal*, Delhi, 1995, updates his many years of research.
6. One such study focusing on rural Bengal is by Rajat Datta, *Economy, Society and the Market: Commercialisation in Rural Bengal*, circa 1760–1800, Delhi, 2000. Looking at somewhat similar problems in the context of Peninsular India is Prasannan Parthasarathi's *The Transition to a Colonial Economy: Weavers, Merchants and Kings in South India*, Cambridge, 2001.
7. Seema Alavi (ed.), *The Eighteenth Century in India*, Delhi, 2002.
8. I have discussed some of these features of internal demand in my book, *Textiles and Weavers in Medieval South India*, Delhi, 2006 (First published, 1985).
9. V.I. Pavlov, *Historical Premises for India's Transition to Capitalism*, Moscow, 1979, section two, pp.163 to 214.
10. See Vijaya Ramaswamy, 'South Indian Textiles: A Case for Proto-Industrialization?' in Deepak Kumar, ed. *Science and Empire*, New Delhi, 1991, pp. 41–58.
11. I had raised some of these conceptual issues in the context of early medieval period which coincides with the Chola and Chalukya dynasties in my article 'Visvakarma Craftsmen in Early Medieval Peninsular India', *Journal of the Economic and Social History of the Orient*, Vol. 47, Part 4, 2004, pp. 548–582.
12. *Inscriptions of Andhra Pradesh*, Cuddapah district, Vol. II, no.107.
13. See E. Sivanagi Reddy, 'Shilpins in Early and Medieval Andhra: Epigraphical Study from 200 B.C. to 1800 A.D', Published by the Organisers of The Second International Seminar on Mayonic Science and Technology held in Jan 1997 at Thiruvananthapuram, Kerala, p.7 for the contextual citing of this inscription.
14. *Annual Report of Epigraphy* (henceforth *A.R.E.)* 309 and 378 of 1916; Report 1917, para 55.
15. *South Indian Inscriptions* (henceforth *SII*), Vol. XVII, no.603, Nagapattinam Taluq, Tanjavur district.
16. *A.R.E.*, 479 of 1908 from Uyyakondan Tirumalai, Tiruchchirapalli taluq and district.

17. *A.R.E.*, 575 of 1909. The inscription which is on a Naga pillar in the courtyard of the Chennakesavaswami temple records gift of land to the temple of Adityesvara.
18. *SII*, Vol. VI, no. 439.
19. *SII*, Vol.III, Pt. 3, no. 205.
20. *A.R.E.*, 331 and 332 of 1936-7. The first is from Repalli in Tumkur district of Mysore dated 882CE and the second record from Palnad taluq of Guntur district is dated in the 7th century CE.
21. A sixth-century inscription from Badami written in archaic Telugu refers to Vidyadharan Kalgabharana Achrya *SII*, Vol. XII, no. 23 A.
22. *SII*. Vol. XVII, no. 603, Tiruvarur, Nagapattinam taluq, Tanjavur district.
23. *A.R.E.*, 479 of 1908 from Uyyakondan Tirumalai, Tiruchchirapalli taluq and district.
24. A. Appadorai, *Economic Conditions in Southern India*, 1000–1500 A.D., Madras, 1936, Vol. I, pp. 357 ff.
25. Karl Marx in *Capital*, Vol. I, the English translation of the third German edition by Moore and Aveling, ed. F.Engels, Moscow, 1958, pp. 339–40.
26. *Ibid*.
27. Irfan Habib, 'Potentialities of Change in the Economy of Mughal India', *Socialist Digest*, no. 6, Sept. 1972.
28. Morris D. Morris, 'Reinterpretation of Nineteenth Century Economic History', *Indian Economic and Social History Review*, Vol. V, No. I, March 1968, pp. 5–6ff.
29. Karl, Marx, *Capital*, Vol. I, p. 340.
30. 'Potentiatities of Change', p. 105 ff. See specially p.105 ff.
31. K.N. Chaudhuri, *The Trading World of Asia and the English East India Company*, Cambridge, 1978, p.274.
32. K.N. Chaudhuri, 'The Structure of Indian Textile Industry in the Seventeenth and Eighteenth Centuries', in *Indian Economic and Social History Review*, (Hereafter, *IESHR*)Ibid., 1974, p.152.
33. *Ibid*, pp.180–81.
34. *The English Factories in India* (henceforth *EFI*) ed.William Foster, 1606–1669, 13 volumes, Oxford 1906–1927, letter dated 25th June 1629, p. 342.
35. *Ibid*, 26th Oct. 1646, p. 52.
36. *Ibid*, 4th April 1954, p. 256.
37. This point was discussed at some length in my book, *Textiles and Weavers*, pp. 151–2.
38. J. Brouwer, 'A Matter of Liminalities: A Study of Women and Crafts in South India' in *Man in India*, Vol. 67, no. I, March 1987, p. 6.
39. The details of women's participation in the handloom sector during the Sangam age (roughly from circa third century BCE to third century CE, is to be found in my article 'Aspects of Women and Work in Early South India', *IESHR*, Vol. XXVI, no.I, Jan–March, 1989, pp. 85–87.
40. Sharanacharitramu p. 223 cited in J.K. Kamat, *Social Life in Medieval Karnataka*, New Delhi, 1980, p. 119.
41. For the powerful poetry within the Virasaivite tradition by women spinners, see my book *Divinity and Deviance: Women in Virasaivism*, Delhi, 1996, pp. 53–54.

42. Vijaya Ramaswamy 'Women and Work', p. 86.
43. *Ibid*, p. 88. The translation from the original Tamil is mine.
44. The published version of Kreedabhiramamu in Telugu was edited by Vetturi Prabhakara Sastry – Muktiyala, 1952. See verse 67. A recent translation of the same text has been brought out by the Oxford University Press.
45. *Ibid*, verses 101 to 105.
46. Published by the Government of Karnataka, Bangalore, 1975, pp. 207–9.
47. *Parasara Madhaviyam,* vide A. Appadorai *Economic Conditions in Southern India,* Chennai, 1990, Vol. I, p. 236.
48. *Parasara Madhaviyam*, Vol. I, p. 432 cited in *Ibid*, Vol. I, p. 235, fn. 616.
49. Hamilton Buchanan, *A Journey from Malabar through the Countries of Mysore, Canara and Malabar,* three volumes, edited by T. Cadell, W. Davis and Black, London 1807, Vol. I, p. 100.
50. Colonial Alexander Walker's comment on the Malabar plough is from a detailed report on the subject, the full text of which is published in Dharampal, *Indian Science and Technology in the Eighteenth Century.* The above passage is taken from Claude Alvares, *Homo Faber: Technology and Culture in India, China and the West* – 1500 *to the Present Day*, New Delhi , 1979, p. 50. This book also contains an excellent discussion on the issue of appropriate technology.
51. *Ibid*, p. 49.
52. Vijaya Ramaswamy, *Textiles and Weavers*, Chapter V.
53. Elijah Hoole, *Madras, Mysore and South India*, London, 1844.
54. *Visvakarma Puranam,* Mackenzie Manuscripts, Wilson Collection, no. 72, p. 6–7.
55. Although multiple oral versions of this community tradition exist, an excellent textual analysis is to be found in Jan Brower, 'The Story of the Magnetic Fort' published in his book *Makers of the World,* Delhi, 1995. Also see 'The Story of the Magnetic Fort' by the same author in A de Ridder and J.A.J. Karremans eds. *Tradition in Structural Anthropology,* Netherlands, 1987. This is not to say that this is the only authentic version since other oral traditions differ from it in significant respects.
56. Hamilton Buchanan, *A Journey*, Vol. I, p. 42.
57. This forms the exclusive focus of my essay 'Artisans in Vijaynagar Society', *IESHR,* Vol. XXII, no. 4, Oct.-Dec., 1985. Noboru Karashima has explored the theme of rise of craft groups in his book, *Towards a New Social Formation: South Indian Society under Vijayanagar Rule,* Delhi, 1992, pp. 159–169.
58. See Vijaya Ramaswamy, *Textiles and Weavers,* op cit Chapter IV, pp. 103–107.
59. *A.R.E.*, 65 of 1922–23, Report, para 54.
60. *SII,* Vol. II, no. 25.
61. *Pudukottai State Inscriptions*, Nos. 690 and 694.
62. *A.R.E.*, 293 of 1928–29.
63. *Nellore District Inscriptions*, Vol. 3, Udayagiri, no. 20.
64. *A.R.E.*, 293 of 1928-29, Report, para. 54; 273 of 1939-40, Report, para. 101.
65. *A.R.E.*, 293 of 1928-29.
66. *A.R.E.*, 309 and 378 of 1916–17, Report, para. 55.

67. See, for example, *A.R.E.*, 216 of 1917-18; 489 of 1937-38; 92 of 1918, para. 18 and 355 of 1950-51.
68. *A.R.E.*, 59 of 1914-15. The very lengthy set of rates fixed on land and various varieties of crops has been omitted here.
69. *Devanga Puranam* of Mambala Kavirayar, ed. N. Sadasivayya, Madras, 1893.
70. R.N. Nandi, 'Origins of the *Vira Satva Movement*', *Indian Historical Review*, Vol. 2, no. 1, July 1975, p. 32. The Virasaivite movement both in terms of its artisanal roots and the strong presence of women has been discussed in my book *Divinity and Deviance*. The role of the untouchables in the Vira Saiva and Srivaishnava movement is also well discussed in K.R. Hanumanthan, *Untouchability: A Historical Study*, Madurai, 1979, pp. 165–74.
71. Abdur Razzaq's account of his travels in R.H. Major ed., *India in the Fifteenth Century*, Delhi, 1974, p. 17. M.N. Srinivas, *A Note on Sanskritisation and Westernisation*, Bombay, 1962, while quoting the Lingayats as a leading example of Sanskritisation has himself pointed out that the more orthodox Lingayats did not eat food touched or cooked by Brahmins. He has however neither clearly defined nor emphasised this reverse process of Sanskritisation.
72. 'In fact, certain Southern school Brahmins (Tengalai Srivaishnavas) can be identified as former Sudras from their manners and customs',—Burton Stein, 'Social Mobility and Medieval South Indian Hindu Sects,' in J. Silverburg ed., *Social Mobility in the Caste System in India—An Interdisciplinary Symposium*, The Hague, 1968, p. 90.
73. The verse has been quoted in Burton Stein, 'Social Mobility,' op. cit., p. 83.
74. Arjun Appadorai, 'Kings, Sects and Temples in South India—A.D. 1350-1700' in *IESHR*, Vol. 14, no. 1, 1977, pp. 47–73.
75. N. Jagadisan, *History of Srivaishnavism in the Tamil Country, Post Ramanuja Period*, Madurai, 1977, pp. 86,91–92 ff.
76. Burton Stein, 'Social Mobility,' p. 87.
77. Arjun Appadorai, 'Kings, Sects, and Temples', p. 67.
78. This in fact constitutes the main theme of Arjun Appadoria's 'Kings, Sects and Temples'.
79. The *Valangai Charitram*, Mackenzie Manuscripts, no. 71, Wilson Collection, is replete with reference to various types of *amman* or mother goddess. Matangi, for instance, is said to be the consort of Siva and the *Sudra* saint Nandanar is said to be their son! Burton Stein has made a special study of the proliferation of *amman* shrines in 'Temples in the Tamil Country' in Stein ed., *South Indian Temples*, Delhi, 1978.
80. This phrase occurs often in the Company correspondence but one significant instance is the letter dated 1696 regarding the musters to be sent to the Coromandel weavers through their Agent Mr. Ongley, India Office Records, Letter Book IX,466 cited in John Irwin, 'Indian Textile Trade in the Seventeenth Century: South India', in *Studies in Indo-European Textile History* ed. John Irwin and P.R.Schwartz, Ahmedabad, India, 1966, p.37.
81. John, Fryer, *A New Account of the East Indies and Persia*, London, 1909-15, Vol. I, Chapter 3, p. 82.

Chapter 12

Contesting Hegemony: State and Peasant in Late Medieval Rajasthan

Dilbagh Singh

For long, peasant uprisings in Mughal India have commanded much academic interest. With the publication of Irfan Habib's *Agrarian System of Mughal India* in 1963, a major change was introduced in our perception of the medieval Indian rural society. Habib portrayed the excessive exploitation, which the medieval peasantry was subjected to and proceeded to analyze spontaneous uprisings against excessive and intolerable exploitation.[1] In his subsequent writings too, Habib continued to examine the explicit forms of peasant resistance and dissent. Habib writes of the range of resistance right from subtle to armed resistance: from refusal to pay tax to flight from the village.[2] However, the focus is on armed resistance and other variables in this context are not given adequate attention.

Harbans Mukhia has tried to view the notion of resistance as being both silent and explicit. He has suggested that peasant protest could take many forms, depending upon the production system. Lethargy, carelessness, haggling over tax payment, concealment, petitioning, migration, abandonment of cultivation, violent upheavals have all been seen as alternatives. In this context, he argues that the peasants accept only a part of the ruling class ideology and that the peasantry possessed a certain power to resist and a considerable degree of dynamism irrespective of the basic fact of their exploitation.[3]

Two images of the peasantry emerge. On the one hand we have the image of an utterly oppressed, absolutely hapless and helpless peasantry ultimately taking recourse to armed rebellion. On the other hand, it has been suggested that the peasantry cannot be treated as forever at the receiving end of exploitation. Peasants are not seen as an utterly passive and powerless lot. They resist the claims of the ruling class in myriad ways and contest space in more ways than we usually concede.[4] I have made an attempt to examine the subtle forms of resistance in late medieval rural Rajasthan on the basis of archival records pertaining to revenue-related offences. These records among other things highlight the level of state intervention in rural society and the ways and means developed by the members of the village community to contest the claims of the superordinate class over their surplus produce.

It is perhaps, most appropriate to open the discussion with an examination of the precise meaning of the term 'resistance'. In social science terms a definition of the terms is problematic, in that there exist two broad strands of opinion. One sees it as explicit and the other as hidden and subtle. Resistance is viewed as 'antagonism' or the *'desire to oppose'*, and hence to exert oneself so as to withstand or counteract the force or effect of another. Yet, is this necessarily an overt expression or does it include the hidden and subtle forms of withstanding pressure or counteraction?

Perhaps the question most crucial to peasant resistance is whether individual acts such as theft of crop or concealment of crop qualify as resistance, even though there is herein, an obvious lack of collective action. Moreover, can actions which are not aimed at or constitute, nor do they pose an open challenge to the existing socio-economic and political structure (which is inclusive of power relations and structures of property and domination) be construed as 'resistance', when at best they serve self-interest?

James Scott views class resistance as 'any act(s) by member(s) of a subordinate class that is or are intended either to mitigate or deny claims (e.g. rent, taxes, labour) made on that class by superordinate classes.[5] The definition, though admittedly not all-encompassing and rigid, focusses on the material basis of class relation and class struggle. It allows for both individual and collective actions of resistance. Moreover, it is not dismissive of the ability of the subordinate classes to question the ideological base of the hegemony of the state/ruling classes. The definition also does not constrict resistance to only the obvious or overt attempts to change the status quo. A central aspect of this view of resistance is its emphasis on intentionality and not consequences; so that each action which is intended to withstand or counteract the pressures exerted (in the shape of claims made) qualifies as 'resistance' irrespective of the eventual outcome.

The question of intentionality is however not without its share of problems. For one, acts such as tampering with the sealed sacks of grain belonging to the state as its share of produce, pilferage or petty theft of grain may be viewed as being merely prompted by self-interest. One cannot substantially argue against such a view, since the intentions in such cases will not be proclaimed for obvious reasons of survival.

Second, the problems that arise in this connection, are part of broader issues of definition and analysis. Resistance is commonly perceived as action, which involves some 'short run individual or collective sacrifice' in the pursuit of a higher goal, which is usually meant to yield long-term benefits. In such a paradigm, petty theft or pilferage is found wanting for the sheer self-interest in the immediate context by which it is apparently propelled. Hence a dichotomy emerges between overt resistance and what are seen as acts of 'self help'. Whereas the former presupposes a level of organisation and systematic coordination, together with an explicit objective, which negates the very basis of domination; the latter on the contrary is seen as an action implicitly expressing accommodation with the system at large, being token, incidental, unsystematic and individual.

Such an approach, however, misconstrues what are in effect 'every day forms of resistance', and constitute the basis of 'economic and political struggle conducted daily by subordinate classes'. To deny these the status of resistance on the grounds that these lack 'intrinsic revolutionary consequences' is a weak line of argument, considering that if occurring on a large scale and following a clearly discernable pattern, they form the building blocks of the revolutionary process, when viewed over a time frame.

It may safely be said that everyday forms of peasant resistance flow from *fundamental materials needs*. Scott sees these as the needs of survival.[6] I would however, add to it the enhancement of income for reasons that will become evident later in the discussion. Moreover, these seemingly trivial acts of self-interest have implications for the surplus appropriating authority. When a peasant hides part of his crop or conceals part of his land under cultivation (as in late medieval eastern Rajasthan) to avoid payment of taxes, he not only secures a larger part of the produce for himself but correspondingly deprives the state of its share of produce. Thus this act, apart from conferring immediate advantages on the peasants, also denies the state its resources. Apart from the material implication, everyday forms of resistance implicitly contest the justification and rationale behind a claim, so that the hegemony and legitimacy of the state/ruling class, as appropriator of surplus in questioned.

Having broadly outlined the paradigm through which peasant resistance is being viewed in the present study, an enumeration of the various forms of resisting and contesting the state's claim to peasants surplus produce is presented in this study.

The present study is based on information contained in systematically arranged series of annual revenue records prepared *pargana* wise and termed *arhsattas*, which were compiled from a variety of notations. The *arhsattas* contain interesting information under the revenue head *hasil farohi*, i.e. details of fine imposed and collected from defaulters. The *farohi* account described a wide range of crimes, offences, violation of established social norms, the social groups involved and how these were viewed by the state. Analysis of the relevant *farohi* accounts is restricted to those parganas which were included in *tankhwah* and *watan jagirs* of the Kachwaha rulers of Amber-Jaipur and the period covered is from 1680 to 1790.

It is quite evident from the documents that almost all sections of the rural society including its dominant groups were adopting ways and means to avoid paying what the state demanded from the village as tax, thereby raising the question of real magnitude of land revenue and the relationship between the state's claim over the surplus produce and its actual payment in practice. These include concealment of the area under cultivation, non-discloser of actual number of tax payers, area under cultivation, area under cash crops, inter-cropped plants, and irrigated lands. Also included could be tampering with measured areas figures, false declarations regarding the rate of assessment applicable, and crops planted, removal of standing crop before payment of tax, consumption of crop yet to be extracted in the field itself, stealing of grain before actual division of grain between the state and taxpayer, tampering with the *chak* or seal affixed on stored sacks of grain and so on.

The concealment of area under cultivation was a means adopted to evade payment or revenue to the state. In village Gabhira, *pargana* Malarna, *patel* Deepchand and other cultivators did not get their fields measured, the produce of which they (mis) appropriated. In the same village Nathya Jat, Narayan Jat and the wife of Duda Jat evaded measurement of parts of their respective holdings under cash crop cultivation. Similarly, the *patel* of village Hasanpur concealed two fields belonging to him under cotton and *moth* cultivation from the measuring party.[7] Govinda Meena of village Kharkari in *pargana* Toda Bhim was accused of not disclosing his holding to the *tapdar* who had gone to the village to assess the areas under *zabt*. The recorded charge is that of '*jamin ki chori*' (theft of land). Jado and Hirde Ram, etc. —cultivators of the same village—got away without getting land under vegetables cultivation during the *rabi* (spring) harvest measured.[8] Ghasi and Karma *patels* of village Mirzapur falsified the measured area figures by declaring *khalisa* land as *udik* land, which was exempted from assessment.[9] In village Ajitpur, the *patel* and *patwari* by a collusion with Mani Ram Bohra of the same village kept a field measuring six *bighas* unmeasured. The field was actually owned by the *patel* who let it out to Maniram for its cultivation.[10] In village Udaipura, *pargana* Lalsot,

Prahlad Singh Rajput concealed his field measuring thirteen *bighas* under sugarcane from the measuring party.[11] In village Ugarvas, *pargana* Lalsot, Kashi Balahi cultivated *guwar* in his field. However, he managed to conceal half the area under crop from the measuring party. Similarly, in village Jhafda, *pargana* Chatsu the *patel* and *paltis* kept some fields unmeasured at the time of assessment.[12]

The cultivators took advantage of the multiplicity of the methods of assessment adopted by them for different crops raised on the same plot of land. Classification of cultivated land into several categories on the basis of the nature of soil offered ample scope for indulging in fraudulent activities. The *patels* and others rich cultivators often manipulated the recording of different land tenure such as *khalisa, udik, inam* and *sanjha* to escape from the obligation to pay taxes.

In the dry lands of semi-arid eastern Rajasthan, intercropping continued to be the dominant agricultural practice. Such crop combinations created ample scope for the producers to cheat the state by concealing at least one or the other inter-cropped plant in the same field. The following instances are illustrative.

The *patel* of village Dasaro did not disclose to the revenue officials the area under food crops in the same field where cash crops were being grown. Lalkhan Kagdi of *qasba* Malarana intermixed sugarcane and maize in his field. However, at the time of assessment, inter-cropping of maize was not disclosed[13] as it was possible to conceal its plantation in the same field as sugarcane. Neta Patel and other cultivators of village Todri, *pargana* Malpura planted cotton in the same field as under *jowar* cultivation but he managed to get the area under *jowar* measured by the *tapdar*.[14] Kaju Patel of village Sangrampur, *pargana* Niwai cultivated sugarcane and oil-seed in the same field. However, at the time of assessment he tried to conceal the once under oil-seed.[15] In village Upritha of *pargana* Bahatri, Ajaba Bania cultivated cotton and sun hemp in the same field. While getting his field measured he found it convenient to keep quiet about sun hemp.[16] The manner in which the hereditary village officials tampered with assessment records is evident from the example of village Vijalpur, *pargana* Tonk. The *patel* and *patwari*, while preparing *takhmina* (estimate of crops grown) made false entries regarding crop production.[17]

The *patel* of village Vokaravas submitted the *takhmina* for *kharif* (winter) harvest of the year 1724. However, while undertaking measurement of the area under *zabt* crops the *tapdar* located discrepancy amounting to forty *bighas* of land in *takhmina* and actual measurement figures.[18] In village Kacharoli, *pargana* Mauzpur, by a collusion of the *patel* and *raiyat* one hundred and eight *bighas* of land was concealed from the measuring party.[19] Jadu Bania of village Ronija Jat in the same *pargana* made false declarion about his land under *zabt*.[20] Similarly, the actual number of *asamis* (tax payers) was very often concealed by a collusion of the village headman and members of the village community to evade a part of the revenue payment. How the benefits of this evasion were distributed amongst the taxpayers in the village or these were entirely misappropriated by the headman and other dominant members of the community, may have depended on the internal organisation of the village community and its structure of power relations. The following cases illustrate the act of evasion by this means.

The *patels* of village Narayanpur, Qadirabad, Chatrabhujpura, Kiratpur and Kishorpura falsified the number of dwelling huts by not declaring the actual number to the revenue officials. In village Narayanpur there were twenty dwelling huts whereas only seven were declared. Similarly, in village Kishorpur seventeen dwelling huts were not revealed to the officials.[21] While preparing the *khasra* for village Jhirana, the *patel* and *patwari* did not include the names of the *asami* to be assessed according to the *batai* system.[22]

Involvement of other weaker sections of the rural society in hoodwinking the state's revenue officials is also evident. Because of the land-abundant situation and the interdependent character of the village community, the artisan and menials collectively termed as *kamin* were allotted plots of cultivable land for self-cultivation. As per the customary practices, they were assessed at concessional rates partly to induce them to engage in cultivation and partly to make cultivation affordable. The *kamin* also cultivated land as tenants of the holders of *udik* and *inam* grants. Notwithstanding a favourable tax schedule, the *kamins* often tried to evade payment of tax at full rate. This is evident from the instance of *qasba* Phagi where Hira Balahi and other *kamin asamis* managed to get away from the assessment of their land holdings.[24] Likewise, the *kamins* who were engaged in their caste-related professions attempted to cheat the state in order to reduce the burden of taxation levied upon their professions. In village Mohikalam, *pargana* Bahatri the actual number of tax papers belonging to *lohar* (blacksmith) caste was twenty-six. However, at the time of tax payment it was declared that there existed only four such *asamis*.[25] Gariba Nilgar (indigo dyer) of village Chandlai in *pargana* Chatsu owned four indigo vat (*kund*), which he did not report to the revenue official to escape tax payment.[26] Land allotted to the *kamins* in lieu of services rendered to the village community was also taxed at concessional rate. How the *kamins* tried to escape assessment is evident from the instance of *qasba* Phagi where Hira Balahi evaded *lata* of land holdings cultivated by the *kamin asamis*.[27]

Other forms of reducing the state's fiscal burden on the cultivators were the false claims of exemption from payment, the claim of low yield as also claims to concessional rates of assessment on account of privileged status as cultivators. These also included fraudulent declaration of the entire land under *sanjha* cultivation as belonging to the privileged partner of the holding. Harji, Poora, Duda, Dayaram, etc. *patels* were found guilty of declaring number of fields to be assessed at the rate of one-fourth and one-third of the produce whereas they were liable to be assessed at the normal rate.[28] In village Bhurtya Khurd, Parbrahm Brahman's son got his holding assessed at the rate of one fourth of the produce on the false claim that he recited the Gayatri hymn.[29] Thakarsi *qanungo* cultivated land in *sanjha* along with Daya Ram Meena in village Mirzapur in pargana Toda Bhim. However, the Qanungo, declaring the *sanjha* holding as belonging to himself, made the entire payment of land revenue at a concessional rate. He misused his official position to help Daya Ram Meena to escape assessment of his share of produce on the basis of the normal rate of assessment. In village Trisul of the same *pargana* the Patel, while undertaking measurement of the area under *kharif* crops, deliberately omitted the measurement of *sanjha* holdings.[30]

In village Alipur, *pargana* Hindon, the *patel* forged the revenue records to give benefit of concessional rate of assessment to the cultivators. Also, he tampered with records pertaining to the extent of area under cotton cultivation.[31] In village Shankarpur of the same *pargana,* land holdings of the *patel* and *paltis* were declared as belonging to the Qanungo.[32] In village Banavirpur, the *patels* Amar Singh and Kashiram showed land under continuous indigo cultivation as cultivated once in three years. Here they took advantage of the crop rotation widely practised by the peasants.[33]

Maharam Jat of village Jasreta in *pargana* Kathumbar petitioned to the state that he had not been able to cultivate his holding. It was later found that contrary to the claim, he did cultivate his land and obtained its produce.[34] A number of cultivators belonging to village Sitarampur in *pargana* Bahatri cheated the state by falsifying their tax obligation. Mana Brahman was entitled to pay one-third share of the crop as tax whereas he got himself assessed at the rate of one-fourth. Khiva Gujar, instead of paying tax at the rate of fifty per cent paid twenty-five per cent and Amara Mahajan who cultivated land in *sir* (*sanjha*) along with Chatra did not reveal the nature of holding at the time of assessment.[35] Ramu Patel of village Niwli in *pargana* Naraina who got his holding cultivated in *sir* (*sanjha*) did not disclose the name of his Jat partner and declared it as his *gharu hala* holding.[36] In village Datano, *parganes* Tonk, the *patel* in order to evade tax payment showed the entire crop belonging to his tenants as the stock of grain belonging to the holders of *aima* grants (tax free land grant)[37].

Tampering with the measurement of land and concealing cultivated fields that were subject to assessment by way of *lata*, *kankut* and *batai* were yet other means by which revenue payment was sought to be mitigated. In village Kotari of *pargana* Malarna, the *patel* and *patwari,* while assisting the *tapdar* to undertake assessment of revenue by *lata* method deliberately kept several fields outside the scope of *lata*.[38] Similarly, Hathu Patel of village Nangal Puran avoided assessment of land on the basis of *kankut*.[39]

In Qasba Niwai three brothers—Kanta, Meda and Teja Mali—cultivated eighteen *bighas* of land near the pond the entire produce of which they divided among themselves.[40] The *patel, patwari* and Rajput cultivators of village Guda Ramdas managed to get the *lata* assessment of their fields in the absence of the *chaudhari, qanungo* and *tapdar*, a mandatory requirement.[41] The *thakurs, patel, patwari* and the *raiyat* of village Israda were charged with manipulation of assessment under *kankut*.[42]

How the dominant sections of the village were able to take advantage of the multiple methods of revenue of assessment existing side by side in the same village is evident from the example of village Sewa, *pargana* Hindon. Here the *patel* did not reveal correct information about the cultivated land to be assessed according to the *zabt* and *lata*.[43] Harkishan Brahman cultivated seven *bighas* of land under *moth* in the village Shahijahanpur, *pargana* Lalsot. However, he escaped *latai* of his crop and appropriated it.[44] We find the involvement of the entire village community including *panch, patel* and *palti* belonging to village Idawer in *pargana* Lalsot in manipulating assessment on the basis of *kankut* by declaring a lower number of *asamis*.[45]

Irrigated lands were assessed at higher rates and therefore, often attempts who made to declare these as non-irrigated. The rate of assessment on irrigated lands was determined on the basis of the source and method of lifting water out of it. The *patel* of village Vidoli in *pargna* Lalsot declared forty *bighas* of well-irrigated land under sugarcane as irrigated by river water, subject to assessment at a lower rate.[46] Likewise in village Morada, *pargana* Naraina the *patel* and *raiyat* cultivated *gorma* land but at the time of assessment it was shown as *magra* land, which was less productive and attracted assessment at a lower rate.[47]

Dominant sections of the village also took advantage of the peasant stratification to mitigate the state's claim. In village Dungrisil, *pargana* Chatsu, the *patel* managed to get *gavati* cultivators assessed as *pahis*. The old resident cultivators of village Dariyapur in the same *pargana* were declared by the *patel* as recently migrated *pahis* and got assessment of their holdings at the rate of two-fifth of the produce.[48] Similarly, Kheta Patel of village Azizpur, *pargana* Toda Bhim got *gaveti* tax payers listed as *pahis* in the *khasra*.[49] Moni Brahman of Udehi Khurd undertook cultivation in village Kashipur. However, in the *khasra* a Rajput was entered as the taxpayer.[50] The benefits accruing from such acts, if successful in hoodwinking the state, were probably divided amongst the concerned parties. Perhaps a share of the benefits would also be given to the headman since it was he who assisted the state revenue officials in the task of measurement of land in the respective village, whose community was so well-known to him.

Apart from the assessment-related frauds, there existed other means by which personal shares in the produce of land were sought to be augmented by reducing the state's claims to the produce. Instances of tampering with the *chak* or official seal on the stored crop in order to remove (steal) part of the contents of the sacks constituted another manner of increasing the cultivator's share in the produce and correspondingly, of reducing the state's share. The sealing of the reaped crop was itself evaded at times through deception. In village Darhara Hindgi, *pargana* Tonk, the *patel*, *patwari* and all cultivators were found tampering with the seal and removing the state's share of grain. A collective fine of Rs.42,000 was imposed upon the village.[51] In village Nadneri of the same *pargana*, Thakarsi Brahman shifted grain from the state heap to his own heap. In village Kathmana the entire *raiyat* were charged with removing grain from yet-to-be-divided heaps of grain.[52] In village Sewa of *pargana* Mauzabad, Jodha Ahir was caught while breaking the seal of stocked grain. He tried to bribe the *sahna*.[53] Sukha Rajput of the same village was caught red-handed by the *sahna* while stealing grain from the heap. In village Srivasdevpur of *pargana* Lalsot, the *patel* was found tampering with the seal. In village Shivsinghpur of the same *pargana*, Jaita Brahman evaded his stock of grain from being officially sealed.[54] These may be viewed as examples of petty theft to serve self interest, yet considering their widerspread prevalence cutting across all sections of the rural society, they had implications for the state, as has been discussed above.

Other acts of 'self-help' comprised the direct consumption of crop in the field itself or its consumption in the household before meeting the tax obligation. The standing crop was also used for celebrations at the expense of the tax appropriating authority. Lalu Chamar of *qasba* Malarna stole sugarcane from the field.[55] In village Sirsali, *pargana* Malarna, Vija, Nanak, Kushla and Valu were found using sickles to remove the standing crop of gram from the field.[56] Bhikha, Saif, Vadu Muslim and Mukunda Khati, all of *qasba* Toda Bhim were caught while chewing on ears of corn in the field itself.[57] There are numerous instances of cultivators' involvement in the 'theft' of one or the other crop from their own fields. Involvement of all sections of the rural society is evident from the documents. For instance, in village Putugaon, pargana Chatsu, Poora *hali,* who ploughed the field of Man Singh Nathawat was held guilty of removing sheafs of grain from the field.[58] Godha Patel of village Pathraich was guilty of the same offence.[59] Peasants used all conceivable means to steal standing crop or threshed grain well before meeting their tax liability.

In village Murlia Joga, *pargana* Chatsu, Deepa Jat's wife took away sheafs of *jowar* on the pretext of cutting grass.[60] Similarly, in village Raghunathpur, Parsa Mali was caught with stolen *chola* crop, which he kept inside leaves of *moth*.[61] In village Titaria, Tara *patel* misappropriated three *maunds* of grain while harvesting his crop of *moth*.[62] In village Bhimpur, *pargana* Malpura, Kishan Aheri quietly collected cotton from his field.[63] In village Sirag, *pargana* Malpura, Anada Jat cultivated *khalis* land as tenant. Oilseed (*till*) was also grown along with other crops. However, he removed 4½ *maunds* of *til* from the field in the full knowledge of the *patel* and *patwari* of the village and the *sahna* appointed by the state.[64] In village Nagar of the same *pargana*, Rupa Jat, Deva Gujar, Chkha Jat, Bhopati Gujar, Gidha Teli, Bakhat Chandel, Kahar Parihar, Rama Papariwal's *hali* and Savalya Jat removed *jowar* and cotton from their fields. They were caught by the *sahna*.[65] In a subsequent record, Bakhta Chandel is again shown as the culprit of stealing grain at the time of getting *lata* done of his field.[66] In village Lahan, *pargana* Tonk, Mona, etc. four cultivators removed and consumed sheafs of grain under the pretext of weeding.[67] In village Murtza Nagar of the same *pargana* the *patel, patwari* the *raiyat* kept aside part of the harvested grain to mitigate their tax burden.[68] In village Churani, *pargana* Gaji Ka Thana, a cultivator of the village Aasa removed sugarcane and *til* from the field which was also under paddy cultivation.[69] Baking of sheafs of grain was a common practice for its direct consumption in the field or for celebration of Holi, etc. In *qasba* Mulpara, Dayaram Baragavan and Sabla Jat used part of their standing crop for Holi celebrations.[70]

Theft of the crop yet to be harvested by members of the rural society was so rampant that the state was constrained to conduct a house-to-house search to detect such acts. In village Dhudhra, *pargana* Mulpura the *patel, patwari* and entire *raiyat* were held guilty of stealing fresh grain.[71] The *patel* and entire *panchayat* of village Kahar and Adilpur, *pargana* Malarna were charged with a similar offence.[72] Daya Ram and Bhaisa Muslim of *qasba* Phagi removed much of the crop from their fields and stored it in their dwelling huts. Subsequently stolen grain was recovered after a routine search of the households of the *qasba*.[73] A large number of villagers were involved in consumption of freshly harvested grain before payment. In village Bisanpur, *pargana* Bahatri, cooked *jowar* and *ragi* were recovered from Deva Brahman's house.[74] Gudra Patwari, Jai Ram Gujar and Rati Ram *qanungo* of *qasba* Malarna were caught by the *sahna* while consuming bread made of *bajra* in the field.[75] Kusla *patel* of village Thikarya *pargana* Dausa shifted grain to his residence prior to the division of the standing crop.[76] The *sahna* of village Dahtana, *pargana* Malpura recovered bread made of gram from the house of Hira Mali.[77] In village Varkhari Bujurg, *pargana* Tonk, fresh wheat flour was recovered from the house of Kalu Mahajan. In the same village, gram pulse was found in the house of Chatra *patwari*.[78]

Repeated attempts on the part of the state to tighten its control over the rural taxpayers to ensure maximum realisation of revenue within the customary limits is manifest in other instances also. *Lawni* of the crop without prior approval of the state was considered to be an offence. The *patel* of village Gopalpura in *pargana* Chatsu was punished by the state for undertaking *lawni* without permission.[79] Residents of village Vasnoli in *pargana* Bayana were charged with performing *lawni* without having any instruction from the state to this effect.[80] The state look a serious view of the act of Mana Brahman of Baragaon, who cultivated *bajra* in *qasba* Niwai. He did not take requisite care of the field and his negligence led to the ruination of the crop.[81]

All these instances indicate the growing extraneous interference and control over the process of production evidently to safeguard the interest of the ruling class. The high level of state's intervention in the village and its ability to penetrate below the village is a factor that comes across rather clearly from some instances of charges made against cultivators or the village community as a whole, including the *panchayat*. The state endeavoured to promote agriculture and extend patronage to the producers. However, at the same time it tended to subordinate all other interests to its own revenue interest. The ongoing tussle between the state and the members of rural society to outwit each other is also evident from the repeated attempts of the individual cultivators as well as the village community to market their share of grain obtained from the current harvest despite injunctions from the state to refrain from such acts until such time as the state was able to sell its share of grain realised in revenue. The *patel, raiyat* and Rajputs of village Vanahere, *pargana* Lalsot marketed their fresh stock of grain without prior approval of the state. A collective fine of Rs. 161 was imposed upon the village.[82] Maluk Teli of *qasba* Naraina was held guilty of selling fresh grain.[83] Despite allowing freedom in the choice of any existing mode of payment of revenue, the marketing of grain by the primary producers without prior permission of the state was construed as an offence. First, bulk of the state's share of revenue was paid in kind and its marketing was the concern of the state. During a good harvest season, if fresh stock of grain was marketed, it could lead to a glut in the market, pushing prices downwards. Under such a condition the state's revenue would also drop, owing to the low price its share of produce would command.

Second, the state wished its share of stock to be marketed first for the reasons cited above as also because of the poor storage facilities, which could cause the reaped crop to spoil. Hence the state insisted upon its prior approval of the sale of grain by any member of the village community including the *mahajan*. This manifests the extent of control exercised by the state over the cultivators beyond its concern for the collection of revenue and even after the division of produce between the state and taxpayers. The extent of control exercised by the state is manifest in the instance of village Abhaneri in *pargana* Lalsot. The *patel* and cultivators of the village were collectively fined for uprooting the barley crop and replacing it with mustard at sapling stage. The objection here was to the substitution of crop without prior permission of the state even though there was no loss being incurred by the state. It is interesting however, that a continued subversion of this control occurred continuously.

In the realm of ideology, the state's claim to a part of the peasants' produce was contested. At times this was openly expressed in the form of argumentation with the state officials.

It is interesting that one finds herein an alliance of sorts, between all categories of peasants and rural elites in the seemingly common objective of evading payment of revenue to the state. In a number of cases, the *patel* and *panchayat* were involved. These also constituted the dominant sections of the village community, whose being embroiled in the cheating of the state, indicates that the primary objective was not the securing of a bare subsistence level in order to meet the needs of survival, but clearly an attempt to increase personal income. There was also no crisis of production in this region up to the first half of the eighteenth century. Therefore, it was not impoverishment and deprivation, which caused the various means of evading the states claims, rather, the objective was to strengthen the individual's economic base.

The state was well aware of the capability of the peasant community to indulge in what the state perceived as '*hasil ki chori*' (theft of revenue). The *patels* were required to give an undertaking that they would not misappropriate the state's revenue. Despite repeated injunctions to this effect, the state could not arrest the temptation on the part of the *patels* to under-cut its share of the produce. The *patel* of village Rampur in *pargana* Dausa failed to honour his undertaking that he would not misappropriate the *hasil* in future. Such acts, apart from being an expression of resistance are manifestations of the extent of intervention of the state in the life of the village community. The extent of state intervention is important in that it often determines the modes of protest that are adopted by the peasantry. In Skocpol's view, if peasants are to be capable of 'self initiated rebellion (explicit) against the state/ruling class they must have (a) autonomy from direct day-to-day supervision (control) by landlord and state official and (b) an institutionalized collective solidarity'[84]; however, notwithstanding this high degree of intervention, the rural community was able to resist the claims of the state to demand a share in the surplus produce in mundane ways.

With respect to pre-colonial India (Mughal India/Rajasthan) the level of state intervention in the affairs of the village was considerable, as has been shown in the course of discussion somewhat in contrast to the notion of a 'free peasant economy'.

In so far as peasant solidarity is concerned, it was confined to village, caste and clan affiliations; each village community had by and large, a multiplicity of castes ordered into a social and economic hierarchy with a well-defined structure of power relations. The end result was a lack of 'class consciousness' among the peasantry, as Irfan Habib has also argued. The agrarian uprisings in Mughal India were based upon a solidarity effected on caste or clan lines under the banners of powerful zamindar (e.g. Jats); zamindars also took over peasant grievances, forming a military organisation (e.g. Marathas) implying therefore a degree of mobilisation while uprisings such as the Sikhs were the result of organisation under a common religious ideology and community solidarity. On the whole therefore, institutionalised peasant solidarity was absent.

Under such a condition the day-to-day passive forms of resistance best suited to the social structure of the peasantry, a class scattered across the countryside lacking formal organisation, and socially and economically stratified. Moreover, all ranks of people of the rural society colluded for a common objective: the evasion of tax obligation. On the whole, Popkin's view of 'the peasants as a rational problem solver, with a sense both of his own interests and of the need to bargain with other to achieve mutually acceptable outcomes'[85] seems tenable.

REFERENCES

1. Irfan Habib, *The Agrarian System of Mughal India*, second revised edition, Delhi, 1999, p. 378.
2. Irfan Habib, 'Forms of Class Struggle in Mughal India', Reprinted in *Essays in Indian History: Towards a Marxist Perception*, Delhi, 1995, pp. 109–160. Also see R.P. Rana, 'Agrarian Revolts in Northem India during the late 17th and Early 18th century", *Indian Economic and Social History Review*, Vol. XVIII, no. 3 & 4, p. 305.

3. Harbans Mukhia, *Perspectives on Medieval History*, Delhi, 1993, p. 159.
4. Shalini Mishra, 'Everyday Forms of Peasant Resistance in 18th century Eastern Rajasthan', Ph.D. Thesis, Jawaharlal Nehru University, 2004.
5. James C. Scott, *Weapons of the Weak: Everyday Forms of Peasant Resistance*, Delhi, 1990, pp. 28–41.
6. *Ibid*, pp. 41–47.
7. *Arhsatta pargana,* Malarna V.S. 1769/1712, Historical Section, Jaipur Records, Rajasthan State Archives, Bikaner.
8. *Arhsatta paragana,* Toda Bhim V.S. 1769/1712.
9. *Ibid,* V.S. 1768/1711.
10. *Ibid,* V.S. 1804/1747.
11. *Arhsatta pargana,* Lalsot V.S. 1769/1712.
12. *Ibid,* V.S. 1770/1713.
13. *Arhsatta pargana,* Malarna V.S. 1771/1714.
14. *Arhsatta pargana,* Malpura V.S. 1794/1737.
15. *Arhsatta pargana,* Niwai V.S. 1795/1738.
16. *Arhsatta pargana,* Bahatri V.S. 1722/1665.
17. *Arhsatta pargana,* Tonk V.S. 1818/1761.
18. *Arhsatta pargana,* Chatsu V.S. 1781/1724.
19. *Arhsatta pargana,* Mauzpur V.S. 1770/1713.
20. *Ibid,* V.S. 1747/1690.
21. *Arhsatta pargana,* Chatsu V.S. 1802/1745.
22. *Ibid,* V.S. 181/1761.
24. *Arhsatta pargana,* Bahatri V.S. 1722/1665.
25. *Arhsatta pargana,* Chatsu V.S. 1768/1711.
26. *Arhsatta pargana,* Phagi V.S. 1798/1741.
27. *Arhsatta pargana,* Chatsu V.S. 1802/1745.
28. *Ibid,* V.S. 1783/1726.
29. *Arhsatta pargana,* Toda Bhim V.S. 1814/1794.
30. *Arhsatta pargana,* Hindon V.S. 1779/1722.
31. *Ibid.*
32. *Ibid,* V.S. 1787/1730.
33. *Arhsatta pargana,* Kathumbhar V.S. 1774/1717.
34. *Arhsatta pargana,* Bahatri V.S. 1763/1706.
35. *Arhsatta pargana,* Naraina V.S. 1788/1731.
36. *Arhsatta pargana,* Tonk V.S. 1765/1708.
37. *Arhsatta pargana,* Malarna V.S. 1801/1744.
38. *Ibid,* V.S. 1769/1712.
39. *Arhsatta pargana,* Nawai V.S. 1773/1716.
40. *Arhsatta pargana,* Tonk V.S. 1765/1708.
41. *Ibid,* V.S. 1818/1761.
42. *Arhsatta pargana,* Hindon V.S. 1809/1752.
43. *Arhsatta pargana,* Lalsot V.S. 1816/1759.
44. *Ibid,* V.S. 1770/1713.
45. *Ibid,* V.S. 1797/1740.
46. *Arhsatta pargana,* Naraina V.S. 1787/1730.
47. *Arhsatta pargana,* Chatsu V.S. 1781/1724.

48. *Arhsatta pargana,* Toda Bhim V.S. 1772/1715.
49. *Arhsatta pargana,* Udehi V.S. 1773/1716.
50. *Arhsatta pargana,* Tonk V.S. 1768/1711.
51. *Ibid,* V.S. 1794/1737.
52. *Arhsatta pargana,* Mauzabad V.S. 1789/1732.
53. *Arhsatta pargana,* Lalsot V.S. 1796/1739.
54. *Arhsatta pargana,* Malarna V.S. 1769/1712.
55. *Ibid.* v.S. 1768/1711.
56. *Arhsatta pargana,* Toda Bhim V.S. 1769/1712.
57. *Arhsatta pargana,* Chatsu V.S. 1774/1770.
58. *Ibid.*
59. *Ibid,* V.S. 1785/1728.
60. *Ibid,* V.S. 1768/1711.
61. *Ibid,* V.S. 1795/1738.
62. *Arhsatta pargana,* Malpura V.S. 1788/1731.
63. *Ibid,* V.S. 1794/1737.
64. *Ibid.*
65. *Ibid,* V.S. 1798/1741.
66. *Arhsatta pargana,* Tonk V.S. 1794/1737.
67. *Ibid.*
68. *Arhsatta pargana,* Gazi ka Thana V.S. 1824/1767.
69. *Arhsatta pargana,* Malpura V.S. 1788/1731.
70. *Ibid,* V.S. 1798/1741.
71. *Arhsatta pargana,* Malarna V.S. 1801/1744.
72. *Arhsatta pargana,* Phagi V.S. 1771/1714.
73. *Arhsatta pargana,* Bahatri V.S. 1722/1665.
74. *Arhsatta pargana,* Malarna V.S. 177/1718.
75. *Arhsatta pargana,* Dausa V.S. 1807/1750.
76. *Arhsatta pargana,* Malpura V.S. 1788/1731.
77. *Arhsatta pargana,* Tonk V.S. 1790/1733, V.S. 1796/1739.
78. *Arhsatta pargana,* Chatsu V.S. 1819/1762.
79. *Arhsatta pargana,* Bayana V.S. 1750/1643.
80. *Arhsatta pargana,* Niwai V.S. 1773/1716.
81. *Arhsatta pargana,* Lalsot V.S. 1794/1737.
82. *Arhsatta pargana,* Naraina V.S. 1813/1756.
83. Theda Skocpol, *The State and Social Revolutions: A Comparative Study of France, Russia and China,* Cambridge, 1979.
84. Samuel L. Popkin, *Rational Peasant: the Political Economy of Rural Society in Vietnam,* Cambridge, 1979.

Chapter 13

Worthies and the Worth of their Land: Revenue Farmers and the Company's State in Early Colonial Bengal

Ujjayan Bhattacharya

Farming of land revenue involves both the initiatives of the state and the intermediaries. Though the process implies a certain mode of assessment and collection of revenue that could be resorted to by either, the crucial point that has been debated by historians is the choice of social group that had been made by the state, at different times, in vesting responsibility of the management of revenues. This is borne out by historical literature that has often debated the point whether certain landed-proprietors of early eighteenth-century Bengal, had in origin been tax-farmers or not.[1] It implies that while tax-farmers operated with extremely limited objectives, the zamindars or landed proprietors functioned with broader and longer-term interests in view. This paper discusses the subject of revenue farming in the light of the institutional innovations[2] that the fledgling Company's state in Bengal attempted, in order to establish a standard of revenue assessment and pre-emp defaults in revenue payment. It also takes into account the farmer's response to the entire question of agrarian management which they had to shoulder after the contracts were made.

A General Formulation of the Problematic

Under 'ideal' conditions, revenue or tax farming would mean that the revenue farmer would agree to make a fixed payment to the government in exchange for the residual claim to any tax revenues collected above the fixed amount. Thus it would also be expected that such farms should have defined rates of transactions, which would be judicially negotiable.[3] Given the political and economic setting of Bengal in the second half of the eighteenth century, such as normal or ideal state of affairs was far from attainable.

We can draw this inference from a letter addressed to Harry Verelst by Richard Becher, the Resident at the Nawab's Darbar. The beginning of political turbulence and fiscal crisis for the state, according to Becher, dates back to the Maratha raids of the 1740s, but the deleterious condition in the economy had set in a definite manner since the early 1760s, especially with the initiation of the *amildari* system. What Becher pointed out was that though the appointment of the *amil* was made upon an agreement to pay a fixed sum, this agreement was neither based on any fixed administrative principle nor any fixed valuation or defined rates of transaction. Becher wrote:

> These aumils on their appointment agree with the Ministers to pay a fixed sum for the districts they are to go to and the man that has offered most has generally been preferr'd.[4]

Regarding the uncertainty in the rates of transactions, he pointed out the lack of fixity in evaluation modes, procedures and standards, and also the judicially non-negotiable nature of the problem:

> There is no fixed hustabood by which they [*amils*] are to collect, nor any likelihood of complaints till the poor ryot is really drove to necessity by having demanded of him [more] than he can possibly pay.[5]

It appears from the above and other accounts that the state of affairs in Bengal's agrarian society was rather unhinged as far as norms and procedures were concerned at the point of transition in the late eighteenth century. Whatever the historical causality behind such a state of affairs, the accounts of various authorities regarding the period elapsing between Murshid Quli Khan's death and 1757 describe more or less the same reality. That is, the state levied expedient taxes on the zamindars who passed that on to the entire agrarian society to tide over their fiscal crisis.[6] Also, by the 1760s the zamindars were no longer 'men of substance' or of credit from whom balances could be recovered by any means other than the 'sale of their lands'.[7]

The state of affairs does point to a considerable degree of anomie within the system, particularly during the 1760s. But in spite of a lack of conviction that the government was capable of credibly enforcing property rights, one finds that there was an increase in the propensity to acquire assets in land and revenue farms during the first two decades of the mid-eighteenth century. Much of such property was bought *benami*, probably to protect it from uncertain actions of the state or changes in political climate.[8] Families like that of the Ghoshals of Calcutta and the Nandis of Murshidabad prefaced their ventures to obtain revenue farms by substantial accumulation of landed assets, directly through purchases, to establish their reputation as men of substantial wealth, credit and goodwill in society. The Nandis had been acquiring gardens and houses since 1742, the year of Maratha invasion, when the government of the Nawab at Murshidabad and the business house of the Jagat Seth as well, were vulnerable to the attacks by Marathas.[9] From 1754 onwards the Nandis had enjoyed the close friendship with servants of the East India Company like Warren Hastings and others posted at Murshidabad and Kasimbazar and this proximity helped them to secure portfolios of political and administrative nature.[10] Such connections were even more pronounced in the case of Nabakrishna Deb of Calcutta, who, though refusing to farm the lands in Calcutta in 1766, was appointed as intendant of revenue and finances of the declining zamindaris like Nadia and Burdwan in early 1770s.[11]

Such families rose to prominence as landed-property owners through already developed institutional structures for transactions relating to landed property. But a puzzling fact is that such acquisitions of landed-property in the 1740s and 1750s, and later the offers of pre-guarantee for land-revenue farms in the 1760s were not backed by legal-institutional structures clearly defining property rights in land and credibly enforcing those. That had not yet fully evolved. The state's agreement to farm out the right of collection reciprocated by the farmers' agreement to bid for it and offer of a pre-guarantee of payment could not have rested merely on the basis of a social contract that would always be subject to the hazards of violation by the state.

It is also important to remember that the Company's state was intrusive politically and economically, and was cautious in securing its prerogative. The government imposed terms on which the farms were held, and its officials from Becher to Hastings underscored the necessity of a fixed valuation of land, or an exact *hustabood*, in conditions that were extremely fluctuating. In 1772, when farming of revenue was adopted as a general policy of revenue management, the government admitted a reserve in its favour 'for making during the course their actual lease, an exact *hustabood* ...... or a measurement of their possessions, in order to ascertain the true value at a future settlement, should the present accounts be found fallacious or concealment suspected'.[12] This meant that the state would have the power to alter settlements at any point of time. Also, the *amilnamahs* subjected the farmers to penalties if the state had reasons to believe that the farmer had disturbed the possession of the cultivator's land.[13]

These points became all the more crucial as many of the undertakers were men who had accumulated substantial capital from commerce. These were the leading families, with whose aid the early colonial state extended its base of credibility to attract further pre-guarantees for payment of land-revenue. So, the question remains: whether the Company was able to raise its credibility as ruler, de facto or de jure, during days when disturbed political conditions since Maratha raids had added to the stress of revenue burden, and, institutional structures in revenue management had come under heavy strain due operation of *amildari* system? Thus, it is important to consider the motivations from the point of view of agrarian management that accounted for the several bids to acquire revenue farms.

In the historiography of eighteenth-century Bengal, an answer to this question can be found. The answer would be that the Company's credibility ought to be understood in terms of its social and political liaison with these men, who in different capacities had rendered valuable service to the Company and its servants, in commerce as well as in politics.[14] That is to say, the Company dealt with them as a social group, whom they chose to engage with for revenue.[15] To fit this argument a more economically-oriented argument is that in the mid-eighteenth century, the traditional landlords of Bengal or the ancient territorial aristocracy was on the wane due to competition faced from outsiders. This argument traces the origin of revenue farming to exogenous causation, that is the accumulation of commercial capital and its investment in revenue management.[16]

But neither of these would be complete without seeking an explanation endogenously. For example, the first point regarding credibility has to answer why the farmers were ready to engage despite constraints and restraints, which would inevitably lead one to an enquiry into the social and economic value of landed estates to men of wealth and substance who enjoyed wide options with regard to their investments and careers. In addition, one needs to address the point regarding strategies of the state to prevent defaults, or spreading out its risk from one to many. Second, the more economically-oriented argument needs to take into consideration the changes in the economic value of land, the market value of its produces, its productivity, etc. making revenue farming a commercial proposition.

The Company's State and its Revenue Agents

The choice of social agency in the 1760s to partner the Company's fiscal business fell on the farmers of revenue due to a belief that zamindars were incapable of meeting revenue targets. Apprehensions recorded in the minutes and correspondences regarding recurrent defaults and accumulating arrears, conjures up a picture of a nervous Company on a maximisation drive. The Nizamat revenue system epitomised by the *amildari* seemed cumbersome, oppressive and prone to default. But a replacement formula was still absent. Thus the question of partnering the newly revenue business of the new acquired province remained open for some time, till new institutional strategies were worked out.

Based on the argument that relations between landed interests and the state were clearly defined only at the moment of zamindari/ permanent settlement, historical explanations have hitherto suggested that this choice inevitably fell on the farmers, as the Company was on a revenue maximisation drive, impelled by commercial and military requirements. But a second and closer look at the relation between the government and the farmers suggests that institutional strategies of the state and responses to it by the farmers played as crucial a role as the agency's social background. Though revenue augmentation was an aspect of Company's policy, the farmers were by no means constrained by this factor alone to bid and operate the revenue farms. A number of other factors played an important role regarding which various strategies had been worked out.

Such features of state–farmer relation had implications for the overall agrarian situation. We have to keep in mind an expanding agrarian economy, within which acquisition of property on a substantial scale meant a greater degree of power to control rental receipts. The other important element in this situation was the attempt by the state to put in place an institutional structure to govern the agrarian society and estimate its fiscal receipts on the basis of value of land. We can make two substantial points in this regard.

First, one does notice that the Company tried to contain the competition for bids of revenue estates as much as possible within the ambit of its knowledge and scope for action. As the farming policy evolved and took shape, the risk of revenue default spread from one to many. Thus, it could spread its net wider to bring in more farmers to make offers for engagement through the outcry method or through sealed applications.

The recurrent defaults by the zamindars in the 1760s made the Company apprehensive, and they were convinced that the problem lay in not knowing the real value of land whose revenue they were to collect.[17] It is this belief that made them choose the native agency, as farmers of revenue, but the Company did not intend to foreclose the option of intervention by transferring any degree of secure rights or status within the agrarian set-up, to the farmers. It viewed the engagement with the farmers as a settlement, more tentative than final. Rather, it intended to hold the 'ring',[18] at least in principle, in the relation between revenue farmers and the ryots.[19]

The farming settlements of lands in the 24-Parganas (also referred to as lands southward of Calcutta[20]) and Nadia show evidence of containing the competition for auction bids and risk of revenue defaults, and how it spread its net wider to bring in more farmers. In the 24-Parganas, farming of land was a fairly old issue, since Nawab Mir Jafar made the grant to the Company in 1760. The grant was made for collection of revenue that would 'equal' their requirement for maintenance of troops and other military needs, but on condition that hereditary possessions would not be disturbed.[21] After fairly detailed surveys and frequent bidding for farms between 1760 and 1766, the Company 'discovered' 'diverse tracts' of consequence to the Company's interest and also 'persons the most responsible and whose character and services merit consideration' with whom an agreement could be made, the Company found the climate favourable for renewing leases.[22] As the competitive atmosphere strengthened, with the number of bidders increasing, it seems that the Company had adopted the imperative of stimulating bids through informal channels, bypassing procedures.[23] Though this made Richard Barwell accuse the Board of breaching faith, those who lost out in the bid represented that they would have certainly won the deal had they been given an opportunity.[24] There was a confidence in the ability of the farmers to raise the required sum engaged for, in a climate of rising value of land's resources, as the Revenue Board noted, 'the most reasonable expectation of proportionable improvements in the cultivation and value of the neighbouring lands'.[25] However, of all the *parganas* let out to the farmers, four were found to be over-rated and re-let out at the Khalsa. In the case of one Calcutta farm the difference due to over-rating amounted to 25 per cent of the ultimately settled amount.[26]

The failure of the Committee of Circuit's farming settlement in Nadia by itself shows that such events were not necessarily due to the adverse agrarian impact that the policy was supposed to have created. In fact, it was not even due to the failure in discovering hidden *mofussil* resources that were supposed to have led to their eventual bankruptcy. The Collector of Nadia reported that the local moneylenders had a crucial role to play behind the defaults and accumulation of arrears:

> I have good reason to believe that all the farm except Kishnagur and Belia are in so good a state that if the present Izaradars had not appropriated the Revenue to the payment of all old debts to the merchants they would not at this time have been anything in arrears. The merchants have also been one occasion of the present balance and they have acted with extraordinary cunning and precaution. For till they received the full amount of the old loans they kept up the appearance of being as willing as ever to continue in the same practice, but they no sooner recovered their they immediately withheld their hand...[27]

Regarding the farm held by one of the farmers, Rasbeharry Chaudhury, he wrote:

> The farm is in so good state that there are many candidates for it.[28]

The Collector expressed hope that several people of Calcutta might come forward to farm the *parganas*, and he mentioned Nabakrishna Deb and Sobharam Basak as being amongst them.

In Midnapur the Company introduced the farming settlement through publication of advertisement and received offer of farming only five *parganas*, and that too at no more than 11 per cent collecton of the previous year. Moreover, due to the peculiarities of the agrarian structure the zamindars claimed a large proportion of it as current charges 'for the support of himself and family and dependants'.[29] The Collector queried:

> I beg leave to ask whether the present zamindars and talukdars of the province may be permitted to turn farmers, for if they are not there is nobody in the country to make proposals. The whole of it being into the hands of hereditary zamindars who derive their right from original sunnuds granted to their ancestors.[30]

The country, it was reported was in the same state since 1765, when an earlier attempt at farming under Clive's orders had failed.[31] Here the Company was quick to withdraw and turned the possession of lands to zamindars and talukdars on the basis of the previous year's engagement. The Board remarked: 'upon the whole... the proposals offered by the farmers are considerably [more] than the surplus revenue demanded by zamindars for the defraying expenses'.[32]

In Rajshahi the *parganas* suffered much due to droughts and inundation in 1769-70, which was followed by a period of low grain prices that made fulfilment of revenue obligations difficult.[33] The apprehension was that the yield of revenue for that and the next few years would not reach the standard of revenue that existed in the years before the famine.[34] The question was not only one of realising the value of land but also one of seeking out people who would engage with the government for payment of revenue. Deserted lands were held *khas*—and this was the situation in many neighbouring districts like Rajmahal and Rangpur—and the government's options were either to send farmers or to turn those over to the *amil* or *shikdar*.[35] Rous preferred the former mode:

> it was needless for me... to enumerate the benefits I think must accrue from letting the lands in farm, in preference to the most favourable method of collecting the revenue under the superintendency of government[36]

He expressed satisfaction at being able to 'procure farmers' to farm almost all the *parganas* of Bhaturia. However, the proposal that he sent to the Council embodied a general plan for the improvement of revenue, based on growth of cultivation, in which the central point was the extension of the years of lease that would be required to cover the deficiency or shortfall from the former standard. Ducarel formulated a similar plan for Purnea.[37]

Thus, in Rajshahi the early colonial state or its field officer acted out of very different consideration than that of those who recommended farming settlements in the 24-parganas or Nadia a few years earlier. However, the important point to note is that by 1772, the state could reckon the policy of revenue farming as an approach in dealing with the agrarian question, which had presented itself to the state mainly as a revenue problem. The state could also conceive of it as an alternative to the policies and procedures of the Nizamat.

Second, one notices that as the policy of revenue farming took shape or unfolded, the farmers, that is those who staked their and their securities money often combined or acted collectively to bargain with the state over different issues to demand deductions. Such instances, though limited, were significant as they involved issues of local importance, like inundation by rivers and maintenance of embankments or the level of grain prices. However, fortuitously perhaps, such collective representations were also occasions when important state policies having a bearing on the internal economy were enunciated. But, from the farmers' point of view, these were gradual steps to strengthen claims generally, especially as the prospect of 'discovery' of hidden assets in the *mofussil* began to emerge.

The farmers of Nadia represented in 1771 that they were at a considerable loss because the 'dutys [Sic] from every article being much decreased, that they are not able without a considerable loss to themselves to pay the rents'.[38] They complained that they suffered greatly because the duty from every article passing through the *ghat* had reduced considerably. The Supravisor, thus, cautioned the Council of the prospect of a low *sair* (non-agricultural) collection. In 1772, that is after the proclamation of the abolition of the zamindari *ghat* duties and *sair chalanta* the Burdwan farmers complained 'in a body' to the Collector that since then their rents had fallen considerably.[39] These rents also included the collections of the ground rent at *haats* and special duty on clothes called *chilkee*. The Board however stood firm on its decision regarding not granting remission of rent to Burdwan farmers as the Collector reported that their demands were heavy and unreasonable.[40] Such demands could be quite normal in the initial years of farming, as from the petitions of the Burdwan and Nadia farmers it appears that collections in the *parganas* were irregular and low. In addition, as both districts were situated close to the major arterial river, *sair* collections at the *ghats* ought to have formed a major component of the collection.[41]

Though in the cases discussed above the government did not take much cognisance of the combination of farmers and their representations, as it went against the general line of their policies, they acted with some degree of concern when it was reported to them that the farmers of Dinajpur 'in a body' had represented to the Collector that owing to a plentiful supply of grain in the markets a very low price had prevailed.[42] Thus, the ryots were not able to procure enough money to pay revenue to the farmers. This was however, a general situation prevailing all over the province[43] and to remedy its effects the government resorted to some extraordinary measures to obviate the loss of revenue. It was decided to suspend the levy of duty—collected by the government—upon grain 'to facilitate the transportation of it from the interior parts of the province' from the 1st of *poos* (15th December) to 1st of *bhadon* (14th August) and facilitate exportation of it outside the province by taking off duty at Hooghly and Murshidabad.[44] The measure was intended to facilitate the ryot in harvesting and selling the grain, and, procure the necessary amount of cash required for payment of revenues to the farmers. The period was also important for the farmers for payment of revenue to government and renewal of leases of those held on a short-term basis. The decision to lift duties was thus a major decision of the early colonial government, which immediately activated the network of internal trade in grain. Two Company servants, George Bogle and John Stuart submitted a plan for purchase of grain from ryots in northern Bengal against receipts that could be used for payment dues to farmers.[45]

In the other instance of such combination, the Collector of Burdwan reported that farmers had represented to him 'in a body' that *bunds* on the rivers had suffered or broken due to severity of rains and required urgent repair before the next swelling of river.[46] For this they requested an advance for commencement of work. They Collector strongly recommended that the advance be given to the farmers instead of the *poolbundy daroga*, and this signifies again a switchover from the methods of Nizamat. Instead, he proposed that the entire project be under the supervision of the Collector.[47]

In the petitions discussed above, it is noticeable that pleas of the farmers were urgent, that there was already a substantial balance to be paid and that the places from where such complaints originated—Dinajpur and Burdwan—were at a distance from Calcutta. This suggests that the farmers were not sure of making good their engagement even if they had a three-year lease. In cases of a year's lease or temporary leases, such pleas must have been even more urgent. However, though we find that the Company decided on its policy regarding who should be given the advance for repairs, there was no policy regarding extending the leases for such purpose. Such and other instances of the farmers' collective action and government's response had significance for the years 1772–1777 when the farmers were the main agency of revenue collection in the *mofussil* and the government had to depend on them for realising the current revenue as well as for future augmentation. After 1777, when preference for engagement shifted to zamindars, such combinations became rare.

This could possibly be because the equation in the tussle between the farmers and the government had changed by then. Combinations were useful when risk of default was spread over a number of agents who, by combining, could hold down the cost of risking a default, while the state always wanted to keep the cost high for individual defaulters by spreading the net over a number of farmers.[48] In this tussle, therefore, by resorting to combinations the farmers tried to compel the state to make compensatory allowances for the causes behind the defaults or into admitting that defaults could be possible, particularly in a situation where an idea regarding the resources in the *mofussil* was not perfect. The state on the other hand moved away by 1777 from the policy of spreading its net over numerous agents to a few on whom it could depend.

The Ghoshals as Revenue Farmers

So far, we have discussed the revenue farmers as agency of the early colonial state in its fiscal domain. They were the vehicles of implementation of Company's policies, and evidence suggests that selection of farmers was based on the amount of security that they offered, and obviously many revenue farmers were in need of securities. But the relation between revenue farmers and the state was also based on more enduring interests and over a longer span of time. The prerequisite here was an involvement in the overall administrative and economic arrangements of the Company on the part of the revenue farmer and possession of wealth or capital. Here they were not merely instruments of state policy, but collaborators in a project, which in other words can be described as implantation of a new state in Bengal.

The policy of the government regarding revenue farming and the attitudes and responses of the farmers has been reviewed in the light of the situation that shaped the economy of mid-eighteenth century Bengal. One needs to look at their role as collaborators with the early colonial state, in a distinct phase of historical transition during the late-eighteenth century. They were referred to as the new zamindars who made fortunes during 'the confused conditions of the time, say from

1760 to 1790', that 'offered ample opportunities for getting rich quick to all those who had a control over the new administrative machinery'.[49] They also acquired substantial fortunes through collaboration with the East India Company in trade and have been identified as 'fortune-makers and family-founders' in the urban setting of the new metropolis of Bengal, that is Calcutta.[50] These families were the Singhs or Sinhas of Kandi, the Nandis of Kasimbazar, the Ghoshals of Bhukailash, and the Debs of Shovabazar, and, from such viewpoints as mentioned above, these families appear to be men of substantial commercial wealth encroaching on the rural landed property from an urban perch.

Here we will focus on the Ghoshals as collaborators and rural estate managers who assiduously cultivated their rural estates as secure footholds. In fact, the family history of the Ghoshals over a century between 1750 and 1850 indicates a transitory phenomenon. Starting out as salt contractors under the monopoly of the Nizamat, they diversified their business as *banias* of an important Company official and as benefactors to many others. They continued their business in salt under the changed regime, but their prominence owed much to extensive acquisitions of landed property, which they secured not through mere investment, but through their operation as revenue managers. However, once acquired, they tenaciously held on to these possessions, through many disputes with the agrarian strata they had subordinated. In this struggle, however abject, the family displayed unity and cohesion amongst stakeholders, who were related through kinship ties, and retained the landed possessions throughout the Hastings' era, and for thirteen years beyond that.

The fortunes of the Ghoshals had soared during the lifetime of Gokul, the founder of the Bhukailash family's prosperity. He had inherited the salt business from Kandarpa, his father, and moved from Baksara near Howrah to Kidderpore in Calcutta.

Gokul's death in 1779 does not seem to have brought about any change in the good relations with the Company's government. However, in the next ten years reference to disputes between the Ghoshals and tenurial-right holders became more frequent in the proceedings of the Revenue Board and the Council and the government seemed to be adopting a more objective approach in investigating the reasons behind such disputes and in accounting the landed assets of the Ghoshal family in eastern Bengal. The Revenue Board had taken up Ghoshal's assets and liabilities for examination in 1784. The tone and the official mood, as can be gauged from these records, did not acknowledge the social standing of the family as it had been found in the records of the Controlling Council and the Superintendent of the Khalsa.

The drop in status in the 1790s seemed marginal initially, as the Ghoshal brothers displayed a rallying power to save their titles and estates by contesting other's claims. But there were signs of weakness that were visible in the records. To begin with, they were in debt, owing money to individuals like Krishnaprasad Bidyalankar, son of Joyram Panchanan. This led to the sale of land at Selimabad for the recovery of debts.[51] In 1789 the Sadar Dewani Adalat decreed that the judges of Krishnanagar, Rangpur, Islamabad (Chittagong), Moorley (Jessore), and 24-Parganas should hold under sequestration eight zamindaris located in different *tarafs* and *parganas* of these districts.[52] The judges were directed to open public advertisement 'calling upon all persons who may have claim upon the said zamindaris under mortgage deeds or otherwise, to produce to establish (before) respective Courts of adalat, on or before the 25th day of February' 1790. In the same year, a little earlier, the Collector of Chittagong reported to the Board that the revenue of *pargana* Joynagar would fall short of *jamabandi*, while Ghoshal's agent represented that it was due to the inaccuracies in the measurement papers of the *noabad* lands made by the *amin*, that had thus prevented them from making over lands to the *talukdars* who had consequently fallen in arrears.[53] The Collector of Rangpur reported to the Board in 1789 that a balance of revenue from the zamindari of pargana Coondy that the Ghoshals had purchased was irrecoverable. This purchase was 'in the name of his (Joynarayan's) guru Jagannath Bhattacharjee'. The Collector requested the Board to call upon him in Calcutta, but the Board wrote that he was 'absconding'.[54] Also, by the end of 1789 one of the constituents of the Ghoshal family, Bishnucharan, had relinquished his share of a zamindari in Chittagong for farming of revenue by the government.[55]

Around the time of Decennial Settlement the Collectors of some districts of eastern Bengal and the Revenue Board expressed concern regarding their title to property in some cases and also their balances in revenue payment. One location of their proprietary possession was *pargana* Selimabad in the Collectorate of Dacca. Here the descendants of Gokul Ghoshal were in possession of the 5 *annas* and 5 *gundahs* division, one part of which was sold in 1782 by the Collector to realise a revenue balance.[56] The other part they continued to hold through a contrivance, perhaps expeditiously, that only suggested a straitened circumstance. A balance of revenue due to embezzlement allegedly by a *naib* had accrued,[57] but the Ghoshals continued to hold on to this estate even after their sale by re-purchasing it in the name of Kashinath Choudhury.[58] With regard to this balance, the Collector and the Board initially made attempts to recover it from the 'former proprietor' in Calcutta, during whose possession the embezzlement had taken place.[59]

But finally both agreed that to liquidate another estate at 8 *anna* division of Bandarkhola to make good the amount 'collected by their agents from the current year's assets prior to the sale of their division of Selimabad at the Khalsa'.[60] Curiously, Kashinath Choudhury represented that the 'former zamindar' had not made any payment of his collections on account of revenue. But this collection which had actually been made had been retained as a part of the engagement with him by the Collector.[61] In 1791 the Roy Royan reported to the Board that the zamindari was in the possession of Ghoshals through re-purchase. It gave a sketch of the division of the Ghoshals' properties and heirs in Dacca and Chittagong. Two brothers, Ramnarain and Harinarain were entrusted with the management of the estate, of whom the former left for his zamindari in Chittagong and died there in 1790.[62] Two other brothers, Lakhsminarain and Ganganarain Ghoshal denied any involvement in the management of Selimabad estate.

Petitions from the Ghoshal brothers regarding Sundarban *taluks*—which were under the Collector of Jessore and within their zamindari of Selimabad—show how they had been able to stall alienation of property to the *talukdars*. These Sundarban *taluks*, probably on the outskirts of their holding, had been taken over by *talukdars* on the strength of *patta* granted by the Collector of Jessore. The Ghoshal brothers, describing themselves as the 'Managers of the estate of Gokul Ghoshal deceased', alleged that the three of the *patta* holders had taken over 27 villages and *haat* in the Sundarban areas, preventing the collection of revenue.[63]

One needs to look also at the fortunes or misfortunes of the Ghoshals in the overall context of the transition in British policy that came about not only through a re-formulation of administrative principles, but also a steady intrusion of their administrative mechanism into the heart of the province. In 1760, the amount of land from which revenue could be collected was uncertain. In districts like Chittagong, where the proportion of uncultivated land was high, this was a very much a matter of conjecture, because fresh assessment was necessary. Thus individuals like Gokul Ghoshal could prove their worthiness to the Company and were held in high esteem and trust for very obvious reasons. But by the time of the Decennial Settlement the policy of the Company had changed its track. It was less hinged on the question of hunt for sources that could be augmented, because over the course of thirty years that had gradually unfolded to them. It was now fastened on the question of potential for the increase of profits of cultivation. In Chittagong and Dacca the situations differed to an extent, but the overall thrust of the early colonial policy remained the same. The basic idea was to look for productive assets within a small area through measurement that could secure the *talukdar*'s profits and facilitate collection of revenue without incurring high costs. Therefore the settlement officers urged the government not to divide the zamindaris by dividing their *jama*, and 'a general measurement of the zamindari(s) be made in order that (partners) each may share equally of the productive and unproductive land.'[64] Thus while the government had to create 'distinct and compact' share for each *talukdari* partner to facilitate collection of revenue and supervision of agriculture, the mode of creating such units had to be different from the pre-colonial one.[65] The pre-colonial system had created 'exclusive' properties in the hands of zamindars like Pitambar Sen, 'whose object was to retain the exclusive possession of lands he claimed as *neej* taluks and ... hoping if the division could be prevented, to retain the exclusive management of the zamindari as the only surviving descendant of Maharaja Rajballabh.'[66] In Chittagong, such extensive and exclusive zamindaris were not the rule during the Mughal period. Conditions for that were laid only after Verelst and Gokul Ghoshal intervened.

Settlement operations for the creation of new *taluks* were in the process of implementation around the same time—1789-90—in the same region. The Board's policy with regard to *neej taluks* was that the *taluks* formed out of the estate of the partners of the estate—as for example, the Ghoshal brothers and kin— could be 'considered the exclusive property of those partners or the joint property of all'.[67] In the zamindari of Rajnagar, the estate of Rajballabh, there were claimants and counter-claimants to various portions of the estate. These zamindaris, 'contiguous to Sundarbans where a custom prevails of constituting taluks in virtue of *pottahs* from the zamindar, termed *jangalbari*...' were exposed to *batwara* and distraint of the private *taluks* 'as if the co-heirs advanced any claim thereon'. Rajchandra Sen, the *gomasta* of Pitambar Sen, represented:

> ...what representations on the part of the co-heirs that gentleman may have forwarded to the Board, I do not presume to conjecture, but he now produces an order conformable to which he declares his intention of extending the *batwara* to the private *taluks* and including them in division of the 5 co-heirs.[68]

But in the case of the Ghoshal family—in Selimabad, Chittagong or Jessore—the united stand of its members in petitions and representations saved the estates from encroachment of their rights by the settlement authorities, which in general were moving towards a settlement with *talukdars*.

Differing histories of the formation of *taluks* in the *noabad* tracts of Chittagong—the stronghold of the Ghoshals—and of that in the Sundarban tracts also gives a clue regarding the reason why the

Ghoshals could present a united front, especially in Chittagong. The key to the operation in Chittagong was Gokul Ghoshal's collaboration with the Company that gave him the virtual monopoly over *noabad* lands, and future assessment of the lands and creation of under-tenancies. In the Sundarbans, the *jangalbari taluk* holders enjoyed the land brought into cultivation as heritable property, and there were many such holders who contested other's claims. The *talukdars* and co-sharers of property of Rajnagar—Kebalram Sen, Ramkissen Sen, Kalisankar Sen and Nilmani Sen—alleged that Roy Gopalkissen who was a partner and manager of the zamindari 'caused much of the lands in Buzurgumedpore to be granted to himself in *talukdari* leases in the names of Pitambar Sen, Mahades Sen and others'.[69] Thus differential origin and the nature of *taluk* formation, compounded by a policy in favour of the *talukdars* that appeared to be equitable, could make a dent in the ancient proprietorial structure in Dacca. In Chittagong, where there was an equal, if not greater resistance by the subordinated *talukdars* to the Ghoshals' landed acquisitions, such a dent could not be created because acquisitions and titles, though of similar nature, were more recent than in the Dacca region.

We find a continuation of a similar effort in Chittagong made by the Ghoshals to preserve their titles and acquisitions. Here the involvement of the state was greater, as it was complicit in Ghoshal's acquisition of their zamindari title, and, actually the formation and foundation of the zamindari called Joynagar owed much to it. Moreover, they were, in a sense, obliged to the family, and particularly its main persona, Gokul, and his heir, Joynarayan, to ensure continuity of their patrimony, which they had tenaciously held on to for decades. The title held by Gokul and Joynarayan for the Joynagar zamindari was confirmed by a *sanad* that suppressed rights and privileges that were conferred on others by the previous regimes, and created afresh new ones that made up the patrimony of the Ghoshals.

The core of the property was the grant of *lakharaj* and *nijjot* lands, which amounted to 200 *dhones* at the measurement, and assessment of 1764. These 200 *dhones* were left un-assessed under the denomination of *nijjot*.[70] Though the Sadar Board of Revenue proposed later that it should be summarily subjected to assessment, in 1833 the Government directed that it should be considered exempt from assessment till it had been declared liable to payment of revenue after investigation. In 1842, the order was virtually repeated and land was ordered to be released free of assessment, on the estate's being finally settled and made over to the zamindars.[71]

These lands, cultivated, cleared and measured in 1764, designated *noabad*, including the lands of Joynagar *noabad* estate were held under a *sanad* of Chittagong council of 12th May 1761. In 1797, the Ghoshals were dispossessed of all their lands, rightfully held and usurped 'in consequence of the discovery of extensive usurpation by means of a forged deed'.[72] In August 1815, the Sadar Dewani Adalat decreed 'to mark off and separate and assess and settle with the Ghoshals the Joynagar *noabad* lands measured in 1764 as their property',[73] and also that the assessments on lands to be restored should bear the same proportion to the measurement made in 1126. It was further directed 'that such portion of the original lands as might not be capable of identification from the existing *chittas* of 1126 should be made up by an equal portion from the Government *noabad* lands.'[74]

From the records of the government, a general idea regarding the mode of appropriation of landed property by the Ghoshals can be made out. Gokul had the lands measured for his estate along with that of the rest of the district in 1764. But by using the *sanad* that was granted to him in a fraudulent manner, he was able to subvert the entire assessment procedure in the district that 'concerned nearly every village; in each of those villages people must have been suborned by his agents to endeavour to mislead the collector's officers respecting the land he claimed'.[75] This led to an extraordinary distribution of lands within the estate of Ghoshal that was explained later by the Commissioner in 1848 as 'parties having possessed themselves by clearing the jungle or by buying cleared spots of lands in various directions, caused such a number of those spots they farmed (?) to be measured in 1764 as one estate'.[76] Obviously, this was an enormous expansion in holding that was much beyond the intent of the original *sanad* of 1761. The Collectors of Chittagong had stated this even earlier, in 1789 and 1791. In 1789 the Collector reported to the Board that:

> since finding that major part of the claims exhibited are for annexation of certain charity lands, some of which have been long alienated from the *jama* ... obliges me to apply for your instructions on a matter of this importance which ... affect the property of a large body of individuals ... it is hardly necessary for me to acquaint the Board that the *sanad* granted by the government of Bengal in favour of Gokul Chand Ghoshal comprehends with very little exception the whole of the wastelands of this province.[77]

Ghoshal's penchant for ascertaining the charity lands and consolidating those is reflected here and in other records. In January 1789, three heirs of Gokul's property, including Joynarayan petitioned the Board to push forward their claim for *nijjot* lands in the Sandeep Island. The Collector wrote back that vast quantities of it had been secreted. He however considered himself not competent enough to determine how much of *nijjot* land they should be allowed and enjoined the Board to take a decision.[78]

The other detail that comes to light is that this *sanad* grant of 1761 and subsequent monopolisation of all *noabad* had a bearing on the hitherto existing structure of property and grants. The Collector in 1789 asked the Board whether, in 'cases where the lands shall appear to have been measured in his (Joynavain's) name .... is the *sanad* of Joynagar to supersede the *sanads* given by the Mughal government, which the proprietor neglected to produce at the time of the government?'[79] Moreover, we notice that in the case between Mirza Bakar and Joynarayan Ghoshal at Chittagong the claim of the plaintiff, Bakar was that his lands granted as charity to him by the Mughal government and one Sugdie Roy was superseded by the land acquisitions of the Ghoshals.[80] The Ghoshals made every attempt to prevent encroachment of their rights, even if it had the sanction of the state. Collector Batesman had granted *patta* to some immigrants from Arakan on the wastelands that the Ghoshals claimed were their own. The Collector had made the grant on the ground that Ghoshals had not improved or cultivated the lands or given any amount to the government. The government took a decision in their favour ordered the *naib* of one of the immigrants to represent.[81]

Finally, the *sanad* itself became the ground for contestation of rights. In 1787, the Collector enclosed a copy of the *sanad* without much doubt about its validity.[82] But in 1791 the Collector commented that 'the origin of the grant is not clear', but finally added a statement in the nature of a qualifier: 'The grantee I conceive to be in full possession of the privileges conveyed by the *sanad*, if we except some partial alienation made by former Collectors in favour of individuals'.[83] Most probably he was referring to the *patta* issued by Collector Batesman.

These were encounters with the colonial government who received numerous complaints from subordinated agrarian strata in Chittagong and adjacent Sandeep Island. These came about mainly after the first promulgation of orders respecting the Decennial Settlement. The Collector reported that on one part these complaints were from the zamindar about the difficulty he experienced in realising revenue, and on the other from individuals complaining of the grievances they suffered from inaccuracies in the measurement and assessments.[84] Similar problems with subordinated tenure holders and *talukdars* were in evidence in Sandeep Island too. Here however, as the Collector reported, the problem was the indigent circumstance of the lands, which were subjected to heavy revenue demand.[85]

Acquiring Estates: The Revenue Farmer as Collaborator

The role of farmers had an obvious connotation of collaboration with the state and that has been emphasised in historical research. This was through rendering of service and acceptance of assignments as rewards. For example, the services rendered by Gokul Ghoshal in Chittagong as the *dewan* of Harry Verelst had an obvious quid pro quo in the acquisition of the estate called Joynagar and other lands in Sandeep and Chittagong.[86] But this instance as a fact in itself neither suggests the nature of collaborative relation between the Ghoshals and Company officials, nor the earnestness with which such farmers nurtured their agrarian acquisitions. The modes of acquisition of such rewards, and that of nurturing those were far more ingenious than what would be suggested by a mere barter of services against assignments. Very often the services were rendered to a private individual, as in the case of *bania*'s services to Company servants. Sometimes these were public services too, as in the case of Gokul Ghoshal's role in assessment and collection of revenue in Chittagong on the occasion of its takeover by the Company in 1760 under Harry Verelst.[87] But, while men like Gokul Ghoshal were quick to realise the economic potential of their agrarian assignments and acquired as much as they could, the Company assisted their ventures with sufficient legal cloaks, unless stretched beyond the limits set by their own norms. Through these processes of rapid accumulation of revenue assignments and proprietorial holdings, and vexed and long-drawn deliberations at the Councils and Board, which brought about surprising disclosures, a commitment or a stake in the acquired resources took shape. This is probably best reflected in the fact that even after admitting that the *sanad*, by which the Ghoshals had acquired *noabad* lands in Chittagong, was a fraud and that they had manipulated the rates of assessment of land-revenue to their advantage at the time of acquisition of Chittagong by the Company, the Dewani Adalat recognised their proprietorial rights.[88]

Such collaboration worked itself out as the historical process of the consolidation of the Company's rule.

The initial accumulation of property came about during the period of Gokul Ghoshal's Chittagong assignment. During this phase one notices a marked emphasis on acquiring titles to property and protecting those with claims of purchase. These were settled estates with definite sale prices, and the purchase of those placed him in a position to bargain for revenue collecting rights in an extensive manner. This in turn allowed him to encroach on more settled estates.

Gokul Ghoshal purchased the *taluk* or *turuff* of Krishnaram Majumdar in the *pargana* of Bhuluah in 1762.[89] He defended the acquisition of the *taluk* by right of purchase based on a bill of sale.[90] He stated that until 1772 he had paid revenue to the *wadadar*. It also appears from the records that Ghoshals in partnership with Brijoo Dalal, a commercial magnate of Dacca, became the Naibs of the zamindari of

Husthhazary in the same *pargana* of *sarkar* Sonargaon.[91] However, the turning point came about with the appointment of the Ghoshals as *wadadar* in 1773.[92] By this time, the association of the Ghoshals with Company's officers had also thickened. The petition of the Chaudhuries of Bhuluah in 1776 stated that in the Bengal year 1180 or 1772-73, Richard Barwell, the Chief of the Provincial Council of Dacca 'contrary to all justice found means to alienate the *turuff* of Gopalnagar and *talook* of Kishenram, Daulut Roy, Ramballabh, Perwish Mahomed and many others.... and erected them under the title of Joynagar into an independent estate'.[93]

The method by which the Ghoshals acquired lands in Bhuluah was very ingenious. Subsequent to obtaining the *turuff* of Gopalnagore, Gokul Ghoshal purchased land on a number of occasions between the years 1765-66 and 1771-72. The sale prices ranged between Rs.15 and Rs.3001.[94] This gave Gokul Ghoshal an advantage as landholder in the area and allowed him to step in as *wadadar* of Chowdahazary.[95] From then onwards, he procured, very rapidly—as the records show—13 *taluks* with a total *jama* of Rs. 20,890, but paid into the *sadar cutcherry* less than half of the assessed amount as revenue collection. Subsequently he transferred the responsibility or burden of meeting this balance on the *mofussil talukdars* of the *pargana*, by obtaining a government order for separation of a part of the revenue assessed on him from Bhulua to Dacca. Thus he could subsequently dispossess the *talukdars* on whom 'consequently an additional burthen' fell. In December 1775, Ducarel, the Superintendent of Khalsa noted:

> He had possessed himself of more land than the amount of his purchases allowing them to be valid vizt. that he has purchased only 2 talooks under cover of which he possessed 53, and further that he has brought the ½ of another talook on pretence of which he has possessed himself of the whole of it.[96]

It is possible that such modus operandi in *taluk* acquisition could work because the dimensions of the estates and the value of land therein were undetermined. This can be gauged from the representations made by the zamindars of Husthhazary and Chowdahazary:

> ....it is the custom of the pargana and those adjacent for the zamindars to grant proportions of their lands in talooks by pottahs either for the support of their family or dependents or as is most common to induce people bring the waste and jungle lands of the zamindari into cultivation. For this last purpose they are generally held for the first two or three years free of rent, afterwards made subject to pay their proportion of the general rent of the pargana.... The talooks are inheritable by the family of the grantee but cannot be alienated from the zamindari without the consent of the zamindar...[97]

At Bhuluah in 1787, the complaints against Gokul Ghoshal were thus: (a) as *wadadar* he had 'by ill treatment of several talookdars compelled them to sell their land' without the consent of the zamindars; (b) under the pretext of purchases he had usurped much more land in the *pargana* than the amount of the purchases themselves; (c) had alienated those lands from the zamindari, formed a separate zamindari of them and obtained a *sanad* for it[98], and (d) for such lands as thus acquired he did not pay his proportion of the general rent of the zamindari by which means the burden fells so much heavier on the remaining portion.

The modus operandi of acquiring land and the title to it was different in areas where revenue potentials of lands were not assessed, or where the task of initial assessment was left to Gokul Ghoshal. This happened in Chittagong, where he acquired *noabad* lands, that Gokul Ghoshal was taking advantage of this rather fluid nature of assessment and indeterminacy is apparent from the Collector of Chittagong's letter in 1787 about the Joynagar zamindari:

> It is not possible to acquaint the Board of Revenue with the present state of the zamindari as it has not been completely measured or surveyed since 1132 Muggy, since which 16 years have elapsed. Doubtlessly in this time much land has been brought under cultivation and profits thereof enjoyed by the zamindar without further demand made on him by the government. A thorough investigation should be made into the state of the zamindari by a general survey and measurement of lands, which have not been assessed, may be brought into account.[99]

The lands held by Ghoshal were described by the Collector as *beet kholah, madut kholah, janglah, charbastah, omed chur,* and *juljullah* and could occur anywhere within the *jaidah* [*Jaidad*] or the surveyed area, and could remain outside the assessment or *jama*.[100] The state of these lands were described in the *sanad* granted to Gokul Ghoshal by Harry Verelst:

> that for the improvement of lands, the woody waste and fallen to decay or *charbustee* unincluded in the *jamabandi* and those already granted, situated in the parganas according to *chakbandi*, contained in the *sanad* of the chowdhury are given under the name of the district of Joynagar to Gee Narain Ghoshal.... He will according to agreement bring the new cultivated lands within the *jamabandi*.

The role of the Ghoshals as agrarian proprietors initially and primarily derived from Gokul's official role as the native assistant to the Company's regime. In this capacity, he was laying down the format for future *jamabandi* and revenue administration of Chittagong, and acting as a buffer between a turbulent peasantry and the new regime of the Company.

The country was exposed to incursions and violence, which had an impact on land settlements and revenue collection. The Collector reported that men of means did not settle in the district and thus 'needy' persons on application to 'men in office' procured charity grants for such lands whose cultivation had declined.[101] Many parts of the province were also held with a view to repel the attacks of the enemy.[102] The Nizamat had attempted to raise the pitch of assessment here, with no definite results, and since the Company's first settlement in the district in 1761, the assessment remained high but steady till 1766, though not even in one instance it was realised.[103] But, since 1767 the rate of assessment increased leading to an addition of rent to the total assessed figure.[104] The Company officials stationed in Bengal reported to the Court of Directors that lands cleared since 1760 were considerable and had begun to pay rent. However, the new settlement and imposition of demand brought about a violent reaction from the existing proprietors of land, and the assessed amount could scarcely be collected without pacifying the countryside.

In this pacification drive, the role played by Gokul Ghoshal was to settle the question of revenue collection within the *jamabandi* area of the district, particularly where resistance was high. Resistance was encountered at Sandeep under the leadership of Malkhan Singh, who, according to Sandeep zamindars, was a tenure-holder and head of corps established for the protection of the country.[105] Nizamat and Company officials, however, called him a free-booter.[106] The zamindars who combined against the intrusions made by Ghoshal and his agents for the purpose of collection of revenue were Abu Jerab Chowdhury, Muhammad Bakhar Chowdhury, Muhammad Knawf (?) and Jaffir Chowdhury.[107] Their combined resistance was broken through an application of force and persuasion to draw them into the more institutionalised channel of grievance redressal before the Committee of Circuit at Dacca in 1772. The complaints against Ghoshal were similar to the ones discussed earlier. First, that the *talukdaris* were usurped and the *talukdars* displaced under the pretence of bringing lands under *jamabandi*. The second complaint was that Bishnu Charan Ghoshal, having obtained the *wadadari* of the district, wrote out *brahmottar sanads* in the name of his brother for some lands, seized them and send agents to collect more than the stipulated rent. Encroachment on the rights of the revenue-free landholders was another area of tussle between the revenue farmer and the landholding strata in many parts of the province.[108]

Between 1772 and 1787, the tide of fortune turned away from the Ghoshals. But, they had their patrimonial inheritances scattered over the province as valued landed property. They were, thus, in a sense revenue farmers at large, operating across the length and breadth of the province. His properties in Selimabad *pargana* of Dacca, Sandeep of

Chittagong and Palaspai in Burdwan were substantial in 1790. Gokul thus attempted to entrench his property wherever he could, leaving for posterity substantial inheritances. The only problem was that he did not create this property merely through the institutional channels that the colonial state was attempting to put in place, but instead believed that state patronage and wealth could be used to create rightout claims over property. He however tried to maintain the procedural forms.

Comparisons can be made between Gokul Ghoshal and Krishnakanta Nandi, both having been contemporaries and engaged in similar endeavour of creating landed estates. However, the Nandis created property in the more densely populated regions of the province where landed estates were already in existence, for example, in the Murshidabad district. In contrast, Gokul created property in rather sparsely populated regions where the value of land had to be ascertained first, be it in Dacca, Chittagong or Burdwan.[109] Nabakrishna Deb was a frequent collaborator of Gokul as surety, which is evident from the records relating to Gokul's acquisitions in Burdwan.[110]

List of abbreviations used:

BRP – Proceedings of the Board of Revenue
CCDa – Proceedings of the Committee of Circuit at Dacca.
PCCRM – Proceedings of the Controlling Council of Murshidabad
PRBWC – Proceedings of the Revenue Board of the Whole Council
PKSR – Proceedings of the Suprintendent of the Khalsa Records
RD: GGinC – Revenue Department: Governor-General in Council
SCP – Select Committee Proceedings

REFERENCES

1. Jadunath Sarkar,*The History of Bengal Vol.II, Muslim Period 1200–1757*, pp. 408–17. This point was contested by Abdul Karim, *Murshid Quli Khan and his Times*, Dacca, 1963, p. 92.
2. The idea that the farming settlements were institutional innovations was first discussed by Binay Bhushan Chaudhuri, in Dharma Kumar (ed.), *Cambridge Economic History of India,* Vol. II, Cambridge, 1982, p. 91.
3. Noel Johnson, 'Banking on the King: The Evolution of Royal Revenue Farms in Old Regime France' (Draft), Washington University, Economics Department.
4. Select Committee Proceedings, 24th May 1769, quoted in W.K. Firminger, Introduction to the *Fifth Report from the Select Committee of the House of Commons,* Calcutta, 1917, pp. clxxvi-clxxvii.
5. However, fixity of tenures or transaction rates between the state and its agents were not the exact problems that Becher was addressing. These, very crucial points no doubt, came up while he was addressing a more

vexed question of the late 18th century, that is the down-turn in the economy since the early 1760s, and the perceived drop in the credibility of governments—the Nizamat under Mir Kasim, the Company under successive Governors, and the joint rule—that made 'zamindars, shroffs, merchants etc.', as Becher put it, unreliable partners in the revenue administration of Bengal. The point of comparison regarding the drop in credibility was the government under Alivardi Khan, when revenue was more forthcoming into the treasury 'even under arbitrary government and at a time when a large tract of it was for years together invaded by the Morattoes (Marathas), who burnt and destroy'd all they could come at, the poor inhabitants flying for shelter to the principal cities, European factorys etc.' Firminger, *Fifth Report*, p. clxxvii.

6. John Shore, *Fifth Report from the Select Committee on the Affairs of the East India Company, Appendix No.1,* Minutes dated 18th June 1789, para 37 in Firminger (ed.) *Fifth Reprint*, Vol. II.
7. Hastings, RD: GGinC, 22nd April 1775, his observations were made in 1775, but pertained to the conditions prevailing in the 1760s. The term 'sale of lands' actually refers to public auction of their estates.
8. S.C. Nandee, *Life and Times of Cantoo Baboo,* Calcutta, 1978, pp. 9, 10, 11,19.
9. *Ibid*, pp. 9–10.
10. Committee of Circuit at Kasimbazar, 7th August 1772, Krishnakanta Nandy executed the official responsibility of receiving financial statements from the Nizamat regarding their arrears on behalf of the Company.
11. Select Committee Proceedings, 26th August 1766, Nabakrishna Deb's deposition regarding the Treaty of Restitution. He was a *moonshy* to Clive and also close to the Nawab; SCP, 29th August 1766, in this deposition he stated that in 1763 he was with Company's army in the service of Major Adams, a *faujdar* in 1764, and a go-between amongst Mir Jafar, Vansittart, Hugh Tinker and other officials.
12. Letter from Hastings to the Committee of Circuit, 3rd November 1772, in Firminger, *Fifth Reprint,* Introduction, p.ccxvii.
13. Committee of Circuit at Krishnanagar 10th–28th June 1772, *amilnamahs* to the farmers of Nuddeah.
14. The origin of this argument is in the British records, which greatly focused—perhaps expectantly—on men of wealth in the commercial world to play role in revenue management. But, later this was turned into a general nationalist critique of the policies of the Hastings' period. See N.K. Sinha, *Economic History of Bengal,* Vol. II, Calcutta, 1968. It can be said originally it began with R.C. Dutt.
15. Binay Bhushan Chaudhuri, *Cambridge Economic History of Bengal,* Vol. II. p. 91, Chaudhuri's argument expanded the space of a rather narrow argument.
16. Ranjit Sen, 'Landlords of Calcutta in early Colonial Period', *Bengal Past and Present,* Vol. cvii, 1988.
17. This point makes it appearance in most correspondences between the Company authority in Bengal and the Court of Directors.
18. P.J. Marshall discussed the idea that the Company was holding the ring between ryots and the zamindar.

19. The Company's posture was always pro-ryot. Evidence of this can be found in the concern expressed by them for the ryots and under-tenants rights while farming lands in the 1760s, Public Proceedings (PP) 11th June, 1759; PP 26th September 1759; PP 20th August 1767.
20. Mentioned in Richard Becher's minutes as Muragatcha and Azimabad, SCP, 24th April 1758.
21. *Ibid*, 4th January 1758, this was the beginning of what Holwell described as the 'hunt' for revenue.
22. *Ibid*, 4th November 1766.
23. PRBWC, 27th October 1772, Petition of Jagatram Das.
24. *Ibid*, petition of Jagmohan Gose.
25. *Ibid*, Barwell's minutes 15th October 1772.
26. *Ibid*, Superintendent of the Khalsa's minutes, 20th November 1772.
27. *Ibid*, Letter from Collector of Nadia, 24th November 1772.
28. *Ibid*, Letter from Collector of Nadia, 24th November 1772.
29. *Ibid*, Proceedings of the Board, 30th October 1772.
30. *Ibid*, Letter from Collector of Midnapur, 4th November 1772.
31. *Ibid*, Enclosure in the letter dt. 4th November 1772, letter from Mr. Graham to the Select Committee dated Midnapur 14th September 1765.
32. *Ibid*, 30th October 1772, Minutes of Proceedings.
33. PCCRM, 14th December 1771, Bhaturia was the most affected hoodah (a revenue circle) and Rous was reporting to the Controlling Council about the farming settlement here.
34. *Ibid*, 30th November 1771.
35. *Ibid*, 6th November 1770.
36. *Ibid*, 30th November 1771.
37. For a discussion on Rous' and Ducarel's measures and principles on which the measures were based, see Ranajit Guha, *A Rule of Property for Bengal*. However, Guha's contention was that Rous had rejected the farming system.
38. PCCRM, Letter from Supravisor of Nadia, 3rd December 1771.
39. PRBWC, Letter from Collector of Burdwan, 1st December 1772.
40. *Ibid*, Letter from Board to the Collector of Burdwan 1st December 1772; Letter from Collector of Burdwan, 22nd December 1772.
41. BRP, 15th April 1790, Letters and enclosures from Collector of Burdwan.
42. PRBWC, Letter from Collector of Dinajpur, 17th November 1772.
43. PCCRM, letter from Supravisor of Rajshahi, 14th December 1771; PRBWC, Board to Collectors of Purnea, Burdwan and Chief of Patna, 17th November 1772.
44. *Ibid*.
45. For details of the plan, see *Ibid*, 24th November 1772.
46. *Ibid*, Letter from Collector Burdwan, 1st December 1772.
47. *Ibid*.
48. An interesting case of collective action by the farmers to demand revenue abatement for inundation and changes in the course of the river—*nadee shikast* and *balloo parah*—occurs in 1773 when Gokul Ghoshal, a high-profile farmer, joined a host of others. Gokul had a number of farms,

many of which had accrued balances as he had defaulted time and again but was able to avoid penal action because of his connections with high officials, PRBWC, 14th September 1773.

49. Binay Bhushan Chaudhuri, 'Land Market in Eastern India, 1793–1940 Part II: The Changing Composition of the Landed Society', *IESHR*, Vol. 12, no. 1, Jan–March 1975, p. 140.
50. Pradip Sinha, *Calcutta in Urban History*, Calcutta 1978; For evidence regarding *bania-ship* and collaboration in Company officer's private trade, see P.J. Marshall, *East Indian Fortunes: The British in Bengal in the Eighteenth century*, Oxford, 1976.
51. BRP, 20th July 1789.
52. *Ibid*, 24th December, 1789.
53. *Ibid*, 30th November, 1789.
54. *Ibid*, 29th June 1789, Vol. 71, part II, Letter from Collector of Rangpur, and the Board's resolution.
55. *Ibid*, 28th December 1789.
56. *Ibid*, 16th June 1790, Petition of Kalishankar zamindar of 2 *anna* 17 *gundah* division of Selimabad.
57. *Ibid*, 18th March 1790, Vol. 86, Report on the Balances of the Towjee accounts of the districts of Bengal.
58. *Ibid*, 4th July 1791, Vol. 115 part I, Roy Royan's report on embezzlement in 5 anas 15 gundahs division of Selimabad.
59. *Ibid*, 22nd February 1790, Letter from Collector of Dacca, and Letter to Collector of Dacca, and BR resolution.
60. *Ibid*, 22nd February 1790 and BRP, 21st May 1790.
61. *Ibid*, 8th April 1789, Vol. 89, Petition from Kashinath Choudhury zamindar of 5 *annas* 15 *gundahs* of *pargana* Selimabad.
62. *Ibid*, 4th July 1791, Bol. 115, part I, Roy Royan's report on embezzlement in 5 *anas* 15 *gundahs* division of Selimabad.
63 *Ibid*, 13th January 1789, Petition from Joynarayan, Ramnarayan, and Harinarayan Ghoshal; BRP, 4th May 1789, Letter from Commissioner of Dacca and Letter from BR to Collector of Jessore; BRP 18th June 1789, Letter from Collector of Jessore.
64. *Ibid*, 24th November 1790, Letter from Mr. Thompson to William Douglas, Collector of Dacca. Thompson argued that if the division of the landed property was done by dividing the *jama*, there would be great inequality. If the amount payable to the zamindar by the *talukdar* was fixed, many objections would come up because 'the talukdar had no other funds than the produce of his lands for the discharge of revenue.... Thus the ability of the taluk to pay such a revenue ought to be ascertained first because in the event of a failure the partner in whose share he may be placed would be made responsible for his deficiency; and ...ascertainment of the present assets of the taluk alone will not suffice, the quality and extent of the land are requisite considerations, ...as future improvement depends much on the character and disposition of the talukdar.' Where the revenue is not fixed and the *talukdars* possess the land under various tenures, 'all derived from their zamindars or their predecessors' a annual measurement is

necessary to enable the zamindar to ascertain his just due and where a period of 30 years have elapsed since the last measurement was done.

65. *Ibid*, There were obstacles to government's plan of dividing the zamindaris of Buzurgumedpore, Rajnagar and Kartikpur because of inheritances from past. Mr. Thompson, the settlement officer reported that the subdivisions of the *pargana* was so scattered, that there was scarcely a *taluk* which was not composed of small parcels of land lying in different situations at a distance from each other and inter-mixed with other *taluks*.
66. *Ibid*.
67. *Ibid*, 24th November 1790.
68. *Ibid*, 21st September 1791, Petition from Rajchandra Sen.
69. *Ibid*, 21st September 1791, Letter from Collector of Dacca.
70. *Correspondences of the Settlement of Noabad Lands in the District of Chittagong* (henceforth *Correspondences)* p. 8.
71. *Ibid*, p. 8.
72. *Ibid*, pp. 6, 33–34.
73. *Ibid*, p. 2.
74. *Ibid*, p. 3.
75. *Ibid*, p. 6, The Commissioner noted that the rates of assessments established in 1848 were fictitious, as most proprietors held more land than had been measured.
76. *Ibid*, p. 34.
77. BRP, 4th May, 1789, Letter from Collector of Chittagong.
78. *Ibid*, 3rd April, 1789, Letter from Collector of Chittagong.
79. *Ibid*, 4th May, 1789, Letter from Collector of Chittagong.
80. *Ibid*, 11th March, 1791, Letter from Collector of Chittagong.
81. *Ibid*, 14th May, 1789, Petition from Ramkanta Chowdhury *vakil* of Joynagar zamindar.
82. *Ibid*, 30th January, 1787, Letter from Collector of Chittagong.
83. *Ibid*, 6th May 1791, Letter from Collector of Chittagong.
84. *Ibid*, 29th July 1791, Letter from Collector of Chittagong.
85. *Ibid*, 19th May 1790 and BRP, 13th January 1789, Petition of Joynarayan, Ramnarayan and Harinarayan Ghoshal.
86. The conferment of the *sanad* of the *chaudhury*-ship of Joynagar to Gokul Ghoshal is practically in the nature of a proclamation, which is rather conspicuous because in 1763 it was too early for them to issue it in that style.
87. This instance can be compared to the services rendered to Warren Hastings by Krishna Kanta Nandy, or to the services rendered by Nabakrishna Deb to Robert Clive.
88. *Correspondences on Noabad,* p. 35.
89. RD: GGinC, 2nd October 1776.
90. In practically all representations to the government, the Ghoshals and their *vakils* defended their right to the *taluks* on the basis of the bill of sale.
91. PSKR, 3rd and 4th January 1776, Petition of Narnarain Chaudhury states that Gokul and Brijoo undertook the station of Naib of his zamindari in the names of Joynarayan, nephew of the former and Nandkishore, son of

the latter. The petition of Gokul Ghoshal states that zamindars of Bhuluah (?) entreated them to take *naib*-ship because they were not able to pay the rents.

92. PSKR, 4 December 1775, Gokul procured the *wadadari* in the name of his servant Kirparam.
93. RD: GGinC, 2nd October 1776; PSKR, 5th January 1776.
94. RD: GGinC, 29th October 1776, most of these lands were purchased in Joynarayan Ghoshal's name and a few in the name of Haranarayan Ghoshal.
95. PSKR, 29th January 1776.
96. *Ibid*, 4 December 1775.
97. *Ibid*, 29th January 1776.
98. *Ibid*, 4th January 1776, the *vakil* of Ghoshal delivered in a copy of a *sanad* under the seal of the *Qazi*, received at Dacca, creating him zamindar of the lands in dispute—"the chowdrieship of Gopalnagar and the and the talooks of Kishen Narain Ram having been purchased by Joynarain have been since the year 1180 B.S. agreeable to the endorsation on the back of the present deed separated from the pargana and having obtained the appellation of Joynarayan has been appointed chowdhury thereof'.
99. BRP, 30th January 1787, Vol. 9.
100. *Ibid*, also petition from Ramsaran Ghosh BRP, 4th May 1789, Vol. 67 part I.
101. *Ibid*, 9th January 1789, Letter from Collector of Chittagong, Vol. 58 part II.
102. *Ibid*, also 4th May 1789, Letter from Collector of Chittagong, Vol. 67, part I.
103. *Ibid*, also 14th May 1789, petition from vakil of Gokul Ghoshal.
104. *Ibid*.
105. Proceedings of the CCDa Arzee from zamindars of Sandeep, 13th October 1772.
106. *Ibid*, Representation of Muhammad Tahir, *vakil* of Gokul Ghoshal, 4th November 1772.
107. *Ibid*, Representation of Muhammad Tahir, 14th November 1772.
108. BRP, 31st January 1791, Letter from Collector of Jessore, reports decline of the *jama* since 1772 and farmers's oppression; see also 30th July 1789, vol. 73 (2).
109. For reclamation of wasteland by Gokul in Burdwan, see representation of Bhowanicharan Mitra, *dewan* of Burdwan 27th September 1773, PRBWC, 1st October 1773.
110. *Ibid*, 30th July 1773; PRBWC, 23rd November 1773.

Chapter 14

Was there Capitalism in Early Modern India?

Prasannan Parthasarathi

INTRODUCTION

One of Harbans Mukhia's greatest contributions to medieval Indian history was his essay 'Was there Feudalism in Indian History?' Published in the *Journal of Peasant Studies* in 1981, the article launched a major debate with responses to the essay coming from the pens of many prominent medievalists, including Irfan Habib, Burton Stein, R.S. Sharma, Frank Perlin, Chris Wickham, and others.

In the essay, Mukhia defined feudalism in Europe as a set of social relations in which the peasant was unfree in economic terms. For Mukhia, the free peasant was one 'who, quite independently of his social or juridical status, earns his and his family's subsistence off his own (including his family's) material resources and labour.' The free peasant, in other words, 'does not render labour to any one else either in performances of labour services or for wages.' (p. 275) In medieval Europe, peasants were not free in this sense. As a consequence, the labour potential of the European peasant household 'was always in excess of the resources on which it could be fully expended.' (p. 275) This excess supply of labour enabled the feudal lord to have access to workers for the cultivation of his demesne. As Mukhia put it: 'non-economic coercion by the feudal lords, then, consisted of a system of exploitation of the structural labour surplus, or excess of the labour potential of the peasant family over its resources.' (p. 276)

The combination of an unfree peasantry and the severe technical constraints under which agriculture operated bequeathed to European feudalism a dynamics for change, which culminated in the rise of capitalism. The unfree status of peasants created dynamism because peasants were forced to devote a portion of their labour time to the lands of lords and away from their own fields. This laid the foundation for a 'silent class struggle . . . in the actual process of tilling the soil' between lord and peasant. (p. 276) The other source of dynamism was the severe technical deficiencies of medieval European agriculture, which led to enormous pressures for agricultural innovation and improvement. Superior agricultural performance was achieved through technological breakthroughs in implements, manuring, and cultivation practices. Although the dynamic of change was by no means continuous or uninterrupted, by late medieval times European agriculture was certainly on a very different footing, with greater technical capabilities and the beginnings of new social relations on the land, according to Mukhia.

From this understanding of feudalism in Europe, Mukhia rejected its appropriateness for medieval India for two reasons. First, agriculture in medieval India was conducted on the basis of a free peasantry, which meant that the dynamics of conflict between lord and peasant was not found in the Indian subcontinent. This was not meant to imply that the Indian countryside was free of conflict, but rather that the lines of tension lay between peasant and state. Second, medieval Indian agriculture was far more productive than European, with efficient tools, sophisticated cultivation practices, and climatic conditions for double and even triple cropping. These differences between Europe and India lent great structural stability to agricultural society in the subcontinent:

> The characteristics of agrarian history discussed above—high fertility of land, low subsistence level and free peasant production—also explain the relative stability of India's social and economic history. It is, after all, true that there has hardly been any concentrated social effort caused by acute social tensions to change completely the means, the methods and the relations of production. . . In India, unlike Europe, there appears to have been no prolonged and acute scarcity either of labour or production; the routine increase in demand could perhaps have been met by the routine extension of agriculture. (p. 292)

Further contributing to the relative stability of medieval India was the absence of 'acute social tensions which might have necessitated significant changes in the entire system of production. The conflicts that characterised the economic history of pre-British India were conflicts over the distribution and redistribution of the surplus rather than over a redistribution of the means of production, which had changed the face of the medieval European economy.' (p. 293)

Mukhia's reconstruction of medieval social relations and agricultural conditions, both European and Indian, brilliantly showed the limited applicability of European historical categories to Indian conditions. It also provided an analytic framework that explained the dynamism of Europe and the stability of India, but did this without falling prey to special constructs for the Indian case, including some time worn categories such as the Asiatic mode of production. In reaching such a conclusion, Mukhia is in agreement with Irfan Habib who, because of these very conceptual difficulties in categorising India, has settled upon the neutral phrase 'Indian medieval economy' in a discussion of north India in the period of the Delhi Sultanate. In a similar vein, Irfan Habib has also rejected the label of capitalism for a later period, specifically the sixteenth and seventeenth centuries when north India was under the political rule of the Mughals, but we will have more to say about these arguments about capitalism shortly.[1]

CAPITALISM AND EARLY MODERNITY

Despite Harbans Mukhia's and Irfan Habib's conclusions on the limited applicability of European categories to the Indian past, in the last two decades there have been several historians who have attached the label capitalism to the three centuries between 1500 and 1800. Frank Perlin has argued for the use of proto-capitalism to describe pre-colonial India on the grounds that 'it avoids the dualist assumption that India, or any other region, must have possessed economies of a different order from those in which capitalism was generated.'[2] Christopher Bayly has pointed to a profound social transformation in the eighteenth century, in which 'the petty kings, the revenue and military entrepreneurs, the great bankers and warrior peasant lords of the villages' of the subcontinent 'all represented forms of indigenous capitalism.'[3] And David Washbrook has insisted that 'in a great many ways, South Asia was involved in 'the social history of capitalism' from a very early period and underwent many of the same types of social development as those taking place in Western Europe.'[4]

The use of capitalism to describe the social and economic changes in these centuries stems from three major developments in medieval history writing. First, there is growing discomfort with the longstanding periodisation of Indian history, with a medieval period stretching somewhere from the eighth or ninth centuries to the rise of British power in the closing decades of the eighteenth century. Second, there is also discomfort with the view of long-term stability that Mukhia so well described and greater emphasis is being placed on very far-reaching changes in the social and economic world of the Indian subcontinent after 1500, most critically, it would seem, a long and sustained commercial boom. These changes also presaged the development of an indigenous Indian 'modernity.' Finally, a number of historians, building upon these changes that overtook many parts of India from the sixteenth century, are viewing India, not as the 'other' of Europe which constructions such as the Asiatic mode of production imply, but as having experienced historical developments that ran in parallel with the changes overtaking Europe in these centuries.

To describe the economic and social order that emerged in India between 1500 and 1800 as capitalist, however, raises a number of problems that are familiar to many historians. One that has been perennial and seems particularly intractable is the correct, or even acceptable, definition of capitalism. The protagonists in this definitional debate may be divided roughly into two camps. The first, conforming closely to the usage of Marx and Engels defines capitalism as a system of generalised commodity production in which labour itself is a commodity, to be bought and sold in return for wages. The second, while acknowledging the importance of the commodification of labour, writes perhaps more in the spirit of Marx and tends to focus on markets and exchange in its definition of capitalism. The most prominent exponent of this approach in recent years has been Immanuel Wallerstein and his followers within the world systems theory, who see the essence of capitalism as production for profit in a market system.

Although there has not been much engagement with these debates on how to define capitalism, the historical work that categorises early modern India as capitalist focuses predominantly upon markets and exchange, with far less research undertaken on labour and class relations. Frank Perlin, for instance, has devoted much scholarly energy to describing and analyzing the development of money use. Similarly, Christopher Bayly portrays class formation, especially the emergence of powerful merchant groups across the subcontinent as a product of widening commercial networks and the accumulation of financial resources that accompanied this process. It is upon this basis that Bayly and Sanjay Subrahmanyam have argued for a transformation in the nature of the state after 1500, with a growing interpenetration of commercial interests and political power. According to their research on north and south India, political authorities entered the sphere of commerce, using political power to support their trading ventures, and commercial figures translated their economic clout into political power, especially by becoming key players in revenue collection.[5]

Some historians would dismiss this characterisation of early modern India as capitalist on the grounds that commerce is insufficient to define capitalism as a mode of production. The complex and contentious debate over this question may be sidestepped, however, by observing that even from the point of view of labour, although this is a topic that has not received as much attention as markets and money, that as late as the eighteenth century there are important parallels between the Indian and European systems and conditions of labour. Even in Britain, widely acknowledged to have been the most advanced capitalist economy in Europe, the social relations in which labourers found themselves possess more than a passing resemblance to those found in the Indian subcontinent.

As an ideal type, capitalism severs the connection of the producer to the means of production and creates a new social class, the proletariat, the members of which own nothing but their ability to work, in other words their labour-power. In reality, however, the conditions of eighteenth-century Britain were far from this ideal type. In both agriculture and in manufacturing, large numbers of workers continued to possess property rights of various sorts. In the British countryside, there were still large numbers of peasants who survived by cultivating small holdings of arable land and by exploiting the resources of the commons.[6] Similarly, in manufacturing, large numbers in eighteenth-century Britain continued to own their means of production, exerted enormous control over the organisation of work, working either in their homes or in small workshops, and received not a market-determined wage but a customary payment for their efforts.[7] These conditions of ownership and work were broadly similar to those in the Indian subcontinent.

Yet what was different in eighteenth-century Britain was the direction of change in the position and conditions of labourers, and in this respect there were profound differences between Britain and India. First, although the majority of British workers were still not wage-labourers, the property rights that British labourers possessed had been far reduced in comparison with previous centuries. In other words, many of their rights were beginning to appear vestigial by the late eighteenth century as they had been substantially hacked down from what had existed until even fairly recently. Of course, this process of hacking would continue into the nineteenth century, when a more fully proletarianised workforce emerged in Britain. Second, the setting of wages was increasingly being turned over to the market and the forces of supply and demand as opposed to custom, a process that was accompanied by a great deal of state violence and coercion. Finally, the autonomy and independence of the worker was giving way to new systems of work organisation that gave employers more control. Peter Linebaugh has brilliantly analyzed many of these changes.[8]

In the Indian subcontinent, by contrast, what is striking is the relative stability in social relations after 1500. Although there was certainly a very extensive commercialisation of life, there are no signs of change towards a system of wage labour. In fact, in the Indian case, the commercialisation of life may have strengthened the positions of labourers—the peasants, artisans, dependent cultivators, and others who worked with their hands and bodies—as the demand for their services soared in the sixteenth, seventeenth and eighteenth centuries. Therefore, commercialisation had very different outcomes in Europe and the Indian subcontinent with respect to working people and class relations.

Another significant difference between the two regions of the world has to do with the revolution in the means of production that took place in Europe, most markedly in Britain, in the eighteenth century. The spread of new technologies and the diffusion of new forms of work organisation, and the corresponding explosion in productive capacity, are often seen as the hallmarks of capitalism. In fact, much Marxian historical work has been devoted precisely to this problem of trying to account for the shift from feudal forms of production to revolutionary forms of capitalist production. Robert Brenner, for example, in his seminal contribution to the debate on the problem of transition from feudalism to capitalism saw his analysis as a contribution to explaining the industrialisation of England: 'What distinguished the English industrial development of the early modern period was its continuous character, its ability to sustain itself and to provide its own self-perpetuating dynamic. Here, once again, the key was to be found in the capitalist structure of agriculture... It was indeed, in the last analysis, an agricultural revolution, based on the emergence of capitalist class relations in the countryside which made it possible for England to become the first nation to experience industrialization.'[9] And Eric Hobsbawm, writing two decades earlier, explored the crisis of the seventeenth century as 'the last phase of the general transition from a feudal to a capitalist economy.' He argued that the crisis led to a 'considerable concentration of economic power,' which 'directly and indirectly served the ends of future industrialization.'[10]

The linking of industrialisation and capitalism has also influenced writing on India. Irfan Habib, in his very important essay, 'Potentialities of Capitalistic Development in Mughal India' is reluctant to apply the label of capitalism to India because the subcontinent did not undergo any transformation in the means of production. Indeed, Habib treats capitalism and industrialisation as synonymous: 'In the present paper we are, formally speaking, concerned not with the potentialities of growth, but specifically with potentialities for capitalistic development. It is a reasonable assumption, however, that for all societies other than those of our own day, the only possible road to modern industry lay through capitalism; and it may therefore be taken for granted that the proximity to or distance from true capitalistic relations that a given premodern or modern society maintained offers a valid criterion for judging its capacities of growth, so that in essence, the two questions may be treated as identical.'[11]

This connection between capitalism and industrialisation dates to the writings of Karl Marx. As Marx wrote, 'The bourgeois relations of production are the last antagonistic form of the social process of production; at the same time the productive forces developing in the womb of bourgeois society create the material conditions for the solution of that antagonism. This social formation brings, therefore, the prehistory of human society to a close.'

For Marx, capitalism was both an analytic category as well as a political category. His account of the rise and development of capitalism was infused with a deep belief in capitalism's historical and political necessity. Therefore, Marx's understanding of capitalism combined seamlessly an interpretation of the past, an analysis of the present, and a vision of the future. For Marx, capitalism, like feudalism, was a transitional phase in human history. He believed firmly, at least in his younger years, that capitalism was a historical necessity as it would revolutionise the technology of production, which was a prerequisite for a communist society and it would give rise to the proletariat, the class whose dissolution would mean the dissolution of all forms of class society. Marxism, therefore, provided a unified theory of historical change as well as setting a political agenda for the present. In both historical and political modes, therefore, capitalism and industrialism were intertwined as capitalism simultaneously created the material preconditions for communism and gave rise to the revolutionary class which would usher in the new mode of production.

This unification of past, present and future was Marxism's greatest strength and it gave its adherents a powerful sense of certainty: they possessed the secret to unlocking the direction of historical change, which placed them at its cutting edge. At the same time, this unification was a grave weakness. In political terms, too much was expected of capitalism as a precursor to a post-capitalist Utopia. In historical terms, the analysis delivered too little because capitalism had to carry the burden of explaining the profound economic transformations of the modern period, especially industrialisation. And all too often the link between capitalism and industrialisation was assumed rather than explored in rigorous historical detail. As a consequence, important features of economic and social life after 1500, and many that contributed to industrialisation, were either excluded from the framework—the world market, for instance—or treated in a reductive manner. A striking and repeated example of reductionism may be seen in the Marxian treatment of the state.

Some of these dissatisfactions with prevailing approaches to capitalism led Immanuel Wallerstein to shift the focus of enquiry to the global dimension of modern economic activity and to analyze capitalism as a world system of exchange and production. Wallerstein's discontent with existing approaches in part stemmed from the need to integrate imperialism into story of capitalism's development, from the Spanish empire in the Americas of the sixteenth through eighteenth centuries to the rise of British power in Asia in the eighteenth century. Giving central place to imperialism, however, and the broadening of the definition of capitalism to accommodate many regions of the world in a single field of analysis shattered any necessary link between capitalism and industrialisation. As Wallerstein argued, 'Since the intellectual debate between the liberals and the Marxists took place in the era of the industrial revolution, there has tended to be a *de facto* confusion between industrialism and capitalism.' Wallerstein rejected this link, arguing that for nearly three centuries, from the early sixteenth century to the late eighteenth century, capitalism existed but industrialisation had not yet taken place. Therefore, for Wallerstein industrialisation cannot be taken as the hallmark of the appearance of capitalism. Rather, capitalist relations are defined by exchange for profit on the market.[12]

Where do Wallerstein's intellectual moves leave us? In terms of politics, the clarity of the Marxian analysis of capitalism and the political projects it gave rise have clearly disappeared. Wallerstein is certainly aware of this and he has devoted some energy to recapturing some sort of revolutionary vision from his understanding of capitalism on the global scale and he has argued repeatedly for revolutionary transformation and socialism on a world scale. In fact, Wallerstein has produced a very substantial body of writing on political issues of the day.

In terms of historical analysis, the elegance of the Marxian model of historical change has been lost, as the historical canvas has been broadened, and therefore, been made much messier. Wallerstein has sought to recapture some analytic simplicity, but in the process becoming simplistic in his approach. The dynamics of change in Marxist accounts of history, most important, the key role played by class conflict, has been obscured, only to be replaced by a crude functionalism in which historical change is too often reduced to the needs of the world capitalist system. In addition, Wallerstein's Eurocentric view of the world completely rules out the possibility of global capitalism possessing multiple cores in the period before 1800, with regions of Asia representing important nodes in the global economy. Nonetheless, the failure of many Marxian analyses of capitalism to deal with the importance of the world market from the sixteenth century and the problematic equation of capitalism and industrialisation that Wallerstein has pointed to are path-breaking interventions, even if his reinterpretations of Marxism are inadequate in important respects.

AN ALTERNATIVE FRAMEWORK

This section builds upon the deficiencies in the Marxian narrative that Wallerstein has identified and offers an alternative framework for analyzing the early modern world. The framework moves beyond the Eurocentrism of Wallerstein's account and rests upon the fact that the rapid commercialisation of economic life, as well as social and cultural changes that may be characterised as early modernity, were not isolated to Europe, but took place after 1500 across much of Eurasia. In other words, it does not treat the world east of the Mediterranean as the Oriental Other. At the same time, the framework offers an explanation for the apparent stability in economic and social life in the Indian subcontinent, while explaining the rapid transformation life in western Europe, but without reducing explanation to capitalist teleologies of industrialism or Wallersteinian functionalism. Whether this framework should be labelled capitalism will be taken up subsequently.

This framework operates on three registers: the world market, the state and class relations. It argues that the interactions and conjunctures produced by these three elements shaped paths of historical development in Europe and the Indian subcontinent between 1500 and 1800.

'The history of all hitherto existing society is the history of class struggles,' Marx and Engels declared in the *Communist Manifesto* in 1848. And much Marxian history has been written upon this premise, building not only upon this dictum but also following the seminal forms of analysis Marx developed in countless texts, from *The Eighteenth Brumaire* to the *Class Struggles in France*. Even non-Marxian historians have been influenced by this approach. Marc Bloch, for instance, in a brilliant section of his *French Rural History* accounts for the divergent paths of agrarian development in late medieval England, France and central Europe to different outcomes in the struggle between peasants and seigneurs.[13] It was, of course this insight that Robert Brenner later developed in his 'Agrarian Class Structure and Economic Development in Pre-Industrial Europe.'

As Bloch recognised in his account, however, class conflicts are fought through the institutions of the state. In his case, the juridical regimes that existed in different areas of Europe played a major role in conflicts over land and of particular importance was the relative power of kingly courts in relation to lordly courts. In the first volume of *Capital,* Marx himself gave great weight to the state in the development of capitalism in England beginning in the fifteenth century with legislation on land and labour. Enclosure by Acts of Parliament, for instance, were the means by which land was expropriated from peasants and a proletariat created. Acts of Parliament also forced down the wages of the expropriated, through rigorous punishment of begging and vagrancy.

The state not only played a role in the class struggle, but also mediated between local markets and world markets, in this way regulating the impact that producers in other regions of the world had upon local producers. This brings us to the world market, the final element of the three in this alternative framework. In the writings of Marx and Engels the world market is perhaps the least analyzed of these elements. Nevertheless, Marx certainly concurred with Adam Smith's assessment that the creation of the world market, which followed from the 'discovery' of the Americas and the circumnavigation of Africa, were of revolutionary importance. As Smith put it in *The Wealth of Nations,* 'The discovery of America, and that of the passage to the East Indies by the Cape of Good Hope, are the two greatest and most important events recorded in the history of mankind . . . By uniting, in some measure, the most distant parts of the world, by enabling them to relieve one another's wants, to increase one another's enjoyments, and to encourage one another's industry, their general tendency would seem to be beneficial.'[14] And Marx echoed these words in *The German Ideology,* where he wrote, 'Manufacture and the movement of production in general received an enormous impetus through the extension of commerce which came with the discovery of America and the sea-route to the East Indies.'[15]

Certainly, there are important Marxian accounts of European development between 1500 and 1800, which give an important role to the world market. One of the most influential was Eric Hobsbawm's 'Crisis of the Seventeenth Century,' which spawned a long series of responses in the pages of *Past and Present* in the late 1950s and early 1960s. For Hobsbawm, the world market, or overseas and colonial market as he put it, played a major role in the revival from crisis, and northwestern Europe was particularly well-positioned to profit from that trade, in the case of his essay chiefly from the Atlantic market.

The growing importance of the world market after 1500 suggests that agricultural conditions alone, which was the focus of Mukhia's contribution on feudalism, is not sufficient to explain the greater dynamism of Europe after 1500, in contrast to the relative stability of the Indian subcontinent. What is required is a more complex account that considers the world, the region and the locality and this is what follows.

ECONOMIC CHANGE IN EUROPE, 1500–1800

In Marxian accounts, class relations in the countryside have been crucial for explaining the revolutionary changes in production that unfolded in Europe after 1500. In particular, the emergence of the classic capitalist class structure of landlord, yeoman farmer and wage labourer in the English countryside has been seen as central to England's unique path of economic development. With this structure of class relations, agriculture was primed for improvement, a revolution even, as there were powerful incentives to invest in the land and in other ways raise productivity. These greater efficiencies in the countryside were crucial for industrial growth as they made it possible to feed the burgeoning manufacturing population, supplied the labour for these new manufacturing jobs, and created a market of newly prosperous rural dwellers for the goods being produced on an ever expanding scale with new industrial methods.

More recent research, however, has questioned the extent to which there was a revolution in English agriculture as a forerunner for the later revolution in industry. First, improvements in agriculture did not supply labour for manufacturing. In 1800, England had a substantial peasantry as well as very large ranks of unemployed and underemployed in the countryside. There was no simple labour transfer from agriculture to industry before the nineteenth century. Second, although agricultural productivity went up in the seventeenth century, it appears that this was not primarily the result of greater investment in the land. Rather, Robert Allen has shown that much of the more efficient use of land and capital stemmed from the intensification of work which enclosure made possible. The creation of widespread rural distress—with rampant shortages of jobs—that followed the creation of enclosed estates meant that employers could demand from workers a more disciplined and intense pace of work, which greatly increased yields and output. Third, even if labour productivity went up through intensification of work, domestic agriculture was unable to keep pace with growing food requirements from the late eighteenth century. The food gap came to be filled in part by imports, first from Ireland and Europe and then from the New World and eastern Europe. The gap was also met through a decline in standards of living as workers were forced to make do with smaller quantities of food. Finally, and perhaps most important, even if there was a transformation of agriculture, as Robert Allen has observed, it cannot explain the technological change in manufacturing and the rise of modern industry.[16]

Therefore, changes in the agrarian economy appear to be less crucial for explaining industrialisation than many accounts have believed. What then were the forces that propelled change in European industry?

To answer this question, it is essential to bring in the state and the role that political power played in shaping industrial activity. On the one hand, one of the key functions of states in Europe was to regulate the labour market. This function was most advanced in England, where elaborate measures, including the Statutes of Artificers of 1563, regulated apprenticeship, wages, and employment contracts. This sixteenth-century Act was modelled on earlier regulations, most important kingdom-wide regulations that sought to put a limit on wage increases after the Black Death of the fourteenth century. The scale and scope of English labour market regulations were unparalleled in Europe from the fourteenth century onwards.

European states also used political power to both encourage local manufacturing as well as to spark manufacturing ventures in entirely new areas. This was certainly the case in England, where, according to Joan Thirsk, starting from the sixteenth century the state lent crucial support to a series of projects that sought to reduce imports of manufactured goods, including woad, fustians, linen, iron, and metal goods. The aim of state policy was not to prohibit the consumption of these goods, but rather to encourage their manufacture locally with imported raw material. According to Thirsk, this English policy may have been modelled on several such manufacturing successes that Englishmen had observed in Europe. For example, silk makers in Antwerp and Italy flourished on the basis of imported raw silk and English wool was exported to Flanders, woven into cloth, which was then returned to England for sale. It was in this period of manufacturing projects that a number of key industries had their beginnings or received great impetus in the British Isles, including cotton and iron.[17]

The adoption of policies to discourage imports of manufactured products was shaped in part by bullionist thinking on the sources of wealth. What is perhaps even more significant about these policies, however, is that they reflect a keen understanding of England's inferior position within the international market and the reality that its manufactures could not compete in a number of trades. The inability of the English, and more generally western Europeans, to compete in world markets became even more apparent from the mid-seventeenth century when Indian calicoes and muslins began to be imported into Europe on a large scale. By 1700, these textiles had been shut out of most European markets, again in the name of mercantilist principles on the importance of bullion and employment for a nation's wealth.[18] Nevertheless, as historians have shown, protectionist ideas translated into very different policy prescriptions in the different nations and kingdoms of seventeenth-and eighteenth-century Europe.

Some of these striking differences in policy are evident from a comparison of the restrictions that were placed on cotton cloth in France and Britain in the eighteenth century. Although both nations sought to restrict Indian imports, France did so by prohibiting the wearing of cotton altogether, which hindered the development of an indigenous cotton industry. Britain, by contrast, in the opinions of Patrick O'Brien, Trevor Griffiths, and Philip Hunt, followed a more pragmatic policy that allowed domestic cotton manufacturing to develop and mature with some modicum of protection and insulation from Indian competition.[19] Cotton was not the only industry that received protection and encouragement in eighteenth-century Britain. There is a similar story about iron where British manufacturers were unable to compete with far cheaper imports from Sweden and Russia. Iron manufacturers received very substantial tariff protection over the course of the eighteenth-century, and this was an important impetus to technological breakthroughs in British iron production.[20]

To sum up, between 1500 and 1800, states in Europe played a pivotal role in mediating the effects of the world market upon merchants and producers. Although policies varied widely from state to state, the goal was at a minimum to protect local producers from the competition of world markets and more ambitiously, as was the case in the British Isles, to transform the process of production. Therefore, the commercialisation of Europe after 1500 produced dramatic economic and social changes, but these did not stem directly from the expansion of markets, whether local or global, but were a product of active state intervention in the functioning of global markets. In the Indian subcontinent, by contrast, there was a similar commercial boom, which has already been noted in this paper. But there, the dramatic development of the commercial economy was accompanied by the apparent stability of the both the agrarian and manufacturing economy. And this point of the relative stability of agrarian life, albeit mainly for the period before 1500, was noted by Harbans Mukhia in his essay on feudalism.

ECONOMIC CHANGE IN THE INDIAN SUBCONTINENT, 1500–1800

In some respects, the level of commercial activity in the Indian subcontinent was far greater than that in Europe in the period between 1600 and 1800. In eighteenth-century England, a nation that had achieved a very high level of commercial activity both in European and global terms, there was an acute shortage of coins and credit. Pat Hudson has documented the desperate measures that manufacturers in Yorkshire had to pursue in order to make up for their inability to obtain coin and credit.[21] These included paying workers in chits and tokens that could be used in local stores, what was known as truck, because of the shortage of small coins in eighteenth-century Britain. By contrast, there is little indication of shortages of coin or credit in eighteenth-century India. The abundance of money appears to have been characteristic of the subcontinent for several centuries. According to Sanjay Subrahmanyam, 'by the mid-sixteenth century, even North India appears relatively well-supplied with coin.'[22] And the large quantities of copper, cowries and other inferior monetary media that were imported into India suggest that low-level transactions were amply supported with plentiful supplies of monetary media.

Although in the centuries after 1500, trade boomed and commercial networks expanded, there is a remarkable sameness to economic life in the subcontinent between the sixteenth and eighteenth centuries. The scale certainly changed, with a steady growth in population and and the location of activity shifted—with the rise and fall of states and regions—but one is pressed to identify the dramatic transformations in class structure or technology that overtook Europe in these centuries. In part it was this stability, combined with Orientalist prejudice, that led Marx to proclaim, 'Indian society has no history at all, at least no known history.' Of course, Marx attributed this fact to the torpor of the village community, but from our vantage point today, we may offer a different explanation for stability.

Harbans Mukhia noted that a major source of stability in medieval times was the fertility of agriculture, which he attributed in part to the climatic and ecological conditions of the subcontinent. Also crucial to the fertility of Indian agriculture, however, were the political institutions of the Indian subcontinent, which played a key role in the maintenance of agricultural systems through sustained and high levels of investment. Satish Chandra has noted that in Mughal north India the state was a major source of investment funds for agriculture, along with the village community and the individual cultivator.[23] Although it is difficult to assess the share of the state in total investment, political authorities had enormous incentives to invest in agricultural improvement as a means to attracting and securing scarce supplies of labour.

Between the sixteenth and eighteenth centuries, the Indian subcontinent was characterised by shortages of labour, which led to intense competition for it. Exacerbating this competition was the mobility of agriculturalists, who routinely picked up and moved to new lands in new locations. In this economic climate, investment in agriculture—whether it was systems for water control, the clearing of high quality land or encouragement for the cultivation of high value crops—helped to attract and settle labourers in a political territory. Since Mughal times, if not earlier, rulers offered such inducements to cultivators and these may be found from the *farmans* of Aurangzeb. 'If the peasants are well off, [the 'amils] should arrange that all of them try to increase (the area under) sowing and bring about an enlargement in the area cultivated and, while shifting from the inferior crops to high grade, not leave waste any cultivable land, so far as they can. If any one from amongst the cultivators has fled, they should find out the reason thereof and try hard in the matter of his return to his native place. Similarly, they should use praiseworthy endeavour and much effort at soothing and conciliation, to gather cultivators from all sides and directions'.[24] The revenue regulations of Tipu Sultan sound a very similar note in which a tax farmer who was unable to collect the sum he had engaged for was instructed to 'procure new Reyuts, whom he shall provide with new ploughs, and by advancing Tucavee [cash advances] to them, enable them to complete the cultivation'. Similar instructions were given to revenue officials, who were to 'give Tucavee [advances], at the rate of three or four pagodas for every plough' to enable 'Reyuts who are needy to purchase ploughs and to cultivate the lands'. Individuals who undertook investments such as digging tanks and wells were to receive a quantity of ground as inam [tax-free].[25] Therefore, investment and improvement in agriculture became a means by which political authorities and dominant classes managed conflict in the Indian countryside.[26]

In contrast to its active intervention in agricultural production, states in the Indian subcontinent were less involved in managing the impact of the world economy. This, of course, does not mean that state officials in their private capacity were not involved in long-distance trade. But there was no counterpart in the Indian subcontinent to the massive state regulation of imports or pushes to replace goods from abroad with home production, policies which became common in Europe from the sixteenth century. Nor did the Indian subcontinent develop bullionist thinking of the sort that became very prevalent in early modern Europe.

Although some historians have argued for South Asian forms of mercantilism, analogous to policies of early modern European polities, most prominently Burton Stein, state regulation of trade and state commercial monopolies made their appearance in the subcontinent largely in the eighteenth century.[27] And these policies, it would appear, were instituted to compete against the market power of the European trading companies, and later to resist the political expansion of the British. In Malabar, for example, the early eighteenth-century pepper monopoly was created in part to resist the growing power of the Dutch East India Company.[28] In Mysore, Tipu Sultan's elaborate commercial system was developed to amass state resources for the military battles against the expanding British presence in South India. In these policies, there is no attempt to mitigate the impact of the world market on local production systems or to transform the relationship of local producers to the world market, both of which were hallmarks of European mercantilism.[29]

Indian states were unconcerned about these issues because local production in a wide range of goods was in a commanding position in world and regional markets. In agriculture, rice from the subcontinent was traded from the Persian Gulf to the islands of Southeast Asia. Spices, most important black pepper, were traded at profitable margins and demanded throughout the world. In manufacturing, Indian cotton textiles, calicoes, muslins, plain cloth, printed cloth, painted cloth, bleached white, or dyed blue, had their avid customers from Mexico to Russia to mainland and island Southeast Asia. The subcontinent was self-sufficient in iron and even exported the metal to the Persian Gulf and Southeast Asia. And there was no need for bullionist thinking as the subcontinent was awash in gold, silver, copper and other commodities that were the basis for money. There was no need for state regulation to conserve the stuff as there were no shortages of monetary media.

To conclude, the worldwide commercial boom from the sixteenth century in which the Indian subcontinent was a key participant reinforced the agrarian stability that Harbans Mukhia argued as characteristic of medieval India. These factors were complemented by states that accommodated themselves to these conditions, which actually flourished for much of the period between 1500 and 1800. After all, one can hardly label the Mughal state a political failure, and its decline in the late seventeenth century had a great deal to do with its success in maintaining the high pace of agricultural activity as well as booming Indian participation in world trade.

Conclusion

Two decades ago, Harbans Mukhia rejected the description of medieval India as feudal on the grounds that the social relations as well as the conditions of production in agriculture were profoundly different in India and Europe. Nonetheless, shortly thereafter several historians, focusing on the period from 1500 to 1800, began to attach the label of capitalism to the transformations of Indian society that occurred in this early modern period. By applying a historical category derived from the European experience to India, these historians rejected the view that India is the 'other' of Europe and argued that the subcontinent's historical development was not fundamentally different from that of

Europe. Of course, a problem with this argument is that by the late eighteenth century the paths of economic development in Europe had begun to diverge from that of the Indian subcontinent and other Asian countries, as regions of Europe, commencing in Britain, began to industrialise.[30]

For most Marxist writings on capitalism, there is an implicit connection between the emergence of capitalist relations of production and industrialisation. This connection has been challenged in recent years in order to broaden the historical terrain, so to speak, upon which capitalism may be applied. The broadening of capitalism, as done most prominently by the historical sociologist Immanuel Wallerstein, however, has raised the problem of how to explain Europe's industrialisation. And this question Wallerstein has largely sidestepped.

At issue, therefore, is a set of problems larger than the appropriateness of capitalism for describing early modern India. These have to do with the extent to which the similarities between Europe and India between 1500 and 1800 may be incorporated into a single analytic framework that can at the same time account for divergences. In other words, can sameness and difference be brought under a single theoretical structure? This essay has proposed one such approach, which operates on three registers: the world economy, the state and class relations.

And what of capitalism? This essay has suggested that capitalism is not an appropriate category for the analysis of early modern India because the range of issues it brings into its analysis are too narrow to comprehend what made Indian society work from the sixteenth to the eighteenth centuries. At the same time and for much the same reasons, however, this essay has argued that capitalism is an inadequate category for the analysis of early modern Europe as well. Some years ago, Gareth Stedman Jones wrote that it is time for historians to gain inspiration from Marx, but not to slavishly follow his theoretical pronouncements.[31] It is in this spirit that I call for an end to the search for capitalism.

REFERENCES

1. Irfan Habib, 'Potentialities of Capitalistic Development in the Economy of Mughal India', *Journal of Economic History*, 29, 1969, pp. 32–78.
2. Frank Perlin, 'Proto-Industrialization and Pre-Colonial South Asia', *Past and Present*, no. 98, 1983, p. 59.
3. C.A. Bayly, *Indian Society and the Making of the British Empire*, Cambridge, 1988, p. 47.
4. D.A. Washbrook, 'Progress and Problems: South Asian Economic and Social History c. 1720–1860', *Modern Asian Studies*, 22, 1988, p. 72.

5. Sanjay Subrahmanyam and C.A. Bayly, 'Portfolio Capitalists and the Political Economy of Early Modern India', *Indian Economic and Social History Review*, 25, 1988, pp. 401–24.
6. J.M. Neeson, *Commoners: Common Right, Enclosure and Social Change in England, 1700–1820*, Cambridge, 1993.
7. John Rule, *The Experience of Labour in Eighteenth Century Industry*, London, 1981.
8. Peter Linebaugh, *The London Hanged: Crime and Civil Society in the 18th Century*, London, 1991. Also see Rule, *Experience of Labour*.
9. Robert Brenner, 'Agrarian Class Structure and Economic Development in Pre-Industrial Europe', *Past and Present*, no. 70, 1976, pp. 67–8.
10. E.J. Hobsbawm, 'The General Crisis of the European Economy in the 17th Century', *Past and Present*, nos. 5 & 6, 1954.
11. Habib, 'Potentialities of Capitalistic Development', p. 33.
12. Immanuel Wallerstein, 'The Rise and Future Demise of the World Capitalist System: Concepts for Comparative Analysis', in his *The Capitalist World Economy*, Ch. 1.
13. Marc Bloch, *French Rural History: An Essay on its Basic Characteristics*, trans. Janet Sondheimer, Berkeley, California, 1966.
14. Adam Smith, *The Wealth of Nations*, ed. R.A. Campbell and A.S. Skinner, Oxford, 1976, Vol. 2, p. 626.
15. Karl Marx and Friedrich Engels, *The German Ideology*, New York, 2001, p. 74.
16. Robert C. Allen, *Enclosure and the Yeoman*, Oxford, 1992. Also see Neeson, *Commoners*.
17. Joan Thirsk, *Economic Policy and Projects: The Development of a Consumer Society in Early Modern England*, Oxford, 1978.
18. P. J. Thomas, *Mercantilism and East India Trade*, London, 1926.
19. Patrick O'Brien, Trevor Griffiths and Philip Hunt, 'Political Components of the Industrial Revolution: Parliament and the English Cotton Textile Industry, 1660–1774', *The Economic History Review*, new series, 44, 1991, pp. 395–423.
20. Charles K. Hyde, 'Technological Change in the British Wrought Iron Industry, 1750-1850', *Economic History Review*, new series, 27, 1974; Charles K. Hyde, 'The Adoption of Coke-Smelting by the British Iron Industry, 1709–1790', *Explorations in Economic History*, x, 1972–3.
21. Pat Hudson, *The Genesis of Industrial Capital: A Study of the West Riding Wool Textile Industry, c.1750–1850*, Cambridge, 1986.
22. Sanjay Subrahmanyam ed., *Money and the Market in India 1100–1700*, Delhi, 1994, p. 19.
23. Satish Chandra, 'Some Institutional Factors in Providing Capital Inputs for the Improvement and Expansion of Cultivation in Medieval India', *Indian Historical Review*, 3, 1976, pp. 83–97.
24. 'Aurangzeb's Farman to Rasikdas', in Irfan Habib ed. *Medieval India*, 1, Delhi, 1992, pp. 202–3.
25. Burrish Crisp, *The Mysorean Revenue Regulations*, Calcutta, 1792, in

C.B. Greville, *British India Analyzed*, London, 1793, Articles 2, 10 & 36.

26. Prasannan Parthasarathi, *The Transition to a Colonial Economy: Weavers, Merchants and Kings in South India, 1720–1800* and David Ludden, *An Agrarian History of South Asia*, Cambridge, 1999.
27. See, for instance, his 'Eighteenth Century India: Another View', *Studies in History*, 5, n.s., 1989; and even more explicitly in his 'Class and Pre-Colonial Indian Mercantilism', paper presented at the Workshop on Early-Modern Empires and Economies, Harvard University, Cambridge, Mass., March 1990.
28. Ashin Das Gupta, *Malabar in Asian Trade*, Cambridge, 1967.
29. See, for example, Ashok Sen, 'A Pre-British Economic Formation in India of the Late Eighteenth Century: Tipu Sultan's Mysore', in Barun De ed., *Perspectives in Social Sciences I*, Calcutta, 1977.
30. On this see Kenneth Pomeranz, *The Great Divergence: China, Europe, and the making of the Modern World Economy*, Princeton, 2000.
31. Gareth Stedman Jones, 'The Determinist Fix: Some Obstacles to the Further Development of the Linguistic Approach to History in the 1990s', *History Workshop Journal*, 42, 1996, pp. 19–35.

Harbans Mukhia: A Historian's Journey through a Millennium

Rajat Datta

As I write the last essay of this festschrift, I reflect on my long association with Harbans Mukhia as teacher, friend and historian in no orderly sequence. Many of the views he later developed in his writings germinated in discussions which he so unselfconsciously shared with us in the classroom, in the smoke-filled university cafeteria over cups of lukewarm coffee, or in the convivial atmosphere of his home. As a teacher he was convincing without being pushy; open to questions without being patronising in his responses; demolishing long-cherished shibboleths without being arrogant. All these traits he applied in his writings, and since he ceaselessly questioned, and compared, he could never rest satisfied with any given version of history, or of his own explanations to counter these versions. In this sense he was a historian truly journeying through his favourite terrain: the history of India in the millennium between the eighth and the eighteenth century.

As a professional medievalist, Harbans Mukhia has innovatively explored that epoch without being overtly sequential in his choice of themes. Historiography, the development of technology, economic trends over the long term, modes of social control and ideology, and social institutions and practices—these comprised some of the historical labyrinths though which Mukhia traversed over four decades. The temporal range of his scholarship has been vast and the choice of themes courageous. Though trained as a historian of the Indo-Persian genre of historical sources, he successfully blended them with vernacular sources and from documents in the regional archives. Taken together, these constitute a highly complex and formidable body of scholarly output.

In the following pages I will attempt to trace some of the broad routes of this journey.

The Intellectual Journey

Mukhia's career as a professional historian dates from 1960, when he was appointed lecturer in Delhi University's Kirori Mal College, after having been trained as a historian of medieval India in the same university. By that time, the strands of medieval Indian historiography stood at a crossroads, and Mukhia's initial historiographical engagement germinated here.

One strand of this historiography, deriving principally from the Nationalist tradition, was oriented towards political, principally dynastic and empire-centric history where the main thrusts of the narrative were the reigning dynasties and their rise and fall. The dominant explanatory variable was human nature—the strong or weak ruler being the fountainhead of stability or instability. Since the sources were the Indo-Persian court chronicles, the main historiographical bias of this strand was the centrality of a state, particularly a strong state, as the bulwark of the nation. Mukhia's first scholarly attempt, his doctoral dissertation, subsequently published[1] was a throwback to this tradition. Significant departures were nevertheless visible. Instead of the celebratory assessment of the Persian chronicles that had characterised the writings of historians like Muhammad Habib[2], Mukhia was deeply sceptical of viewing history from the 'foot of the throne' that was the hallmark of such chronicles. Instead of seeing an inevitability and immanence of imperial centralisation from the thirteenth century onwards, Mukhia pointed to the deliberate attempts in some of these chroniclers to *construct* such a state by a one-sided accentuation of facts, by a generous alteration and misrepresentation of sources, and by being unabashedly subservient courtiers while writing, sometimes even inventing, histories to suit their patrons.

The other strand, which was to introduce a paradigmatic shift in the writing of Indian history, was Marxism. The works of D.D Kosambi, R.S. Sharma and Irfan Habib profoundly turned the writing of history from the political to the social and the economic. From the personality-oriented, Indian history now moved to a class-oriented framework of analysis, and from an obsession with dynastic stability and instability, the dynamic of history was henceforth located in cumulative series of seething tensions between the exploiters and the exploited. Suddenly history mattered, not merely as a tool to look at our past, but as a possible instrument of change. As a historian, this engagement with Marxism led Mukhia into a three-tracked movement: first, as a matter of praxis, to explore the possibilities and pitfalls of secularising the writing of medieval Indian history; second, to see how ideologies function or impede social conflict and protest; and third, to consider the possibilities and limitations of applying an explicitly Marxian framework to Indian history.

In an essay published in 1969 (subsequently revised in 1983)[3], Mukhia explicitly saw 'structural analysis' as the only framework of historical inquiry which could impart an 'integrated pattern' to all 'historical events', and thus enable the historical record to rise above the randomness of human (or divine) volition. For Mukhia, the marginalisation of communalist history-writing was possible only when socio-economic history, which he defined as 'a study of the actual labour processes in the field and the workshop' would come to occupy prime focus in the historian's imagination. With this frame of reference, Mukhia turned to the question of subaltern ideology and social protest in his 1978 essay 'Ideology and the Bhakti Movement: the Case of Dadu Dayal'[4]. Reflecting on the failure of these popular protests to dismantle the double oppressive pillars of caste and denominational religions, Mukhia concluded that the internalisation and assimilation of the ideology of the ruling classes by these protestors weakened these movements, thereby giving his seal of approval to Marx's dictum that 'the ideas of the ruling class are in every epoch the ruling ideals'[5].

While accepting the Marxian position regarding the ideological hegemony of the ruling classes, Mukhia was more circumspect with regard to the applicability of Marx's views on the structural processes in pre-colonial India. In his 1985 essay, 'Marx on Pre-colonial India: An Evaluation'[6], he distanced himself from Marx's central arguments about pre-colonial Asiatic formations: the self-sufficiency of Asiatic economies, the absence of private property in land, and the innately despotic nature of the Oriental states. In a somewhat revisionist mode, he concluded that

> Both Marxism and the historiography of India will be the richer if some of these problems which had occupied Marx, are subjected to a far more detailed examination than has yet been done, even if Marx's own observations have to be modified in the end or abandoned altogether.[7]

Though this was a significant critique indeed, and constituted some of the organising principles of Mukhia's subsequent researches on the question of feudalism in Indian history (on which there is more later), there is no escaping the fact that Mukhia still functioned within the dominant Eurocentric *historical* paradigm as laid out by Marx in so far as he accepted, without any reservations, Marx's prescriptions about the *exceptional* nature of European history. For Marx, the exceptional conditions of European history were to be seen in a neat linear sequence of progress to higher forms of economic activity, which he spelt out in the following words: '...the ancient, feudal and modern bourgeois modes of production may be designated as epochs marking progress in the economic development of society'[8]. For Mukhia,

> Europe's stages of development—slavery, feudalism and capitalism—are clearly enough marked and almost universally accepted. It is also universally accepted that in India the changes that occurred in the production system and social organization, important as these are, do not mark comparable distinct discontinuities.[9]

If the Marxist framework continued to exist in a somewhat attenuated form in Mukhia's historical consciousness, it was being constantly modified and altered by his engagement with the historians of the Annales school, particularly Marc Bloch, George Lefebvre, Georges Duby and Jacques Le Goff. The origins of this engagement lay in the new set of courses for graduate students he devised after his appointment in the Centre for Historical Studies of the Jawaharlal Nehru University in 1971. One of these lecture courses entitled 'Feudalism' (later transformed into the 'Medieval World') proved to be the entry point for Mukhia into the world of medieval European history. In 1988 and 1990, this resulted in a two-volume collection of essays (jointly edited with Maurice Aymard) called *French Studies in History*[10] where the 'multi-dimensional' thrust of Annales historiography was subjected to detailed and critical scrutiny. The ability of the Annalists to create 'ruptures and conflicts between generations and schools of thought' without 'resulting in major clashes', and to incorporate 'a surprising combination of sympathy and caution towards Marxism' were highlighted as its obvious strengths. In methodological terms, the combination of economic history with sociology and cultural anthropology, meant that economic trends, 'major conjunctural movements, beginning with the longest ones' (using long-term price data) could henceforth be combined with the use of other sources (like marriage deeds or testaments) to 'reconstruct units of social structure' and to 'discern the mechanisms by which social hierarchies were formed or renewed...'. Further, Annales historiography, 'in envisaging the reconstruction of "total history" both collaborated and competed with the Marxist 'historical vision', therefore making them singularly compatible with each other, but liberating because now history could 'transgress the reassuring frontiers of its own province and to discard the host of divisions which further fragmented it'.[11]

It was this competitive compatibility of/between the Annales and Marxist traditions that seems to have rooted itself in Mukhia's craft from the 1990s. These were reflected in the kind of courses he designed for his students at the CHS[12] and in his writings.[13] A close scrutiny of these writings reveals both subtle and explicit shifts in methodology in two directions. First, the notion of historical truth is not valorised as an objective reality (as it is in the positivist premise or in his older writings), but (in a more Foucaldian sense) as the existence and mobilisation of social power in a multiple set of intersections, manifestations and inversions, all occurring simultaneously. Therefore every social act (including that of reckoning time) becomes an act in the social negotiation of power, and every institution is implicated in such negotiations. Thus as they modify, they become simultaneously modified.[14]

The second methodological shift occurs in his reckoning of the historical dynamic. Instead of seeing conflict through the older dialectical opposition between two contradictory elements (for instance, between classes), Mukhia henceforth sees opposition, conflict and accommodation as a part of a historical continuum. Continuum conjures up a trajectory in which contradictory elements move together, constantly modifying each other. This approach does not foreclose a linearity of perspective (which remains a historian's Achilles heel, no matter what), but it restricts privileging one agency over another in a nuanced historical perception.

The Historical Journey

Keeping in mind the complexities which these shifts involve, I now turn to some specific examples of the 'craft' of history as practised by Mukhia. In my mind, the corpuses of Mukhia's writings lend themselves to three blocs: the structural, the cultural-conceptual, and a combination of the structural with the cultural.

Mukhia explored the structural realm in two seminal essays: 'Was there Feudalism in Indian History' (in 1981)[15] and 'Peasant Production in Medieval India' (in 1985).[16] These articles constitute, in my view, the culmination of his long-engagement with the Marxist/materialist framework: histories of material structures, production and reproduction. These essays involved three methodological steps: (a) the construction of a rigorous theoretical approach to the problem of feudalism as a form (mode) of production which drew from the rich and diverse experiences of western European feudalism; (b) the application of these constructs in order to establish the initial contours of the discourses of feudalism in non-European societies[17]; and (c) to develop an alternative typology for the medieval in such societies.

Once the methodology was in place, the specifics followed. First, feudalism was defined not blandly as a system characterised by extra-economic coercion, but through its labour process, which was a 'structured dependence of the entire peasantry on the lord', caused initially, by the hiatus between the 'labour potential of the peasant family and its resources', which, subsequently became located 'in the production-process' and therefore in the 'very conditions of labour'.

Second, he found the model inadmissible for India because of the differences in the labour-processes involved in production, in the modes of surplus appropriation, and in the forms of social conflicts which occurred in the countryside. Third, an alternative was proposed, which he argued, set the specific difference between the medieval Indian and medieval European situation, viz. 'the free peasant production' which characterised the labour process of pre-colonial India, contrasted to the structured dependence of their European counterparts. In India, 'free peasant production' was characterised by the 'economic freedom' of the peasants over their instruments of production, including land and labour (the means of production in the classic Marxian sense), and by the absence of 'extraneous controls' both of appropriation and ownership over them, the presence of which in medieval Europe, he saw, as the primary distinguishing feature of the feudal system.

These formulations attracted a lot of attention and flak from various historians. Criticism came from a variety of perspectives. Both Burton Stein (who was actually quite sympathetic to Mukhia's position), and R.S. Sharma (a severe critic) seriously questioned the effectiveness of the typology of a 'free peasant production' for medieval India. Sharma drew attention to a wealth of evidence regarding the imposition of forced labour upon the peasantry in early medieval north India in an attempt to reinforce his definition of feudalism as a system characterised by non-economic coercion (akin to the *corvee* rent in medieval Europe). Stein drew attention to the virtual absence in Mukhia's framework of the state in the workings of the medieval Indian economy, a position which inhered so centrally in Irfan Habib's contribution to the debate.[18]

To a great extent Mukhia's contrast between the European peasant and the Indian 'free peasant' is warranted in Marx's own conceptualisation of serf labour 'as a moment of property in land itself, [as] appendage of the soil' in contrast to the 'free' labourer whose 'labour capacity appears to him as his property... which he maintains by expanding it'.[19] But a question, which was largely elided in that discussion remains: irrespective of freedom or subservience of a producer, can a mode of production (in a strictly Marxian frame) be equated or demolished by *a description of a labour process*? In a particularly incisive moment, Marx indicated that some common features shared by all pre-capitalist forms of labour were the domination of a 'rural patriarchal system', and the predominantly 'communal' (i.e. communitarian) form of existence, which caused individual labour to appear rather as the 'direct function' of a collectivity rather than as the labour of an individual.[20] The *laboratores*, as the third estate (order) in medieval Europe or *jatis* (endogamous caste-groups) in India would express this communal-collectivisation of the labour process, not its freedom. To be sure, Mukhia is deeply aware of caste as a collective mode of appropriation in Indian history,[21] and argues correctly that caste was in no way a hindrance to the peasants' access to means of production (land) or social stratification[22], but it still does not take away from the twin facts that production was overwhelmingly in the form of a 'rural patriarchal system' and that the producers, albeit stratified, *belonged* to a larger communitarian edifice. The notion of a 'free peasant production' therefore does not elaborate a *modal* difference for India's pre-colonial history.

Mukhia's other argument concerning appropriation, that 'coercive power was... never rooted in the production process' but was situated extraneous to it opens the question of modes of appropriation in pre-capitalist formations. It does indicate a structural difference between Europe and India since the appropriators here were not owners of the means of production, and that tax and revenue (in India) was dissimilar to feudal rent (both in its labour and money forms) in Europe. Since 'appropriation of rent is that economic form in which landed property is realized'[23], the existence and continuous elaboration of revenue as the dominant mode of appropriation shows the unambiguous existence of peasant-property—the 'consolidation of petty peasant production' in Mukhia's words— but only as one variant in convergent systems of non-economic exploitation prevailing in the pre-capitalist world. Mukhia's prescription does not help in breaking out of the older problematic of non-economic coercion as the characteristic feature of appropriation in all pre-capitalist formations since force (political, cultural or communitarian) determined systems of appropriation and also fixed their boundaries.[24]

However, the importance of the concept of a 'free peasant production' lies not so much in explicating the differences between medieval Europe and India, but in ways it directs our attention to certain specifics of medieval Indian history. By situating peasant-labour and the peasant-household as the fulcrum of social reproduction and of property, Mukhia draws our attention to the fact that autonomous peasant-production propelled both the domestic and the national economies in pre-colonial India towards more highly developed systems of cultivation and more valuable products. By imparting this singular agency to peasant history, Mukhia significantly modifies a very influential view of medieval Indian history in which the peasant is more or less an inert victim of the state's caprices, and all productive impulses, including that of conflict, emanate from the state's propensity to consume larger and larger portions of the surplus.[25]

The second major historical revision Mukhia commands is in the connection between appropriation through revenue and the nature of social conflict in medieval India. I have already drawn attention to Mukhia's early views about ideological thralldom as a cause of the failure of protest movements spearheaded by petty-artisans and tertiary producers. Now, in a more class-oriented explanation, he tells us that

> Once exploitation of the peasantry had come to be pivoted on revenue collection, conflicts between peasants and the state came to the fore only after the production process had been completed, for the conflict related to the quantum of revenue demand. In other words the conflict remained extraneous to the production system.

This meant that in medieval India, social conflicts tended to remain at the level of 'distribution and redistribution of the surplus' and did not lead to a reappropriation of the means of production. The latter he identifies as the principal difference between India and medieval Europe, where 'conflict inhered in the very process of production', and a 'resolution of it was possible only in the transformation of the production system and redistribution of the means of production, giving rise to new classes'.[26] One may quibble with the implicit inevitability of the European path in Mukhia's framework. It took European peasants nearly six centuries to achieve such an end; economic changes were piecemeal and never dramatic over these centuries; the period of economic expansion after the eleventh century also saw the most intense feudal exploitation of the medieval serf; and there were large areas of Europe where peasant passivity continued in the face of peasant rebellions elsewhere. However, these caveats do not detract from the fact that his is a powerful formulation and opens up the possibility of locating both dynamism and passivity at the doorstep of the medieval Indian peasant.

The establishment of the *Medieval History Journal* (*MHJ*) in 1998, with Mukhia as its founder-editor, constituted a benchmark. It marked a culmination of his restlessness with older categories and issues of medieval history, which converged with a similar dissatisfaction of his editorial collaborators. What was intended instead was a forum which would force a rethinking on the very notion of the 'medieval' or its numerous manifestations in a genuinely open-ended and comparative perspective. True to this desire, the inaugural issue of the *MHJ* was a special issue on 'Contextualizing the "Medieval"', which provided Mukhia with an opportunity to rethink the categories, assumptions and biases which had gone into the ascription of ***a*** 'medieval' period to Indian history. This introspective exercise was an essay entitled '"Medieval India": An Alien Conceptual Hegemony?'[27], which also marked the beginning of what I call the conceptual-cultural turn in his writings.

In this essay, Mukhia drew attention to the fact that the 'medieval' for India was an intellectual construction derived by our colonial rulers from the European triptych of antiquity, the middle ages and modernity, but applied in India bereft of its secular overtones, except in the case of British rule when the 'modern' was written into colonial rule. 'Medieval' historians had no such tripartite divisions in mind. For them, history was a linear progression with 'the birth of Islam as the hegemonic temporal divide [the end of *jahiliya* or unreason] in history'.[28] Thus the concept of the medieval period in Indian history was a derivative discourse, initially associated with Islamic rule in India by British historians, and later, after Independence, incrementally secularised by the insertion of class instead of religion as the dominant analytical category. The 1990s were seen as a new 'threshold' for Indian historiography 'with emphasis on social and cultural profiles, power relationships manifest in everyday life... and the study of space and time in historical contexts'.[29]

The study of economic relations, which had been such a powerful corrective to the older categories of periodisation, seems to have retreated from Mukhia's scheme of the new threshold.

In 1999, Mukhia opened a new window to look at the world of the medieval mentalité in his essay 'The Celebration of Failure as Dissent in Urdu *Ghazal*'[30]. I rate this essay as one of the most important written by him as it is a highly nuanced exposition of a genre of poetry which had so far been seen only as an exposition of unrequited love which arose 'at a point of decadence of the [Mughal] empire', a 'form of poetry which, given the sexually repressive nature of society, could only be a celebration of illicit love'. Mukhia's intervention is multilayered and highly nuanced. First, he challenges the notion of a sexually repressive society, pointing instead to a 'long libertarian tradition' in India from the time of Vatsayayana's *Kama Sutra*.[31] But the *ghazal* is not about corporeal love. It is instead 'the concealment of one's love, keeping it a *raz*. The more the lover suppresses the manifestation of his love, the more he internalises it, the more he suffers the intense loneliness and sadness of love—that for him is the ultimate ecstasy, the supreme *gham* (the joy of eternal longing)'.[32]

Second, Mukhia explores a double-derivation of the *ghazal*'s antecedents from the Perso-Islamic, particularly the Sufic traditions, and from the Indian folkloric tradition—thereby making it a unique synthesis of the mystical (Sufic) and the sensuous (folkloric). A significant point here is the way in which one strand of the *ghazal* is traced to the Indian folkloric milieu—an artifact of the pluralism characteristic of the cultural milieu of medieval India.

Third, he locates the *ghazal* as part of a long genealogy of dissent in the Islamic tradition, particularly the *khirad* versus *junoon* (the head versus the heart, rationality versus the emotion) dichotomy which also 'implicated a dichotomy of elite vs. popular cultures'[33]. Therefore the Urdu *ghazal* in Mukhia's view is a medium of inversion, where failure and despair are celebrated as forms of dissent. A good example of this inversion is the way in which the categories *kufr* and *kafir* are used in the denominational Islam and in the Urdu *ghazal*. From the quintessential unbeliever and enemy of the faith, these terms metamorphose into 'the greatest terms of endearment' in the *ghazal*.[34]

The argument is both innovative and provocative and the reader is left demanding more. The folkloric element in the *ghazal* is tantalisingly posited but not fully elaborated. Mukhia sees the folkloric in the celebration of life and love (*ishq*), which this genre of poetry espoused, and in the linguistic mode of these couplets in the language of the bazaar. Does this not equate folkloric with popular culture? And are the two interchangeable? Would it not have been more pertinent if Mukhia had explored the imageries and idioms in these *ghazals* to see whether there was actually an attempt to incorporate the various *rasas* (moods) in the folkloric traditions in his explication of *ishq* and *gham* in the Urdu language?

Another question relates to the play of gender in this form of poetry. If we argue, following Carla Petievich that, in the *ghazal*, 'it is conventional for both the *'ashiq* and the *ma'shuq* to bear grammatically masculine gender, though the emotions expressed in the *ghazal* are not thought to be exclusively male'[35], then it is vital to explain why this is so? One is reminded of another genre of masculine poetry, that of Courtly Love in medieval Europe where the construction of the female 'subject' and the man's love/lust for her are its explicit intentions. The man constructs the 'lady' and in doing so gets gendered simultaneously.[36] Is there a female subject in the imagination of the Urdu poet? If so, who is she? Or is the *ghazal* an expression of a masculine, homo-erotic love? This, if true, would indeed be a great example of dissent.

Finally, Mukhia takes another issue only half way after raising it as a starting point of his essay. This is the issue of 'decline' in eighteenth-century India. The pungency of his critique of the modern protagonists of the decline theory (correctly identified by him as the 'Aligarh' historians) does not dilute the fact that there was a great deal of anxiety among the eighteenth-century Indo-Persian *Ashraf* that their 'world' had been turned upside down. It was in midst of this that *Rekhta* literature in the eighteenth century saw the emergence of a specific kind of lament known as the *Shahr Ashob*, which wove together an atavistic concern with a deep melancholy about the present.[37] In my view, this reflected a restlessness born of a medley of inversions happening at that time: the decline of the Mughal empire, the demise of a genteel, urbane way of life of the elite, and the aggressive assertion of people of 'low' culture: the *razil qaum.*[38].

The cultural-conceptual stream of Mukhia's writings culminated in two essays, 'Time, Chronology and History: the Indian Case' in 2001, and 'Time, Religion and History in India' in 2002[39], exploring the notions of time in Indian history in a comparative framework. In these essays Mukhia makes an important point that the binary juxtaposition between the division of historical time into the linear (the Occidental model) and the cyclical (the Oriental model) is a positivist invention to juxtapose the supposed dynamic nature of western civilisations against the changelessness and stagnation of the Orient. In India, Mukhia argues, the notion of cyclical time is at best one of several notions and, even here it does not implicate closure of social change. In classical Hindu philosophy, the notions of *kryā bhed* and *parināma* reckon time not in its own terms but in relation to individual action and volition. In other words, change through action already implicates in it the possibilities of breaking through these cyclical notions of time.

Islam, the other strand in India's medieval culture, as a legatee of the Judaic-Christian tradition inherited the concept of linear (i.e. historical) time, but combined it with a strong infusion of eschatology. The combination of these two brought a new 'vision' of history to India. History now became a narrative of events in actual time, very precisely measured in years, months and days, starting from a temporal dividing line of 622 CE, the beginning of the Hijri era. However, even within this tradition there were 'dissenting voices', voices which envisioned historical time as an uninterrupted flow either from the beginning of the universe or from the beginning of humanity from the time of Adam. Abul Faz'l was a great exponent of this voice of dissent, as were certain sects, like the Ismailis, who perceived time as eternal and infinite.

Like much of his other writings, Mukhia gives us a multi-layered explanation of perceptions and *mentalités* existing both complimentarily and in dynamic opposition to each other. Dominant paradigms, like the reckoning of time, are simultaneously perpetuated and subverted in both the Hindu and Islamic traditions, thus leaving no ground for complacency about the immutability of certain categories. Yet one cannot leave the discussion without a niggling doubt that it tends to remain largely an explication of the normative structures (notwithstanding the dissenting undertones) as it does not get into two very important arenas: (a) the modes, including the technology for the physical reckoning of time in order to see how that changes time into a measurable category, subject to precise divisions and intervals; and (b), the social (i.e. class) specific differences in approaches to such reckonings of time, which would make time a contested territory—a source of tension in society.[40]

Mukhia combined the structural with the cultural in his last major study, *The Mughals of India*[41] published in the same year he retired from Jawaharlal Nehru University (JNU). This book marks the apogee of his engagement with the cultural realm of medieval India since the 1990s, and establishes a new benchmark in that area. The four chapters of the book—Legitimacy, Religion and Political Culture; Etiquette and Empire; The World of the Mughal Family; and Folklore and Mughal Culture—explicitly ground the Mughal empire within a new *problematique* where the structural and the cultural intersect in mutually sustaining ways to generate a system of rule which was absolutist in theory and intent and Islamic in spirit, yet had to negotiate its way through entrenched Indian traditions and was continuously reshaped in the process. This is a refreshing departure from an influential orthodoxy which views the Mughal Empire as a centralised system, standing firm on the twin pillars of a strong military-bureaucratic apparatus (the *mansabdari*) and a successful system of fiscal (mainly land revenue) appropriation.[42] Instead of a 'monocentric' explanation, like the one above, Mukhia posits 'varying and varied sources of legitimacy' composed of 'durable' structures, 'plastic' elements and 'fleeting' moments which yet leave a lasting impress on history'[43].

With the possible exception of Akbar in his later years, the Mughals were devout Muslims and the demands of Islam did loom large in the scheme of ruling over a country where the majority of subjects were non-Muslims. The solution to this conundrum didn't take the shape of an orthodox, Islamic view of the state (though there were ideologues baying for precisely such a turn) or repression of the unbelievers (in spite of of many examples of desecration of temples and conversions to Islam, which Mukhia candidly discusses).[44] Regardless of these countervailing pressures, the Mughals found a workable solution by experimenting with multiple and 'expansive' strands of legitimacy, among which the 'ideology of paternalism'[45] and that of 'universal sovereignty' were the most innovative. The Muslim state in medieval India had many limitations and shortcomings, but religious fundamentalism and proselytising zeal were not part of that list. India remained firmly pluralistic despite an overwhelmingly Hindu majority at the end of Mughal rule, as it continues to be even today! Mukhia helps us trace the lineages of that pluralism back into the sixteenth and seventeenth centuries.

The major strength of this book is the way it moves into unknown historiographical paths. One such path is the chapter on 'Etiquette and

Empire', a completely novel way of constructing the Mughal court through an elaborate chain of spoken and unspoken codes of demeanour and deportment in the Mughal court. Court etiquette encapsulated hierarchy and power expressed in a multitude of ways. Genuflection, postures, proximity to the emperor, gift-exchange and the celebration of festivals comprised a bundle, the semiotics of which was the constant reinvention of royal power. Akbar's *Din-i Ilahi* was another innovation which blended the Sufic *pir-murid* (master-disciple) relationship (also, perhaps the *guru-bhakta* relationship from the Bhakti tradition) demanding unquestioning loyalty to the person of the emperor. Mukhia also indicates a subtle change in court etiquette in the seventeenth century when a more formal structure of courtly life emerged 'in which solidity of structures grew at the expense of personal space'[46]. The Mughal court was as a powerful weapon of both imperial organisation and social regulation as it synthesised idioms from high governance with quotidian forms of existence; it successfully blended exalted theories of divine kingship with idioms extracted from the popular Sufic and Bhakti traditions, thereby making it the fulcrum of interaction 'between social and imperial layers'[47].

A similarly innovative departure marks Mukhia's attempt to reconstruct 'The World of the Mughal Family'. In an empire where the ideology of paternalism was vital to governance, the family and the household became forms of social organisation and pivots of imperial authority. Families clustered around two axes—the expansive and extended, at least among the Mughal elite because of the prevalence of multiple marriages (polygamy) and concubinage. Families were patriarchal but not yet patronymic, the latter being an invention of the 'modern-colonial regime'[48]. A significant dimension of Mukhia's analysis lies in its gendered perspective on the family. From a relatively open system in its early stages, where women enjoyed a fair degree of autonomy, Mukhia detects a significant closure and conservatism towards the freedom of women, especially their sexuality, from the time of Akbar. For instance, the increasing preoccupation from Akbar onwards with the chastity of women, the emergence of the harem as a site of gender-segregation, the sacralisation of marriage and growing restrictions on widow-remarriage[49] arose, in Mukhia's views, from the 'long shadow' cast by Rajput morality over the Mughal ethos. Unfortunate as this was for the position of women, this is a clinching example of Indianisation: the Mughals in India now truly became the Mughals *of* India.

Finally, Mukhia looks at the empire as a cultural phenomenon. In a significant departure from his early understanding of the inevitable hegemony of ruling class culture and ideology, Mukhia now sees the cultural phenomenon as a two-way process riddled with ambivalences and seepages. While Persian flourished as the language of attainment, refinement, and of high politics[50], Mughal culture, according to Mukhia, had Persian and folkloric genealogies. Seeking the benediction of Sufi shaikhs and Hindu ascetics as the medium of divine transference, believing in omens and auguries, consulting astrologers for finding the propitious moment, and sitting in the *jharoka* so that subjects could get a glimpse (*darshan*) of their emperor—each one was derived from folk culture and charismatically reified.. 'Yet another form of folk culture—overt sensuality—rose high up in the social ladder'[51] and found expression on special occasions like the spring festival of Holi which was celebrated at the imperial court along with Dussehra and Diwali.

While one would, following Marx's grand prescription about the hegemony of ruling ideologies, expect the shadow of high-culture to cover those below it, what is not always obvious is how elite cultures appropriate from the 'subaltern'. Georgs Duby demonstrated this tellingly in his study of the feudal nobility in Europe[52] and Jacques Le Goff drew our attention to this seepage within the medieval European clergy[53]. Mukhia has done the world of medieval Indian history a great service by drawing our attention to this phenomenon in India.

Seminal works such as the *Mughals of India* inspire a sense of awe in the reader. They also give rise questions as well as a niggling sense of incompleteness. I go along with Mukhia in his dissatisfaction with the framework which has so far dominated medieval studies in India. Based almost exclusively in Persian language sources generated by the court, these studies have privileged the empire over every other aspect. There is an obsession with stability and a great fear of instability in these studies, which mirror the biases of those texts themselves. Mukhia successfully demonstrates how those same texts can be read differently to yield an almost contrary picture. But following Mukhia's own methodology, one cannot but help ask the counter-question: is it possible to study an empire without grappling with its institutional foundations? One area which Mukhia refuses to enter is that of the state's fiscal system, perhaps because this occupies centre-stage in the older historiography. Mughal revenue terminologies bristle with terms like *dastur*, *qarar* and *rusum*. These are usually translated as established rates of revenue, agreements and fiscal perquisites by historians[54]; but don't these terms also mask customary practices and deeply entrenched cultural codes which had to be carefully negotiated through in each locality of the empire? Otherwise, how does one explain the prevalence of a myriad forms of non-monetised assessment in an empire obsessed with extracting its revenue in cash; or understand the emperor Aurangzeb's anxieties that his revenue officials not only be fair but also appear to be fair while dealing with the cultivators; or understand, as Dilbagh Singh shows, the existence of seething contests over the quantum of revenue itself?[55] I am also reminded of the ceremony of the *punya* (literally, a virtuous act) held in eighteenth century eastern India on the first day of the Hindu month of Baisakh (April-May) when landed proprietors would assemble at the Mughal subahdar's (governor's) court to submit their annual accounts and pay the final *kist* (instalments) of revenue due from them. An apparently fiscal operation was marked by festivities, celebrating the closure of a financial year and the beginning of a new one, much like the regeneration of a life-cycle, thus simultaneously 'converting every power relationship into a personal one'[56]. Is it therefore not possible to read cultural practices even in matters like assessment, collection and redistribution of revenue?

On the question of the Mughal family, Mukhia's analysis turns more on the *working* of the family rather than on its structure. We see the Mughal family as a lattice of agnatic descent perpetuated primarily, though not exclusively, through marriage. But what we don't see is the historic form of the Mughal family despite the strong indication that it was patriarchal and situated somewhere in between a joint and an extended family. Primogeniture was there but could never be assured as can be seen in the bloody struggles for succession to the throne which erupted between competing sons irrespective of the familial pecking order. This is not to say that family structures had not taken shape as evidence exists to show the crystallisation of a patriarchal joint-family among business communities in northern India[57], and among land-based communities western India[58], while in Bengal the patriarch (*korta*, literally, master) was the functioning head of a joint family of landed proprietors.[59] The nebulous nature of the Mughal family seems enigmatic in this context. The history of the family in medieval Europe may suggest some oblique answers. Here the salient feature from the eleventh century was the consolidation of the nucleated family among the nobility in order to prevent fission of their landed properties from competitive claimants in a joint family set-up. Thus single-stem feudal 'houses' arose in western Europe in order to consolidate their estates under strict laws of primogeniture, restrictive inheritances, patronymic filiations, monogamous marriages and growing limitations on the marriages of younger male siblings.[60] Did the Mughal family remain unstructured because it possessed a huge empire but did not belong to any class of property owners?

Finally, while one may be circumspect, as Mukhia is, in assigning definitive labels to social formations, as historians we cannot escape dealing with such categories (for instance, feudalism, capitalism or colonialism) almost on a daily basis. Shouldn't an attempt be made to develop a typology for a state too? In the Marxian framework, the state is an instrument of the ruling class, and a device to protect and reproduce oppressive forms of private property, whereas in a Weberian framework the state exists because of its monopoly on the legitimate use of force in a given territory.[61] For Marx, the class nature of the state is an immanent phenomenon applicable to all social formations, while for Weber the power of the state derives from 'the basic *legitimations* of domination' which change temporally and spatially. The pre-modern state and the modern state are differentiated in Weber's views by the latter appearing as a rational-legal institution by virtue of the belief in the 'validity of the legal statute'.[62]

Problems arise in the social explication of a pre-modern state. Here, Weber's notion of the 'patriarch and the patrimonial prince of yore', enjoying power through 'mores sanctified through the unimaginably ancient recognition and habitual orientation to conform'[63] may be used as one strand of a possible framework. The other strand may be derived from the Marxian conceptualisation of an absolutist state as 'ostensible mediator' between 'warring classes', thereby acquiring 'for the moment, a certain degree of independence of both'.[64] Further features of this state are 'salaried state functionaries', 'a standing army', and substitution 'for the checkered anarchy of conflicting medieval powers the regulated plan of a state power with a systematic and hierarchic division of labour'.[65]

Many of the features of Mughal rule which Mukhia discusses straddle the Weberian and Marxian frameworks of the state, as outlined above. Multiple strands of legitimation, paternalistic and familial notions of governance and the personal charisma associated with the monarch were blended with secular institutions of absolutist authority: a standing army, a paid semi-bureaucratic apparatus and elaborate fiscal regulations. Can then one classify the Mughal state as a form of absolutist-patrimonialism of the early modern world? Mukhia does not engage with this question. One can only wish he had, while simultaneously realising that some historical reconstructions attain great heights, not because they raise all questions, or offer all the answers, but because they enable readers to derive their own inferences, even if they are sometimes, as they are in my case, half-baked.

REFERENCES

1. *Historians and Historiography during the Reign of Akba*r, New Delhi, 1976.
2. On this, see Raziuddin Aquil's essay 'On Islam and Kufr in the Delhi Sultanate: Towards a Reinterpretation of Ziya 'al-Din Barani's *Fatawa-i Jahandari*' in this volume.

3. 'Medieval Indian History and the Communal Approach', revised as 'Communalism and the Writing of Medieval Indian History– a Reappraisal', *Social Scientist*, 1983. All citations are from the 1983 version.
4. In D.P. Chattopadhyay (ed.), *History and Society: Essays in Honour of Professor Nihar Ranjan Ray*, Calcutta, 1978, reprinted in Harbans Mukhia, *Perspectives on Medieval History*, Delhi, 1993.
5. *Ibid*, p.93, citing Karl Marx, *The German Ideology*, in Marx and Engels, *Selected Works*,Vol.1, Moscow, 1969, p. 47.
6. In Diptendra Banerji (ed.), *Marxian Theory and the Third World*, Delhi, 1985, reprinted in Harbans Mukhia, *Perspectives on Medieval History*.
7. *Ibid*, p. 83.
8. Karl Marx, A *Contribution to the Critique of Political Economy*, London, 1970, (original, 1859), p. 21.
9. 'Marx on Pre-colonial India', p. 78. Though Marx incorporated the 'Asiatic' as one of the modes of production in his sequence of economic progress, it was used more as a differentiator of the European experience than its purveyor.
10. Maurice Aymard and Harbans Mukhia (ed.), *French Studies in History, Vol. 1: The Inheritance*, Delhi, 1988; and *French Studies in History, Vol. II: The Departures*, Delhi, 1990.
11. Aymard and Mukhia (ed.), *French Studies in History, vol.I*, Introduction, pp. 1–26.
12. In a major refashioning of the history syllabus which took place in the Centre for Historical Studies in the 1990s, Mukhia developed a slew of courses like 'Festivity and Culture', 'Symbols and Rituals of Sovereignty', 'Legitimacy and Political Culture' and 'Community Formation and Identities' for students of medieval history. The older course 'Feudalism' was transformed (with my collaboration) into a completely new 'Medieval World'.
13. 'Medieval India': An Alien Conceptual Hegemony?', *The Medieval History Journal*, Vol. 1 (1), 1998; 'The Celebration of Failure as Dissent in Urdu *Ghazal*', *Modern Asian Studies*, Vol. 33 (4), 1999; 'Time, Chronology and History: the Indian Case' in Sølvi Songer, ed., *making Sense of Global History*, Universitetsforlaget, Oslo, 2001; 'Time, Religion and History in India', *Historical Inquiry*, (Taipei) 29, 2002; *The Mughals of India*, Blackwell Publishing, Oxford, 2004.
14. Mukhia, *The Mughals of India*, pp. 1–13, esp. pp. 11–12.
15. *The Journal of Peasant Studies*, Vol. 8, no. 3, 1981.
16. *Ibid*, Vol. 12, no. 2–3, 1985, special issue on 'Feudalism and Non-European Societies', ed. Terry Byers and Harbans Mukhia.
17. In this he departed significantly from the approach of R.S. Sharma and his followers, whose understanding of feudalism was predominantly taxonomic—an enumeration of its characteristics and their selective application to the Indian situation.
18. See Harbans Mukhia and Terry Byers (ed.), *Feudalism and Non-European Societies*, London, 1985; and Harbans Mukhia (ed.), *The Feudalism Debate*, New Delhi, 1999 for these discussions. All references to Mukhia's writings on the question of feudalism are from this latter book.

19. Karl Marx, *Grundrisse: Foundations of the Critique of Political Economy*, (ed. and translated by Martin Nicolaus), Penguin, Harmondsworth, 1974, p. 405.
20. Marx, *Critique of Political Economy*, pp. 33–34.
21. See, 'Marx on Pre-colonial India: An Assessment'; and 'Peasant Production in Medieval India'.
22. Mukhia, 'Peasant Production', pp. 251, 255.
23. Karl Marx, *Capital*, Vol. 3, Moscow, 1974, p. 634.
24. Harbans Mukhia, 'Illegal Extortions from Peasants, Artisans and Menials in Eighteenth Century Rajasthan', *The Indian Economic and Social History Review*, 14, 2, 1977. Also see Dilbagh Singh's essay in this volume.
25. See Irfan Habib, *The Agrarian System of Mughal India, 1556–1707*, Delhi, 1999 for this influential view.
26. Mukhia, 'Peasant Production', pp. 258–59.
27. *The Medieval History Journal*, vol. 1 (1), 1998.
28. *Ibid*, p. 99.
29. *Ibid*, p. 105.
30. *Modern Asian Studies*, Vol. 33 (4), 1999.
31. Also see Asim Roy, 'Sexuality—an Islamic historical perspective with special reference to South Asia', *South Asia: Journal of South Asian Studies*, Vol. 13 (2), 1990.
32. Mukhia, '*Ghazal*', p. 868.
33. *Ibid*, p. 873.
34. *Ibid*, p. 878.
35. Carla Petievich, 'Gender Politics and the Urdu Ghazal: Exploratory Observations on Rekhta vs. Rekhti', *Samyukta : A Journal of Women's Studies*, Vol. III, No.1, Jan 2003 (http://www.museindia.com/showfocus3.asp?id=663).
36. Georges Duby, *Love and Marriage in the Middle Ages*, Oxford, 1994, (first published, 1988).
37. For examples of such angst, see Khurshidul Islam and Ralph Russell, *Three Mughal Poets: Mir, Sauda, and Mir Hasan*, Delhi 1991.
38. I investigated some of these elements in my paper, 'A City in Decline: Perception and Social History in Eighteenth Century India', presented at a workshop on 'The City and the Idea of a City', Centre for Historical Studies, JNU, 12 April 2007.
39. In Sølvi Songer, (ed.), *Making Sense of Global History*, Universitetsforlaget, Oslo, 2001; and in *Historical Inquiry*, (Taipei) 29, 2002.
40. I have Carlo Cipolla's, and Jaques Le Goff's seminal discussions on both these aspects in mind while making this point (see Cipolla, *Clocks and Culture*, London, 1967; Jacques Le Goff, *Time, Work and Culture in the Middle Ages*, Chicago, 1982).
41. Oxford, Blackwell Publications, 2004.
42. This orthodoxy, propounded almost single-handedly by Irfan Habib, remains a hallmark of the historians at the Aligarh Muslim University.
43. *Mughals of India*, p.16.
44. *Ibid*, pp. 23–27. This is in refreshing contrast to the propensity within Nationalist and Marxist historians to remain silent on these embarrassing

episodes, thereby learning the issue open to misrepresentations by communal historians.

45. *Ibid*, pp. 41–43.
46. *Ibid*, p. 100.
47. *Ibid*, p. 106.
48. *Ibid*, p. 128.
49. *Ibid*, pp. 135–146.
50. *Ibid*, p. 159; see also Muzaffar Alam, 'The Pursuit of Persian: Language and Mughal Politics', *Modern Asian Studies*, Vol. 32 (2), May 1998.
51. *Mughals of India*, p.169.
52. 'Diffusion of Cultural Patterns in Medieval Europe', *Past and Present*, no. 39, April 1968.
53. Jacques le Goff, 'Clerical Culture and Folklore Traditions in Merovingian Civilization', in Le Goff, *Time, Work and Culture in the Middle Ages*, pp. 153–159.
54. See Habib, *Agrarian System;* also Shireen Moosvi, 'Akbar's Farman to Rasikdās on Problems of Revenue Administration', in Irfan Habib (ed.), *Medieval India 1: Researches in the History of India, 1200–1750*, Delhi, 1999.
55. 'Contesting Hegemony: State and Peasantry in late Medieval Rajasthan' in this volume.
56. John R. McLane, *Land and Local Kingship in Eighteenth Century Bengal*, Cambridge, 1993, p. 49.
57. This is the impression one gets from reading the description of the family life and business ventures of a seventeenth century Oswal jeweller, Banarasidas in the *Ardha Kathanak*, in *Indica*, Vol. 7, nos. 1 and 2, March and September 1970.
58. Dilbagh Singh, 'Notes on the Domestic: Notes on the Pre-colonial Family', *Studies in History*, vol.19 (1), January–June 2003.
59. Ronald Inden and Ralph Nicholas, *Kinship in Bengali Culture*, Chicago, 1977.
60. Georges Duby, *Love and Marriage in the Middle Ages;* David Herlihy, 'The Making of the Medieval Family: Symmetry, Structure and Sentiment', *Journal of Family History*, Vol. 8, 1983; Frances and Joseph Gies, *Marriage and the Family in the Middle Ages*, 1987.
61. H.H. Gerth and C. Wright Mills, *From Max Weber: Essays in Sociology*, London 1970 (first published, 1948)
62. *Ibid*, pp. 78–79; emphasis in original.
63. *Ibid*, p. 79.
64. Friedrich Engels, 'On the Origins of the State', in Robert C. Tucker (ed.), *Marx-Engels: A Reader*, New York, 1972, p.653.
65. Karl Marx, 'On the Civil War in France', in Karl Marx, *The First International and After. Political Writings*, vol. 3, (ed. David Fernbach,), Penguin, Harmondsworth, 1974, p. 246; for an exceptionally lucid exposition of some of these ideas, see Perry Anderson, *Lineages of the Absolutist State*, London, 1974.

Selected Publications of Professor Harbans Mukhia

Books:

Historians and Historiography During the Reign of Akbar, Vikas, New Delhi, 1976.

Perspectives on Medieval History, Vikas, New Delhi, 1993.

Feudalism and Non-European Societies, co-edited with T.J. Byres, Frank Cass, London, 1985.

French Studies in History, 2 vols., co-edited with Maurice Aymard, Orient Longman, New Delhi, 1988 and 1990.

Religion, Religiosity and Communalism, co-edited with P. Bidwai and A. Vanaik, Manohar, New Delhi, 1996.

The Feudalism Debate, edited, Manohar Publications, New Delhi, 1999.

The Mughals of India, Blackwell Publications, Oxford, 2004.

The History of Technology in India, vol. II, (Medieval India), edited, Indian National Science Academy, New Delhi, (projected for 2008).

Articles:

'Medieval Indian History and the Communal Approach' in Romila Thapar, Harbans Mukhia, Bipan Chandra, *Communalism and the Writing of Indian History*, first published, People's Publishing House, New Delhi 1969.

'Communalism: A Study in Historical Perspective', *Social Scientist*, 1, 1972.

'Illegal Extortions from Peasants, Artisans and Menials in Eighteenth Century Rajasthan', *The Indian Economic and Social History Review*, vol.14 (2) 1977.

'Ideology of the Bhakti Movement: the Case of Dadu Dayal' in D.P. Chatopadhyay, ed., *History and Society: Essays in Honour of Professor Nihar Ranjan Ray*, K.P. Bagchi, Calcutta, 1978.

'Maurice Dobb's Explanation of the Decline of Feudalism is Western Europe—A Critique, *The Indian Historical Review*, Vol. 6 (1–2), 1979–80.

'Was there Feudalism in Indian History?' Presidential Address, Medieval India Section, Indian History Congress, 40th Session, Waltair, 1979. Later published in *The Journal of Peasant Studies*, Vol. 8 (3), 1981.

'Communalism and the Writing of Medieval Indian History—a Reappraisal', *Social Scientist*, no. 123, 1983.

'Social Resistance to Superior Technology: The Filature in Eighteenth Century Bengal', *The Indian Historical Review*, vol.11 (1), 1984–85.

'Marx on Pre-Colonial India: An Evaluation' in Diptendra Banerji, ed., *Marxian Theory and the Third World'*, Sage Publications, New Delhi, 1985.

'Agricultural Technology in Medieval North India' in A. Roy and S.K. Bagchi, eds., *Technology in Ancient and Medieval India*, Sundeep Publications, New Delhi, 1985.

'Peasant Production and Medieval Indian Society', *The Journal of Peasant Studies*, Vol. 12 (2–3), 1985.

'The *Risâla-i Zirâ't* [An Eighteenth Century Treatise on Agriculture]', tr. from Persian in Harbans Mukhia, *Perspectives on Medieval History*, Vikas, New Delhi, 1993.

'The Rama Janmabhoomi-Babri Masjid Dispute: Evidence from Medieval India', in L. Gopal. ed., *Ayodhya: History, Archaeology and Tradition*, All-India Kashiraj Trust, Varanasi, 1994.

'La violence communautaire et la transmutation des identités' Violence et politique (Colloque de Cerisy, 1994), *lignes*, 25, mai, 1995 (sous le direction des Etienne Balibar et Bertrand Ogilvie).

'Témoignages étrangers' in *L'histoire et le métier d'historien en France 1945-1995*, sur le direction de François Bédarida, MSH, Paris, 1995.

Entretien avec Georges Duby, *Etudes Rurales*, no. 145-146, EHESS, Paris, janvier-décembre 1997.

'Medieval India': An Alien Conceptual Hegemony?' *The Medieval History Journal*, vol.1 (1), 1998.

'The Celebration of Failure as Dissent in Urdu *Ghazal*', *Modern Asian Studies*, vol.33, (4), 1999.

'Liberal Democracy and its Slippages', in Okwui Enwezor, et al. (ed.), *Democracy Unrealized. Documenta 11_Platform 1*, Kassel, 2000.

'Time, Chronology and History: the Indian Case' in Sølvi Songer, ed., *Making Sense of Global History*, Universitetsforlaget, Oslo, 2001.

'Time, Religion and History in India', *Historical Inquiry*, (Taipei) 29, 2002.

'Historiography of Medieval India: A Retrospective of Evolving Contours', and 'Time in Abul Fazl's Historiography and the Construction of New Dichotomies', 42nd Heras Memorial Lectures, *Indica*, 43, 1, 2006.

List of Contributors

Daud Ali is Senior Lecturer, Department of History, School of Oriental and African Studies. His areas of research are the evolution of religious practices and ideas in classical and medieval India, the growth and spread of courtly culture, and the relationship of ethics, politics and aesthetics among Indian elites in early medieval India. His publications include *Courtly Culture and Political Life in Early Medieval India.*

Raziuddin Aquil is Fellow, Centre for Studies in Social Sciences, Kolkata. His areas of research are state and society in medieval north India, and religion and politics in medieval India. His publications include *Sufism, Culture, and Politics: Afghans and Islam in Medieval North India.*

Catherine Asher is Professor, Department of Art History, University of Minnesota. Her areas of research are art and architecture of the Indian subcontinent from the twelfth century to the present. Her publications include *The Architecture of Mughal India* and *India Before Europe* (co-authored with Cynthia Talbot).

Ujjayan Bhattacharya is Reader, Department of History, Vidyasagar University, West Bengal. His areas of research are the fiscal history of eighteenth-century India, and the social and institutional history of early colonial India with specific focus on Bengal. He has published papers on this theme in journals and has contributed to the Proceedings of the Indian History Congress.

Stephen P. Blake is Senior Research Fellow, Centre for Early Modern History, University of Minnesota. His areas of research are the political systems and practices in medieval South Asia, the nature of imperial cities, and a comparative history of the three early modern Islamic empires: the Mughal, Safavid, and Ottoman. His publications include *Shahjahanabad: The Sovereign City in Mughal India, l639-l739* and *Half the World: The Social Architecture of Safavid Isfahan, 1590-1722.*

Ranabir Chakravarti is Professor, Centre for Historical Studies, Jawaharlal Nehru University. His areas of interest are social and economic history of early India, especially the maritime history of the Indian Ocean between 600 and1500 CE. His publications include *Trade in Early India; Trade and Traders in Early Indian Society;* and *Indo-Judaic Studies in the Twenty-first Century* (co-edited).

Richard Eaton is Professor, Department of History, University of Arizona, Tucson. His areas of research are the social history of pre-modern South Asia and the history of Islam in medieval South Asia. His publications include *Social History of the Deccan, 1300–1761: Eight Indian Lives; Essays on Islam and Indian History* (edited); *India's Islamic Traditions, 711-1750* (edited); and *Slavery and South Asian History* (co-edited with Indrani Chatterjee).

Sumit Guha is Professor, Department of History, Rutgers University. His areas of interest are the economy of western India in the colonial period, state and society in pre-colonial western India and histories of environment and communities. His publications include *The Agrarian Economy of the Bombay Deccan, 1818-1941; Environment and Ethnicity in India, c.1200-1991; Health and Population in South Asia from Earliest Times to the Present*; and *Growth, Stagnation or Decline? Agricultural Production in British India* (edited).

Dirk Kolff is Emeritus Professor, Department of South Asian History, Leiden University, the Netherlands. His areas of interest are the history of India's peasantries and their relationship to the Mughal and British states; colonial law, and the comparative history of the Dutch East Indies and British India, His publications include *Naukar, Rajput and Sepoy: the Ethnohistory of the Military Labour Market in Hindustan, 1450-185;* and *Warfare and Weaponry in South Asia, 1000-1800* (co-edited with Jos Gommans).

Sunil Kumar is Professor, Department of History, Delhi University. His areas of research are politics and state-formation in the thirteenth and fourteenth centuries, communities and identities in medieval India, and the history of medieval Delhi His publications include *The Present in Delhi's Pasts* and *The Emergence of the Delhi Sultanate, 1192-1286.*

Prasannan Parthasarathi is Associate Professor, Department of History, Boston College. His areas of research are the economic history of early modern South Asia, labour history, and the history of the British Empire in the eighteenth century. His publications include *The Transition to a Colonial Economy: Weavers, Merchants and Kings in South India, 1720-1800.*

Vijaya Ramaswamy is Professor, Centre for Historical Studies, Jawaharlal Nehru University. Her areas of research are artisanal communities and crafts and the histories of gender in pre-colonial South India. Her publications include *Textiles and Weavers in Medieval South*

India; Divinity and Deviance: Women in Virasaivism; Walking Naked: Women, Society, Spirituality in South India; and *The Historical Dictionary of the Tamils.*

Dilbagh Singh is Professor, Centre for Historical Studies, Jawaharlal Nehru University. His areas of research are rural society in medieval India, and the social and economic history of western India in the eighteenth century. His publications include *State, Landlords and Peasants: Rajasthan during the Eighteenth Century.*

Madhu Trivedi is Reader, School of Open Learning, Delhi University. Her areas of research are cultural history, and the history of performing arts in medieval North India. She has published articles in various journals and has contributed to the Proceedings of the Indian History Congress.

Plate 1 : Jagatsiromani Temple

Plate 2 : Palace Pavilion – Amber

Plate 3 : Rajasamand Pavilion

Plate 4 : Nathani Haveli

Plate 5 : Ram Temple at Nathani Haveli

Plate 6 : Sita Vallabha Temple

Plate 7 : Ramchandra Temple

Plate 8 : Govindadeva Temple

Figure 1 : Relief sculpture depicting Viṣṇu as Varāha rescuing the earth as Bhūdevī from the waters, with a Nāga king, the Gupta monarch and a courtier in postures of obeisance. Cave 5, Udayagiri, Madhya Pradesh, c. early fifth century, CE.

Figure 2 : Gold stater of Kaṇiṣka standing in rigid posture (see Robert Göbl, *System and Chronologie der Münzprägung der Kusanreiches* [Wien: Verlag der österreichischen Akademie der Wissenschaften, 1984], type 71). Photo courtesy Department of Oriental Antiquities, British Museum.

Figure 3 : Gupta gold coin, depicting King Candragupta standing with bow (see John Allan, *Catalogue of the Coins of the Gupta Dynasties and of Śaśāṅka, King of Gauḍa.* [London: British Museum, 1914], archer type, no. 63). Photo courtesy Department of Oriental Antiquities, British Museum.

Figure 4 : Gupta gold coin, depicting King Samudragupta seated on couch, playing lyre (see John Allan, *Catalogue of the Coints of the Gupta Dynasties and of Śaśāṅka, King of Gauḍa.* [London: British Museum, 1914], archer type, no. 51). Photo courtesy Department of Oriental Antiquities, British Museum.

Figure 5: Gupta gold coin, depicting King Chandragupta seated on couch with foot dangling on footstool (see John Allan, *Catalogue of the Coins of the Gupta Dynasties and of Śaśāṅka, King of Gauḍa.* [London: British Museum, 1914], couch type, no. 102). Photo courtesy Department of Oriental Antiquities, British Museum.

Figure 6 : Early depiction of seated courtier in relaxed posture. Frieze fragment, Mathurā region, late Kūṣāṇa period, 2nd–3rd centuries CE (National Museum of Scotland, Edinburgh) A.1975.265.